The tragic vision of politics

Ethics, interests and orders

Is it possible to preserve national security through ethical policies? Richard Ned Lebow seeks to show that ethics are actually essential to the national interest. Recapturing the wisdom of classical realism through a close reading of the texts of Thucydides, Clausewitz and Hans Morgenthau, Lebow argues that, unlike many modern realists, classical realists saw close links between domestic and international politics, and between interests and ethics. Lebow uses this analysis to offer a powerful critique of post-Cold-War American foreign policy. He also develops an ontological foundation for ethics and makes the case for an alternate ontology for social science based on Greek tragedy's understanding of life and politics. This is a topical and accessible book, written by a leading scholar in the field.

RICHARD NED LEBOW is the James O. Freedman Presidential Professor of Government at Dartmouth College. He is the author, co-author and editor of eighteen books, many of them about international conflict and its management. He is currently President of the International Society of Political Psychology.

The tragic vision of politics

Ethics, interests and orders

Richard Ned Lebow

Dartmouth College, New Hampshire

PUBLISHED BY THE PRESS SYNDICATE OF THE UNIVERSITY OF CAMBRIDGE
The Pitt Building, Trumpington Street, Cambridge, United Kingdom

CAMBRIDGE UNIVERSITY PRESS
The Edinburgh Building, Cambridge, CB2 2RU, UK
40 West 20th Street, New York, NY 10011–4211, USA
477 Williamstown Road, Port Melbourne, VIC 3207, Australia
Ruiz de Alarcón 13, 28014 Madrid, Spain
Dock House, The Waterfront, Cape Town 8001, South Africa

http://www.cambridge.org

First published 2003

Printed in the United Kingdom at the University Press, Cambridge

Typeface Plantin 10/12 pt. *System* LaTeX 2_ε [TB]

A catalogue record for this book is available from the British Library

Library of Congress cataloguing in publication data
Lebow, Richard Ned.
The tragic vision of politics : ethics, interests, and orders / Richard Ned Lebow.
p. cm.
Includes bibliographical references and index.
ISBN 0 521 82753 1 – ISBN 0 521 53485 2 (pb.)
1. National security – Moral and ethical aspects. 2. International relations – Moral and ethical aspects. 3. Realism – Political aspects. 4. Thucydides. 5. Clausewitz, Carl von, 1780–1831. 6. Morgenthau, Hans Joachim, 1904–7. United States – Foreign relations – 1989– I. Title.
UA10.5.L43 2003
172′.4 – dc21 2002041445

ISBN 0 521 82753 1 hardback
ISBN 0 521 53485 2 paperback

To everyone who has defied authority
to maintain *nomos*

To everyone who has defied *nomos*
to promote equality

Contents

Preface *page* ix
Acknowledgments xv

1. Nixon in hell 1
2. Tragedy and politics 14
3. Thucydides and war 65
4. Thucydides and civilization 115
5. Carl von Clausewitz 168
6. Hans J. Morgenthau 216
7. The wisdom of classical realism 257
8. Running red lights and ruling the world 310
9. Tragedy and scholarship 360

Name index 393
Subject index 399

Preface

In 1959, in a Western civilization course at the University of Chicago, I read Thucydides' *History of the Peloponnesian War* for the first time. I read it a second time in a literature course, and yet again in a philosophy course. Each time, we approached the text with a different set of questions in mind: Thucydides was a wonderful vehicle for making students aware of multivocality. Approaching a rich text from different disciplinary perspectives also encouraged me to reflect back on the several disciplines, and to understand divisions among them as having more institutional than intellectual justification. Scholarship is, or ought to be, holistic, but such an approach, I soon learned, runs counter to the fragmentation and specialization of knowledge within the university.

I read Thucydides at what we now know to have been the highwater mark of the Cold War. My three readings spanned two Berlin crises and Cuba. The parallels between the Cold War and the run-up to the Peloponnesian War were unsettling, and all the more so because of my overly literal reading of I.23.5–6 and its apparent assertion that war was inevitable because of the rise to power of Athens and the fear it inspired in Sparta. In addition to scaring me, Thucydides' history, as I came to understand it more fully, provided a new purchase from which to approach the Cold War. It drew me back from the emotional and short-term perspectives that tend to dominate the untrained mind's response to dramatic contemporary events. It encouraged me to think about hegemonic conflict as a generic phenomenon and to develop a more detached and analytical approach to the Cold War. I emerged with a new set of questions with which to interrogate American and Soviet foreign policy, explore the role of third parties and assess the efficacy and possible consequences of arms races, alliances, deterrence and the emerging emphasis in the Kennedy administration on crisis management and low-intensity warfare.

Thucydides offers readers a double vision. His narrative, speeches and dialogue place readers in the midst of human decisions and actions in political assemblies and battlefields. His text orders and shapes events in a manner that fosters a broad, conceptual understanding of the processes at work. Readers experience the unresolved tension between agency and structure; the way in which certain outcomes seem preordained but nevertheless depend upon decisions and actions of individuals that appear highly contingent. They also experience the tension between the seeming requirements of security and the values that people are ultimately fighting to preserve. This contradiction becomes painfully apparent in the Melian Dialogue and the parallel Spartan slaughter of Plataeans; both events illustrate how acute conflicts can develop a powerful and self-defeating logic. The reader is not merely told about these developments, but watches them unfold in the mind's eye, and accordingly feels the pain more acutely. Thucydides thus drew me back from contemporary emotional commitments only to involve me in human dramas of ancient provenance. His purpose in doing so, I suspect, was to make me and other readers confront the human consequences of political decisions and the ethical dilemmas to which they give rise.

It was an easy transition from Thucydides to Hans Morgenthau's course on international relations. He shared Thucydides' tragic understanding of politics, reflected in their belief that order was fragile, that human efforts to control, or even, reshape, their physical and social environments were far more uncertain in their consequences than most leaders and intellectuals recognized, and that hubris – in the form of an exaggerated sense of authority and competence – only made matters worse. Morgenthau attempted to frame his theory of international politics within the limits of human understanding and action. He recognized that even something so fundamental to politics as the balance of power was only a general tendency and not a law. It provided a general frame of reference, a starting point for analysis by statesmen and scholars. The same was true of bipolarity. Whether it constrained the superpowers and goaded them into nuclear preemption would depend on the moral qualities of leaders. Like Thucydides, Morgenthau put great emphasis on the determining choices of leaders, and those decisions in turn reflected their vision, character and ethical commitments. His writings aimed not only to help shape their vision, but to make them more aware of the ethical choices they confronted. He never flagged in efforts to use his conceptual skills to help improve the human condition despite his deep pessimism at times about the willingness of leaders and people alike to learn from experience, control their passions and rise above momentary calculations of narrow self-interest.

Morgenthau's commitment was shared by other scholars who influenced my intellectual and personal development, among them, Herman Finer, Karl Deutsch, John Herz and Ivo Duchacek. They were European refugees, and their close-up experiences of war, ethnic cleansing and authoritarian regimes intensified their efforts to understand the causes of domestic and international conflict and instability and what might be done to alleviate them. They characterized themselves as realists because they rejected as naive and dangerous, far-reaching proposals for transformations of domestic or international orders, but still believed that the world might be made a better place through incremental changes, instituted through consensus by people who had an enlightened sense of self-interest. They were interested in theory, not as an end in itself, but as a means of understanding and responding to the pressing problems of the age. One of theory's goals was to influence policymakers by helping to shape their understanding of the political world.

In the course of the last fifty years the study of international relations, like all the branches of the social sciences, has been deeply affected by the behavioral revolution. One consequence is that the study of theory and policy have increasingly gone their separate ways with, at best, sporadic contact between the communities engaged in each enterprise. International relations theory is ignored by most policymakers, and often considered irrelevant by those few who make the effort to familiarize themselves with the literature. A former national security advisor once confided to me his frustration after reading Kenneth Waltz. Even granting Waltz's claims that bipolar systems were more stable, he observed, such a statement was probabilistic and said nothing about the likely outcome of the one bipolar conflict that interested him: the Cold War. Nor did it offer any policy guidance.

To an even greater degree, theory and policy have both become divorced from ethics. For theoreticians, ethics is a largely extraneous concern, of interest only in so far as ethical commitments influence the calculations of actors whose behavior they are trying to predict or explain. For many policymakers, ethics at best provides a useful rationalization for policies they are committed to for other reasons, and at worst, imposes constraints (most often in the form of laws and regulations) that they lack the power to ignore. Ethical language has largely disappeared from the foreign policy discourse, and people who advocate policies on ethical grounds generally find that their arguments do not resonate within the policy community. Realism, the principal paradigm for both theorists and practitioners, gives priority to interests. Many formulations of realism see ethics as a competing value, and one, moreover, that is only feasible to consider in a society or world made secure by a hard-headed focus on capabilities and interests. The dominance of realism in turn appears to justify the lack of interest in ethics for theorists.

Orientations of this kind are not going to be changed by a single book, no matter how compelling its arguments. I too am a realist, and have far more modest expectations. In the tradition of my intellectual forebears, I would like to stimulate reflection, initially by scholars, about the relationships between theory and policy and interests and ethics. The latter relationship gets very little attention in the literature, and much of the discussion is premised on the realist assumption that interests and ethics routinely conflict. The "dirty hands debate" examines the circumstances in which it may be acceptable to violate ethical norms for purposes of survival, security or other goals.[1] Thucydides recognized this dilemma, and his Melian Dialogue has remained an unsurpassed statement of the competing claims of justice and security. I nevertheless intend to show that Thucydides believed that justice and security, and interest and ethics, could be reconciled at a more fundamental level; that substantively and instrumentally rational interests could not be constructed outside of the language of justice and the communities it enabled. His understanding was shared by other classical realists – Machiavelli, Clausewitz, Morgenthau – and is particularly pertinent to our time.

Heads of governments, institutions and companies routinely finesse moral dilemmas by convincing themselves that the ethical codes that govern personal behavior do not apply to behavior intended to advance or safeguard the organizations over which they have authority. This logic often goes unchallenged unless the behavior in question rebounds against the interests of stakeholders in the organization or the public at large. I open my book with a short story, "Nixon in Hell," that challenges this morality of convenience in the starkest way. It sets the stage for a more reflective consideration of the question in subsequent chapters that draws on the writings of classical realists, ancient and modern philosophers, and social scientists. This analysis, which makes for the case that justice enables interests, provides the foundation for a critique of post-Cold War American foreign policy.

Modernists, among them Joyce, Pound and Eliot, recognized that no single epoch had a monopoly on experience, understanding or wisdom. Recovery of the past was accordingly essential to human fulfillment. They embraced poetry as the appropriate vehicle for giving voice to events, feelings and language of the past to make them alive to us.[2] By doing so, they not only enriched our understanding of life, but offered vantage points from which to reflect on the present. I want to use the texts of classical realists for much the same purpose. By recapturing the perspectives,

[1] See, for example, Michael Walzer, "Political Action: The Problem of Dirty Hands," *Philosophy and Public Affairs*, 2 (Winter 1973), pp. 160–80; Christopher Gowens, *Moral Dilemmas* (Oxford: Oxford University Press, 1987); Peter Digesser, "Forgiveness and Politics: Dirty Hands and Imperfect Procedure," *Political Theory*, 26 (October 1998), pp. 700–24.

[2] Charles Taylor, *Sources of the Self: The Making of Modern Identity* (Cambridge, Mass.: Harvard University Press, 1989), p. 465; James Longenbach, *Modernist Poetics of History: Pound, Eliot, and the Sense of the Past* (Princeton: Princeton University Press, 1987), ch. 10.

emotions and language of Thucydides, Clausewitz and Morgenthau, I hope to enrich our understanding of politics and, more generally, of the post-Cold War world. This task is critical because the conceptual language of modern realism has become so impoverished that it almost precludes asking, let alone answering, some of the most important questions about our interests, the nature of influence and the dangers and opportunities that hegemonic powers confront.

Like the modernists – who here, hark back to Plato – I envisage all forms of expression and inquiry as parts of the broader human project of understanding whose ultimate purpose is to help us lead the good life. Compartmentalization of knowledge obviously has its practical benefits, but it also involves a price that we may not fully appreciate. The metatheme of my book is the need – and benefits – of escaping from parochial perspectives; in this case, by bridging to the humanities and creative arts and using their insights to reflect back upon problems that we consider within the purview of social science. I hope to show that by getting outside of our customary language and related concepts we can develop a new understanding of the nature and sources of cooperation and order, domestic and international.

Chapter 2 provides a more detailed overview of my argument and describes the structure of the book. As the chapter that follows is a short story, I thought it imperative to say something in advance about the nature of my project, why it is appropriate to begin with a work of fiction and how it helps to set up my subsequent inquiry. Let me conclude with a few mundane words about sources and transliteration.

I transliterate the Greek directly into English, not via Latin as was formerly done. So nature is rendered *phusis*, not *physis*. The exception is for the Greek letter 'chi', represented by 'ch' as in *technē*. For most proper names I use the Latin transliteration (e.g., Achilles not Achilleus, Ajax not Aias, Cimon not Kimon), as they are more familiar to the reader. Quotes and references to Homer and Herodotus refer to the book and chapter, and in the case of Thucydides to book, chapter and line. Citations to Plato's dialogues give the section (number) and subsection (letter). This is the standard form in Greek texts and in most English translations. With Aristotle, I also follow the standard numbering procedure. *Politics* 1253a2–3 refers to section 1253, "a" to the subsection, and 2–3 to the lines. Fragments from pre-Socratics, unless otherwise noted, are cited in the form they are given in the "Diels–Krantz" bilingual Greek–German edition, the most comprehensive collection.[3] Fragments are identified by author and number and are followed by the letters A or B. B fragments

[3] Hermann Diels and Walther Kranz, *Die Fragmente der Vorsakratiker*, 7th ed. (Berlin: Weidmannsche Verlagsbuchhandlung, 1956).

are considered by Diels and Krantz to be actual texts and translations. A fragments are paraphrases. Most of the numerous English quotations from Thucydides are from the Richard Crawley translation as reproduced in the *Landmark Thucydides*.[4]

[4] Robert B. Strassler, ed., *The Landmark Thucydides: A Comprehensive Guide to the Peloponnesian War* (New York: Free Press,1996).

Acknowledgments

This book has been a stretch for me. I had to reach out to other fields and disciplines to reconstruct the thought of three representatives of what I call the classical realist tradition. Colleagues in classics, Greek literature, history, political theory and philosophy were extraordinarily forthcoming. They helped with translation and transliteration, bibliography and interpretation and provided useful commentary on successive drafts. There is no way I could have written this book without their knowledge, interest and extraordinary generosity. So heartfelt thanks to June Allison, John Champlin, Val Dusek, Peter Euben, Claudio Fogu, Victor Hanson, Bruce Heiden, Holger Herwig, Jim Murphy, Nick Onuf, Allan Silverman, Niall Slater, and Barry Strauss. And extra special thanks to Dorry Noyes who nurtured, watered and pruned, when necessary, my growth as a humanist.

I began this project when I was director of the Mershon Center at Ohio State University. Like salmon swimming upstream, my colleagues and I struggled against powerful University currents to transform Mershon into an open, collegial, anti-hierarchical, collaborative and interdisciplinary enterprise. For a while, we succeeded, and I would like to acknowledge the effort, unflagging spirit and good-will of my still, for the most part, unindicted co-conspirators. They include Richard Herrmann, then associate and now director of the Center, Matthew Keith, assistant director, Oded Shenker (business), Judy Andrews (Chinese Studies), David Hahm (classics), Steve Cecchetti, Eric Fisher and Nori Hashimoto (economics), Dorothy Noyes, Army Shuman and Chris Zacher (English), Alex Stephan (Germanic Languages), Claudio Fogu, Allan Millett and Geoffrey Parker (history), Mary Ellen O'Connell (law), Allan Silverman (philosophy), Tim Frye, Dick Gunter, Clarissa Hayward, Ted Hopf, Bill Liddle, John Mueller, Brian Pollins, Don Sylvan (political science), Marilynn Brewer and Phil Tetlock (psychology), Ed Crenshaw, Richard Hamilton and Craig Jenkins (sociology) and Halina Stephan (Slavic Studies). Visitors and post-doctoral fellows also made a major contribution to the Center, and I would like to express special appreciation for the contribution made by Steve Bernstein, Manu Castano, Pete Furia, Azar Gat, Ofer Feldman Hatani, Wulf Kansteiner, Fritz Kratochwil, Steve Remy, Norrin Ripsman and Niall Slater and Peter Suedfeld.

I was fortunate to escape from my administrative responsibilities to spend a month in residence at the Rockefeller Conference Center in Bellagio and a quarter in the political science department of the University of California at Irvine. I am grateful to Susan Garfield and the Rockefeller Foundation fo their support, and to the intellectual stimulation and companionship I found at Bellagio from Elizabeth Neuffer, Daniel Javits, Dick and Debbie Samuels, Przemyslaw Urbanczyk and my wife, Carol Bohmer. Elizabeth, a reporter for the Boston Globe, was tragically killed while covering the war in Iraq. For making my stay in Irvine so pleasant, productive and intellectually challenging, I am especially indebted to David Easton, Cecelia Lynch, Kristi Monore, Pat Morgan, Mark Petracca, Shaun Rosenberg, Etel Solingen, Wayne Sandholtz and my former Cornell colleagues, Robin and Marguerite Williams.

Colleagues at these institutions and elsewhere also provided useful thoughts and commentary on my project and manuscript. In this connection, I would like to thank Pete Furia, Ted Hopf, Peter Katzenstein, Fritz Kratochwil, David Lebow, Cecelia Lynch, John Mueller, Brian Pollins, Pat Morgan, Shawn Rosenberg, Wayne Sandholdz and Janice Stein. In the course of writing the manuscript I was invited to present various chapters as talks at colloquia at Columbia, Dartmouth, Georgetown, New Mexico State University and the University of California at Berkeley and Irvine. Colleagues and students at these several institutions provided thoughtful feedback and much-needed encouragement. The Dickey Center at Dartmouth organized an afternoon seminar around my manuscript, where I received extraordinarily thoughtful criticism from Jenny Lind, Gene Lyons, Mike Mastanduno, Jim Murphy, Daryl Press, Alan Stam and guest participants Val Dusek, Chris Harth and Martin Heisler. Joe Lepgold, my host at Georgetown, good-natured friend and thoughtful critic, subsequently died with his family in a fire in a Paris hotel. Joe, you are missed.

I finished the manuscript during and after my move to Dartmouth. I have already acknowledged the assistance of those new colleagues who attended the Dickey seminar. In addition, I received very thoughtful feedback from Rogers Masters and Lucas Swaine. I also want to thank chairs Dick Winters and Mike Mastanduno and Deans Richard Wright and Jamshed Barucha for their tactful recruitment and warm welcome to the campus.

John Haslam of Cambridge University Press, who expressed interest in my manuscript well before I had anything to show him on paper, was extraordinarily helpful at every step of the process from writing to publication. I am also indebted to Sheila Kane, who did the most thoughtful and professional job of editing my manuscript. Thanks too to Ann Powers, my former assistant at the Mershon Center, Pat Glenn, former systems director, and Kathleen Donald, administrative assistant in the Dartmouth Department of Government, all of whom rendered invaluable technical and administrative assistance.

Finally, I acknowledge with enormous pleasure the support and love of my family. Carol, my wife, Kate, my daughter, my two sons, David and Eli, and my son-in-law, Andrew remain my toughest critics and my biggest supporters. And a big kiss to my granddaughter Naomi, working on her first article: "the."

1 Nixon in hell

Hell was nothing like Richard Nixon thought it would be, not that he had thought much about it when he was "upside." That was the term everyone here used to describe the world in which they had once lived. It was an ironic reference to the ancient and erroneous belief that Hell was subterranean. As far as anyone could figure out, it wasn't anywhere in relation to earth. But in every other way it was undeniably the "downside," so the term stuck.

On the few occasions that Nixon had thought about Hell – usually during interminable church services that presidents feel compelled to attend – he imagined fire and brimstone and little red devils with spears and evil grins, swishing their tails in delight when they made tortured souls writhe in agony. Hell may once have been like that – opinion among "lifers" was divided – but over the centuries it had evolved to reflect lessons the devil and his assistants had learned from observing life on earth. Not that they lacked imagination, but when it came to torture, human beings showed an ingenuity and dedication that the devil found inspiring. So Hell was frequently remodeled to take advantage of the latest in human innovation. Some time back, the devil had installed an ornate, wrought-iron gate with the words *Arbeit macht frei* [work makes you free] across the top. Scuttlebutt had it that his assistants were now upgrading modules to incorporate the latest in computer graphics technology. Virtual torture would free more assistants for administrative tasks, always a crushing burden in eras of extraordinary growth.

Nixon entered Hell through the devil's gate, and being a well-read man, understood its significance all too well. Inside, his attention was drawn to an officer in a smartly tailored SS uniform barking out orders to *Kapos* – prisoners who worked for the camp authorities in return for special privileges. They used their bull whips to separate terrified newcomers into two groups and herd them off in different directions. Nixon and about twenty other souls were marched off through the mud to one of the hundreds of squat, wooden barracks that formed a grid on the seemingly endless plain. The sky was gray and the fast moving, low clouds gave the camp something of a two-dimensional quality. Dressed in a tropical weight suit Nixon began to shiver.

The barracks smelled something fierce, but they were warm. The SS guard escorting them shouted something in German that Nixon did not understand. An old man, lying on one of the bottom bunks, looked up and explained in heavily accented English that Nixon was expected to undress and change into one of the blue and white striped uniforms stacked in two neat piles in a corner of the barracks. Nixon looked around and saw a few of his group beginning to shed their clothes. He had always been uncomfortable about undressing in front of other people, and in his student days had usually managed to find some ruse to avoid changing in locker rooms. The whip exploded in the air in front of Nixon's face and involuntarily he jumped back in fright. The guard shouted at him, and Nixon took off his jacket and fumbled with his tie.

The two-piece uniform was stiff and uncomfortable, but had been freshly laundered. The pants were too tight, and the jacket was at least two sizes too large. The contrast with his argyle socks and supple Italian shoes was striking. The old man told him that the bunk above his was unoccupied, and that he should take it. To Nixon, all the bunks looked unoccupied, but then he realized that nobody came here with luggage or personal effects. He wondered how he would brush his teeth; he looked around and noticed there was no sink.

"Where do I wash up?" he asked.

The old man smiled. "You don't."

"What did I do to deserve this? I'm not a Jew! Why have they sent me here? There must have been a mistake . . . unless one of those reporters was responsible for this."

"Relax," the old man said. "Nobody here is Jewish or Gypsy. Beelzebub is sadistic but not insensitive."

"Or else he has a wicked sense of humor," volunteered another man.

Nixon turned to address him. "What do you mean?"

"Think about it," he said. "No Jews or Sinta, but a permanent work force of former guards or petty officials at Nazi concentration camps, or people somehow connected with Hitler's campaigns of extermination. They are treated like shit, and there's no hope of liberation." He shook his head. "Endless cycles of hard labor and beatings. Freezing in the winter, roasting in the summer."

"I'd slit my throat," Nixon volunteered.

"You can't," the second man said. That's the beauty of it. Nobody dies here, because you're already dead! There's no way out unless they ship you off somewhere."

Nixon's voice grew animated. "You mean some people leave here alive?"

"Alive? Let's not get into that one. But yes, people, most of them, leave. The place looks like Auschwitz–Birkenau, but it is a processing center, not a death camp. Most new arrivals stay here no longer than a week or two. They get shoved into cattle cars for resettlement elsewhere."

Nixon gave him a quizzical look. "So it's Auschwitz in reverse?"

"More or less. It's a devilishly clever scheme, don't you agree?"

The conversation was interrupted by the return of the other inhabitants of the barracks. They passed through the door one at a time, trudged across its floor of bare wooden planking and sought out their bunks in silence. Nixon looked at them in horror.

"It's OK," said the old man reading his thoughts. "They're sinners like you and me."

"Sinners, you say?"

"Mass murderers."

"Murderers? I'm not a murderer!"

The door opened again and a detail of *Kapos* pushed through a wheelbarrow that contained two large, covered, metal cauldrons. Inmates rose from their bunks, grabbed their tin bowls and quickly lined up to be served a thin gruel and chunks of stale, pale-gray-colored bread. Nixon was hungry but revolted by the smell of the gruel and could not bring himself to go through the chow line. He stood in front of his bunk thinking about suppers on his terrace overlooking the Pacific. "What I wouldn't give for a bowl of cottage cheese and ketchup!" he said to himself.

The old man consumed his gruel with enthusiasm and used a piece of bread to soak up whatever liquid was left in the bottom of his bowl. Nixon watched him in amazement. Just like an animal, he thought. The old man popped the last piece of bread into his mouth and replaced his empty bowl on a nail sticking out from the side of his bunk. Nixon waited from him to get into his bunk before resuming their conversation.

"You said this is a camp for mass murderers?"

"That's right. Everyone here is guilty of it in some way, directly or indirectly. I could have saved Jews during the Holocaust. The man who spoke to you earlier helped to plan the fire bombing of Tokyo." The old man pointed to the bunk above Heinrich. "They're inseparable buddies."

"I didn't kill anybody!"

"Nobody wants to think of himself as a murderer."

A *Kapo* arrived with a footstool and positioned it under one of four naked bulbs that provided illumination to the windowless barracks. He had to unscrew each bulb from its socket; they were very hot and he could only give them a quick twist before removing his hand. It took five or six tries before the first bulb flickered and went out. The *Kapo* blew on his fingers to ease the pain before moving the stool into position under the next bulb. When the barracks was dark, the *Kapo* left, and Nixon heard the sound of a padlock being attached to the door.

"They lock us in for the night?" he asked the old man.

"Not that there's anywhere to go."

"What if I have to go to the bathroom? I have a weak bladder."

"You'd better learn to control it."

"There's no john in the barracks?"

"I think you should go to bed," the old man said.

Nixon gingerly raised his foot and put it on the wooden frame of the old man's bunk to get a better purchase on his own bunk. He grabbed the side board above and tried twice without success to pull himself up. He waited to catch his breath before trying again.

The old man suggested that he grab one end of the frame and hook his leg over the other end. "Then you should be able to pull yourself up and roll over on to the mattress."

"Maybe I'll just sleep on the floor."

"Go ahead . . . if you don't mind the rats."

Nixon thought about this for a minute, and decided to give it one more try. He followed the old man's instructions and after some effort made it into the bunk. He eased his tired body on to the lumpy, straw-filled mattress. There was no pillow.

The days that followed were miserable. Nixon was infested with lice and fleas, and scratching his bites only made them itch more. He ate nothing for two days and tried to ignore his hunger pangs. On the third day, cramps and severe stomach pains forced him into the chow line. He had been assigned to a work team that dug holes for the foundations of new barracks. It was back-breaking work, especially for somebody out of shape and suffering from phlebitis. After his first fifteen minutes of digging, he thought he was going to faint. He let his shovel drop and tried to steady himself while gasping for air. One of the *Kapos* in charge of the work detail, a round-faced Asian, shouted at him in a language Nixon thought might be Chinese. He understood that he was supposed to resume work, but he was unable to move. The *Kapo* addressed him again and then lashed out with his coiled whip. Nixon felt its leather tip draw across his buttocks and was then overcome by an intense burning sensation. Somehow, his body found the energy to bend down to pick up the shovel.

Nixon struggled to come to terms with his situation. At first he hoped it was just a particularly vivid nightmare. He gave that idea up after being abruptly awakened from a real dream the next morning by a *Kapo* marching through the barracks shaking a cow bell. He was mustered out of his bunk and the barracks and marched to the common latrine and showers. No dream, he decided, could have a smell so ugly and penetrating.

Nixon responded with anger. The devil had no right to punish him this way. He was not a mass murderer; character assassination was his biggest sin. If he was here, where were Kennedy and Johnson? Those two were real criminals, he told himself. Kennedy had stolen the White House from him in 1960 by having the Daley machine stuff all those ballot boxes in Cook County. He was a fool for persuading his supporters that it was against the national interest to challenge the election in the courts. And that egomaniac Johnson dragged the country into a useless war in Vietnam. It took him and Henry four years to get out with honor, and we would have done it sooner too if those [expletive deleted] Democrats hadn't stirred up the hippies and tried to block our every move in Congress. Nixon began to think that Kennedy had bested him again. He had carefully cultivated his relationship with Billy Graham, but the Kennedy clan had all those cardinals eating out of their hands, even the Vatican. Maybe they got the pope to pull strings to send him here? Just the kind of thing they would do!

Nixon was also unhappy about the way he was being treated in Hell. Maybe he was a sinner, although assuredly not a murderer, but he was also a VIP. Nobody had met him at the gate, not that he expected old Lucifer himself. But the devil could have sent a couple of his chief assistants. Brezhnev must be here – Mao too. The thought was strangely comforting. He would have to ask them what kind of reception they had received. He wondered how they were holding up; he had difficulty imagining either of them digging ditches. For the first time since he had entered Hell, Nixon broke into a grin.

The old man with the Italian accent aside, nobody had briefed him about Hell. That would have been one of the perks of VIP treatment. He allowed himself to remember how attentive, well-dressed assistants and officers in crew cuts and perfectly pressed uniforms had fawned over him, anxiously soliciting his approval for memos, schedules and itineraries, even what to serve at state dinners. In Hell he was anonymous and powerless. Nobody deferred to him or told him anything, unless it was an order, and then it was usually barked in German or Chinese. Once Nixon had screwed up his courage to talk back. He had demanded that the *Kapo* marching his group off to a work site take him to whoever was in charge. The *Kapo* told him to shut up – or so Nixon assumed from his tone of voice – but he continued to insist that he speak to someone in authority. The *Kapo* shrugged his shoulders and summoned a colleague to take over the work detail. He led Nixon off in a different direction to a small hut at some distance from any of the barracks. Nixon rehearsed the speech he would make, but never got the chance. Two *Kapos* appeared from nowhere with and began to beat him with rubber hoses. Nixon remembered absorbing a number of painful blows before losing consciousness.

After his beating, Nixon withdrew from camp life as much as possible and sought refuge in memories of pleasant upside moments. He went through the motions of morning ablution, work, meals, free time, until he found release in sleep. His social interactions were limited to perfunctory conversations with the old man. Inner exile helped Nixon to preserve his dignity, and he almost convinced himself that reality was his mental reveries, not servitude in a concentration camp. Every afternoon when his work detail finished, Nixon always managed to lead the procession back to the barracks. He would walk smartly up the steps and nod his head ever so slightly in acknowledgment to an imaginary band leader who struck up "Hail to the Chief" as soon as the president came into view.

Nixon's coping strategy was ultimately defeated by curiosity. He had an alert and inquiring mind that could only be suppressed for so long. It surreptitiously stored and processed information from his new environment, awaiting a propitious moment to intrude on his inner self. Nixon was vaguely aware that part of his mind was insubordinate and impossible to control fully. He nicknamed this corner of his mind "Henry," and chose to tolerate it as long as it did not interfere with his fantasy life. This uneasy accommodation lasted for some time; Nixon really did not know for how long, nor did he care. Time's arrow was a tool used by the mind to order memories and expectations to cope with the world that Nixon had rejected.

He was brought back to reality by recognition of a familiar face. He had been digging an irrigation trench alongside a newly constructed barracks when another work detail passed by struggling to push wheelbarrows laden with bags of cement across the damp and uneven ground. The high-pitched scraping sound of the wheels was as penetrating as it was unpleasant, and Nixon involuntarily looked up to identify the source of the annoyance. His subconscious mind registered the scene and the face of the *Kapo* hurrying the work detail along and filed it away for subsequent analysis. Later that afternoon Nixon was resting in his bunk having just finished a long replay of the banquet Mao Tse-tung had held in his honor in the Great Hall of the People. He had not enjoyed the food – too much spice and too many vegetables – but he reveled in being the center of attention, not only of Mao, but of the entire world. He was especially pleased that Mao had directed most of his questions about America to him rather than to Henry, and that this had been picked up by the press.

Nixon's mind went blank while his memory banks uploaded scenes from his favorite film, *Around the World in Eighty Days*. His subconscious chose this moment to intervene, and signaled Nixon that it had sighted someone he knew. Nixon summoned up the image of the work detail in preference to the movie. The *Kapo's* face was indeed familiar, but he could not put a name to it. He had never been good at recalling names, and it was always more difficult to do so when he encountered people out of context. Nixon wondered if anyone would recognize him. He had grown leaner, and as far as he could tell – there was no mirror in the barracks – he had lost most of his double chin. For some reason, neither his hair nor nails had grown, and he pulled his fingers across his cheek to confirm that his skin was smooth and lacking his tell-tale afternoon stubble. For the next hour or so he played over the scene in his mind's eye. The long, angular face with deep-set eyes was definitely somebody he knew from his political past, when they were both much younger, he thought. It bothered him that he could not identify the man, and decided to do what he could to get another glimpse of him.

To do this, Nixon had to take a more active interest in camp life and began to engage the old man in more animated discussion.

"I was worried about you," the old man confided.

"About me?," Nixon asked.

"Yes. A lot of people never come out of withdrawal. They don't want to face the truth."

"What truth?"

"You need to find the answer to that yourself, my son."

Nixon began to wonder if he was the only sane person in the barracks. He absent-mindedly plucked a louse from beneath his shirt and calmly crushed it between his fingers. "How long have you been here old man?"

"Not very long. Twenty or thirty years. I don't rightly know."

"You don't know?"

"No. It's not important."

Nixon pondered his answer and decided not to pursue the line of questioning any further in the expectation that he would find any clarification even more depressing. Instead, he guided the conversation toward the camp and the work detail he had witnessed that morning. He learned that it contained upward of 50,000 souls, who provided the labor force used to maintain and expand the camp. Ever since he had arrived, the old man explained, expansion had been under way, and there were rumors that this was only one of many concentration camps.

Nixon still hoped he might be one of the fortunate people in transit. Where would they send him? He remembered a newspaper column by that bastard Buchwald that proposed he be sentenced to an eternity in high school as punishment for Watergate. That would be just fine, he thought. There would be no back-breaking labor in high school, but recesses and hot school lunches. He salivated at the thought of the latter. Were there still hot lunches, or was it one of the programs his administration had cut? Nixon felt an unusual pang of guilt.

The old man interrupted his reverie. "If you were in transit, you would have been out of here already. You're one of us."

"What do you mean, one of us?"

"I told you when you first arrived. Everyone here is guilty in some way of mass murder."

"Now let me say this about that. . . ."

The old man raised his hand with an air of practiced authority and Nixon stopped in mid-sentence.

"As far as I can tell," the old man explained in a matter-of-fact tone of voice, "we have been divided into three groups. The largest number of people are those who abetted mass murder indirectly. They are people like Lou, who knew at the time it was wrong to calculate the distribution of incendiaries most likely to create a massive firestorm over Tokyo. Or, Hwang-ho, who, for a small bribe, told the Chinese authorities where anti-communist refugees were hiding. They were all slaughtered. There's even the odd spy who sold or gave away secrets that led to peoples' deaths. They work as laborers or do chores around the camp, like serving food and doing laundry."

"Laundry," Nixon said. "I've been in these clothes since I arrived. They're absolutely filthy!"

"*Piano, piano*," the old man said, using his mother tongue with Nixon for the first time. "Everything here takes time, and you have lots of it before you."

At a loss for words, Nixon looked down at his feet. His favorite shoes were all but unrecognizable. If only he had known, he would have been buried in Goretex-lined hiking boots. The Egyptians had the right idea, he thought. They buried their dead with everything they were expected to need in the afterlife, although sandals would not last long here. He wondered why he had seen no Egyptians; everybody here was modern, although they came from every corner of the globe. In due course, he would have to ask the old man.

"Some people ultimately leave; where they go I don't know." The old man made the sign of the cross. "The second group consists of people who actually committed atrocities. They do hard labor; I explained that to you earlier. The third group are the most serious offenders. They ordered or planned mass murder, or, like me, were in a position to stop it at little risk to themselves and failed to do so. They spend some time as *Kapos*, and are compelled to beat and torture other inmates."

"What sort of punishment is that?," Nixon asked.

"Think about it," the old man suggested. "For the most part these are people who see themselves, or used to anyway, as decent, even god-fearing folk. Many of them were caring parents, respectful of their neighbors and invariably kind to their pets. Did you ever notice that people are on the whole kinder to animals than they are to each other? Even when we slaughter animals for food, we try to do it as quickly and painlessly as possible."

"There are animal activists who would disagree," Nixon suggested.

"I know. There are people here who killed people to protect animals. Also people who killed to prevent abortion."

"You were telling me about punishment," Nixon reminded the old man.

"You're right, I digress. But there's really no reason to hurry. Some mass murderers are Sadists. But most are not, and pride themselves on having led exemplary lives. The violence they committed was never first-hand, so it was easy for them to deny responsibility. To the extent they thought about it, they convinced themselves they were merely cogs in the wheel or, if they were near to the apex of authority, that their behavior was compelled by reasons of state."

"It often is."

The old man ignored Nixon's comment. "Here in Hell, they get the opportunity to experience violence first-hand."

"I know. I've been beaten."

"No, you still don't understand. *You* get to beat people."

"What do you mean?," Nixon asked.

"In due course, they'll teach you to beat and torture people without doing too much damage to their internal organs. Just like medical school, you practice on dummies before you do it to real people."

"You're kidding!"

"I never joke," the old man said. "I wish I could. I think I would have had a happier life."

"I'm not known for my sense of humor either."

The old man lowered his voice, not that anybody was listening. "You get to beat other inmates, usually with truncheons or rubber hoses, but sometimes with your bare fists."

"I couldn't do that."

"Oh yes, you can," the old man insisted. "You will not only pummel people but burn them with cigarettes and shock them with cattle prods and metal clamps you attach to their nipples and testicles."

"I'll refuse!"

The old man shook his head and regarded Nixon with a look of pity. "It won't work. I said no at first. They frog-marched me to the outskirts of the camp and forced me into a hole just wide enough to accommodate me standing up. They kept me there for two days, without food or water, while water seeped in up to the level of my knees. I was still recalcitrant, so they thrashed me. I held out until they explained how they were going to force a glass catheter up my urethra and then manhandle my penis so that the catheter splintered into numerous fragments. They said the pain would be excruciating for years to come whenever I urinated."

Nixon shuddered and tried to push from his mind the image of a glass tube being rammed up his penis. He wouldn't even wish such a fate on the owners of the *Washington Post*.

The old man shook his head. "I even lack the courage to be a martyr. So I agreed to do what they wanted. At first it wasn't too awful. I worked over some newcomers with hoses. I tried not to hit them too hard, but the *Kapos* saw that I was holding back and threatened me with the catheter unless I lashed out with all my strength. It was awful. I beat the victims into unconsciousness."

"I know what that feels like," Nixon said.

"Believe me, it's pretty terrible on the giving end too. I thought they would let me go after a few beatings, but it only got worse. Each time I was pushed into doing something worse. They made me do unspeakable things." The old man crossed himself again.

"How long did this go on?"

"I don't know. In the end, they had me garrotte a young man until his face turned blue and he collapsed. They told me I had killed him."

Nixon frowned. "I thought you said nobody died here?"

The old man shrugged his shoulders. "Every night I see his contorted face with his tongue sticking out and hear the gurgling sound he made as he struggled unsuccessfully to draw in air. Now I know what it means to be a murderer."

Hard labor, simple food and the absence of coffee and alcohol had worked wonders for Nixon's body. He had lost weight and his blood circulation had improved. He had also became increasingly inured to the fleas and lice that colonized his mattress and hair, and rarely bothered to scratch his bites. That night, Nixon lay awake in his bunk – into which he now easily climbed – thinking about what the old man had told him. He did not want to torture anybody, and he certainly did not want it done to him.

The next morning Nixon gave a perfunctory hello to the old man, and was relieved to throw himself into the numbing mindlessness of hard, physical labor. The work went quickly and Nixon was not the least perturbed by the rain that splattered him during a brief late morning shower. He wondered if the devil was able to control the weather. The winter season was perennially gray with only rare glimpses of the sun. It rained or snowed almost every day; never enough to make work impossible, but enough to keep the ground wet and muddy and make work difficult. Nixon kept a sharp lookout for the *Kapo* he had seen the day before. He was absolutely certain it was somebody he knew.

When Nixon returned to the barracks he found the old man lying in his bunk and anxious to resume their conversation. He decided to do his best to keep it away from the topic of the previous evening. The old man must have sensed his anxiety, and to Nixon's relief, talked about his adjustment to the routine of Hell.

"Most of the men here miss women," he told Nixon, "but I've never been troubled by their absence in the camp. I was a priest and celibate even when I was young."

"I don't miss women either. But I do miss my wife. She did a good job of looking after me and never judged me. I'm glad she's not here. I wouldn't want her to see me now."

"What do you miss?

"Music. Music and books. I played the piano. I wasn't great, but I played well enough to enjoy it, show tunes and the like. Life – or whatever this is – is going to be Hell without music."

"Nietzsche said there is no life without music." The old man reached up with his right hand to scratch his bald pate. "Little did he know."

"I had no idea Nietzsche said anything like that. I always thought of him as one of those nihilists."

"There is that side of him," the old man conceded.

"Damn...". Nixon stopped himself. "I probably shouldn't say that here."

The old man chuckled. "I don't think it can do you any harm."

"What I meant to say, is that I may have an eternity in front of me without music and books. I might enjoy reading Nietzsche, and certainly all the history and literature I never had time for upside. I'd give anything for a good book... especially if it were printed in large type."

"Don't be so sure," the old man said. He turned his back on Nixon and reached around and behind his mattress to pull out a bible. Nixon could tell immediately what it was from the gold cross embossed on the black, pseudo-leather cover.

The old man held it out to Nixon to inspect. "They gave me this a couple of days before they took me off for torture training."

Nixon took the bible and stared at it for several seconds. He wiped one hand and then the other on the cleanest part of his pants before fingering its pages. It would not have been his first choice of books, but he was overjoyed to see any book – a sign of the life he once knew. Tears welled up in his eyes.

"May I read it?"

"Of course. How could a priest refuse anyone a bible? Just be furtive about it. I don't know how the *Kapos* would respond if they caught you with it. You'd better stash it under your mattress."

"What about you? Don't you want to read it?"

"Not really. It's another one of the devil's little jokes."

"I don't understand."

The old man swallowed hard and scrunched up his leathery face. "I was a priest. I rose to a position of high authority in the church during difficult times. Secularism and materialism were luring people away from the faith, and much of Europe fell into the hands of two Godless regimes that had declared war on Christianity. Italy was occupied by the Germans in September 1943, and the Bolsheviks were advancing daily in the East. The Church had no choice but to reach some accommodation with the Germans, and I thought them the lesser of the two evils."

"Statesmanship requires compromise," Nixon said.

"I went too far. In looking after the interests of the Church I lost sight of the principles on which it was based." The old man paused, and Nixon stood silently shifting his weight from foot to foot waiting to see if he would continue.

The old man braced himself against the bunk frame and resumed his story. "Not long after the Germans occupied Rome the order came from Berlin to round up and deport the city's Jews. Many of them sought refuge in the Vatican, and I only allowed in those who had converted to Christianity, had a Christian parent or were somehow well connected or otherwise useful. In October the SS put 1,023 Jews on a train destined for here, for Auschwitz-Birkenau. Two of my associates pleaded with me to join them and stand in front of the train in our robes and miters in protest. They insisted that the Nazis would never dare move the train in our presence, and that our action would galvanize opposition to them all over Italy. I said no, and forbade them to take any action by themselves. I made only the weakest protest to the German ambassador. I later learned that the SS had orders to back off from any deportations if the Vatican expressed any serious opposition. All the people on the train died, and some of them were only children." The old man crossed himself.[1]

"You can see why I don't want to look at the bible, let alone read it. All it does it remind me of my moral failings. Perhaps one day when I have come to terms with my guilt I will be able to take solace in the good book again."

Nixon realized that he was still holding the bible, and not wanting to give his friend any offence, reached over to stash it under his mattress. He noticed several bed bugs jump when he lifted up the corner of the mattress. He turned back to face the old man but was at a loss for words.

His embarrassment was only momentary, because the door of the barracks opened and he and the old man looked across to see a *Kapo* enter. As the *Kapo* walked under one of the light bulbs, Nixon got a good look at his face. A chill ran down his spine and beads of sweat instantly appeared on his hands and forehead. It was the *Kapo* he had seen yesterday, and now Nixon knew who it was. He approached his bunk, smiled and handed him a book. Without thinking, Nixon reached out to accept it. By the time he had second thoughts and tried to withdraw his arm, it drew back with the book clasped in his hand. Alger Hiss turned on his heels and strode out of the barracks.[2] Nixon stood motionless and watched him depart. After the door banged shut, he looked down at the book. It was a cloth edition of William Shawcross, *Sideshow: Kissinger, Nixon and the Destruction of Cambodia*. Its dog-eared, red dust jacket had a picture of a B-52 disgorging packets of cluster bombs.

[1] For sources concerning Pope Pius XII and the Holocaust, see Susan Zuccotti, *Under His Very Window: The Vatican and the Holocaust in Italy* (New Haven: Yale University Press, 2000), and *The Italians and the Holocaust: Persecution, Rescue, and Survival* (Lincoln: University of Nebraska Press, 1996); Michael Phayer, *The Catholic Church and the Holocaust, 1930–1965* (Bloomington: University of Indiana Press, 2000); John Cornwell, *Hitler's Pope: The Secret History of Pius XII* (New York: Viking, 199).

[2] For the information of younger or non-American readers, Alger Hiss was a high-level State Department official convicted of perjury in 1950. The original charge against Hiss, made during hearings before the House Committee on Un-American Activities in 1948, was that he was a communist agent. Richard Nixon, then a freshman Congressman from California, played an important role in these hearings and later efforts to pillory and try Hiss. Nixon used his campaign against Hiss and other alleged communists to attract national attention, and later admitted that he never would have been tapped for the vice-presidency had it not been for the Hiss affair.

2 Tragedy and politics

> The great events, they are not our loudest, but our stillest hours. Not around the inventors of new noises, but around the inventors of new values does the world revolve. It revolves inaudibly.
>
> Friedrich Nietzsche[1]

Many readers may feel uneasy about dispatching Richard Nixon and Pope Pius XII to hell, and to its innermost circle at that. In the Western world, there is a widely accepted distinction between public and private morality. We consider it wrong to lie, but smile knowingly when we first hear the old adage that a diplomat is an honest man who lies to foreigners in the interest of his country. But how do we feel about leaders who lie to their own people in the name of national security, or actively support murderous dictatorships because they are anti-communist or protect American interests? Is any action defensible if it enhances national security or the national interest? And how do we know what they are? Is the distinction between public and private morality a useful, perhaps necessary, one in a world where hostile forces plot our destruction? Or, is it merely a convenient rationalization for unscrupulous and self-serving behavior?

Realism purports to have answers to these questions, or at least a framework for thinking intelligently about them. Modern realism, derived from the seminal mid-century works of E. H. Carr, Frederick Schumann, John Herz and Hans J. Morgenthau, has been the dominant paradigm in international relations for the last fifty years.[2] Realism comes in a variety of flavors, but its adherents acknowledge a core set of assumptions. First and foremost, is the anarchic character of the international environment that makes international relations a self-help system in which survival ultimately depends on a state's material capabilities and alliances with other

[1] Friedrich W. Nietzsche, *Thus Spake Zarathustra* (New York: 1924), p. 158.

[2] Frederick L. Schumann, *International Politics: An Introduction to the Western State System* (New York: McGraw-Hill, 1933); E. H. Carr, *The Twenty Years Crisis, 1919–1939: An Introduction to the Study of International Relations* (New York: St. Martin's Press, 1952 [1946]); Hans J. Morgenthau, *Politics Among Nations: The Struggle for Power and Peace* (New York: Alfred A. Knopf, 1948).

states.[3] Robert Gilpin, a leading realist theorist, explains that this does not imply a world of constant warfare, only the recognition that "there is no higher authority to which a state can appeal for succor in times of trouble."[4] It follows that states must make power a priority, but here realists disagree among themselves about whether states should conceive of their power in absolute or relative terms, that is, as a goal in and of itself or in comparison to the power of other states.[5] Because of their emphasis on the importance of power, many realists have tried to erect a firewall between foreign affairs and domestic politics in the tradition of European *Realpolitik*.[6] These same realists dismiss ethics as a form of weak sentimentality that has no business in the affairs of state.[7] International anarchy makes it a dog-eat-dog world in which states must convince others that they will behave like pit bulls if challenged.[8]

As currently formulated, there is no way to adjudicate between competing claims of ethics and security.[9] The demand for ethical foreign

[3] Kenneth N. Waltz, *Theory of International Politics* (Reading, Mass.: Addison-Wesley, 1979), pp. 103–04; Robert Gilpin, *Global Political Economy: Understanding the International Economic Order* (Princeton: Princeton University Press, 2001), p. 16, writes that "all realists share a few fundamental ideas such as the anarchic nature of the international system and the primacy of the state in international affairs."

[4] Gilpin, *Global Political Economy*, p. 17. Waltz, *Theory of International Politics*, p. 113, offers a more extreme characterization of the differences between domestic and international life: "In international politics force serves, not only as the *ultima ratio*, but indeed as the first and constant one."

[5] Waltz, *Theory of International Politics*; Joseph M. Grieco, *Cooperation Among Nations: Europe, America, and Non-Tariff Barriers to Trade* (Ithaca: Cornell University Press, 1990).

[6] The term *Realpolitik* was coined by disillusioned German liberals after the failure of the revolutions of 1848. It was intended to represent the polar opposite to Kant's idealist *noumena*, and was a reaction to the universal, rationalist criteria of the Enlightenment. The concept of the national interest can be traced back to Machiavelli, who wrote about *interesse* and *ragione di stato*. These terms gained wide currency in the sixteenth century. According to Friedrich Meinecke, *Die Idee der Staatsräson in der neuerer Geschichte* (Munich: Oldenbourg, 1924), p. 85, their use was indicative of a search for a "sophisticated, rational will, untroubled by passions and momentary impulses" that could guide state policy.

[7] Drawing on their reading of Thucydides, moderate realists like Michael Doyle, *Ways of War and Peace: Realism, Liberalism and Socialism* (New York: Norton, 1997), pp. 33, 83, acknowledge the importance of ethics, but insist that it must play a "constrained" role for "responsible heads of state."

[8] For a recent crude statement of this thesis, see Robert D. Kaplan, *Warrior Politics: Why Leadership Demands a Pagan Ethos* (New York: Random House, 2001).

[9] The distinction between ethics and security must be tempered by the recognition that physical safety and national security are ethical concerns, but not the only concerns of ethics. Nor is the contrast between ethics and interests strictly one of duties to others and to ourselves, for we also may be considered to have ethical duties to ourselves. The dilemma involved in the choice between moral action and behavior that may be necessary or advantageous to the community (violation of deontological principles for some other-regarding consequentialist end) is given thoughtful treatments by Cicero and Machiavelli. In our time, it is known as the problem of "dirty hands," after the communist leader in

policies is rebuffed by the assertion that physical security is the essential precondition for the kind of society that makes ethical life possible.[10] The counter-argument that one cannot produce or sustain an ethical society by immoral means provokes the rejoinder that international politics does not allow this kind of luxury. The argument quickly returns to its starting point. But are the imperatives of security really at odds with the canons of ethics? Is hard-nosed egoism the most efficient way of protecting one's interests in an intensely competitive world? If it can be shown that ethical behavior is more conducive – perhaps even essential – to national security, the advocates of *Realpolitik* could be challenged on their home turf. This is one aim of my book. I hope to persuade readers that ethics are not only instrumentally important, but that it is impossible to formulate interests intelligently outside of some language of justice. To do this, I turn to three of the foundational texts of realism in an attempt to show that "classical" realism, as represented by Thucydides, Carl von Clausewitz and Hans J. Morgenthau, was very much concerned with questions of justice. All three realists believed that it was essential, if only for practical reasons, that foreign policies conform to the ethical standards of their day.[11]

Realism is not just another arcane academic doctrine. As currently formulated, it offers an intellectual justification for a range of policies at odds with core democratic and humanitarian values. American presidents, secretaries of state and national security advisors have used – mostly in private or off-the-record – the language of realism to defend their least palatable policies: coups, bombings, interventions and support of oppressive dictatorships. Realism cannot be held directly responsible for any of these actions. The Cold War was the principal catalyst for what I shall call "expedient foreign policies," in the absence of a better term. In

Sartre's play of the same name. For recent discussions, see Michael Walzer, "Political Action: The Problem of Dirty Hands," *Philosophy and Public Affairs*, 2 (Winter 1973), pp. 160–80; Christopher Gowens, *Moral Dilemmas* (Oxford: Oxford University Press, 1987); Peter Digesser, "Forgiveness and Politics: Dirty Hands and Imperfect Procedure," *Political Theory*, 26 (October 1998), pp. 700–24.

[10] Chris Brown, "Ethics, Interests and Foreign Policy" in Karen E. Smith and Margot Light, *Ethics and Foreign Policy* (New York: Cambridge University Press, 2001), pp. 15–33, correctly points out that all sophisticated variants of realism see states as egoists in the last resort, but recognize that enlightened self-interest is not necessarily incompatible with a concern for principle and the common welfare. It is only what he calls "pop realism" that conceives of interests in terms of narrow *Machtpolitik*.

[11] The core of the book argues for a reformulation of the concept of security, but it also recognizes that ethics is equally problematic. Alasdair MacIntyre, *After Virtue*, 2nd ed. (Notre Dame, In.: University of Notre Dame Press, 1984), pp. 6–12, reminds us that there are numerous rival claims about the substance of ethics, and that this controversy is unresolvable for these competing sets of premises are based on different normative and evaluative concepts. Concepts of ethics are shaped by culture and historical experience and must be considered in context.

the immediate aftermath of World War II, US officials in Europe coopted Nazi war criminals to help them gather intelligence on communists, provided the necessary transportation and logistics for France to reestablish colonial rule in Indochina and looked the other way while its strongman in South Korea murdered or imprisoned his democratic opposition.

These initiatives, and others like them, took place more or less out of public view. Truman and Eisenhower administration officials were careful to couch major foreign policies like the Marshall Plan, NATO and intervention in South Korea in language they thought likely to evoke a positive response from the Congress and public opinion. Building and strengthening democracy and upholding the principle of collective security and the rule of law may not have motivated these initiatives, but they undeniably helped in garnering public support and winning the votes necessary for budget appropriations and treaty ratification. La Rochefoucauld observed that "hypocrisy is an homage that vice renders to virtue."[12] By justifying our behavior in terms of core values, we signal the importance of these values and may reinforce their legitimacy. Hypocrisy can become extreme and transparent, as it did during the war in Indochina, where the contrast between rhetoric and behavior demonstrated the centrality of these values at the same time as it undermined them. It would have been inconceivable for a president to have told the American people that he was intervening in Vietnam, not, as proclaimed, to save a "fledgling democracy," but to demonstrate resolve to Moscow. And it would have been equally out of the question for him to have unleashed an air war against North Vietnam in the absence of a pretext; in this case an attack against American destroyers that probably never took place. Mendacity helped to mobilize and initially sustain support for military intervention in Indochina. However, growing recognition of the contradiction between the proclaimed purpose of American intervention and its apparent character fueled a growing and ultimately successful anti-war movement.

In retrospect, Vietnam appears to have been the catalyst for an important transition in the evolution of American values. Hypocrisy is the hallmark of transitions. It is most pronounced when old values have broken down but are still honored publicly because the new values that guide behavior have not yet been articulated or legitimated. By the time the Cold War ended, self-interest had become a publicly acceptable goal and, in the realm of foreign policy, found ready expression and justification in the language of realism. This language has become so entrenched that it has

[12] La Rochefoucauld, *Maximes et Réflexions Diverses*, ed. Jean Lafond, 2nd ed. (Paris: Gallimard, 1976 [1665]), *Réflexion* 218, p. 79.

proven very difficult to gain public support for goals, like humanitarian intervention and economic development, that are neither intended to advance short-term economic interests nor cope with immediate threats to national security. In fifty years we have come full circle in our foreign policy discourse.

The Cold War ended more than a decade ago, but the discourse it empowered continues to exercise its hold over American foreign policy. The Clinton and Bush administrations have refracted almost every important foreign policy decision through the prism of narrow self-interest, and have had no compunction – quite the reverse – about publicly justifying their policies on this basis. In its first year in office, the Bush administration acted against the coordinated efforts of many of its closest allies, and often, a sizeable part of the world community, on fourteen issues ranging from its unilateral withdrawal from the Anti-Ballistic Missile Treaty to its scuttling of the 1997 Kyoto Protocol intended to forestall global warming.[13] The White House also evoked horror at home and abroad by broaching the possibility of using limited-yield nuclear weapons in

[13] In December 2001, the United States officially withdrew from the 1972 Anti-Ballistic Missile Treaty, gutting the landmark agreement. This is the first time in the nuclear era that the US renounced a major arms control accord; in July 2001 the US walked out of a London conference to discuss a 1994 protocol designed to strengthen the 1972 Biological and Toxin Weapons Convention (ratified by 144 nations including the United States) by providing for on-site inspections. At Geneva in November 2001, US Undersecretary of State John Bolton stated that "the protocol is dead," at the same time accusing Iraq, Iran, North Korea, Libya, Sudan and Syria of violating the Convention but offering no specific allegations or supporting evidence; in July 2001, the US was the only nation to oppose the UN Agreement to Curb the International Flow of Illicit Small Arms; in April 2001, the US was not reelected to the UN Human Rights Commission, after years of withholding dues to the UN (including current dues of $244 million) – and after having forced the UN to lower its share of the UN budget from 25 to 22 percent. In the Human Rights Commission, the US stood virtually alone in opposing resolutions supporting lower-cost access to HIV/AIDS drugs, acknowledging a basic human right to adequate food, and calling for a moratorium on the death penalty; the International Criminal Court (ICC) Treaty was signed in Rome in July 1998, and approved by 120 countries, with 7 opposed (including the US). It set up a court in The Hague to try political leaders and military personnel charged with war crimes and crimes against humanity; in October 2001 Great Britain became the 42nd nation to sign. In December 2001 the United States Senate again added an amendment to a military appropriations bill that would keep US military personnel from obeying the jurisdiction of the proposed ICC; the Land Mine Treaty, banning land mines, was signed in Ottawa in December 1997 by 122 nations. The United States refused to sign, along with Russia, China, India, Pakistan, Iran, Iraq, Vietnam, Egypt and Turkey. President Clinton rejected the Treaty, claiming that mines were needed to protect South Korea against North Korea's "overwhelming military advantage." He stated that the US would "eventually" comply, in 2006; this promise was disavowed by President Bush in August 2001; the Kyoto Protocol of 1997, for controlling global warming was declared "dead" by President Bush in March 2001. In November 2001, the Bush administration shunned negotiations in Marrakech (Morocco) to revise the accord, mainly by watering it down in a vain attempt to gain US approval; in

future combat situations. As I write, the Bush administration is now preparing to go to war in Iraq in the face of opposition from some of its closest allies and without authorization from the United Nations' Security Council. Domestic opposition to these moves was muted, and largely limited to the elite press and liberal professional associations and lobbying groups. The United States has power to "go it alone," and its leaders, with the apparent backing of the Congress and electorate, have no compunction about doing so even on issues where no serious national interests appear to be at risk.

When Henry Kissinger was awarded the Nobel Peace Prize, Tom Lehrer announced his retirement on the grounds that satire could no longer compete with reality. The logic of the Nobel Peace Committee is indeed hard to fathom, but one of the consequences of their double award – Le Duc Tho of North Vietnam was co-recipient – was undeniably to increase the stature of one of the country's leading realists, and to legitimize the Nixon–Kissinger approach to Indochina and international relations more generally. All the more reason then to pursue our inquiry into the nature of realism, and the important differences between the classical realism of Thucydides, Clausewitz and Morgenthau, and the cruder, modern realism, more properly described as *Realpolitk*, of Nixon and Kissinger and their academic and policy successors.

I analyze the principal works and thought of these three realists in historical sequence. This makes sense, for the obvious reason that Thucydides influenced the thinking of subsequent realists and

May 2001, the United States refused to meet with European Union nations to discuss, even at lower levels of government, economic espionage and electronic surveillance of phone calls, e-mail, and faxes (the US "Echelon" program); the United States refused to participate in talks sponsored by the Organization for Economic Co-operation and Development (OECD) in Paris, May 2001 on ways to crack down on off-shore and other tax and money-laundering havens; in February 2001, the United States refused to join 123 nations pledged to ban the use and production of anti-personnel bombs and mines; in September 2001, the US withdrew from International Conference on Racism, bringing together 163 countries in Durban, South Africa; in July 2001, the US was the only one to oppose the International Plan for Cleaner Energy, sponsored by the G-8 group of industrial nations (US, Canada, Japan, Russia, Germany, France, Italy, UK); in October 2001, the UN General Assembly passed a resolution, for the tenth consecutive year, calling for an end to the illegal US embargo of Cuba, by a vote of 167 to 3 (the US, Israel, and the Marshall Islands in opposition). The US refused to comply. In November 2001, the US forced a vote in the UN Committee on Disarmament and Security to demonstrate its opposition to the Comprehensive [Nuclear] Test Ban Treaty. Signed by 164 nations and ratified by 89 including France, Great Britain and Russia; signed by President Clinton in 1996 but rejected by the Senate in 1999. The US is one of thirteen countries that have nuclear weapons or nuclear power programs that have not ratified the Treaty. Also in November, the United States scuttled the negotiations sponsored by the World Health Organization to reduce worldwide use of tobacco.

Morgenthau in turn was influenced by the writings of Clausewitz, and more broadly, by the German philosophical tradition of which he was an important representative. There is a less obvious reason too, which has to do with Greek tragedy, whose high point, represented by the works of Aeschylus, Sophocles and Euripides, occurred during the lifetime of Thucydides. In contrast to modern realists, who claim Thucydides as their founding father, I argue that Thucydides conceived of his history as a tragedy, and is appropriately described as the last of the great tragedians. Viewed as a tragedy, his portrayal of the Peloponnesian War leads us to a very different set of questions, understandings of politics and of knowledge itself. Clausewitz and Morgenthau did not write tragedy but shared Thucydides' tragic perspective on life and politics. Their works must also be read in the tragic tradition, and doing so offers more complex, and, I believe, more accurate understandings of their respective approaches to war, politics and their study.

Tragedy is something with which we are all too familiar. Terrible things happen all the time to people who did nothing to deserve such fates. As I write this chapter, the nation is still reeling from successful attacks against the World Trade Center and Pentagon, and I am coming to terms with the loss of a colleague and friend, and his wife and son, in a Paris hotel fire. Greek tragedy was rooted in the empirical observation that there is no relationship between justice and suffering. It advanced a counterintuitive thesis: that efforts to limit suffering through the accumulation of knowledge or power might invite more suffering. Tragedy confronts us with our frailties and limits, and the disastrous consequences of trying to exceed them. *Antigone* explores the limits of power, and *Oedipus Tyrannus* those of reason. All tragedies remind us of our mortality and how it differentiates us from the gods. Mortality also imparts a poignancy and intensity to life, and encourages us to take special satisfaction in its simple pleasures, to participate constructively in family and community, and it allows a few unusual individuals to achieve heroic status by becoming themselves through losing everything that superficially seems to define them and by sacrificing their lives in defense of their values. Tragedy encourages us to develop and use our analytical facilities, but to be equally attentive to our imagination and feelings, to balance inference with prophecy and to recognize that the world is full of contradictions that we cannot resolve.

Homer, Shakespeare and modern authors have employed narratives to develop a stance on virtues because they envisaged human life as a dramatic narrative. Their characters act out moral philosophies. In the course of confronting dangers and challenges, successful strategies are associated with virtue, reveal the nature of virtue to us and enable us to judge ourselves as well as the characters we read about.[14] Tragic characters thus embody individual characteristics and social roles. In fifth-century tragedies, we shall see, they are focal points for exploring the limits of these roles, conflicts between them and the ever-fluid boundaries between man and beast, nature and convention and household and polis.

In Greek thought, literature preceded and informed philosophy. Thucydides drew heavily on epic poetry and tragedy to construct his history, which not surprisingly is also constructed as a narrative. Plato (427–347 BCE) wrote his dialogues in opposition to existing forms of literary expression, poetry especially, but they are quasi-narratives conceived of as works of literature and include passages that are decidedly poetical.[15] Aristotle was more self-consciously informed by literature, but like Plato, did not distinguish it from politics as we routinely do in the modern era. For Greeks, literature expressed truths that could not be conceptualized, a kind of wisdom that went beyond words.[16] Thucydides and Plato were deeply influenced by this precedent, which became a model for their own writings. They encouraged readers to aspire to wisdom, which they conceived of as something general and universal, that speaks to our life force or soul (*psukhē*) and comes to shape our behavior and view of the world. Conceptual knowledge was merely a means to this more important end. Here too, their writings drew on the literary tradition. All three thinkers were deeply concerned with the meaning of justice, and took as their starting point conceptions of justice found in Homer, Hesiod and Solon and subsequently problematized in the tragedies of Aeschylus and Sophocles.

In my own fumbling way, I imitated this tradition, albeit unintentionally. A short story I wrote in the autumn of 1998 turned out to be the unexpected catalyst for key arguments of my book. "Nixon in Hell" was prompted by a flurry of newspaper articles commemorating the thirtieth anniversary of the Tet Offensive, an event etched in my memory, as I had inspected the ruins of Hue not long after the Viet Cong had been repulsed in some of the bloodiest fighting of the war. I was in Vietnam

[14] Anne Righter, *Shakespeare and the Idea of the Play* (London: Chatto and Windus, 1962); MacIntyre, *After Virtue*, pp. 28, 143; James Olney, *Memory and Narrative: The Weave of Life-Writing* (Chicago: University of Chicago Press, 1998).

[15] See his *Phaedrus*, 274b–278b, on the limitations of the written word and the superiority of speech as a vehicle of teaching and learning. Written works, 275c–276a, leave questions unanswered, cannot be tailored to the audience, degrade the memory, and most importantly, circumvents dialogue. Plato nevertheless acknowledges, in 276d, that writing can aid the memory, especially of one enfeebled by old age.

[16] Adam Parry, "Thucydides' Use of Abstract Language," *Yale French Studies* 45 (1970), pp. 3–20.

giving talks critical of Washington's policy. I had been an anti-war activist since the summer of 1963, which I spent at the Sorbonne and was made aware of the nature of American involvement in their country by Vietnamese friends. I had despised Richard Nixon for almost as long as I could remember, and went into a prolonged depression when he won the presidency in 1968. I anticipated the Nixon–Kissinger escalation of the war, but was appalled by their utterly callous and destructive invasion of Cambodia. I thought at the time – and still do – that both men deserved to be tried as war criminals. My story was initially a vehicle for me to work through and express my still festering anger.

My story wrote itself in the sense that I did not know where it was heading once I pushed Nixon through the gates of hell. To my surprise, he began to emerge as a more complex and sympathetic character. From his initial expressions of anger and subsequent retreat into denial, he somehow mobilized the emotional strength and commitment to stage a comeback – much as he had after his 1960 electoral defeat. To my annoyance, Nixon began to reveal other qualities that I had to admire: love for music and learning, and warmth and affection toward his long-suffering wife. To the extent that he rose to the challenge of hell and became more human in the process I found him harder to hate.

The Nixon of my story can be read as a tragic figure. In a highly regarded study of Greek theater, Bernard Knox offers us a description of the generic Sophoclean hero. He is someone faced with a choice between compromise or certain disaster, who recognizes that any compromise would betray his conception of himself, his rights and his duties. His decision to stand firm is announced in emphatic, uncompromising terms – and it is always put to the test. He is subjected to emotional pleas from loved ones, appeals to reason from advisors, all with the goal of encouraging him to yield. The hero grows increasingly angry and even irrational in response to this pressure, and he in turn is seen as stubborn and uncompromising by others. Heroes are awesome and terrifying because they lack any sense of moderation.[17] Nixon conformed to this pattern.[18] He repeatedly escalated the war in the hope of compelling concessions from Hanoi, and persevered with this strategy in the face of growing criticism from friendly and hostile quarters. His rhetoric became more uncompromising in the face of opposition, just as his policy led in the end to the

[17] Bernard W. Knox, *The Heroic Temper: Studies in Sophoclean Tragedy* (Berkeley and Los Angeles: University of California Press, 1964), pp. 1–27.

[18] Lyndon Johnson might also qualify for this role. He met with more opposition from his family and inner circle of advisors, became just as testy in the face of opposition, but also had more self-doubts about the wisdom of intervention. He lacked the unidimensional and unquestioning commitment of Nixon, and in many other ways, to me at least, was a far more sympathetic figure, personally and politically.

very disaster he had worked so hard to avoid: the collapse of America's puppet regime and American influence in Southeast Asia. The image, televised around the world, of Americans shoving aside their desperate local hangers-on to board helicopters on the roof of the embassy and escape from Saigon, was a positively Sophoclean *dénouement*.

Tragedy often explored conflicts between opposing systems of values. Antigone and Creon personify extreme and seemingly irreconcilable commitments to family and religious obligations on the one hand and paternal authority and civil order on the other. In *Philoctetes*, Neoptolemus and Odysseus stand for different conceptions of honor, justice and wisdom. Nixon can be cast readily as a powerful and committed representative of *Realpolitik*, a well-established, if not unchallenged, value system for the conduct of foreign policy. His application of *Realpolitik*, while it benefited from Kissinger's tactical brilliance, was nevertheless deeply flawed strategically. It arguably left the United States worse off than it would have been if Nixon had arranged for a de Gaulle-like retreat from Indochina at the outset of his administration. Nixon's behavior is in many ways reminiscent of Creon, ruler of Thebes, whose heavy-handed defense of civil authority ended up undermining that authority as well as his own. Like Creon, Nixon seemed to be motivated as much by stubbornness and petulance as he was by his commitment to a vision of the national interest.

There are, of course, significant differences between Nixon and tragic heroes. Nixon's defense of his commitment to Vietnam never rose to heroic proportions. He belatedly chose to cut his losses, and allowed Kissinger to cut a face-saving deal with Hanoi to allow a withdrawal of American ground forces. Of all the figures in tragedy, Nixon may come closest to Ajax, but here too the analogy is incomplete. Ajax courageously fell on his sword to preserve his honor after he had run amok in a fit of delusion and killed some herdsmen and their animals, convinced they were Odysseus and his comrades. "The man of noble birth," he declares, "must live well or die well."[19] Nixon, under siege because of Watergate, prodded his underlings to fall on their swords in the false hope that it would preserve his hold on office. His ultimate resignation lacked the dignity of Ajax's suicide.

My story put me in touch with a different Nixon, and I began to think of him as at least in part a tragic figure. The tragic frame of reference offered me a new – although no more favorable – perspective on his foreign policy, and on the relationship between private and public morality and ethics and interest. It became an incentive and a vehicle for me to

[19] Sophocles, *Ajax*, 473–80.

work these problems through in an extended analysis of classical realism and its similarities and differences from its contemporary counterpart. I understand now that my story expressed truths – or, at least, ways of thinking about politics – that I had not yet thematized. Of equal importance, it appeared to serve the more important purpose Hannah Arendt attributed to tragedy: allowing the audience – or, in this case, the author – to widen their intellectual and emotional horizons in a manner conducive to political tolerance and reconciliation.[20]

Greek tragedy flourished in a unique and short-lived moment – the second half of the fifth century in Athens – when drama, politics and philosophy were intimately connected. The Athenian Dionysia, held every year in late March, was its venue. Tragedies and other plays were performed in a large, open-air amphitheater on the southern slope of the Acropolis before an audience of Athenians, resident aliens and foreigners of all classes. The generals (*stratēgoi*) poured the libations to open the festival, followed by a public display of allied tribute, an announcement of the names of the city's benefactors, including those who underwrote the cost of producing the plays, and a parade of state-educated boys, now men, in full military panoply provided by the city. The plays themselves were organized as a contest (*agōn*) in which playwrights competed with words the same way personal and political disputes were transformed into verbal contests in the law courts and assembly. Jean-Pierre Vernant speculates that tragedy could only exist when the distance between the heroic past and its religious values was great enough to allow new values based on the polis and its juridical structure to have emerged, but close enough to the past for the conflict in values to have been painfully real. "For tragic man to appear, the concept of human action must have emerged but not acquired too autonomous a status. By the first decade of the fourth century, that moment had passed. Athenians had lost a war and an empire, and perhaps, the inner strength and confidence necessary to confront, let alone relish, critical portrayals of themselves and the human condition."[21]

[20] Hannah Arendt, *The Human Condition* (Chicago: University of Chicago Press, 1958); Robert C. Pirro, *Hannah Arendt and the Politics of Tragedy* (DeKalb: Northern Illinois University Press, 2000), for an exploration of this aspect of Arendt's thought.

[21] Jean-Pierre Vernant, "Greek Tragedy: Problems of Interpretation," in Richard Macksey and Eugenio Donato, eds., *The Structuralist Controversy: The Languages of Criticism and the Sciences of Man* (Baltimore: Johns Hopkins University Press, 1972), pp. 273–88, and "Tensions and Ambiguities in Greek Tragedy," in Jean-Pierre Vernant and Pierre Vidal-Nacquet, *Myth and Tragedy in Ancient Greece*; trans. J. B. Lloyd (New York: Zone Books, 1990); Charles Segal, *Oedipus Tyrannus: Tragic Heroism and the Limits of Knowledge*, 2nd ed. (New York: Oxford University Press, 2001), pp. 15–18, 20–22; Simon Goldhill, *Reading Greek Tragedy* (Cambridge: Cambridge

Tragedy can be understood as a response to modernization – and I use the term in its broadest sense. Economic, political and social changes threaten traditional values and encourage the emergence of new ones that tend to emphasize the individual over the community, achieved over ascribed status, the future over the past and material over spiritual well-being.[22] The tragedies of Aeschylus, Sophocles and Euripides, the history of Thucydides and the philosophical inquiries of Socrates and Plato all address the conflict between the old and the new and search for ways of reconciling or accommodating them in a more stable and just society. Czeslaw Milosz observes that "People always live within a certain order and are unable to visualize a time when that order might cease to exist. The sudden crumbling of all current notions and criteria is a rare occurrence and is characteristic of only the most stormy periods of history." Milosz suggests that "the only possible analogy" to our own age "may be the time of the Peloponnesian War, as we know it from Thucydides."[23] The twentieth century undeniably witnessed enormous upheavals, but so did other epochs. I contend that there is an equally striking connection between fifth-century Greece and Europe of the late eighteenth and early nineteenth centuries. The Enlightenment and Counter-Enlightenment, while undeniably modern phenomena, nevertheless recapitulated in important ways intellectual developments and currents that took place in fifth-century Greece. The change and uncertainty wrought by this sea-change in thinking, the French Revolution and Napoleonic Wars prompted German writers and philosophers to turn to ancient Greece, and Greek tragedy in particular, for appropriate responses. Tragedy has also been central to efforts by writers and thinkers to come to terms with World War II and the Holocaust. My *Leitmotiv* of tragedy is neither arbitrary nor coincidental, but the key to understanding the thinking of major philosophers, historians and political scientists addressed in this volume.

University Press, 1986), and "The Great Dionysia and Civic Ideology," in John J. Winkler and Froma I. Zeitlin, *Nothing to Do with Dionysos?: Athenian Drama in its Social Context* (Princeton: Princeton University Press, 1990), pp. 97–129; John J. Winkler, "The Ephebes' Song: *Tragōidia* and Polis," in Winkler and Zeitlin, *Nothing to Do with Dionysos?*," pp. 20–62; Froma I. Zeitlin, "Thebes: Theater of Self and Society in Athenian Drama," in J. Peter Euben, ed., *Greek Tragedy and Political Theory* (Berkeley and Los Angeles: University of California Press, 1986), pp. 101–41; J. Peter Euben, *The Tragedy of Political Theory: The Road Not Taken* (Princeton: Princeton University Press, 1990), pp. 50–59.

22 Karl W. Deutsch, *Nationalism and Social Communication* (Cambridge, Mass.: MIT Press, 1953) for a classic discussion of this transformation.

23 Czeslaw Milosz, *The Witness of Poetry* (Cambridge, Mass.: Harvard University Press, 1983), p. 81.

Realism and modernization

Why do I choose these three realists? Why not Machiavelli, Hobbes or Morgenthau's contemporary, E. H. Carr? Thucydides requires little justification. He is the first writer to analyze the origins of war, the role of power in international affairs, the relationship between domestic and foreign politics, the process by which civil and international orders unravel and what might be done to restore them. His insights into these matters are profound, and his history has long been regarded as one of the great works of Greek literature and philosophy. Thucydides is credited with introducing the concept of the balance of power and the distinction between underlying and immediate causes of war. His Melian Dialogue remains the starting point of discussions about the relative role of ethics and interests in foreign affairs. Because Thucydides emphasized the role of power in international relations, he is regarded by realists of all persuasions as the founding father of their paradigm.[24]

Carl von Clausewitz is the preeminent theorist of war and arguably the leading realist thinker of the nineteenth century. His magnum opus, *On War*, has been read by generations of strategists, and along with Thucydides' *History of the Peloponnesian War*, remains required reading at staff and war colleges around the world. Like Thucydides, Clausewitz understood political history as an endless cycle of growth and decline, of the rise and fall of political units that advanced civilization but also threatened it through their overreaching ambitions and the destructive wars they provoked. While not an historian-philosopher on a par with Thucydides, he addressed many of the same questions as his illustrious predecessor. One of his most important theoretical contributions was the analysis of the implications of different organizing principles of societies for the conduct of warfare and international stability.

Hans J. Morgenthau is the most influential postwar theorist of international relations. His *Politics Among Nations*, which appeared in 1948, sought to discredit "idealism" and its putative misplaced faith in the ability of international law and organization to constrain state behavior. It offered "realism," which defined the national interest in terms of power, as the appropriate starting point for foreign policy. *Politics Among Nations* was far and away the most widely read international relations text of the next two decades. It helped to educate a generation of future policymakers and provided the intellectual underpinning for the Cold War national security state. By the time of the Vietnam War, Morgenthau

[24] Doyle, *Ways of War and Peace*, for these different approaches to realism and their indebtedness to Thucydides.

had become disillusioned with American-style realism and ironically had come to adopt much of the agenda of his former idealist opponents.

One of the principal reasons I choose these three realists is that they wrote their most notable works in the aftermath of catastrophic wars that had destroyed or seriously threatened the survival of the old order. They sought to understand the origins of these wars, the reasons why they became so brutal and what could be done to prevent their recurrence or destructiveness. The wars in question – the Archidamian and Peloponnesian, French Revolutionary and Napoleonic, and World Wars I and II were all at least in part the result of processes of modernization. All three thinkers understood that the intellectual, economic and political changes that helped to bring about these wars, had on the whole been accelerated by them and greatly complicated the problem of conflict prevention and management. Leaders and theorists confronted a novel set of domestic and international conditions and challenges.

My claim about modernization in fifth-century Greece may strike some readers as enigmatic because we tend to think of modernization as a unique attribute of the "modern" world and a cause and product of the industrial revolution. Modernization has taken many forms over the millennia, and these include transitions from a nomadic, hunter-gatherer existence to life in more settled, agricultural communities; from small, relatively isolated and self-supporting communities to larger political units centered on cities with a division of labor, written records, money and some means of long-distance transport. Nor should we consider industrialization and its consequences the final stage of modernization. Advances in information science and bio- and nano-technology could dramatically extend human longevity and potential, and transform political, economic and social relations and our conceptions of ourselves in even more far-reaching ways than the Enlightenment and industrial revolution.

Economic and technological modernization is only one dimension of what might be called modernity. Bernard Yack identifies four distinct conceptions of modernity: philosophic, sociological, political and aesthetic.[25] Philosophic modernity represents a self-conscious break with authority, initiated by Bacon, Descartes and later Enlightenment philosophers. It is a project whose roots can be traced back to the Renaissance. The sociological conception describes changing social relationships and conditions, and is generally thought to have been ushered in by the development of capitalism in the late eighteenth century and the break it initiated with traditional forms of authority. The political conception of modernity focuses

[25] Bernard Yack, *The Fetishism of Modernities: Epochal Self-Consciousness in Contemporary Social and Political Thought* (Notre Dame: University of Notre Dame Press, 1997), pp. 32–35.

on the emergence of egalitarian and democratic forms of political legitimacy, and the corresponding decline of aristocratic political hierarchies. The watershed here is the French Revolution. The aesthetic conception of modernity is associated with styles of art and literature that understand beauty and meaning as ephemeral, and are opposed to the orthodoxy of the moment regardless of its content. Modernism in this sense did not appear until the late nineteenth century. The proto-Enlightenment of fifth-century Greece was characterized by many aspects of philosophic and political modernity, in addition to economic change.

One important difference was that the ancient philosophical enterprise was characterized by an effort to understand nature and human life in the hope that such knowledge might reduce the frequency of pain and suffering. The modern enterprise is devoted, in the words of Francis Bacon, to "the conquest of nature for the relief of man's estate."[26] The goal is no longer to understand nature, but to conquer it.

The Peloponnesian War (431–404 BCE) is the first war associated with modernization and for which good documentation is available. Population growth, specialization of labor, writing and written records, and far-flung trade made possible by improvements in maritime technology gave rise to commerce-oriented cities like Athens, Corinth and Syracuse. Athens established an empire that stretched from the Aegean to the Black Sea that made it the most powerful state in the Mediterranean basin. Athenian wealth, culture and military power threatened Sparta's claim to hegemony and, more importantly, its way of life, based as it was on physical isolation and a self-sufficient agricultural economy. Athens and Sparta fought an indecisive war that ended with the Thirty Year Truce of 446, and two subsequent wars – the Archidamian (431-421) and Peloponnesian (414-404) – that engulfed most of Hellas, including *Magna Graecia*, and non-Greek states, most notably, Persia. Sparta emerged the nominal victor, but could not maintain its position against other challengers (e.g., Macedon and Syracuse) who exploited new technologies to develop siege engines and catapults, which when combined with better logistics, allowed both states to triumph easily over hoplite armies and reduce resisting cities without long sieges.[27] Both states grew powerful and wealthy through conquest, which fueled further expansion. The ancient revolution in military affairs put an end to the polis as a political unit.

Modernization and the discourses associated with it are mutually constitutive. Shifts in discourses are often essential preconditions for

[26] Cited in Roger Masters, *The Nature of Politics* (New Haven: Yale University Press, 1989), p. 147.

[27] Plutarch, *Moralia*, 219a on how siege technology put an end to hoplite warfare.

economic, technological and political change. Modernization in turn changes the ways in which people think and speak about the world, themselves and their communities. The Enlightenment and the industrial revolution went hand-in-hand and gave rise to a long-standing controversy about the relative importance of the transformative potential of modes of production (Karl Marx) and ideas (Max Weber). A similar argument developed about modernization in ancient Greece. There is general agreement that the individual gradually replaced the extended household (*oikos*) as the fundamental economic unit, and that the goal of production and exchange increasingly became the pursuit of profit (*kerdos*). But scholars disagree about whether these changes were a response to the emergence of the polis, introduction of money and expansion of trade, and whether they were preconditions for these developments or something that occurred simultaneously and reinforced the pace of economic and political change.[28]

The Enlightenments of fifth-century Greece and eighteenth-century Europe share many similarities.[29] Both movements were fundamentally projects about using the power of reason to unlock the secrets of nature, emancipate people from the constraints of the past and allow them to realize their potential in just, ordered and secure societies. The Greek belief in the power of reason inspired an array of projects in the fifth and eighteenth-nineteenth centuries leading to impressive accomplishments in domains as varied as science, medicine, philosophy, art and architecture and constitutional engineering.[30] The power of reason also

[28] For an overview, see Max Weber, *Economy and Society: An Outline of Interpretative Sociology*, ed. Guenther Roth and Clauss Wittich, trans. Ephraim Fischoff *et al.*, 3 vols. (New York: Bedminster Press, 1989), I, pp. 370–85; Marcel Mauss, *The Gift: The Form and Reason for Exchange in Archaic Societies*, trans. W. D. Halls (New York: Norton, 1990 [1925]); Karl Polanyi, "Aristotle Discovers the Economy," in Karl Polanyi, Conrad Arensberg and H. C. Pearson, eds., *Trade and Market in the Early Empires* (Glencoe: Free Press, 1957), pp. 65–94; Joseph Schumpeter, *History of Economic Analysis*, ed. Elizabeth Brady Schumpeter (Oxford: Oxford University Press, 1954), pp. 53–54; Moses I. Finley, *The Ancient Economy*, 2nd ed. rev. (Berkeley and Los Angeles: University of California Press, 1999); Sarah C. Humphreys, "History, Economics and Anthropology: The Work of Karl Polanyi," in Humphreys, *Anthropology and the Greeks*, 2nd ed. (Boston: Routledge & Kegan Paul, 1983), pp. 31–75; Christopher Gill, Norman Postlethwaite and Richard Seaford, *Reciprocity in Ancient Greece* (Oxford: Oxford University Press, 1998); Albert O. Hirschman, *The Passions and the Interests: Political Arguments for Capitalism before its Triumph* (Princeton: Princeton University Press, 1977), on how profit making came to be a highly valued activity.

[29] Intellectual developments in fifth-century Greece, but especially Athens, are commonly referred to as an "Enlightenment." W. K. C. Guthrie, *A History of Greek Philosophy* (Cambridge: Cambridge University Press, 1969), III, p. 48.

[30] René Descartes, *Discourse on Method*, in *The Method, Meditations, and Philosophy of Descartes*, trans. J. Veitch (London: M. W. Dunne, 1901), p. 192; Charles Taylor, *Hegel* (Cambridge: Cambridge University Press, 1975), pp. 6–7; James Schmidt, ed., *What is Enlightenment? Eighteenth Century Answers and Twentieth Century Questions* (Berkeley and Los Angeles: University of California Press, 1996).

encouraged skepticism, as it revealed the arbitrary nature of knowledge and beliefs.[31] Modernization confronted Greeks with a choice between the values of an archaic past, preserved in mythic form, and those associated with the new political, juridical and cultural life of the polis. The unity of Greek thought broke down and the resulting tension between the old and the new led to a "split consciousness" born of the feelings of man against himself.[32] German idealist philosophers described similar feelings of disorientation and inner conflict arising from modernity. The two epochs are also connected in that it was the repudiation of Aristotelian thought by the modern Enlightenment that triggered the search for new foundations on which to base morality.[33]

The early optimism of both Enlightenments foundered on the shoals of revolutionary excess and destructive wars. Reacting to these events, counter-Enlightenment writers developed a darker picture of the world and began to represent it as complex, contradictory, conflict-prone and in a state of constant flux. They rejected the Enlightenment conception of the individual person as a *tabula rasa,* and emphasized instead the imaginative, emotional, spiritual – and often disruptive – qualities of people, and the need to understand them in their totality and highly specific cultural contexts. Something similar occurred in the late fifth century. For Sophocles, writing in the later stages of the Peloponnesian War, reason and human agency are powerful but highly suspect because of that. The dramatic reversals of fortune (*peripeteia*) Oedipus undergoes from king to beggar, from hero to pitiable figure and from ruler to exile demonstrate the self-destructive consequences of intelligence

[31] In the proto-Enlightenment, this problem arose from the effort to discover first principles that would provide a firmer foundation for the verities associated with myths which had become scientifically absurd. Something similar happened in the Enlightenment, where revealed truth and traditional religion became equally unacceptable, but all efforts to find sound first principles on which to base their ethical codes were open to challenge as arbitrary. The problem was further confounded by the investigations of Descartes, Locke, Berkeley, Hume Condillac, Leibniz and Kant, which suggested that knowledge is conditioned and mediated by the act of cognition. Our ideas of things are not the same as things themselves. The resulting "veil of perception" encouraged skepticism about knowing anything.

[32] The quote is from Jean-Pierre Vernant, "Tensions and Ambiguities in Greek Tragedy" in Vernant and Vidal-Nacquet, *Myth and Tragedy in Ancient Greece*, pp. 29–48; Charles S. Singleton, ed., *Title Interpretation: Theory and Practice* (Baltimore: Johns Hopkins Press, 1969), pp. 100–04. See also Werner Jaeger, *Paideia: The Ideals of Greek Culture*, trans. Gilbert Highet, 2nd ed. 3 vols. (New York: Oxford University Press, 1945 [1939]), I, p. 151, for earlier development of this theme.

[33] MacIntyre, *After Virtue*, p. 117; J. G. A. Pocock, *Barbarism and Religion: I: The Enlightenment of Edward Gibbon, 1737–1764* (Cambridge: Cambridge University Press, 1999), pp. 7–9, reminds us that the modern Enlightenment was inextricably connected with the emergence of the state system and sustained efforts to reduce the power of the churches.

and knowledge cut loose from their traditional familial and communal moorings.[34]

"Enlightenment" and "counter-Enlightenment" are loose, catchall terms that refer to general tendencies rather than to specific schools of thought. Even so, it is difficult to place Thucydides, Clausewitz and Morgenthau unambiguously in either philosophical tradition. Thucydides appeals to the intellect, but also to the emotions, of his readers to make them recognize the dangers of constructing identities outside of communities. He wants readers to recognize the critical importance of language and rituals that shape communal identities and create the conditions for constructive political dialogue. Clausewitz embarked upon a quintessential Enlightenment project: the search for a universally valid theory of war. He nevertheless denied that war could be reduced to a science or that theory could guide a campaign. These limitations reflected counter-Enlightenment perspectives, as did his emphasis on the emotions, personality and ability of genius to make its own rules.

Morgenthau came of age in the 1920s, at a time when the controversy between the Enlightenment and its critics appeared to have been all but won by the former. He began his career as a liberal humanist, committed to using law and reason to improve the lot of humankind. The Nazis and World War II transformed his world view and turned him into an outspoken critic of the Enlightenment. His early postwar books attributed the horrors of the twentieth century to man's misplaced faith in the power of reason. Like Thucydides, he developed a tragic perspective on life and searched for ways of strengthening the values and conventions that might restrain the worst human impulses. In the last decade of his life, he became more optimistic about the possibility of a fundamental transformation of the international system.

Thucydides, Clausewitz and Morgenthau start from the Enlightenment assumption that readers can adopt universalist, culture-free perches from which to reason their way to better understandings of the problems of war and peace. But the understandings they have in mind embody the distinctively counter-Enlightenment focus on the social practices embedded in cultures. All three thinkers nevertheless recognized that those

[34] I am thinking here of *Oedipus at Colonus*. Aristotle, *Poetics*, 11.1452a32 and 24.1460a27–31, considered *Oedipus* the finest tragic plot because the principal reversal coincides with Oedipus' recognition of the truth. For modern interpretations, see Bernard Knox, *Oedipus at Thebes: Sophocles' Tragic Hero and His Time* (New Haven: Yale University Press, 1998 [1957]), p. 99; R. P. Winnington-Ingram, *Sophocles: An Interpretation* (Cambridge: Cambridge University Press, 1980); Jean Pierre Vernant, "Oedipus without the Complex," in Vernant and Vidal-Nacquet, *Myth and Tragedy in Ancient Greece*, pp. 85–112; Charles Segal, *Sophocles' Tragic World* (Cambridge, Mass.: Harvard University Press, 1998), pp. 138–60.

practices had broken down, could not be restored in their old form but had to be reformulated and combined with emerging practices to form the basis of a new order. They also had to be restored by artifice. Their projects accordingly combined counter-Enlightenment respect for tradition with Enlightenment faith in the efficacy, or at least the possibility, of social engineering. They also revealed a counter-Enlightenment influence in their emphasis on holistic understandings in lieu of instrumental knowledge, the kind of wisdom that Greeks described as *sophia* – a distinction to which I shall return.

The cycle of war, breakdown and reconstruction has engaged the attention of philosophers, policymakers and international relations scholars.[35] Modernization adds another wrinkle that complicates reconstruction and how one thinks about it. There appear to be three generic responses: restoration of the *ante bellum* social and political order; construction of new domestic or international orders on novel or untried principles; or of hybrid orders that attempt to blend the best of the old and the new. The first strategy is often appealing to policymakers. Sparta tried and failed to restore the old order at the end of the Peloponnesian Wars.[36] Metternich created the Holy Alliance for the same purpose in the aftermath of the Napoleonic Wars.[37] Thucydides has been portrayed – wrongly, I believe – as anti-democratic and committed to the old aristocratic political order.[38] Plato has also been described by some as an upholder of more traditional values. But he defies simple characterization because he attempted to restore traditional values by novel, even radical means, in the form of conscious institutional design.[39] In modern times, Edmund Burke can fairly be characterized as an advocate of the "turn back the clock" strategy.

[35] Robert Gilpin, *War and Change in World Politics* (New York: Cambridge University Press), refers to this process as "systemic change."
[36] W. G. Forrest, *A History of Sparta*, 3rd ed. (London: Duckworth, 1995), pp. 122–31.
[37] G. John Ikenberry, *After Victory: Institutions, Strategic Restraint, and the Rebuilding of Order after Major Wars* (Princeton: Princeton University Press, 2001), pp. 80–116, for an insightful analysis of these efforts and discussion of the relevant literature.
[38] This question is addressed at length in Chapter 3.
[39] Plato might be read as a conservative trying to turn the clock back. His *Republic* envisaged a Spartan-like society somewhere on Crete, considered the most backward of Greece, without money, industry or poets. He can be considered a radical because he rejected traditional practices as the basis for order, and sought instead to lay entirely rational and deductive foundations for conventions. His use of novel means to achieve traditional ends allows a third reading of him as a synthetic thinker. All three interpretations are problematic because it seems unlikely that he ever intended the *Republic* as a practical project. For some of the relevant literature, see Jaeger, *Paideia*, II; A. E. Taylor, *Plato: The Man and His Work*, 3rd ed. (New York: Dial Press, 1929); Arendt, *The Human Condition*; Sheldon Wolin, *Politics and Vision: Continuity and Innovation in Western Political Thought* (Boston: Little, Brown, 1961); Leo Strauss, *The City and Man* (New York: Rand McNally, 1964); T. H. Irwin, *Plato's Moral Theory* (Oxford: Oxford University Press, 1977); Hans-George Gadamer, *Dialogue and Dialectic: Eight Hermeneutical Studies on*

Burke wrote his best-known works as a reaction to the French Revolution, and argued that a political and social order that had developed naturally and found expression in a complex pattern of rights and obligations was more stable and superior to one derived from first principles and then imposed on society.[40] Leo Strauss attributed the wars and barbarism of the twentieth century to the Enlightenment, and, following his idiosyncratic understanding of Plato, sought to resurrect natural law (*phusis*) as the foundation for a stable political order.[41]

The second variant is represented by Immanuel Kant, Karl Marx and Woodrow Wilson. They advocated radical breaks with the past, or at least an accelerated development of existing trends. Thomas Paine, John Cobden, Marx, Friedrich Engels, V. I. Lenin and Wilson all attempted to put their radical ideas into practice.

The three realists I examine envisaged a hybrid order that would maintain or resurrect the best features of the old system but accommodate the kind of changes that were either unavoidable or held out the prospect of benefits. This strategy is hardly surprising as all three men straddled the Enlightenment and counter-Enlightenment, and struggled to reconcile these clashing world views into some kind of synthesis. Thucydides abandoned the aristocratic mindset of his youth and came to recognize the old order as doomed by the economic, intellectual and political changes that had transformed Athens in the course of the fifth century. Pericles and Hermocrates were the statesmen he held in the highest esteem; each in his own way had created an amalgam of the old and new that worked to the advantage of their societies. Clausewitz hoped that gifted leaders might create a workable synthesis by exploiting the potential of the modern state to enhance the physical and spiritual well-being of its citizens without sacrificing older, core values that encouraged patriotism, restraint and prudence. Morgenthau sought to provide leaders and the educated public with the intellectual tools and moral commitments they

Plato, trans. P. Christopher Smith (New Haven: Yale University Press, 1980); Martha Nussbaum, *The Fragility of Goodness: Luck and Ethics in Greek Literature and Philosophy* (Cambridge: Cambridge University Press, 1986); Euben, *The Tragedy of Political Theory* pp. 235–80; Allan Silverman, *The Dialectic of Essence: A Study of Plato's Metaphysics* (Princeton: Princeton University Press, 2003).

40 Edmund Burke, *Reflections on the Revolution in France* (Oxford: Oxford University Press, 1993 [1790]); Peter J. Stanlis, *Edmund Burke: The Enlightenment and Revolution* (New Brunswick: Transaction Publishers, 1991).

41 Alan Udoff, ed., *Leo Strauss's Thought: Toward a Critical Engagement* (Boulder: Lynne Rienner, 1991); Ted V. McAllister, *Revolt Against Modernity: Leo Strauss, Eric Voegelin, and the Search for a Postliberal Order* (Lawrence, Ka.: University Press of Kansas, 1996); Kenneth L. Deutsch and John A. Marley, eds., *Leo Strauss, the Straussians, and the American Regime* (Lanham, Md.: Rowman & Littlefield, 1999); Robert C. Bartlett, *The Idea of Enlightenment: A Postmortem Study* (Toronto: University of Toronto Press, 2001).

needed to think more effectively about the national interest and thereby reduce the threat of nuclear war.

Clearing away the underbrush

Original thinkers are frequently misunderstood, and this has certainly been the fate of our three realists. Thucydides' account of the Peloponnesian War has been interpreted very differently by generations of political philosophers and scholars. Since the time of Thomas Hobbes, his most prominent early translator into English, Thucydides has been praised as someone who exposed the calculations of power and advantage that motivated successful political actors.[42] In the nineteenth century, Leopold von Ranke and his followers installed him in their pantheon as the first serious historian because of his valorization of evidence, explicit rules for evaluating it and interest in "high politics," that is, questions of war and peace. During the Cold War, realists embraced the Hobbesian interpretation to justify their power-based approach to foreign policy. For neorealists, Thucydides had the additional appeal of a seeming interest in parsimonious, universal generalizations. They celebrated him as the first power transition theorist because of his statement in Book I.23.6 that "the growth of the power of Athens, and the alarm which this inspired in Sparta, made war inevitable."[43]

Post-modernists portray Thucydides as an artist and political partisan who carefully structured his text to evoke a desired set of responses.[44] Postmodernist readings build on an alternative tradition that goes back to the mid-nineteenth-century efforts of Jacob Burckhardt to debunk Hegel's romantic picture of Athens as the cradle of democracy and home

[42] J. B. Bury, *A History of Greece to the Death of Alexander the Great* (London: Macmillan, 1914); Jaeger, *Paideia*, I, pp. 397–402; G. E. M. de Ste Croix, *The Origins of the Peloponnesian War* (London: Duckworth, 1972), pp. 11–25; Russell Meiggs, *The Athenian Empire* (Oxford: Oxford University Press, 1972), p. 388; Donald Kagan, *The Outbreak of the Peloponnesian War* (Ithaca: Cornell University Press, 1969).

[43] Thucydides, I.23. On power transition, see A. F. K. Organski, *World Politics*, 2nd ed. (New York: Knopf, 1968); A. F. K. Organski and Jacek Kugler, *The War Ledger* (Chicago: University of Chicago Press, 1980); Robert Gilpin, *War and Change in World Politics* (Cambridge: Cambridge University Press, 1981), p. 198; Charles F. Doran, "War and Power Dynamics: Economic Underpinnings," *International Studies Quarterly* 27 (December 1983), pp. 419–41; Charles Doran and Wes Parsons, "War and the Cycle of Relative Power," *American Political Science Review* 74 (December 1980), pp. 947–65; Wosang Kim and James D. Morrow, "When Do Power Shifts Lead to War?." *American Journal of Political Science* 36 (November 1992), pp. 896–922.

[44] W. P. Wallace, "Thucydides," *Phoenix* 18 (1964), pp. 251–61; Glen P. Bowersock, "The Personality of Thucydides," *Antioch Review* 35: 1 (1965), pp. 135–45; Hans-Peter Stahl, *Thucydides: Die Stellung des Menschen im geschichtlichen Prozess* (Munich: C. H. Beck, 1966); W. Robert Connor, *Thucydides* (Princeton: Princeton University Press, 1984).

of the proto-Enlightenment.[45] For Burckhardt, ancient Greece was a battleground of conflicting forces in art as well as politics.[46] In recent decades, avowedly revisionist works have attempted to show how the Greek tradition was manipulated by Western scholars for nationalist and racist ends and how earlier scholarly treatments ignored women, homosexuals and slaves, or portrayed them in conformity with the social and political values of the day.[47]

For international relations scholars, the realist interpretation remains dominant. It is the one I will primarily engage. I contend that realists err by reading Thucydides in a non-reflexive manner. Thucydides structures his text to provide readers with a vantage point outside of the "current events" and narratives of his day, something realists recognize and take as the starting point for their transcendent reading of him. They typically fail to recognize that their own framework is temporally and culturally bound, that it is a quintessential "insider" perspective. They are correspondingly blind to the inherent contradiction of using such a framework to infer a universally valid interpretation and set of associated lessons.

Interpretations of Clausewitz have been equally plastic. The posthumous publication of his works in 1832–37 made little impact until Germany's stunning triumphs over Austria in 1866 and France in 1870–71. When Field Marshal Helmuth von Moltke, the architect of those victories, announced that *On War* had been a principal influence

[45] The nineteenth-century understanding of Greece was not only highly romantic, it exaggerated enormously the intellectual level of life in fifth-century Athens. See, for example, Thomas Macaulay, "On the Athenian Orators," in G. M. Trevelyan, ed., *Complete Works of Lord Macaulay*, 12 vols. (London: Longmans, Green, 1898), VIII, pp. 153–55; George Grote, *A History of Greece from the Earliest Period to the Close of the Generation Contemporary with Alexander the Great*, 12 vols. (New York: Dutton, 1907 [1850–65]), IV, pp. 59–67.

[46] Selections from Burckhardt's lectures on ancient Greece, have been published in English as Jacob Burckhardt, *The Greeks and Greek Civilization*, ed. Oswyn Murray, trans. Sheila Stern (New York: St. Martin's Press, 1998); Dennis J. Schmidt, *On Germans and Other Greeks: Tragedy and Ethical Life* (Bloomington: University of Indiana Press, 2001), pp. 192–93.

[47] Sarah Pomeroy, *Goddesses, Whores, Wives and Slaves: Women in Classical Antiquity* (New York: Shocken Books, 1975); Martin Bernal, *Black Athena: The Afroasiatic Roots of Classical Civilization*), I: *The Fabrication of Ancient Greece, 1785–1985* (London: Free Association Books, 1987); Eva C. Keuls, *The Reign of the Phallus: Sexual Politics in Ancient Athens*, 2nd ed. (Berkeley and Los Angeles: University of California Press, 1993 [1985]); Gregory Vlastos, "Was Plato a Feminist?," and Mary Lefkowitz, "Only the Best Girls Get To," *Times Literary Supplement*, 17–23 March 1989, pp. 276, 288–89, and 5–11 May, pp. 484, 497; David M. Halperin, John J. Winkler and Froma I. Zeitlin, eds., *Before Sexuality: The Construction of Erotic Experience in the Ancient Greek World* (Princeton: Princeton University Press, 1990); Danielle S. Allen, *The World of Prometheus: The Politics of Punishing in Democratic Athens* (Princeton: Princeton University Press, 2000); Helene P. Foley, *Female Acts in Greek Tragedy* (Princeton: Princeton University Press, 2001).

on him, Clausewitz became an overnight sensation and his work was translated into a score of European languages.[48] He was read primarily by military officers who approached *On War* as they would an operation manual. Not surprisingly, their narrow frame of reference led to serious misunderstandings, among them the mistaken belief that Clausewitz valued the offensive over the defensive and thought that the goal of war was the destruction of enemy forces in a battle of envelopment (*Vernichtungsschlacht*). Clausewitz was mobilized for more progressive ends by younger, freer-thinking German officers to put an end to strategies based on geometric conceptions of maneuver and to introduce greater flexibility and initiative at every level of command.[49] The French army was understandably reluctant to adapt the precepts of their enemy's chief strategist, but by 1900 Clausewitz had become *de rigeur*, largely because his emphasis on moral force appeared to support the emerging military doctrine of *élan vital*. In 1903, General Ferdinand Foch, who would become generalissimo of the Allied armies in World War I, published his *Principles of War*.[50] Foch drew heavily on Clausewitz, and, like his German counterparts, ignored his admonition that defense was the stronger form of war.[51] French and German students of Clausewitz were oblivious to his warnings that wars were hard to limit or control once popular passions were aroused, and to his implicit warning that a future continental war could shake the foundations of European civilization.

Marx, Engels and Lenin were drawn to Clausewitz for his characterization of war as an instrument of policy. Clausewitz's contention that war was an expression of deeper social forces, and the corollary that military doctrine and strategy had to be based on an appreciation of these forces, could readily be incorporated into their materialist philosophy. Lenin urged party functionaries to read Clausewitz. Trotsky and Stalin cited him, and made *On War* required reading for generations of Soviet

48 Eberhard Kessel, *Moltke* (Stuttgart: K. F. Koehler, 1957), p. 108.

49 Peter Paret, "Clausewitz and the Nineteenth Century," in Michael Howard, ed., *The Theory and Practice of War* (London: Cassell, 1965), pp. 21–42.

50 Ferdinand Foch, *Des principes de la guerre: conférences faites en 1900 à l'École Supérieure de Guèrre*, 5th ed. (Paris: Berger-Levrault, 1918 [1903]); Azar Gat, *The Development of Military Thought: The Nineteenth Century* (Oxford: Oxford University Press, 1992), pp. 116–72, on the influence of Clausewitz in France; Christopher Bassford, *Clausewitz in English: The Reception of Clausewitz in Britain and America, 1815–1945* (New York: Oxford University Press, 1994), pp. 116–50 on Britain; Beatrice Heuser, *Reading Clausewitz* (London: Pimlico, 2002), for a more general description of the response to Clausewitz; Jack Snyder, *The Ideology of the Offensive: Military Decisionmaking and the Disasters of 1914* (Ithaca: Cornell University Press, 1984), more generally on the cult of the offensive.

51 Colmar von der Goltz, *Das Volk in Waffen: ein Buch über Heerwesen und Kriegführung unserer Zeit* (Berlin: R. V. Decker, 1884), insisted that if Clausewitz were still alive he would have changed his mind on this point.

staff officers.[52] If the Soviets were attracted to Clausewitz, the British were in equal measure repelled. Following World War I, British strategists demonized Clausewitz as a bloodthirsty Prussian. B. H. Liddell Hart, who failed to distinguish Clausewitz from his ill-informed interpreters, dismissed him as "the Mahdi of mass and of mutual massacre."[53] The Anglo-American vilification of Clausewitz continued into the post-World War II era.[54] Anatol Rapoport rejected Clausewitz's formulation of war as an extension of politics by other means and denied that war was an inescapable element of human life.[55] Rapoport went after Clausewitz in a round-about effort to discredit nuclear strategists like Thomas Schelling, Henry Kissinger and Herman Kahn who considered nuclear weapons usable. Kahn actually thought nuclear war was winnable, and the title of his principal work, *On Thermonuclear War*, implied an attempt to apply Clausewitz to the contemporary strategic environment. Kahn in fact made few references to the Prussian strategist, and his argument was not significantly influenced by his thought.[56] The mistaken belief that Clausewitz advocated the offensive also remained alive. In 1976, Edward Luttwak chided the Romans for their "seemingly ineradicable Clausewitzian prejudice against defensive strategies."[57] More recently, John Keegan has engaged in extensive Clausewitz bashing, accusing him of designing a "pernicious" political philosophy that provided the foundation for the totalitarian state.[58] Victor Hanson portrayed Clausewitz as seeing the real purpose of war as "the absolute destruction of the enemy's armed forces" in support of his contention that the Western way of war is unique by reason of its "desire for a single, magnificent collision

[52] Gat, *The Development of Military Thought*, pp. 226–46, contends that the influence of Clausewitz on Marx, Engels and Lenin has been exaggerated.

[53] B. H. Liddell Hart, *The Ghost of Napoleon* (New Haven: Yale University Press, 1934), pp. 120–21; Azar Gat, *Fascist and Liberal Visions of War: Fuller, Liddell Hart, Douhet, and Other Modernists* (Oxford: Oxford University Press, 1998), for Clausewitz's reception in the first half of the twentieth century.

[54] Bassford, *Clausewitz in English*, pp. 197–212, for a good overview of this literature.

[55] Anatol Rapoport, *Strategy and Conscience* (New York: Harper & Row, 1964). Rapoport also edited an abridged English edition of Clausewitz, *On War* (Harmondsworth: Penguin Books, 1968).

[56] Henry A. Kissinger, *Nuclear Weapons and American Foreign Policy* (New York: Harper Bros., 1957); Herman Kahn, *On Thermonuclear War* (Princeton: Princeton University Press, 1961), and *Thinking About the Unthinkable* (New York: Horizon Press, 1962); Thomas C. Schelling, *The Strategy of Conflict* (New York: Oxford University Press, 1963), and *Arms and Influence* (New Haven: Yale University Press, 1966).

[57] Edward Luttwak, *The Grand Strategy of the Roman Empire: From the First Century A.D. to the Third* (Baltimore: Johns Hopkins University Press, 1976), p. 61.

[58] John Keegan, *War and Our World* (New York: Vintage, 2001 [1998]), pp. 41–43; *A History of Warfare* (London: Key Porter, 1993), pp. 3, 23, 40, 46–47, 58, seriously misreads Clausewitz.

of infantry, for brutal killing with edged weapons on a battlefield between free men."[59] Like Thucydides, Clausewitz has become a powerful symbol, and his interpreters, with few exceptions, read him in a manner consistent with their outlook and goals.[60]

More serious studies also appeared, beginning with Robert Osgood's study of limited war. It was based on an accurate reading of Clausewitz's views and made the case for treating him as a sophisticated thinker, even a philosopher.[61] The real turning point came in 1976 with the publication of Peter Paret's carefully researched intellectual biography of Clausewitz and a new English edition of *On War*, translated and edited by Paret and Michael Howard.[62] Both volumes, but especially the translation, sparked renewed interest in Clausewitz and were the catalyst for a series of subsequent studies of his thought or intelligent applications of it to problems of contemporary strategy.[63]

Morgenthau was subject to a different pattern of misrepresentation. His early postwar works – *Scientific Man versus Power Politics* (1946), *Politics Among Nations* (1948) and *In Defense of the National Interest* (1951) – were broadsides against an approach to international relations that put great stock in the power of law and international institutions to restrain and resolve conflict. It is not surprising that the targets of Morgenthau's criticism, whom he disparaged somewhat unfairly as "idealists," were both hostile and insensitive to the nuances of his arguments. Some replied in kind and called him immoral and "Machiavellian." They misread his insistence on the enduring and central importance of power in all political

[59] Victor David Hanson, *The Western Way of War: Infantry Battle in Classical Greece* (Berkeley and Los Angeles: University of California Press, 1989), p. 9.

[60] Important nineteenth-century exceptions were Wilhelm Rüstow, a Prussian lieutenant (and grandfather of the late political scientist, Dankwart Rustow), who was a prolific writer and became chief-of-staff to Garibaldi, and historian Hans Delbrück. The latter's *Geschichte der Kriegskunst im Rahmen der politischen Geschichte* (Berlin: de Gruyter, 200 [1920]), IV, pp. 439–44, made accurate use of Clausewitz's concept of limited war.

[61] Robert E. Osgood, *Limited War: The Challenge to American Strategy* (Chicago: University of Chicago Press, 1957), pp. 21–13; Samuel P. Huntington, *The Soldier and the State: The Theory and Politics of Civil-Military Relations* (Cambridge, Mass.: Harvard University Press, 1957), also contain more sophisticated references to Clausewitz.

[62] Peter Paret, *Clausewitz and the State: The Man, His Theories, and His Times* (Princeton: Princeton University Press, 1976); Clausewitz, *On War*, trans. and ed. Michael Howard and Peter Paret (Princeton: Princeton University Press, 1976).

[63] Examples include, James E. King, "On Clausewitz: Master Theorist of War," *Naval War College Review* 30 (Fall 1977), pp. 3–36; Barry D. Watts, *The Foundations of US Air Doctrine: The Problem of Friction in War* (Maxwell Air Force Base, Al.: Air University Press, 1984); Richard Ned Lebow, *Nuclear Crisis Management: A Dangerous Illusion* (Ithaca: Cornell University Press, 1987); Stephen J. Cimbala, *Clausewitz and Escalation: A Classical Perspective on Nuclear Strategy* (Portland: Frank Cass, 1991), and *Clausewitz and Chaos: Friction in War and Military Policy* (Westport, Conn: Praeger, 2001); Gat, *The Development of Military Thought*.

relationships as an endorsement of European-style *Realpolitik* and its corollary that might makes right. By the time of the Korean War, the battle with the so-called idealists had been won and realism had become the conventional wisdom of the American foreign policy establishment. To Morgenthau's consternation, prominent representatives of that establishment came away with more or less the same understanding of *Politics Among Nations* as had idealists, only they endorsed its emphasis on power and alleged disparagement of ethics.

Realism faced a different kind of threat within the academic community where Kenneth Waltz and his neorealist disciples sought to translate Morgenthau's understanding of international relations into a set of deductively derived and empirically falsifiable propositions.[64] Waltz asserted that classical realism was indistinguishable from *Realpolitik*, and that there was an unbroken line of descent from Machiavelli through Friedrich Meinecke and Morgenthau. For all three thinkers, he insisted, good policy was whatever advanced the interests of the state.[65] Morgenthau and Thucydides remain foundational texts for international relations scholars, and are cited more frequently than their counterparts in other social sciences.[66] Perhaps this is because international relations is still a young field and feels the need – as indeed it should – to justify itself intellectually. There is all the more reason then to have lucid, defensible readings of these texts, readings, moreover, that build reliable bridges between them and the kinds of problems that are, or should be, of interest to contemporary scholars.

Interpretations

Thucydides wrote his account of the Peloponnesian War to recapture the meaning of words and the conventions they sustained. These conventions were necessary to restore the community (*homonoia*) on which stable domestic and international orders depended. I have a similar, if far more modest, ambition. By analyzing the writings of Thucydides, Clausewitz and Morgenthau, I want to recapture the language of classical realism and the discourse it sustains. It offers us a subtle and supple set of concepts for the study of international relations and the conduct

[64] Waltz, *Theory of International Politics*. [65] Ibid., p. 117.

[66] Economists rarely cite Ricardo, Adam Smith or Karl Marx, and none of them, as far as I know, are required readings in North American Ph.D. programs. Psychologists, as distinct from psychiatrists, do their best to distance themselves from Freud, and rarely mention William James. Tocqueville is similarly slighted in articles on American politics that appear in top behavioral journals; he has been relegated to political theory. Sociology may come closest to international relations in its ritual genuflections to Max Weber.

of foreign policy. I begin by situating these thinkers in their respective historical and intellectual settings and analyze their writings as responses to the problems of their respective eras. I provide the most thorough grounding for Thucydides because his political and cultural context is least well known to modern readers. It is also the most critical to understanding his writing. I provide somewhat less context for Clausewitz because the early nineteenth-century German setting is better known. His principal ideas can be grasped without as much background knowledge of the Prussian and wider German and European political and intellectual scene. In the case of Morgenthau, there is an additional reason to omit an introductory section on the setting. His life experiences bring politics, culture and scholarship together in the most pronounced way, and the necessary context can be brought in through a discussion of his life and writings.

My most striking finding is the extent to which they share remarkably similar understandings of power and influence, the relationships between interests and justice, agency and structure, domestic and international politics, and the importance of community for domestic and international order. These commonalities constitute the core wisdom of a philosophical tradition that transcends time, context and place in a different sense than understood by neo-positivist social science. Their arguments are heavily context-dependent but provide access to a deeper wisdom.

I devote two chapters to Thucydides because he is the most important and complex of the three thinkers. The first of these chapters addresses the outbreak of the Peloponnesian War and what it reveals about Thucydides' understanding of the relationship between ethics and interest. It offers an interpretation sharply at odds with conventional realist ones. I contend that the Peloponnesian War was not inevitable, and that shifts in relative military capabilities were at best an indirect cause of war and by no means the most important one. The debates in Sparta on the eve of the war indicate that the "war party" did not fear Athenian power; they expected to wage a brief and victorious campaign. More realistic Spartans favored a diplomatic settlement because of their accurate assessment of Athenian power and concern that any war they started would be inherited by their sons. The most important underlying cause of war was Spartan fear for their way of life, under growing threat from the political-economic-cultural transformation of Greece spearheaded by Athens. Spartan identity, not power, was the issue for both the war and peace parties. Pressures and constraints at the system and state levels may have made it difficult to prevent the crisis of 433–431 BCE. However, leaders retained considerable freedom of choice. As much as anything else, the war was due to their miscalculations at critical junctures of the crisis, miscalculations that allowed civil strife in a remote and insignificant settlement to escalate into an all-out clash between the two hegemons and their respective allies.

Thucydides was not a sophist, but he was a student of Prodicus and adopted many sophistic rhetorical practices, including the convention of proceeding from simple to complex questions.[67] The more profound the question and the possible responses to it, the less likely it is to be addressed by an explicit argument, especially one in the authorial voice. Readers must infer questions and answers from the progression of the text, its characterization of actors and its seeming contradictions and subversion of earlier arguments, explicit or implied. The history is a layered text, and the first of my chapters, on the outbreak of war, examines only the outermost. It concerns the relationship between interest and justice. Chapter 3 continues the process of unpacking, and describes the three inner layers of the text: Athens as tragedy, the relationship between *nomos* (convention) and *phusis* (nature), and the feedback loop between words (*logoi*) and deeds (*erga*). The fourth and final layer of the history suggests that Greek civilization was made possible by the emergence of communities held together by common conventions. These practices and rituals were sustained in turn by a shared language. In the course of the Peloponnesian War, key words lost their meaning, the conventions they sustained broke down, and the sense of community disappeared. This process led to even more destructive warfare and civil strife (*stasis*). Thucydides' text folds back upon itself. Readers who work their way through its four layers can return to previous levels and their questions with a different and more informed perspective. I conclude Chapter 3 with a second look at the origins of the war and what it reveals about Thucydides' understanding of modernization as the principal underlying cause of war and challenge to the reconstruction of orderly societies

Thucydides' underlying political message is that secure and prosperous societies depend on conventions, and they must be restored and maintained by reason and language. Thucydides is thus not only the father of realism, but of constructivism.[68] There is an unresolvable, and, I believe, deliberate tension between these polar world views. This is typical of many Greek works of the period, and intended to lead readers to a more complex and subtle understanding of human beings and their societies.[69]

[67] Thucydides' relationship to Sophism is discussed in Chapter 3.

[68] Richard Ned Lebow, "Thucydides the Constructivist," *American Political Science Review*, 93 (September 2001), pp. 547–60, makes this point.

[69] My interpretation builds on earlier work of James Boyd White, *When Words Lose their Meaning* (Chicago: University of Chicago Press, 1984); Euben, *The Tragedy of Political Theory*; and Connor, *Thucydides*.

Thucydides was a contemporary of the great Greek playwrights, and his indebtedness to them has long been a matter of discussion.[70] I contend that the similarities between his history and their plays go beyond the plot line and casting of Athens in the role of tragic hero. The entire history is conceived of as a tragedy. Like the playwrights, Thucydides depicts cities and their leaders as archetypical characters confronting archetypal situations.[71] His history is not an exhaustive narrative, but a spare, abstract and artfully constructed account that selects and emphasizes those aspects of the story that serve their author's broader purpose. The words and deeds of his actors often work at cross purposes, just as they might on the stage, alerting readers to contradictions and prompting them to search for hidden meanings. And in the tradition of the tragedians, he uses protagonists who represent opposite interests, values and beliefs. Corcyra and Corinth, Athens and Sparta, Nicias and Alcibiades depend on one another to define their identities, and their conflicts confront them with the moral choices that make some of them tragic figures. Thucydides also exploits the "double vision" of the theater to draw spectators, or readers in his case, into the drama emotionally while distancing themselves from it intellectually to develop a more profound understanding of its dynamics and meaning.

If Thucydides was a tragedian, why did he write a history instead of a play? No doubt, temperament had something to do with his choice. There were substantive reasons as well. The nature and difficulty of his text indicate that he directed his work at a smaller, better educated and more reflective elite. His principal political message – that conventions were arbitrary and periodically reshaped to fit changed circumstances but should nevertheless be treated as gods-given – was too "sophisticated," and perhaps too cynical, for a mass audience. Unlike a play, his history cannot be understood in a linear manner but needs multiple readings. The engaged reader needs to rethink the meaning of earlier passages in light of later ones to grasp their multiple meanings. Thucydides proclaimed his intention of producing a work for all time, and may have reasoned

[70] F. M. Cornford, *Thucydides Mythistoricus* (London: Arnold, 1907); John H. Finley, Jr., *Three Essays on Thucydides* (Cambridge, Mass.: Harvard University Press, 1967); Euben, *The Tragedy of Political Theory*; Hayward R. Alker, "The Dialectical Logic of Thucydides' Melian Dialogue," *American Political Science Review* 82 (September 1988), pp. 806–20; David Bedford and Thom Workman, "The Tragic Reading of the Thucydidean Tragedy," *Review of International Studies* 27 (January 2001), pp. 51–67. Our best estimate is that Thucydides was born in about 460. Sophocles and Euripides were his contemporaries, and he would almost certainly have attended some of their performances, although he was in exile from 424 to 420. Aeschylus was born a generation earlier.

[71] Cornford, *Thucydides Mythistoricus*, pp. 140–47, makes this point.

that a written text held out the greater possibility of transcending time and culture at a time when the oral tradition, the accepted mode of transmission for plays, was becoming problematic.[72] Tragedies reworked old myths, and the power of myths was also declining in the late fifth century. Moreover, they only spoke to a Greek audience. History offered a new foundation for construction of narratives for the same purpose, and narratives that would transcend their specific temporal and cultural settings.

There was a more fundamental reason still for Thucydides' choice of tragedy as a model. As I noted earlier, tragedy encourages us to confront our frailties and limits and the disastrous consequences of trying to exceed them. All tragedies remind us of our mortality. Aristotle maintained that tragedies communicated knowledge by inspiring fear and pity, and the *katharsis* these emotions produce. *Katharsis* is a medical term, and Aristotle used it metaphorically to signify a purge of the soul that restores a healthy balance by removing toxic emotions and ambitions. For Aristotle, the greatness of art, especially tragedy, derived from its ability to expose us to the monstrous possibilities of human behavior without at the same time infecting us with the madness that leads to that behavior. Such an imitation (*mimēsis*) of practice (*praxis*) was no inoculation against disaster, but it might make us more introspective and cautious to the extent that it brings awareness of the potential we all have to make fatal miscalculations. This message could best be driven home by describing the reality of the Peloponnesian War.[73]

Aristotle and Thucydides understood that art could be a more effective teacher than argument. I believe this was the fundamental reason why

[72] Thucydides' decision to embrace the new medium stood in sharp contrast to its rejection by Plato's Socrates. In *Phaedrus*, 275d–276a, Plato has Socrates complain that written words "seem to talk to you as though they were intelligent, but if you ask them anything about what they say, from a desire to be instructed, they go on telling you just the same thing forever. And once a thing is put in writing, the composition, whatever it may be, drifts (*kulindetai*) all over the place, getting into the hands not only of those who understand it, but equally of those who have no business with it." Plato, like Thucydides, champions the written word because it facilitates the triumph of *epistēmē* over *doxa*. Eric Havelock, *Preface to Plato* (New York: Grosset & Dunlap, 1967); James Risser, "The Voice of the Other in Gadamer's Hermeneutics," in Lewis Edwin Hahn, ed., *The Philosophy of Hans-George Gadamer* (Chicago: Open Court, 1997), pp. 389–402.

[73] For Aristotle, *Politics*, 1341b35–1342a20, *Poetics*, 9, 1450a–b, 1452a1–10, 1453b1–2, tragedy (*tragōidia*) is the imitation (*mimēsis*) of a good (*spoudaias*) action. Through pity (*eleos*) and fear (*phobos*) it achieves catharsis. *Eleos*, in the sense of serious or earnest, suggests sympathy and suffering with someone's pain. See also, John Jones, *On Aristotle and Greek Tragedy* (London: Chatto & Windus, 1962); Gerald Frank Else, *Plato and Aristotle on Poetry* (Chapel Hill: University of North Carolina Press, 1986), pp. 158–60; Nussbaum, *The Fragility of Goodness*, pp. 388–90. Thucydides also makes use of medical analogies, an issue I shall address in Chapter 2.

Thucydides dramatized his history as a tragedy and made the most sparing use of explicit arguments. He nevertheless sought to probe and extend the limits of what words could convey. His history might be read as a conscious attempt to close, as far as possible, the gap between what could be known and what could be expressed. Such an experiment required a different mode of presentation than traditional tragedy, and toward this end he developed a syncretic form that blended argument, narrative and debate. He nevertheless adhered to the long-standing classical convention that stories are the principal means of conveying moral lessons.

From the Peloponnesian War, I jump many centuries to the Napoleonic Wars and their implications for strategy and politics as understood by the Prussian soldier, reformer and historian, Carl von Clausewitz. The French Revolution and the wars it unleashed were made possible by a process of modernization that stimulated nationalism while increasing the military capability of states. Clausewitz sought to understand the nature of these changes and their implications, not only for warfare but for the post-Napoleonic political order. Like Thucydides, he regarded political history as an endless cycle of growth and decline, of states that advanced and transformed civilization, but also threatened it through their hubris, overreaching ambitions and the destructive wars to which they gave rise. He also recognized the important role of leaders and tried to develop a more general understanding of the relationship between agency and structure.

My chapter examines his unfinished magnum opus, *On War*. His other books, essays and correspondence provide further insight into his understanding of the Napoleonic Wars, warfare more generally and its relationship to other forms of social activity. The principal problem that engaged Clausewitz for much of his adult career was how to construct a scientific and universally valid theory for a phenomenon that was shaped by the interaction of ever-evolving culture and technology, by individual choices, emotions and pure chance. His solution was to distinguish between the worlds of theory (thesis) and practice (antithesis). The former should aspire to describe the fundamental principles and processes associated with war and use them to deduce general patterns of behavior. Such a conceptual architecture would have pedagogical but not predictive value because principles and processes alike only take on shape in context, and are subject to faulty human understanding and execution and various forms of inefficiency and breakdown that Clausewitz grouped together under the rubric of "friction." All these complications distinguish war in practice from any theoretical representation of it. The best one can do is to get a "feel" for the real world through reading and practice (*Übung*).

Clausewitz's thinking evolved from unquestioning loyalty to the Prussian state and its premodern values to a more cosmopolitan outlook. His mature political agenda rested on his Kantian hope that gifted leaders might exploit the potential of the modern state to enhance the physical and spiritual well-being of its citizens without sacrificing older, core values that encouraged loyalty, restraint and prudence. He was under no illusion that post-Napoleonic warfare would naturally revert to the eighteenth-century pattern of restraint in means and ends. He considered modern warfare a threat to progress and civilization, and all the more so because of the failure of so many of his contemporaries to understand that "national" wars could not easily be limited in scope or duration. A key challenge for nineteenth-century Europe was to bring a society of modern, largely national states into being without provoking catastrophic wars.

One of the striking features of the German counter-Enlightenment was its deep interest in Ancient Greece, and tragedy in particular. Artistically, the appeal of a highly idealized Greece of reason and "noble simplicity" was a reaction against the overblown baroque tastes of the aristocracy. More fundamentally, it expressed a yearning for a time in which it was believed that thought and feeling, reason and expression and man and nature were in harmony. It was also a vehicle for alienated and powerless intellectuals to attempt to restructure their society through a cultural and educational revolution. Johann Joachim Winckelmann, Friedrich August Wolf, Wilhelm von Humboldt and Friedrich Schleieremacher all insisted that classical literature and art – especially Greek literature and art – were foundational components of *Bildung* and university education.[74]

The Renaissance revived interest in Greek tragedy, and the first stage production of a tragedy, Sophocles' *Oedipus*, took place in Vicenza in 1585.[75] Early operas were efforts to reproduce tragedy, on the questionable assumption that all the characters sang their lines, not just the chorus. Translations into the vernacular also provided a model for contemporary drama.[76] Theoretical interest in tragedy became pronounced in the eighteenth century. Beginning with Friedrich Wilhelm Joseph Schelling, German writers and thinkers sought to rejuvenate tragedy,

[74] Suzanne L. Marchand, *Down From Olympus: Archeology and Philhellenism in Germany, 1750–1970* (Princeton: Princeton University Press, 1976); Walter Rüegg, "*Die Antike als Begründung des deutschen national Bewussteins*," in Wolfgang Schuller, ed., *Xenia*, XV (Konstanz, 1985); Taylor, *Hegel*, pp. 25–29.

[75] Peter Burian, "Tragedy Adapted for Stages and Screens: The Renaissance to the Present," in P. E. Easterling, *The Cambridge Companion to Greek Tragedy* (Cambridge: Cambridge University Press, 1997), pp. 151–77.

[76] Ibid.; Martin Mueller, *Children of Oedipus and Other Essays on the Imitation of Greek Tragedy, 1550–1800* (Toronto: University of Toronto Press, 1980).

not as a genre, but as a means of nourishing ethical and political sensibilities appropriate to the time. German Idealists and Romantics from Kant and Herder on were particularly drawn to the way in which tragedy explored in a public forum the conflicts and responsibilities associated with social and political relationships. Tragedy offered a model for thinking through the problem of adapting traditional values to a changing political order. Tragedy, as the German philosophers realized, is a situationally specific political art form and cannot be resurrected to build community. But it provides insight into this problem and suggests another route to establish ethics. The fascination with tragedy also reflected the belief – which Hegel certainly did not share – that philosophy had reached a dead end and that new ways of thinking about the world were accordingly needed. Schelling, Hölderlin and Nietzsche in the nineteenth century, and Benjamin and Heidegger in the twentieth, found inspiration in the beauty of art, but especially in tragedy, which they, like Aristotle, considered its highest embodiment. They were also drawn to tragedy's emphasis on primal emotions, acceptance of suffering and recognition that conflict and contradiction defined the human condition.[77]

If Thucydides conceived of history as tragedy, post-Kantian German philosophers embraced tragedy as a means of understanding history, and thus, their present. Hume and Gibbon – more typical representatives of the Enlightenment – derided history as a record of folly, superstition and oppression. Kant, by contrast, approached history with reverence and as the story of humanity's struggles to uplift itself morally. Hegel adopted this view, and was drawn to tragedy as a model for thinking about historical development. In it he found hidden dynamics that moved social interactions at every level of analysis. He reasoned that history was driven by the same dialectic of conflict and recognition, and came to understand it as the efforts of the spirit to recognize its individuality, by comprehending the universality in terms of which it could come to know and differentiate itself. Like Schelling, he considered history tragic in its inexorability.[78] Clausewitz idealized the state, but differed from Kant and

[77] Walter Kaufmann, *Tragedy and Philosophy*, rev. ed. (New York: Anchor Book, 1969); Hayden White, *Metahistory: The Historical Imagination in Nineteenth Century Europe* (Baltimore: Johns Hopkins University Press, 1973); Schmidt, *On Germans and Other Greeks*, for the role of tragedy in post–Kantian German philosophy.

[78] Hegel did not think much of either Herodotus or Thucydides, both of whom represented *ursprünglich* historiography. Their descriptions, he wrote, "are for the most part limited to deeds, events, and states of society, which they had before their eyes, and whose spirit they shared. They simply transferred what was passing in the world around them, to the real of representative intellect." Hegel's notion of decline is nevertheless reminiscent of Thucydides. It is based on the concept of a widening gap between practice

Hegel in that he regarded neither history nor the state as expressions of some purposeful design. His thinking was nevertheless deeply influenced by Hegel, whom he knew personally, and by other major figures of the German counter-Enlightenment who were his friends, whose works he read and with whom he corresponded.

Clausewitz did not write *On War* as a tragedy. By the time of Aristotle, history, philosophy and literature had already emerged as separate genres governed by their own conventions.[79] Clausewitz was interested in history and philosophy, and *On War* is more self-consciously theoretical than his earlier historical works. But Clausewitz's entire project was informed by tragic sensibilities. He used the dialectic not only to differentiate war in theory from war in practice, but to highlight polarities and the unresolvable tensions between them. War in theory represented what we could understand and control through the application of reason. War in practice was influenced by emotions and chance, whose understanding lay beyond our intellects and were only partially subject to our will. More than other aspects of life, war was complex, unpredictable and subject to dramatic and unexpected reverses in fortune. Paradoxically, the likelihood of such reverses rose in proportion to prior success. Victory did not lead to mastery of war as much as it did to hubris and a resulting *hamartia* (miscalculation, but originally, missing the mark in archery) that set tragic heroes on the road to catastrophe.[80]

German idealist philosophers developed an important implication of Aristotle's conception of *katharsis*: that tragedy, and art more generally, can impart wisdom that goes beyond that which can be expressed in words. Kant depicted beauty as a non-conceptual presentation of a *sensus communis*, as something outside and beyond the ability of words to capture.[81] Hegel rejected this notion – dismissing art as "a thing of the

and the ideals that hold a culture together. *Philosophy of History*, in *The Philosophy of Hegel*, trans. J. B. Baillie, revised Carl J. Friedrich (New York: Modern Library, 1953), pp. 399–519; Walter Kaufmann, *Hegel: A Reinterpretation* (Garden City, N.Y.: Doubleday, 1966); White, *Metahistory*, pp. 98–99.

79 Tragedy itself has fragmented into distinct genres. Greek drama, especially before Euripides, blended music, singing, dance and spoken parts, and the playwright was expected to compose his own music and choreography and train all of the performers.

80 In Homer, *hubrizein* means to wax wanton or run riot, and specifically to overfed asses that bray and run wild. Hubris is also used to indicate the wanton violence of Penelope's suitors. By the late fifth century it has become associated with abuses of power and might be defined as the "wanton disregard for the rights of others." Kaufmann, *Tragedy and Philosophy*, pp. 64–68. See Chapter 4 for a discussion of the concept of *hamartia*.

81 Immanuel Kant, *The Critique of Judgement* (Oxford: Oxford University Press, 1961. Kant's analysis departed from Greek understandings in that it approached beauty as an ethical question. Starting from this premise, Schelling, Hegel and Schlegel went on to argue that the analysis of beauty is more important and on a higher level that the creation of beauty.

past" – prompting Schelling and Kierkegaard to come to its defense.[82] A central question for Kierkegaard was the limits of language and how to find a way to speak that did not betray the deep insights that could be experienced independently of the intellect. Nietzsche, who sided with Schelling and Kierkegaard, maintained that the beauty of art could not be understood or appreciated through "logical insight" or any kind of reasoning. It could only be grasped by "intuition," which, Nietzsche insisted, was "the highest task and the true metaphysical activity of life."[83] Clausewitz, writing some fifty years before Nietzsche, was also rooted in this tradition. He struggled to reconcile conceptual and non-conceptual kinds of knowledge in the domain of strategy and politics, and toward this end borrowed the idea of genius from Kant.[84] For Clausewitz, genius was an innate psychological quality (*ingenium*) that allowed someone to rise above the rules – or what others consider to be the rules – to intuit new possibilities and create a synthesis of war in theory and practice. William Tell, Wallenstein, William of Orange, Gustavus Adolphus, Frederick the Great, but above all, Napoleon, qualified as geniuses because they grasped new possibilities and by implementing them effectively changed the nature of warfare. Like Hegel's "world historical individuals," Clausewitz's geniuses did not have to understand conceptually what they were doing, although some, like Napoleon, he recognized, certainly did.

The German rediscovery of tragedy was intended to serve broader artistic and political ends. Clausewitz also had political goals. He was humiliated by the ease with which Napoleon overwhelmed Prussia and despaired at the inability of King Friedrich Wilhelm to rise to this political-military challenge. He looked to an elite of reformers to provide leadership, appropriate institutions and moral inspiration for the German nation. The war against France provided Prussia, and Germany as a whole, with an opportunity to find unity and purpose. He was elated by the ability of reformers to arouse idealism among Prussia's subjects and bitterly disappointed by the political reaction that set in after Napoleon's defeat.

The link between Morgenthau and tragedy is more self-conscious. In his first postwar book, *Scientific Man vs. Power Politics*, Morgenthau attributed the horrors of the twentieth century to hubris and miscalculation.

[82] G. W. F. Hegel, *Aesthetics; Lectures on Fine Arts*, trans. T. M. Knox (Oxford: Oxford University Press, 1975), p. 11.

[83] Friedrich Nietzsche, *The Birth of Tragedy*, trans. Walter Kaufmann (Mineola, N.Y.: Dover, 1995), pp. 19–23.

[84] Kant, *The Critique of Judgment*, pp. 168 and 181, described genius as "the talent that gives the rule to art." It is the talent "for producing that for which no definite rule can be given." Rothfels, *Carl von Clausewitz*, pp. 23–25, for Kant's influence on Clausewitz.

Hubris took the form of the Enlightenment's misplaced faith in reason and the false belief it engendered that human beings could remake and control the social and physical environments. These beliefs had inspired remarkable advances in technology and social organization and facilitated the emergence of the modern industrial state. And as Clausewitz had hoped, the state became the most exalted object of loyalty on the part of the individual. But the unexpected and powerful transference of private impulses on to the state, Morgenthau lamented, had been exploited by demented leaders like Stalin, Hitler and Mao Zedong for the most murderous of purposes.[85]

Following the Greeks, Morgenthau read history as a struggle between the traditional and modern, reason and passion and life and death. Appreciation of the inescapable and enduring nature of this struggle gave rise to "the tragic sense" and acceptance of the "unresolvable discord, contradictions, and conflicts which are inherent in the nature of things and which human reason is powerless to solve."[86] Like the German idealist philosophers, with whose works he was intimately familiar, Morgenthau believed that the tragic sense found its fullest expression in the Greek tragedies and plays of Shakespeare. He regretted that the owl of Minerva had taken flight in the age of science. The illusion that "the tragic antinomies" of life could be overcome through education and public life blinded modern man, as it had Oedipus in ancient times, to the possibility that his well-intentioned actions could produce outcomes the very opposite of those desired. A case in point was the expectations of many Western leaders and foreign policy experts that international law and treaties could regulate conflict. Instead, these expectations had facilitated the rise of the dictators, delayed recognition of the threat they posed to Western civilization and helped to bring about the most destructive war in history. The dreams of modernity led to the nightmares of World War I, the Russian civil war, forced collectivization and famine, Nazi barbarism, genocide and World War II.[87]

Morgenthau based his theory of international politics on his tragic understanding of the world in the hope that it would help statesmen to avert another major and perhaps fatal war. In keeping with the Greek project, his theory was intended to avert pain and suffering. In an era when *nomos* had lost its ability to constrain, he reasoned that status quo countries had no choice but to base their security on their economic and military capability and the skill of their diplomats. He conceived of power as a

[85] Hans J. Morgenthau, *Scientific Man vs. Power Politics* (Chicago: University of Chicago Press, 1946). Citations refer to the edition published in London by Latimer House in 1947.

[86] Ibid., p. 174. [87] Ibid., pp. 174–77.

psychological relationship that put a premium on the quality of leadership: it was the only mechanism that could transform raw capability into influence and maximize that influence efficiently through a judicious mix of activism and restraint. Like Thucydides, Morgenthau worried that his country's leaders were incapable of acting wisely; they were too willing to sacrifice the enduring interests of their society for putative short-term domestic and foreign gains. They also succumbed to hubris and became arrogant in the exercise of their power. Morgenthau drew a parallel between the Sicilian expedition and Vietnam, both of which he described as manifestations of the decline of the Athenian and American political cultures. In the last resort, security and international order depended on the *moral* qualities of leaders and their ability to practice restraint in the face of pressures on them to use their power in adventurous and unethical ways.

At mid-century Morgenthau identified two key international threats: nuclear war and environmental catastrophe. He doubted the ability of sovereign states to address either problem. He worried that leaders lacked the courage to exercise restraint in an acute crisis or make the near-term sacrifices necessary to preserve the environment. By 1970 he had become guardedly optimistic about the prospects for a far-reaching transformation of the international system. Arms control, the gradual diminution of the Cold War and the first steps toward European integration made it appear more likely that the superpowers could avoid a nuclear Armageddon. The American civil rights and anti-war movements gave him hope that modern, participatory democracy could build an egalitarian society and compel a more prudent foreign policy. If the system of sovereign states was to be superseded, it had to be through traditional political means: leaders and public opinion had to recognize that their interests required some form of supranational authority. The principal task of international relations theory was to make leaders and public opinion aware of this need and lay the intellectual foundations for the required transformation.

Reading texts

From time immemorial religions have considered control over texts and their readings potent sources of legitimacy and authority. The Old Testament was codified with this end in mind, and for over a millennium the Roman Catholic church forbade translations of the Bible into the vernacular. At its core, the Enlightenment was an attempt to use reason to destroy tradition and free the individual, and its proponents envisaged texts as powerful weapons in this struggle. It was not a coincidence that

Hobbes saw himself as providing a rational foundation for the experience-derived truths that Thucydides had discovered. Assertions of some post-modernists that elites shape the discourses used to interpret texts to strengthen their hold on power is old wine in new bottles. It also ignores the equally effective use of discourses and texts by those who wish to supplant them.[88] Christian and Muslim fundamentalists offer a striking contemporary example of how radical discourses and the interpretations of texts they enable can be used to mobilize political support to the religious and political establishment.[89]

Humanists have long acknowledged that texts are open to multiple readings. Texts are often ambiguous, and the writings of Thucydides, Clausewitz and Morgenthau pose formidable problems for even the most open-minded and sophisticated readers. Thucydides' account of the Peloponnesian War and Clausewitz's *On War* are incomplete, contradictory and utilize rhetorical conventions not readily accessible to modern readers. Morgenthau completed the works for which he is principally known, but they also contain contradictions, and, like Clausewitz, his views evolved over time. Ambiguity provides an opening for those with political or intellectual agendas to try to capture these texts to legitimize and advance their goals.

There are more fundamental reasons for interpretive diversity. The answers we find are largely determined by the questions we ask. Those questions in turn reflect who we are, the nature of the problems that interest us and the assumptions or sensitivities we bring to texts. Changes in identities, discourses and interests account for the periodic and often quite radical shifts in how Thucydides has been read over the ages. They also influence interpretation in the shorter term. W. Robert Connor, one of the most distinguished contemporary classical scholars, attributes his initial interest and understanding of Thucydides to the war in Indochina.[90] The end of the Cold War stimulated new readings of Thucydides.[91] As Hans-Georg Gadamer has noted, there is a feedback process between texts and

[88] Michel Foucault, "Nietzsche, Genealogy, History," in Donald F. Bouchard, ed., *Language, Counter-Memory, Practice: Selected Essays and Interviews*, trans. Bouchard and Sherry Simon (Ithaca: Cornell University Press, 1977), pp. 139–64, and "Two Lectures," in Colin Gordon, ed., *Power/Knowledge: Selected Interviews and Other Writings, 1972–1977* (New York: Pantheon, 1980), pp. 93–94, 109–33.

[89] Susan Friend Harding, *The Book of Jerry Falwell: Fundamentalist Language and Politics* (Princeton: Princeton University Press, 2000), shows how fundamentalists use the Bible as a generative text to create new cultural forms. They invoke the Holy Spirit as a unifying interpretive convention that allows ongoing creation. Fundamentalist language is therefore the opposite of a skeptic's literalist reading that searches for contradictions: rather it seeks to integrate, reconcile and generate, and to create hybrid cultural forms rather than separatist ones.

[90] Connor, *Thucydides*, pp. 6–8.

[91] Chapter 3 discusses this literature.

identities. Our understanding of ourselves shapes our understanding of texts, but these interpretations in turn alter our understanding of ourselves and our world.[92]

Nietzsche regretted that attempts to understand the Greeks on their own terms were doomed to failure even though he considered this an all-important task. The very idea of Greece, he believed, had become so contaminated by German conceptions of Germany that it was impossible to separate one from the other. Nietzsche understood that the wealth of texts far exceeds the intentions of their authors and the cultures that produced them.[93] More recently, Stanley Fish has noted that good texts point away from themselves to ideas and feelings they cannot capture. They invite readers to enter into a dialogue and to create a "community" between author and reader that transcends generations.[94] Peter Euben believes that Thucydides deliberately sought to create such a community with future readers because he wrote at a time when acute factional conflict made it difficult to create a fellowship with his contemporaries.[95] From Schelling through Hegel, Hölderlin, Nietzsche and Heidegger, several generations of German writers and philosophers engaged in "dialogues" with Aeschylus and Sophocles in their search for a discourse appropriate to their epoch.[96]

[92] Hans George Gadamer, *Truth and Method* (New York: Saber, 1975 [1960]) and "Text and Interpretation," in Diane Michelfelder and Richard Palmer, eds., *Dialogue and Deconstruction* (Albany: State University of New York Press, 1989), pp. 21–51; Jacques Derrida, "Structure, Sign and Play in the Discourse of the Human Science," in *The Structuralist Controversy*, pp. 247–64.

[93] Nietzsche, *The Birth of Tragedy*, pp. 73–75; Pierre Vidal-Nacquet, *The Black Hunter: Forms of Thought and Forms of Society in the Greek World*, trans. Andrew Szegedy-Maszak (Baltimore: Johns Hopkins University Press, 1986), p. 252, offers the same judgment about the last century of Hellenic studies. Hanson, *The Western Way of War*, pp. 6–7, criticizes contemporary scholars for creating a false image of Athens as a rarefied world of intellectuals and artists. Nietzsche was a great admirer of Jacob Burckhardt, who was trying to reclaim Greece from the romantic historians. For their relationship, see Oswyn Murray, "Introduction" to Burckhardt, *The Greeks and Greek Civilization*, pp. xxv–xxvii.

[94] Stanley E. Fish, *Self-Consuming Artifacts: The Experience of Seventeenth Century Literature* (Berkeley and Los Angeles: University of California Press, 1972), ch. 1, and *Is There a Text in the Class? The Authority of Interpretative Communities* (Cambridge, Mass.: Harvard University Press, 1980), pp. 323–24, 347–48. White, *When Words Lose Their Meaning*, pp. 18–20, 286–91, recognizes that such communities exist in practice, but warns that the claims of such communities can be overstated if they destroy the distinction between the kind of communities that are free to do whatever they wish and those that regard themselves "as bound by external fidelities or authorities," as, for example, the meaning of a literary text. See also Wolfgang Iser, *The Implied Reader: Patterns of Communication in Prose Fiction from Bunyan to Beckett* (Baltimore: Johns Hopkins University Press, 1974).

[95] Euben, *The Tragedy of Political Theory*, pp. 172, 214.

[96] Schmidt, *On Germans and Other Greeks*, *passim.*

If multiple readings are possible, what criteria can we use to distinguish good from bad ones? Hermeneutic philosophies recognize two traditions of interpretation. The first, common to many religions, aims to reconstruct the original text with the goal of discovering G-d's message. Marxism and psychoanalytic theory have undertaken similar efforts to elucidate their founders' beliefs. The second tradition arises out of Roman Law and the Talmud. It acknowledges that the objectives of original legislators, even if they are discoverable, may no longer be relevant. Interpretations must be adapted, or new ones devised, that are appropriate to contemporary circumstances. The case law tradition, which describes the Talmud and the Anglo-American legal system, is particularly malleable in this manner. Over time, such a process enriches and expands the meanings of texts, as it has for the American constitution.[97]

Most readings of historical documents and literary texts are motivated by contemporary concerns, and, for this reason, historiography and literary criticism share much in common with the Roman law and Talmudic traditions. Some of these readings use texts as Rorschach inkblots on which to project their own meanings. Hegel's interpretation of *Antigone* – which stresses the different ethical positions of man and woman, and how events in the tragedy unfold to reveal the need of the spirit to recognize itself in its radical individuality – offers a novel interpretation of the play that may tell us more about Hegel than it does about Sophocles.[98] So does Nietzsche's projection of Enlightenment individualism on to aristocratic heroes, or his contention that *Antigone* and *Oedipus at Colonus* are at their core struggles between the sexes and the Apollonian and Dionysian.[99] Greek tragedy was a catalyst for Nietzsche's imagination and led him to ideas that he subsequently read back into texts. He used his interpretations to make his insights and concepts resonate more effectively with its intended audience. It would not be productive to evaluate the interpretations of either Hegel and Nietzsche in terms of the tragedies they

[97] On hermeneutics, see Peter L. Berger and Thomas Luckmann, *The Social Construction of Reality* (New York: Free Press, 1964); Gadamer, *Truth and Method*, and "Text and Interpretation"; Jürgen Habermas, *On the Logic of the Social Sciences* (Cambridge, Mass.: MIT University Press, 1994); Paul Ricoeur, *Freud and Philosophy: An Essay in Interpretation* (New Haven: Yale University Press, 1970), and "The Model of the Text: Meaningful Action Considered as a Text" (originally published in 1971) in Fred Dallmayer and T. McCarthy, eds., *Understanding and Social Inquiry* (Notre Dame: Notre Dame University Press, 1977); John R. Searle, *The Construction of Social Reality* (New York: Free Press, 1995); Gary Shapiro and Alan Sica, eds., *Hermeneutics* (Amherst: University of Massachusetts Press, 1984). For an overview and the controversies surrounding hermeneutics, see Paul Diesing, *How Does Social Science Work? Reflection on Practice* (Pittsburgh: University of Pittsburgh Press, 1991), pp. 104–48.

[98] Georg Wilhelm Friedrich Hegel, *The Phenomenology of Mind*, ed. George Lichtheim, trans. J. B. Baillie (New York: Harper & Row [1967]), paras. 457, 463–466.

[99] Nietzsche, *The Birth of Tragedy*.

wrote about.[100] Sigmund Freud's reading of *Oedipus Tyrannus* is even more inattentive to textual detail and historical context, but nobody denies the psychoanalytic utility of the "Oedipal complex" on the grounds that Oedipus himself clearly did not have such a complex.[101] The appropriate yardsticks for all of these readings are their originality, richness and philosophical, literary or medical utility.

Other readings, also motivated by contemporary concerns, nevertheless attempt to justify themselves on the basis of what they reveal about texts and the intentions of their authors. Most of the interpretations of Thucydides, Clausewitz and Morgenthau that we will encounter in this volume claim our attention on this basis. There are many criteria, some general, and some specific to the texts in question, for making comparative evaluations of such readings. Classicists have used the language and structure of Thucydides' history, the nature or repetitions and omissions, explicit and implicit arguments and their partial or total subversion elsewhere in the text, the selective use of authorial voice, narrative, debate and dialogue, how the text mimics, differs from or plays off against the epics, tragedies and history of Herodotus, and how these patterns highlight the author's themes and purposes.[102] As in the hard sciences, an evolving set of practices rather than a set of formally specified rules determines what gets taken seriously.[103] These criteria are not foolproof, and radical innovation may encounter the kind of resistance the impressionists met from those responsible for admitting paintings to the salon. In the field of

[100] Ulrich von Wilamowitz-Moellendorff, the *éminence grise* of German philology in the second half of the nineteenth century, accused Nietzsche of seriously misinterpreting Greek texts.

[101] Sigmund Freud, *The Interpretation of Dreams*, ed. and trans. James Strachey, 3rd ed. (New York: Basic Books, 1955), "Dostoevsky and Parricide" in James E. Strachey, ed., *The Standard Edition of the Complete Psychological Works of Sigmund Freud* (London: Hogarth Press, 1961), XXI, p. 188, and *A General Introduction to Psychoanalysis*, trans. Joan Riviere (New York: Liverwright, 1935), p. 291, for Freud's evolving understanding of the Oedipal complex and the play. For a discussion, see Kaufmann, *Tragedy and Philosophy*; Juliet Mitchell, *Psychoanalysis and Feminism* (New York: Pantheon, 1974); Vernant, "Oedipus without the Complex," in Vernant and Vidal-Nacquet, *Myth and Tragedy in Ancient Greece*, pp. 85–111; Charles Segal, "Freud, Language, and the Unconscious," in Segal, *Sophocles' Tragic World*, pp. 161–79; Pietro Pucci, *Oedipus and the Fabrication of the Father: Oedipus Tyrannus in Modern Criticism and Philosophy* (Baltimore: Johns Hopkins University Press, 1992), pp. 44–48.

[102] The modern study of classics began with the appointment of August Böckh to the chair of rhetoric in Berlin in 1811. He recognized that Greek texts could only be understood in their broader cultural and political context, and that interpretation accordingly required mastery of arts, law, politics and religion in addition to philology. This approach led to the emergence of *Sachphilologie* and *Realphilologie,* in contrast to *Wortphilologie* that concerned itself with only Greek vocabulary and grammar.

[103] Roy Bashkar, *A Realist Theory of Science* (Leeds: Leeds Books, 1975); Rom Harré, *Varieties of Realism* (Oxford: Blackwell, 1987); Steve Fuller and William R. Shadish, *The Social Psychology of Science* (New York: Guilford Press, 1993).

classics, there was considerable initial resistance to the "linguistic turn" as a mode of analysis. But the community became more receptive once the analytical utility of the approach had been demonstrated.

Hans-Georg Gadamer differentiates surface from depth hermeneutics. The former addresses the overt and readily accessible messages of texts, and the latter, those that are concealed from readers, and perhaps from their authors as well.[104] Classical realist texts, and especially the history of Thucydides, carry, at the very least, concealed messages of the first kind. To decode them, we must rely on our general understanding of genres and specific information about the authors and their cultures. There is no knowledge without foreknowledge, but, as Gadamer reminds us, we must consider our foreknowledge provisional because it may be incomplete, flawed or otherwise misleading. It will direct our attention to certain passages as the most important keys to understanding. These passages may suggest interpretations that can be sustained by additional passages, and ultimately allow us to construct a complex narrative about the overall text and its meaning.[105] Not all passages may support this narrative or be explicable by it. They should prompt us to consider alternative or multiple interpretations, which we put together by searching for other passages and relevant contextual knowledge just as we did to construct the initial narrative. These interpretations may lead us to reconsider the validity or utility of our original foreknowledge and begin again on the basis of different assumptions and hypotheses. This back-and-forth process, sometimes called "tacking" or "feedback," constitutes the hermeneutic circle.[106] For Gadamer, tacking is more than a research tool, but a means of broadening one's own horizons: "Hermeneutics is above all a practice, the art of understanding and of making something understood to someone else. It is the heart of all education that wants to teach how to philosophize. In it what one has to exercise above all is the ear, the sensitivity for perceiving prior determinations, anticipations, and imprints that reside in concepts."[107]

Interpretation is easier when the reader and the author of the text share the same culture, language and life experiences. My reading of Morgenthau builds on many such commonalities, including almost two decades

[104] Gadamer, *Truth and Method*, pp. 236ff.

[105] Knox, *Oedipus at Thebes*, pp. xi–xii, on his efforts to acquire appropriate foreknowledge.

[106] Gerhard Radnitzky, "Justifying a Theory Versus Giving Good Reasons for Preferring a Theory," in Radnitzky and Gunnar Anderson, eds., *The Structure and Development of Science* (Boston: D. Reidel, 1979), pp. 213–56; Wolfgang Stegmüller, *The Structure and Dynamics of Theories*, trans. William Wohlhueter (New York: Springer-Verlag, 1976), pp. 8–10; Diesing, *How Does Social Science Work?*, pp. 108–10.

[107] Gadamer, "Reflections on My Philosophical Journey," in *The Philosophy of Hans-George Gadamer*, p. 17.

of personal interaction as his student, research assistant, and later, as his friend and colleague. Foreknowledge becomes more problematic as cultural and temporal distance from a text increases.[108] Homer and Thucydides do not critique their societies by developing a competing language of motive and value, as we expect of contemporary writers. They do so through their ordering of their texts, by arranging scenes, speeches and dialogues to highlight inconsistencies and lead the reader to feelings and judgments at odds with those the material superficially appears to suggest. Homer actually exploits the inability of his characters to develop a language appropriate to their feelings as a means of subverting heroic values.[109] Modern readers lacking appropriate foreknowledge would be likely to miss this dimension of Greek texts, or misinterpret their authors' intentions.

There are compensating advantages to temporal distance. Generations of engagement with a text identify anomalies, draw out hidden meanings and find new questions that result in fuller, more varied and complex readings. Over time, these interpretations, which include commentary and criticism of earlier interpretations, establish a tradition that provides readers with insights and understandings that were unavailable to their predecessors or even to the author.[110] The claim that we can understand a text better than its author sounds arrogant but rests on solid ground. Historical distance puts an author and his or her ideas into perspective by allowing us to situate them along broader trend lines and to see implications of their arguments or sensibilities that the authors could not have envisaged. "Depth hermeneutics" acknowledges that authors may purposely embed meanings for readers to tease out, as I argue is true for Thucydides. But this process can also be unconscious and reflect contradictions in the author's mind or culture. The surface meaning of the text may represent a kind of "false consciousness" that requires interpreters to search for more significant hidden meanings – as I tried

[108] John Jones, *On Aristotle and Greek Tragedy* (London: Chatto & Windus, 1962), pp. 11–16, 66–72, makes a compelling case of how subsequent exegesis of Aristotle, especially by the Romantics and post-Romantics, led us to read the tragedies through inappropriate modern lenses. Jean-Pierre Vernant, "Tensions and Ambiguities in Greek Tragedy," in Vernant and Vidal-Nacquet, *Myth and Tragedy in Ancient Greece*, on the difficulty of acquiring the necessary foreknowledge to approach the corpus of Greek tragedies.

[109] In Book IX of the *Iliad*, Achilles spurns the gifts of Agamemnon offered to him by Odysseus. In effect, he rejects the war, and, with it, honor and the other motives that have spurred him to action in the past. He gives vent to rage because he lacks a vocabulary that would let him conceptualize a new identity and articulate its values. In its absence, he is more easily drawn back into the fray once his rage subsides.

[110] Roy Schafer, *The Analytic Attitude* (New York: Basic Books, 1983), ch. 13, on how dreams and narratives about the past help to create a case history. A case history, in turn, can prompt other, more repressed layers of childhood.

to do with my story. Marx, Nietzsche and Freud, each in his own way, advocated what Paul Ricoeur called a "hermeneutics of suspicion," to ferret out meanings buried deeply in an author's unconscious but conveyed by their texts.[111] Hermeneutic philosophers are divided in their opinion about whether the search for hidden meanings leads to better understandings, as Apel and Habermas believe, or merely, as Gadamer insists, to different interpretations.[112]

Where do I situate myself in the hermeneutic tradition? I read the texts of Thucydides, Clausewitz and Morgenthau to discover their intended meanings and their authors' intentions. I do not approach these texts as inkblots *à la* Hegel, Nietzsche and Freud to stimulate my creative juices. Many realist discussions of Thucydides, like so many nineteenth- and twentieth-century references to Clausewitz, consist of lapidary cites to justify conclusions reached by other means. They are more ritual genuflections than readings. I have done my best to offer convincing readings. I approach all three authors and their texts with appropriate foreknowledge, that includes familiarity with the literature that influenced them. On this basis I developed provisional interpretations that I subsequently refined by considering anomalies and questions that could not be subsumed or answered by these interpretations.[113] Over the course of time – decades in the case of Thucydides – this kind of "tacking" has led me to interpretations that go beyond and are, in important ways, at odds with my earlier takes.[114] I also accept Mikhail Bakhtin's contention that

[111] Paul Ricoeur, *Freud and Philosophy: An Essay in Interpretation* (New Haven: Yale University Press, 1970), pp. 32–35; Jürgen Habermas, *Knowledge and Human Interests*, trans. Jeremy J. Shapiro (Boston: Beacon Press, 1971 [1968]), pp. 214–45, argues that Freud thought he was practicing science but was actually engaging in hermeneutics. See also Jacques Lacan, *Ecrits: A Selection*, trans. A. Sheridan (New York: Norton, 1977), and *Speech and Language in Psychoanalysis*, trans. A. Wilden (Baltimore: Johns Hopkins University Press, 1968); Diesing, *How Does Social Science Work?*, pp. 129–38.

[112] Jürgen Habermas, "Der Universalitätsanspruch der Hermeneutik," and Karl Otto Apel, "Szientismus oder Transzendentale Hermeneutik?," in Rüdiger Bübner, Konrad Cramer and Reiner Wiehl, eds., *Hermeneutik und Dialektik* (Tübingen: J. C. B. Mohr, 1970), II, pp. 73–104, 105–44.

[113] Isaiah Berlin, "The Concept of Scientific History," in William H. Dray, ed., *Philosophical Analysis and History* (New York: Harper & Row, 1966), pp. 40–51, calls such a strategy "colligation," as it attempts to find the "threads" that connect an individual, text or institution to its broader socio-political context and account for changes in one or the other.

[114] The evolution and, I believe, the increasing sophistication of my understanding of Thucydides' understanding of the origins and meaning of the Peloponnesian War can be traced through three earlier publications: "Thucydides, Power Transition, and the Causes of War," in Richard Ned Lebow and Barry S. Strauss, eds., *Hegemonic Conflict: From Thucydides to the Nuclear Age* (Boulder: Westview Press, 1991), pp. 125–68; "Play it Again Pericles: A Non-Realist Reading of Thucydides," *European Journal of International Relations*, 2 (June 1996), pp. 231–58; "Thucydides the Constructivist," *American Political Science Review*, 95 (September 2001), pp. 547–60.

texts have "potential" to speak beyond the context of their creation, and so, I believe, did Thucydides and Clausewitz.[115] They looked to a more receptive reading from future generations, and Thucydides, in his only direct comment on his work, described it as a "possession for all time." I read all three authors in this light.

Tragedy, ethics and politics

The modern academy has introduced a false dichotomy between political and moral behavior and political and moral theorizing. They were one and the same in ancient Israel and Greece, and remained so until the twentieth century.[116] Traditional Greek culture looked to the poets, and especially to Homer, for insights into the nature of a healthy soul (*psuchē*). Plato was concerned that poetry and tragedy could also arouse unhealthy emotions and were a threat to the authority of reason, but Aristotle believed that tragedy nurtured an ethical sensibility.[117] The German idealists and romanticists were drawn to tragedy for much the same reason. So were Thucydides, Clausewitz and Morgenthau, for whom it was an appropriate starting point for any exploration of interests, individual or "national."

The concern of classical realists for ethics was only one facet of their engagement with the world and its problems. They conceived of their writings as meta-level responses to those problems. Thucydides and Plato hoped to encourage the emergence of conditions conducive to moral deliberation and meaningful political discourse by establishing dialogues with future readers.[118] To engage a text is to open oneself up to changes, and authors can aspire to change the world by changing the collective understandings their readers have of that world. Clausewitz and Thucydides

[115] Gary Saul Morson and Caryl Emerson, *Mikhail Bakhtin: Creation of a Prosaics* (Stanford: Stanford University Press, 1990), pp. 284–90. Bakhtin contends that the full meaning of texts cannot be found either in the text itself or in the author's original intentions. Works take on additional meaning in the course of time, and many authors genuinely intend for their writings to have meanings beyond those they intended. Bakhtin nevertheless denies that meaning is entirely the product of the interpreter.

[116] MacIntyre, *After Virtue*, p. 61.

[117] In Book II, from 377b to Book III, 399e of the *Republic*, Plato expresses serious concern, and some jealousy, about the influence of poets. He considers Homer and most poetry to be works of *mimēsis* that illuminated only the surface, and not the underlying unity and harmony of life. Philosophy, as he conceived of it, had the potential of turning the soul toward justice, defined as recognition of underlying harmonies. For Plato and the poets, see Gadamer. *Dialogue and Dialectic*. Plato acknowledged that poetry could arouse good emotions, but was not certain how one could determine this in advance. Aristotle developed his concept of *katharsis* as a response to Plato's doubts.

[118] White, *When Words Lose their Meaning*; Connor, *Thucydides*; Euben, *The Tragedy of Political Theory*.

are heirs to this tradition, and so is Morgenthau, although his works are directed to a decidedly contemporary audience.[119]

Social science believes that knowledge should be explicit, and, when possible, stated in the form of propositions and theories, preferably in mathematical symbols. Greek tragedy and classical realists had a different understanding of knowledge. In the words of Charles Segal, "The kind of intellect tragedy encourages is one mindful of incoherence, respectful of the contradictions of experience, and conscious that questions about justice and politics do not yield their significance to terse hypotheses."[120] Tragedy and classical realism do not so much solve problems as they deepen our understanding of them by engaging our intellect and emotions. They produce what Michael Polanyi has called "tacit political knowledge."[121]

Greeks distinguished between *technē* and *sophia*. The former described practical knowledge, of the kind that enabled people to fashion things, cure illnesses and reach concrete goals.[122] By *technē*, one of the tragic poets wrote, "we master that to which we are subject by nature."[123] Socrates applied *technē* more broadly to the social realm. Plato's Socrates maintained that dialectic (as opposed to sophistic rhetoric) was the true art of politics (*technē politikē*) because it facilitated meaningful discourse.[124] In his search for knowledge, Socrates professed to be greatly impressed by

119 In *Gorgias*, Plato explores the possibility of reconstituting community through collective reconstitution of language. For modern explorations of these themes, see Jean-Paul Sartre, *Qu'est-ce que la littérature?* (Paris: Gallimard, 1948); J. L. Austin, *How to Do Things with Words* (Cambridge, Mass.: Harvard University Press, 1962); John R. Searle, *Speech Acts: An Essay in the Philosophy of Language* (London: Cambridge University Press, 1969); Jürgen Habermas, *Communication and the Evolution of Society*, trans. Thomas McCarthy (Boston: Beacon Press, 1979).

120 Charles Segal, *Tragedy and Civilization: An Interpretation of Sophocles* (Norman, OK: University of Oklahoma Press, 1999), p. ix.

121 Michael Polanyi, *Personal Knowledge* (Chicago: University of Chicago Press, 1958).

122 The word descends from the Indo-European stem *teks-* that meant woodwork or carpentry. In ancient Greek, *tektōn* initially meant master builder, but later expanded its field to encompass the art associated with every kind of production. The concept of *technē* was a favorite subject of Greek philosophers, especially Aristotle, and came to occupy an intermediate position between ordinary know-how (*empeiria*) and theoretical knowledge (*epistēmē*). *Technē* differs from *epistēmē* in that it refers to productive knowledge as opposed to primary knowledge like mathematics that is immutable and exists outside of any human experience of it. Wolfgang Schadewaldt, "The Concepts of *Nature* and *Technique* According to the Greeks," *Research in Philosophy and Technology*, 2 (1979), pp. 159–71.

123 Antiphon as quoted by pseudo–Aristotle, *Mechanical Problems*, 847a21.

124 In *Gorgias*, Plato argues that the goal of rhetoric, which he denigrates as the knack (*empeiria*) of public speaking, is to persuade (*peithein*), and thereby to make others responsive to one's will. Rhetoric treats others as means to an end, but dialogue treats them as ends in themselves and appeals to what is best for them. See also, the *Republic*, 509d–511d, 531d–534c.

the genius of craftsmen (*technikos*). Some of them nevertheless made the mistake of presuming to know everything, or of thinking themselves capable of judging everything on the basis of their specialized knowledge.[125] Modern social science aspires to produce knowledge in the form of *epistēmē*. As understood by Aristotle, *epistēmē* consisted of propositions and theories that facilitate explanation and prediction.[126] Unlike Aristotle, social science mistakenly considers *epistēmē* the final goal of knowledge. This is a variant of the error of ancient craftsmen who equated limited forms of knowledge with wisdom (*sophia*). For the tragedians, Thucydides and Socrates and Plato, *sophia* describes an understanding of life that goes beyond discrete knowledge to grasp and integrate deeper meanings.[127] Plato even had a definition of *sophia* appropriate to international relations. It is the knowledge, possessed by the rulers of his *Republic* "that takes counsel about the city as a whole as to how it would best order its relations to itself and to other cities."[128] And as Aristotle reminds us, the most universal things are the hardest to know, for they are furthest from the senses. For the playwrights, tragic wisdom starts from the premise that suffering cannot fully be explained by justice. Recognition of this truth, and of the limited ability of either knowledge or power to protect us from suffering, is the first step toward acquiring wisdom.[129]

[125] Plato, *Apology*, 22c–d, whose interest in craftsmen reflects the high regard in which they were held by Greeks. They were acknowledged masters of *technē*, and so linked nature to science.

[126] The Greeks distinguished *poiēsis* from *praxis*. For Aristotle, *Nichomachean Ethics*, 114b3–7, *poiēsis* is any kind of activity intended to achieve a goal, often associated with crafts (its sense is conveyed by the English verbs making or producing), *praxis*, signified action. *Poiēsis* was a means to an end, while *praxis* was an end in itself. Efforts to lead a good life are a form of *praxis*, regardless of their effects, and a good life is in any case always an elusive goal. Modern theories of social science tend to conflate the two concepts, but they are closer to *poiēsis* because of their concern for the positive, productive results of theories.

[127] In the sixth century BCE, *sophia* signified knowledge about the world and human experience. By the later fifth century, due to Sophist influence and claims, it had taken on a more professional connotation in the sense of being associated with the teachings of philosophers. Plato aspired to restore its earlier, and more general meaning. Plato attempted to provide a more formal definition based on the premise that each part of the soul is functionally specific and finds expression in a different virtue. Reason imposes restraint on bodily appetites: the virtue of *sōphrosunē*. It also responds to physical dangers with courage: the virtue of *andreia*. When disciplined by mathematical and dialectical inquiry, reason can grasp the meaning of beauty and justice, and all forms of the Good: the virtue of *sophia*. These three virtues depend on the fourth virtue of *dikaiosunē*, which allocates and restricts each part of the soul to its proper function.

[128] Plato, *The Republic*, 428c12–d3, also 429a1–3.

[129] Aristotle, *Metaphysics*, 982b–983a, *Politics*, 1341b35–1342a20, *Poetics*, 1452a1–10, 1450a–b; Winnington-Ingram, *Sophocles*; H. D. Kitto, *Sophocles, Dramatist and Philosopher* (Westport, Conn.: Greenwood Press, 1981); Charles Segal, *Interpreting Greek Tragedy: Myth, Poetry, Text* (Ithaca: Cornell University Press, 1986).

I noted earlier that one of the reasons why Clausewitz was misunderstood was that military officers approached *On War* as an operational manual. They read it as instrumental knowledge, for rules they could apply to the planning and conduct of warfare. In doing so, they misconstrued Clausewitz's arguments and remained oblivious to the wisdom accessible through his text. Many modern political scientists commit the same error with Thucydides and Morgenthau. They read their works as operational manuals of politics, and search for rules and propositions appropriate to the conduct of foreign policy or the theory of international relations. To be fair, *Politics Among Nations* does invite this kind of reading, but it also operates on a deeper level, as do *On War* and *The Peloponnesian War*.

International relations theorists who read Morgenthau for *technē* or *epistēmē* find him frustrating because his generalizations are hedged in with caveats and some of them appear to operate at cross-purposes. Kenneth Waltz attempted to "clean up" Morgenthau and construct a deductive theory of international relations based on some of Morgenthau's insights.[130] Such a theory, whatever its merits, does not do justice to Morgenthau's understanding of politics, nor can it motivate readers to embark on the path to *sophia*. Toward this latter goal, I offer a different kind of reading of Thucydides, Clausewitz and Morgenthau. Instead of simplifying their texts, I revel in their complexity and exploit the countless oppositions on the surface level – what Plato called *gignomenon* (literally, the becoming) – to get at their deeper meanings and the subtle wisdom they impart.[131] By doing so, I hope to show, among other things, that there is no fundamental contradiction between ethics and interests in their thinking.

Chapters 3 through 6 are devoted to this task. They examine the writings of Thucydides, Clausewitz and Morgenthau in their political, social and intellectual milieus. Alasdair MacIntyre warns us against reading philosophers as contributors to a single debate and as contemporaries of each other and of ourselves. Such an approach imparts a false independence to their thought and encourages us to make false distinctions between history and philosophy and between political theory and behavior.[132] This caveat is equally applicable to our three realists, each of whom must be read in context: Thucydides as a fifth-century Athenian general and exile, Clausewitz as a nineteenth-century Prussian and Morgenthau as a twentieth-century German and American intellectual and refugee. They addressed similar problems but in different

[130] Waltz, *Theory of International Politics*.
[131] Plato, *Republic*, Book 19, 603b. [132] MacIntyre, *After Virtue*, p. 11.

cultural settings. Clausewitz, who may not have read Thucydides, nevertheless had the benefit of nearly 2 millennia of additional history and philosophy, while Morgenthau was familiar with Thucydides, Clausewitz and another century of history and philosophy. There are nevertheless striking similarities in the thought of all three realists about the nature of international relations and its study. Chapter 7 looks at the three authors comparatively in an effort to distill the core wisdom of classical realism.

Chapter 8 builds on the argument of the previous chapter to critique existing theories of cooperation (e.g., tit-for-tat, institutionalism, the democratic peace), and the underlying utilitarian ontology on which they are based. They assume egoistic, autonomous actors who respond to the constraints and opportunities of their environment. All these assumptions mistake Enlightenment ideology for social reality, and – as Hobbes made clear by example – it is an oxymoron to try to construct social order on the basis of actions by fully autonomous actors.

In contrast to modern social science, many philosophers, ancient and modern, have sought the explanation for cooperation *within* the minds of actors. Plato, Aristotle and Kant all emphasized the central role of the mind in producing knowledge and self-enforcing ethics. For Kant, social antagonism provides an incentive for us to develop our rational faculties. We use these faculties to advance our own selfish ends, primarily by means of calculation and communication with others. When our reason fully develops, it grasps the fundamental law of humanity: the absolute equality and dignity of all human beings. Reason becomes the vehicle for helping us to overcome our competitive propensity and to cooperate with other human beings on the basis of equality to achieve common goals. The liberal philosophers made similar claims. Grotius, Pufendorf, Hobbes and Smith all started from the assumption that human beings need each other to achieve their individual goals, and that recognition of this need impels them toward society and the social life. Hobbes considered "fellow-feeling" and the sympathy for others it engendered as natural proclivities of human beings.

Cooperation is possible when people recognize that it is in their interest. This recognition is not brought about so much by external constraints and opportunities as it is by introspection and inductive learning. Reason and experience bring some of us – individuals and states – to a better understanding of our interests. At every level of interaction, from personal relationships to civic participation, we become willing to forgo short-term gains to sustain these relationships, and the longer-term and more important rewards they make possible. Viewed in this light, the emergence of the European Community, the end of the Cold War and the survival of NATO represent triumphs of higher-order learning. American foreign policy in the Clinton and Bush administrations, by contrast, represents a retrogression to an earlier, less sophisticated and largely counterproductive way of thinking about ourselves and the world.

Classical realism is an expression of the tragic understanding of politics, and of life more generally. Chapter 9 returns to the theme of Greek tragedy and suggests how it is an appropriate foundation for an alternative ontology for social science that starts from the premise that the human condition is defined by a series of polarities that are always in tension. Social theories must build on this recognition and struggle to represent, not to suppress, the diversity and inherent instability of human identities, interests and motives, and their complex interactions with the discourses, social practices and institutions they generate and sustain. The individual and social levels of identity and interest are mutually constitutive, and evolve in tandem, or, if they diverge, generate pressures to find a new basis for reconciliation. The dynamism of social life deserves special emphasis. The accommodations individuals and societies make with the tragic polarities are never stable. They are uneasy compromises that can never be adequately justified by logic, may be difficult to legitimize politically and are likely to be challenged by a succession of moral and political dilemmas. Like the moon's tug and pull on the oceans, they give rise to inner tides that find outward expression in breaking waves of conflicting obligations and loyalties. I conclude by suggesting that social science needs to move closer to humanities and the arts, not in the sense of copying their methods, but using them as a source of fruitful images and a purchase from which to examine itself critically.

A final word about reading the chapters that follow. One of my meta-objectives is to bridge the gap between the social sciences and the humanities, and to show how they can both profit from closer collaboration. My short story is intended to be a step in this direction. I use it to involve the reader emotionally, as well as intellectually, in the problem of ethics and foreign policy, and to raise questions to which my subsequent investigations attempt to respond. I revisit the story at the end of the book, making use of my analysis to rephrase the problem and offer some insights about the relationship between interest and ethics. These insights grow out of my analysis of Thucydides, and his understanding of the underlying reasons for the decline of Athens. They find further resonance in Clausewitz's analysis of the Napoleonic Wars and Morgenthau's understanding of great power politics.

My short story is followed by more traditional intellectual biography and social science. But here, too, the influence of the humanities is apparent. My three thinkers functioned to varying degrees in the interstices of literature, philosophy, history and political science, and my analysis attempts to bring these domains together and to use methods of analysis appropriate to each. Nor is my narrative linear in the traditional sense. The principal arguments can be grasped and assimilated at one reading, but I have employed a muted variant of the Sophist mode of presentation that Thucydides found so useful. My argument is layered, and makes some seemingly contradictory statements that are at least in part reconciled later in the narrative. One example, quite appropriately, is my treatment of Thucydides' understanding of the origins of the Peloponnesian War. Chapter 2 shows that his one authorial statement about the origins of the war (I.23.5–6) is properly read as a judgment about who was most responsible for the war. The narrative of Book 1 tells a different story, and encourages the reader to conclude that the war was the result of the peculiar political cultures of Athens and Sparta, the machinations of third parties and a series of miscalculations made by their leaders. At the end of Chapter 3, I revisit the problem of the war's origins and show how Thucydides conceived of its deepest underlying cause as the process of what we would call modernization that made Athens so powerful. Both the political culture of Athens and the miscalculations of Pericles might be understood, at least in part, as epiphenomena, as products, or reflections, of the modernization process. On this and other issues (e.g., the question of ethics), readers are urged to keep a sharp eye out for tensions and their possible resolutions.

3 Thucydides and war

'The Prince to whom the oracle at Delphi belongs neither speaks nor conceals: he gives a sign.'

Heraclitus[1]

All great texts are refracted through some version of *Zeitgeist*, and Thucydides is no exception. During the Cold War, international relations scholars saw parallels between the bipolarity of late fifth-century Greece and the postwar world and between the superpowers and Athens and Sparta. The greatest naval power once again confronted the greatest land power in a struggle that pitted the democracy against the "garrison polis." The burning question was whether the superpowers, unlike Athens and Sparta, could avoid a mutually destructive war. The Vietnam War heightened interest in Thucydides. It undermined the Cold War consensus in the United States, and raised questions of morality and foreign policy to the forefront of public consciousness. W. Robert Connor, one of the great contemporary Thucydides scholars, was drawn to the subject by a March 1968 *New Yorker* essay by Jonathan Schell that described the destruction he had witnessed in Vietnam in detached language reminiscent of Thucydides' account of the suffering at Mycalessus.[2]

Cold War interest in the origins of the Peloponnesian War drew attention away from the consequences of that war for Athens and Greece more generally. To be sure, the Melian Dialogue, which took place during the sixteenth year of the war, appeared regularly on college reading lists and is still hailed by realists as evidence of Thucydides' realism. From the vantage point of the twenty-first century, Thucydides' insights into the rise and fall of hegemons, and what this says about the relationship between justice and interest, has more contemporary relevance. This chapter and the next tease out these insights by examining the origins and course of

[1] Hermann Diels and Walther Kranz, *Die Fragmente der Vorsokratiker*, 7th ed. (Berlin: Weidmannsche Verlagsbuchhandlung, 1956), fragment 93. All Greek fragments cited are from this edition unless otherwise noted.

[2] W. Robert Connor, *Thucydides* (Princeton: Princeton University Press, 1984), pp. 6–8.

the Peloponnesian War. They develop a critique of realist readings and explore tensions in the text that point toward a more complex, subtle and evolving interpretation.

Since the time of Thomas Hobbes, who produced an early and important English translation of his history, Thucydides has generally been described by many classicists and historians as someone who stripped away all moral pretenses to expose the calculations of power and advantage that, of necessity, motivated successful political actors.[3] Neorealists claim that his history vindicates their emphasis on the system level and belief that norms and conventions cannot preserve peace under conditions of international anarchy.[4] They celebrate him as the first power transition theorist because of his statement in Book I.23.6 that "the growth of the power of Athens, and the alarm which this inspired in Sparta, made war inevitable."[5] Contemporary power transition theories are based on this insight, and some of their proponents acknowledge their debt to Thucydides.[6] More nuanced realist readings also put great stock in I.23.6. For Michael Doyle, it illustrates the truth of the "security dilemma": how international anarchy makes states fearful for their

[3] David Grene, ed., *The Peloponnesian War: The Complete Hobbes Translation* (Chicago: University of Chicago Press, 1959 [1628]). The first English translation, in 1550, was made by Thomas Nicolls. For modern realist interpretations of Thucydides, see J. B. Bury, *A History of Greece to the Death of Alexander the Great* (London: Macmillan, 1914); Werner Jaeger, *Paideia: The Ideals of Greek Culture*, trans. Gilbert Highet, 2nd ed., 3 vols. (New York: Oxford University Press, 1945[1939]), I, pp. 397–402; Jacqueline de Romilly, *Thucydides and Athenian Imperialism* (Oxford: Blackwell and Motto, 1963); Donald Kagan, *The Outbreak of the Peloponnesian War* (Ithaca: Cornell University Press, 1969); Arthur G. Woodhead, *Thucydides on the Nature of Power* (Cambridge, Mass.: Harvard University Press, 1970); G. E. M. de Ste. Croix, *The Origins of the Peloponnesian War* (London: Duckworth, 1972), pp. 11–25; Russell Meiggs, *The Athenian Empire* (Oxford: Oxford University Press, 1972), p. 388; Edmond Lévy, *Athènes devant la défaite de 404: Histoire d'une crise idéologique* (Paris: Bocard, 1976); June W. Allison, *Power and Preparedness in Thucydides* (Baltimore: Johns Hopkins University Press, 1984); Henry Immerwar, "Pathology of Power and the Speeches of Thucydides" in Philip Stadter, ed., *The Speeches of Thucydides* (Chapel Hill: North Carolina University Press, 1973), pp. 16–31; Steven Forde, "Thucydides on the Causes of Athenian Imperialism," *American Political Science Review* 80 (June 1986), pp. 433–48.

[4] Kenneth Waltz, *The Theory of International Politics* (Reading, Mass.: Addison-Wesley, 1979), p. 186; Robert Gilpin, "The Richness of the Tradition of Political Realism" in Robert O. Keohane, ed., *Neorealism and its Critics* (New York: Columbia University Press, 1986), p. 306.

[5] Thucydides, I. 23.

[6] A. F. K. Organski, *World Politics* 2nd ed. (New York: Knopf, 1968); A. F. K. Organski and Jacek Kugler, *The War Ledger* (Chicago: University of Chicago Press, 1980); Robert Gilpin, *War and Change in World Politics* (Cambridge: Cambridge University Press, 1981); Charles F. Doran, "War and Power Dynamics: Economic Underpinnings," *International Studies Quarterly* 27 (December 1983), pp. 419–41; Charles Doran and Wes Parsons, "War and the Cycle of Relative Power," *American Political Science Review* 74 (December 1980), pp. 947–65; Wosang Kim and James D. Morrow, "When Do Power Shifts Lead to War?," *American Journal of Political Science* 36 (November 1992), pp. 896–922.

security and encourages them to act in ways that make their fears self-fulfilling. It also reveals that Thucydides understood that moral choices can only play a "constrained role" in the options available to "responsible statesmen." Security comes first.[7]

A close reading of Book I indicates that Thucydides did not describe the Peloponnesian War as inevitable, and considered shifts in relative capabilities at best an indirect cause of war, and by no means the most important one. The debates in Sparta indicate that the "war party" did not fear Athens; they were confident of waging a brief and victorious campaign. The "peace party" sought an accommodation because of their accurate assessment of Athenian power and concern that any war they started was likely to be inherited by their sons. Spartiates went to war primarily to preserve their honor and standing in Greece, which was threatened by the political, economic and cultural changes spearheaded by Athens. Spartan identity, not power, was the issue for both the war and peace parties.

Realists are not wrong in drawing attention to the security dilemma. It features prominently at the outset of Thucydides' account of the origins of the War, and indicates that the crisis of 433–431 BCE would have been difficult to prevent. Book I also suggests that pressures and constraints at the state level (really polis level, in ancient Greece) were at least as important in the calculus of leaders, but that leaders everywhere still retained considerable freedom of choice. As much as anything else, war was the result of their reinforcing miscalculations at critical junctures of the crisis. They allowed civil strife in a remote and insignificant settlement to escalate into an all-out clash between Athens and Sparta and their respective allies.[8]

How do we account for the apparent contradiction between Thucydides' explicit statement about the cause of war in I.23.6 and the more complex, albeit implicit arguments he develops in the rest of Book I? It is in part an artifact of translation. Proper renderings of key words and phrases in I.23.6 – *dunamis, anangkē* and *hē alēthestatē prophasis* – go some way toward reconciling these arguments. They suggest that Thucydides

[7] Michael Doyle, *Ways of War and Peace: Realism, Liberalism and Socialism* (New York: Norton, 1997), pp. 33, 51–52, 83.

[8] Donald Kagan, *The Outbreak of the Peloponnesian War* (Ithaca: Cornell University Press, 1969), also challenges the structural explanation of I.23. 5–6. Kagan maintains that there was no increase in Athenian power between the end of the First Peloponnesian War and the beginning of the Second in 431 B.C. He further contends that the second war was not inevitable but the result of bad judgment by Pericles. I agree that miscalculation was the immediate cause of war, but argue that Pericles' miscalculations were only part of a chain of bad judgments made by leaders and factions of all of the parties to the war crisis, and that these misjudgments themselves had, to a certain degree, structural causes.

is answering two different questions: who was responsible for war, and what caused it. A real tension nevertheless exists, one that I believe is deliberate and intended to lead thoughtful readers to deeper levels of analysis and understanding.

My interpretation builds on the seminal insight of W. Robert Connor who suggests that Thucydides uses omissions, repetitions and inconsistencies in the form of arguments and judgments that are "modified, restated, subverted, or totally controverted" to tell a more complex story about the human condition.[9] I read the history as a layered text that raises four different sets of questions, each of which lays the foundation for the next. For Connor, omissions, repetitions, inconsistencies and subverted sentiments and arguments are the catalysts that move readers to more complex understandings. I see them as playing this role *within* levels – as I hope to demonstrate in my analysis of the origins of the war. Thucydides uses the structure of his narrative, choice of language and implicit references to other texts to move readers from one level to the next. He also relies on the emotional impact of his story to question, even subvert, some of his arguments and to move us between levels.[10] I analyze the overall structure of the history in the next chapter, so here I note only that Thucydides' treatment of the origins of the war resides at the first of the four layers of his history. This level addresses the relationship between justice and interest.

Son of Olorus

Our knowledge of Thucydides is sketchy at best. His father's name, Olorus, is Thracian and royal, and Thucydides was probably a member of the wealthy and conservative Philaidae clan. If so, he was closely related to Miltiades, the father of Cimon. In about 512, Miltiades married a Thracian princess, daughter of Olorus, after whom Thucydides' father may have been named. The best guess is that Thucydides was born around 460 and died sometime in the first decade of the fourth century. He was a generation younger than Pericles and his illustrious contemporaries, Sophocles, Herodotus, Anaxagoras and Phidias.

Thucydides' praise of Pericles is indicative of his intellectual independence given the long-standing antagonism between the Philaidae and the Alcmaeonidae clan, to which Pericles belonged. Themistocles, the victor

[9] Connor, *Thucydides*, quotes, pp. 15, 18.

[10] Charles Segal, "Logos and Mythos: Language, Reality, and Appearance in Greek Tragedy and Plato," unpublished manuscript, cited in J. Peter Euben, *The Tragedy of Political Theory: The Road Not Taken* (Princeton: Princeton University Press, 1990), p. 170.

of Salamis, was ostracized in 471. Cimon, his successor, continued his policy of naval and imperial expansion and the use of ostracism to remove political enemies from the scene. Possibly an aristocrat, he nevertheless built up a clientele among the *dēmos* by providing employment in the navy and building an early version of a political machine that looked after their personal needs. In 462, Cimon persuaded the Athenian assembly (*ekklēsia*) to honor its alliance with Sparta and send forces to assist in subduing the helot rebellion. Sparta welcomed the Athenian forces but subsequently expelled them, embarrassing Cimon and leading to his banishment in 461. His successor, Pericles, seized the opportunity to have the assembly approve a key democratic reform: transfer of key powers from the aristocratic Areopagus to popular juries. Pericles suffered a series of foreign policy reverses and lost power to Thucydides, the son of Melesias, who wanted to maintain the peace and undo many of his predecessor's democratic reforms. The *dēmo*s was unprepared to give up its new rights and authority, and the son of Melesias was ostracized and Pericles restored to power.

John Finley, author of the most extensive biography, thinks the young Thucydides imbibed the aristocratic political views of his clan, then became a democrat and supporter of Pericles and more conservative in old age.[11] A recent study describes Thucydides as a tepid supporter of democracy whose preferred form of government was moderate oligarchy.[12] Other authorities contend that Thucydides favored a limited and controlled democracy. I will address this question in Chapter 7.[13]

Thucydides provides little information about himself. We know he was born in Athens, grew up as the Parthenon was being constructed on the Acropolis and reached maturity at the height of Athens' golden age. He suffered from but survived the great plague that broke out in 430 after the residents of Attica took refuge in the city to escape the Peloponnesian invasion.[14] In the eighth year of the Peloponnesian War, in 424, he was elected a general (*stratēgos*) and sent to the island of Thasos in Thrace

[11] John H. Finley, Jr., *Thucydides* (Ann Arbor: University of Michigan Press, 1963), p. 32.

[12] Josiah Ober, *Political Dissent in Democratic Athens: Intellectual Critics of Popular Rule* (Princeton: Princeton University Press, 1998), p. 70. For a contrasting view of Thucydides as someone with no constitutional preferences, see Hartmut Leppin, *Thucydides und die Verfassung der Polis: Ein Beitrag zur politischen Ideen geschichte des 5 Jahrhunderts v. Chr.* (Berlin: Akademie Verlag, 1999), pp. 81–82.

[13] Gregory Vlastos, *Socrates, Ironist and Moral Philosopher* (Ithaca: Cornell University Press, 1991); J. Peter Euben, "Democracy and Political Theory: A Reading of Plato's Gorgias" in J. Peter Euben, John R. Wallach and Josiah Ober, eds., *Athenian Political Thought and the Reconstruction of American Democracy* (Ithaca: Cornell University Press, 1994), pp. 198–226.

[14] Thucydides, II.48.3.

where he had the right to work the local gold mines. He tells us that he "had great influence with the inhabitants of the mainland." Sparta's ablest general, Brasidas, was campaigning in Thrace, and made a lightning move on the city of Amphipolis, where he offered its inhabitants generous terms if they would turn the city over to him. Thucydides and his small fleet arrived too late to prevent the city's surrender, and put in to the coastal port of Eion to protect it against attack. The loss of Amphipolis caused consternation in Athens because of the city's strategic location and economic importance, and fear that this setback would encourage other allies to rebel.[15] Thucydides appears to have been made a scapegoat for the more serious defeat of Cleon at Delium, and was exiled from Athens for twenty years. He used this opportunity to observe the war more closely, largely from the Peloponnesian side.[16]

Reading Thucydides

Thucydides' text presents numerous problems for the scholar. It is incomplete, ending abruptly in the summer of 411, seven years before the defeat of Athens. It is difficult to know which books, if any, represent a finished text. And the book divisions are not the author's, but the invention of subsequent Greek editors. Thucydides appears to have died unexpectedly, and his work was prepared for publication by his literary executor, identified as Xenophon by a later and questionable source. Xenophon did begin his narrative of the war, *Hellenica*, almost precisely where Thucydides left off. The absence of a conclusion – we do not know if Thucydides intended to write one – deprives us of a useful signpost for inferring his overall intent. There are no contemporary histories to which Thucydides can be compared. Later accounts, by Ephorus, Diodorus Siculus and Plutarch, are incomplete and partly based on Thucydides, although they include some contemporary material not used by him. We have no choice but to evaluate Thucydides' history largely on the basis of information that he provides. This is something akin to a jury having to decide the guilt or innocence of a defendant solely on the arguments and evidence presented by the defense.

Thucydides undeniably had political and personal preferences. He repeatedly contrasts the *dēmos*, the majority of citizens who pursue primarily selfish ends, with the *dunatoi*, influential political men more likely to govern in the interests of the *polis*.[17] He describes Pericles as the very

[15] Ibid., IV.105–109. [16] Ibid., V.26.5.
[17] Ibid., II.65.2, III.47.3, V.4.3, VIII.2.1, VIII.73.2, VIII.90.1; Ober, *Political Dissent in Democratic Athens*, p. 70.

exemplar of the leader (*dunatōtatos* – literally, the most able man) who was able to win the support of the *dēmos* because they held him in high esteem (*axiōsis*), valued his integrity and knew that he put the interests of the polis above his own.[18] Thucydides has been accused of exaggerating the virtues of Pericles, of being too critical of his successors, most notably, Cleon, and too soft on the oligarchic opposition in Athens.[19] His account of the war is based on the implicit counterfactual that if Pericles had survived the plague he would have persevered with his limited, defensive military strategy, and it would have succeeded. This is by no means self-evident.[20]

Defense attorneys often try to select jurors who know as little as possible about the case, and in a high-profile trial, jurors are sequestered to keep them from being contaminated by media coverage. To the extent that defense and prosecution are kept honest it is by one another. If either counsel ignores important evidence or makes arguments patently at variance with the facts, the other will hasten to introduce the evidence, put its own spin on it and point out the alleged fallacies in their adversary's reasoning. Thucydides as barrister faced a double constraint. Contemporary readers – his jury, so to speak – had lived through the war, or knew about it from their parents or other first-hand witnesses. They had heard the case against Pericles, made by able prosecutors, among them, Aristophanes.[21] Thucydides could not play fast and loose with the facts without exposing himself and his arguments to ridicule. He was compelled to provide evidence that does not always support interpretations he appears to advance. Like all good defense attorneys, Thucydides makes the best case

[18] Thucydides, II.34.6, II.65.8.

[19] M. I. Finley, "Athenian Demagogues," *Past & Present* 21: 1(1962), pp. 3–24; G. E. M. de Ste. Croix, "The Character of the Athenian Empire," *Historia* 3 (1954), pp. 1–41, and *Origins of the Peloponnesian War*; Virginia Hunter, *Thucydides the Artful Reporter* (Toronto: Hakkert, 1973); Donald Kagan, *The Archidamian War* (Ithaca: Cornell University Press, 1974), pp. 156–60; A. J. Woodman, *Rhetoric in Classical Historiography: Four Studies* (London: Croom, Helm, 1988). W. Robert Connor, *The New Politicians of Fifth-Century Athens* (Princeton: Princeton University Press, 1971), pp. 174–75, suggests that Cleon offended members of the old elite not because he was upwardly mobile and willing to take any short-cut to power, but because he showed contempt for the established system of political and social mores.

[20] Thucydides, II.65.7. Pericles told Athenians that they would win the war if they remained on the defensive, maintained their fleet, resisted any temptation to make new conquests and did nothing to endanger their city. George Cawkwell, "Thucydides' Judgment of Periclean Strategy," *Yale Classical Studies* 24 (1975), pp. 53–70, and *Thucydides and the Peloponnesian War* (New York: Routledge, 1997). While it is undoubtedly true that bad leadership was an important cause of Athens' defeat, it was not the only cause. Sparta pursued the war more seriously after the collapse of the Peace of Nicias, and with Persian financial support.

[21] Aristophanes, *Acharnians*, 534–28, 618–15, signals his belief that the war was the result of Pericles' Megarian Decree. The play was produced at the Lenaean festival in 425.

for his client consistent with the evidence. But a careful reading of the text reveals that he, like many defense attorneys, harbored second thoughts about his "client," Pericles.[22]

Even the ancients found Thucydides difficult to read. His Greek is very abstract and filled with neologisms and antitheses. He uses more abstract nouns than any other fifth-century author, also more *hapax legomena* – words found only once in the corpus of Greek literature.[23] Greek exposition in general relies on *men... de* constructions (on the one hand... on the other), which encourage the juxtaposition of opposites. Thucydides takes antithesis to a new level, and uses it not only in clauses but in pairs of speeches and even in units of discourse that span books.

How we read Thucydides determines what we find. Positivistically inclined social scientists look for clear statements of argument and method, followed by data and conclusions that summarize the findings and relate them to broader arguments in the field. Reading his history this way gives undue weight to the arguments in the introductory section of Book One, including the discussion of the origins of the war in I.23.5–6. Thucydides wrote in the sophistic tradition. In addition to antilogies – sets of arguments advanced by paired and opposing speeches – he develops his arguments in stages that lead readers from simple to more complex questions and understandings. In contrast to Herodotus, he is sparing in his use of authorial interjections.

Texts, then and now, often reflect upon their artifice or encourage readers to do so. They may self-consciously suspend, distort or otherwise misrepresent reality in the hope of enhancing our understanding of that reality. This possibility was routinely exploited by the Greek playwrights.[24] Thucydides also presents a highly stylized and selective version of events, and one that is shaped to lead readers to conclusions he wants them to draw. He admits as much in Book I.22.1 where he tells readers in one of his few first-person statements that "my habit has been to make the speeches say what was in my opinion demanded of them by the various occasions, of course adhering as closely as possible to the general sense of what they really said." Contemporary readers would also have recognized that he omitted any description of a number of key events, among them

[22] David Grene, *Greek Political Theory: The Image of Man in Thucydides and Plato* (Chicago: University of Chicago Press, 1965 [1950]), pp. 70–79, and Finley, Jr., *Thucydides*, pp. 312–15, argue that one of the purposes of the history is to vindicate Pericles. Connor, *Thucydides*, p. 6; and Victor Hanson, "Introduction" in *The Landmark Thucydides*, pp. ix–xxiv, contend that he is more critical of Pericles.

[23] June W. Allison, *Word and Concept in Thucydides* (Atlanta: Scholar Press, 1997).

[24] Charles Segal, *Oedipus Tyrannus: Tragic Heroism and the Limits of Knowledge*, 2nd ed. (New York: Oxford University Press, 2001), pp. 60–62, commenting on Sophocles' choice to present the life of Oedipus in reverse.

the second assembly called by Pericles to convince an initially reluctant assembly to approve an alliance with Corcyra. The sophist Gorgias, a contemporary of both Sophocles and Thucydides, observed in connection with tragedy that "He who deceives is more just than he who does not deceive, and the one deceived is wiser than the one who is not deceived."[25] Readers of Thucydides can become wiser still by recognizing when and why they are being deceived.

At the outset (Book I.1), Thucydides introduces his work in the third person with the phrase *xunegrapse ton polemon*, "he wrote up the War."[26] The verb *xungraphein* was routinely used to describe medical, architectural and cooking texts.[27] Some authorities consider this seeming self-deprecation to be a reaction to Herodotus, who calls his own work a history (*historia*), but is described by Thucydides as a storyteller (*logographos*).[28] I believe Thucydides had a more fundamental intellectual purpose in mind.

The Greeks came close to identifying knowledge with what could be learned by the senses, especially through visual perception (*opsis*).[29] The Greek word for "I know," is *oida*, a perfect form that literally means "I have seen." What I know is not what I currently see, but what I have seen and what I could recognize if I saw it again, and what I can recount because I was an "eyewitness." Sung speech in the form of poetry had this capacity for truth-telling because the poets were thought to have religious powers that gave them direct access to past and future events.[30] Thucydides relies upon eyewitness accounts, his and others, and is obviously proud of it,

[25] Gorgias, frg. 82 B23, cited in Segal, *Oedipus Tyrannus*, p. 61.

[26] Thucydides, I.1; Eric Vogelin, *Order and History*, II, *The World of the Polis* (Baton Rouge: Louisiana State University Press, 1957), pp. 349–51; Connor, *Thucydides*, p. 248; Ashley J. Tellis, "Reconstructing Political Realism: The Long March to Scientific Theory," in Benjamin Frankel, *Roots of Realism* (Portland, Or.: Frank Cass, 1996), p. 17.

[27] Connor, *Thucydides*, p. 248.

[28] Thucydides, I.21–22. In the middle of his account of Egypt, Herodotus, II.99, says that he has relied on sight (*opsis*), his judgment (*gnōmē*) and inquiry (*historiē*); Rosalind Thomas, *Herodotus in Context: Ethnography, Science and the Art of Persuasion* (Cambridge: Cambridge University Press, 2000), pp. 190–200.

[29] Bruno Snell, *The Discovery of Mind*, trans. T. G. Rosenmeyer (Cambridge: Harvard University Press, 1985 [1924]), pp. 4–6; Hermann Fränkel, "Xenophanesstudien" in Fränkel, *Wege und Formen frühgriechischen Denkens*, 2nd ed. (Munich: Beck, 1955). Edward Hussey, "The Beginnings of Epistemology: From Homer to Philolaus," in Stephen Everson, ed., *Epistemology* (Cambridge: Cambridge University Press, 1990), pp. 11–38, maintains that the Snell–Fränkel thesis is an overstatement and misses the gradual evolution of Greek thought from Homer on toward a more sophisticated position that is increasingly cautious about the validity of sensory perception.

[30] Plato, *Meno*, 99c–d, has Socrates say with irony that gods lead poets to correct beliefs. Hesiod, and the Eleatic and Plato all considered the evidence of the senses misleading. Parmenides in frg. 7 warns against being deceived by the senses and conventional beliefs. Melissus, in frg. 8, develops a clever argument against the value of sight and hearing. The nature of "poetic truth" for Greeks is the subject of increasing debate today. See,

but he tells a cautionary tale about the reliability of sight as the basis for knowledge. Early in Book I, he speculates that if Sparta were ever reduced to ruins, observers would never credit it with having been a great power, when in fact it controlled two-fifths of the Peloponnese and had numerous tributaries and allies elsewhere in Greece. If Athens suffered this fate, its monumental architecture and urban sprawl would convince observers that it had been twice as powerful as it was.[31]

Hearsay, or second-hand knowledge, was traditionally disparaged. Homer appeals to the goddesses to help him make a list of the leaders of the Argive forces because men "hear only rumor and know nothing."[32] Homeric heroes routinely ignored this injunction and say or report things they heard from others who witnessed them or learned about them from witnesses.[33] By the fifth century, hearsay was an acknowledged form of knowledge, especially in the law courts where its credibility was thought to depend on the number and quality of those speaking and the extent to which their stories were supported by independent evidence. *Historia* in Greek refers to second-hand knowledge, and the *histōr* is one who knows by having heard or asked. When a *histōr* appears in an epic it is always in the context of a dispute, and usually as an arbiter, never as an eyewitness. He will reveal what has happened or serve as the guarantor of whatever decision is made.[34]

Experience was recognized as a third form of knowledge. When people use what they have seen as a sign or index they may infer authentic knowledge that was not directly accessible to the senses. In Sophocles' *Electra*, a messenger from Phocis arrives with the news that Electra's brother, Orestes, has been killed in a chariot race. Orestes then appears in disguise, and Chrysothemis, Electra's sister, infers that he is still alive because she discovers newly spilled rills of milk, a wreath of flowers and a lock of hair that resembles hers at their father's grave. Posing as an envoy bringing his ashes to his mother, Orestes subsequently shows Electra their father's

for example, Louise Pratt, *Lying and Poetry from Homer to Pindar* (Michigan: University of Michigan Press, 1993); Jacques Brunschwig, "Epistemology" in Jacques Brunschwig and Geoffrey E. R. Lloyd, trans. Catherine Porter, *Greek Thought: A Guide to Classical Knowledge* (Cambridge: Harvard University Press, 200), pp. 72–93; Marcel Detienne, *The Masters of Truth in Archaic Greece*, trans. Janet Lloyd (New York: Zone Books, 1996), pp. 42–44.

[31] Thucydides, I.10.1–2. [32] *Iliad*, II.484–90.

[33] Ibid., XX.203ff., for a long chain of witnesses concerning genealogy.

[34] François Hartog, "Herodotus," in Brunschwig and Lloyd, *Greek Thought*, pp. 642–48: Bernard Knox, *Oedipus at Thebes: Sophocles' Tragic Hero and His Time* (New Haven: Yale University Press, 1957), p. 121, notes that *historein* is also associated with the Ionian physicists for whom it seems to have meant to give a causal account. Herodotus, who embodies their investigative spirit, uses the word to mean "to question" and "to know as a result of questioning."

signet ring, which she accepts as proof of his identity.[35] In his version of the play, Euripides has some fun at Sophocles' expense, and uses these episodes to show the fallibility of signs. Electra initially denies the meaning of the hair and matching footprint, reasoning that people who are unrelated can look alike, and how odd it would be for brother and sister to have identical footprints. But she is ultimately convinced by the definitive sign of her brother's childhood scar.[36]

Signs, like witnesses, must be treated with caution, and Greeks sometimes distinguished, as did Euripides, between a sign (*sēmeion*) and a definitive sign (*tekmērion*).[37] For rationalists, signs (*sēmata*) are the key to knowledge because they are the only means of discovering the hidden causes of phenomena, and through them, the real nature of things. Hippocratic doctors used the outward, observable symptoms of diseases to infer what was going on inside the body and the outcome to which it would lead (*prognōsis*). They classified symptoms by the diseases with which they were associated (*diagnōsis* means distinction) and developed treatments appropriate to each. They repudiated the earlier conception of medicine as a deductive science based on philosophical principles. Thucydides relies heavily on signs to reconstruct the past, especially the distant past, and at several places in the so-called *Archeology* (Book I.2–21), shows how they can be used to discredit the conventional wisdom associated with hearsay. For Thucydides, type three trumps type two learning.

The three kinds of learning correspond to the three master words of the Hippocratic physicians: *autopsia* (witnessing oneself), *historia* (second-hand reports), and *prognōsis* (inference).[38] Thucydides relies on all three for his account of the Peloponnesian War: he was an eyewitness to many key events, sought evidence from witnesses about other events and weighed their accounts against each other and whatever independent evidence was available. He reports that his research was labor intensive and required considerable judgment on his part because of "the want of

[35] Sophocles, *Electra*, 877–930, 1098–124.

[36] Euripedes, *Electra*, 511–36, 573–80. There is considerable scholarly debate about whether Sophocles' *Electra* was written before or after Euripides wrote his *Electra*. It is generally recognized that Euripides' recognition scene is poking fun at the version Aeschylus offers in *The Libation Bearers*.

[37] Gregory Nagy, "*Sēma* and *Noēsis*: Some Illustrations," *Arethusa* 16 (1983), pp. 35–55, uses examples from the *Odyssey* to argues that *sēmata* are necessary for recognition (*anagnōrisis*).

[38] *Historia*, which was associated with observation, occupies an important place in the history of philosophy. It was originally used to counter attributions of causation to deities. By the fifth century it was replaced by *autopsia*. *Historia*, associated with second-hand accounts, gradually evolved in to our modern conception of history.

coincidence between accounts of the same occurrences by different eyewitnesses, arising sometimes from imperfect memory, sometimes from undue partiality for one side or the other."[39] To label his account a "history" would be a misleading and narrow characterization, and identify it only with the second type of knowledge.

Greeks distinguished between information and knowledge. People had to use their minds to understand what they had seen, heard, smelled, tasted or felt. At a minimum, this consisted of organizing the experience conceptually and expressing it in words that others could understand. Some experiences require more complex elaboration and new vocabulary and concepts to make them intelligible. A Greek word for understand (*xuniēmi*) means "throw together," that is, to organize experiences in accord with the structures that constitute reality. Heraclitus of Ephesus, who lived in the late sixth century, taught that "eyes and ears are bad witnesses to men, if they have souls that do not understand the language."[40] In *Oedipus Tyrannus*, Sophocles offers a more radical critique by equating sight with ignorance. His Oedipus is an astute analyst who uses his powerful intellect to recognize problems and work out solutions to them that escape others who use only their eyes.[41]

Insight (*nous*) is the result of an intellectual process that deciphers the meaning of experience.[42] Greek thinkers struggled to devise some kind of general framework in terms of which the natural world and social interactions could be interpreted. Plato developed his theory of *a priori* knowledge and its recollection to address this need. He posited a soul that has experienced multiple lives in the course of which it has seen and learned all the forms, knowledge that can be recovered with the help of a dialectic "midwife" who asks appropriate questions.[43] We can assume that Thucydides was familiar with this problem, although not with the

[39] Thucydides, I.22.2–3.

[40] Frg. 107; Martin Heidegger, "Logos (Heraclitus Fragment B 50)," in D. F. Krell and F. A. Capuzzi, *Early Greek Thinking* (San Francisco: Harper & Row, 1984), pp. 59–78; C. H. Kohn, *The Art and Thought of Heraclitus: The Cosmic Fragments* (Cambridge: Cambridge University Press, 1979); Edward Hussey, "Epistemology and Meaning in Heraclitus," in Malcom Schofield and Martha Nussbaum, eds., *Language and Logos: Studies in Ancient Greek Philosophy Presented to G. E. L. Owen* (Cambridge: Cambridge University Press, 1982), pp. 33–59; Edward Hussey, "Heraclitus," in Brunschwig and Lloyd, *Greek Thought*, pp. 631–41.

[41] Euben, *The Tragedy of Political Theory*, p. 101.

[42] *Nous* in Athens was associated with scientific and philosophical inquiry, in part because of the widely discussed theories of Anaxagoras, who made *nous* the moving force (*archē*) of the universe. Aristotle, *Nicomachean Ethics*, 1177b27, suggested that *nous* makes us partially divine, for when we formulate our actions in an intelligent way we act like gods.

[43] Plato, *Meno*, 86b1–2, and *Cratylus*, 400c, for his theory of rebirth and its connection to knowledge. Speusippus, Plato's nephew and successor at the Academy, thought that Plato's theory of recollection led to the paradox that one had to know everything to know anything.

solution that Plato would propose. His strategy for tackling this problem was to analyze the war in terms of a broader political perspective, and to nest this perspective within a more general treatment of the rise and fall of civilization. By this means, the particular could be understood – as it had to be – with reference to the general. And knowledge, retrieved and transcribed, could become "a possession for all time."[44]

Thucydides' goal militated against calling his work a history. For Aristotle (384–322 BCE), the critical distinction between history and tragedy was not that the one is written in prose and the other in verse. History described particular events, while philosophy and poetry (including tragedy) had the potential to convey general truths.[45] Aristotle considered the plot (*muthos*) the most important part of tragedy because it represents a clarification of events (*sunthesis tōn pragmatōn*). The tragedian composes his story to bring out the universal features of human action so that we might come to recognize ourselves.[46] Thucydides wanted his work to be seen as a possession for all time, as a text that conveyed general lessons that transcended his historical epoch. He accordingly had every reason not to call it a history.

The truest cause of war

The conventional wisdom of fifth-century Greece was that the Peloponnesian War had been provoked by the aggressive policies of Pericles, especially the Megarian Decree that excluded the produce of Megara from the markets of Athens and its empire. This relatively novel form of economic warfare flatly contradicted Athens' commitment to open commerce and both worried and antagonized other *poleis*. Thucydides presents these incidents as superficial manifestations of a deeper process that brought the two hegemons of fifth-century Greece to blows. In his discussion of the origins of war in Book I.23.6, he distinguishes among grounds for complaints (*aitiai kai diaphorai*), accusations (*engklēmata*) and precipitants (*prophaseis*), and "the truest precipitant or precondition" of war

[44] Thucydides, I.22.4.

[45] According to Aristotle, *Poetics*, 1451a36–b11, poetry does not describe what happens, but what might happen. It is more philosophical and worthwhile (*spoudaioteron*) than history because it deals with universals, not particulars. Aristotle, moreover, has a very wide definition of history, which includes all kinds of knowledge, in addition to knowledge about the past discovered through research and inquiry. P. Louis, "Le mot 'ΙΣΤΟΡΙΑ' chez Aristote," *Revue de Philologie*, series 2, 29 (1955), pp. 39–44; G. E. M. de Ste. Croix, "Aristotle on History and Poetry (*Poetics*, 9, 1451a36–b11)" in Rorty, *Essays on Aristotle's Poetics*, pp. 23–32.

[46] Aristotle, *Poetics*, 1450a12, 1450a18, 1451b8. For Plato, myths and legends are the icons around which tragedy is composed. Aristotle understands these legends as a mere conveniences for poets and tragedians. They add weight to the drama, but are unnecessary. What is important is that the plot have reversals and discoveries.

(*alēthestatē prophasis*). He makes little mention of the Megarian Decree, but describes the creation and consolidation of the Athenian empire and the concern on the eve of war, common to Athens and Sparta, that one would increase its power at the other's expense. The implicit inference – and grist for realist mills – is that the "security dilemma" drove the two greatest powers of ancient Greece into a war that neither desired.

Thucydides uses paired speeches by Corcyrean and Corinthian representatives to the Athenian assembly to suggest that the alliance with Corcyra (Corfu) was motivated by fear of loss. If Athens rejects the alliance, the Corcyrean envoy warns, Corcyra could go down in defeat, and their fleet, the third largest in Hellas, would fall into Corinthian hands. The Corinthian spokesman makes a counter-threat: an Athenian–Corcyrean alliance will lead to war with Corinth, and probably with Sparta as well. Thucydides tells us that the assembly voted for the alliance because "it began now to be felt that the coming of the Peloponnesian War was only a question of time, and no one was willing to see a naval power of the magnitude of Corcyra sacrificed to Corinth."[47] As the Corinthians predicted, the alliance drew an Athenian naval squadron into a battle between the Corcyrean and Corinthian fleets. Corinth then appealed successfully to the Spartan assembly for military assistance against Athens.

Sparta's decision for war also appears to have been motivated by loss aversion. Paired speeches again provide arguments for and against belligerency. The Corinthian spokesman berates the Spartan assembly for its consistent failure to respond to Athenian aggrandizement and warns of the consequences of allowing Athens to grow stronger. The Athenian speaker offers no defense beyond his assertion that his city's policy has been motivated by a combination of self-interest and fear of the consequences of giving up its empire. He warns Spartans against challenging a confident, rich, powerful and self-sufficient adversary. Thucydides tells us that the Spartans voted for war "not so much because they were influenced by the speeches of their allies as because they were afraid of the further growth of Athenian power."[48]

Athens on the eve of war

On the eve of war, Athens was a bustling metropolis whose city walls enclosed a space a little less than a square mile and connected with those of the port of Piraeus, which enclosed another square mile. Attica was

[47] Thucydides, I.32–43, for the speeches, and I.44, for Thucydides' analysis of the Assembly's decision.

[48] Ibid., I.68–78, for the speeches, and I.88, for Thucydides' analysis of the Spartan decision.

some 40 miles long from north-west to south-east, and contained several other large settlements. Population estimates are controversial, and run on the high end of perhaps 300,000 people.[49] The empire consisted of some 160 tributaries. By virtue of its cosmopolitan population and largely seaborne trade, Athens was open to goods and ideas from diverse cultures. Literature and philosophy flourished, the profits of empire supported reconstruction of the Acropolis and other public monuments and public structures, and attracted to the city philosophers, writers, architects, artisans and charlatans from all over Greece.

Solon's reforms (*c.*594–593), and those of Cleisthenes (510–500), made every Athenian a freeman and citizen.[50] The restriction of the powers of the Areopagus Council in 462 had the effect of vesting political authority in the assembly (*ekklēsia*). By 431, large numbers of citizens took an active role in government through participation in the assembly and the courts (*dikastēria*) where they served as judge and jury. Athens was a democracy in that final authority was vested in an assembly in which all male citizens could vote. The assembly's agenda was prepared by the *boulē*, which provided day-to-day government of the city along with ten chief magistrates, or archons. The members of the *boulē*, the archons and all jurors were chosen annually by lottery. The only elected officials were ten generals (*stratēgoi*), the office to which Pericles was repeatedly elected.

Athens was Greece's greatest democracy and naval power, and the two were closely related.[51] The fleet required large numbers of artisans to build and maintain its ships.[52] Poorer citizens (*ponēroi*), some of them landless (*thētes*) and many residents, or metics, found employment in the fleet, dockyards or chandleries, and were essential to the security of the city and the expansion of its empire. Traditional Greek ideology justified political authority on the basis of the contribution citizens made to defense of the polis, and service in the fleet provided a strong claim for participation in the affairs of state by the large class of citizens who could not afford a hoplite panoply.[53] The importance of the fleet, and service in

49 Mogens H. Hansen, *Demography and Democracy: The Number of Athenian Citizens in the Fourth Century B.C.* (Herning, Denmark: Systime, 1986).

50 Christian Meier, *The Greek Discovery of Politics* (Cambridge, Mass.: Harvard University Press, 1990), pp. 53–81 on the reforms of Cleisthenes and the development of a civic culture.

51 Relatively little is known about other Greek democracies, see R. K. Sinclair, *Democracy and Participation in Athens* (Cambridge: Cambridge University Press, 1988), pp. 218–19.

52 Thucydides, I.142.

53 Josiah Ober, *Mass and Elite in Democratic Athens: Rhetoric, Ideology, and the Power of the People* (Princeton: Princeton University Press, 1989), pp. 83–84.

it for some hoplite infantry, may also have made the upper classes more receptive to these demands.[54]

Athens played a leading role in repelling two Persian invasions of Greece. The first invasion was halted at the Battle of Marathon in 490, where the Athenians defeated a larger Persian army. The second invasion compelled Athenians to evacuate their city and seek refuge on a nearby island. Their navy and allied squadrons engaged and destroyed the numerically superior Persian fleet at the battle of Salamis in 480.[55] In the following decade, Cimon led Athenian and allied forces in a series of successful engagements against Persia and its allies that carried Athenian arms to the Bosporus and beyond. In and around the Ionian Sea, Athens consolidated its hold over its allies, transforming its *hēgemonia* into an *archē*.[56] It also tried to expand its influence in mainland Greece. This brought Athens into conflict with Sparta and led to the First Peloponnesian War, fought in a desultory way, from 461 to 445 BCE.

Athenian expansion was brought to a halt by a series of military and political disasters: the complete annihilation in 454 of its expedition to Egypt, the revolt of Erythrae and Miletus in 452, and the defeat at Coronea in 446. These setbacks compelled the Athenians to recognize the limits of their power. In 449, Athens made peace with Persia and, in the summer or early autumn of 446, Athens and Sparta concluded the Thirty Years Peace. Under the leadership of Pericles, Athens devoted its energies to consolidating its sprawling empire.[57]

By the terms of the Thirty Years Peace Athens gave up its continental conquests, most of which had already been lost, and agreed to withdraw from the strategically valuable Megarid, which controlled the overland route between Attica and the Peloponnese.[58] In return, Athens received official Spartan recognition of its empire and a free hand to govern it as it wished. Allies of the two powers were forbidden to change sides

[54] Aristotle, *Politics*, 1297b16ff., 1305a18; Kurt A. Raaflaub, "Equalities and Inequalities in Athenian Democracy" in Josiah Ober and Charles Hedrick, eds., *Dēmokratia: A Conversation on Democracies, Ancient and Modern* (Princeton: Princeton University Press, 1996), pp. 139–74, on the connection between naval service by *thétes* and attainment of political rights. Victor D. Hanson, "Hoplites into Democrats: The Changing Ideology" in Ober and Hedrick, *Dēmokratia*, pp. 289–312, suggests that service of "middling" hoplites on Athenian warships created solidarity with rowers and support for their incorporation into the body politic. Barry S. Strauss, "The Athenian Trireme, School of Democracy," in Ober and Hedrick, *Dēmokratia*, pp. 313–26, makes the case from the perspective of the *thétes*, arguing that trireme service created a sense of class solidarity and entitlement which translated into political influence.

[55] Peter Green, *The Greco-Persian Wars* (Berkeley and Los Angeles: University of California Press, 1996, offers a good account.

[56] Chapter 4 elaborates on the distinction between *archē* and *hégemonia*.

[57] Thucydides, I.104, 109–10; Meiggs, *Athenian Empire*, chs. 5–9.

[58] On Megara, Ronald P. Legon, *Megara: The Political History of a Greek City-State to 336 B.C.* (Ithaca: Cornell University Press, 1981).

but neutrals could join either alliance. Disputes were to be settled by arbitration.[59] From 446 to 433 Athens made no conquests and added no new allies to its confederacy. Most of its colonizing efforts consisted of cleruchies – colonies set up on territory taken from rebellious allies and designed to maintain a constant military presence. Other colonies were established at Erythrae, Hestiaea, Astacus, Brea and Ennea Hodoi (Amphipolis), all with the purpose of fortifying strategic locations or protecting vital trade routes between Athens, Chalcidice, the Hellespont and grain-producing areas along the Black Sea. Even the Corcyrean alliance of 433 was technically defensive, not in violation of the Thirty Years Peace, and undertaken entirely at the initiative of Corcyra.[60]

Athens gave other indications of its acceptance of the status quo. In 434–433, the town of Thurii was torn apart by civil strife. Athens and Sparta both claimed it as a colony but Athens agreed to let the pro-Spartan oracle at Delphi mediate the dispute and deferred to her judgment that Apollo had been the founder and that Thurii accordingly belonged to all of Greece. By respecting the political fiction that the settlement was pan-Hellenic, Athens gave up its claim to a strategically situated outpost in the west that was likely to side with Sparta in the case of war.[61]

Thucydides reports that after 446 both sides marshaled their strength in preparation for a decisive showdown.[62] But his account also indicates that scrupulous observance of the terms of the Thirty Years Peace by Athens belied its reputation for *pleonexia* (greediness) and encouraged at least some Spartiates to see it as a sated power.[63] Not everyone felt this way. A sizeable faction wanted to go to war in 441–440 to take advantage of Athens' vulnerability at the time of the Samian rebellion. But cooler heads prevailed, just as they had in Athens at the time of the helot rebellion when many Athenians would have preferred to make war against Sparta instead of coming to its aid. Spartiates would not have been so restrained in 441 if they had regarded Athenian ambitions as unlimited and war as inevitable.[64]

[59] Thucydides, I.35, 40, 44–45, 67, 78, 140, 144–45; Meiggs, *Athenian Empire*, ch. 10.

[60] Meiggs, *Athenian Empire*, chs. 11–14.

[61] Ibid., p. 368; Ste. Croix, *Origins of the Peloponnesian War*, pp. 154–66.

[62] Meiggs, *Athenian Empire*, pp. 197–98, 201–08, makes similar claims.

[63] For the traditional point of view, see W. G. Forrest, *A History of Sparta, 1950–192 B.C.* (New York: Norton, 1968), p. 108, and Ste. Croix, *Origins of the Peloponnesian War*, passim, who accept Thucydides' contention that Spartans were consistently hostile to Athens and took as a given that the two hegemons would sooner or later come to blows.

[64] The existence of a "peace party" in Sparta is controversial, and part of a larger debate over the relative role of Athens and Sparta in bringing about the war, and the respective reasons for doing so. Cawkwell, *Thucydides and the Peloponnesian War*, pp. 20–39, reviews some of the relevant literature.

Sparta's reaction to the events of 433–431 provides further evidence that its leaders hoped to keep the peace and considered it as a feasible objective. From the beginning of the Corinthian–Corcyrean conflict, Sparta urged caution on Corinth and may have asked its allies not to assist or participate in Corinth's punitive expedition.[65] Following the first naval battle at Leucimme, Sparta pleaded with Corinth to settle its dispute by negotiation or arbitration, as proposed by the Corcyreans. Spartan envoys accompanied the Corcyrean mission that went to Corinth to propose arbitration.[66] Spartan peace efforts foundered on the rock of allied and Athenian stubbornness.

Third parties

Thucydides' narrative makes it apparent that Sparta succumbed to allied pressure. The most rabid war-monger was Corinth, who desperately needed Spartan military backing to compensate for Athenian naval support of Corcyra. Megara and Aegina also had grievances against Athens. Corinth readily enlisted them in its campaign to goad Sparta into war and sent envoys to other allies to drum up fear of Athens and complain about the lack of Spartan support.[67]

Sparta had two royal houses and two kings. They performed ritual functions, but in wartime, one of them was chosen as commander-in-chief. Their power was balanced by five annually elected ephors who had the right to call the *gerousia*, or council of elders, into session. It was composed of the two kings and twenty-eight men over the age of sixty. The kings also arranged for meetings of the assembly, where all Spartiates voted, usually without debate on proposals put before them. In August 432, the Spartan ephors convened an assembly at which the Corinthians, other allies and friendly states were invited to voice their grievances. Despite an eminently sensible plea for caution by King Archidamus, the Spartan assembly voted that the treaty had been broken and war must be declared. Thucydides' account of the assembly reveals that it was carefully orchestrated by the ephors to achieve the maximum political effect. In addition to Sparta's allies, they invited "others who might have complaints to make about Athenian aggression." They allowed the Corinthians to speak last, after the other envoys had worked the crowd to inflame anti-Athenian sentiment.[68]

[65] A. W. Gomme, *A Historical Commentary on Thucydides*, 3 vols. (Oxford: Oxford University Press, 1950–56), I, p. 178; Kagan, *Outbreak of the Peloponnesian War*, p. 246.
[66] Thucydides, I.28. [67] Ibid., I.67, 119. [68] Ibid., I.66–88.

The Corinthians made a masterful appeal.[69] Analyses of it usually emphasize the Corinthian portrayal of Athenians as restless, ambitious and intent on subjugating all Hellas.[70] The Corinthians argue that Athens must be stopped while it was still possible to do so, which seems consistent with Thucydides' claim that Sparta went to war because it feared the growing power of Athens. But the context of the speech indicates that this argument was a rationalization for a war Corinthians and their Spartan backers sought for other reasons.

The Corinthian motive for war was entirely selfish. An oligarchy located on the isthmus connecting the Peloponnesus with the rest of Greece, Corinth was a wealthy commercial metropolis and transit route for east–west trade. By off-loading goods, transporting them across the narrow isthmus in either direction and reloading them at the other side, shippers could avoid the long, perilous sea route around the Peloponnesus. Corcyra was an obstacle to Corinth's ambition to establish a sphere of influence in the north-west corner of Greece. Unwilling to submit its dispute with Corcyra to arbitration or renounce its ambition to regain great power status by means of colonial expansion, Corinth sought to use Spartan power to humble Corcyra, and Athens for supporting Corcyra. Prior to their imbroglio with Corcyra, Corinth evinced no hostility to Athens or fear of its power. In 441–440, Corinth opposed Spartan and allied intervention in support of the Samian rebellion against Athens.[71] They would not have done this if they had been alarmed by Athenian power. Nor would they have sent a delegation to Athens in 433 to seek support after their first naval encounter with Corcyra; if they had regarded Athenian imperial ambitions as unlimited, they would have considered an Athenian–Corcyrean alliance as a foregone conclusion. The Corinthian arguments indicate their belief that alliance with Corcyra would represent a sharp departure from the policy that Athens had followed since 446.[72] This is how Athenians viewed the matter at first; they heeded the advice of the Corinthians and voted it down. It required a second assembly and the intervention of Pericles to bring them around.[73]

The Corinthian speech was a frontal assault against accommodation. The effort to which the ephors went to orchestrate a series of appeals to the assembly culminating in the Corinthian presentation indicates that even after Megara and Potidaea, many Spartiates must have favored peace with

[69] Ibid., I.119–25.

[70] Gregory Crane, *Thucydides and the Ancient Simplicity: The Limits of Political Realism* (Berkeley: University of California Press, 1998), pp. 93–113, for a good overview of this literature.

[71] Thucydides, I.40. [72] Ibid., I.42.

[73] Ibid., I.46, p. 27; Plutarch, *Pericles*, Book XXIX.

Athens. The Corinthians told the assembly that the Thirty Years Peace had been exploited by Athens to become powerful enough to threaten the peace and security of Greece. Athens would become too strong to oppose if it extended its dominion over Sparta's allies. The Corinthians recognized that this argument was unlikely to persuade because they followed it with a threat: if Sparta allowed Athens to humble Megara and subjugate Potidaea, it would "sacrifice friends and kindred to their bitterest enemies, and drive the rest of us in despair to some other alliance."[74] Modern authorities have generally treated this threat as a significant cause for alarm in Sparta.[75] Corinth was Sparta's wealthiest ally and the second naval power of Greece, and its defection from the Lacedaemonian Confederacy would have dealt a severe blow to Spartan power and influence. Even if the Corinthians were bluffing – and there is reason to believe that they were – Sparta's rejection of Corinth's plea for support would have seriously weakened the alliance and might have been interpreted as a sign of weakness by Athens.[76]

The Corinthian threat was a cleverly calculated appeal to the Spartan's self-image. Spartiates prided themselves on their virtue, honor and loyalty. The Corinthians sought to shame them for their failure to come to the aid of Potidaea and Megara, defenseless in the face of Athenian aggression. The Corinthians warned Spartans that if they failed to intervene, their standing in Greece would "degenerate from the prestige that it enjoyed under that of your ancestors."[77] The Spartan assembly was full of impressionable and illiterate young men with little knowledge of the wider world, no experience of serious warfare and no previous

[74] Thucydides, I.71.

[75] Ste. Croix, *Origins of the Peloponnesian War*, p. 60, in a personal communication to the author, argues that Corinth might have cut a deal with Athens. Marta Sordi, "Scontro di Blocchi e Azione di Terze Forze nello Scoppio della Guerra del Peloponneso" in Richard Ned Lebow and Barry R. Strauss, *Hegemonic Rivalry: From Thucydides to the Modern Age* (Boulder: Westview, 1991), pp. 87–100 also finds the Corinthian threat convincing. Kagan, *The Outbreak of the Peloponnesian War*, pp. 292–93, argues against the seriousness of the Corinthian threat, as does P. A. Brunt, "Spartan Policy and Strategy in the Archidamian War," *Phoenix* 19 (Winter 1965), pp. 255–56. Brunt dismisses the Corinthian threat as "an empty threat and known to be such at Sparta." Argos, the only strong uncommitted city in Greece, was the enemy of Sparta and linked to Athens by ideology. Nor was Argos strong enough to offset the loss of Sparta. Crane, *Thucydides and the Athenian Simplicity*, p. 215, concludes that it is impossible to know if Corinth was bluffing, but thinks that Sparta's position would have been considerably weakened if Corinth and other allies had left the alliance.

[76] According to Forrest, *A History of Sparta*, p. 108, "The choice appeared to lie between a technically unjustified war and a serious risk of seeing the alliance disintegrate, a nasty dilemma." Brunt, "Spartan Policy and Strategy in the Archidamian War," pp. 256–57, argues that rejection of Corinth might have had "incalculable results on the cohesion of the Peloponnesian League."

[77] Thucydides, I.71.

exposure to this kind of emotional pressure.[78] There can be little doubt that they had already been made to feel uncomfortable by the speeches of the allies and friendly states, who had harangued them about Athenian high-handedness and pilloried them for their passivity. By the time the Corinthians rose to speak, the Spartan audience had been suitably "softened up" for their appeal. The Corinthian speech had its intended effect. Spartan anger and shame were intensified and together with the jealousy many Spartiates had long harbored toward Athens, prompted a vote for war. The Athenian attempt to explain and defend their policy was dismissed with a short, derisive speech by one of the ephors, who simply asserted that "we have good allies whom we must not give up to Athens."[79] Emotion triumphed over reason.

Did Sparta fear Athens?

After the Athenian speech and before the vote for war, Sparta dismissed all foreigners and consulted among themselves. In another pair of revealing speeches, supporters and opponents of war offer divergent predictions of what such a conflict would be like. King Archidamus, spokesman for what we might call the peace party, or more accurately, the party of caution, addressed the assembly first. He implored his fellow Spartiates, especially the young men who had never experienced a military campaign, not to romanticize war or minimize the sacrifice it would entail. Athens' wealth, navy, large population, and many tribute-paying allies, made its power unrivaled in the Greek world. Sparta's greatest asset, its heavy infantry, could be used to devastate Attica but could not prevent Athens from importing everything it needed by sea. To bring Athens to its knees, it would be necessary to defeat its navy or destroy its empire to deny the navy the revenues on which it depended for ships, sailors and food. This would be a long and hazardous undertaking, Archidamus warned, one "that we may leave . . . as a legacy to our children; so improbable is it that the Athenian spirit will be the slave of their land, or Athenian experience be cowed by war."[80] It is significant that his strategic estimate exactly matches those of both Pericles and Thucydides.[81]

Thucydides describes Archidamus as intelligent (*xunetos*).[82] This is the highest word of praise in his lexicon, and suggests sympathy and support

[78] Diodorus (11.50) cites an earlier instance of Spartan youth moved by spirit instead of reason. He describes meetings of the Gerousia and assembly at which "the younger men and most of the others" were anxious to resume the hegemony by force until Hetomaridas succeeded in dissuading them, and they "abandoned their impulse to make war on Athens." Cited in Ste. Croix, *Origins of the Peloponnesian War*, p. 170.

[79] Thucydides, I.86.

[80] Ibid., I.80–85.

[81] Ibid., I.144 for Pericles, and II.65 for Thucydides.

[82] Ibid., I.79.2.

for his argument. However, Archidamus' words fell on deaf ears, and the implication is that his audience was not as thoughtful or intelligent. The war party had no understanding of naval power and nothing but contempt for Athenian infantry. Sthenelaïdas, one of the ephors, brushed aside his arguments with the claim that the Athenians were in the wrong and deserved punishment. Athenian power also got short shrift. "Others have much money and ships and horses," the ephor exclaimed, "but we have good allies." At his urging, the Lacedaemonians voted that the treaty had been broken and that war must be declared.[83] Power transition theories explain hegemonic war with reference to changes in the relative distribution of power between hegemon and challenger. These theories assume that leaders have a reasonably accurate understanding of the power of the relative actors. The Greek experience belies this expectation and undercuts Thucydides' apparent explanation for war in I.23.6.

Sthenelaïdas' speech and the several years of unsuccessful military campaigning that followed demonstrate the extent to which the Spartan war party misjudged Athenian resolve and power. They seriously underestimated Athenian military capability, and the ease with which the Athenian economy could sustain that capability in a long war. They expected to invade Attica, overwhelm the Athenians in a single battle, dictate the terms of settlement and return home to bask in the glory of their victory.[84] But, as Archidamus had predicted, the Athenians refused to come out from behind their walls, and used their fleet to harass the Peloponnese and attack Spartan allies in other theaters of war. Lack of respect for Athenian power, not fear of it, was a principal precondition and incentive for war. King Archidamus and the peace party had a far more accurate grasp of military and economic realities, and their assessment made them cautious of war and anxious to reach an accommodation with Athens.

A final bid for peace

Sparta voted for war in the summer of 432, but made no immediate effort to begin hostilities. Messengers were sent to Delphi to solicit the approval of the oracle. Receiving favorable omens, Sparta summoned its allies to a congress to vote on war.[85] They then sent three successive diplomatic

[83] Ibid., I.86–88.

[84] Brunt, "Spartan Policy and Strategy in the Archidamian War," pp. 255–80, describes all the formidable obstacles that stood in the way of the success of this strategy and speculates that Spartans were relatively insensitive to them because of the success of their invasion of Attica in 446, the catalyst for the Thirty Years Peace.

[85] Thucydides, I.80–81.

missions to Athens, two of which can be interpreted as serious attempts to reach a settlement and make war unnecessary.[86]

The most interesting Spartan proposal was the second embassy. War could be avoided, the Spartans suggested, if Athens lifted the siege of Potidaea, respected the independence of Aegina and revoked the Megarian Decree.[87] From the Spartan perspective, the key condition was revocation of the Megarian Decree; it was the only Athenian initiative that was an unambiguous violation of the Thirty Years Peace. It was also the most controversial act of Pericles, so the domestic political cost of reversing himself might not have been so great.

Aegina and Potidaea posed problems of a different kind. Both states had cross-alliance ties. Aegina was an old enemy of Athens, deeply resentful of its rise to prominence, and had fought against it in the First Peloponnesian War. After being defeated in a great sea battle, its city was reduced by siege. In the spring of 457, Aegina was compelled to tear down its walls and join the Athenian league as a tribute-paying member.[88] The Aeginetans chafed at their vassalage and were among the most vitriolic critics of Athens. They voiced their complaints out of the public eye for fear of Athenian reprisal.[89] Potidaea was a strategically important settlement on the isthmus connecting the Pallene Peninsula with Chalcidice. It was a Corinthian colony and a tribute-paying ally of Athens. The Potidaeans valued their close ties to the mother country and received Corinthian magistrates every year. In the winter of 433–432, immediately after the naval battle of Sybota, Athens ordered the city to tear down its defensive wall facing the sea, hand over hostages and send home its Corinthian magistrates.[90] When Potidaea rejected these demands, Pericles sent an expedition to impose these terms. Athenian forces encountered unexpected resistance and were compelled to reduce the city by means of a long and costly siege.

Of all the Spartan demands, ending the siege of Potidaea would have been the most difficult to accept. Potidaea was strategically located on the grain route to the Black Sea and it controlled access to Chalcidice, a region of some importance to Athens.[91] It is possible that a pledge of Potidaean neutrality in an Athenian–Corinthian war would have provided Athens with a face-saving justification for ending its costly siege. Equally significant is what the Spartans left unsaid. Their emissaries made no

[86] Ibid., I.126–39.

[87] Ibid., I.139. For opposing views of these overtures and the latitude that Pericles had in responding to them, see Kagan, *Outbreak of the Peloponnesian War*, pp. 317–31, and Crane, *Thucydides and the Athenian Simplicity*, pp. 187–95.

[88] Thucydides, I.105, 59–60; Diodorus, 2.78. [89] Thucydides, I.67.

[90] Ibid., I.56. [91] Kagan, *Outbreak of the Peloponnesian War*, p. 278.

public mention of Corinth, and this omission can only be interpreted as willingness to let Corinth fend for itself in return for Athenian concessions on Megara, Potidaea and Aegina. Such a settlement made sense from the Spartan perspective. Some Spartiates at least resented Corinth for its uncompromising antagonism toward Corcyra and seemingly successful effort to drag them into an unwanted war with Athens. To avoid that war, they needed some concessions from Athens to placate other allies and Spartan opinion. Revocation of the Megarian Decree, some symbolic gesture toward Aegina and termination of the Potidaean siege, would have satisfied this need and have left Corinth isolated.

It was not naïve for Sparta to have hoped that Athens would accede to their demands, or at least accept them as the basis for negotiation. Megara and Aegina were minor issues. Control of the Megarid, which the Decree did nothing to bring about, was critical if there was to be war with Sparta, but moot in the aftermath of an accommodation. Potidaea would have been the major stumbling block. But Athens might have seen it in its interest to end the siege even without a pledge of Potidaean neutrality because it would have left Corinth isolated. Without Spartan backing, Corinth would have been unlikely to challenge Athens because it surely would have been defeated. The arrangement Sparta proposed did not demand termination of the Corcyrean alliance, so Athens would have gained at least as much as it gave up.

There was considerable support in Athens for rescinding the Megarian Decree. Thucydides reports that after the third Spartan embassy, "There were many speakers who came forward and gave their support to one side or the other, urging the necessity of war, or the revocation of the decree and the folly of allowing it to stand in the way of peace."[92] Once again it took a masterful speech by Pericles to convince Athenians to persevere in the hazardous course he had set.[93]

In effect, Sparta sought accommodation with Athens at Corinth's expense. Sparta's willingness to sacrifice Corinth on the altar of hegemonic accommodation is the strongest possible evidence that many Spartiates did not view Athenian ambitions as unlimited or a Spartan–Athenian war as inevitable. If they had, they most assuredly would not have tried to make peace at the expense of their most important military ally. Sparta's peace initiatives also indicate second thoughts about the wisdom of war. We may speculate that with time for reflection and internal debate more Spartans saw the merit of King Archidamus' arguments or came to appreciate that Corinth was out to manipulate them for its own ends. There may have been enough of a backlash to permit Archidamus and his followers to

[92] Thucydides, I.139. [93] Ibid., I.140–44.

insist that some effort be made to reach a diplomatic settlement. Athenian repudiation of the Spartan proposals strengthened the hand of the war party, which now prepared to invade Attica.[94]

Was war inevitable?

Corinthian, Spartan and Athenian illusions about the likely consequences of their policies suggest that the Peloponnesian War was the result of an improbable series of remarkably bad judgments made by the leaders of the several powers involved. The most critical decisions, from the Corcyrean rejection of Epidamnus' appeal for assistance to Pericles' stubborn rejection of Sparta's final peace overtures, were contrary to polis interests and based on inaccurate understanding of military and political realities. Most of these decisions seem to have been a response to narrow situational pressures, not to deeper strategic realities.

The first link in this chain was Corcyra's decision to turn a deaf ear to appeals from the Epidamnian envoys for help in defending their city against local tribesmen in league with their exiled nobles.[95] Thucydides does not tell us why the Corcyreans spurned these pleas, so scholars have ventured their own opinions.[96] The most persuasive hypothesis is that Epidamnus, a colony of Corcyra, had become powerful in its own right and the Corcyreans welcomed the prospect of having it reduced to relative impotence by civil strife.

Corcyra's dismissal of the Epidamnian ambassadors encouraged them to turn to Corinth for assistance. The Corinthians responded with alacrity, Thucydides tells us, because of their hatred of Corcyreans (*misei tōn Kerkuraiōn*), who failed to show them the respect and honor due a founding city.[97] What happened next is well known. Corinth sent a large force to Epidamnus. The Corcyreans, outraged by Corinthian intervention, promptly laid siege to Epidamnus. Corinth readied a fleet to come to the aid of the city. Fearful of war with Corinth and its allies, Corcyra proposed negotiations and then arbitration. Corinth refused, and sent its fleet toward Epidamnus, where it was defeated by Corcyra at Leucimme.

[94] Ibid., I.126–30. [95] Ibid., I.24.

[96] Kagan, *Outbreak of the Peloponnesian War*, pp. 208–09.

[97] Herodotus, III.49.1, reports that Corinth and Corcyra had been hostile toward each other almost since Corcyra's founding. Thucydides, I.13.4, reports that they fought a sea battle *circa* 664, the first encounter of its kind known to Thucydides. In I.25.3, he notes that Corinthian hatred of Corcyra was attributable to the latter's failure to honor its founder. A. J. Graham, *Colony and Mother City in Ancient Greece*, 2nd ed. (Chicago: Ares Publishers, 1983), pp. 4–8, observes that failure to honor a mother city was as shocking to Greeks as failure to honor one's parents. See pp. 118–53, on Corinth and its colonial empire.

Corinth now prepared for war in earnest, and Corcyra appealed to Athens for support.

The Corcyreans had not foreseen any of these developments when they refused aid to Epidamnus.[98] That Epidamnus would turn to Corinth for support should have come as no surprise. The city had been a Corcyrean colony. Following custom, Corcyra chose a "founder" (*oikiotēs*) from its Corinthian metropole, and this provided the basis for its appeal. And despite strenuous past efforts to preserve its independence, Epidamnus was now desperate enough to seek support in any quarter. Corinth was motivated to intervene by practical as well as emotional reasons. For some years it had been building a sphere of influence in north-west Greece at the expense of Corcyra. By 435, Corinth had gained control of all the mixed Corinthian-Corcyrean colonies in the region except for Epidamnus.[99] The Epidamnian appeal for assistance was seen by many in Corinth as a gods-sent opportunity to consolidate their influence in the region.

The Corinthians made a double miscalculation: they did not realize their expedition to Epidamnus would provoke war with Corcyra, and when it did, they were overconfident of victory. They might have behaved more cautiously if they had had a better appreciation of Corcyrean resolve and naval prowess. Following their defeat at Leucimme, the Corinthians thought only of revenge and their judgment became more clouded by emotion. They spurned Corcyrean and Spartan pleas for negotiation or mediation, although it was likely that they would have emerged with considerable gains from either process. Instead, they spent two years preparing for a renewed round of fighting.

The second Corinthian expedition also ended in failure. With Athenian assistance, the Corcyreans beat back the Corinthian attack. Once again the Corinthians had miscalculated; they failed to consider at first that Corcyra would turn to Athens for assistance and secure a defensive alliance. After the alliance, Corinth still persevered with its plans for war. Corinthian emotions ran so high that leaders and people alike were unwilling to recognize the foolishness of risking war against both Athens and Corcyra.

The decisive step in this tragic chain of events was the Athenian decision to ally with Corcyra. Thucydides tells readers to believe that the alliance was a foregone conclusion and a wise strategic decision because the Corcyrean fleet might otherwise have been captured by Corinth. His

[98] Crane, *Thucydides and the Ancient Simplicity*, pp. 95–100, provides a good review of the background to this dispute.

[99] Kagan, *Outbreak of the Peloponnesian War*, p. 218.

narrative indicates the alliance was extremely controversial. After listening to the speeches of the Corcyreans and Corinthians, the Athenian assembly rejected the Corcyrean plea for support.[100] Thucydides offers no explanation for this decision, but it seems likely that a majority of those present worried that the proposed alliance would lead to war with Corinth and Sparta. Moreover, Athenians had no affection for the Dorian Corcyreans.[101] We can surmise that Pericles was busy drumming up support behind the scenes and reconvened the assembly when he had enough votes for the alliance.[102] Pericles probably addressed the second assembly; Plutarch reports that he "persuaded the people to send aid" to Corcyra.[103]

Thucydides tells us nothing about the Athenian *volte face*, although he acknowledges that it was the point of no return on the road to war. Reproducing speeches for and against the alliance would have drawn attention to the division of Athenian opinion and the fact that a majority of the first assembly opposed the alliance with Corcyra. It would have revealed that the alliance that was ultimately approved was a strictly defensive one, a restriction intended to keep Athens from violating the Thirty Years Peace. Concern to avoid war may also explain why Pericles sent only ten ships to Corcyra. If his objective was to deter Corinth, a force of 50 or 100 ships would have been much more effective.[104] The inescapable conclusion is that the alliance was a near thing. It took all of Pericles' considerable political and rhetorical skills to convince a pacifically inclined citizenry to vote for it. Without his intervention, the Corcyrean appeal would have been rejected. This is not a novel judgment; it was conventional wisdom in ancient Greece.[105]

The next step toward war was the Spartan assembly's vote on the grounds that Athens had broken the Thirty Years Peace. I have already analyzed this decision and the faulty assessment of Athenian power on which it was based. A more accurate appraisal of Athenian power would have dictated caution, as King Archidamus urged. The final step toward war was Athens' refusal to respond favorably to the second and third Spartan emissaries. These proposals offered a reasonable basis for negotiation and accommodation. They evoked a positive response from many

[100] Thucydides, I.44.
[101] The Corinthian speech to the Athenian assembly opens with an attack on the character and policy of the Corcyreans. It is reasonable to assume that the speaker expected to evoke some sympathy in his audience, which suggests that the Athenians themselves were not particularly well disposed toward Corcyra. Thucydides, I.37–38, pp. 23–24.
[102] Plutarch, *Pericles*, 29. [103] Ibid., 29.1.
[104] Kagan, *Outbreak of the Peloponnesian War*, pp. 242–45.
[105] Plutarch, *Pericles* 29, p. 196; Connor, *Thucydides*, p. 39n.

Athenians. Once again, Pericles felt the need to speak out. He opposed repeal of the Megarian Decree and succeeded in deflecting Athenian opinion away from peace.[106] His policy is puzzling. Thucydides implies that he saw war with Sparta as unavoidable and took Corcyra into alliance to augment Athenian naval power. Like Cimon before him, Pericles had consistently supported a policy of accommodation with Sparta. Both leaders had worked hard to undo the damage done by Themistocles' policy of unlimited expansion. They had ended the war with Persia, signed the Thirty Years Peace with Sparta, and consolidated the Athenian empire. Under Pericles, Athens had scrupulously adhered to the terms of the Thirty Years Peace. In 433 there was every reason to believe that Sparta would continue to uphold the peace if unprovoked by Athens. For Pericles to jettison his decades-old policy for a naval alliance with Corcyra seems odd indeed.

Pericles may have acted on the basis of subtle calculations. One possibility was an interest in western expansion. He may have believed that sooner or later Athenians would once again demand a policy of conquest or colonization. By directing these energies toward Italy and away from Greece, he could hope to maintain amicable relations with Sparta. As Greek ships made their crossing to Italy from Greek ports along the Adriatic coast, Corcyra was ideally situated to act as a staging point for Athenian commercial and military ventures in the west. A more likely possibility is that Pericles perceived the Corinthian–Corcyrean conflict as a low-cost opportunity to enhance Athenian power. In politics as well as business, Athenians were famous for making the most of an opportunity (*kairos*), and Pericles may have calculated that Athenian support of Corcyra would be sufficient to deter Corinth from attacking. If so, Athens would gain a valuable ally and at the same time impede Corinthian plans for expansion in the north-west.[107]

Pericles was an experienced politician and must have considered the possibility that his policy could fail and lead to war with Corinth. He may have viewed this risk as acceptable because he thought it likely that Sparta would stand aside. A successful campaign against Corinth in this circumstance had much to recommend it. Athens would humble a naval and commercial rival who was also Sparta's most important ally. Corinth's defeat would tip the balance of power in Greece further in Athens' favor. After Sybota, where the Corinthians were turned back the second time, it became apparent that Corinth was spoiling for a fight. Instead of attempting to resolve the conflict through diplomacy, Pericles issued

[106] Thucydides, I.139–145, pp. 80–86.
[107] Kagan, *Outbreak of the Peloponnesian War*, pp. 222–50, makes this argument.

the Megarian Decree and sent an ultimatum to Potidaea, actions that his Greek contemporaries understood as preparations for, indeed, as provocations for, war with Corinth.

At Sybota, the Athenians, by dint of skill and fortune, had light losses. The Corinthians, who lost a substantial part of their fleet, fled when they saw Athenian reinforcements on the horizon. Pericles, and Athenians more generally, seem to have become emboldened by their easy victory. Their ensuing demands on Potidaea and the Megarian Decree, also forms of coercive diplomacy, may have been initiated in the hope that, once again, they would achieve their ends without leading to war. But like the Athenian effort to deter Corinth, these initiatives quickly got out of hand, each in a different way. The principal reason for the failure of coercive diplomacy was that Athenian demands struck at the core interests of Megara, and the core identity of Potidaea, and were thus unacceptable. Instead of prompting the desired concessions, they provoked anger and a desire for revenge among the target states and Sparta's allies.

Pericles' expectation that Sparta would remain neutral in an Athenian–Corinthian war may have been based on Spartan behavior up to the time of the alliance with Corcyra. King Archidamus and the "peace party" had tried to discourage Corinth from its expedition against Corcyra, had urged their allies to refrain from coming to Corinth's assistance and had sent their emissaries to Corinth to lend weight to the Corcyrean offer of negotiation or arbitration. Sparta gave every indication of being piqued with Corinth and anxious to avoid being drawn into a private and unnecessary quarrel. Pericles may also have derived false confidence from his friendship with Archidamus, a man known for his commitment to the Thirty Years Peace and the preservation of harmonious relations with Athens. Spartiates were reasonably alarmed by the prospect of the defeat of their most powerful ally. Corinth's defeat would put them and their other allies at the mercy of Athens, who would now control the Gulf of Corinth as effectively as it did all the seas to the east. As Thucydides' account of the Spartan assembly indicates, the majority were not prepared to stand aside; for this, and other reasons, they voted for war.

Pericles had a final fallback position. He planned to fight the most limited war against Sparta. He would not contest the expected Spartan invasion of Attica, but conduct a low-key campaign of naval harassment in and around the Peloponnese. Pericles expected Spartiates to become increasingly frustrated by their inability to engage Athens, tire of war and return the peace party to power. Pericles and Archidamus between them would then conclude a more enduring peace. Once again, Pericles miscalculated. His strategy and the assumptions on which it was based bear an uncanny similarity to German calculations in 1914, all of which were equally flawed. German leaders supported Austria's démarche with Serbia in the expectation that it would deter Russia from intervening. If Russia refused to stand aside and allow Serbia to be subjugated, they were unreasonably confident that France would not come to the aid of its Russian ally. If both countries defied German expectations and went to war, Britain was expected to remain neutral. In the unlikely event that it did not, Germany counted on defeating both of its continental adversaries in a short campaign before British sea power could have any effect on the war.

In 1914, the short war illusion was attributable in part to the general failure to understand the ways in which modern technology had transformed warfare.[108] But its deeper cause was political. European statesmen ignored Clausewitz's prescient warning that war between peoples is extraordinarily difficult to control. When peoples' passions become engaged, Clausewitz wrote, "a reciprocal action is begun" that tends to carry war to its most extreme expression regardless of any intention of leaders to keep it in check. Once this spiral begins, war is most likely to end in the exhaustion of one or both sides.[109] This was true of the Peloponnesian War and World War I. In 431 and 1914 there were individuals like King Archidamus and Sir Edward Grey who foresaw what lay ahead. Had there been more of them, war might have been averted.

Thucydides' account indicates that leaders had considerable freedom of choice. This is most clearly demonstrated by the success of key individuals to shift the direction of state policy in the face of considerable opposition. The ephors and the allied representatives did this in Sparta, and Pericles' intervention convinced his compatriots to reverse themselves and ally with Corcyra. Without Pericles, Athens would not have concluded its fateful alliance. It might be argued that Pericles' success in swaying the Athenian assembly is the ultimate confirmation of relative gains and the balance of power. Pericles assumed that war with Sparta was unavoidable in the long term, and therefore worth risking in the short term for the sake of an alliance that would significantly enhance Athenian military capability. His belief in the inevitability of war made those additional capabilities more important. The fact that Pericles could impose

[108] Lancelot L. Farrar, Jr., *The Short-War Illusion: German Policy, Strategy and Domestic Affairs, August–December 1914* (Santa Barbara, Ca.: ABC-Clio, 1973); Fritz Fischer, *War of Illusions: German Policies from 1911 to 1914*, trans. Marian Jackson (New York: Norton, 1975); Jack Snyder, *The Ideology of the Offensive: Military Decision Making and the Disasters of 1914* (Ithaca: Cornell University Press, 1984).

[109] Carl von Clausewitz, *On War*, ed. and trans. Michael Howard and Peter Paret (Princeton: Princeton University Press, 1976), pp. 119–21.

his policy on a pacifically inclined citizenry which at first rejected alliance with Corcyra could be said to demonstrate the determining influence of deeper strategic realities. This argument verges on the tautological. It assumes that war was inevitable because of Athens' rise to power and the fear that this inspired in Sparta, and offers the Peloponnesian War as proof of the thesis. It makes Pericles appears prescient and his policy a triumph of strategic reason, even if it led to a long and disastrous war. But if a more restrained Athenian foreign policy could have kept the peace, as seems likely, Pericles' actions must be judged the product of a flawed vision that led to a war from which Athens, and Greece more generally, never recovered. Thucydides makes no effort to hide his admiration for Pericles, but as I will show in Chapter 4, he considered Pericles' war policy a serious miscalculation.

Like most tensions in Thucydides, that between agency and structure exists at multiple levels. Actors in Thucydides, like heroes in most Greek tragedies, represent an amalgam of traits. They are not interesting because of their uniqueness, but for what they share with other people. Sthenelaïdas and Pericles are intended to represent the defining qualities of their respective cultures. The decisions they take are as much the expressions of these cultures as they are the choices of individuals. In this sense, actors express the imperatives of structure, or at least of culture, and their miscalculations have general as opposed to idiosyncratic causes.

The speeches, most of which are in Book 1, might be read as further support for the responsibility of individuals and the indeterminate nature of their choices, and undercut Athenian claims in the Melian Dialogue that they have no choice but to act as they do. The importance of agency is further driven home by Thucydides' counterfactual that if only Pericles had lived, things would have turned out differently.[110] Thucydides may have modeled his text on Homer, who also uses a counterfactual to lend poignancy to his ensuing account of the war. Because the siege of Troy was proving difficult, the frustrated Argives went down to their ships to sail for home. "A homecoming beyond fate might have been accomplished, had not Hera spoken a word to Athene." The grey-eyed Athena sped down the peak of Olympus and instructed Odysseus to prevent the departure of the Argives, which he did, with horrendous consequences for both sides.[111] Athena's intervention was out of the question in the fifth century, but death by plague accomplished the same end.

[110] Thucydides, II.65.

[111] *The Iliad of Homer*, trans. Richard Lattimore (Chicago: University of Chicago Press, 1951), Book II, lines 135–210, pp. 80–81.

These parallels indicate a continuity in tradition that begins with Homer and extends through Aeschylus and Sophocles to Thucydides.[112] Homeric and tragic heroes make disastrous choices because of their natures (*phusis*), but these choices are freely entered into because they have the power to act otherwise.[113] Tragedies raise the question of foreknowledge and predetermination as a problem, not as dogma. According to Charles Segal, Oedipus "is both free and determined, both able to choose and helpless in the face of choices that he has made in the past or circumstances (like those of his birth) over which he had no power of choice."[114] Philip Vellacott suggests that Oedipus reveals choice and predetermination to be "a box of mirrors."[115] Thucydides leaves his readers with the same impression, with the difference that the tension in his account is between agency and structure rather than agency and the gods.

Levels of analysis

Thucydides shows us that leaders played important independent roles and brought war about through a series of reinforcing miscalculations. But these miscalculations did not take place in a political vacuum. They were conditioned at least in part by systemic and polis-level constraints.

[112] E. R. Dodds, *The Greeks and The Irrational* (Berkeley and Los Angeles: University of California Press, 1951), pp. 3–7, 17, argues that Homer and his characters appear to attribute much to the gods and little to agency. But *atē* is an excuse for behavior that would otherwise appear shameful. They did not frame the question as one of actor and agency, but distinguished between normal actions and those performed in a state of *atē*.

[113] Bernard Knox, "Introduction" to Homer, *The Iliad*, trans. Robert Fagles (New York: Viking Penguin, 1990), pp. 39–40, observes that Homer gives the appearance of the gods pulling the strings, but they often only encourage actors to do what is in character. A typical example is in Book I, 1.224–29, Achilles refrains from killing Agamemnon because Athena grasps him by the hair and forbids it. But Achilles had already considered restraint, and was undecided about what course of action to follow when Athena appears. She represents his decision to act cautiously, rather than being the cause of it. She uses the word *pithē*, which is a form of the verb, "to persuade," further evidence that Achilles had made up his own mind. Williams, *Shame and Necessity*, pp. 21–49, uses this example to make the same point. Albin Lesky, "Decision and Responsibility in the Tragedy of Aeschylus," *Journal of Hellenic Studies* (1966), pp. 78–85, argues that tragic decisions are rooted in *ēthos* (character) and divine power (*daimōn*). An aspect of submission is clearly present, but the decision is also a reflection of character. Knox, *Oedipus at Thebes*, pp. 3–14, rejects the view that tragic heroes are governed by fate and do not have the same will as Hamlet, but his *The Heroic Temper: Studies in Sophoclean Tragedy* (Berkeley and Los Angeles: University of California Press, 1964), pp. 5–6, contrasts Euripidean heroes, who suffer what the gods mete out, with Sophoclean heroes, who are largely responsible for their own fates.

[114] Ibid.

[115] Philip Vellacott, *Sophocles and Oedipus* (Ann Arbor: University of Michigan Press, 1971), p. 108.

At the systems level, the most important constraint was the existence of several dissatisfied middle-rank powers with ties to one or the other hegemon. Conflicts between these middle-rank powers, or between them and smaller powers, set in motion the chain of events that led to war. The Epidamnus–Corcyra conflict evolved into a confrontation between Corcyra and Corinth, which then escalated into a Corinth–Athens conflict. Thebes' long-standing conflict with Plataea also drew in the hegemons on opposing sides.

War was made more likely by the vulnerability of Athens and Sparta to third-party pleas for assistance. Militarily, the Athenian and Spartan alliances were roughly equal, but had different force structures. The Spartan army was the most powerful ground force in Greece, a status also accorded to the Athenian navy. The Spartan hoplites, with their purple cloaks, crested helmets and polished shields, advanced slowly in perfect order to the sound of the flute. Their skill in lance and sword, commitment to return home victorious or carried on their shields, struck fear into the hearts of their adversaries, some of whom fled at the prospect of engagement.[116] There were a relatively small number of Spartiates, maybe 4,000 at the outbreak of war. Sparta had to rely on Corinth for naval forces and the money to finance a long campaign. Athens was largely self-sufficient; it was wealthier than Corinth, and, with approximately 50,000 men of military age, could muster an impressive contingent of hoplite and lighter infantry and rowers for its fleet.[117] Its land and naval forces were augmented by those of the empire and independent allies.

The rough military balance between the two alliances was a source of stability, but that stability was fragile. It could be undermined by the addition or defection of one or more middle-rank powers. Both considerations came into play with the Athenian alliance with Corcyra. "Can you conceive of a stroke of good fortune more rare in itself, or more disheartening to your enemies?," the Corcyreans ask in making their bid for alliance.[118] Some Athenians undoubtedly relished the prospect of the Corcyrean navy added to their own. But Thucydides reports that the Athenians were moved more by fear that the Corcyrean fleet would end up in Sparta's service through a Corinthian victory: "no one was willing to see a naval power of such magnitude as Corcyra sacrificed to Corinth . . ."[119]

Unlike the Athenian empire, in which Athenian will was law, Sparta was *primus inter pares* in a much looser confederacy; it could dictate policy to

[116] Herodotus, IX.53.2, 55.2; Plutarch, *Moralia, 241;* Xenophon, *Lacedaemonion Politeia* [The Spartan Constitution], 11.3.
[117] Meiggs, *The Athenian Empire*, p. 196. [118] Thucydides, I.33. [119] Ibid., I.44.

weaker, nearby cities like Phlius and Orchomenus, but had to woo more powerful allies like Corinth and Thebes.[120] Often, these allies succeeded in mobilizing Spartan arms in support of their parochial ends.[121] This happened in 431 and again in 421, when Corinth and Thebes succeeded in sabotaging the Peace of Nicias and rekindling war between Athens and Sparta.

International relations theorists have long debated the relative stability of multipolar versus bipolar international systems.[122] Greek politics on the eve of the Peloponnesian War contained important elements of both. There were two hegemons, each dominating a major alliance system, which gave the system its bipolar characteristics. But second-rank powers like Corinth, Thebes, Corcyra and Argos, the last two unaffiliated with either alliance, were powerful enough to play important, independent roles on the stage of Greek politics. Other major powers on the periphery of the system, most notably Persia and Syracuse, also affected the balance. This distribution of power and a certain fluidity in alliances – the decisive political events were Athens' alliance with Corcyra, which gave rise to the war, and Sparta's much later alliance with Persia, which made its ultimate victory possible – imparted multipolar characteristics to the system.

Greek city states were for the most part oligarchies or democracies, and the two great alliance systems reflected this ideological and interest-based division.[123] In some of *polei*s (e.g., Epidamnus, Plataea, Mytilene), the balance of power between the elite of rich and influential men and the masses of citizens was uncertain, and coups or revolutions, or fear of them, encouraged factions to seek support from outside powers sympathetic to their cause. Civil war in Epidamnus led to war between Corcyra and Corinth when they were drawn in on opposite sides, and in turn led to war between Athens and Sparta when they came to the aid of their respective allies. Thucydides leads us to the conclusion that allies were also a principal cause of the renewal of war in 414. Given the reinforcing cleavages between domestic and international politics, and the tight links between the two realms, internal cleavages in any strategically located polis were highly destabilizing to the system as a whole.

[120] On the Peloponnesian League and Sparta's position in it, see Ste. Croix, *Origins of the Peloponnesian War*, ch. 4.

[121] Kagan, *Outbreak of the Peloponnesian War*, pp. 22–25, offers several examples.

[122] Karl W. Deutsch and J. David Singer, "Multipolar Power Systems and International Stability," *World Politics* 16 (1964), pp. 390–406; J. David Singer, Stuart Bremer and John Stuckey, "Capability Distribution, Uncertainty and Major Power War, 1820–1965" in Bruce Russett, ed., *Peace, War and Numbers* (Beverly Hills, CA: Sage, 1972); Kenneth Waltz, "The Stability of a Bipolar World," *Dædalus* (Summer 1964), pp. 881–909.

[123] Thucydides, I.19, observes that the Spartans made sure that their allies were governed by oligarchies.

Had the Greek world been unambiguously bi- or multipolar, some of these problems might have been avoided. In a bipolar system, the capabilities of the hegemons *vis-à-vis* other states would have been significantly greater. They would not have been so much at the mercy of their allies and important third parties as the support or defection of these powers would have mattered less. A multipolar system would have offered different advantages. With more independent players possessing a greater variety of capabilities, the support or defection of any one of them would have been less important because of the possibility of compensating for this change from the pool of uncommitted states. Nor is it likely that any single alliance system would have developed the capabilities to challenge the rest of the system.

The mixed system of fifth-century Greece combined the worst features of bi- and multipolarity. The addition or defection of a middle-rank power could have profound strategic implications; it made Athens willing to risk war for the sake of Corcyra, and Sparta for Corinth. And there were enough independent and quasi-independent powers around to make it likely that such changes would occur from time to time. The instability of Greek international relations was further aggravated by the different nature of hegemonic capabilities. Sparta's strength derived from the unsurpassed skill and self-confidence of its heavy infantry. Spartiate males devoted most of their lives to military training and service; they were the property of the state, and on military call until age sixty, if they were fortunate enough to live that long. Hoplite warfare put a premium on individual skill and group discipline, and gave Spartiates a decisive edge over the part-time, non-professional forces of their adversaries. Full-time military and physical training was made possible by a slave economy that produced enough agricultural surplus to free Spartiates from any requirement of labor and enabled them to live in relative isolation from the rest of Hellas. Sparta's unbalanced force structure and undeveloped economy made it particularly vulnerable to the pleadings of its allies.

The peculiar character of Sparta was also responsible for the *hubris* so apparent in the assembly's vote for war. Because of Sparta's self-imposed isolation, its citizens had little experience of the wider world and little appreciation of the power of their adversary, based as it was on entirely different political and economic foundations. Socialized from childhood into believing in the invincibility of their army and that manliness (*andreia*) was established through pugnacious bravery, Spartiates were ill-prepared, intellectually and emotionally, to make the kind of considered judgments the situation required.

Sparta's isolation and traditional values contributed to its decision for war in a less obvious way. The Spartan political system rested on the twin pillars of a slave economy and a social order that emphasized martial valor at the expense of material affluence. To maintain its way of life, Sparta tried as far as possible to isolate its citizens from social intercourse with the rest of Hellas, and to some extent from the rest of Lacedaemon.[124] At the age of seven, a male Spartiate left his mother to live in a barracks at a military school. He was allowed to marry at age twenty, but remained a resident of a barracks and could never live with his wife and children. At thirty he became a citizen. This double isolation was the source of Sparta's greatest strength and its greatest weakness. It permitted a social order in which individual interests were successfully subordinated to state interests. Isolation nevertheless made Spartans particularly vulnerable to the contaminating influences of foreign contact. Pausanias, who led Greek forces at Plataea in 479 and later conquered Byzantium, had to be recalled when he succumbed to sexual and material temptations. Fear that it would be impossible to keep Sparta's young men "down on the farm after they've seen Paree" was probably the single most important reason for the otherwise surprising decision to withdraw from the campaign. It was undoubtedly instrumental in the decision to expel Cimon and his Athenian hoplites (*circa* 461) at the time of the helot uprising.[125]

Sparta was vulnerable in a second sense. Helots vastly outnumbered Spartiates, and had periodically risen in rebellion. To guard against internal uprisings, their greatest fear, young Spartiates did service in a secret police (*krupteia*), which spied on the helots and periodically intimidated them by liquidating members of their class who displayed independence or initiative. The need to guard against uprising by the oppressed and vastly more numerous helot slaves limited the ability of Spartan forces to engage in extended campaigns at any significant distance from home.[126] Athens would exploit this manpower weakness and compel Sparta to sue for peace to regain the 120 Spartiates who surrendered at Sphacteria in 424.[127]

Spartan recognition of their peculiar vulnerability engendered great caution about entering into foreign entanglements to the point of near isolationism. The peace party was particularly sensitive to the danger of social contamination; this accounts for their extreme caution and conservatism in foreign policy. But Spartiates were also moved to action by their exaggerated concern for honor.

[124] Forrest, *A History of Sparta*, and Ste. Croix, *Origins of the Peloponnesian War*, pp. 89–94.

[125] Thucydides, I.94–96, pp. 55–56; Plutarch, *Aristides* 23, *Cimon* 6, pp. 134, 146–47; Ste. Croix, *Origins of the Peloponnesian War*, p. 179, on the Spartan motives for expelling the hoplites.

[126] Herodotus, IX.10.1, 28.2, 29.1; Thucydides, VIII.40.2.

[127] Thucydides, IV.38.5 and IV.117.2.

Striving for honor (*timē*) was a central preoccupation of Greece in the heroic age, at least as it is portrayed by Homer. His warriors seek honor above all other goals. Achilles, "the best of the Achaeans," chooses an early death with honor over a long but ordinary life. The plot of the *Iliad* is propelled by two slights of honor. Paris runs off with Helen, compelling Menelaus and the Greeks to go to war against Troy to restore his honor. Agamemnon appropriates the desirable Briseis for himself, although she had been awarded to Achilles as his share of the booty from an earlier raid. Achilles withdraws from the struggle against Troy, and much of the *Iliad* revolves around the consequences of his inactivity and efforts to bring him back to the fight.

Greeks were fed Homer with their mother's milk, and nowhere was the diet so rich as in Sparta where respect for the past and its values were actively fostered by the state. Spartan customs, as the Corinthians hastened to point out, were positively antidiluvian (*archaiotropa*) and unchanging (*akinēta nomima*). Spartiates rejected a money economy and material goods, and its citizens were prohibited from engaging in commerce or becoming artisans. They were full-time soldiers and judged on the basis of their bravery, courage, honor and other personal attributes like wisdom (*euboulia*) and self-control (*sōphrosunē*).[128] For centuries, Spartans had been driven by a fierce ambition to achieve and then maintain hegemony in Hellas. Spartiates lived to serve their *polis* and internalized its goals. Their self-esteem was inextricably connected with Sparta's honor and international standing and respect for the bravery and accomplishments of its hoplites. Spartiates were deeply offended by the power and confidence of Athens, and charges by their allies that they had left them to fend for themselves. They sought honor and glory, aims that had little to do with, and were often adverse to, more tangible interests. The Spartan decision for war had less to do with security than it did with Spartan values and identity.

War party and peace party alike recognized that Athens posed a serious threat to their self-esteem and way of life. Unable and unwilling to transform their society, they advocated diametrically opposed but equally unrealistic strategies to cope with this threat. The war party wanted to assert its military superiority and puncture the appeal of Athenian style commercial democracy by overwhelming its army. The peace party sought an accommodation that would allow Sparta to pursue its conservative, agrarian lifestyle in relative isolation, protected in part by

128 Thucydides, I.119–25, pp. 65–69; Crane, *Thucydides and the Ancient Simplicity*, ch. 8, for a good discussion of the Corinthian speech and the two Spartan speeches that followed, and Kagan, *Outbreak of the Peloponnesian War*, pp. 304–06, for a contrasting view on the Spartans.

Athenian power. Peace would have preserved Sparta's authority and way of life in the short term, but accelerated the transformation of Greece in the longer term.[129] A quick victory, the goal of the Spartan war party, would only have slowed the pace of changes associated with the growth of commerce and accumulation of surplus wealth. Nor must we forget that Corinth, Sparta's most important ally, was also an engine of economic development. Sparta's power, based on a highly trained army drawn from a diminishing population base, was doomed, and so was its way of life. Sparta could only have maintained its power in the longer term by moving away from its subsistence economy and extending the benefits of citizenship beyond the aristocracy. This was anathema to Spartiates of all persuasions. Archidamus insisted that they remain steadfast to the ways of their fathers (*meletai*), and Sthenelaïdas concurred. In the course of the war that followed, Sparta proved extraordinarily reluctant to make the kinds of changes that victory required. Brasidas, the one Spartan who thought and acted like an Athenian, was the exception who proved the rule.

Archidamus and Sthenelaïdas not only made different estimates of Athenian capabilities, they were motivated by different goals. Sthenelaïdas was intent on upholding Sparta's honor and international standing, and Archidamus on preserving Sparta's way of life, although he too recognized the central place honor held in Spartan society.[130] There is reason to suspect that understandings and goals were related, and that

[129] The analogy here is to the Soviet Union, another garrison state on the decline, hobbled by its command economy and authoritarian political system, and increasingly unable to compete with the democratic, capitalist West. Neither Brezhnev nor Gorbachev was prepared to confront the real source of the problem and they pursued unrealistic and ineffective panaceas instead. Brezhnev tried and failed to rectify the Soviet economic situation through a series of limited reforms intended to "rationalize" planning and investment. He supported détente to gain access to advanced foreign technology and make the West the co-guarantor of the political-territorial status quo in Eastern Europe. In doing so, he merely forestalled the final reckoning. Gorbachev implemented more radical reforms, but sought until the end to preserve the Communist Party and the command economy. He also sought a more far-reaching accommodation with the West – an Archidamian strategy – whose very success hastened the demise of communism and the Soviet Union. As in Sparta, domestic problems generated imperatives for action but did not dictate the policies, domestic or foreign, that leaders pursued. For an elaboration of the argument see Richard Ned Lebow, "The Long Peace, the End of the Cold War, and the Failure of Realism," *International Organization* 48 (Spring 1994), pp. 249–78; Robert D. English, *Russia and the Idea of the West: Gorbachev, Intellectuals and the End of the Cold War* (New York: Columbia University Press, 2000); Richard K. Herrmann and Richard Ned Lebow, eds., *Learning From the Cold War* (New York: Palgrave, 2003).

[130] Archidamus notes that "We are both warlike and wise, and it is our sense of order that makes us so. We are warlike, because self-control contains honor as a chief constituent, and honor bravery." Thucydides, I.84.3.

policy preferences shaped strategic assessments. The war party desperately wanted to uphold Sparta's honor and international standing, but was also committed to its isolation and unique way of life. These nearly contradictory goals could only be served by a quick, victorious war that could be fought with existing forces, would not make Sparta dependent on Corinth and would avoid prolonged contact with foreigners. Hence, the war party's unquestioning belief that Athens could be overwhelmed in a single season of campaigning. The peace party eschewed war because it was more sensitive to the threat it posed to Sparta's internal structure. They were motivated to see Athens as a placable foe, and one, moreover, whose power might be used to guarantee Spartan isolation and security. Thucydides' juxtaposition of the speeches of Archidamus and Sthenelaïdas brings out the emotional bias of the war party's position. Sthenelaïdas fails to respond in any substantive way to the arguments of Archidamus, or to propose a military strategy for coping with Athenian naval supremacy and economic self-sufficiency.

Archaic Sparta is a good foil for thoroughly modern Athens. But here too, honor played a role. In their speech to the Spartan assembly, the Athenians explain that "the nature of the case first compelled us to advance our empire to its present height; fear being our principal motive, though honor and interests afterwards came in." Fear, they assert, is once again their principal concern: "And at last, when almost all hated us, when some had already revolted and had been subdued, when you had ceased to be the friends that you once were, and had become objects of suspicion and dislike, it appeared no longer safe to give up our empire, especially as all who left us would fall to you."[131] Thucydides tells a somewhat different story. The Athenian assembly ultimately backed Pericles' appeal for an alliance with Corcyra because

> it began now to be felt that the coming of the Peloponnesian War was only a question of time, and no one was willing to see a naval power of such magnitude as Corcyra sacrificed to Corinth; though if they could let them weaken each other by mutual conflict, it would be no bad preparation for the struggle which Athens might one day have to wage with Corinth and the other naval powers. At the same time the island seemed to lie conveniently on the coasting passage to Italy and Sicily.[132]

There may well have been an element of fear in the background, but if we credit Thucydides' account, Athenians were moved by the kind of complex calculations we associate with strategic and economic interests.

A first reading of Book I suggests the pessimistic conclusion that states are doomed to make catastrophic decisions. Spartan fixation on honor led

[131] Ibid., I.75.3–4. [132] Ibid., I.44.2–3.

them to ignore their other interests and vote for war on largely emotional grounds. Athenians did the reverse. Guided initially by their emotions – in this case, an understandable desire to avoid war – they rejected the proposed alliance with Corcyra. In a second assembly, they were persuaded by Pericles, whose speech – in contrast to that of Sthenelaïdas – must have been a masterpiece of cool logic. If Thucydides' account of Athenian thinking can be read as paraphrase of that speech, the much-respected *stratēgos* laid out a series of reasons why alliance with Corcyra could only enhance Athenian security. Greek culture valued the middle way, an ethical and political orientation that found expression in the aphorisms of the Seven Sages and the often-quoted precept of the Delphic Oracle: nothing in excess (*mēden agan*). Thucydides is very much rooted in this tradition, as are the other great tragedians. Book I can be read as a plea for balance. Emotions need to be held in check by reason, and alarms should sound when we hear arguments that make us feel uncomfortable because they go against what we intuitively feel is right. Honor needs to balanced by healthy concerns for security and material interests, but they in turn must be constrained by the limits of ends and means imposed by honor.

Is Thucydides inconsistent?

Detailed unpacking of Thucydides' text in the mid-nineteenth century called into question its consistency and unity. This research gave rise to the *thukydideische Frage*, a controversy about how many distinct parts there were to the history, the order in which they had been written and what this revealed about the evolution of its author's thinking over approximately two decades of research and writing. Thucydides was considered a detached and dispassionate rationalist, a scientist in the tradition of Hippocrates, in search of an "objective" and timeless understanding of politics and war. As ordered thought and presentation were absolutely essential to such an enterprise, scholars assumed that if Thucydides had lived long enough he would have "cleaned up" his manuscript to remove all of its seeming inconsistencies.[133] "Unitarians" – the term is Connor's – attempt to reconcile these inconsistencies. Simon Hornblower, a recent exemplar, thinks he has found the real Thucydides lurking in the speeches of Pericles and other key actors.[134] "Separatists" contend

[133] W. R. Connor, "A Post Modernist Thucydides?," *The Classical Journal* 72 (April–May 1977), pp. 289–98; Clifford Orwin, "Thucydides," *The American Scholar* 55 (Winter 1985–86), pp. 128–30.

[134] Simon Hornblower, *Thucydides* (Baltimore: Johns Hopkins University Press, 1987), pp. 155–90.

that there are too many inconsistencies and differences in style to reconcile. Peter Pouncey suggests that Thucydides advances inconsistent points of view because he never settled on a single position.[135] Gregory Crane believes that Thucydides deliberately chose to speak in several voices, and it is a mistake to try to reconcile them.[136] The problem of Thucydides' inconsistency might be more productively addressed by distinguishing between his putative intentions and his rhetorical strategy. Following Connor, I argue that Thucydides' rhetorical strategy leads him to advance seemingly inconsistent arguments with the purpose of provoking us to reason our way to an underlying and somewhat more uniform understanding.

The explanation for war offered in I.23.6 represents Thucydides' initial defense of Pericles. If war was indeed inevitable, or even highly likely, then Pericles was justified in wanting to fight it when Corcyra's navy would augment, not diminish, Athens' military might. Thucydides also wants readers to conclude that if Pericles was responsible for war, he was not responsible for Athens' defeat. He died of plague in 429, his defensive strategy was jettisoned by the leaders who followed him and they pursued policies that advanced their personal and political ambitions at the expense of the state. Even then, Thucydides suggests, Athens might still have come out on top if only the assembly had supported Alcibiades and sent to Sicily the reinforcements requested by Nicias.

Pericles was undeniably an extraordinary leader, and Thucydides rightly contrasts him to demagogues like Cleon and Alcibiades. But Pericles' probity, dedication and rhetorical skill did not make him immune to hubris and error; his push for the Corcyrean alliance, the Megarian Decree and dispatch of inadequate forces to subdue Potidaea were all misguided and ultimately unsuccessful policies. The alliance put Athens on a collision course with Sparta, while the Megarian Decree and Potidaean siege inflamed opinion throughout Hellas, making it easier for Corinth to mobilize allies and, with their assistance, persuade Spartans to vote for war. The ultimate irony may be that the Corcyrean navy turned out to be of no account in the war; it remained in home waters and rendered no meaningful assistance to Athens. This member of the jury votes with his fifth-century peers to hold Pericles responsible for the war.

The contradiction between Thucydides' statement in 1.23.6 and the narrative that follows is sharpened by the use of the English word "inevitable" in several widely used translations, including that of Richard

[135] Peter A. Pouncey, *The Necessities of War: A Study of Thucydides' Pessimism* (New York: Columbia University Press, 1980), pp. ix–x.

[136] Crane, *Thucydides*, pp. 294, 301.

Crawley.[137] In Greek tragedy, *anangkē* conveys a constraint or external pressure, but still leaves the agent with choice. It implies compulsion but not determinacy.[138]

A more fundamental objection can be raised to the Crawley and Warner translations of I.23.[139] The key words and phrases here are *aitiai kai diaphorai*, usually translated as "complaints," *engklēmata*, as "accusations" and *prophaseis* as "precipitants," "causes" or "motives."[140] *Alēthestatē prophasis* is translated by Crawley as "the real cause," and by Warner as "the real reason for war." *Prophasis* entered the Greek lexicon with Herodotus who used it to signify that a statement of self-justification, not necessarily of true intention, is about to follow.[141] A *prophasis* (rationalization) is essential to mask unacceptable motives. Herodotus reports that Miltiades sailed against Paros with a fleet of seventy ships because of a grievance he had against the Parians. Miltiades is careful to offer a *prophasis*: the Parians provided one ship to reinforce the Persians at Marathon. This ridiculous justification is necessary because Greeks did not level cities to settle personal scores.[142] *Prophasis* underwent a parallel development with the Hippocratics, students of medicine who emerged in south Italy and Ionia in the fifth century, and coined new words to fill in gaps in medical terminology. The Hippocratic corpus, a collection

[137] The Landmark edition is based on the Crawley translation. See also, *The Peloponnesian War*, the Crawley translation, rev. and ed. T. E. Wick (New York: Modern Library, 1982), p. 14.

[138] Ste. Croix, *The Origins of the Peloponnesian War*, pp. 60–63; K. J. Dover, Appendix 2 to A. W. Gomme, A. Andrews and K. J. Dover, *Historical Commentary on Thucydides*, 10 vols. (Oxford: Oxford University Press, 1945–81), V, p. 419; C. Schneider, *Information und Absicht bei Thukydides* (Göttingen, 1974), pp. 101–10; A. W. Gomme, *The Greek Attitude to Poetry and History* (Berkeley: University of California Press, 1954), pp. 156–58; Hunter Rawlings III, *A Semantic Study of Prophasis to 400 B.C., Hermes: Einzelschriften* 33 (Wiesbaden: Franz Steiner, 1975), pp. 92–95; Thomas G. Rosenmeyer, *The Art of Aeschylus* (Berkeley and Los Angeles: University of California Press, 1982), p. 302; Connor, *Thucydides*, p. 32.

[139] For the 1954 Rex Warner translation, see Thucydides, *History of the Peloponnesian War* (London: Penguin Books, 1972).

[140] According to Bernard Williams, *Shame and Necessity* (Berkeley and Los Angeles: University of California Press, 1993), p. 58, Homer used *aitia* to mean "cause" or "explanation." Herodotus, I.1. and Thucydides, I.23.5–6, used it in both senses as well. Gomme, *Historical Commentary on Thucydides* I, pp. 153–54, and Ste. Croix, *Origins of the Peloponnesian War*, pp. 51–54, read it in this context to refer to grounds for complaint and the immediate cause of war.

[141] R. Sealey, "Thucydides, Herodotus, and the Causes of War," *Classics Quarterly* 57 (1957), pp. 1–12; Robert Browning, "Greek Abstract Nouns in *-sis, -tis*," *Philologus*, 102 (1958), pp. 60–74; Rawlings, *A Semantic Study of Prophasis to 400 B.C.*, pp. 22–24.

[142] Herodotus 6, 133. Democritus, DK 68 B83, used *aitia* twice, in the sense of "reason" or "motive." For Gorgias, DK 82 B11, it signified "culpability." Mario Vigetti, "Culpability, Responsibility, Cause: Philosophy, Historiography, and Medicine in the Fifth Century," in A. A. Long, ed., *The Cambridge Companion to Early Greek Philosophy* (Cambridge: Cambridge University Press, 1999), pp. 271–89.

of medical treatises attributed to Hippocrates of Cos, and largely written between 430 and 420, addressed, among other things, the stages of diseases.[143] *Prophasis* is used repeatedly to describe a "precondition" or "something that appears before a disease." It suggests association, but not causation. There are many passages in which the Hippocratics acknowledge the onset of diseases without their associated *prophaseis*.[144]

Hunter Rawlings III makes a compelling case against the traditional view of *prophasis* as one word that took on two meanings (polysemy) in favor of two words with different origins and meanings but the same phonological form (homonymy). Thucydides appears to have been aware of this distinction and used the two meanings systematically to distinguish between Spartan and Athenian propaganda and the conditions that led to both stages of the Peloponnesian War. Rawlings contends that Sparta's peace overtures are unambiguous examples of the former. Pericles properly understood Sparta's demand that he rescind the Megarian Decree as a false issue intended to provide a pretext for war. He tells the assembly "not to submit to either a great or small *prophasis*. If you give way to Sparta's demand you will instantly have to meet some greater demand. . . ."[145] In I.118, after concluding the *Pentēkontaëtia*, Thucydides returns to his discussion of the origins of the war. Here and in the conclusion to Book I (I.146), *prophasis* is used in the second, Hippocratic sense. The *aitiai kai diaphorai* refer back to the events that began with Epidamnus and Corcyra and culminate with the Megarian Decree and siege of Potidaea; they represent these events as seen from the vantage points of the several actors, and collectively constitute a *prophasis* for the war.[146] Viewed in this light, Thucydides' statement in I.23.6 about the growth of Athenian power and Sparta's concomitant fears should be read as neither pretext nor motive, but as a *precondition* for war. There was no Greek word to express the difference between precipitant and precondition, so Thucydides borrowed *prophasis* from the Hippocratics. To mark the different use of the word in this context, he used the superlative form of the adjective *alēthestatē*.[147] Like a physician, Thucydides was

[143] G. E. R. Lloyd, ed., *Hippocratic Writings* (London: Penguin, 1978); Eustace D. Philipps, *Greek Medicine* (London: Thames and Hudson, 1978); Jaeger, *Paideia*, I, p. 293.

[144] Browning, "Greek Abstract Nouns in *-sis, -tis*," pp. 66–71; Rawlings, *A Semantic Study of Prophasis to 400 B.C.*, pp. 36–48.

[145] Rawlings, *A Semantic Study of Prophasis to 400 B.C.*, pp. 64–65; Thucydides, I.140, pp. 80–81.

[146] Rawlings, *A Semantic Study of Prophasis to 400 B.C.*, pp. 69–70; Thucydides, I.118 and I.146.

[147] Rawlings, *A Semantic Study of Prophasis*; George B. Kerford, *The Sophistic Movement* (Cambridge: Cambridge University Press, 1981). For a dissenting view, see A. Heubeck, "Πρόφασις und Keine Ende (zu Thuk. I 23)," *Glotta* 58 (1980), Nos. 3–4, pp. 222–36.

making a clinical observation, in this case about the political symptoms that preceded the onset of crisis.

This double meaning of *prophasis* and its specific use in I.23.6 and I.146 has important implications for my broader argument. It indicates that Thucydides was not suggesting that the rise to power of Athens was the truest cause of war, only that it was the most important precondition. To the extent that Thucydides addresses causation, as we understand the concept, his take on the causes of war must be inferred from the text, especially its detailed examination of the multiple preconditions, the *prophaseis* offered by the two sides, and the interaction among them.[148]

Let us turn to *dunamis* and its meaning. *Dunamis* and *kratos* are often used interchangeably and invariably translated as power. To modern readers, realists especially, power is associated with material capabilities. For Homer, *kratos* is the physical power to overcome or subdue an adversary as well as what one acquires from such action. In the fifth century, according to Woodhead, *kratos* was understood to be the basis for *dunamis*. Or, as June Allison puts it, power confers power. One who achieves dominance (*kratos*) through some action achieves a recognized ability or capability (*dunamis*) to exercise that dominance. *Dunamis* is thus an "abstract power," something latent that exists in a thing, as opposed to *kratos*, which is the power that is exerted in action.[149] By Thucydides' time, *dunamis* had as wide a semantic field as any word in the Greek lexicon, and its meaning may be best captured by our concepts of authority and influence.

Authority and influence, personal and political, derive from status and obligations as well as from coercive mechanisms, whether economic or military. The growth of Athenian power that Thucydides refers to in I.23.6 should be read to include all the attributes that made the polis influential, including its cultural accomplishments, wealth, energy, civic pride and commitment of its citizens, as well as its empire, treasury and military power. This conception of *dunamis* is consistent with my contention that Book I leads us to the conclusion that the most fundamental cause of war was the set of changes in thinking, values and economics, of which Athens was the cutting edge, that threatened the status and perhaps the survival of Sparta. Translation in context goes a long way toward reconciling introduction and text.

[148] And here we must exercise caution because Greeks prior to Aristotle did not reflect on causation and its nature.

[149] Woodhead, *Thucydides on the Nature of Power*; personal communication from June Allison, 25 April 2002.

Inconsistency is also made to appear more acute by reason of our expectations about scholarly works. Modern readers, especially social scientists, expect authors to state their thesis in the introduction, develop and document it in the narrative or "data section" and conclude with a recapitulation of the argument and a discussion of its wider implications. Fifth-century Greeks, and sophists in particular, wrote in a different tradition.[150] They considered themselves teachers, and intended their works as courses of study. They introduced the idea that every argument had a contrary thesis, and that all ideas were open to criticism. Their works started with simple arguments or statements of a problem and went on to develop increasingly complex and sophisticated arguments. Their deeper level arguments were generally left implicit in the expectation that readers whose intellects and emotions became engaged would draw these conclusions for themselves.[151]

There are sound historical and textual reasons for reading Thucydides this way. Sophists dominated Athenian philosophy during the second half of the fifth century and had considerable political influence. Pericles was their principal patron and chose Protagoras to write the laws for the colony of Thurii, founded in 444, hired Hippodamus of Miletus to lay out the streets of Piraeus on a grid pattern, and is reported to have spent an entire day debating Protagoras.[152] Sophists were distinguished by their beliefs, commercialization of philosophy and style of instruction. Radical sophists questioned the underpinnings of the polis by emphasizing that conventions were arbitrary and not based on nature. They were subversive of the old aristocratic order in the deepest sense for they maintained that *aretē* (excellence, and especially the kind that made a man a respected leader) could be acquired through study, not only though breeding and lifelong association with socially prestigious men (*chrēstoi*) of wealth and good families.[153] Thucydides rejected some Sophistic teachings – he was clearly troubled by the social consequences of Sophist ridicule of objective standards of justice, and perhaps, like Socrates, put off by their efforts to turn a profit from their claims to knowledge. He nevertheless accepted

[150] James Boyd White, *Acts of Hope: Creating Authority in Literature, Law, and Politics* (Chicago: University of Chicago Press, 1994), p. 6.

[151] Mario Untersteiner, *The Sophists*, trans. Kathleen Freeman (New York: Philosophical Library, 1954); W. K. C. Guthrie, *The Sophists* (Cambridge: Cambridge University Press, 1971); Kerferd, *The Sophistic Movement*; Jacqueline de Romilly, *Les grands sophistes dans l'Athènes de Périclès* (Paris: Editions de Fallois, 1988); Barbara Cassin, *L'effet Sophistique* (Paris: Gallimard, 1995); Marcel Détienne, *The Masters of Truth in Archaic Greece*, trans. Janet Lloyd (Cambridge, Mass.: Zone Books, 1996).

[152] Plutarch, *Life of Pericles*, 5, describes close relations between Protagoras, the Sophists and Pericles. Euripides is also supposed to have studied with Protagoras and Prodicus. Thucydides is alleged to have been a disciple of Gorgias, Prodicus and Antiphon.

[153] This theme will be explored at greater length in Chapter 7.

the sophist antithesis between nature and convention, and would explain human behavior with reference to both.[154] He was also greatly attracted to the sophistic style of argument, including the use of opposed speeches, which he adopted for his own quite different purposes.[155]

Sophistic rhetoric was a reaction against contemporary political oratory, and was thought to be a more effective way of teaching. The ancients knew and modern scholars confirm that people everywhere are more convinced by lessons embedded in stories than by mere arguments, and by conclusions they reach themselves instead of those laid out before them.[156] Thomas Hobbes was among the first to recognize this aspect of Thucydides.[157] W. Robert Connor builds his highly regarded post-modernist reading of Thucydides around this insight. He suggests that Thucydides uses his narrative to draw readers into the war and in the process broadens and deepens their assessments and understandings. "We should be prepared to consider the text itself as a progression, that is the first part of the work may reflect attitudes, assumptions, and ideas that are eventually modified, restated, subverted, or totally controverted."[158]

Thucydides' treatment of the origins of the war can best be understood as an adaptation of Sophistic rhetorical strategy. He opens his history

[154] Sophists opposed *phusis* to *nomos*, which allowed them to justify social and political change. As we will see in Chapter 7, Plato sought to reveal *phusis*-based *nomoi*. Aristotle found an accommodation between the two positions. In the *Nicomachean Ethics*, V, 1134b19, 26, he argues that what is determined by nature is everywhere the same, while convention reflects chance variations.

[155] Felix Heinemann, *Nomos und Physis* (Darmstadt: Wissenschaftliche Buchgesellschaft, 1965), ch. 3, sec. 1–2; Untersteiner, *The Sophists*, p. 3; Kerferd, *Sophistic Movement*, p. 18; Arlene W. Saxonhouse, "Nature & Convention in Thucydides' History," *Polity* 10 (Summer 1978), pp. 461–87; On Socrates, see Xenophon, *Memorabilia*, I:2.6, I:6.5.

[156] For relevant psychological research, Ulric Neisser, "John Dean's Memory: A Case Study," *Cognition*, 9 (1981), pp. 1–22; D. P. Spence, *Narrative Truth and Historical Truth: Meaning and Interpretation in Psychoanalysis* (New York: Norton, 1982); Jerome Bruner, "Life as Narrative," *Social Research* 54 (1987), pp. 11–32; R. T. White, "Recall of Autobiographical Events," *Applied Cognitive Psychology* 18 (1989), pp. 127–35; D. E. Polkinghorne, "Narrative and Self-Concept," *Journal of Narrative and Life History* 1 (1991), pp. 135–53; Ulric Neisser, ed., *The Perceived Self: Ecological and Interpersonal Sources of Self-Knowledge* (Cambridge: Cambridge University Press, 1993); Ulric Neisser and Robyn Fivush, *The Remembering Self: Construction and Accuracy in the Self Narrative* (Cambridge: Cambridge University Press, 1994); Katherine Nelson, *Language in Cognitive Development: Emergence of the Mediated Mind* (New York: Cambridge University Press, 1996). On the humanist side, see Paul John Eakin, *How Our Lives Become Stories* (Ithaca: Cornell University Press, 1999).

[157] *The Peloponnesian War: The Complete Hobbes Translation*, ed. David Greene (Chicago: University of Chicago Press, 1989), "To The Readers," p. xxii.

[158] Connor, *Thucydides*, pp. 15–19, 236. Also Wolfgang Iser, *The Implied Reader* (Baltimore: Johns Hopkins University Press, 1974), p. 58; J. Peter Euben, "Creatures of a Day: Thought and Action in Thucydides," in Terence Ball, ed., *Political Theory and Praxis: New Perspectives* (Minneapolis: University of Minnesota Press, 1977), pp. 28–56.

with a discussion of responsibility for the war. He explores the accusations Athens and Sparta made against each other and their justifications for drawing the sword. He engages the question of the war's origins at the most superficial level, but so did ordinary citizens, consumed, as were Europeans in the aftermath of World War I, by the *Kriegschuldfrage* – the war guilt question. Those interested only in right and wrong need not read any further: Athens was somewhat more responsible for the war than Sparta. In this connection it is interesting to note that *prophasis*, in its first, legal meaning, was widely used by the time Thucydides wrote to describe the claims parties made against each other in court.[159] Book 1 presents Athens and Sparta, on the eve of the war and immediately afterwards, making their respective cases in speeches before the court of public opinion. Thucydides signals to more sophisticated readers that charge and counter-charge were little more than propaganda and obscured the real causes of the war. The subsequent narrative and paired speeches investigate these preconditions in more detail, and use them to address the more interesting question of causation.[160]

After World War I, diplomatic historians debated the relative responsibility of the various Europeans powers for the war; it took a follow-on generation to ask how that conflict could have happened and what lessons its origins might have for future conflict prevention. Thucydides' text is remarkable for many reasons, and surely one of the most important is his ability to see beyond the question of responsibility. He deals with it succinctly at the outset and encourages us to move on to more interesting and important questions.

Thucydides requires a patient, clever and thoughtful audience. Readers must be willing to recognize multiple levels of analysis, arguments specific to these levels, and ponder the reasons for the apparent contradictions between them. They cannot work their way through the history in a linear manner, but must move back and forth between sections of the text to grasp the contrasts and ironies embedded in structure and language and the ways in which different contexts and order of presentation code insights and interpretations. Not all inconsistencies can be resolved in this manner, and those that remain are intended to draw attention to tensions inherent in the situation and the possibility of an underlying truth that goes some way toward reconciling them. Heraclitus taught that the world was a battleground between opposing forces and

[159] I am indebted to Bruce Heiden for bringing this use to my attention.

[160] Protagoras is credited with having begun the tradition of thrashing out ideas in "opposed speeches." He taught his pupils how to make arguments for one side and then the other. These double arguments (*dissoi logoi*) take the form of paired speeches in Thucydides. Diogenes Laertius, IX.51 and Clement of Alexandria, *Stromates*, VI.65.

that philosophers had to look beneath the surface to find the deeper unity (*harmonia*) that united them. Plato developed his concept of forms to capture this hidden meaning, and the form of the good to lead to knowledge of all the forms.[161] Thucydides wrote in this binary tradition.[162] His history is a dialogue among opposite pairs: rational decision (*gnōmē*) and chance (*tuchē*), speech (*logos*) and deed (*ergon*), law (*nomos*) and nature (*phusis*) and peace and war. At the most fundamental level, the tension – not contradiction – between I.23.6 and the rest of Book I leads to the conclusion that structure is important but not determinate, and that the origins of the Peloponnesian War must be understood as a confluence of causes at multiple levels of analysis. Moreover, the structures that were important had little to do with the balance of power.

Is Thucydides a realist?

This may strike the reader as a surprising if not impertinent question. From the time of Hobbes, realists have claimed descent from Thucydides, and the international relations community has recognized their claim.[163] So have many classicists, one of whom writes that "Few would deny that Thucydides was, in some sense, 'a realist' – indeed, perhaps, the first such author whose work survives in the tradition of European writing."[164]

Realism claims to describe the world as it is, not as it ought to be. Thus its emphasis on the role of power, which many realists consider both the ends and means of international relations. There are different strands of realism, according to Michael Doyle, but they are built around a common, irreducible core: realism "discounts any claim to system-wide international order other than that based ultimately on power or

[161] Plato, *Republic*, 505a–509c.

[162] On the binary tradition in Greece, see Pierre Vidal-Naquet's "Foreword" to Détienne, *The Masters of Truth in Archaic Greece*, and Pierre Vidal-Naquet, *The Black Hunter: Forms of Thought and Forms of Society in the Greek World*, trans. Andrew Szegedy-Maszak (Baltimore: Johns Hopkins University Press, 1986), pp. 259 and 241.

[163] Hans J. Morgenthau, *Politics Among Nations*, 4th ed. (New York: Knopf, 1967), p. 8; Waltz, *Theory of International Politics*, p. 186; Robert Gilpin, "The Richness of the Tradition of Political Realism," in Keohane, *Neorealism and its Critics*, p. 306; Joseph S. Nye, Jr., "Neorealism and Neoliberalism," *World Politics* 40 (January 1988), pp. 235–51; Robert Jervis, "Realism, Game Theory, and Cooperation," *World Politics* 40 (April 1988), pp. 317–49; Michael W. Doyle, *Ways of War and Peace* (New York: Norton, 1997), pp. 18, 49.

[164] Crane, *Thucydides and the Ancient Simplicity*, pp. 38–39, proposes four criteria for realism, all of which, he avers, fit Thucydides. See also J. B. Bury, *The Ancient Greek Historians* (London: Macmillan, 1909), pp. 75–149; Russell Meiggs, *The Athenian Empire* (Oxford: Oxford University Press, 1972), p. 38; Ste. Croix, *Origins of the Peloponnesian War*, pp. 11–25.

force."[165] In a recent, collaborative study of the roots of realism, Ashley Tellis contends that Thucydides fits squarely in this tradition because he regards human nature as egoistic, recognizes that the pursuit of power and material gain leads to disorder, violence and decay, and thus "the logic of domination cannot be avoided or subdued."[166] Michael Doyle identifies three kinds of realism: complex, fundamentalist and structuralist. He considers Thucydides a complex realist because his interpretative insights are implicit, embedded in an historical account and contingent. Like other complex realists, Thucydides assumes nothing about the rationality of states or how they set their goals, and recognizes the possibility that international law and society can provide some constraints on state behavior.[167]

Key actors in Thucydides' history are driven by concerns for their security that make them sensitive to their power, especially military power. The fear of military disadvantage played a significant role in the outbreak of war; it was one motivation for Pericles to ally with Corcyra, and Spartiates voted for war at least in part from fear of losing Corinth and other allies. Military power and its consequences are a main theme of the narrative that follows, which after all is an account of a war. Nor in the circumstances is it surprising that the expedient (*sumpheron*) often triumphs over the just (*dikaion*).[168] The most striking example of this phenomenon is, of course, the Melian Dialogue, which I analyze in Chapter 4. But there are many other examples of interest trumping ethics that involve major and minor powers on both sides. These are so common, especially late in the war, that Peter Fliess reads the history as an "affirmation of the value of military power over any mitigating principle."[169]

So in what way is Thucydides not a realist? For a start, he is equally sensitive to a range of non-power-based motives and causes: domestic structure, culture and identities and the idiosyncracies of leaders, considerations that are largely ignored or downplayed by contemporary realists. According to Doyle, these qualities make him a complex realist, and distinguish him from Machiavelli, Morgenthau (more about him later) and Kenneth Waltz. But Thucydides stretches Doyle's definition in ways that take him beyond realism, or make any definition of it so embracing as to deprive it of meaningful analytical substance. If the reader accepts

[165] Doyle, *Ways of War and Peace*, p. 43.
[166] Tellis, "Reconstructing Political Realism," appendix.
[167] Doyle, *Ways of War and Peace*, pp. 45, 52–53.
[168] Crane, *Thucydides and the Ancient Athenian Simplicity*, p. 62.
[169] Peter J. Fliess, *Thucydides and the Politics of Bipolarity* (Baton Rouge, La.: University of Louisiana Press, 1966), pp. 85–106; Tellis, "Reconstructing Political Realism," pp. 12–25.

my interpretation of 1.23.6, power was a secondary consideration, and changes in the power balance only a manifestation of more fundamental causes of war. Honor and identity were central for Spartans, and interest for Athens. The priority of different values for different actors resulted in different foreign policy preferences.

Thucydides' history indicates that emotion, in the form of appetite and spirit (honor), was as important as reason. We have already examined this phenomenon in the case of Sparta. Emotions were also fundamental to the choices of Epidamnus, Corcyra and Corinth, and were a major cause of the miscalculations that led to war. Corinth was in many ways the prime mover of the conflict. Thucydides says nothing about Corinth's interest in consolidating its influence in north-west Greece; we know about this from other sources. But he does tell us that Corinthians welcomed the opportunity to come to the aid of Epidamnus in order to best Corcyra, a former colony that had slighted them by not acknowledging them properly at local sacrifices and Panhellenic festivals. The Corinthians were moved by considerations of honor and above all, by their hatred (*misei*) for Corcyra.[170] Even their interest in north-west Greece appeared to be less a matter of economic interest than a means of achieving higher status in the eyes of other Greeks. At the deepest levels of interest formation, appetite and spirit rode roughshod over reason.

What should we to conclude? Was Thucydides a realist – or perhaps, a proto-constructivist? Let us withhold any judgment until we explore the deeper levels of his text, which, I contend, allow us to make analytical sense of the tensions and seeming contradictions that we have discovered.

[170] Ibid., I.25, 3 and I.103.

4 Thucydides and civilization

Zeus shows man the way to think,
Setting understanding securely in the midst of suffering.
In the heart there drips instead of sleep
A labor of sorrowing memory;
And there comes to us all
Unwilling prudent measured thought;
The grace of gods who sit on holy thrones
Somehow comes with force and violence.

Aeschylus[1]

This chapter examines the consequences of the Peloponnesian War for Athens and Greece. In the course of this analysis I develop the outline for a "quasi-unitarian" reading of Thucydides. I describe four levels to the history, each of whose questions and answers move readers to the next level. To access the deeper levels of the text we must go beyond the explicit and implicit arguments of the narrative, speeches and dialogues to "signs" (*sēmata*) embedded in their language and structure. Thucydides must also be read against the Greek oral tradition and fifth-century writings, including Herodotus' history, the Hippocratic corpus and the tragedies of Aeschylus, Sophocles and Euripides.

The first level of the text is about interest, justice and their relationship. The analysis of the origins of war in Book I introduces a tension between interest and justice that becomes increasingly pronounced as the war unfolds. The Corcyrean and Corinthian speeches to the Athenian assembly on the eve of the war and the subsequent exchange between Cleon and Diodotus over the punishment of Mytilene, the Sicilian debate and the Melian Dialogue reveal how foreign policy became divorced from considerations of justice and correspondingly unlimited in its aims. For many present-day realists, whose analysis is largely restricted to this level of the text, Thucydides' history is a primer on strategy and alliances and how they are shaped, or should be, by considerations of power. This

[1] Aeschylus, *Agamemnon*, 176–83.

is a serious misreading of Thucydides, who understood influence as a psychological phenomenon, and who considered material capability to be only one component of power, and not necessarily the most important one. Books 2 through 5 can be read as an insightful analysis of the changing basis of Athenian influence that reveals how over-reliance on military power eroded that influence and made survival of the empire increasingly problematic. The siege of Melos and subsequent extermination or enslavement of its citizens and the ill-fated expedition to Sicily are symptomatic of this decay. Thucydides regarded the crude exercise of power as pathological, as something to be shunned, not emulated.[2]

His account of Athens reads like a tragedy, and this is the second level of the text. Fifth-century tragedies dramatized the lives of individuals to convey more general insights into human beings and their societies. Thucydides wanted readers to experience the rise and fall of the Athenian empire as a tragedy and to move from emotional involvement with the story to contemplation of its wider lessons, just as they would with a play by Aeschylus, Sophocles or Euripides. The tragic hero, like his Homeric predecessor, is often a self-centered, narcissistic figure who revels in his own importance and comes to believe that he need not temper his actions by taking into account the needs and commitments of other. Success intoxicates the hero and leads him to an inflated opinion of himself and his ability to impose his will on man or nature. He becomes susceptible to risky adventures and places his faith in hope (*elpis*), when reason would dictate caution and restraint. The Greeks called this kind of seduction *atē*, and associated it with *hamartia* (miscalculation, but literally, missing the mark). *Hamartia* leads to *nemesis*, the wrath of the gods. The Athenian victory over Xerxes at Salamis marks the emergence of Athens as a military power and sets the cycle in motion. For Thucydides, the initial *hamartia* – alliance with Corcyra – leads to war, plague, Pericles' death, a prolonged war and abandonment of Pericles' defensive strategy. A second *hamartia* – the Sicilian expedition – leads to *nemesis*. Thucydides could assume that his readers were familiar with the works of Herodotus and the tragic playwrights, and would recognize his personification of Athens as a tragic hero and the mordant comparison he intended between Athens and Persia.[3]

[2] This has long been the dominant view among classicists. See, for example, Werner Jaeger, *Paideia: The Ideals of Greek Culture*, trans. Gilbert Highet, 3 vols. (Oxford: Blackwell, 1939–45), III, pp. 401–02; John H. Finley, Jr., *Thucydides* (Ann Arbor: University of Michigan Press, 1967 [1942]), p. 89; A. B. Bosworth, "The Humanitarian Aspect of the Melian Dialogue," *Journal of Hellenic Studies* 113 (1993), pp. 3–44, for a review of the literature and a contrary point of view.

[3] Aeschylus' *Persians* was produced in the spring of 472, when Themistocles was at the height of his fame, and offers a cautionary tale about the consequences of hubris.

Thucydides' framing of Athens' rise and fall as a tragedy leads the reader to his larger political-philosophical project: the relationship between *nomos* (convention, custom, law) and *phusis* (nature), and its implications for the development and preservation of civilization.[4] At this third layer of the text, Thucydides mines the history of Greece, not only the Peloponnesian War, for insights into the conditions under which the most constructive and destructive human impulses find expression. He finds that *nomos* – a concept that also encompasses values, norms, expectations and obligations embedded in relationships – shapes identities and channels and restrains the behavior of individuals and societies. But *logos* (speech, story, explanation, argument, line of reasoning) makes *nomos* possible, because all conventions depend on shared meanings.[5] The speeches in the history suggest a two-way interaction between *logoi* and *erga* (deeds). Speech shapes action, but action transforms speech. It prompts new words and meanings, and can subvert existing words by giving them meanings diametrically opposed to their original ones. The positive feedback loop between *logoi* and *erga* made Greek civilization possible, and its unraveling was responsible for the most destructive forms of civil strife (*stasis)* that befell Hellas as a consequence of the Peloponnesian War.

This understanding directs our attention to the fourth layer of the text and the meta-theme of Thucydides' narrative: the rise and fall of Greek civilization, and the circumstances in which different facets of human nature come to the fore. If speech and reason weakened and undermined many of the conventions essential for civilized discourse, they might also be used to restore these conventions, or create new ones appropriate to the changed circumstances of fourth-century Greece. By this means, destructive impulses might be restrained and constructive and creative ones tapped and exploited. The underlying message of the

[4] Charles Segal, *Tragedy and Civilization: An Interpretation of Sophocles* (Norman: University of Oklahoma Press, 1981), pp. 2–3. Civilization has no single word equivalent in Greek. The closest representations are *nomos* and *ta nomima*, which refer to the customs of society; *politeia*, which refers to government, especially of the constitutional kind; and *paideia*, which describes the kind of culture that is transmitted through poetry and other forms of art. Greeks conceived of civilization in spatial terms. Human beings occupy a middle ground between the savage life of the beasts and the immortal life of the gods. People are threatened from below and illuminated from above. Greeks considered order precarious, and the result of man's never-ending struggle to assert his humanity against the impersonal forces of nature and the violence he himself unleashes. In classical Athens, the focus of civilization was the polis. The plays of Aeschylus and Sophocles, and Aristotle's *Politics*, come close to equating civilization with the polis.

[5] *Logos* in its simplest meaning was "word" or "story." It nevertheless assumed a much wider range of meanings pertaining to language and its expression, thought and mental processes and attempts to describe the physical and social worlds. It also came to signify proportion, measure, mathematical ratio, and by extension "proper reckoning."

history is that the restoration and maintenance of secure and prosperous societies must be approached through *logoi*, not through the exercise of power.[6]

Having worked my way through the four levels of the text, I attempt to demonstrate the analytical utility of my reading by returning to the original question of the war and its origins. I reconsider the structure and opposed speeches of Book I in light of the argument of this chapter and suggest that Thucydides considered the on-going economic, political and social transformation of Greece – what we would call modernization – the most fundamental cause of the Peloponnesian War. It altered the culture of Athens in a way that encouraged an expansionist foreign policy, and made Sparta more intent on opposing Athens.

My reading of Thucydides indicates that his commitment to realism has been exaggerated, and that he might with equal justice be considered the father of constructivism. Like all key contradictions in the text, this one is also amenable to at least partial resolution at another level of analysis. Such an understanding suggests the possibility and, indeed, the necessity, of a symbiotic and productive partnership between two currently antagonistic research traditions.

Engaging the literature

The linguistic turn was a catalyst for classicists to rethink their understanding of Thucydides. Articles by W. P. Wallace and G. Bowersock, in 1964 and 1965, and a 1966 book by Hans-Peter Stahl, directed attention to Thucydides the artist. They made the case for a passionate and politically engaged writer, in contrast to previous portrayals of Thucydides as the father of the scientific approach to history.[7] Robert Connor's *Thucydides*, published in 1984, represented an equally dramatic break with the past in that it attempted to restore what its author called a "unitarian" reading of the *History*. Connor's Thucydides is a masterful

[6] We must distinguish between Athens, Greek civilization and civilizations more generally. Thucydides had in mind the restoration of civil society in Athens and Greece. Did he look beyond Greece geographically or historically? Fifth-century Greeks were aware of other civilizations (e.g., Egypt, Persia) and past (Mycenaean and Homeric). As Thucydides had a clear sense of the rise and fall of civilizations, and describes his history "as a possession for all time," it is reasonable to infer that he looked to a future readership beyond the confines of Athens, and, probably, of Greece.

[7] W. P. Wallace, "Thucydides," *Phoenix* 18 (1964), pp. 251–61; Glen P. Bowersock, "The Personality of Thucydides," *Antioch Review* 35, 1 (1965), pp. 135–45; Hans-Peter Stahl, *Thucydides: Die Stellung des Menschen im geschichtlichen Prozess* (Munich: C. H. Beck, 1966), and "Speeches and Course of Events in Books Six and Seven of Thucydides," in Philip A. Stadter, *The Speeches of Thucydides* (Chapel Hill: University of North Carolina Press, 1973), pp. 60–77; W. Robert Connor, "A Post Modernist Thucydides?" *Classical Review* 72 (1977), pp. 289–98.

postmodernist who carefully structured his text to evoke an intended set of responses.[8]

Thucydides' attention to language is the starting point for another seminal study published in 1984: James Boyd White's, *When Words Lose Their Meaning*.[9] White contends that, for Thucydides, words construct and maintain the character of individuals, communities and cultures. Thucydides is interested in how words acquire, hold or lose their meanings, a process that he explores in his speeches, debates and dialogues. They reveal that at the outset of the war, the terms of discourse functioned in intelligible ways. As the War progresses, the discourse shifts and changes until the language and community (*homonoia*) it constituted deteriorate into incoherence. Athenians can no longer use the traditional language of justification for their foreign policy. Struggling to find an alternate language, they resort to assertions of pure self-interest backed by military clout. Such a language is not rooted in ideas, is unstable and deprives its speakers of their culture and identities. In using it, Athenians destroy the distinctions among friend, colony, ally, neutral and enemy, and make the world their enemy through a policy of limitless expansion. By the time of the Sicilian debate Athenians can no longer speak and act coherently, and this failure is the principal cause of the catastrophe that follows. For Thucydides, and for White, the history of the Athenian empire indicates the tension between justice and self-interest, but also reveals how they validate and give meaning to one another.

Daniel Garst employs White's formulation to demonstrate that neorealists define power too narrowly and improperly project their understanding onto Thucydides.[10] For Thucydides, material capabilities are only one component of power. Hegemony also requires persuasion. Athenian imperialism was successful when power was exercised in accord with well-defined social conventions governing Greek speech and behavior. Thucydides documents the decline of these conventions from their high point at the time of Pericles' funeral oration through the debate over Mytilene, the Melian Dialogue and the Sicilian debate. The speeches and dialogues reveal how the Athenians destroy the rhetorical culture in terms of which their interests as an imperial power were formulated and expressed. Their foreign policy has become based instead on violence, coercion and limitless expansion. For Garst, this process illustrates the

[8] W. Robert Connor, *Thucydides* (Princeton: Princeton University Press, 1984), quotes on pp. 15, 18.

[9] James Boyd White, *When Words Lose Their Meaning: Constitutions and Reconstitutions of Language, Character, and Community* (Chicago: University of Chicago Press, 1984).

[10] Daniel Garst, "Thucydides and Neorealism," *International Studies Quarterly* 33, 1 (1989), pp. 469–97.

power of agency and demonstrates that foreign policy is rarely, if ever, a mechanical response to a balance of power.

For Gregory Crane, Thucydides' history is a classic of realist analysis because it offers an unvarnished portrayal of how the strong dominate the weak and how interests ride roughshod over considerations of justice.[11] But Crane acknowledges that Thucydides considered such behavior a fundamental departure from traditional Greek practice in which foreign policy was an extension of aristocratic family connections and enmeshed leaders and their *poleis* in a web of mutual obligations. The Corinthian plea to the Athenian assembly not to ally with Corcyra, based on Corinth's prior restraint during the Samian rebellion, reflects this approach and uses the time-honored language and arguments of reciprocity.[12] The Athenians reject their appeal because they formulate their interests and foreign policy on the basis of immediate interests. They treat alliances as market transactions: short-term exchanges unaffected by past associations. Thucydides considers this approach to politics destructive of the relationships that are the true source of security and prosperity. The single-minded focus on self-interest, typified by Alcibiades, was the underlying cause of discord at home and reckless expansionism abroad. Crane contends that Thucydides' goal was to reconstitute the "ancient simplicity" (*euēthēs*) of the aristocracy in a new, rationalized form.

Paul Rahe also sees two sides to Thucydides: the hard-headed analyst of power politics and the critic of realism.[13] His portrayal of post-Periclean Athens shows how lust (*erōs*) for power ultimately made prudent calculation of advantage and calibration of means and ends impossible. In the Melian Dialogue and the debate over the Sicilian expedition, Athenians lose all sense of measure and proportion, become impervious to reasoned argument and the risks inherent in their initiatives. Thucydides wants readers to recognize that moral boundaries are essential to limit ambitions. The sober construction of self-interest requires restraint, and this only happens when leaders and peoples internalize the claims of justice and human decency.

Justice is central to the critiques of Steven Forde and Clifford Orwin, both of whom approach Thucydides from a Straussian perspective.[14]

[11] Gregory Crane, *Thucydides and the Ancient Simplicity: The Limits of Political Realism* (Berkeley: University of California Press, 1998).

[12] Thucydides, I.37–44.

[13] Paul A. Rahe, "Thucydides' Critique of Realpolitik," in Benjamin Frankel, *Roots of Realism* (Portland, Or.: Frank Cass, 1996), pp. 105–41.

[14] Leo Strauss, *The City and Man* (Chicago: University of Chicago Press, 1964); Steven Forde, "Varieties of Realism: Thucydides and Machiavelli," *Journal of Politics*, 54: 2 (May 1992), pp. 372–93, and *The Ambition to Rule: Alcibiades and the Politics of Imperialism in Thucydides* (Ithaca: Cornell University Press, 1989); Clifford Orwin, *The Humanity of Thucydides* (Princeton: Princeton University Press, 1994.

Forde criticizes neorealists for ignoring justice, a concern that he rightly observes was paramount for early postwar realists like Hans Morgenthau and John Herz. He contends that Thucydides, like Plato, recognized the possibility of reconciling justice and interest through the citizen's love for and identification with his *polis* – the principal theme of Pericles' funeral oration. In post-Periclean Athens, citizens put self-interest first, leading to acute discord and domestic instability.[15] For Orwin, Thucydides paints an "unflinching" portrait of harshness, and even brutality, to show how man through his "humanity" can transcend the security dilemma and crippling domestic discord.

Josiah Ober blends the traditions of classical and international relations scholarship, and might be considered a postmodern realist.[16] He uses Austin's conception of performative speech acts and Searle's understanding of social reality to analyze Athenian politics. He contends that Searle's all-important distinction between social and brute facts became blurred in the context of the awesome power wielded by the Athenian assembly. Their debates and decisions became "social facts," which allowed skilled orators to impose their preferred speech-dependent meanings on brute facts. As brute facts and social meanings diverged, the latter became the basis for disastrous foreign policies. In this conflict between acts (*erga*) and words (*logoi*), he contends, Thucydides sided with the former. His history attempts to reconstruct *erga* through the application of scientific methods of data collection and evaluation (*technē*) to the past, and points the way to a restructuring of everyday politics.

My analysis is deeply in debt to these several works, but differs from them in important respects. I take issue with some of their interpretations, or with respect to the relationship between interest and justice, reach some of the same conclusions by a different route. My biggest difference with my political science and classical colleagues concerns the purpose of the history; I contend that at its core it is about the rise and fall of civilizations and what can be done to restore civilizations. My analysis builds on Connor's insight that Thucydides might be read as a layered text and many of its seeming inconsistencies thereby reconciled. For Connor, omissions, repetitions, inconsistencies and subverted

[15] For a similar argument, see Laurie M. Johnson, *Thucydides, Hobbes and the Interpretation of Realism* (De Kalb: Northern Illinois Press, 1994). An earlier piece, "The Use and Abuse of Thucydides in International Relations," *International Organization* 48 (Winter 1994), pp. 131–53 under the name of Laurie M. Johnson Bagby, argues that Thucydides, unlike neorealists, thought the character of states, their leaders and ethical judgments all critical to foreign policy.

[16] Josiah Ober, *Political Dissent in Democratic Athens: Intellectual Critics of Popular Rule* (Princeton: Princeton University Press, 1998), and *Mass and Elite in Democratic Athens: Rhetoric, Ideology, and the Power of the People* (Princeton: Princeton University Press, 1989).

sentiments and arguments are the catalysts that move readers to deeper understandings. I see them as playing this role primarily *within* levels, and argue that Thucydides uses the structure of his narrative, his choice of language and implicit references to other texts to move readers between levels.

Power, interest and justice

Most of the works I have described address primarily questions of interest and justice at the first level of the text. There is a consensus that Thucydides does not approve of the harsh realism of the Athenians. He considers justice important because it provides a sensible framework for formulating interests. When interests are constructed outside the language of justice they will be equated with power and encourage policies of aggrandizement. Several of the studies I cited develop this thesis from an "inside out" perspective: from the vantage point of Athenians looking at the world and attempting to manage, protect and expand their empire. Thucydides also develops an "outside in" perspective that shows how allies, enemies and neutrals understand and respond to Athens and its policies. He not only documents the process by which Athens succumbs to a foreign policy of limitless expansion, but the reasons why such a policy is bound to fail.

Thucydides distinguishes *hēgemonia* and *archē*, both of which are generally translated into English as hegemony. For fifth- and fourth-century Greeks, *hēgemonia* was a form of legitimate authority and was associated with *timē* – the gift of honor. *Timē* meant "esteem" in the abstract, but also referred to the "office" to which one was therefore entitled.[17] Sparta and Athens earned *timē* by virtue of their contributions to Greece during the Persian Wars. *Timē* was also conferred on Athens in recognition of its literary, artistic and intellectual, political and commercial accomplishments that had made it, in the words of Pericles, the "school of Hellas."[18] *Archē* meant "control," and initially applied to authority within a city state, and later to rule or influence over other city states.

The years between the Battle of Salamis (480) and the outbreak of the Peloponnesian War (431), known as the *Pentēkontaëtia*, witnessed the gradual transformation of the Delian League into the Athenian empire. Athens removed the treasury from Delos, imposed its silver coinage and

[17] Russell Meiggs, *The Athenian Empire* (Oxford: Oxford University Press, 1972); Shalom Perlman, "Hegemony and *Archē* in Greece: Fourth-Century Views," in Richard Ned Lebow and Barry S. Strauss, *Hegemonic Rivalry: From Thucydides to the Nuclear Age* (Boulder: Westview, 1991), pp. 269–88.

[18] Thucydides, II.4.

weights and measures on most of its allies, and made the Great Panathenaia an empire festival. It intervened in the domestic affairs of allies to support democratic factions, and did not hesitate to use force to extract tribute from recalcitrant allies. With these funds, Athenians built the Parthenon, Parthenos and the Propylaea. By 430, Pericles acknowledged that the Athenian empire had many attributes of a tyranny, but he could proclaim, and not without justification, that "We Athenians obey the laws, especially those which are designed for the protection of the oppressed, and those which are unwritten but bring acknowledged shame on those who break them."[19] Athens still retained a high degree of popular support among subject governments and peoples, and there were few revolts in the early stages of the Peloponnesian War. They became more frequent after Sparta's successes in Chalcidice, and there was a rash of defections after Athens' defeat in Sicily.[20]

The cultural vitality of Athens was much admired throughout the Greek world, and especially by fellow Ionians, many of whom were proud to be allies. Self-interest also entered the picture. Athenian support was often decisive for democrats, who remained loyal to Athens if for no other reason than to keep oligarchs from returning to power.[21] Most allies greatly valued access to the large and expanding Athenian market and benefited from Athenian suppression of piracy. Many poor men found employment as rowers in the Athenian fleet, and the lower classes as a whole profited from the many jobs created through expanded trade and commerce.[22]

Change in leadership led to changes in military strategy, and after 427 Athens entered a new stage in its relations with its allies. Pericles had urged his countrymen "to wait quietly, to pay attention to their fleet, to attempt no new conquests, and to expose the city to no hazards during the war."[23] Cleon and his successors spurned Pericles' advice in favor of an offensive strategy aimed at imperial expansion. As Pericles had foreseen, this offensive strategy aroused consternation throughout

[19] Ibid., II.63. Tyrants were people who achieved the ambitions of many nobles in the archaic period and many politicians in the fifth century. They surpassed all rivals in their power and used it to lead a luxurious lifestyle. By describing Athens as a tyranny, Pericles is again conferring a status on average citizens usually reserved for the elite. Kurt A. Raaflaub, "Equalities and Inequalities in Athenian Democracy," in Josiah Ober and Charles Hedrick, eds., *Dēmokratia: A Conversation on Democracies, Ancient and Modern* (Princeton: Princeton University Press, 1996), pp. 139–74.

[20] Meiggs, *The Athenian Empire*, pp. 188–92, on the Samian revolt.

[21] Ibid., p. 208. There were still oligarchies in the alliance in the 430s, but only a few of them.

[22] Thucydides, 6.43; Boromir Jordan, *The Athenian Navy in the Classical Period*. Classical Studies, XIII (Berkeley: University of California Press, 1975).

[23] Thucydides, II.65.7.

Greece and appeared to lend substance to Sparta's claim that Athens was an oppressor while it was the "liberator of Hellas." The new strategy required more resources and compelled Athens to demand more tribute from its allies, and this too provoked resentment and, occasionally, armed resistance. Allied rebellion elicited a harsh response, and several cities were starved into submission. Siege operations required considerable resources, making it necessary to extract more tribute, triggering a downward spiral in Athenian-allied relations that continued for the duration of the war.[24]

By 416, the year the assembly voted to occupy Melos and subdue Sicily, the Athenian empire was an *archē* based primarily on military might. The structure and language of the Melian Dialogue mark a radical break with past practice. The Melians deny the Athenian envoys access to the people, granting them only a private audience with the magistrates and a small elite (*oligoi*). The resulting exchange consisted of *brachylogies*: short, blunt, alternating verbal thrusts, suggestive of a military encounter.[25]

The Athenian generals, Cleomedes and Tisias, dispense with all pretense. They acknowledge that their invasion cannot be justified on the basis of their right to rule or as a response to provocations. They deny the relevance of justice, which they assert only comes into play between equals. "The strong do what they can and the weak suffer what they must," and the Melians should put their survival first and submit.[26] The Melians warn the Athenians that their empire will not last forever, that if they violate the established norms of justice and decency their fall "would be a signal for the heaviest vengeance and an example for the world to meditate upon." The Athenians respond that they live in the present and must do what is necessary to preserve their empire. The Melians attempt to address this concern by arguing that their mutual interest is best served by a neutral and friendly Melos. The Athenians explain that their empire is held together by power (*dunamis*, the broader meaning of power) and the fear (*phobos*) it inspires. Other island states would interpret Melian neutrality as a sign of Athenian weakness and it would therefore serve as a stimulus for rebellion. "The fact that you are islanders and weaker than others renders it all the more important that you should not succeed in baffling the masters of the sea."[27] Fifth-century Greeks would have been shocked by Athens' failure to offer any justification (*prophasis*) for their

[24] Meiggs, *The Athenian Empire*, pp. 205–54.

[25] Connor, *Thucydides*, p. 148, observes that a similar exchange is alluded to in II.71–74, which describes the negotiations between King Archidamus of Sparta and the Plataeans prior to the investiture of their city. An obvious parallel is intended here, and in III.53–68. Like the Athenians at Melos, the Spartans violate their obligations and execute the Plataeans to satisfy their Theban allies.

[26] Thucydides, V.89. [27] Ibid., V.91–99.

invasion, and even more by their rejection of the Melian offer of neutrality on the grounds that "your hostility (*echthra*) cannot so hurt us as your friendship (*philia*)."[28] Fifteen years into the war the Athenians have repudiated, indeed inverted, core Greek values.

The rhetorical style of the Athenian generals reinforces the impression conveyed by their words. Dionysius of Halicarnassus judged their language "appropriate to oriental monarchs addressing Greeks, but unfit to be spoken by Athenians to Greeks whom they liberated from the Medes."[29] Thucydides appears to have modeled his dialogue on a passage in Herodotus where the Persian King Xerxes discusses the wisdom of attacking Greece with his council of advisors.[30] The language is similar and so are the arguments; Xerxes also alludes to the law of the stronger and the self-interest of empires. Later in his account, Herodotus describes an offer of peace and friendship that Xerxes makes to Athens and Sparta on the eve of his invasion. The Athenians spurn his olive branch and accept the danger of confronting a seemingly invincible force in the name of Greek freedom, just as the Melians reject Athens' offer of alliance because of the value they place on their freedom.[31] These parallels would not have been lost on contemporary readers. For Thucydides, as for many Greeks, the Athenians of 416 have become the Persians of 480 and the symbol of rank despotism.[32]

Thucydides is using the Dialogue to tell us that raw force can impose its will at any given moment, but no empire has the military and economic capability to repress its subjects indefinitely. Allies who regard themselves the objects of exploitation will rebel when the opportunity arises. Oppression also leaves memories that inhibit future attempts at empire building. In 378, most of Greece resisted efforts by Athens to revive its empire in the form of the Second Athenian Confederacy.[33] *Hēgemonia* is an essential precondition of sustainable empire.

[28] Ibid., V.95.

[29] Dionysius of Halicarnassus, *On Thucydides*, trans. William K. Pritchett (Berkeley: University of California Press, 1975), ch. 38, p. 31, quoted in Connor, *Thucydides*, p. 155.

[30] Herodotus, VII.8; Francis R. B. Godolphin, ed., *The Greek Historians*, contains the complete and unabridged historical works of Herodotus, trans. George Rawlinson (New York: Random House 1942); Connor, *Thucydides*, pp. 155–57; Henry R. Immerwar, *Form and Thought in Herodotus* (Atlanta: Scholars Press, 1966), p. 22, n. 40; F. M. Cornford, *Thucydides Mythistoricus* (London: Arnold, 1907), pp. 176–82; Crane, *Thucydides and the Ancient Simplicity*, pp. 241–46; Tim Rood, "Thucydides' Persian Wars," in Christina Shuttleworth Kraus, ed., *The Limits of Historiography: Genre Narrative in Ancient Historical Texts* (Leiden: Brill, 1999), pp. 141–68, on the parallels between Herodotus and Thucydides.

[31] Herodotus, VIII.140, 144; Thucydides, V.91; Connor, *Thucydides*, pp. 156–57.

[32] This point is made by Crane, *Thucydides and the Ancient Simplicity*, pp. 246ff.

[33] Thucydides, who died around 399, did not live to see this development, so it must be considered a logical but unintended consequence of his argument. It is a good example of how texts speak beyond the intentions of their authors.

Realists define the national interest in terms of power.[34] Many consider international law and its associated norms impediments to state interests unless they provide rhetorical cover for interest-based policies.[35] Realists on the whole urge statesmen to resist popular pressures to bend foreign policy to ideological or humanitarian causes. Thucydides rejects any narrow construction of interest. He contrasts foreign policies based on enlightened conceptions of interest with those driven by momentary constraints and opportunities and unduly influenced by fear, domestic politics and popular passions. Pericles was praiseworthy because his foreign policies were intended to serve the interests of the community (*Athēnaioi*), and used his personal standing and oratorical skill to win popular support for them. The leaders who followed him were at best successful tacticians. They advocated policies calculated to appeal to the masses (*homilos*), and were more interested in their own fortunes than those of their polis. Pericles understood that the overriding foreign policy interest of Athens was preservation of its empire, and that this required naval power *and* legitimacy. To maintain its *hēgemonia* Athens had to act in accord with the principles and values that it espoused, and offer positive political and economic benefits to allies. Post-Periclean leaders consistently chose power over principle, and, by doing so, alienated allies and third parties, lost *hēgemonia* and weakened Athens' power base. Viewed in this light, the Melian Dialogue and the Sicilian expedition are radical departures from rational self-interest.

Athens as tragedy

In Chapter 2, I suggested that the three classical realists whose writings I analyze in this book shared a tragic vision of politics. They are critical of overreliance on reason and sensitive to the ways in which its untempered application to political and social affairs can produce outcomes diametrically opposed to those that are sought. They have little faith in the ability of individuals or societies to safeguard themselves against suffering through the application of power or knowledge. None of them wrote tragedies. Thucydides nevertheless makes use of tragic conventions and constructs the rise and fall of Athens as a tragedy.

Following White, I argued that the progression of speeches from Pericles' funeral oration through the debate over Mytilene and the Melian Dialogue to the Sicilian debate tracks the breakdown of language and

[34] The classic statement is Hans J. Morgenthau, *Politics Among Nations: The Struggle for Power and Peace* (Chicago: University of Chicago Press, 1948), ch. 1.

[35] Edward Hallet Carr, *The Twenty Years Crisis, 1919–1939: An Introduction to the Study of International Relations*, 2nd ed. (New York: Harper & Row, 1946), ch. 5.

the community it sustained. Acting outside the bonds of community, Athenian citizens and their polis became unrestrained in the pursuit of short-term advantage. Fifth-century readers would have recognized this pathology as a core theme of tragedy. In Sophocles' *Ajax*, the armor of the dead Achilles is awarded to Odysseus. Convinced that he should have been honored, Ajax seeks revenge against Odysseus, the Atridae clan and the Greek army. Athena intervenes and deludes Ajax into believing that he is killing Greeks, when in fact he is slaughtering their flocks and herdsmen. He drags a ram back to his dwelling to torture, convinced that it is Odysseus. When Ajax comes to his senses and realizes what he has done, the only way he can preserve his honor, he concludes, is by falling on his sword. The Parodos – the ode sung by the chorus – points us toward the underlying lesson of the play: the importance of community and the destructive consequences of acting outside of it. Ajax has family – a wife, an infant son, a half-brother and loyal companions-in-arms – all of whom reach out to him in the course of the play. But he distances himself from them emotionally, and does the same with Agamemnon and other Greek chieftains. In the absence of restraining emotional ties and commitments, Ajax carries his quest for honor to the extreme and overreacts to an imagined sleight in a violent way that leads to his destruction.[36]

Greek tragedy examines the place of man in the broader scheme of things, and explores the tensions between traditional life, epitomized by the *oikos* and kingly rule, and the modern civic culture. Our best guess is that Thucydides was born in about 460, two years before the production of *Oresteia* in 458. Sophocles and Euripides were his contemporaries, and he would almost certainly have attended some of their performances, although we must remember that he was in exile from 424 to 403. Cornford and Euben, among others, have discussed Thucydides' relationship to tragedy and the structural similarities between his history and the tragedies. There is a long-standing controversy about which playwright he most closely resembles.[37] The more important question is why Thucydides models his history on tragedy and portrays Athens as

[36] R. P. Winnington-Ingram, *Sophocles: An Interpretation* (Cambridge: Cambridge University Press, 1980), pp. 18–24.

[37] Cornford, *Thucydides Mythistoricus*, makes the case for Aeschylus. John H. Finley, Jr., *Three Essays on Thucydides* (Cambridge, Mass.: Harvard University Press, 1967), finds a stronger parallel with Euripides. For a general discussion, see J. Peter Euben, *The Tragedy of Political Theory: The Road Not Taken* (Princeton: Princeton University Press, 1990), pp. 171–73; Hayward R. Alker, "The Dialectical Logic of Thucydides' Melian Dialogue," *American Political Science Review* 82 (September 1988), pp. 806–20, and the expanded version in *Rediscoveries and Reformulations: Humanistic Methods for International Studies* (Cambridge: Cambridge University Press, 1966); David Bedford and Thom Workman, "The Tragic Reading of the Thucydidean Tragedy," *Review of International Studies* 27 (2001), pp. 51–67.

an archetypical tragic hero. The answer, I think, is that he wants readers to move from intellectual and emotional involvement with the story he tells to contemplation of its meaning and implications, just as they might with a theatrical production. This is the second layer of the history.

In the only first-person statement about his intent, Thucydides offers his work as "an aid for the interpretation of the future, which in the course of human things must resemble it if it does not reflect it."[38] The cycle he has in mind is not limited to the growth and decline of empires. It is an illustration of a more general human pattern: success spawns greater ambitions, overconfidence and self-defeating behavior. Homeric and tragic heroes are driven by self-aggrandizement (*pleonexia*), ambition (*philotimia*), and the desire (*erōs*) for wealth and dominance (*archē*).[39] These are the same impulses that drive political actors in Thucydides' real-world tragedy. The *oikos* was the usual setting for tragedies, and by personifying Athens as a tragic hero, Thucydides was able to exploit a well-developed and understood set of concepts to order and explain behavior at a different level of social interaction. Part of his originality lies in his extrapolation of the values and pathologies of the *oikos* to the polis, and beyond, to the wider community of Hellas.[40]

Greek literature developed gradually out of oral tradition. A fully phonetic alphabet was in use around 775, and the first prose tract, by Anaximander, was written in about 546. Some genres, notably philosophy, made the shift from poetry to prose in the course of the late sixth and fifth centuries.[41] Heraclitus, Anaximander and other Ionian physicists wrote narratives. Herodotus, who died around 425, had contemporaries who wrote prose, among them Hekataios of Miletos, Akousilaos of Argos, Charon of Lampsakos. We have only fragments of their writings, or, sometimes, just titles. Like Herodotus, a Dorian from Halicarnassus, they all appear to have written in the Ionian dialect regardless of the native tongue. Herodotus chose his words with their sounds in mind, and his style, *lexis eiromenē* (literally, speech strung together), is related

[38] Thucydides, I.22.

[39] The individual and community were supposed to value the excellence demonstrated by the victor. Excellence was to be its own reward, and this is why victors received only a laurel wreath. *Pleonexia* represents a perversion of the spirit of competition; prizes and rewards became the goal, and excellence merely a means to this end. Agamemnon provides a prototypical display of *pleonexia* in the *Iliad*; he is only interested in the fruits of victory and unwilling to share them with others. Nietzsche effectively captured the sense of *pleonexia* when he translated it into German as *haben und mehrwohlhaben*.

[40] The analogy between *oikos* and polis was a long-standing one by the end of the fifth century, but the extension of community to *Hellas* as a whole was still relatively novel.

[41] On tragedy's role in the transition to a written culture, see Charles Segal, "Tragedy, Orality, Literacy," in Bruno Gentili and Guiseppe Psioni, eds., *Oralità: Cultura, Litteratura, Discorso* (Urbino: Edizione dell'Atheneo, 1980), pp. 199–226.

to epic poetry. He introduces an idea or action, defines it by approaching it from different perspectives, and expands its meaning through the apposition of words, phrases and clauses. Fifth-century Greeks typically recited from memory, and heard rather than read their literature. "I read" (*ana-gignōskō*) means, literally, "I recognize again."[42] Herodotus is reported to have received a stipend in Athens for publicly reciting part of his history, and he undoubtedly expected his work to be read aloud before an audience.[43]

Writing some twenty to twenty-five years after Herodotus, Thucydides worked at a time when the oral tradition was declining. Opinion about his intentions are divided.[44] His speeches are oral presentations and lend themselves to dramatic reading, as do large parts of his narrative, including the Melian Dialogue. Thucydides can be appreciated in a public reading, but it would be difficult to grasp deeper layers of meaning.[45] His writing is complex and idiosyncratic and requires careful analysis to discover and work through its purpose. He makes extensive use of parallels in setting, structure and language with other passages in his history and those of other writers, and offers a more abstract and decontextualized account than Herodotus. This suggests that he intended his history to be read and studied.

In the *Iliad*, from which so much of Greek tradition derives, paired and group speeches are vehicles for arousing compassion and encouraging recognition of ethical complexity. Homer also uses them to mark fateful decisions and turning points.[46] So does Thucydides, for whom speeches highlight critical junctures, suggest their contingency, and provide justifications for opposing courses of action.[47] Heraclitus maintained that nature (*phusis*) tended to conceal itself, and that its seemingly contradictory manifestations had an underlying unity (*harmonia*) that could

42 Paul Cartledge, *Spartan Reflections* (London: Duckworth, 2001), p. 43.

43 T. J. Luce, *The Greek Historians* (London: Routledge, 1997), p. 19. Historical narrative existed prior to Herodotus. In the sixth and seventh centuries, narratives were written about the foundation of cities, mythic traditions, genealogies of heroes and recent events, and were probably read aloud at festivals. Fragments of the "Elegy on the Battle of Plataea" by Simonides indicate a gradual shift from poetry to prose.

44 On the Greek oral tradition, see Eric A. Havelock, *Preface to Plato* (Cambridge, Mass.: Harvard University Press, 1963); Pedro Lain Entralgo, *The Therapy of the Word in Classical Antiquity*. ed. and trans. E. J. Rather and John M. Sharp (New Haven: Yale University Press, 1970); Jesper Svenbro, *Phrasikleia: An Anthology of Reading in Ancient Greece*, trans. Janet Lloyd (Cornell: Cornell University Press, 1993), introduction.

45 I use this term because reading in the ancient world was done aloud, even that done privately. In the late fourth century, Augustine of Hippo was stunned to see Ambrose reading silently to himself.

46 Examples include the exchange between Poulydamas and Hector, the council of Achaean leaders and the Trojan assembly. The *Iliad*, XII.195–250, XIV.1–132 and XVIII.242–313.

47 For a discussion, Stadter, *The Speeches of Thucydides*.

be discovered by reflection.[48] The double and superficially conflicting nature of the divine is a concept with deep roots in Greek myth, and consistently invoked by the tragedians to prompt audiences to recognize truths about the human condition.[49] Thucydides uses speeches for the same end. They track the descent of Greece from a community of relatively secure *poleis* bound together by conventions, mutual obligations and common interests to disorder and anarchy, a transformation to which I shall return.

Another similarity with tragedy is Thucydides' use of heroes to provide continuity and structure to the text.[50] Modern writers on the origins, course and consequences of wars frequently acknowledge the prominent role of key actors, but they almost always provide readers with some kind of general, sociological framework to understand and assess the decisions and behavior of these people.[51] Herodotus and Thucydides do the reverse; like Homer and the tragedians, they rely on the words and deeds of actors to move their narratives along and give them meaning. Herodotus gives great play early on to the story of Croesus which sets readers up for the ensuing saga of Xerxes.[52] Solon warns Croesus to recognize his

[48] Dennis Sweet, *Heraclitus: Translation and Analysis* (Lanham, Md.: University Press of America, 1995), frgs. 51, 54, p. 23. Martin Heidegger, "Logos (Heraclitus Fragment B 50)," in D. F. Krell and Charles H. Kahn, *The Art and Thought of Heraclitus* (Cambridge: Cambridge University Press, 1999); C. H. Kohn, *The Art and Thought of Heraclitus: The Cosmic Fragments* (Cambridge: Cambridge University Press, 1979); Edward Hussey, "Epistemology and Meaning in Heraclitus," in Malcom Schofield and Martha Nussbaum, eds., *Language and Logos: Studies in Ancient Greek Philosophy Presented to G. E. L. Owen* (Cambridge: Cambridge University Press, 1982), pp. 33–59; Edward Hussey, "Heraclitus," in Brunschwig and Lloyd, *Greek Thought*, pp. 631–41.

[49] Mario Untersteiner, *The Sophists*, trans. Kathleen Freeman (New York: Philosophical Library, 1954), pp. 22–23, contends that Aeschylus gives this concept powerful form in *Supplices*, *Prometheus*, *Seven Against Thebes* and the *Oresteia*.

[50] Bernard W. Knox, *The Heroic Temper: Studies in Sophoclean Tragedy* (Berkeley: University of California Press, 1964), observes that since Aristotle the traditional view of tragedy is that it is centered on the tragic hero, with Oedipus being the quintessential example. This is true for Sophocles, six of whose seven extant plays are named after their chief character. But the reverse is true for Aeschylus. Walter Kaufmann, *Tragedy and Civilization* (Princeton: Princeton University Press, 1968), p. 77n., calculates that eight of the fourteen extant plays of Aeschylus and Sophocles are without tragic heroes. The remaining six revolve around a hero, but three of them (Orestes in *The Libation Bearers* and Sophocles' *Electra* and *Oedipus*) cannot be said to have tragic flaws.

[51] For a case in point, Holger H. Herwig, *The First World War: Germany and Austria-Hungary, 1914–1918* (London: Arnold, 1997); Gerhard L. Weinberg, *A World At War: A Global History of World War II* (Cambridge, Mass.: Harvard University Press, 1994); Williamson Murray and Allan R. Millet, *A War to Be Won: Fighting the Second World War* (Cambridge, Mass.: Harvard University Press, 2000).

[52] Herodotus was a contemporary and friend of Sophocles. His account of Croesus and the Achaemenids (Cyrus, Cambyses and Xerxes) all follow tragic form. Oracles are misinterpreted, and mistaken choices lead to personal and political catastrophes. Pierre Vidal-Nacquet, "Oedipus in Athens," in Jean-Pierre Vernant and Pierre Vidal-Nacquet, *Myth and Tragedy in Ancient Greece*, trans. J. B. Lloyd (New York: Zone Books, 1990), pp. 301–2.

limits and restrain his ambitions, and Xerxes receives similar advice from Artabanus. Both men spurn caution and embark upon ambitious military ventures that end in catastrophe. Early in Book I, Thucydides uses the story of Agamemnon and the Trojan War – a war triggered by an exaggerated concern for honor in which an alliance held together by naval power confronted a major land power – to provide an introduction to the Peloponnesian War that follows.[53] Within the history, the stories of individuals and cities prefigure the fate of more important personages and major powers, especially Athens.

There is a more fundamental difference in the way ancient Greek and modern historians approach heroes. Most contemporary works dwell on the particular mix of background, personal qualities and experience that make people unique as individuals. They do so even when these figures are intended to be emblematic of a class, movement or set of shared life experiences.[54] Herodotus and Thucydides hardly ever take note of idiosyncratic attributes; like the authors of epic poetry and drama they use individuals to create archetypes. They stress the qualities, especially the strengths and weaknesses, their heroes have in common with other heroes. The typicality, not the uniqueness, of actors and situations, is a central convention of fifth-century poetry, tragedy and prose. Even Pericles, whom Thucydides offers as the model of a modern man of politics, is a stereotype. He is the sum of qualities that make him an ideal leader in a transitional democracy, and a benchmark for his successors. All subsequent leaders possess different combinations of his qualities, but never all of them – to the detriment of Athens. Nicias displays honesty and dedication, but lacks the skill and stature to dissuade the assembly from the Sicilian expedition. Alcibiades has intelligence and rhetorical skill, but no moderation, and uses them to advance his career at the expense of his city.

Greek tragedies consist of archetypical characters confronting archetypical situations. The tragic hero, like his Homeric predecessor, is a self-centered, even narcissistic figure who revels in his own importance and comes to believe that he is no longer bound by the laws and conventions of man. These manifestations of ego and their consequences are often explored through a standard plot line: success carries with it the seeds of failure. Success intoxicates heroes and leads them to inflated opinions of themselves and their ability to control man and nature alike. They trust in hope (*elpis*), and become susceptible to adventures where reason would dictate caution and restraint. The Greeks used the word *atē*

[53] Thucydides, I.9–11.
[54] For example, Carl E. Schorske, *Thinking with History: Explorations in the Passage to Modernism* (Princeton: Princeton University Press, 1998); Fritz Stern, *Einstein's German World* (Princeton: Princeton University Press, 1999).

to describe the aporia this kind of seduction induces, and the *hamartia* (miscalculation) it encourages.[55] *Hamartia* ultimately leads the hero to catastrophe by provoking the wrath of the gods (*nemesis*).[56] The *Persians* of Aeschylus, produced in the spring of 472, at the height of Themistocles' power, is an early example of this genre, and was intended as a cautionary tale about the consequences of hubris.[57]

The tragedians may have conceived some of their characters as personifications of Athens. Bernard Knox contends that *Oedipus*, performed in the late 420s, is a thinly veiled portrayal of Periclean and post-Periclean Athens. Oedipus' intellectual prowess becomes impulsiveness, his decisiveness thoughtlessness, and his sense of mastery finds expression as intolerance to opposition. Oedipus' fall may be intended to presage that of Athens, and for the same reasons.[58] Other scholars have described Antigone as a personification of Athens; she champions the right of her brother to an appropriate burial in Thebes as the Athenians did for the unburied seven warriors who died in the unsuccessful assault on that city.[59] If Sophocles could use a tragic hero to represent the polis, Herodotus and Thucydides could do the reverse and portray the polis as a tragic hero.

[55] English translators of Aeschylus often render *atē* as delusion, but it also suggests a more ominous connotation suggestive of the potential for self-destruction. R. D. Dawe, "Some Reflections on *atē* and *hamartia*," *Harvard Studies in Classical Philology* 72 (1967), pp. 89–123; R. E. Doyle, "The Objective Character of *Atē* in Aeschylean Tragedy," *Traditio* 28 (1972), pp. 1–28.

[56] Aristotle once again overstates the case, this time in his claim that *hamartia* is the defining characteristic of tragedy. Antigone is innocent of any *hamartia*. Oedipus' downfall is not caused by any *hamartia*. Philoctetes rises rather than falls as a result of his. The *Persians* of Aeschylus is the one play that is squarely based on *hamartia*. The very focus on the hero is distorting for understanding tragedy. H. D. F. Kitto, *Form and Meaning in Drama: A Study of Six Greek Plays and of Hamlet* (London: Methuen, 1956), p. 233; Bernard Knox, *Oedipus at Thebes: Sophocles' Tragic Hero and His Time* (New Haven: Yale University Press, 1970), p. 31.

[57] Homeric heroes are all subject to failure and sooner or later in the suffering come to recognize their limits. Their acceptance of their mortality prompts them to establish, or reestablish, more intimate relationships with other human beings. This is not always true of the heroes of Greek tragedy. Robert Fagels, "Introduction" to Homer, *The Iliad*, trans. Robert Fagels (New York: Viking, 1990), pp. 3–64.

[58] Knox, *Oedipus at Thebes*, pp. 61–106. Charles Segal, *Oedipus Tyrannus: Tragic Heroism and the Limits of Knowledge*, 2nd ed. (New York: Oxford University Press, 1986), pp. 11–13, suggests that *Oedipus* was a response to the war and great plague of 429–425. Victor Ehrenberg, *Sophocles and Pericles* (Oxford: Blackwell, 1954), pp. 67–69, argues that *Oedipus* was Sophocles' warning about the consequences of Periclean rationalism. See also Froma Zeitlin, "Thebes: Theater of Self and Society in Athenian Drama," in J. Peter Euben, *Greek Tragedy and Political Theory* (Berkeley and Los Angeles: University of California Press, 1986), pp. 101–41.

[59] Larry Bennett and William Blake Tyrrell, "Sophocles' *Antigone* and Funeral Oratory," *American Journal of Philology* 111 (1990), pp. 441–56; Nicole Loraux, *The Invention of Athens*, trans. A. Sheridan (Cambridge, Mass.: Harvard University Press, 1986), pp. 48–52, 65–68.

Herodotus clearly exploits the tragic plot line for his stories of Croesus and Xerxes. Intoxicated by his riches, Croesus misinterprets the oracle who tells him that a great empire will be destroyed if he invades Persia. He is defeated and only saved from being burned alive by the mercy of his adversary. Xerxes is an ambitious but cautious leader who accumulates enormous power through his skill and good fortune. His exaltation and pride grow in proportion to his success, and *atē* leads him to a *hamartia*. At first, he resists Mardonius' suggestion to exploit the revolt of the Ionians to invade Greece and add Europe to his empire. Dreams subsequently lead him to change his mind and make an enormous misjudgment. His sense of omnipotence is apparent in his attempt to punish the Hellespont for washing away his bridge across it in a storm. His *nemesis* at Salamis is inevitable, and from the perspective of Herodotus and Greek tragedy, the destruction of the Persian fleet, and later, of the expeditionary force, represents less a triumph of the Greeks than it does a fitting punishment of Xerxes.[60]

Thucydides distances himself from Herodotus at the outset of his history by telling readers that they will encounter no romance, only a narrative of events put together from eye-witness accounts.[61] Thucydides nevertheless begins where Herodotus leaves off, and shifts the locus of the narrative from Persia to Greece. The Athenians, the principal agents of Xerxes' *nemesis*, now repeat the cycle of success, overconfidence, miscalculation and catastrophe. Indeed, the Athenian victory over Xerxes at Salamis marks the emergence of Athens as a military power and sets the cycle in motion. Athens achieves a string of victories until ambition and overconfidence are responsible for a string of military and political disasters: the annihilation in 454 of its expedition to Egypt, the revolt of Erythrae and Miletus in 452 and defeat at Coronea in central Greece in 446.[62] These setbacks temporarily compelled Athenians to recognize the limits of its power. In 449, Athens made peace with Persia and, in the summer or early autumn of 446, Athens and Sparta agreed to the

[60] Herodotus, I.204, I.108–13, I.207, I.212, VII.9–10, VII.15, VII.34. Aeschylus offers a similar reading in the *Persians*, 353–432, where the Messenger attributes Xerxes' defeat to the cunning of the Greeks, but explains that his invasion of Greece was a "set up" by the gods. Herodotus (IX.78.9) describes the restraint of the Spartan general Pausanias after the Battle of Plataea. The Athenian Xanthippos (IX.120), by contrast, allows the citizens of liberated Sestos to crucify the Persian commander and stone his son to death in his presence. Leslie Kurke, "Charting the Poles of History: Herodotos and Thoukydides," in Oliver Taplin, ed., *Literature in the Greek and Roman Worlds: A New Perspective* (New York: Oxford University Press, 2000), pp. 115–37, argues that it is probably not coincidental that this incident, and other signs of Greek adoption of barbarian practices, take place at the Hellespont, where Europe meets Asia. Herodotus may be intimating that this is Athens' first step toward behaving like the barbarians.

[61] Thucydides, I.22. [62] Ibid., I.104, 109–10.

Thirty Years Peace. Under the leadership of Pericles, Athens devoted its energies to consolidating its sprawling empire. Like Xerxes, Pericles is unable to exercise restraint in the long term. Convinced of his ability to control events at home and abroad, he persuades an initially reluctant assembly to seize the opportunity of alliance with Corcyra in the erroneous expectation that the worst possible outcome would be a short war in which Sparta would discover the futility of opposing Athens. His initial *hamartia* leads to war, plague, his death and abandonment of his defensive strategy. A second *hamartia*, the Sicilian expedition, urged on the assembly by Alcibiades, led to *nemesis*.

Cleon, intended to represent a figure intermediate between Pericles and Alcibiades, shows none of Pericles' caution or thoughtfulness. He is as unscrupulous as Alcibiades, and surpasses other politicians in his spreading of largesse in return for political support. Thucydides calls him "the most violent man at Athens," and he was parodied by Aristophanes in two of his plays.[63] Cleon launches a stinging verbal attack on Nicias, accusing him and his troops of cowardice in facing the Spartans in Pylos. Nicias offers to stand aside and let Cleon assume command of his forces. Cleon discounts this as rhetorical posturing, but Nicias then resigns his command. Cleon tries desperately to back down, but the assembly, remembering his earlier bravura, will not let him.[64] Cleon is forced to sail for Pylos, where he and Demosthenes – much to Cleon's surprise and relief – succeed in overwhelming the Spartans in short order.[65] In the aftermath of his victory, Sparta sued for peace to secure the return of its hostages, and the Archidamian phase – the first ten years of the Peloponnesian War – came to an end.

Alcibiades was not content with the peace, and convinced the assembly to renew the war and embark upon a policy of imperial expansion. Thucydides sees the decisions to ally with Corcyra and conquer Sicily as the most fateful decisions of the assembly; each is a *hamartia*, and together they lead to *nemesis*.[66] The decision to ally with Corcyra required a second debate in which the assembly reversed itself. This also happened in the punishment of Mytilene and the Sicilian expedition.[67] But the most important similarity, that really sets the Corcyra and Sicilian decision apart from other events in the history, is that they are preceded by

[63] Plutarch, *Nicias*, III; Thucydides, III.36.6; Aristophanes, *Wasps* and *Knights*; W. Robert Connor, *The New Politicians of Fifth-Century Athens* (Princeton: Princeton University Press, 1971), pp. 20–21, 129–34; Victoria Wohl, *Love Among the Ruins: The Erotics of Democracy in Classical Athens* (Princeton: Princeton University Press, 2002), pp. 73–79.

[64] Thucydides, IV.24–29. [65] Ibid., IV.29–42.

[66] Ibid., I.44; 4.65. [67] Ibid., I.44; III.36; VI.8.

"archeologies" that establish the background for the momentous events that will follow.[68]

In the Sicilian debate, Nicias does his best to dissuade the assembly, utterly ignorant of the size and population of Sicily, from sailing against an island so large, far away and with such a powerful city as Syracuse. Echoing Artabanus' plea to Xerxes, Nicias urges Athenians not to risk "what is actually yours for advantages which are dubious in themselves, and which you may or may not attain."[69] Alcibiades, cast in the role of Mardonius, makes light of the risks and greatly exaggerates the possible rewards of an expedition to the assembly. He does not attempt to rebut any of Nicias' arguments but makes a calculated, emotional appeal to a receptive audience.[70] Nicias comes forward a second time, and recognizing that direct arguments against the expedition will not carry the day, tries to dissuade the assembly by insisting on a much larger force and more extensive provisions than were originally planned. To his surprise, the more he demands, the more eager the assembly becomes to support the expedition, convinced that a force of such magnitude will be invincible.[71]

There are striking similarities in plot line and language between Thucydides' account of the Athenian assembly and Herodotus' depiction of Xerxes at Abydus. Thucydides describes the Sicilian expedition as more extravagant than any Greek campaign that preceded it by virtue of its *lamprotēs* (splendor) and *tolma* (rashness, daring, audacity).[72] These are words used by Herodotus and other Greeks to describe Xerxes' court and military plans. Thucydides could assume that most of his readers were familiar with the works of Aeschylus, Sophocles, Euripides and Herodotus, and would recognize his personification of Athens as a tragic hero and the mordant comparison he intended between Athens and Persia. This format and analogy would encourage these readers to consider the story of Athens as the basis for generalizations about the human condition.

The link between Thucydides and tragedy goes far beyond his adoption of a tragic plot line. Crafted speeches to political "audiences" in

68 Ibid., I.2–13; VI.2–6. Hunter R. Rawlings, III, *The Structure of Thucydides' History* (Princeton: Princeton University Press, 1981), pp. 62–27, and Connor, *Thucydides*, p. 160, make this point.

69 Thucydides, VI.9; Connor, *Thucydides*, pp. 158–68, for an insightful discussion of the debate, and 159, n. 5 which notes another parallel between the Persian and Sicilian invasions: leaders' lack of experience; Kurt von Fritz, *Die Geschichte Geschichtsshreibung* (Berlin: Walter de Gruyter, 1968), I, p. 728, on Nicias as advisor.

70 Thucydides, VI.6–18.

71 Ibid., VI.20–24; Crane, *Thucydides and the Ancient Simplicity*, pp. 147–48.

72 Thucydides, VI.12, 15–16; Rahe, "Thucydides' Critique of Realpolitik," p. 133.

the assembly, council and law courts lay at the heart of the democratic process in Athens. As I noted in Chapter 1, the stage was an integral part of the civic-political culture of Athens, and understood as such by citizens. At the Great Dionysia, libations were poured by the *stratēgoi*, tribute from allies was on public display and there was a parade of state-supported orphans who had reached manhood and were presented with a full military panoply. Plays were performed under the supervision of the magistrates, who selected the victors by secret ballot. Acting had the same status as pleading in court or speaking before the assembly.[73] The city used tragedies to build an identity and encourage solidarity across class and other social divides.[74] And the playwrights used their works to explore contemporary issues, albeit in distant settings.

Aeschylus wrote during the democratization of Athens, from the 480s to the 450s. In his *Oresteia*, revenge gives way to the law, self-reliance to citizenship, and the polis becomes an expression of the entire community, not just an extension of a royal *oikos*. The *Oresteia* also makes references to the Argive alliance. In the *Suppliant Women*, Aeschylus dramatizes democratic decision making by an assembly and has the king acknowledge what he calls the sovereign hand of the people (*dēmou kratōusa cheir*).[75]

[73] Jean-Pierre Vernant, "Greek Tragedy: Problems of Interpretation," in Richard Macksey and Eugenio Donato, eds., *The Structuralist Controversy: The Languages of Criticism and the Sciences of Man* (Baltimore: Johns Hopkins University Press, 1972), pp. 273–88, and "Tensions and Ambiguities in Greek Tragedy," in Vernant and Vidal-Nacquet, *Myth and Tragedy in Ancient Greece*; Segal, *Oedipus Tyrannus*, pp. 15–18, 20–22; Simon Goldhill, *Reading Greek Tragedy* (Cambridge: Cambridge University Press, 1986), and "The Great Dionysia and Civic Ideology," in John J. Winkler and Froma I. Zeitlin, *Nothing to Do with Dionysos?: Athenian Drama in its Social Context* (Princeton: Princeton University Press, 1990), pp. 97–129; John J. Winkler, "The Ephebes' Song: *Tragōidia* and Polis," in Winkler and Zeitlin, *Nothing to Do with Dionysos?*," pp. 20–62; Froma I. Zeitlin, "Thebes: Theater of Self and Society in Athenian Drama," in Euben, ed., *Greek Tragedy and Political Theory*, pp. 101–41, and *The Tragedy of Political Theory*, pp. 50–59.

[74] Nicole Loraux, *The Invention of Athens* (Cambridge, Mass.: Harvard University Press, 1987), contrasts the ways the funeral oration and tragedy encouraged unity. Josiah Ober and Barry Strauss, "Drama, Political Rhetoric, and the Discourse of Athenian Democracy," in Winkler and Zeitlin *Nothing to Do With Dionysos?*, pp. 237–70, offer an analogy to Clifford Geertz's description of a Balinese cockfight. Tragedy was a setting in which the "tactics" of symbols could be devised and used to create a cultural strategy that fostered harmony. Goldhill, "The Great Dionysia and Civic Ideology," in Winkler and Zeitlin, *Nothing to Do with Dionysos*?, pp. 97–129, observes that tragedies were embedded in rituals, all of which were intended to reinforce communal identity and solidarity.

[75] Aeschylus may have been the first author-playwright to try to make his arguments acceptable to political authorities by presenting them in a distant setting. *Suppliant Women* was produced in 463 and clearly about Athens, but safely set in Argos during the heroic period of the bronze age. The anachronistic king is something of a constitutional monarch who consults and accepts the judgment of the Argive assembly. The phrase, the sovereign hand of the people, would have been understood by his audience to mean *dēmokratia*.

In Antigone, produced in 441, Sophocles pits civil authority against religious tradition in the guise of a conflict between Creon, the Theban ruler, and his niece Antigone. Creon, a secular man intent on maintaining order, violates divine law by insisting that the body of his nephew Polyneices, a traitor to the state, be left out as carrion for birds and animals. Moved by religious feeling and familial duty, Antigone buries her brother and provokes Creon's wrath. Thebes is wracked by civil strife as two conceptions of justice clash. Sophocles may have been warning Athenians that this is the kind of *stasis* they will suffer if civil authority is not constrained by tradition and *nomos*.

Euripides wrote during the Peloponnesian War and witnessed Athens' defeat and the short-lived aristocratic counter-revolution of 404–403. His tragedies display little of the civic pride and cautious optimism of Aeschylus. The *Suppliant Women*, performed between 424 and 420, warns of the dangers, already evident, of the increasing tendency in Athens to make decisions on the basis of anger, pride and personal and family interests.[76] The play stresses the importance of democratic values and procedures, freedom of speech, the equality of citizens and the publication of laws.[77] His *Trojan Women* of 415 is avowedly anti-imperialist, and leaves his audience with a discomforting sense that argument and debate are unlikely to lead to justice. In the prologue of his lost *Philoctetes*, Odysseus reveals his disenchantment with the political process – widely shared in Athens – by speculating about the advantages of private life.[78] *Hecuba*, *Trojan Women*, *Electra*, *Orestes* and *Bacchae* document the dissolution of civilization and the regression to bestiality and barbarism.

Not all tragedies tell the story of a single hero. *Antigone* has a "double center of gravity."[79] It is built around the interactions of two protagonists who are "demonically bound" in the sense that each is necessary to bring out the identity and character of the other.[80] Antigone's

[76] Especially lines 476–510, 728–30, 736–44, the last stressing how victory incites ambition.

[77] Euripides, *Suppliants*, 350–53, 405–08, 429–34 and 438–41; Raaflaub, "Equalities and Inequalities in Athenian Democracy."

[78] Thomas G. Rosenmeyer, *The Art of Aeschylus* (Berkeley: University of California Press, 1982); Goldhill, *Reading Greek Tragedy*; Euben, *The Tragedy of Political Theory*, pp. 67–130; Charles Rowan Beye, *Ancient Greek Literature and Society* (Ithaca: Cornell University Press, 1975), pp. 173–97; Paul Cartledge, "Utopia and the Critique of Politics," in Jacques Brunschwig and Geoffrey E. R. Lloyd, *Greek Thought: A Guide to Classical Knowledge*, trans. Catherine Porter (Cambridge, Mass.: Harvard University Press, 2000), pp. 163–79; Peter Wilson, "Powers of Horror and Laughter: The Great Age of Drama," in Taplin, *Literature in the Greek and Roman Worlds*, pp. 88–132.

[79] C. M. Bowra. *Sophoclean Tragedy* (Oxford: Oxford University Press, 1944), pp. 66–67.

[80] The term is from Karl Reinhardt, *Sophokles*, 3rd ed. (Frankfurt: Klosterman, 1947), p. 74. See also C. H. Whitman, *Sophocles: A Study of Heroic Heroism* (Cambridge, Mass.: Harvard University Press, 1951), p. 86.

insistence that divine laws (*nomima*) take precedence over human decrees (*kērugmata*) puts her on a collision course with Creon, who defines justice in terms of the polis, its laws and interests. Antigone's uncompromising behavior provokes an equally extreme response from Creon: he compels her to choose between compliance and death. Antigone's decision to die in defense of her values gives her identity and tragic stature. Creon and Antigone might be said to form part of a greater whole, and the conflict between them to encapsulate key fault lines of fifth-century Athens: woman's emotional commitments versus man's abstract rationality, human versus divine law, private versus public morality, individual freedom versus the interests of the state and tyranny versus the rule of law.[81]

In the *Women of Trachis*, Sophocles sets up a deadly conflict between Heracles and Deianira, tied together by bonds of matrimony, to explore the incompatibility but equal necessity of "heroic" and modern values, of primitive, self-centered animal drives and the more refined feelings, commitments and selfless caring associated with civilization.[82] Thucydides also exploits antinomies (e.g., Corcyra versus Corinth, Athens versus Sparta, Archidamus versus Sthenelaïdas, Cleon versus Diodotus, Nicias versus Cleon) for much the same purposes. They provide human drama and frame conflicting attributes of human nature, conceptions of society and visions of justice. They also create identities: Athens would not be Athens without Sparta, and vice versa. As with Sophocles, all the tensions generated by conflicting pairs are left unreconciled, and spectators and readers are encouraged to recognize their inherent incompatibility – but also the need to work out compromises in the interests of order and civilization. In this sense, Thucydides departs radically from his predecessor, Herodotus, whose only real link with tragedy is his plot line.

Hegel revolutionized the study of tragedy by directing our attention away from tragic heros to tragic collisions. He observed that tragedies place their characters in situations where they have to choose between competing obligations and associated conceptions of justice. Their choices propel them into conflicts with characters who have made opposed choices. Conflicts arise not only as a result of these choices, but even more from the inability of the characters to empathize. They

81 Charles Paul, "Sophocles' Praise of Man and the Conflicts of the *Antigone*," *Arion* 3 (Summer 1964), pp. 47–66; Charles Segal, *Sophocles' Tragic World: Divinity, Nature, Society* (Cambridge, Mass.: Harvard University Press, 1995), pp. 119–67; Winnington-Ingram, *Sophocles*, p. 128.

82 Bowra, *Sophoclean Tragedy*; Victor Ehrenberg, "Tragic Heracles," in K. F. Stroheker and A. J. Graham, eds., *Polis und Imperium; Beiträge zur alten Geschichte* (Zurich: Artemis, 1965), pp. 380–98; T. F. Hoey, "The *Trachiniae* and the Unity of Hero," *Arethusa* 3:1 (1970), pp. 1–22; Segal, *Sophocles' Tragic World*, pp. 26–68.

understand the other's position as a reality without justification [*rechtlose Wirklichkeit*].[83] Antigone's loyalty to her brother and the gods bring her into conflict with Creon, who is just as committed to upholding civic order and his authority as head of the family. There are lesser collisions between Antigone and her sisters, Creon and his son and Creon and Teiresias, each of them equally emblematic.[84] This plot structure was pioneered by Aeschylus, who adapted the Homeric precedent of the contest (*agōn*) to have his characters defend, often to the death, the extreme representations of justice to which they are committed. Collisions are central to his *Suppliant Women* and the *Oresteia*, and this tradition was carried on and refined by Euripides. E. R. Dodds observes that his "favorite method is to take a one-sided point of view, a noble half-truth, to exhibit its nobility, and then to exhibit the disaster to which it leads its blind adherents – because it is after all only part of the truth."[85] Tragedy does not always require a collision, and Sophocles' *Oedipus* achieves the same effect by having its eponymous character respond to a series of external challenges arising from diverse sources.

Tragedy derives much of its power from its spareness. It addresses complex political and moral issues through personal dramas involving a small number of key individuals. Their complex stories are told in a few episodes that are presented in their barest essentials. Color, complexity and ambiguity are provided by the astute use of language to conjure up images and emotions and play off against well-known scenes and tropes from the epic tradition.[86] Thucydides' narrative is more complex but also consists of a series of a carefully constructed scenes, chosen and presented as stylized abstractions of reality. His prose is as evocative as poetry, and, like the playwrights, his words expand the meaning of events by invoking settings and scenes from earlier works of history and literature.

[83] Hegel, *Phenomenology of Spirit*, p. 332; Walter Kaufmann, *Tragedy and Philosophy* (Princeton: Princeton University Press, 1968), pp. 201–02; Charles Taylor, *Hegel* (Cambridge: Cambridge University Press, 1975), p. 175. Dennis J. Schmidt, *On Germans and Other Greeks: Tragedy and Ethical Life* (Bloomington: University of Indiana Press, 2001), on how Hegel's interpretation of Antigone related to his broader philosphy.

[84] Ibid., p. 138.

[85] E. R. Dodds, "Introduction" to Euripides, *Bacchae* (Oxford: Oxford University Press, 1944), p. xliii.

[86] There are striking parallels, largely unexplored, between tragedy and memories. The latter are typically simplified and condensed in their representation. Their details are reduced and simplified, and certain aspects of them are emphasized so they can be assimilated to a broader narrative scheme. Memory also adapts itself to the conventions of the age. See Gordon W. Allport and Leo Postman, *The Psychology of Rumor* (New York: Henry Holt, 1947); Frederic C. Bartlett, *Remembering: A Study in Experimental and Social Psychology* (Cambridge: Cambridge University Press, 1932); M. H. Erdelyi, "Repression, Reconstruction and Defense: History and Integration of the Psychoanalytic and Experimental Frameworks," in J. L. Singer, *Repression and Disassociation* (Chicago: University of Chicago Press, 1990), pp. 1–31.

Tragedies use tensions in vocabulary to bring to light discrepancies and contradictions. In *Oedipus*, words take on opposed meaning for speakers.[87] Words and actions are often reinforcing, but they can also be cross-cutting, and another means of communicating tensions or problematizing values and behavior.[88] When action on the stage subverts the meaning of what is said on stage, it encourages spectators to look for some way of reconciling word and deed at another level of understanding. *Ajax* ends with a eulogy to its eponymous hero, who has thrown himself on his sword. It is delivered by Odysseus, his sworn enemy. His praise for the most valiant of heroes, and by extension for the warrior life, is magnanimous but jarringly at odds with the reality of that life, symbolizes the ignominious death of Ajax and the ugly sight of his bloodied corpse. *Antigone* draws to a climax when Creon's effort to have the city commemorate Haemon's death are halted by his wife's cries and curses, reminiscent of Antigone's wailing after her brother's death. The chorus, which tries to make sense of a cruel world, proclaims that the gods mete out punishments to teach wisdom to proud men in their old age – a message undercut by the horrible and unwarranted suffering of the young.

Once again, Thucydides more closely resembles Aeschylus, Sophocles and Euripides than he does Herodotus. Beginning with the opening speeches of Book I – the appeals of Corcyra and Corinth to the Athenian assembly – his speakers deconstruct and reconstruct the meaning of words – (*dikē*, *nomos*, *philia*, *sophia*, *gennaios* (nobility) and *kalos* (good)) – that are central to justice and civil order. He puts words in the mouths of speakers that are belied by their behavior and that of their cities. This becomes so routine, that when in Book 5 the Athenians finally resort to *parrhēsia* (utter frankness) in the Melian Dialogue it comes as a double shock. Contradiction and reinforcement of words and deeds are *sēmata* (signs) that encourage readers to enter into a dialogue with the text in search of more complex meanings.

Tragedy offered a double vision in another sense. The citizen was both participant and observer. He took part in the affairs of state, generally

[87] On this point see Vernant, "Greek Tragedy: Problems of Interpretation"; Robert G. Goheen, *The Imagery of Sophocles' Antigone* (Princeton: Princeton University Press, 1951); Charles Segal, "Sophocles' Praise of Man and the Conflicts of the *Antigone*," *Arion* 3:2 (1964), pp. 46–60, and *Tragedy and Civilization: An Interpretation of Sophocles* (Norman, Ok.: University of Oklahoma Press, 1999), p. 55.

[88] Winnington-Ingram, *Sophocles*, pp. 11–72, 304–29; P. E. Easterling, "The Tragic Homer," *Bulletin of the Institute of Classical Studies*, 31 (1984), pp. 1–8; Goldhill, "The Great Dionysia and Civic Ideology," in Winkler and Zeitlin, *Nothing to Do with Dionysos?*, pp. 97–129. Vernant, "Tensions and Ambiguities"; V. Turner, *The Ritual Process: Structure and Anti-Structure* (Chicago: Aldine, 1969); P. E. Easterling, "The Tragic Homer," *Bulletin of the Institute of Classical Studies* 31 (1984), pp. 1–8.

through attendance at the assembly and jury service in the courts. Actors in a political drama see only part of what is going on, but the tragic audience is offered the full picture, presented to them, moreover, in a format intended to focus attention on its core dynamics and significance. In *Ajax*, Athena renders Odysseus invisible and brings him on stage to stand alongside her and observe how pitiful the once powerful Ajax has become. Odysseus recognizes that Athena's *technē* has given him the kind of vision normally available only to gods. The playwright's *technē* gives the audience the same omniscient and quasi-divine perspective.[89] Tragedy sought to arouse spectators emotionally not just intellectually. Both forms of engagement were intended to catalyze spectators to think more abstractly about their polis and themselves.[90] Thucydides uses the same methods for the same ends. His history, I will argue, encourages Athenians and other Greeks to relive their political traumas in the most vivid way and provides an intellectual structure to work through their meaning and implications for their lives and societies.

Nomos versus *Phusis*

Separated from each other and the wider world by mountain ranges and large bodies of water, Greek city states lived in relative isolation until the fifth century when economic growth, immigration and improvements in ship-building enabled them to expand their horizons and learn more about each other and other peoples. The diversity of customs they encountered led some Greeks to question the traditional belief that social practices were gods-given, and move toward a position of cultural relativism. In Athens, there was a century-long controversy about the relative importance of human nature (*phusis*) and convention (*nomos*).[91] Pindar, who declared that custom is the master of us all (*pantōn basileus*), and

[89] Segal, *Sophocles' Tragic World*, pp. 18–19, and "Spectator and Listener," in Jean-Pierre Vernant, ed., *The Greeks*, trans. Charles Lambert and Teresa Lavender Fagan (Chicago: University of Chicago Press, 1994), pp. 184–217, on the importance of vision and spectacle in tragedy and fifth-century Athens.

[90] Christian Meier, *Die Entstehung des Politischen bei dem Griechen* (Frankfurt: Suhrkamp, 1980); Euben, *The Tragedy of Political Theory*, p. 56; Rosenmeyer, *The Art of Aeschylus*, p. 83–84.

[91] The lexical field of *nomos* encompasses customs, mores, conventions, norms and laws. For Greeks, *nomos* as law was officially prescribed behavior, and *nomos* by convention, socially prescribed behavior. *Nomos* originally pertained to customs and conventions (but only those regarded as normatively beneficial) before some of them at least were written down in the form of laws. Hesiod is the first written reference, and Plato later wrote a treatise, *Nomoi*, in which he suggests that long-standing customs have higher authority than laws. *Nomos* can refer to all the habits of conforming to an institutional and social environment, whether these are the conglomerate of accumulated customs, the arbitrary rule imposed by leading classes to advance their interests or a rational system of law

Herodotus, who cited Pindar and offered a detailed and non-judgmental account of the diversity of human practices, represented one pole of this debate.[92] Sophocles railed against agnosticism and relativism. In his *Protagoras* and *Republic*, Plato, like Thucydides, attempted to transcend the opposition.[93]

The *nomos–phusis* controversy problematized moral and political obligations. Realists and some classicists consider Thucydides a believer in the primacy of *phusis*.[94] In support of this interpretation, they cite speeches that invoke universal laws of human behavior.[95] The Athenian envoys justify their empire this way before the Spartan assembly on the eve of the war. Their city has done nothing more than to act in accord with "human nature" (*hē anthrōpeia phusis*) that "the weaker should be subject to the stronger."[96] The Athenians later offer the same justification to the Melians. If realists and their classical allies are right, human drives for dominance (*archē*), ambition (*philotimia*) and self-aggrandizement (*pleonexia*) will sooner or later defeat any effort to construct an international order based on norms, conventions, laws and underlying common interests.[97] Is this pessimistic reading of Thucydides warranted?

that Greeks believed distinguished them from barbarians. *Phusis* is routinely translated as nature. It was used by Homer to designate things that are born and grow and retained its dynamic quality as its meaning shifted to describe the inherent characteristics of things. For fifth-century Ionian "physicists," it described all of nature or reality, or its constituent parts. Felix Heinemann, *Nomos und Physus* (Darmstadt: Wissenschaftliche Buchgesellschaft, 1965 [1942]), ch. 3, sec. 1–2; Untersteiner, *The Sophists*, p. 3; G. B. Kerferd, *The Sophistic Movement* (Cambridge: Cambridge University Press, 1981), p. 18; E. R. Dodds, *The Greeks and the Irrational* (Berkeley and Los Angeles: University of California Press, 1951), pp. 182–83; Arlene W. Saxonhouse, "Nature & Convention in Thucydides' History," *Polity* 10 (Summer 1978), pp. 461–87; on Socrates, see Xenophon, *Memorabilia*, 1.2.6, 1.6.5.

92 Herodotus, III.38, offers a wonderful, if probably apocryphal passage describing inquiries made by King Darius of Persia of Greeks and Indians and how each was horrified by the others customs for disposing of their dead. The most thorough study of this question is Heinemann, *Nomos und Physus*.

93 John H. Finley, Jr., *Thucydides* (Ann Arbor: University of Michigan Press, 1967) [1942], ch. 2; Kerferd, *The Sophistic Movement*, ch. 10.

94 G. E. M. de Ste. Croix, *The Origins of the Peloponnesian War* (London: Duckworth, 1972), p. 29; Saxonhouse, "Nature & Convention in Thucydides' *History*" pp. 461–87; N. G. L. Hammond, "The Particular and the Universal in Thucydides with Special Reference to that of Hermocrates at Gela," in Stadter, *The Speeches of Thucydides*, pp. 49–59; Jacqueline de Romilly, *La construction de la vérité chez Thucydide* (Paris: Julliard, 1990); Crane, *Thucydides and the Ancient Simplicity*, p. 297.

95 Crane, *Thucydides and the Ancient Simplicity*, pp. 297–98, for a good overview of the speeches and principles that they elucidate.

96 Thucydides, I.76. Other examples include III.45, III.82, III.84.

97 See especially, Kenneth N. Waltz, *Theory of International Politics* (Reading, Mass.: Addison-Wesley, 1979), p. 186; Robert Gilpin, "The Richness of the Tradition of Political Realism," in Robert O. Keohane, ed., *Neorealism and its Critics* (New York; Columbia University Press, 1986), p. 306.

Thucydides was deeply interested in the relationship between *nomos* and *phusis*, and his account of the Peloponnesian War can be read in part as an elaborate inquiry into this question. Thucydides modeled this aspect of his inquiry on medical research.[98] Hippocrates and his followers had charted the course of diseases in the human body, noting the symptoms that appeared at their onset and how they built up to a critical moment or crisis stage (*kairos*) that led to death or recovery. Thucydides followed this procedure with the social diseases of revolution and war; he described their manifestations and charted their course through the body politic to the point of social strife (*stasis*) and the disintegration of civil society. As physicians sought to learn more about the nature of the body from studying the progression of illness, so Thucydides hoped to learn about the mind.[99]

Thucydides made the link between physical and social diseases explicit in his parallel analysis of the Athenian plague of 430–428 and the Corcyrean revolution of the 420s. He uses the same Hippocratic word, *metabolai* (upheavals), to describe both events. In the case of the plague, he reports the widespread belief that it arrived in Athens via Africa, but refuses to speculate about its origins. In keeping with the Hippocratic tradition, he tells readers that "I shall simply set down its nature, and explain the symptoms by which perhaps it may be recognized by the student, if it should ever break out again." He describes in clinical detail the onset of the disease, subsequent symptoms, variation in the course of the illness, the suffering and fatalities it caused and how survivors were disfigured. "The plague-filled city was crowded with dead and dying, with bodies accumulating and decaying in houses, half-dead creatures roaming the streets in search of water and sacred places full of the corpses of those who had come there seeking relief."[100] As rich and poor died off in large numbers, the social fabric began to unravel. "Men, not knowing what was to become of them, became utterly careless of everything, whether sacred or profane." Family responsibilities were ignored in violation of the most fundamental ethical principle of Greek society: the obligation to help one's own *philoi*. People were increasingly afraid to visit each

[98] Charles Cochrane, *Thucydides and the Science of History* (London: Oxford University Press, 1929), ch. 3.

[99] On the Hippocratics, see Geoffrey E. R. Lloyd, *Magic, Reason and Experience: Studies in the Origin and Development of Greek Science* (Cambridge: Cambridge University Press, 1979); D. Wesley Smith, *The Hippocratic Tradition* (Ithaca: Cornell University Press, 1979); Jacques Jouanna, *Hippocrate*, 2nd ed. (Paris: Fayard, 1995); Jacques Jouanna, "The Birth of Western Medical Art," in Mirko Grmek, ed., *Western Medical Thought from Antiquity to the Middle Ages*, trans. Antony Shugaar (Cambridge, Mass.: Harvard University Press, 1998), pp. 22–71.

[100] Thucydides, II.47–50.

other, causing many sufferers to die from neglect. Sacred rituals were ignored, burial rites were dispensed with, and corpses were disposed of in any which way. "Lawless extravagance" became increasingly common, with men "coolly venturing on what they had formerly done in a corner." Those who suddenly inherited wealth "resolved to spend quickly and enjoy themselves, regarded their lives and riches as alike things of the day." Finally, fear of the gods and human laws all but disappeared as "each felt that a far severer sentence had been already passed upon them all and hung over their heads, and before this felt it was only reasonable to enjoy life a little."[101]

The other *stasis* Thucydides describes is the political and moral disintegration of Corcyra.[102] Once again, he begins with a detailed, almost day-by-day description of what transpired that sets the stage for a more impressionistic account that leads to some general observations. He concludes with a chilling description of the most gruesome atrocities.[103] Violent conflict between democratic and oligarchic factions, intervention by the foreign allies on both sides and civil war culminated in seven days of "butchery" in which Corcyreans, consumed by hatreds arising from private and political causes, tortured and killed any of their enemies they could lay their hands on. Every convention was violated: "sons were killed by their fathers, and suppliants dragged from the altar or slain upon it, while some were even walled up in the temple of Dionysus and died there." After Corcyra, Thucydides tells us, "the whole Hellenic world" was convulsed as democratic factions sought to assume or maintain power with Athenian help, and oligarchs attempted to do the same with the support of Sparta.[104] "The sufferings which revolution entailed upon the cities were many and terrible, such as have occurred and always will occur, as long as the nature of mankind remains the same, though in a severe or milder form, and varying in their symptoms, according to the variety of the particular cases."[105]

These extreme situations brought out the worst in human beings, and the passage quoted at the end of the last paragraph could be read as support for the universality of human nature. But Thucydides modifies his generalization in the next sentence: "In peace and prosperity states and

[101] Ibid., II.53.

[102] Similarities in Thucydides' analysis of the plague and Corcyrean revolution have been noted by Cochrane, *Thucydides and the Science of History*, pp. 133ff., and L. A. Losada, "Megara and Athens," *Classica et Mediaevalia* 30 (1969), p. 157, n. 31; Connor, *Thucydides*, p. 99; Clifford Orwin, "Stasis and Plague: Thucydides on the Dissolution of Society," *Journal of Politics* 50 (November 1988), pp. 831–47.

[103] Connor, *Thucydides*, pp. 100–01, notes a corresponding progression in the language from simple to complex and the syntax becomes more convoluted.

[104] Thucydides, III.70–81. [105] Ibid., III.82.

individuals have better sentiments because they do not find themselves suddenly confronted with imperious necessities; but war takes away the easy supply of daily wants, and so proves a rough master that brings most of men's characters to a level with their fortunes."[106] The arrow of causation is reversed; *stasis* does not so much reveal the hidden character of people as it shapes that character. People who have little to live for behave differently than people who have much to lose. The qualifier "most" is important because it indicates that not everyone responds the same way to social stimuli, not even in the extreme situation of *stasis*. In his description of the plague, Thucydides uses parallel constructions to describe how some people, fearful of succumbing to the plague, isolated themselves at great cost to friends and family, while others placed honor above survival and "honor made them unsparing of themselves." Some survivors participated in the greatest excesses, while others found "the most compassion" within themselves and were unstinting in administering to the ill and dying.[107] The same bifurcated response can be observed at the other end of the spectrum, in secure and prosperous societies, where the majority adhere to social and religious conventions, but a minority are unconstrained and destructive in their behavior.

Thucydides has a less deterministic understanding of human nature than most modern realists. By removing the constraints and obligations arising from convention, *stasis* encouraged expression of the worst human impulses, but among a minority of people it brought out the best. The plague and Corcyrean revolution – and the other "tests" to which human beings are subjected in the course of the Peloponnesian War – indicate that human nature includes a range of contradictory needs, desires and impulses.[108] People appear driven by needs of self-preservation, pleasure, recognition and power, but also by love, honor and self-esteem. The Melian Dialogue offers a nice counterpoint to the Corcyrean revolution in this connection. Opposition to Athens is futile, but the Melians choose to resist because they value freedom more than self-preservation, as did the Athenians when confronted by Persian invaders.

The Hippocratic physicians on whom Thucydides modeled his inquiry taught that *phusis* varied according to the environment. The author of *The Nature of Man* maintained that every body humor waxed and waned with the seasons, and the author of *Airs, Waters and Places* believed that physical and mental capabilities were shaped by the climate, and especially by

[106] Ibid., III.82. [107] Ibid., II.51.

[108] Nancy Kokaz, "Moderating Power: A Thucydidean Perspective," *Review of International Studies* 27 (2001), pp. 27–49, also makes the case for Thucydides' view of human nature as indeterminate.

the direction of the winds. Other doctors attributed the social characteristics of peoples to their physical environments. It was widely believed that traits acquired through social practice (*nomos*) could, over time, modify nature (*phusis*).[109] Thucydides also recognized that human behavior is a reflection of a complex interaction between *nomos* and *phusis*. Human nature can be harnessed for constructive as well as destructive ends; otherwise civilization could never have developed. This conclusion refocuses our attention on the meta-theme of Thucydides' narrative: the process that governs these outcomes and its implications for Greek civilization.

Logoi and *Erga*

The fourth and final level of the *History* addresses the relationship between *logoi* (words) and *erga* (deeds). Thucydides understood both *erga* and *logoi* are social constructions, and, contrary to many of his contemporaries, gave pride of place to *logoi*, not to *erga*. Social facts and social conventions create the intersubjective understandings on which all action depends. Social facts often misrepresent so-called brute facts, as Ober points out, but Thucydides considered this discrepancy a double-edged sword.[110] It could prove destructive, as it did in the Sicilian debate for all the reasons that Ober gives. But it was potentially beneficial, if not essential, to the maintenance of community. Democratic ideology in Athens exaggerated the equality that existed among classes and downplayed political, economic and social inequalities. It reconciled the *dēmos* to the existing social order and muted the class tensions that led to violent conflict and civil wars in many other *poleis*. The democratic ideology rested on myths: social facts at variance with reality, and on a history that bore only a passing relationship to so-called empirical facts, as the *Archeology* convincingly demonstrates.

It is no coincidence that Thucydides' observations about words in III.82 follow directly on his discussion of the consequences of the Corcyrean revolution for the rest of Hellas. "Revolution ran its course from city to city, and the places which it arrived at last, from having heard what had been done before, carried to a still greater excess the refinement of their inventions, as manifested in the cunning of their enterprises and the atrocity of their reprisals." Language is the vector by which the disease of revolution spreads, but also a contributing cause of

[109] Jacques Jouanna, "Hippocrates," in Jacques Brunschwig and Geoffrey E. R. Lloyd, trans. Catherine Porter, *Greek Thought: A Guide to Classical Knowledge* (Cambridge: Cambridge University Press, 2000), p. 657; Lloyd, *Magic, Reason and Experience*, p. 23.

[110] Ober, *Political Dissent in Democratic Athens*, pp. 57–59.

constant upheaval (*kinēsis*) and destruction.[111] Not only in Corcyra, but throughout much of Greece, "Words had to change their ordinary meanings and to take those which were now given them." Thucydides gives a string of examples, all of them indicative of the extent to which meanings and the values they expressed were subverted:

Reckless audacity came to be considered the courage of a loyal supporter; prudent hesitation, specious cowardice; moderation was held to be a cloak for unmanliness: ability to see all sides of a question, incapacity to act on any. Frantic violence became the attribute of manliness; cautious plotting a justifiable means of self-defense. The advocate of extreme measures was always trustworthy; his opponent a man to be suspected. To succeed in a plot was to have a shrewd head, and to divine a plot still shrewder; but to try to provide against having to do either was to break up your party and to be afraid of your adversaries.[112]

Words are the ultimate convention, and they too succumb to *stasis* in the sense that civilized conversation is replaced by less civilized exchange. Altered meanings changed the way people thought about each other, their society and obligations to it, and encouraged barbarism and violence by undermining long-standing conventions and the constraints they enforced. Thucydides attributes this process to "the lust for power arising from greed and ambition; and from these passions proceeded the violence of parties once engaged in contention." He is more specific in the next sentence. Leaders of democratic and aristocratic factions

sought prizes for themselves in those public interests which they pretended to cherish, and, recoiling from no means in their struggles for ascendancy, engaged in the direct excesses; not stopping at what justice or the good of the state demanded, but making the party caprice of the moment their only standard, and invoking with equal readiness the condemnation of an unjust verdict or the authority of the strong arm to glut the animosities of the hour.

Politicians used "fair phrases to arrive at guilty ends," and so began to degrade and abase the language.[113]

The Melian Dialogue is part and parcel of this process. The Greek words justice and just (*dikaion*) embraced a wide field of meaning, all of which conveyed positive worth.[114] W. K. C. Guthrie observes that

[111] Thucydides, III.83.1 [112] Ibid., III.82. [113] Ibid.

[114] *Dikē* means the order of the universe, and the man who respects that order is *dikaios*. By the latter part of the fifth century, order and justice had become problematized and did not always correspond. In *Antigone* and *Philoctetes*, principal characters have fundamental disagreements about what is just. Neoptolemus and Odysseus both claim *dikaiosunē* for their arguments and disagree as well about the nature of wisdom (*sophia*) and what is disgraceful (*aischros*) (1245–51). Hugh Lloyd-Jones, *The Justice of Zeus* (Berkeley: University of California Press, 1971), p. 161; Alasdair MacIntyre, *After Virtue*, 2nd ed. (Notre Dame: Notre Dame University Press, 1984), p. 134.

"*dikaion* is a word so strongly charged with moral approval, it was difficult for any Greek to say openly that he meant by it simply the interest of the stronger party."[115] But under the pressure of war, this inhibition began to break down, and even the meaning of *dikaion* was transformed. At Melos, the Athenians accused the Spartans of breaking with convention by justifying their actions on the basis of their superior power, but have no qualms about doing the same and asserting that "The strong do what they can and the weak suffer what they must."[116] *Stasis* is the result of a negative, reinforcing cycle of *logoi* and *erga*.

Thucydides follows his introductory remarks in Book I with the so-called *Archeology*, which describes the rise of Hellenic civilization.[117] In contrast to other fifth-century accounts of this process, Thucydides puts less emphasis on agriculture and the development of material technology, and more on the power of tyrants who cobbled together small settlements into larger kingdoms and alliances.[118] He portrays archaic Greece in constant movement (*kinēsis*) as a result of frequent migrations due to population growth, depletion of local agricultural resources and the depredations of pirates and invaders.[119] Civilization, defined as a state of peace and rest (*hēsuchia*), only became possible when communities combined to undertake common action, including the suppression of piracy. Common action required common understanding, and language was the

115 W. K. C. Guthrie, *The Sophists* (Cambridge: Cambridge University Press, 1971), p. 92.

116 Thucydides, V.89.

117 Ibid., I.2–21. An early influential work, E. Schwartz, *Das Geschichtswerk des Thucydides* (Bonn: Friedrich Cohen, 1929), p. 173, saw no rhyme or reason to the *Archeology*, and considered it a distraction from the rest of the history. Later scholars have been kinder, and some even regard it as the key to the history. J. R. Ellis, "The Structure and Argument of Thucydides' Archeology," *Classical Antiquity* 10:2 (1991), pp. 344–75, describes the *Archeology* as an elaborately constructed ring composition. Jacqueline de Romilly, "La crainte dans l'oeuvre de Thucydide," *Classica et Mediaevalia* 17 (1965), pp. 119–27, regards it as a manifesto of rationalism. V. J. Hunter, *Past and Present in Herodotus and Thucydides* (Princeton: Princeton University Press, 1982), pp. 44–45, suggests, as I do below, that it develops indices that can be used to measure the rise and fall of civilization. Finley, *Thucydides*, p. 88; de Romilly, "La crainte dans l'oeuvre de Thucydide," pp. 91, 266, and Connor, *Thucydides*, pp. 33–35 contend that it establishes the importance of power. Finley, *Thucydides*, p. 87, and Connor, *Thucydides*, pp. 33–35, suggest that the emphasis on sea power is intended to create a tension for readers between the actual outcome of the war, which they know, and the expectation, based on logic and power, that the future belongs to Athens, who should have emerged victorious.

118 Euripides, *Suppliant Women*, 201–13, produced *c*. 421, also stresses language. Theseus, who stands for Athenian humanity and the rule of law, blesses the god "who brought our life to order out of beastlike confusion, implanting in us first of all intelligence, then giving us a tongue to be the messenger of speech, that words might be distinguished. . . ."

119 Thucydides, I.2. *hēsuchia* was considered the antonym of *kinēseis politeia* (revolution). It is used by Pindar, *Pythian Odes*, 8.1, to describe the goddess of tranquillity and the calmness of spirit and right to rest earned by the victor in an athletic contest.

vehicle for that understanding and the foundation of political stability and civilization.[120] Civilization is the result of a *positive* reinforcing cycle of *logoi* and *erga*. The *Archeology* sets the stage for the history of decline that follows and helps to make a tragic interpretation plausible.

Greeks distinguished men from animals by their ability to speak and their preference for cooked meat. The word *ōmos* means raw, and is used by Homer to indicate disgust and defilement.[121] Thucydides uses *ōmos* on three occasions: to describe an Aetolian tribe that is so uncivilized that "they speak a language that is exceedingly difficult to understand, and eat their flesh raw"; in the Mytilenian debate, to characterize what many Athenians think about the previous day's decision to execute all the Mytilenians; and to describe the *stasis* that convulsed the Greek world beginning with the revolution in Corcyra.[122] Paul Rahe suggests that Thucydides uses *ōmos* on the last two occasions to indicate that the war, plague and revolutions reversed the process described in the *Archeology*.[123] The measure of rest (*hēsuchia*) and peace civilization brought about was disrupted by the *kinēsis* (literally, movement, but here upheaval and destruction) of war, that undermined *nomoi* (conventions), including those of language, and encouraged the kind of *tolma* (brazen daring) that provoked "raw" and savage deeds. The Greeks became increasingly irrational and inarticulate (*alogistos*) and, like animals, no longer capable of employing the *logos* (rational facilities and language) necessary for communal deliberation.

Is the rise and fall of civilization inevitable? Greek myth and saga portray a largely unalterable world, but one that is only tenuously connected to the time in which the audience dwells. The great playwrights carried on this tradition, and the tragic sense of life depends on the inevitability of *nemesis* and the mutability of things.[124] Like the plots of so much myth and epic, tragedy also relies on the intervention of the gods and the power of situations to generate pressures and psychological states that move the action along and leave limited choice to the individual. In *Agamemnon*, Agamemnon confronts a dilemma from which there is no exit. The chorus tells us that the most he can do is preserve his dignity and learn from his

[120] Ibid., I.3.

[121] *Iliad*, IV.39–42. In his rage, Zeus tell Hera of his desire to have the gates of Troy breached and Priam, his sons and the Trojan armies devoured "raw." Achilles (22.407–9) taunts Hector with the threat that he will "hack your flesh away and eat you raw." Priam's wife (XXIV.253), lamenting the death of her son Hector, exclaims that she could sink her teeth into Achilles' liver and eat him raw.

[122] Thucydides, III.94, III.36, and III.82.1.

[123] Rahe, "Thucydides' Critique of Realpolitik," p. 123.

[124] Beye, *Ancient Greek Literature and Society*, pp. 199, 202.

suffering.[125] Herodotus imported this tradition into prose. His Xerxes has no control over his fate; the power of Persia and the insolence of the Greeks compel him to attempt their conquest. When he has second thoughts, the gods intervene through Mardonius to push him to invade Greece, just as in the *Iliad*, where the Argives are compelled to make war against Troy by Athena who speeds down the peak of Olympus to convince Odysseus prevent their departure.[126]

For Herodotus, the stories of Croesus and Xerxes are concrete manifestations of a timeless cycle of *hubris-atē-hamartia-nemesis* that can be expected to repeat itself as long as humans stride the earth. For many ancients, life alternated between good and bad, but the human condition never changed. Thucydides reflects this view, and it is articulated by some of his characters. The Athenian envoys at Sparta portray themselves as prisoners of history and seem to understand that they are playing roles in a grand, historical drama, although not yet framed as a tragedy.[127] Pericles warns his countrymen that one day they too will be forced to yield "in obedience with the general law of decay."[128]

Thucydides was nevertheless not as pessimistic as many realist readings suggest. Why would he have invested decades in the research and writing of his history and offered it as a "possession for all time" if he had thought human beings and their societies were prisoners of circumstance and fate? He must have believed that people possess at least some ability to control their destinies. The appropriate analogy is to psychotherapy.[129] Freudian therapy assumes that people will repeatedly enact counterproductive scripts until they confront and come to terms with the experiences that motivate their behavior. This can only be achieved through regression; patients must allow themselves to relive painful experiences they have repressed and come to understand how they shape their present behavior. Sophists relied on a somewhat similar process. Their works were offered as courses of study that engage the emotions and mind. By experiencing the elation, disappointment, anguish and other emotions a story provoked, and by applying reason to work through its broader meaning and implications, readers could gain enlightenment. Hippocratic physicians put great store in the curative power of words. Euripides' Phaedra

[125] Aeschylus, *Agamemnon*, 176–83.

[126] *The Iliad of Homer*, trans. Richard Lattimore (Chicago: University of Chicago Press, 1951), Book II, lines 135–210, pp. 80–81.

[127] Ibid., I.75. [128] Thucydides, II.64.

[129] This kind of Freudian healing should not be confused with the healing of false beliefs that Martha Nussbaum, *The Therapy of Desire: Theory and Practice in Hellenistic Ethics* (Princeton: Princeton University Press, 1994), finds at the core of Hellenistic philosophy.

and Andromache describe words as sources of power and psychological compensation. Aeschylus' plays are based on the maxim of *pathei mathos*, of learning and transcending one's situation through the pain associated with understanding that situation. The chorus in *Agamemnon* explains that "Zeus shows man the way to think, setting understanding securely in the midst of suffering. In the heart there drips instead of sleep a labor of sorrowing memory; and there comes to us all unwilling prudent measured thought; the grace of gods who sit on holy thrones somehow comes with force and violence."

There is ample Greek precedent for Thucydides' project.[130] Neither sophists, tragic playwrights nor analysts *tell* readers or analysands what lessons to learn; all believe that genuine understanding (*saphōs skopein*) can only be internalized and influence behavior if it arises out of a process of cathartic self-discovery.[131] As I noted earlier, this was one of the purposes of Greek theater. Actors in a political drama can only observe part of it, but the audience in a drama can get a sense of the broader picture, especially if it is presented to them in a stylized format deliberately intended to highlight its core dynamics and significance. Tragedy involved spectators emotionally, but also made them think more abstractly about themselves and their polis.[132] Thucydides wrote in this tradition. His history encourages Athenians and other Greeks to relive traumatic political experiences in the most vivid way and to work through their meaning and implications for their lives and societies. I believe he harbored the hope that such a course of "therapy" could help free people of the burdens of the past and produce the kind of wisdom that could enable societies from time to time to transcend their scripts. The cycle of good and bad would continue, but some of the bad might be averted, or at least postponed.

[130] Entralgo, *Therapy of the Word*, pp. 48–49, 66–95, on "logotherapy" in ancient Greece; Stephen Halliwell, *Aristotle's Poetics* (London: Duckworth, 1986), pp. 198–201; Elizabeth S. Belfiore, *Tragic Pleasures: Aristotle on Plot and Emotion* (Princeton: Princeton University Press, 1992), pp. 257–60.

[131] Kerferd, *The Sophistic Movement*.

[132] Meier, *Die Entstehung des Politischen bei dem Griechen*; Euben, *The Tragedy of Political Theory*, p. 56. Bennett Simon, *Mind and Madness in Ancient Greece: The Classical Roots of Modern Psychiatry* (Ithaca: Cornell University Press, 1978), pp. 142–43, contends that tragic knowledge and knowledge through suffering is a kind of therapy that is different from and antithetical to catharsis. The tragic playwright's approach comes closer to that of modern psychotherapy, which has long since rejected the idea that catharsis has curative potential. Segal, *Tragedy and Civilization*, p. 48, suggests that confrontation with chaos is a profoundly civilizing experience. Under the protective umbrella of the Great Dionysia, tragedies could express, and allow spectators to feel, emotional states that were otherwise taboo and suppressed. These included loss of control, the breakdown of conventions and the release of the most primal human passions.

Transcending old scripts requires an alternative vocabulary. Crane argues that Thucydides wanted to reconstruct the aristocratic ideology, the "ancient simplicity"(*euēthēs*) to which he was born and raised.[133] Thucydides was undeniably attracted to the "ancient simplicity." Evidence for this is the location of his discussion of it in the text, which follows his description of *stasis* at Corcyra.[134] The intended inference is that religion, honor and aristocratic values promoted a tranquil and secure social and political order, and their decline removed restraints to unprincipled self-aggrandizement.

The passage discussing the ancient simplicity is unabashedly nostalgic but also brutally realistic. The ancient simplicity had not merely declined, it had been "laughed down and disappeared."[135] Here and elsewhere Thucydides recognized the gulf that had opened between the old and the new, and how the lifestyle associated with the ancient simplicity had passed and could not readily be restored. Greece, and especially Athens, had been transformed by what can only be called a process of modernization. Population growth, coinage, trade, the division of labor, major military undertakings and empire had given rise to new classes, new ideas and values and new social and political practices to cope with a more complicated and competitive world. The Athenian empire had become so powerful that it no longer needed to rely on the standard pattern of client–patron relations based on obligation and the mutual exchange of favors and services. Success made the traditional system of political relationships and the values on which it rested look old-fashioned and unnecessary, even a hindrance. The fate of Sparta also testified to this change. Its influence in Greece derived largely from the symbolic capital it had accumulated in the form of reliability in the eyes of others, especially allies. Spartans had gone to war to preserve this capital and in the vain hope that defeat of Athens would stave off the changes that threatened their traditional way of life.[136] Sparta emerged as the victor in the war, but it was no longer the same polis. Spartans had to become more like their adversary to defeat it, perhaps the most compelling evidence that the old ways were doomed.

Thucydides recognized the impracticality of trying to turn the clock back; the aristocratic order and its values had become anachronistic, and the effort to reimpose oligarchic rule at the end of the Peloponnesian War had failed miserably. I believe he had a subtler project in mind: adaptation of older values and language to present circumstances to create a

[133] Crane, *Thucydides and the Ancient Simplicity*.
[134] Thucydides, III.83. [135] Ibid., III.83.
[136] See the discussion in Chapter 2 of the Spartan decision for war.

more workable synthesis that would accommodate progress but mitigate its excesses. Ober contends that Thucydides looked back at Periclean Athens for his model. It functioned well because of the balance of power that existed between the masses of citizens (*dēmos)* and the elite of rich and influential men (*hoi dunatoi*). The need of each group to take the other into account, and the presence of leaders like Pericles, who mediated and muted these class-based tensions, led to policies that more often reflected the interest of the community (*hoi Athēnaioi*) instead of merely their democratic or aristocratic factions.[137] In Book I, Thucydides portrays Pericles as someone who personified the ancient simplicity but had mastered the new arts of oratory and statecraft. His success in governing Athens under the most trying circumstances may have convinced Thucydides that such an amalgam was desirable and possible. But his praise of Pericles is another one of his judgments that is partly subverted later in the text. In Book IV, Thucydides offers Hermocrates of Syracuse as another role model. He is intended to be a counterpoint to Pericles and a more accurate guide to how foreign policy restraint can be sold to the public, and a more peaceful international order maintained. This may be the closest that Thucydides comes to revealing his own approach to security.

In his appeal to Sicilians for unity against Athens, Hermocrates inverts key realist tenets of foreign policy that are associated with Pericles.[138] As Connor observes, the "law of the stronger" becomes an injunction for the weaker to unite, and Hermocrates goes on to exploit the widespread fear of Athens to justify forethought and restraint but also common defensive action.[139] On the eve of war, Pericles sought to inspire confidence in his fellow citizens, but Hermocrates aims at intensifying their fears. The Athenians and their enemies attributed Athenian success to their ingenuity, speed of execution and confidence in their ability to face challenges.[140] Hermocrates finds strength in the restraint and caution that come from recognition of the limits of knowledge and power and contemplation of the future (*promēthia*) with an eye toward its unpredictability. Pericles had urged his countrymen to spurn Sparta's peace overtures, but Hermocrates favored accommodation and settlement. Pericles' successors, especially Cleon and Alcibiades, encouraged the Athenians to contemplate the rewards that would come from imperial expansion.

[137] Ober, *Political Dissent in Democratic Athens*. [138] Thucydides, IV.59–64.

[139] Ibid., IV.62; Connor, *Thucydides*, pp. 123–26; S. Sara Monoson and Michael Loriaux, "The Illusion of Power and the Disruption of Moral Norms: Thucydides' Critique of Periclean Policy," *American Political Science Review* 92 (June 1998), pp. 285–98.

[140] Thucydides, I.68–71, on the Corinthian speech to the Spartan assembly on the eve of war, and II.35–46, for Pericles' funeral oration.

Hermocrates implicitly urges his audience to consider the advantages they already possess and the loss that war could entail. Hermocrates – and Thucydides – had an intuitive grasp of prospect theory, which is based on the robust psychological finding that people will take greater risks to prevent loss than they will to make gains.[141]

Sophists pioneered the rhetorical strategy of "antilogic."[142] Zeno silenced his opponents by showing how their arguments also implied their negations and were thus contradictory.[143] Thucydides makes extensive use of antilogic. He examines every so-called law of politics, appears to validate it, but ultimately subverts it by showing the unintended and contradictory consequences that flow from its rigorous application. This is most obvious with the principles espoused by "demagogues" like Cleon, but it is also true of Pericles.[144] Thucydides did not spoonfeed conclusions to his readers; they had to reflect on his narrative, speeches and dialogues. Hermocrates' speech is his most overt attempt to point readers in the right direction. By emotions and thought – feeling the pain of Athens' decline and grasping the reasons why – readers could experience his history as a course of "logotherapy." Its larger purpose was to make readers wary of the sweet and beguiling words of demagogues, but also of any politician who advocated policies at odds with conventions that facilitate domestic and international order.[145] This caution was the first and essential step toward the restructuring of language and the

[141] Prospect theory also indicates that people are more willing to accept risks to prevent loss than to make gain, which would cut against the grain of Hermocrates' argument. For an overview, see, Amos Tversky and Daniel Kahneman, "Advances in Prospect Theory: Cumulative Representation of Uncertainty," *Journal of Risk and Uncertainty* 5 (1992), pp. 297–323; Jack S. Levy, "An Introduction to Prospect Theory," *Political Psychology* 13 (June 1992), pp. 171–86, and "Loss Aversion, Framing, and Bargaining: The Implications of Prospect Theory for International Conflict," *International Political Science Review* 17 (1996), pp. 179–95.

[142] Protagoras is credited with having begun the tradition of the contest (*agōn*) for thrashing out ideas in "opposed speeches." He taught his pupils how to make arguments for one side and then the other. These double arguments (*dissoi logoi*) take the form of paired speeches in Thucydides. Diogenes Laertius, 9.51 and Clement of Alexandria, *Stromates*, 6.65.

[143] Kerferd, *The Sophistic Movement*, p. 85.

[144] The word demagogue, which today has a pejorative connotation, was neutral when *dēmagōgos* (from the root, to lead) first came into use in the fifth century. Moses I. Finley, "The Athenian Demagogues," *Past and Present* 21:1 (1962), pp. 3–24, Connor, *The New Politicians of Fifth-Century Athens*, pp. 9–10, 109–10.

[145] Monoson and Loriaux, "The Illusion of Power and the Disruption of Moral Norms," suggest that Thucydides also had Pericles in mind. Niall W. Slater, *Spectator Politics: Metatheatre and Performance in Aristophanes* (Philadelphia: University of Pennsylvania Press, 2002), pp. 236–37, advances a parallel thesis about the parodies of Aristophanes. Slater contends that *Acharnians, Knights* and *Wasps* teach their audiences "performance criticism," with the goal of making Athenians less vulnerable to rhetoric in the assembly and law courts by understanding how it is constructed.

reconstitution of conventions that would permit economic and intellectual progress but maintain political order.

Modernization

The feedback loop between *logoi* and *erga* made possible Greek civilization, but also the most destructive forms of war and civil strife. The so-called "Archeology" of Thucydides describes the positive side of this interaction and how it went hand-in-hand with a process of modernization. Political stability was a by-product of tyrants who were gradually replaced by kings and then by oligarchies.[146] The development of seagoing ships encouraged trade, the division of labor, introduction of coinage and the accumulation of wealth. By the mid-fifth century, modernization had transformed many of the coastal regions and islands of Greece, linking them together economically. Cities sprung up and became the center of political and cultural life. These changes marginalized agricultural communities, or drew them into the market economy as suppliers of produce to nearby cities. Spartiates felt understandably threatened, and their desire to preserve their traditional way of life was an important underlying cause of their decision for war. Economic development was equally unsettling to cities on the cutting edge of change because it exacerbated class conflict and gave rise to lifestyles and ways of thinking at odds with the traditions that sustained civic order.

Athens was the most populous, wealthiest and cosmopolitan city. The produce of the world was drawn into its harbor and wealth, generated through agriculture produce, artisanal production and trade, permitted its elite to lead lives of unrivaled elegance and comfort. Thucydides tells us that the city's wealth enabled Pericles to carry out an extraordinary program of monumental building.[147] Wealth and empire, and the intellectual and artistic flowering that came in their wake, confronted Athens with a series of challenges to traditional ways of conceptualizing identities and social relations at every level of interaction. In both economics and politics, this conflict focused on the importance of reciprocity as the basis of social relations.[148] For Thucydides, this conflict came to a head in the debate over Corcyra.

[146] Thucydides, I.18, notes that Sparta's achievement of internal political stability at an early date gave it an advantage over its neighbors and enabled it to intervene in their affairs. Chester G. Starr, "The Decline of the Early Greek Kings," *Historia* 10 (1961), pp. 257–72.

[147] Thucydides, II.38.

[148] L. Pearson, "Popular Ethics in the World of Thucydides," *Classical Philology* 52 (1957), pp. 226–44; A. W. H. Adkins, *Moral Values and Political Behavior in Ancient Greece: From Homer to the End of Fifth Century Greece* (London: 1972), pp. 133–39; P. Karavites,

The first pair of speeches in the history, those of the Corcyrean and Corinthian ambassadors to the Athenian Assembly, confront Athenians with their most critical decision since the commitment to oppose Persia sixty years before. The speeches serve an obvious dramatic purpose: they set in motion the chain of events that leads to war with Sparta. They also convey a subtle and significant message. Corcyreans and Corinthians alike insist that justice (*dikē*) is on their side. But the Corcyreans emphasize expediency (*to sumpheron*) over justice. They assert at the outset that a party seeking alliance must demonstrate why it will be advantageous (*hōs kai sumphora deontai*) to its partner. The Corcyreans repeat this assertion three times in an obvious effort to establish short-term interest as the relevant frame of reference for their actions and the Athenian response. They go on to describe the military advantages of alliance; how it will forestall any possibility of Corinth being able to challenge Athenian naval supremacy by laying its hands on the Corcyrean fleet. They not only subvert the traditional meaning of justice, but of friendship and generosity (*charis*) by using it to refer to a favor calculated to obtain a specific return.[149] In retrospect, it is apparent that this very first speech of the history begins the process of deconstructing language and the values its sustains.

The Corinthians emphasize justice as the basis for their claim and the Athenian response. They use eighteen words with the stem *dik-* to make the case that Corcyra has acted unjustly and that Athens would behave justly by remaining neutral.[150] Corcyra, they insist, is an outlaw state living in isolation. The unspoken reference here is to the Greek norm that all social relations, including those among poleis, are embedded in a web of interlocking relationships and obligations. People who are not members of communities, and not bound by their conventions, are dangerous and unreliable because they are driven by the basest of impulses – and this is how the Corinthians portray the Corcyreans. In contrast, the Corinthians characterize themselves as responsible neighbors; they remind the Athenians that they sent twenty ships to participate in their

"'*Euergesia*' in Herodotus and Thucydides as a Factor in Interstate Relations," *Revue internationale des droits de l'antiquité*, 3rd series, 27 (1980), pp. 69–79; Nicole Loraux, *L'Invention d'Athènes: Histoire de l'oraison funèbre dans la cité classique* (Paris:1981), p. 81; Anna Missiou, "Reciprocal Generosity in the Foreign Affairs of Fifth-Century Athens and Sparta," in Christopher Gill, Norman Postlethwaite and Richard Seaford, *Reciprocity in Ancient Greece* (Oxford: Oxford University Press, 1998), pp. 181–97.

149 Thucydides, I.32–36 for the speech. Hooker, "χάρις and ἀρεΐή in Thucydides," *Hermes* 102, 1 (1974), pp. 164–69. and Crane, *Thucydides and the Ancient Simplicity*, p. 106, for the Corcyrean emphasis on advantage.

150 Thucydides, I.37–43. Crane, *Thucydides and the Ancient Simplicity*, p. 106, for the word count.

war against Aegina and dissuaded Sparta from coming to the aid of the rebellious Samians. These "gifts" (*dōra*) created the expectation of repayment, and the Corinthians assert their claim for reciprocity.[151] If Athens allies with Corcyra, the Corinthians imply, their decision would not only rupture a long-standing friendship, but put Athens outside the Greek community and invite classification as another outlaw state. By remaining neutral Athens would act justly, and, the Corinthians insist, what is just is in the long run also expedient (*sumphora*).

The next debate, before the Spartan assembly, pits the Corinthians against the Athenians. Earlier, I argued that the Corinthian appeal was intended to shame a naive and unworldly lot of Spartiates into declaring war. The speech can also be read as a commentary on the old and the new ways of thinking about political relationships, and points to an even more fundamental explanation for the Athenian alliance with Corcyra. According to the Corinthians:

> The Athenians are addicted to innovation, and their designs are characterized by swiftness alike in conception and execution; you have a genius for keeping what you have got, accompanied by a total want of invention, and when forced to act you never go far enough. Again, they are adventurous beyond their power, and daring beyond their judgment, and in danger they are sanguine; your wont is to attempt less than is justified by your power, to mistrust even what is sanctioned by your judgment, and to fancy that from danger there is no release. Further, there is promptitude on their side against procrastination on yours; they are never at home, you are most disinclined to leave it, for they hope by their absence to extend their acquisitions, you fear by your advance to endanger what you have left behind. They are swift to follow up a success, and slow to recoil from a reverse . . . Thus they toil on in trouble and danger all the days of their life, with little opportunity for enjoying, being ever engaged in getting: their only idea of a holiday is to do what the occasion demands, and to them laborious occupation

[151] Marcel Mauss, *The Gift: The Form and Reason for Exchange in Archaic Societies*, trans. W. D. Halls (New York: Norton, 1990 [1925]), focused academic attention on how gifts build relationships between donors and recipients. Marshall Sahlins, *Stone Age Economics* (Chicago: Aldine-Atherton, 1972), conceives of exchange and reciprocity as the glue of pre-political social organizations, and documented how gift exchange is usually unequal, creating a hierarchical chain among donors and recipients. W. Donlan, "Reciprocities in Homer," *Classical World* 75 (1981–82), pp. 137–75, distinguishes between "balanced" reciprocity, in which a return is stipulated, and "general" reciprocity, in which only the expectation of return is established. Jonathan M. Parry and Maurice Bloch, eds., *Money and the Morality of Exchange* (Cambridge: Cambridge University Press, 1989), pp. 64–93, suggest that there are two kinds of transactions: those concerned with the well-being of individuals and those that maintain the social and metaphysical order. In the modern age, production, consumption and distribution are focused on the individual and his or her advancement, but in ancient Greece, as in other traditional societies, they were often envisaged as social or ritual exchanges that established, cemented and maintained relationships within or across families, communities and generations. Gill *et al.*, *Reciprocity in Ancient Greece*, elaborates on this theme.

is less of a misfortune than the peace of a quiet life. To describe their character in a word, one might truly say that they were born into the world to take no rest themselves and to give none to others.[152]

Like many modern portrayals of national character, the Corinthian descriptions are stock stereotypes, and would have been immediately recognized as such by contemporaries familiar with the plays of Aeschylus and Aristophanes.[153] The Spartans represent the traditional way of life based on subsistence agriculture in which *apragmosunē* and *hēsuchia* (rustic peace and quiet) were the highest goals to which people could reasonably aspire. Efforts to improve one's material lot were disparaged as hubris – considered an attempt to transcend human limits and become like the gods – and behavior that was dangerous to the individual and community alike.[154] There was no escaping the cruelty of life, and *sōphrosune* (self-control, but also acceptance of one's fate) is the highest form of wisdom. The Athenians are a parody of modernity and its commercial, materialist culture. They are driven by *polupragmosunē*, literally, trespass, but widely used in the late fifth century by critics of modernity to signify a kind of metaphysical restlessness, intellectual discontent and meddlesomeness that found expression in *pleonexia* (envy, ambition, search of glory, monetary greed, lust for power and conquest).[155] Many stereotypes capture an element of truth, and the Athenian stereotype reflected widespread recognition that its civic culture and wealth represented something novel and bewildering, admirable and frightening. Greeks were divided in their opinion about whether Athens should be shunned or emulated.

Thucydides is telling us that the qualities that made Athenians different were both a cause *and* an expression of modernity. His subsequent narrative makes apparent that he thought that ambition and restlessness on the one hand, and modernity on the other, were mutually constitutive

[152] Thucydides, I.70.

[153] William Arrowsmith, "Aristophanes' BIRDS: The Fantasy Politics of Eros," *Arion* 1, 1 (1973), pp. 119–67, makes a compelling case for the convergence between the Corinthian description of the Athenians and Aristophanes' Pisthetairos, the quintessential Athenian man.

[154] Lloyd-Jones, *The Justice of Zeus*.

[155] Thucydides, VI.87.3, uses *polupragmosunē* only once in his text, to characterize Athenians as "hyperactive," but is widely used by other authors to describe Athens. See Victor Ehrenberg, "*Polypragmosyne*: A Study in Greek Politics, *Journal of Hellenic Studies* 67 (1947), pp. 46–67; John H. Finley, "Euripides and Thucydides," *Harvard Studies in Classical Philology* 49 (1938), pp. 23–68; June W. Allison, "Thucydides and *Polypragmosyne*," *American Journal of Ancient History* 4 (1979), pp. 10–22; Kurt A. Raaflaub, "Democracy, Power and Imperialism in Fifth-Century Athens," in J. Peter Euben, John R. Wallach and Josiah Ober, eds., *Athenian Political Thought and the Reconstruction of American Democracy* (Ithaca: Cornell University Press, 1994), pp. 103–48.

and reinforcing. Athenians could not resist the prospect of gain held out by alliance with Corcyra. Spartiates, moved by shame, envy and honor, could not refuse their allies' request for assistance. If defense of tradition was the "truest precondition" (*alēthestatē prophasis*) of Sparta's vote for war, embrace of modernity was the truest condition of Athenian willingness to challenge Sparta. The Peloponnesian War was a contest between Athens and Sparta, but they are personifications of the old and the new, and the conflict between conflicting identities, discourses and ways of life.

In Chapter 2, I suggested that Thucydides' one authorial statement about the origins of the war is best understood as a judgment about who was most responsible for the war. The subsequent narrative of Book I attributes the war to the peculiar political cultures of both hegemons, the machinations of third parties and a series of miscalculations made by their leaders. In this chapter, I suggest that Thucydides wants us to consider modernization the most fundamental cause of war; it made Athens the most powerful political unit in Greece, transformed its political and intellectual culture and threatened Sparta's way of life and core identity. The hyperactive and aggressive political culture of Athens, the miscalculations of Pericles and the overconfidence of the Spartan war party might all be understood, at least in part, as epiphenomena of the modernization process. Seemingly diverse, if reinforcing, causes of war are thus linked and give a new meaning to Thucydides' assertion in Book I.23.6 that "the growth of the power of Athens, and the alarm which this inspired in Sparta, made war inevitable."

Thucydides the constructivist?

Fifth-century Greece experienced the first *Methodenstreit*. "Positivists" insisted on the unity of the physical and social worlds and the existence of an ordered reality that could be discovered through the process of inquiry. They were opposed by "proto-constructivists" who regarded the social world as distinct and human relations as an expression of culturally determined and constantly evolving conventions.[156] Early Greek thinkers

[156] I do not want to make too facile comparisons and exaggerate the parallels between ancient and modern philosophies of social inquiry; there were important differences in the ideas of these schools and their relative timing of advances in science and philosophy. In the modern era, advances in mathematics made modern science possible, and ultimately, social science too. In Greece, the age of mathematical discovery came after these philosophical debates were under way. Athenian interest in mathematics really began a generation after Thucydides. Euclid did not write his *Elements* until the end of the fourth century, and Archimedes made his contributions almost a century later. Lloyd, *Magic, Reason and Experience*, offers a good overview.

accepted the divine nature of the world and considered human customs as part of an overall, unified scheme of nature.[157] The goal of the Ionian proto-physicists was to discover the original principle, the *archē*, that determined all the other regularities, social and physical, of the universe. Reality was out there, waiting to be described in terms of impersonal forces and agency which also expressed those forces. In the fifth century, sophists directed their inquiry away from nature to human beings. According to Werner Jaeger, "The concept of *phusis* was transferred from the whole universe to a single part of it – to mankind; and there it took on a special meaning. Man is subject to certain rules prescribed by *his own* nature."[158]

This shift coincided with closer Greek interactions with alien cultures and the discovery, previously noted, that their practices and beliefs differed markedly from their own. Discovery of cultural diversity influenced philosophical inquiry and encouraged a subjectivist epistemology in which *nomos* was contrasted with *phusis*, which was considered by many to be the more important determinant of human behavior. "The deeds themselves" (*auta ta erga*) and a concept of the "real world" became problematic, as did the assumption that either could be understood through observation. Thucydides' contemporary, Democritus, proclaimed that things were "sweet by convention, bitter by convention, hot by convention, cold by convention," and went on to reason that all observation was illegitimate. Democritus was nevertheless an upholder of *nomos*, and did his best to put it on a firmer philosophical foundation. He taught that law benefits everyone, and by obeying it we come to recognize its excellence (*aretē*). Philosophers should accordingly encourage "the *nomos* of the soul," the self-respect and sense of shame that discourages wrongdoing.[159]

Philosophical scepticism encouraged the belief that truth was relative.[160] Sophist epistemology even spawned a cognate to postmodernism. Its representatives – Protagoras (490–420) is the best known – proclaimed man "the measure of all things," and dismissed most claims to knowledge as rhetorical strategies of self-aggrandizement.[161] Plato's

[157] The roots of the Greek Enlightenment go back to sixth-century Ionia, to the path-breaking thinkers Hecataeus, Xenophanes, Heraclitus and speculative physicists like Anaxagoras and Democritus. Hecataeus, frg. 1, is the first known Greek to have ridiculed myths about the gods.

[158] Jaeger, *Paideia*, I, p. 306.

[159] Democritus, frgs. 1, 25.9–11, 181. The only things not conventions for Democritus were atoms and the void.

[160] Lloyd, *Magic, Reason and Experience*, pp. 236–39. Xenophanes, frg. 15, suggested that "If the ox could paint a picture, his god would look like an ox."

[161] Plato, *Theaetetus*, 152a, quoting Protagoras.

Callicles declared that justice was properly invoked by the powerful to justify their authority and advance their parochial interests.[162] Philosophical nihilism reached its fullest expression in Critias, who defined justice in terms of power, and found justification for this in human practice – the very argument the Athenian envoys made at Melos. Critias would be good grist for the mill of any contemporary critic of postmodernism. He was a politician and one of the "Thirty Tyrants" who briefly ruled Athens after its defeat in 404, and infamous for his corruption and brutality.[163] Plato was critical of the sophists; he opposed their reduction of law to custom, and the equation, by some of them, of justice with tyranny. He nevertheless treated them seriously in his dialogues, especially, *Protagoras*, and argued against their efforts to explain physical and social reality purely in terms of its phenomenal aspects. He sought to restore objectivity and the status of universal laws by discovering an underlying, ultimate reality that would provide a foundation for a universal nation of justice and social order.[164]

Like contemporary constructivists, Thucydides was fascinated by convention (*nomos*) and the role it played in regulating human behavior. The Greek language also made this connection, as the word for lawlessness was *anomia* – the absence of conventions. Thucydides' history makes it apparent that he regarded conventions as more than constraints; conventions, and the rituals they establish, construct reality by providing frames of reference people use to understand the world and themselves. They help define individual and collective identities, reinforce group solidarity and the individual's sense of belonging to the group. It may be going too far to claim that Thucydides initiated the "linguistic turn" in ancient philosophy, but he certainly shared constructivists' emphasis on the importance of language. He thought language enabled the shared meanings and conventions that made civilization possible. His history explored the relationship between words (*logoi*) and deeds (*erga*), and documented the double feedback loop between them. Shared meanings of words are the basis for conventions and civic cooperation. When words lose their meanings, or their meanings are subverted, the conventions that depend on them lose their force, communication becomes difficult and civilization declines. Thucydides exploited the growth and evolution of

[162] Plato, *Gorgias*, 482a2–483d6, 488b8–489b6.

[163] Michael Nill, *Morality and Self-Interest in Protagoras, Antiphon and Democritus* (Leiden: E. J. Brill, 1985), pp. 8–9; W. K. C. Guthrie, *A History of Greek Philosophy*, 5 vols. (Cambridge: Cambridge University Press, 1969), III, pp. 38–39.

[164] Plato, *Republic*, 515a5–6; *Protagoras*, 315c–d, 350c–351b, and *Theaetetus*, 167c. Guthrie, *A History of Greek Philosophy*, 3, pp. 68, 92–93; Kerferd, *The Sophistic Movement*, p. 174.

the Greek language for purposes of expression and precision, and probably coined more neologisms that any other fifth-century author. One of his objectives was the considered restoration of traditional meanings of words to help resurrect the conventions they sustained. In this sense, he anticipated Plato.[165]

The core of constructivism is hard to define because there is so much variation among authors. In a thoughtful analysis of this literature, Ted Hopf suggests that constructivism has two components.[166] The first is appreciation of social structure, whether understood sociologically, as in the thin institutionalist accounts of Martha Finnemore and others, or linguistically, as attempted by John Ruggie, Nicholas Onuf and Friedrich Kratochwil. Second, is the acceptance of the mutual constitution of agents and structures.[167] Constructivism, in its "thicker" linguistic version, is interested in the logic of intelligibility, that is what makes some actions more imaginable and thus more probable than others.[168] The

[165] Well before Thucydides, Greek philosophy debated the importance and meaning of language. There was some recognition that language mediated human understanding of reality, and thus constituted a barrier to any perfect grasp of that reality. One attempted solution to this problem was to assert that names are not arbitrary labels but imitations of their objects. Other philosophers (e.g., Hermogenes) insisted that words are arbitrary in origin, and do not represent any reality. Socrates tried to split the difference, arguing that things have a fixed nature and words attempt to reproduce that nature, but the imitation is imperfect, and this is why languages vary so much. Moreover, all attempts at imitation have become corrupted over time. Considerable effort went into recapturing the meaning of words and names in the late fifth century, and Thucydides must be situated in that tradition. I see no evidence that he believed in the original meaning of words, but certainly wanted to restore earlier meanings, supportive of *homonoia,* that had been subverted. Plato, in *Phaedrus*, 260b, makes a similar argument, where he examines the consequences of a skilled rhetorician convincing someone to use the name "horse" to describe a donkey, and thus transferring the qualities of one to the other. He is clearly tilting at rhetoricians and politicians who advocate evil as good.

[166] Ted Hopf, *Constructing International Relations at Home: Finding Allies in Moscow 1995–1999* (Ithaca: Cornell University Press, 2002).

[167] Nicholas Greenwood Onuf, *World of Our Making: Rules and Rule in Social Theory and International Relations* (Columbia: University of South Carolina Press, 1989); Friedrich V. Kratochwil, *Rules, Norms and Decisions: On the Conditions of Political and Legal Reasoning in International Relations and Domestic Affairs* (Cambridge: Cambridge University Press, 1989); Friedrich V. Kratochwil and John Gerard Ruggie, "International Organization: A State of the Art on an Art of the State," *International Organization* 49 (Autumn 1986), pp. 753–75; John Gerard Ruggie, "What Makes the World Hang Together? Neo-Utilitarianism and the Social Constructivist Challenge," *International Organization* 52 (Autumn 1998), pp. 855–86; Martha Finnemore and Kathryn Sikkink, "International Norm Dynamics and Political Change," *International Organization* 52 (Autumn 1998), pp. 887–918.

[168] According to Nicholas Greenwood Onuf, *The Republican Legacy* (New York: Cambridge University Press, 1998), pp. 141–42, constructivism "holds that individuals and societies make, construct or constitute each other. Individuals make societies through their deeds, and societies constitute individuals, as they understand themselves and each other, through those same deeds." See also, Onuf, *World of Our Making*, pp. 35–65.

"thin" version gives more weight to the role norms play in advancing interests than to the creation of norms by identities.

Thucydides is undeniably a constructivist and may have been the original practitioner of the "thicker" linguistic version. His history examines how language shapes the identities and conventions in terms of which interests are defined. He drives this point home in the most graphic way by showing that it is impossible to formulate interests at all when conventions have broken down and the meanings of language have been subverted. Needless to say, justice is also impossible in these circumstances. Traditional Greek social intercourse, domestic and "international," was embedded in a web of interlocking relationships and obligations and governed by an elaborate set of conventions. When the polis arose in the course of the eighth and seventh centuries, an extensive network of personal alliances linking together households, bands and tribes was extended across Greece. If Homer can be believed, ties of *xenia* (guest friendship) were strong enough to keep warriors from fighting one another when their armies clashed.[169] The city superimposed itself over these earlier linkages, and they remained in existence well after the polis had become the dominant form of political organization. They helped to shape the values of the polis and its foreign relations. Thucydides gave considerable play to three *xenoi*-dyads in his history.[170]

Dealings with foreigners were an extension of domestic relations. It is significant that fifth-century Greeks had no specific word for international relations; like Herodotus, they used *xenia* instead.[171] War was not infrequent, but it was for the most part limited in means and ends, and rarely between cities with common origins or *nomoi*. With rare exceptions, the independence and social system of other city states was respected; wars were waged to establish precedence (not dominance) and settle border disputes.[172] Traditional warfare allowed individuals to gain honor through the display of heroism. Hoplite combat merged the individual into the group, but it too was highly stylized and designed to

[169] Homer, *Iliad*, VI.624, describes how Diomedes and Glaukos were about have a go at each other when they discovered that their grandfathers were bound by ties of *xenia*. Diomedes drove his spear into the ground and urged Glaukos, who promptly agreed, to exchange armor and avoid each other in battle in the future.

[170] They are Pericles-Archidamus, Alkiphron of Argos and King Agis of Sparta, and Alcibiades and Endios of Sparta. Gabriel Herman, *Ritualised Friendship and the Greek City* (Cambridge: Cambridge University Press, 1987), pp. 143–56.

[171] Herodotus, I.69. On *xenia*, see Philippe Gauthier, *Symbola: Les étrangers et la justice dans les cités grecques* (Nancy: Annales d l'Est, 1972), p. 19; Herman, *Ritualised Friendship and the Greek City*.

[172] Thucydides, VII.57; Kurt Raaflaub, "Expansion and Machtbildung in frühen Polis-Systemen," in Walter Eder, *Staat und Staatlichkeit in der frühen römischen Republik* (Stuttgart: Steiner, 1990), pp. 511–45.

minimize casualties. The rules of war, referred to by Thucydides as the common customs (*ta koina nomima*) of the Hellenes, outlawed hostilities at certain times and places, required official declarations of war, limited pursuit of defeated opponents, prohibited mutilation or execution of prisoners of war, and called for obligatory truces to allow both sides to gather their dead for burial and the victor to erect a trophy.[173] Truces were also obligatory during the Olympic games, held every four years beginning in 776 BCE. These rules began to break down during the Peloponnesian War, when participants executed prisoners and committed other atrocities, violated quasi-sacred truces and sanctuaries and tried to undermine adversarial social and economic systems by encouraging slave defections and revolts.[174]

To the extent that they address the breakdown of conventions, realists attribute these changes to the effects of war and innovations in military technology. Thucydides himself observes that "war is a rough teacher."[175] But this structural explanation is not persuasive. The Persian wars were harsh, but many conventions held. Pausanias, the victor of Plataea, resisted pleas to slaughter the surviving Persians and to hang their general's body from a cross, as Xerxes had done to Leonidas at Thermopylae.[176] Modern analogies spring readily to mind. The American Civil War was brutal by any standard, yet both sides observed the conventions of war. Confederate mistreatment of African-American prisoners of war was the principal exception, but even this reflected a convention. Troops on both sides behaved in ways that baffle us today. At Bloody Angle at Gettysburg, New Yorkers refused to fire on the remnant of retreating Alabamians

[173] Thucydides, III.59.1, VI.4.5; F. E. Adcock, *The Greek and Macedonian Art of War* (Berkeley: University of California Press, 1957); Josiah Ober, "The Rules of War in Classical Greece," in Josiah Ober, *The Athenian Revolution: Essays on Ancient Greek Democracy and Political Theory* (Princeton: Princeton University Press, 1996), pp. 53–71. Death in Homer is unalloyed misfortune, but the ultimate evil is desecration of a dead body. It is only through the performance of proper burial rites that family and community maintain their integrity. The strong commitment to burial rites continued down through the fifth century.

[174] Herodotus, VI.113–17. IX.70–45; Thucydides, II.5.7, II.67.4, III.32.1, IV.3–41, V.116.4, VII.19–28, VII.72–87; Ober, "The Rules of War in Classical Greece," pp. 62–63; Victor D. Hanson, *The Western Way of War: Infantry Battle in Classical Greece* (New York: Alfred A. Knopf, 1989), pp. 19–26; Richard J. A. Talbert, "The Role of Helots in the Class Struggle in Sparta," *Historia* 38:1 (1989), pp. 22–40.

[175] Thucydides, III.82.2; Ober, "The Rules of War in Classical Greece," p. 70. Hanson, *The Western Way of War*, pp. 36–38, argues that in the Persian wars. Greeks confronted larger forces with unfamiliar equipment and tactics and specialized forces. The nature of hoplite warfare changed, and with it the conventions governing that warfare.

[176] Herodotus, IX.78. In VII.133, IX.68, reports that the Greeks summarily executed Persian heralds and pursued and slaughtered large numbers of fleeing Persians at Marathon.

and instead threw their caps into the air and cheered them for their bravery. In World War I, German and allied armies behaved on the whole quite honorably toward one another and civilians, in sharp contrast to World War II where warfare on the eastern front approximated Thucydides' depiction of barbarism. The differences were not due to the harshness or duration of war, but to the character of the political systems involved. When language was subverted and conventions ignored or destroyed, as in Nazi Germany, the rational construction of interest was impossible, war aims were limitless and the rules of warfare were disregarded.

Thucydides takes the constructivist argument another step and implies that civil society is also what actors make of it. Following Hobbes, most realists maintain that the distinguishing feature of domestic society is the presence of a Leviathan who overcomes anarchy and allows order to be maintained. For Thucydides, as for Aristotle, law "has no power to compel obedience beside the force of habit."[177] Domestic polities run the gamut from highly ordered, consensual and peaceful societies to those wracked by the anarchy and bloodshed of *stasis*. It is not the presence or absence of a Leviathan that is critical, but the degree to which citizens construct their identities as members of a community (*homonoia* – literally, being of one mind) or as atomistic individuals.[178] When the former prevails, as it did in Periclean Athens and in Greece more generally before the Peloponnesian War, conventions restrained the behavior of actors, whether individuals or city states. When the latter dominates, as it did in Corcyra and almost did in Athens with the short-lived regime of the Four Hundred in 411–410, civil society disintegrates and even a Leviathan cannot keep the peace. The domestic environment in these situations comes to resemble a war-torn international environment, and for the same reasons.

Thucydides drives home the truth that a strong sense of community is equally essential to domestic and international order. Some rational

177 Aristotle, *Politics*, 1269a20.

178 The first reference to *homonoia* is in Democritus, frg. 68B250, for whom it is the quality that enables cities to carry out large projects, including wars. In frg. 68B255, he observes that when the rich advance money and provide benefits for the poor, there is pity, an end to isolation and friendship. This produces like-minded citizens and too many other benefits to be enumerated. Archytas of Tarentum, frg. 47B3, wrote that right reason (*logismos*) prevents stasis and promotes a sense of community (*homonoia*). *Logismos* in turn he defined as sharing with the poor and needy (*penētes*). Antiphon, frg. 87B44a, wrote a work on *homonoia*, and Xenophon, *Memorabilia*, IV.4.16, reports that Socrates described *homonoia* as the greatest good that a city can possess; when it is present, the laws are observed and the city is a good city.

choice formulations – again following Hobbes – acknowledge this reality and recognize that it is necessary to preserve the rules of the game if actors are collectively to maximize their interests. They highlight the paradox that a focus on short-term interests – by individuals, factions or states – can undermine the order or environment on which the rational pursuit of interest depends. Thucydides would regard the tragedy of the commons as an unavoidable outcome in a culture in which the individual was increasingly the unit to which advertisers and politicians appealed and in terms of which social scientists conducted research.

Thucydides' history suggests that interest and justice are inextricably connected and mutually constitutive. On the surface they appear to be in conflict, and almost every debate in the history in one form or another pits considerations of interest against those of justice. But Thucydides, like Democritus, appears to have understood phenomena as visual representations of a deeper reality (*opsis tōn adēlōn ta phainomena*). At this hidden level, his history shows that interests cannot be intelligently considered, formulated or pursued outside a community and the identities it constructs and sustains. The creation and maintenance of *homonoia* depends on respect for other human beings, which is the basis for equality, friendship and justice. Democritus and Archytas of Tarentum singled out the willingness of the rich to look after the needs of the poor as the best indicator of *homonoia.*[179] For Euripides, equality is the bond that unites friend to friend and city to city.[180] For Protagoras, justice "brings order into our cities and creates a bond of friendship and union."[181] In the *Laws*, Plato proposes a variety of measures to guarantee economic, although not political equality.[182] Aristotle favored private property, but thought that citizens, in the tradition of good friends (*philikoi*), should share their wealth to ensure that everyone's basic needs were looked after.[183] In the most fundamental sense, the Greeks understood that justice enables interests.

Materialist interpretations of Thucydides – overwhelmingly realist interpretations – represent a superficial and one-sided portrayal of his history. Constructivist readings must avoid this error. Thucydides is *both* a realist and a constructivist. *Stasis* and *homonoia* represent two faces of

[179] Democritus, frg. 68B255; Archytas, frg. 47B3.

[180] Euripides, *Suppliants*, 404 and *Phoenissae*, 531.

[181] Plato, *Protagoras*, 322c.

[182] Plato proposed to outlaw dowries and restrict the acquisition of disposable forms of wealth. The city should also be some distance from the sea to reduce contact with money and trade. *Laws*, IV.704d–705b, V.739c–745b, IX.855a–856e, 877d, XI.923a–924a, 929b–e.

[183] Aristotle, *Politics*, 1320B7–11, 1329b39–1330a2.

human beings, both are inherent in their *phusis*. Realism and constructivism are thus equally germane to the study of international relations. They need to build on Thucydides's research program: discovery of the conditions underlying *stasis* and *homonoia* and the causes of transitions between them. For this reason alone, his history is as he claims, "a possession for all time."[184]

[184] Thucydides, I.23.4.

5 Carl von Clausewitz

> In mathematics, nothing is lost by abstraction, it fully achieves its purpose. But when abstractions must constantly discard the living phenomena in order to reflect the lifeless form . . . the result is a dry skeleton of dull truths and common places, squeezed into doctrine. It is really astonishing that people waste their time on such conceptualizations . . .
>
> Carl von Clausewitz[1]

The French revolution and the Napoleonic wars ushered in the age of nationalism and transformed the capabilities and roles of states. Clausewitz spent a lifetime pondering these changes and their implications for warfare. Almost alone among his contemporaries, Clausewitz understood the destructive nature of modern warfare and the difficulty of limiting and stopping wars once popular passions became engaged. The challenge to nineteenth-century statesmen was to find some way to allow the major European powers to reorganize themselves into a community of nation states without provoking a catastrophic, continental war. *On War*, Clausewitz's principal work, was intended, in part, to alert contemporaries to this danger, but its author remained deeply pessimistic about its reception and of the ability of leaders to grasp and respond appropriately to the changed nature of warfare.

Clausewitz is considered the preeminent theorist of war, and generations of military officers and strategists have studied his magnum opus. *On War* and the *History of the Peloponnesian War* are the only works written before the twentieth century that are standard fare on reading lists of staff and war colleges around the world. Clausewitz's work is also the starting point of many contemporary studies of warfare.[2] I will make extensive reference to *On War*, but also to Clausewitz's historical works, essays and

[1] Carl von Clausewitz, *Strategie aus dem Jahr 1804, mit Zusätzen von 1808 und 1809*, ed. E. Kessel (Hamburg: Hanseatische Verlagsanstalt, 1937), p. 82.

[2] For an excellent example, see Stephen J. Cimbala, *Clausewitz and Chaos: Friction in War and Military Policy* (Westport, Conn.: Praeger, 2001).

correspondence.[3] These other writings help illuminate his understanding of strategy and warfare and its relationship to other forms of social activity. While Clausewitz is not an historian-philosopher on a par with Thucydides, he addresses some of the same questions as his illustrious predecessor and has interesting and original things to say about them. Many of his insights, substantive and epistemological, remain relevant to the contemporary world.

Clausewitz had political goals and philosophical interests that grew out of the German idealist tradition, to which he made a novel and largely unrecognized contribution. The central intellectual problem with which he grappled was how to construct a scientific and general theory of war when its every aspect was so heavily context-dependent. Warfare was shaped by culture and technology, both of which were constantly evolving, by individual goals, choices and emotions and pure chance. Clausewitz's solution, which came to him only late in life, was to distinguish analytically between the realms of theory and practice. The former could elucidate principles and processes from which general patterns of behavior could be deduced. Such a conceptual architecture would have pedagogical but not predictive value. This is because all human behavior is mediated by context, and attempts to apply principles in practice are often confounded by misunderstanding, flawed execution and various forms of "friction." All of these features make war in practice markedly different from war in theory. The best one can do, Clausewitz insists, is a get a "feel" for war through reading and experience (*Übung*).

The rules of warfare exist to be broken. Periodically, Clausewitz observed, political-military geniuses like Frederick the Great and Napoleon exploited the latent potential of their societies to transform warfare. Genius rises above the rules – or what others consider to be the rules – and reveals most generalizations about warfare to be limited to specific historical epochs. Clausewitz understood genius as an innate psychological quality (*Ingenium*), and sought, without success, to develop a theory of human psychology that would explain both genius and the role of emotions. He considered it a necessary complement to rational theories of war – and of any other social activity.

Clausewitz's interest in war and genius was closely connected to his political project. Here, too, he was a product of his time; with other German idealists he saw revolutionary France as both a challenge and

[3] Carl von Clausewitz, *Vom Kriege* (Bonn: Dümmlers Verlag, 1980). The best English translation is *On War*, ed. and trans. Michael Howard and Peter Paret (Princeton: Princeton University Press, 1976). Page number cites refer to this edition.

an opportunity for the German "nation." Clausewitz idealized the state, but unlike Kant and Hegel, did not consider it the ultimate expression of some purposeful scheme, or, like Fichte, infused by historical and ethical principles. He saw the fate of the individual and the state as inextricably combined; the protective, supportive and regulative power of the modern state made education possible, and, through education, individual improvement and collective cultural expression. In return, the citizen owed the state his loyalty and should be prepared to make sacrifices on its behalf. Clausewitz was humiliated by Prussia's ineffective political and military response to Napoleon and despaired at the inability of King Frederick Wilhelm II to rise to this challenge. He looked to a coterie of reformers to provide leadership, appropriate institutions and inspiration for the German nation. His hopes were dashed – and his military career sidetracked – by the resurgence of absolutism in Prussia following Napoleon's defeat. Clausewitz turned with renewed vigor to his intellectual labors, which provided an alternative form of expression and satisfaction.

Clausewitz's intellectual and political projects informed one another but need to be separated for purposes of analysis. Neither project can be understood independently of Clausewitz's personality, professional experience and the political and cultural influences acting on him. I accordingly begin with an overview of his education and career, which prompted his interest in history and theory and shaped his substantive views on those subjects. Clausewitz's early and whole-hearted commitment to reform did not diminish with age, although he became increasingly circumspect about expressing his views. In his mature years, he reflected on and wrote about the relationship between war and political change. As a young man, Clausewitz regarded war as a vehicle by which Prussia, and Germany as a whole, might find unity and purpose. The older Clausewitz, unlike so many of his contemporaries, came to see war as a threat to progress and civilization.

Thucydides among the Spartans

Clausewitz's career in many ways paralleled that of his illustrious Greek predecessor. Thucydides lived through the entire Peloponnesian War, and briefly held a position of military leadership. Defeat led to exile and a visit to Sparta where he observed the conflict from the perspective of his country's principal adversary. In a military career that spanned four decades, Clausewitz participated in almost all phases of the wars between revolutionary France and its continental adversaries. He began his service in the Prussian army at age twelve in the spring of 1792, and ultimately rose to the rank of general. He was captured and interned in France in 1807, but treated more like a guest of the government; he became acquainted with French provincial society in Nancy and Soissons, and then spent six weeks in Paris where he engaged in extensive discussions with French politicians, military officers, civil servants and savants. He saw service with the Russian army as a volunteer during its struggle to repel Napoleon's invasion, and subsequently returned to the Prussian army and participated in its western advance. He outran pursuing French *cuirassiers* after an unsuccessful cavalry charge at Waterloo. Like Thucydides, he died before completing his master work, and it too lacks a conclusion.[4]

Perhaps the most fundamental similarity between Thucydides and Clausewitz is their deep frustration at being excluded from a central role in the wars in which their societies were engaged. Clausewitz fared somewhat better than his predecessor. He was accepted into the 34th Infantry Regiment, in which his older brother was a private first class (*Gefreiter-korporal*). Early in 1793, the regiment moved up to the Rhine to reinforce the Duke of Brunswick's field army, whose march on Paris was blocked by a major French force in the Argonne Forest. Brunswick tried unsuccessfully to edge his way around the French, and withdrew in confusion when this maneuver failed. Clausewitz went into combat for the first time in February when his regiment shelled a village in the vicinity of Mainz. On 6 June, a few days after his thirteenth birthday, his regiment stormed the village of Zahlbach and engaged in hand-to-hand combat with defending French forces. In the following weeks, Clausewitz was frequently under fire, and on one occasion barely extricated himself from an ambush.[5]

The Treaty of Basel in 1795 ended this phase of the wars with France, and Clausewitz spent the next five years on garrison duty in the small town of Neuruppin. In 1801, the Hanoverian artillery officer and military writer, Gerhard Scharnhorst, entered Prussian military service. He was given the task of transforming the small and moribund Berlin institute of military sciences into the army's premier institution of higher learning,

[4] For many decades the principal secondary work on Clausewitz was Hans Rothfels, *Carl von Clausewitz: Politik und Krieg* (Berlin: Dümmler, 1920). The standard work in German is now Werner Hahlweg, *Carl von Clausewitz: Soldat, Politiker, Denker* (Göttingen: Musterschmidt-Verlag, 1957). Wilhelm von Schramm, *Clausewitz, Leben und Werk* (Esslingen: Bechtle, 1977) is also highly regarded. The best intellectual biography in any language is Peter Paret, *Clausewitz and the State* (New York: Oxford University Press, 1976). Other studies in English include Roger Parkinson, *Clausewitz*, trans. Christine Booker and Norman Stone (New York: Stein and Day, 1971); Raymond Aron, *Clausewitz: Philosopher of War* (Englewood Cliffs, N.J.: Prentice-Hall, 1976); Michael Howard, *Clausewitz* (New York: Oxford University Press, 1983).

[5] Paret, *Clausewitz and the State*, pp. 17–35.

the *Allgemeine Kriegsschule*. Scharnhorst was a distinguished officer, and had performed outstandingly during the War of the First Coalition. He was impressed by the ability of undertrained, poorly led and inadequately supplied French conscripts to learn from their mistakes and ultimately defeat the best professional armies of Europe. Scharnhorst attributed their success to the broader transformation of French society brought about by the Revolution. To defeat the French, he reasoned, it was essential to learn about their society, not just about their army. He established a curriculum for the *Allgemeine Kriegsschule* that included philosophy, literature and history in addition to the usual technical and military subjects.[6]

Clausewitz was admitted into the first three-year course in 1801, and graduated at the top of his class in the spring of 1804. During these years he also participated in the *Militärische Gesellschaft*, a free-wheeling discussion group Scharnhorst organized to consider the implications of the military revolution then under way. Clausewitz greatly admired Scharnhorst for his intellectual sophistication, authority and professional success in spite of his humble origins. Scharnhorst was impressed by his student's mental acuity and broad interests in politics and philosophy. Peter Paret, author of the definitive intellectual biography of Clausewitz, speculates that personal losses in both men's lives drew them closer together. Clausewitz's father died in 1802, and Scharnhorst lost his wife and daughter in the following year. Scharnhorst treated Clausewitz as his son and took a deep interest in his education and career until his premature death in 1813. Clausewitz considered Scharnhorst "the father and friend of my spirit."[7]

After graduation, Clausewitz was appointed adjutant to Prince August, the son of Prince Ferdinand, colonel-in-chief of the 34th Regiment. Through the prince, he made the acquaintance of Marie von Brühl, an educated and thoughtful woman who was a lady-in-waiting to Queen Louise. Her family considered Clausewitz an unsuitable match. Their opposition and the separation brought about by military service led to a seven-year courtship during which the couple carried on an extensive and passionate correspondence in which Clausewitz commented on

[6] On Scharnhorst, see Carl von Clausewitz, "Über das Leben und den Charakter von Scharnhorst," *Historisch-politische Zeitschrift*, I (1832); Max Lehmann, *Scharnhorst*, 2 vols. (Leipzig: S. Hirzel, 1886–87); Rudolf Stadelmann, *Scharnhorst: Schicksal und Geistige Welt* (Wiesbaden: Limes Verlag, 1952); Paret, *Clausewitz and the State*, pp. 55–77 and *passim*; Charles Edward White, *The Enlightened Soldier: Scharnhorst and the Militärische Gesellschaft in Berlin, 1801–1805* (New York: Praeger, 1989); Azar Gat, *The Origins of Military Thought: From the Enlightenment to Clausewitz* (Oxford: Oxford University Press, 1989), pp. 156–67; Klaus Hornung, *Scharnhorst: Soldat, Reformer, Staatsmann: die Biographie* (Munich: Bechtle Verlag, 1997).

[7] Paret, *Clausewitz and the State*, pp. 74–75, 215.

contemporary developments and worked out many of his ideas. Marie became his intellectual partner and the editor of his papers, which she published after his death.

Between 1803 and 1806 Clausewitz had ample time to think and write. He produced his first major historical study, "Gustavus Adolphus's Campaigns of 1630–1632," published posthumously.[8] War with France began again in 1806, to the initial delight of Clausewitz and other Prussian patriots. Napoleon invaded Franconia, brushed aside the Prussian advance guard and advanced toward Leipzig to cut Prussian lines of communication to Magdeburg and Berlin. The twin battles of Jena and Auerstädt, fought on 14 October, were disasters for Prussia, and forced Frederick Wilhelm II to retreat into East Prussia, where, with Russian help, he waged a desperate rearguard action. In July 1808, Frederick Wilhelm II met Napoleon at Tilsit and agreed to a humiliating peace that deprived Prussia of half of its subjects and territory and burdened it with heavy reparations to support a French army of occupation.[9]

Prince August commanded his own battalion and two others at Auerstädt where they were at the mercy of French snipers who made good use of the broken ground for cover. Clausewitz, who had trained his troops in French methods, formed a third of the battalion into skirmishing lines to cover the Prussian withdrawal. He took over command of the battalion when other senior officers were killed or wounded, and led it on an all-night march to escape from the rapidly advancing French. Amidst crumbling resistance and a chain reaction of surrenders of strong points and fortresses, Clausewitz organized surviving veterans into new units that formed the rear guard of a newly organized army under Prince Hohenlohe. On 28 October, between Berlin and the Baltic coast, Prince August, Clausewitz and 240 grenadiers were surrounded by several French regiments and surrendered, but only after repelling seven cavalry charges. Clausewitz was interned in France, first in Nancy, then in Soissons for six months where he learned French, studied mathematics and familiarized himself with the institutions of local government. He was allowed a three-week furlough in Paris, where he took in all the usual sights. What impressed him the most, however, was Abbé Sicard's institute for the deaf and dumb, which, he wrote Marie, demonstrated

[8] Clausewitz, "Gustavus Adolphus Feldzüge von 1630–1632," *Hinterlassene Werke des Generals Carl von Clausewitz über Krieg und Kriegführung*, 10 vols. (Berlin: Dümmler, 1832–37), IX, pp. 1–106.

[9] On these events, see Paul W. Schroeder, *The Transformation of European Politics, 1763–1848* (Oxford: Oxford University Press, 1994), pp. 287–323; Brendan Simms, *The Impact of Napoleon: Prussian High Politics, Foreign Policy and the Crisis of the Executive, 1797–1806* (Cambridge: Cambridge University Press, 1997), chs. 5–8.

the power of education in the face of severe handicaps to create reflective and moral beings. After Tilsit, Clausewitz was released, but spent another two months in Switzerland waiting for his passport to arrive. He passed the time outside Geneva on the estate of Madame de Staël, where he met and had long conversations with August Wilhelm Schlegel and Johann Heinrich Pestalozzi.[10]

Clausewitz was barely reunited with Marie when he had to depart for Königsberg to assist Scharnhorst in reorganizing the Prussian army. He was promoted to captain, drafted numerous memoranda for Scharnhorst and was probably involved in overseeing secret rearmament measures then underway. He used his evenings to write essays on topics ranging from tactics to political philosophy. In the spring of 1812, Frederick Wilhelm II, under pressure from Napoleon, concluded an alliance with France, and allowed a French corps to enter Berlin. Clausewitz was disgusted, and one of approximately thirty officers to submit his resignation. With his friends Karl von Tiedemann and Alexander von Dohna, he entered the Russian service. Frederick Wilhelm II never forgave Clausewitz for this act of independence, and for some time considered confiscating his property. He would later deny Clausewitz a command and reject a recommendation from Field Marshal Gebhard Lebrecht von Blücher that he be decorated for bravery at Grossgörschen.[11]

In the course of the next three years, Clausewitz observed or played an important role in the political and military events that culminated in France's defeat and the double exile of Napoleon. He chafed at the incompetence and rivalries among Russian commanders, urged the czar to conduct a strategic withdrawal to draw the French into the depths of Russia, served as the nominal chief-of-staff of a cavalry corps at the Battle of Borodino, had his horse shot out from underneath him on the retreat to Moscow, watched that city abandoned and burned, was arrested as a French spy by suspicious locals and fought his way back to St. Petersburg with Prince Kutuzov. He was an intermediary in the negotiations at Tauroggen that convinced General Hans David Ludwig von Yorck to defect with his corps to the Russian side. Clausewitz was deeply moved by the human suffering he witnessed and penned a description to his wife of a battlefield after the fighting, filled with "corpses and dying men among smoking ruins, and thousands of ghostlike men [who] pass by screaming and begging and crying in vain for bread."[12]

After Prussia's *volte face*, Clausewitz made his way to Berlin, where the king quashed the legal proceedings against him but refused to readmit

[10] Paret, *Clausewitz and the State*, pp. 123–36.
[11] Ibid., pp. 209–21. [12] Ibid., pp. 222–28.

him into Prussian service. He and his wife were snubbed by the crown prince and other court officials. Friends arranged for him to serve as a Russian liaison officer on Blücher's staff, which allowed him in practice to serve as Scharnhorst's assistant. He helped Scharnhorst raise new armies, a task facilitated by the sense of nationalism then developing among many Prussians. He fought in the inconclusive Spring Campaign, and engaged in desperate hand-to-hand combat at Grossgörschen. In the course of this engagement Blücher suffered a contusion, Clausewitz's friend Grolman was slashed by a bayonet and Scharnhorst was shot in the leg and later died from the infected wound.[13]

Count August von Gneisenau, the new chief-of-staff, tried without success to have Clausewitz appointed his special assistant. In 1814, the king readmitted him to the army but posted him to a unit whose assignment was to protect the lines of communication between northern Prussia and Sweden. Clausewitz soon assumed command of a larger Russo-German force, distinguished himself in the fighting and won promotion to colonel. In April 1815 he was reassigned to the Prussian general staff and then made chief-of-staff of General Johann von Thielmann's III Army Corps. The Corps anchored the left wing of the allied forces in Belgium where throughout the afternoon and evening of 17 April they fought a successful defensive action against a French force twice their size under the command of Marshal Emmanuel de Grouchy. They kept one-third of Napoleon's forces occupied and unable to participate in the main action at Waterloo. The III Army Corp's success was largely attributable to the flexible small-unit tactics that Clausewitz and other reformers had introduced.[14]

After the war, Gneisenau was appointed commander-in-chief of Prussian forces in the west, and Clausewitz became his chief-of-staff. Their headquarters gained a reputation for political and intellectual independence, and both men were brought back to Berlin where they could be monitored more carefully. In September 1818, Clausewitz was made a major-general and shortly afterwards put in command of the *Allgemeine Kriegsschule*, a position he would hold for the next twelve years. His responsibilities were limited to administrative matters, and he could not influence the curriculum, let alone the Prussian army. He had ample time to read and reflect and work on drafts of what would become *On War*.[15]

Clausewitz had no more than drafts of this work completed when in 1830 he was given the command of the 3rd Inspection, a major artillery

[13] Ibid., pp. 229–39. [14] Ibid., pp. 241–50.
[15] Ibid., pp. 255–73; Marie von Clausewitz's introduction to the posthumous edition of her husband's works, reprinted as Preface to Howard and Paret, *On War*, pp. 65–67.

formation in Breslau. Not long afterwards revolutions broke out in Paris and Poland and Clausewitz was recalled to Berlin to serve once more as chief-of-staff to Gneisenau, recently given command of the Prussian army. The threat of war with France receded, and Gneisenau and Clausewitz, operating from a headquarters in Posen, oversaw the surrender of the remnants of the Polish army. A more serious threat arose in the east in the form of a cholera epidemic, to which Gneisenau succumbed in August and Clausewitz in November. He was fifty-one when he died.[16]

Marie acknowledged that her husband was extraordinarily frustrated at never having attained a position commensurate with his abilities and qualifications. Consequently, "all his efforts were directed toward the realm of scientific understanding, and the benefits that he hoped would result from his work became his purpose in life."[17] Clausewitz developed a certain distance from his society while retaining the ability to write about it as an insider. Semi-detachment from the present and a focus on the future may also help explain why *On War*, like the *History of the Peloponnesian War*, sought to mine contemporary experience and historical evidence for insights of universal applicability.

Philosophical roots

Clausewitz learned the fundamentals of grammar, arithmetic and Latin in a provincial municipal school and was later exposed to a more sophisticated curriculum during his three years as a student at the *Allgemeine Kriegsschule*. In France and Berlin, he read a diverse selection of authors, including Ancillon, Fichte, Gentz, Herder, Kant, Machiavelli, Montesquieu, Johannes von Müller and Rousseau.[18] But above all, Clausewitz read history to augment his personal experience and to discover the underlying dynamics of war.

Clausewitz lived through a particularly turbulent era of German and European history that encompassed the French Revolution, the French and Napoleonic Wars, the industrial revolution, the rise of nationalism and the counter-Enlightenment. The latter is a catchall term for a variety of movements and tendencies, including conservatism, critical philosophy, historicism, idealism, nationalism, revivalism and holism, that developed in the late eighteenth and early nineteenth centuries, in large part in reaction to the Enlightenment. The Enlightenment put faith in power of reason to unlock the secrets of the universe and to deduce from

[16] Paret, *Clausewitz and the State*, pp. 396–430.
[17] Marie von Clausewitz, Preface, in Howard and Paret, *On War*, pp. 65–67.
[18] Paret, *Clausewitz and the State*, p. 81.

first principles laws and institutions that would allow human beings to achieve their potential in just, ordered and secure societies. Counter-Enlightenment thinkers considered these expectations naive and dangerous; they saw the world as complex, contradictory, composed of unique social entities and in a state of constant flux. They rejected the Enlightenment conception of a human being as a *tabula rasa,* and the mere sum of internal and external forces, as well as its emphasis on body over soul, reason over imagination and thought over the senses. They insisted on a holistic understanding that built on these dichotomies, and one, moreover, that recognized individuals and social groups as the source of action motivated by their search for expression and authenticity.[19]

The counter-Enlightenment began in France and gained a wide audience through the writings of Rousseau. It found German spokesmen in the 1770s, among them Hamann, Herder, the young Goethe, and Lavater and Möser, the dramatists of *Sturm und Drang*, and the Schiller of his early plays. The French Revolution of 1789, and Napoleon's subsequent occupation of many German territories, provoked a widespread reaction to French cultural and political imperialism and to the Enlightenment more generally. In literature this found expression in the early romanticism (*Frühromantik*) of Novalis (Friedrich Hardenberg), the Schlegel brothers and Christian Friedrich Tieck, in religion with Friedrich Schliermacher, and in the philosophy of Johann Gottlieb Fichte and, later, Georg F. W. Hegel.[20] Clausewitz knew their writings intimately, wrote a letter to Fichte and was personally acquainted with Schlegel, Tieck and Novalis. On more than one occasion he played cards with Hegel at the home of August Heinrich von Fallersleben.[21]

Clausewitz is often described as someone who wholeheartedly embraced the counter-Enlightenment.[22] There are indeed many aspects of his thought that reflect and build upon counter-Enlightenment assumptions, but he owes an equal debt to the Enlightenment. Like Kant, from whom he borrowed heavily, Clausewitz straddled the Enlightenment and

[19] Charles Taylor, *Hegel* (Cambridge: Cambridge University Press, 1975), pp. 3–50.

[20] See M. Frank, "*Einführung in die frühromantische Ästhetik* (Frankfurt: Suhrkamp, 1989); Nicholas Boyle, *Goethe: The Poet and the Age* (Oxford: Oxford University Press, 1992); Frederick Beiser, "The Enlightenment and Idealism," in Karl Ameriks, ed., *The Cambridge Companion to German Idealism* (Cambridge: Cambridge University Press, 2000), pp. 18–36; Daniel O. Dahlstrom, "The Aesthetic Holism of Hamann, Herder, and Schiller," in Ameriks, ed., *The Cambridge Companion to German Idealism*, pp. 76–94; Ernest Behler, *German Romantic Literary Theory* (Cambridge: Cambridge University Press, 1993); Terry Pinkard, *German Philosophy, 1760–1860: The Legacy of Idealism* (Cambridge: Cambridge University Press, 2002), pp. 131–71.

[21] August Heinrich von Fallersleben, *Mein Leben* (Frankfurt: Dietmar Klotz 1998 [1868]), I, pp. 311–12, III, pp. 93–94.

[22] Paret, *Clausewitz and the State*, pp. 149–50; Gat, *Origins of Military Thought*, p. 141.

the German reaction to it. His life-long ambition to develop a theory of war through the application of reason to history and psychology was a quintessential Enlightenment project. His recognition that such a theory could never reduce war to a science nor guide a commander in an inherently complex and unpredictable world reflected counter-Enlightenment views, as did his emphasis on emotive force and personality and the ability of genius to make its own rules. But, in a deeper sense, Clausewitz remained faithful to the Enlightenment. He appropriated many concepts from philosophers of the "German Movement," but stripped them of their metaphysical content. He borrowed their tools of inquiry to subject war to a logical analysis, and looked beyond pure reason to a psychology of human beings to find underlying causes for their behavior.

The same duality marked Clausewitz's political thinking; his unreflexive nationalism and visceral hatred of France coexisted with his belief that education, economic development and good government could bring about a better world. Clausewitz's political beliefs evolved more rapidly than his philosophical ones, and he made little effort to reconcile their contradictions. His thoughts about war were more extensive and productive. One of the remarkable features of *On War* is its largely successful synthesis of assumptions and methods from opposing schools of thought. In this sense too, Clausewitz follows in the footsteps of Thucydides.

Scharnhorst exercised the most direct and decisive influence on Clausewitz's thinking and writing. He was among the leading *Aufklärers* [proponents of the Enlightenment] in the Prussian service.[23] He was born in 1765 to a retired Hanoverian non-commissioned officer and the heiress of a wealthy farmer. He entered the Hanoverian army in 1779, and later taught in a regimental school that he established. In 1782, he founded and edited the first of a series of military periodicals, and wrote two widely read "how to" books for officers before leaving his desk job to fight against revolutionary France.[24] In 1801, he entered the Prussian service, and in 1806, he penned a long essay that summarized and extended his thoughts on the study of war.[25]

Scharnhorst's writing excelled in its detailed reconstruction of historical engagements. He believed that combat experience aside, case studies

[23] On Scharnhorst, see n. 6.

[24] Gerhard Scharnhorst, *Handbuch für Offiziere in dem anwendbaren Theilen der Krieges-Wissenschaften*, 3 vols. (Hanover: Helwingschen, 1787–90), and *Militärisches Taschenbuch zum Gebrauch im Felde* (Hanover: Helwing, 1792).

[25] Gerhard Scharnhorst, "Nutzen der militärischen Geschichte, Ursach ihres Mangels" (1806), reprinted in Ursula von Gersdorff, ed., *Ausgewählte Schriften* (Osnabrück: Biblio, 1983), pp. 199–207.

were the next best way to capture the reality of war. Scharnhorst used his cases to infer "correct concepts" (*richtige Begriffe*) that could order warfare and identify its principal components in a useful way for practitioners. His two books drew extensively on his wartime experience and historical research, but he never succeeded in developing a general theory of war. His case studies provided good evidence for his critiques of mathematical systems to guide the conduct of war developed by Bülow, Dumas, Müller and Jomini.

Peter Paret observes that no military theorist of his time was as conscious as Scharnhorst of the distinction between theory and reality. His lectures at the *Allgemeine Kriegsschule* paid lip service to the conventional wisdom that good theory and good preparation could eliminate uncertainty and chance, but he did not for a moment believe it. In good sophistic tradition, the examples he used to pepper his lectures encouraged perceptive students to conclude that theory might be more effectively used to recognize and exploit departures from the expected. Clausewitz would develop this concept further, making surprise and chance central, positive features of his theory of war, in contrast to many earlier writers on the subject, who treated the unforeseen as an inconvenience, if they addressed it at all. Scharnhorst taught his students that geometry and trigonometry were useful for sharpening the mind, but that any theoretical understanding of warfare had to be based on history. Good history required access to reliable primary sources. This was another lesson the young Clausewitz assimilated, and many of his early writings were historical case studies. Scharnhorst also opened his students' eyes to the broader political, social and intellectual forces that influenced warfare and determined its nature in any historical epoch. He taught Clausewitz that the distinguishing feature of the French revolutionary and Napoleonic Wars was the ability, first of France, and then of the other European states, to extract greater resources and demand greater sacrifices from their populations. Survival in the modern age demanded efficiency in exploiting the physical and social resources at the disposal of the state, and this required a governing elite open to talent and merit independent of class or religious background.[26]

Clausewitz's early writings reveal the influence of Scharnhorst, but also his ability to transcend the conceptual limitations of his mentor. These works span the years 1803–06, and consist of notes and essays on politics and strategic principles, treatments of the Thirty Years War, the Russo-Turkish War of 1736–39, a longer study of Gustavus Adolphus and a review article of one of Heinrich von Bülow's many books on the

[26] Paret, *Clausewitz and the State*, pp. 72–73.

theory of war. Clausewitz reveals an early fascination with power, and qualified acceptance of the rights of states to extend their sway as far as they can. He also emphasizes the interest, indeed the responsibility, of other states to oppose such aggrandizement – especially in the case of France – when it threatens their interests or existence. This principle was so obvious to him that he found it strange that not all statesmen conceived of foreign relations in terms of power. He nevertheless recognized real world constraints on the exercise of power, some of them imposed by domestic political considerations, and others the result of deliberate and wise moderation by many leaders.[27]

Clausewitz's fascination with power may have come from his reading of Machiavelli or Frederick the Great, but it was positively Newtonian in conception. He conceived of power in terms of the latter's Third Law: a body in motion would stay in motion until acted upon by an equal and opposite force. States could be expected to expand their power until checked by an equal and opposite political-military force. This was a law of politics, but, unlike laws of physics, it was tempered in reality by other influences that kept states from expanding as far as their power might allow, and others from checking them as their interests dictated. Paret speculates that it was a short step from Clausewitz's formulation of power to the conception of war he developed in his mature years: that war in theory led to the extreme through a process of interactive escalation, but was constrained in practice by numerous sources of "friction." This concept too was borrowed from Newtonian physics.

Clausewitz's early writings alternated between case studies and more theoretical writings, and the two were related. His cases studies were theoretically informed, more so than those of his mentor, Scharnhorst. He wrote military history to explore the possibilities and limits of theory, and then refined his nascent concepts in follow-up case studies. It is apparent in retrospect that Clausewitz was trying to discover which aspects of warfare were amenable to theoretical description and which were not, and what else he would need to know to construct a universally valid theory. "While history may yield no formulae," he concluded, "it does provide an *exercise for judgment*, here as everywhere else."[28] There is no evidence that Clausewitz began his research program with this insight in mind; it seems to have developed in the course of his reading and writing. It may even represent an unconscious effort to reconcile two distinct and otherwise antagonistic aspects of his intellect: a pragmatic bent that focused his

[27] Carl von Clausewitz, *Politische Schriften und Briefe*, ed. Hans Rothfels (Munich: Drei Masken Verlag, 1922), p. 2, and discussion in Paret, *Clausewitz and the State*, p. 79.
[28] Clausewitz, *On War*, Book VI, ch. 30, p. 517.

attention on concrete issues and problems, and a desire to step back and understand issues and problems as specific instances of broader classes of phenomena.

Clausewitz's case studies addressed campaigns, not engagements, and were more analytical than descriptive. His study of Gustavus Adolphus' campaigns of 1630–32 was the most concrete expression of this approach. He sought to analyze the underlying causes of Swedish strategy during one phase of the Thirty Years War. He ignored the order of battle (the forces at the disposal of the two sides), and gave short shrift to individual engagements, including the Swedish victory at Breitenfeld and the battle of Lützen in which Gustavus Adolphus lost his life. Clausewitz made clear at the outset his intention to focus on the more important "subjective forces," which include the commander's personality, goals, abilities and his own comprehension of them. He produced what can only be described as a psychological study of Gustavus Adolphus, and, to a lesser extent, of his Catholic opponents; he treats the war as a clash of wills, made notable by the energy and courage of the adversaries. He concluded that the Thirty Years War lasted so long because the emotions of leaders and peoples had become so deeply engaged that nobody could accept a peace that was in everyone's interest.[29]

Clausewitz described Gustavus Adolphus as a man of "genius," a concept he picked up from Kant and would develop further in *On War*.[30] William Tell, Wallenstein, William of Orange, Frederick the Great, and above all, Napoleon, qualified as geniuses because they grasped new military possibilities and changed the nature of warfare by successfully implementing them. Genius periodically transformed warfare, and most other social activities, and made a mockery of attempts to create static theoretical systems. The concept of genius was Clausewitz's first step toward a systematic understanding of change. It was based on his recognition, developed more extensively in *On War*, that change could be both dramatic and gradual. Gradual change, in the form of improvements in armaments, logistics and tactics, was an ongoing process, the pace of which varied as a function of political organization, technology and battlefield incentives. Dramatic changes were unpredictable in timing and nature, and transformed warfare – and how people thought about

[29] Clausewitz, "Gustavus Adolphus Feldzüge von 1630–1632."

[30] Immanuel Kant, *The Critique of Judgment* (Oxford: Oxford University Press, 1961), pp. 168 and 181, described genius as "the talent that gives the rule to art." It is the talent "for producing that for which no definite rule can be given." For Kant, fully conscious art had to be created within a system, but to progress beyond a craft, art must constantly reinvent its rule. Rothfels, *Carl von Clausewitz*, pp. 23–25, for Kant's influence on Clausewitz.

warfare – in more fundamental ways. They were somewhat akin to what Thomas Kuhn would later call paradigm shifts.[31]

Clausewitz used the findings of his psychological case studies of Gustavus Adolphus and Frederick the Great to attack existing military theory, especially the work of Heinrich Dietrich von Bülow. Bülow maintained that the outcome of military campaigns was determined primarily by the angle formed by two lines drawn between the perimeters of the base of operations and the objective. Victory was assured if commanders situated their base close enough to their objective and extended their perimeters far enough so that the imaginary lines converged on the objective at an angle of at least 90 degrees. Clausewitz marshaled examples of defeat under these conditions, and of victory in cases where the angle had been less than that prescribed. He attributed both outcomes to the skill of generals, the élan of their forces and simple good luck.[32]

Bülow's system reflected an eighteenth-century preference for wars of maneuver over combat, and was ridiculed by Clausewitz who insisted that war is about fighting. Strategy, he wrote, is "nothing without battle, for battle is the raw material with which it works, the means it employs."[33] The ultimate goal [*Zweck*] of war was political: "to destroy one's opponent, to terminate his political existence, or to impose conditions on him during the peace negotiations." Either way, the immediate purpose [*Ziele*] of war becomes destruction of the adversary's military capability "which can be achieved *by occupying his territory, by depriving him of military supplies, or by destroying his army*."[34] Clausewitz introduced a further distinction, between strategy and tactics: "Tactics constitute the theory of the use of armed forces in battle; strategy forms the theory of using battles for the purposes of the war."[35] The distinctions between *Zweck* and *Ziele*, and strategy and tactics, would become essential components of his later theory of war.[36]

Bülow and Jomini built their systems around the order of battle and relative positioning of deployed forces because they were amenable to quantitative measurement. They considered quantification an essential step in transforming strategy into military science.[37] Clausewitz insisted that science requires propositions that can be validated empirically, and

[31] Thomas Kuhn, *The Structure of Scientific Revolutions* (Chicago: University of Chicago Press, 1970).

[32] Carl von Clausewitz, "Bermerkungen über die reine und angewandte Strategie des Herrn von Bülow," *Neue Bellona* 9: 3 (1805), pp. 252–87; Paret, *Clausewitz and the State*, pp. 89–97, for a useful discussion.

[33] Paret, *Clausewitz and the State*, p. 271. [34] Ibid., p. 51 (emphasis in original).

[35] Ibid., p. 62. [36] Clausewitz, *On War*, Book II, ch. 1, p. 128.

[37] Antoine Henri Jomini, *The Art of War*, trans. G. H. Mendell and W. O. Craighill (Westport, Conn.: Greenwood, 1971).

was struck by how uninterested the leading military theorists of his day were in using historical, or any other kind of, evidence for this purpose. Like Scharnhorst, Clausewitz thought the study of strategy should begin with history, not with mathematics. It had to be rooted in psychology because the motives and means of war were determined by political considerations, and ultimately by human intelligence, imagination and emotions. The study of strategy had "to move away from the tendency to *rationalize* to the neglected riches of the emotions and the imagination."[38] It had to find a systematic way of bringing these more intangible but critical considerations into the picture, while at the same time recognizing that chance, by its very nature, would always defy conceptualization and confound prediction.

Theory

In his review of Bülow, Clausewitz gives us an early and partial statement of his approach to theory. He developed his conceptions of theory and war on parallel and related tracks; his historical writings discuss theory, and his theoretical writings are rich in historical detail. This may be one reason why *On War* went through so many drafts and was still unfinished at the time of his death. As Clausewitz's thoughts about theory progressed, he would return to his growing manuscript to rework its underlying foundations and the manner of presentation.

Clausewitz began from the assumption, already apparent in his essay on Bülow, that social and physical phenomena were fundamentally different. A theory of physics was possible because objects are acted upon. Social actors, by contrast, are independent agents with free will, subjective understandings and independent goals, who act on each other and their environment. Their behavior varied within and across cultures and over time; human nature might be universal but its expression was constantly in flux. Generalizations about war were also of limited utility because the outcomes of battles and campaigns were significantly influenced by "the courage of the commander, his self-confidence, and the effect of moral qualities."[39] These critical but intangible qualities, and the ever-present role of chance, made a mockery of attempts to treat political or military behavior as a predictable, mechanistic exercise.

In keeping with the counter-Enlightenment emphasis on holism, Clausewitz maintained that free will was responsible for a second important distinction between the study of the physical and social worlds.

[38] Carl von Clausewitz, "Historisch-politische Aufzeichnungen," in Rothfels, ed., *Politische Schriften und Briefe*, p. 59.

[39] Carl von Clausewitz, *Strategie und Taktik*, in *Strategie aus dem Jahr 1804*, pp. 78–80.

In physics, he noted, it is possible to isolate and study part of the system and ignore the rest. But human action is an expression of the whole person, and is almost certain to be influenced by aspects of life different from the domain under study. Modern war is an expression of the entire society, an activity that reflects its values, and calls for contributions of one kind or another from most of its members. Unlike mathematics, it cannot be studied apart from these disparate but critical influences.[40] Even if generalizations were possible, they would be short-lived because of the constant evolution of warfare. So-called "laws" that appeared to account for eighteenth-century warfare were inapplicable to the Napoleonic period. It would be just as mistaken, Clausewitz insisted, to generalize on the basis of Napoleonic experience because the future would assuredly be different.[41] History was the key to knowledge, but understanding of the past could not be used to predict the future. Change would come gradually, or dramatically, when men of genius exploited new possibilities.

Clausewitz was equally hostile to the opposite view, expressed most forcefully by Georg Heinrich von Berenhorst, that modern warfare was beyond the realm of rational analysis because it was a manifestation of unknown and uncontrollable spiritual qualities that found expression through will and emotion.[42] Clausewitz sought a middle ground, and gradually came to understand war as something that straddled science and art.

> Rather than comparing it to art, we could more accurately compare it to commerce . . . and it is *still* closer to politics, which in turn may be considered as a kind of commerce on a larger scale. Politics, moreover, is the womb in which war develops – where its outlines already exist in their hidden rudimentary form, like the characteristics of living creatures in their embryos.[43]

Within these limitations theory was possible, but not the kind of predictive theory sought by so many of Clausewitz's contemporaries. The proper goal of social theory was to structure reality and make it more comprehensible by describing the relationship between the parts and the whole. Theory could provide the starting point for working through a problem and standards for evaluation. Theory in art, architecture or medicine – the models Clausewitz had in mind – helped to conceptualize problems, but offered little guidance in practice. An architect would learn a lot from

[40] Clausewitz, *Strategie aus dem Jahr 1804*, p. 82.
[41] Carl von Clausewitz, "Über den Zustand der Theorie der Kriegskunst," reprinted in Walther M. Schering, *Carl von Clausewitz: Geist und Tat* (Stuttgart: A. Kröner, 1941), pp. 52–53, and cited in Paret, *Clausewitz and the State*, p. 155.
[42] On Berenhorst, see Gat, *Origins of Military Thought*, pp. 150–55. Clausewitz shared, and may have been influenced by his critique of scientific theories of war.
[43] Clausewitz, *On War*, Book II, ch. 3, p. 149.

studying the form and function of existing structures, but such knowledge would not enable him to design his own buildings. According to Clausewitz, "Theory is meant to educate the mind of the future commander, or, more accurately, to guide him in his self-education, not to accompany him to the battlefield, just as a wise teacher guides and stimulates a young man's intellectual development but is careful not to lead him by the hand for the rest of his life."[44]

From Galileo, Descartes and Newton, Enlightenment philosophers like Hume borrowed the concept of general laws that could explain concrete instances. The cause of an event was neither its purpose nor its original cause, but its immediate or "efficient" cause – the event prior in time that was responsible for bringing it about. This conception encouraged quantification and the belief that everything could be described by general laws and efficient causes. To impose limits on this process would defy reason. The new physics, accordingly, encouraged the belief that everything was knowable and could be reduced to a set of mathematical laws. If all phenomena were material, there was no room for the independent mind and no foundation for ethics. The mind was either a machine or a ghost. German idealism was a reaction against both the skepticism and materialism of the Enlightenment, and an effort to reassert the centrality of human beings in the overall scheme of things. Kant's transcendentalism sought to show that there is more to human beings than can be discovered by observation and introspection. To understand what we must be like to have the experiences that we have, we must work back from experience to the structure and overall unity of the subject. The world of the subject is distinct from the external world, and motivated by will. Human beings are free in the most radical sense; they are self-determining, not as natural beings, but through their pure, moral wills.[45]

Radical freedom could only be achieved at the expense of man's unity with nature. Kant introduced a division between man and nature, different from, but at least as great, as the dualism brought about by the Enlightenment from which he sought escape. His successors, the generation of the 1790s, sought desperately to overcome this dualism while preserving the radical freedom and the potential they perceived it had to bring about spiritual transformation. They were reacting, as writers and philosophers almost always do, to external developments, and most specifically, the French Revolution. They hoped that Germany could be

[44] Ibid., Book II, ch. 2.

[45] Taylor, *Hegel*, pp. 11–36; Ameriks, "Introduction"; Beiser, "The Enlightenment and Idealism"; Pinkard, *German Philosophy*, pp. 19–81.

the midwife of a spiritual revolution that would succeed where the political revolution of France had failed. This revolution would pave the way for a reintegration of man and nature, and encourage the kind of creative expressiveness that had not been witnessed since fifth-century Athens. The Greeks, Schiller wrote, "are what we were; they are what we shall become again."[46] Various systems toward this end were developed by Fichte, Schlegel, Schleiermacher, Schelling and Hegel.[47]

Clausewitz was familiar with this literature, and shared the political-ethical ideals that motivated its authors. He was particularly drawn to Johann Gottlieb Fichte, because of his belief that citizens had responsibilities to society and the state which they had to fulfill in accord with their own understanding and ability. Clausewitz wrote a warm and complimentary letter to Fichte in response to an essay he published on Machiavelli in 1807.[48] Clausewitz was not a philosopher, and made no systematic effort to address or resolve the dualism introduced by Kant. *On War* can nevertheless be read as an attempt to show how this might be done in a practical, limited way in one important social domain. Its underlying conception is very close to Fichte's "philosophy of striving" (*Strebensphilosophie*), which assumes a self-positing and absolute ego that creates all nature, but has no physical form. The finite ego strives to attain an idea or a goal by shaping nature in accord with its rational demands. It must strive endlessly to control nature, a goal it approximates but never achieves because of the resistance nature offers. Dualism is nevertheless partially resolved because the subject gains limited control over nature. For Clausewitz, we shall see, the soldier-statesmen strives to impose his will on nature by making war a rational expression of his goals. But nature, in the form of "friction," resists that control, and does so in proportion to the degree that rational control is sought. The best the soldier-statesmen can do is to approximate effective control, and, by doing so, create a synthesis in the form of a self-willed, enlightened but uneasy accommodation with nature.

Vom Kriege

In 1816, in Coblenz, after the Napoleonic Wars, Clausewitz returned to scholarship and began to write essays that would form the basis for

[46] Friedrich Schiller, *On Naive and Sentimental Poetry* (New York: Unger, 1966) p. 84.
[47] Taylor, *Hegel*, pp. 34–50; Paul Guyer, "Absolute Idealism and the Rejection of Kantian Dualism," in Ameriks, ed., *The Cambridge Companion to German Idealism*, pp. 37–56.
[48] "Letter to Fichte (1809)," English translation in Peter Paret and Daniel Moran, eds., *Carl von Clausewitz: Historical and Political Writings* (Princeton: Princeton University Press, 1992), pp. 270–84.

On War. The pace of work quickened in 1818 when he was appointed director of the *Allgemeine Kriegsschule* in Berlin. By 1827 he had produced some 1,000 pages divided into eight books.[49] He ceased writing in 1830, when he was transferred to the artillery. Before leaving for his new posting, he arranged his papers and packed them, his manuscript included, in sealed boxes. His literary remains were published posthumously, in the condition in which they were found, although Clausewitz's widow and his friend Major Franz August O'Etzel put a good bit of work into arranging the material.[50]

Clausewitz penned four short commentaries about his evolving manuscript. Between 1816 and 1818, he expressed his belief that analysis and observation, and theory and experience supported one another. He hoped that the propositions of his book would be "like short spans of an arch, and base their axioms on the secure foundation either of experience or the nature of war as such." In this way they would "be adequately buttressed."[51] In a note written around 1818, he explained that his original intention was to lay out his conclusions on the principal elements of war "in short, precise, compact statements, without concern for system or formal connection." But, he confessed, his analytical nature had asserted itself: "The more I wrote . . . the more I reverted to a systematic approach, and so one chapter after another was added." He now intended to revise the entire manuscript "to strengthen the causal connections in the earlier essays," and, if he could, "draw together several analyses into a single conclusion."[52]

Almost ten years later, after extensive writing and rewriting, he continued to express dissatisfaction with his manuscript. The first six books he dismissed out of hand as "a rather formless mess that must be thoroughly reworked once more." His self-criticism was motivated by a positive insight. For some years he had grappled with the anomaly that war in the real world often bore little relationship to the war without limits described by his theory. He finally resolved this discrepancy by recognizing that war could take two forms: general or limited. In the former, the objective is "to *overthrow the enemy* – to render him politically helpless or militarily impotent thus forcing him to sign whatever peace we please." In the latter, it is "*merely to occupy some of his frontier-districts* so that we can annex them or use them for bargaining at the peace negotiations."

[49] Paret, *Clausewitz and the State*, p. x.
[50] Marie von Clausewitz's, Preface, in Howard and Paret, *On War*, pp. 65–67.
[51] Author's Preface, written between 1816 and 1818, reprinted in Paret and Howard, *On War*, pp. 61–61.
[52] Author's Comment, written around 1818, reprinted in Paret and Howard, *On War*, p. 63.

This distinction, based on the different political goals of the two types of war, led Clausewitz to what would become the starting point of his understanding of war as "*nothing but the continuation of policy with other means.*"[53]

In 1830, presumably at the time he packed up his manuscript and notes for safekeeping, he wrote a final note in which he disparaged his draft manuscript "as nothing but a collection of materials from which a theory of war was to have been distilled." He nevertheless expressed satisfaction with the first chapter of Book I, now in finished form, and the overall contents, although not the organization, of the other chapters. "The main ideas which will be seen to govern this material are the right ones, looked at in the light of actual warfare. They are the outcome of wide-ranging study: I have thoroughly checked them against real life and have constantly kept in mind the lessons derived from my experience and from association with distinguished soldiers."[54]

As Clausewitz feared, *On War* is difficult to read. Like the *History of the Peloponnesian War*, it is incomplete, full of apparent contradictions and must be read on multiple levels. Its arguments are best understood in comparison to contemporary and earlier texts by other writers. For all these reasons, Thucydides and Clausewitz lend themselves to misinterpretation, a problem aggravated by the standing both authors achieved. The key to unlocking *On War* is the dialectic, a concept developed by the sophists and Plato, revitalized by Kant and common to subsequent German philosophy. For Kant, Herder, Fichte, Hegel and Marx, the dialectic was imbued with teleological purpose; it was the mechanism that drove history and moved humanity to higher levels of political, economic and social integration and achievement. Clausewitz had little interest in metaphysics, and employed the dialectic purely for purposes of exposition. As early as 1815, his manuscripts show a fascination with the dialectic, and he would ultimately use it to distinguish war in theory (thesis) from war in practice (antithesis) and the possible synthesis of the two in a theory-guided, but experience-based, strategy devised by a soldier-statesman.[55] This solution came to Clausewitz late in his life and is not fully reflected in the text of *On War*.

The dialectic was also appealing to Clausewitz because it could be used to capture the polarity between war in theory and war in practice. Harking back to Empedocles and the Ionian physicists, Goethe conceived of nature as containing opposite forces that might be unified at a deeper

[53] "Note 10 July 1827," in Paret and Howard, *On War*, p. 69. (emphasis in original)
[54] "Unfinished Note," in Paret and Howard, *On War*, pp. 70–71.
[55] Paret, *Clausewitz*, p. 150, on his early interest in the dialectic.

level of understanding. This conception was taken up by Schelling and Hegel, for whom opposites were part of a greater whole because the existence of either pole required the existence of the other. The relationship between opposites was attractive to counter-Enlightenment philosophers because it helped to overcome the seeming differences and antagonism between negative and positive and to suggest an underlying unity of nature and human life. Clausewitz adopted the concept, but once again purged it of any metaphysical content.

The first three chapters of Book I present Clausewitz's theory of war and represent the core statement of his thesis. They develop a critique of existing approaches to theory – a subject I have already touched upon – and an overview of the antithesis he develops later in the book. At the outset of his manuscript, Clausewitz announces his intention to proceed "from the simple to the complex," and chapter 1 opens with a parsimonious and abstract definition of war and its purpose. In keeping with his view of theory, his definition attempts to capture the essence of war and the relationship between the whole and its parts. It is intended to provide the framework for a more detailed examination of the phenomenon in follow-on chapters and to remain valid despite the anticipated evolution of politics and technology.

In Book I, chapter 1, Clausewitz equates war with a duel in which each combatant tries through physical force to compel the other to do his will. "His *immediate* aim is to *throw* his opponent in order to make him incapable of further resistance." Countless duels make a war, but their purpose is the same. *"War is thus an act of force to compel our enemy to do our will."* The use of force is unavoidable and tends toward the extreme because if one side holds back the other will gain an advantage. The use of force sets in motion a process of reciprocal interaction [*Wechselwirkung*], and is the first of three extremes [*Äusserste*] that Clausewitz introduces. The only limiting factors in this reciprocal process of escalation are "the counterpoises inherent in war." These derive from the social conditions of states and the nature of their relationships; they exist *prior* to fighting and are not part of war.[56]

To compel the enemy to do one's will, he must be disarmed or put "in a situation that is even more unpleasant than the sacrifice you call on him to make." The hardships associated with this situation cannot be transient, or at least not give that appearance. Otherwise, the adversary will wait for a more favorable moment to resume fighting. The worst condition is to be defenseless, and that is why the immediate goal of war [*Ziele*] must be to destroy or disarm his forces to make him vulnerable. Because war

[56] Clausewitz, *On War*, Book I, ch. 1, pp. 75–76 (emphasis in original).

is the collision of opposing forces, the enemy will attempt to make you defenseless. "So long as I have not overthrown my opponent I am bound to fear he may overthrow me. Thus I am not in control: he dictates to me as much as I dictate to him." For Clausewitz, this is the second form of interaction and leads to the second extreme of war.[57]

To overcome an adversary you must "match your effort against his power of resistance, and this can be expressed as the product of two inseparable factors, viz. *the total means* at his disposal and *the strength of his will.*" Means encompass forces and their equipment and can be measured. Strength of will is an intangible factor, and usually a product of motive; it tends to increase in proportion to the gravity of interests at stake. In contrast to most of his contemporaries, Clausewitz insists that moral forces are at least as important as material capabilities; courage and morale, which prompt sacrifice and endurance, and largely determine the duration and outcome of wars. "You must calibrate your physical effort to overcome the enemy's will, but the enemy will do the same, and also act to strengthen the will of his forces and people to resist." This competition is the third form of interaction that pushes war toward the extreme.[58]

Clausewitz is adamant that war without fighting is an oxymoron. "Essentially war is fighting, for fighting is the only effective principle in the manifold activities generally designated as war."[59] He disparages as naive the growing hope among "the kind-hearted" that some ingenious way might be found to defeat an enemy "without too much bloodshed" – in German this is even more of an oxymoron as *Schlacht* means both battle and butchery. If wars between modern states "are far less cruel and destructive than wars between savages, the reason lies in the social condition of the states themselves and in their relationships with one another." Modern states do not "devastate cities" or "put prisoners to death" because they are more moral, but because "intelligence plays a larger part" in their warfare and has led them to more effective ways of using force to achieve their goals. He is adamant that so-called civilization has done "nothing practical to alter or deflect the impulse to destroy the enemy, and has stimulated development of increasingly effective means to do this, including the invention of gunpowder and constant improvements in the range, accuracy and rate of fire of rifles and artillery." Arms racing might be considered a fourth kind of interaction that pushes war to its extreme. Clausewitz does not describe it as such, probably because the pace of weapon development in his day was far slower and took place

[57] Ibid., p. 77. [58] Ibid., (emphasis in original).
[59] Ibid., Book II, ch. 1, p. 127, Book VIII, ch. 1, p. 577.

largely *between* rather than during wars. It is nevertheless implicit in his analysis.[60]

Clausewitz acknowledges that his "pure" definition of war represents a logical abstraction and that the human mind is not ruled by such fantasy. War never achieves the extreme posited by his theory. In practice, it is almost always "a pulsation of violence, variable in strength and therefore variable in the speed with which it explodes and discharges its energy." Clausewitz introduces fifteen "modifications in practice," all of them consequences of his recognition that war is never a wholly isolated act; never waged by means of a single decisive act, or set of simultaneous ones; and rarely results in a complete decision. War is never a total effort because neither side is ever able to mobilize all of its resources at the outset of a conflict. The political objective – the motive for war – determines, or ought to determine, the military objectives. It sometimes happens that there is no military objective proportionate to the political concessions sought, so means or ends must be modified. Military action is never continuous, but marked by pauses, some of them lengthy, in which one or both sides seek intelligence, mobilize resources, train and deploy forces and seek allies. Defense is a stronger form of fighting than offense, and the weaker the political motives of the side on the offensive, the more they will be neutralized by the disparity between these two forms of warfare. Nor is the outcome of war final; the defeated state is likely to consider its humiliation transitory and look for political and military ways of regaining what it has lost.[61]

These modifications do not detract from the definitional truth that war is always an act of policy and intended to serve a political goal. If it were a complete, untrammeled, absolute manifestation of violence – as the pure definition suggests – war would override policy considerations and adhere to laws of its own. However, "war is simply a continuation of political intercourse, with the addition of other means."[62] The policy goal must remain the prime consideration, but the political aim "must adapt itself to its chosen means, a process which can radically change it."[63] In general,

> The more powerful and inspiring the motives for war, the more they affect the belligerent nations and the fiercer the tensions that precede the outbreak, the closer will war approach its absolute concept, the more important will be the destruction of the enemy, the more closely will the military aims and the political objects of the war coincide, and the more military and the less political will war appear to be.

[60] Ibid., Book I, ch. 1, p. 76, and Book II, ch. 1, p. 127.
[61] Ibid., Book I, ch. 1, pp. 78–89. Quotes on p. 85.
[62] Book VIII, ch. 6B, p. 605. [63] Ibid., p. 87.

When motives are less intense, "war will be driven further from its natural course, the political object will be more and more at variance with the aim of ideal war, and the conflict will seem increasingly *political* in character."[64]

Clausewitz was struck by how wars vary in intensity and scope. Some of this variation, he reasoned, was a reflection of the differing ideas, capabilities and conditions of the times.[65] But much of it could be traced to the different political goals that motivated warring parties. As early as 1804, he devised the concept of limited war. By distinguishing limited from general or absolute war, conflicts in which the ends and means were constrained – as they so often were in reality – his theory was no longer such an imperfect representation of war in practice.[66] The opening chapter of *On War* introduces this distinction and puts forward the general proposition that "wars vary with the nature of their motives and of the situations that give rise to them." Subsequent chapters, most notably in Book Eight, explore in more detail the different goals and requirements of the two types of war. In absolute war the goal is to overthrow the opposing political unit or its political system, and one must break the will of the adversary to achieve this end. This usually requires destruction of its army and occupation of its capital, but even these punishments may not suffice if the adversary's population is motivated by intense commitment to a cause like nationalism. Clausewitz offers the Napoleonic Wars as his paradigmatic example of general war and proof that warfare can come close to achieving "this state of absolute perfection." Napoleon waged war "without respite until the enemy succumbed," and in the later stages of the war, Russia, Prussia, Austria and Britain "struck counter-blows with almost equal energy."[67]

Limited wars are fought for limited goals, e.g., control of a disputed territory, market or throne, and it is usually necessary only to bend the will of the adversary to obtain such concessions. This may be accomplished by defeating its army and occupying some of its territory. The wars of Frederick the Great are the prototype of limited war. He attacked the Austrian Empire to acquire Silesia, and later, to gain time and strength to solidify his acquisitions. In 1805 and 1806, Prussia and Austria adopted the even more modest aim of driving the French back across the Rhine.[68] The different goals of war not only dictate different military objectives but different strategies to achieve their objectives.[69]

[64] Book I, ch. 1, pp. 87–88. [65] Book VIII, ch. 2, p. 580, and ch. 3, pp. 586–91.
[66] Paret, *Clausewitz*, pp. 377, 381.
[67] Clausewitz, *On War*, Book VIII, ch. 2, p. 580. [68] Ibid., ch. 3, p. 583.
[69] Clausewitz, *On War*, Book I, ch. 1, pp. 87–88, ch. 2, pp. 90–99; Book VIII, ch. 3B, p. 585, and chs. 4 and 5, pp. 595–604.

In Book VI, chapter 26, Clausewitz describes a third kind of warfare: the people in arms. It differs from limited and general war in that its goals are purely defensive and its objective is psychological. Popular uprisings of the kind that occurred in Spain do not engage the principal forces of the invader but rather "nibble at the shell and around the edges." They must operate outside the theater of war, where the invader's forces are not deployed in strength and make occupation of those areas too costly. The enemy's only recourse is to disperse some of his forces to protect convoys, bridges, passes and marshaling areas. For their part, guerrillas must live among the people or in terrain difficult to penetrate with a regular army, and concentrate their forces only temporarily to surprise and overwhelm enemy units, preferably in their rear to threaten their lines of communication and supply. The enemy will have to disperse more of his forces for his own protection, creating more targets for the people to strike, supported perhaps by small formations of the regular army. Success will "arouse uneasiness and fear, and deepen the psychological effect of the insurrection as a whole."[70]

People's war can create the conditions for a successful counter-offensive by the defender's army or, Clausewitz implies, compel a militarily undefeated enemy to withdraw by making the occupation too costly to bear psychologically and politically.[71] In the latter case, guerrilla warfare and insurrection can achieve the same goal as destruction of the enemy's army: making the enemy vulnerable to unacceptable punishment. People's war offers another illustration of the proposition advanced by Clausewitz in chapter 2 that "many different roads can lead to . . . the attainment of the political object," and all of them involve fighting. "Everything is governed by a supreme law, the *decision by force of arms*."[72]

Clausewitz's definition of war and description of its several forms prompted Peter Paret to describe him as a phenomenologist in the sense envisaged by Husserl. Paret maintains that Clausewitz tried to provide a theoretical description of war that revealed its inner and unchanging structure. He sought to discover its "essence" (*Wesenschau*): the core properties something must have for inclusion in the set of a given phenomenon. To do this, Clausewitz attempted to free himself from his time and culture to discover elements common to all wars. He read history and used his imagination to explore endless counterfactual variations of war in his mind to consider which of their features he could subtract without denying war its essence.[73] The definition of war he finally developed, comes close, in my opinion, to what Weber would later call an ideal type:

[70] Ibid., Book VI, ch. 26, pp. 479–83. [71] Ibid.,
[72] Ibid., Book I, ch. 2, p. 99. [73] Paret, *Clausewitz and the State*, pp. 357–58.

an analytical accentuation of aspects of one or more attributes of a phenomenon to create a mental construct that will never be encountered in practice but against which real world approximations can be measured.[74] Clausewitz wrote that "Theory has the duty to give priority to the absolute form of war and to make that form a general point of reference, so that he who wants to learn from theory becomes accustomed to keeping that point constantly in view, to measuring all his hopes and fears by it, and to approximating it *when he can* or *when he must*."[75] By relaxing and elaborating upon his definition, he made it more relevant and descriptive of war in practice. In his antithesis, to which I now turn, he introduced additional principles in tension with the core principles of war, that further distinguished war in practice from war in theory.

The most important of these principles is friction. It makes action in war "like movement in a resistant element." "Countless minor incidents – the kind you can never foresee – combine to lower the general level of performance, so that one always falls short of the intended goal." These difficulties accumulate to produce a kind of friction "that is inconceivable unless one has experienced war."[76] Drawing on his own experience, Clausewitz describes how easy it is for things to go wrong on a campaign. "Fog can prevent the enemy from being seen in time, a gun from firing when it should, a report from reaching the commanding officers. Rain can prevent a battalion from arriving, make another late by keeping it not three but eight hours on the march, ruin a cavalry charge by bogging the horses down in mud. . . ." To these physical impediments must be added the friction generated by inadequate or misleading intelligence, physical exertion and exposure to danger. They combine in synergistic ways to slow down the machine of war.

So long as a unit fights cheerfully, with spirit and élan, great strength of will is rarely needed; but once conditions become difficult, as they must when much is at stake, things no longer run like a well-oiled machine. The machine itself begins to resist, and the commander needs tremendous will-power to overcome the resistance. As each man's strength gives out, as it no longer responds to his will, the inertia of the whole gradually comes to rest on the commander's will alone.

[74] Max Weber, *On The Methodology of the Social Sciences*, trans. and ed. Edward A. Shils and Henry A. Finch (Glencoe, Il.: Free Press, 1949), pp. 90–95. First published in the *Archiv für Sozialwissenschaft und Sozialpolitik* in 1904.

[75] Clausewitz, *On War*, Book VIII, ch. 2, p. 589.

[76] Ibid., Book I, ch. 7, pp. 118–21, and Carl von Clausewitz, *The Campaign of 1812 in Russia (1823–1825)*, in Carl von Clausewitz, *Historical and Political Writings*, ed. and trans. Peter Paret and Daniel Moran (Princeton: Princeton University Press, 1992), p. 165.

Clausewitz warns his readers that "No general can accustom an army to war" because "Peace time maneuvers are a feeble substitute for the real thing."[77]

The second characteristic that distinguishes war in practice is the role of emotions. War is a rational act – it consists of the use of force to attain political ends – but "the emotions cannot fail to be involved." Hostile feelings may not be the source of war, but they are aroused the moment fighting begins. The extent to which they become involved depends on the level of civilization of the warring societies, the nature of the interests at stake and the duration of the conflict.[78] Emotions can retard the spread of violence, when fear of political loss or of one's life makes leaders or soldiers cautious. But hatred and desire for revenge can push war toward the extreme despite the intent of leaders to keep it limited. Clausewitz did not expect this to happen often, but recognized the disastrous consequences of a runaway spiral of escalation.[79]

Although he does not characterize chance as a separate principle, Clausewitz makes repeated references to the significant consequences it has for warfare. "No other human activity," he insists, "is so continuously or universally bound up with chance. And through the element of chance, guesswork and luck come to play a great part in war." The subjective nature of war makes it "more than ever look like a gamble."[80] War in practice is thus a "remarkable trinity – composed of primordial violence, hatred, and enmity, which are to be regarded as a blind natural force; of the play of chance and probability within which the creative spirit is free to roam; and of its element of subordination, as an instrument of policy, which makes it subject to reason alone."[81]

War in theory and war in practice represent polarities than can never be reconciled. Clausewitz nevertheless believed it possible – but extraordinarily difficult – for gifted leaders to achieve a synthesis: they could use theory to structure the problem of war and use the understanding that comes from practical experience and knowledge of history to adapt general principles to specific circumstances. "Theory cannot equip the mind with formulas for solving problems, nor can it mark the narrow path on which the sole solution is supposed to lie by planting a hedge of principles on either side. But it can give the mind insight into the great mass of phenomena and of their relationships, then leave it free to rise into the higher realms of action."[82] Good theory also allows the commander "to see things simply, to identify the whole business of war completely with himself, that is the essence of good generalship. Only if the mind

[77] Clausewitz, *On War*, Book I, ch. 8, p. 122. [78] Ibid., Book I, ch. 1, p. 76.
[79] Ibid., p. 88. [80] Ibid., p. 85. [81] Ibid., p. 89. [82] Book VIII, ch. 1, p. 578.

works in this comprehensive fashion can it achieve the freedom it needs to dominate events and not be dominated by them."[83]

The interplay of theory and practice is apparent in the two principal tasks of generals: the formulation and implementation of strategy. Theory dictates that political goals determine military objectives and the strategies appropriate for achieving them. In practice, this is almost always a dynamic process because of the great differences in the conditions, will and character of peoples. We can never know beforehand how much effort will be required to bend or break the will of a particular adversary. This only becomes apparent in the course of the fighting, and can dictate revisions in strategies or even goals.[84] The most rational strategic plan may be defeated by friction, so strategy must recognize and plan for the physical, logistical, intellectual and psychological impediments likely to interfere with a war plan's execution. Here too, reality may be significantly at odds with expectations. In dealing with these kinds of problems, intellectual activity leaves the field of the exact science of logic and mathematics. It then becomes an art in the broadest meaning of the term – the faculty of using judgment to detect the most important and decisive elements in the vast array of facts and situations. Undoubtedly this power of judgment consists to a greater or lesser degree in the intuitive comparison of all the factors and attendant circumstances; what is remote and secondary is at once dismissed while the most pressing and important points are identified with greater speed than could be done by strictly logical deduction.[85]

Good generalship requires effective responses to rapidly changing political, strategic and tactical circumstances. Assessing all these factors is "a colossal task," and beyond the powers of the normal person. "Rapid and correct appraisals call for the intuition of genius; to master all this complex mass by sheer methodical examination is obviously impossible." Bonaparte insisted, and Clausewitz agreed, that "Newton himself would quail before the algebraic problems it could pose."[86]

Successful commanders solve these problems through a combination of intellect and instinct. "The knowledge needed by a senior commander is distinguished by the fact that it can only be attained by a special talent, through the medium of reflection, study and thought; an intellectual instinct which extracts the essence from the phenomena of life, as a bee sucks honey from a flower. In addition to study and reflection, life itself serves as a source. Experience, with its wealth of lessons, will never produce a *Newton* or an *Euler*, but it may well bring forth the higher calculations of a *Condé* or a *Frederick*."[87]

[83] Ibid., p. 578. [84] Book I, ch. 1, pp. 81, 87.
[85] Book VIII, ch.3B, p. 585. [86] Ibid., p. 586. [87] Book II, ch. 2., p. 146.

War is also distinguished by the magnitude of what is at stake. This does not increase the complexity of the problems commanders face, but it does magnify the value of correct solutions and the costs of incorrect ones. "Responsibility and danger do not tend to free or stimulate the average person's mind – rather the contrary; but wherever they do liberate an individual's judgment and confidence we can be sure that we are in the presence of exceptional ability."[88]

Above all else, the successful commander must understand the political purpose of war. Clausewitz is adamant that war "does not suspend political intercourse or change it into something entirely different."[89] At the highest levels of government, "the art of war turns into policy – but a policy conducted by fighting battles rather than by sending diplomatic notes."[90] The assertion, so often voiced by military leaders, that "a major military development, or the plan for one, should be a matter for purely military opinion is unacceptable and can be damaging. Nor is it sensible to summon soldiers as many governments do when they are planning a war, and ask them for *purely military advice*."[91] At every level of decision, military action must be responsive to the political goals for which the war is being fought.

In an implied criticism of Prussian practice, Clausewitz ridiculed the notion that "a minister of war immersed in his files, an erudite engineer or even an experienced soldier would, on the basis of their particular experience, make the best director of policy." Leadership demands a "distinguished intellect and strength of character."[92] Ideally, the qualities of statesman and soldier should be combined in one person, and Clausewitz had Gustavus Adolphus, Frederick and Napoleon in mind as role models. He recognized that political and military authority were in practice often divided, and that such division gave rise to tensions and conflicts over respective spheres of authority. In this circumstance, it was essential for political leaders to assert authority over their military counterparts, but at the same time make policy with full knowledge of the possibilities and limitations of the military instruments under their control. "If war is to be fully consonant with political objectives, and policy suited to the means available for war . . . the only sound expedient is to make the commander-in-chief a member of the cabinet, so that the cabinet can share in the major aspects of his activities." It was also important to support the authority of the commander-in-chief, and it was "highly dangerous" to let any other soldier influence in the cabinet.[93]

[88] Book VIII, ch. 3B, p. 586. [89] Ibid., p. 586. [90] Ibid., ch. 6B, p. 607.
[91] Ibid. [92] Ibid., p. 608. [93] Ibid.

Clausewitz's conception of leadership is strikingly modern. It is based on the premise that every step up the chain of command makes greater intellectual demands on its office holders. The commander-in-chief

> must be familiar with the higher affairs of state and its innate policies; he must know current issues, questions under consideration, the leading personalities, and be able to form sound judgments. He need not be an accurate observer of mankind or a subtle analyst of human character; but he must know the character, the habits of thought and action, and the special virtues and defects of the men whom he is to command. He need not know how to manage a wagon or harness a battery horse, but he must be able to gauge how long a column will take to march a given distance under various conditions. This type of knowledge cannot be forcibly produced by an apparatus of scientific formulas and mechanics; it can only be gained through a talent for judgment, and by application of accurate judgment to the observation of man and matter.[94]

In contrast to the projects of high modernism, Clausewitz's synthesis recognizes the essential contribution of *mētis* (practical skills) and the limits – and dangers – of theoretical knowledge. This is apparent not only in his discussion of leadership, but his comparison, noted earlier, of war with the professions and politics. Someone with *mētis* is an astute observer of reality and always on the lookout for an opportunity to achieve what the Greeks called *kairos* – an advantage gained by doing the right thing at the right moment. *Mētis* presupposes a fine sense of timing that, in politics, brings success in part because it catches opponents by surprise.[95] Thucydides uses *mētis* in this sense; the best commanders, like Brasidas, combine a good, analytical understanding of the big picture with a superb tactical sense.[96] Clausewitz's understanding of war is much the same.

The old and the new

The Great Elector and his successors had organized the Prussian state to benefit their army. The canton system provided agricultural workers and less prosperous peasants as foot soldiers, and Junker aristocrats served as officers. More prosperous peasants worked on estates and generated the surplus that allowed the king to buy foreign mercenaries who, by 1804, comprised about half the full strength of the army.[97] Aristocrats and foreigners alike staffed an increasingly large civil service which, like

[94] Book II, ch. 2, p. 146.

[95] Andrea Wilson Nightingale, "Sages, Sophists, and Political Philosophers: Greek Wisdom Literature," in Oliver Taplin, ed., *Literature in the Greek World* (New York: Oxford University Press, 2000), pp. 138–73.

[96] Thucydides, I.138.3.

[97] Otto Büsch, *Military System and Social Life in Old Regime Prussia, 1713–1807: The Beginnings of the Social Militarization of Prusso-German Society*, trans. John G. Gagliardo

the army, was closely supervised by the king and had as its primary function the extraction of the resources needed to support a large military establishment. Prussia was only the thirteenth most populous state in Europe, but Frederick the Great inherited its fourth largest army – a force 83,000 strong – which he used to conquer Silesia and achieve a position of near-equality with Austria.[98]

By the time of the Napoleonic Wars, the Frederician army was coasting on the laurels of past victories. Steady bureaucratization had led to a confusing proliferation of command structures with overlapping and ill-defined authorities. Rigidly enforced exclusion of bourgeois sons from the officer corps after 1763 deprived the army of considerable talent. It also required extensive recruitment abroad as the Junker class could provide only a fraction of the needed officers. Their sons usually entered service at the age of twelve or thirteen and received very little in the way of education. The officer corps as a whole was barely literate and largely ignorant of mathematics beyond simple arithmetic. The anti-educational bias of the army functioned to support the authority of the Junkers, who regarded seniority, not performance, as the basis for promotion. Senior commanders were long in the tooth, inflexibly conservative and reluctant to deviate from strategies and tactics that had been successful in the Seven Years War. Prussia's poor performance in the 1792–95 campaigns against France did little to disabuse most commanders of their belief in the army's invincibility.[99]

For a vocal minority of officers these campaigns were an eye-opener. Scharnhorst had been impressed by the mobility and élan of French forces and the ability of their *tirailleurs* to fight as individuals, seek cover wherever they could find it and direct well-aimed fire into the massed ranks of the Prussian line. He informed his readers and students at the *Kriegsschule* that the French were successful because they had become more efficient in mobilizing the resources of their societies and creative energies of their citizens. To preserve its independence, Prussia had to follow suit and

(Atlantic Highlands, N.J.: Humanities Press, 1997 [1962]); Christopher Duffy, *The Army of Frederick the Great* (New York: Hippocrene Books, 1974), for the organization of the eighteenth-century Prussian army.

98 Gordon A. Craig, *The Politics of the Prussian Army, 1640–1945* (New York: Oxford University Press, 1955), pp. 1–14; Gerhard Ritter, *Frederick the Great*, trans. Peter Paret (Berkeley and Los Angeles: University of California Press, 1968).

99 Of a total of 7,166 officers in 1806, some 700 non-aristocrats served in the less prestigious branches of the service. William O. Shanahan, *Prussian Military Reforms, 1786–1813* (New York: Columbia University Press, 1945), pp. 14–34; Carl von Clausewitz, "Prussia in the Year 1806," in *Historical and Political Writings*, pp. 32–84; Craig, *The Politics of the Prussian Army*, pp. 143; Simms, *The Impact of Napoleon*, chs. 2 and 3 on the institutional setting.

introduce radical military and social reforms.[100] Scharnhorst was not alone in urging change. In 1803, Karl Friedrich von dem Knesebeck had drawn up a far-reaching plan for reorganization of the army based on the recognition that war required a national response. The following year, General von Courbière pleaded unsuccessfully for the creation of a cadre system that would allow a rapid wartime expansion of the army.[101]

None of these plans made headway against the deeply ingrained conservatism of the king and a Junker aristocracy intent on preserving its sinecures in the army, absolute control of local government and freedom from taxation. In 1806 Prussia went to war confident of victory, but with antiquated weapons, a disorderly mobilization and without adequate diplomatic preparation. Command was vested in the quasi-senile Duke of Brunswick, who had neither a strategic plan nor any appreciation of the value of good staff work. The duke and king were still debating how to proceed when Napoleon's army unexpectedly appeared on the far side of the Thuringian forest and overwhelmed the Prussian advance guard at Saalfeld on 10 October. The duke ordered a retreat in the hope of protecting his lines of communication, but Napoleon pushed forward at an unheard-of pace and four days later caught up with a destroyed Hohenlohe's corps at Jena. The same day, Davout, with a force half the size of the duke's, attacked his flank at Auerstädt, and won a second decisive victory, largely because another aged general refused to commit his reserves without explicit orders. Only a few commanders, Blücher and Scharnhorst among them, offered any further resistance to the advancing French. Civilian authorities either fled or, like most of the population, willingly collaborated with what now became a French army of occupation.[102]

The king and the remnant of his army waged a war of resistance in East Prussia in alliance with Russia. Napoleon responded by instigating rebellions in Poland and Turkey and launching an offensive against Russia, which culminated in success at the Battle of Friedland. On 9 July 1807, the French and Russian emperors met on a barge in the middle of the Niemen River to sign the peace of Tilsit as a result of which Prussia lost half its territory and population, was forced to pay a large indemnity and support an army of occupation.[103] War, occupation and Napoleonic

[100] Gerhard Scharnhorst, "Entwicklung der allgemeinen Ursachen des Glücks der Franzosen in dem Revolutions-Kriege, und in besondere in dem Feldzuge von 1794. Als Einleitung zur Geschichte dieses Feldzuges," *Neues Militärisches Journal* 8 (1797), pp. 1–154; Paret, *Clausewitz and the State*, p. 73; White, *The Enlightened Soldier*.

[101] Shanahan, *Prussian Military Reforms*, pp. 61–87.

[102] Ibid., pp. 88–126; Craig, *Politics of the Prussian Army*, pp. 28–34.

[103] Schroeder, *The Transformation of European Politics*, pp. 294–323.

blockade had devastating effects. Prussia was ravaged by epidemics of cholera, typhoid and dysentery and famine. Child mortality in Berlin in 1807–08 reached almost 75 percent. Food prices soared and land values plummeted.[104]

In desperation, the king and his advisors turned to the reformers for help. The newly created Military Reorganization Commission, soon dominated by Scharnhorst and his disciples – Gneisenau, Boyen, Grolman and Clausewitz – coordinated their efforts with the new first minister, Freiherr Karl von und zum Stein (1757–1831), a Rhinelander very much influenced by Western ideas and culture. Their goal, as Stein put it, was "to arouse a moral, religious and patriotic spirit in the nation, to instil into it again courage, confidence, readiness for every sacrifice on behalf of independence from foreigners and for the national honor, and to seize the first favorable opportunity to begin the bloody and hazardous struggle." Scharnhorst and his associates worked feverishly to reform the internal structure of the army, to end its draconian and arbitrary justice, purge incompetent officers, impose universal conscription and open the officer corps to qualified commoners – all with an eye toward building bridges between the army and the people. They expected these reforms to go hand-in-hand with abolition of serfdom and estate privileges and improvements in the educational system. In the words of Gneisenau, Prussia had to be restructured as a "triple alliance of arms, science and constitution."[105]

This strategy was made possible by the restraint of German intellectuals, most of whom rejected the radical republicanism of the French Revolution in favor of more limited reform within the structure of the existing estates.[106] Like Karl August von Hardenberg, first chancellor from 1810 until his death in 1822, they tended to conceive of society as an extension of the state. Prussian reformers spoke of creating a citizens' society (*Staatsbürgergesellschaft*), but were reluctant to tamper too much with the existing arrangement (*Staatsgesellschaft*) that recognized under law a

[104] Hans-Ulrich Wehler, *Deutsche Gesellschaftstgeschichte* (Munich: Beck, 1987), I, p. 398.

[105] Shanahan, *Prussian Military Reforms*, pp. 127–50; Craig, *Politics of the Prussian Army*, pp. 37–53; Peter Paret, *York and the Era of Prussian Reform, 1807–1815* (Princeton: Princeton University Press, 1966), pp. 111–52; Thomas Nipperdey, *Germany from Napoleon to Bismarck, 1800–1866*, trans. Daniel Nolan (Princeton: Princeton University Press, 1996), pp. 19–66; quotes from Craig, p. 49 and Nipperdey, p. 38.

[106] Hegel, by contrast, in his *Philosophy of Right*, conceived of civil society as an important sphere of activity in its own right, and sought to liberate individuals from their *ständish* ties. He envisaged commercial society as the arena for individuals to advance their particular needs and interests, while the state would look after the general rights and welfare. *Hegel's Philosophy of Right*, trans. T. M. Knox (New York: Oxford University Press, 1973 [1843–44]).

diverse group of corporate bodies with special rights and privileges.[107] A widespread belief in the possibility of internal harmony encouraged reformers to conceptualize a political system in which the monarch played a central role. Many intellectuals favored maintaining the monarchy, even in its near absolutist form. In the long term, this constitutional outlook hindered the development of the rule of law and development of a parliamentary system. By interjecting a powerful utopian element into Prussian political culture, it also encouraged exaggerated fear of the consequences of domestic discord.[108]

The military reformers succeeded in adapting the structure and tactics of the army to modern warfare, in providing qualified staff officers to assist its commanders and in raising enough volunteers and conscripts to allow Prussia to field a force of 280,000, fully 6 percent of its total population. On 17 March, the day after Prussia declared war on France, the king issued a proclamation, "*An mein Volk*," in which, for the first

[107] Jonathan B. Knudsen, *Justus Möser and the German Enlightenment* (Cambridge: Cambridge University Press, 1986), pp. 4, 86, Matthew Levinger, *Enlightened Nationalism: Transformation of Prussian Political Culture, 1806–1848* (New York: Oxford University Press, 2000), p. 22.

[108] Levinger, *Enlightened Nationalism*, p. viii. The reformist era is the subject of longstanding historical controversy. Hans Rosenberg characterized it as a "revolution from within," that preserved most aristocratic privileges and strengthened the tradition of "bureaucratic absolutism." Similar arguments are made by Walter Simon, *The Failure of the Prussian Reform Movement, 1807–1819* (Ithaca: Cornell University Press,1955); Eckart Kehr, "Zur Genesis der preussischen Bürokratie," in Hans-Ulrich Wehler, ed., *Der Primat der Innenpolitik. Gesammelte Aufsätze zur preussisch-deutschen Sozialgeschichte im 19. Und 20. Jahrhundert* (Berlin: W. de Gruyter 1965), pp. 31–52; Ernst Klein, *Von der Reform zur Restauration: Finanzpolitik und reformgesetzgebung des preussischen Staatskanzlers Karl August von Hardenberg* (Berlin: W. de Gruyter,1965). Elizabeth Fehrenbach, "Verfassungs – und Sozialpolitische Reformen und Reformprojekte in Deutschland unter dem Einfluss des Napoleonischen Frankreich," 228 *Historische Zeitschrift* (1979), pp. 288–316; Bernd von Münchow-Pohl, *Zwischen Reform and Krieg: Untersuchungen zur Bewusstseinslage in Preussen 1809–1812* (Göttingen: Bandenhoeck & Ruprecht, 1987). Reinhart Koselleck, *Preussen zwischen Reform und Revolution: Allgemeines Landrecht, Verwaltung und Soziale Bewegung von 1791 bis 1848*, 3rd. ed. (Stuttgart: Ernst Klett, 1981), offers a more favorable reading of reformers, and portrays Stein and Hardenberg as committed to establishing a free market economy and more liberal institutions. More recent scholarship conceptualizes the reform period as "partial"or "defensive" modernization carried out in response to a range of international and domestic problems, including military defeat, a budgetary crisis, and declining legitimacy. See Herbert Obenhaus, "Verwaltung und ständische Repräsentation in den Reformen des Freiherrn von Stein," *Jahrbuch für de Geschichte Mittel- und Ostdeutschlands* 18 (1984), pp. 130–79; Barbara Vogel, *Preussische Reformen 1807–1820* (Königstein: Anton Hain Meisenheim, 1980); Wehler, *Deutsche Gesellschaftsgeschichte*; Robert Berdahl, *The Politics of the Prussian Nobility: The Development of a Conservative Ideology, 1770–1848* (Princeton: Princeton University Press, 1998); David Barclay, "The Court Camarilla and the Politics of Monarchial Restoration in Prussia, 1848–1858," in Larry Eugene Jones and James Retallack, eds., *Between Reform, Reaction, and Resistance: Studies in the History of German Conservatism from 1789 to 1945* (Providence, RI: Berg, 1995), pp. 123–56.

time, a Prussian monarch offered a justification to his people for war and the sacrifices demanded of them. The new army benefitted from excellent staff work and performed credibly in early engagements and at the Battle of Leipzig, where Napoleon was decisively routed. Bickering among the allies prevented a speedy pursuit and gave Napoleon time to recover, but the balance of resources had shifted against France and the end was now only a matter of time.[109]

Moral renewal was incompatible with absolute monarchy.[110] Reactionaries opposed every change and charged Stein and Scharnhorst with having "brought revolution into the country." Many Junkers felt threatened by the reformers' success in organizing a national uprising against France that encouraged the educated classes, and even some aristocratic youth, to expect dramatic changes at home. After Waterloo, the king became more receptive to their complaints, and was outraged by the nationalist fervor of some of the reformist officers and their desire to fight another war to establish Prussian hegemony in northern Germany. The reformers failed to foresee the extent of the reaction developing against them once the foreign threat receded. They overplayed their hand, quarreled among themselves and by 1819 were driven from office. The aristocracy reasserted its control over the officer corps and sidetracked legislation that would have continued universal conscription, preserved the *Landsturm* and retained the *Landwehr*. The latter was a territorial-based reserve force envisaged by the reformers as the institutional basis for a people's army. For the time being, all hopes were dashed that postwar Prussia might be transformed into a progressive state with a constitution and representative institutions.[111] The rejection of modernity and political change went hand-in-hand with an attempt to deny the revolution in military affairs they had produced. This revolution was equally anathema to the old regime because the reforms necessary to modernize the army

[109] Shanahan, *Prussian Military Reforms*, pp. 179–206.

[110] The role of Frederick William underwent revision with the works of Hans Rosenberg, *Bureaucracy, Aristocracy and Autocracy: The Prussian Experience, 1660–1815* (Cambridge, Mass.: Harvard University Press, 1958); J. R. Gillis, "Autocracy and Bureaucracy in Nineteenth Century Prussia," *Past And Present* 41 (1968), pp. 105–29; Kehr, "Zur Genesis der preussischen Bürokratie," all of whom portray a monarch who was successfully manipulated by his advisors and at the mercy of aristocratic interests. More recently, the pendulum has swung the other way, with the king portrayed as a mercurial but effective arbiter of all important decisions. See, e.g., Thomas Stamm-Kuhlmann, *König in Preussens grosser Zeit. Friedrich Wilhelm III, der Melancholiker auf dem Thron* (Berlin: Siedler, 1992); Simms, *The Impact of Napoleon*.

[111] Shanahan, *Prussian Military Reforms*, pp. 229–33; Craig, *Politics of the Prussian Army*, pp. 54–81; Walter M. Simon, *The Failure of the Prussian Reform Movement, 1807–1819* (Ithaca: Cornell University Press, 1955); Nipperdey, *Germany from Napoleon to Bismarck*, pp. 237–80; Koselleck, *Preussen zwischen Reform und Revolution*, pp. 318–32; Levinger, *Enlightened Nationalism*.

threatened the prerogatives of the aristocracy and the monarchy. In the eyes of many conservatives, the cure was at least as bad as the disease.

This was the political context in which Clausewitz wrote and endlessly revised the manuscript that would posthumously be published as *On War*. In Book VIII, chapter 3, he offers a brief overview of the history of warfare that touches on such diverse societies as the Tartars, the Greek republics, Rome, medieval principalities, the commercial cities of early modern Europe and the modern territorial state. The purpose of the exercise is to challenge the illusion that with Napoleon out of the way war could once again be "tamed" and return to the pattern of limited, restrained and leisurely conflicts that characterized dynastic conflicts of the late eighteenth century. Clausewitz does not imply that limited war is no longer possible, only that it carries a great risk of runaway escalation.

Clausewitz's analysis is thoroughly modern in that it attributes diverse patterns of warfare to the underlying sociopolitical characteristics of the combatants and the external environment in which they operate. The ancient city states were small and their armies smaller still because the mass of the people was excluded from participation. Of necessity, they fought local, limited wars of territorial aggrandizement. Rome was the sole exception, and expanded initially through a series of alliances and assimilation of the peoples of southern Italy to its language and culture. This base provided adequate wealth and population for a strategy of military conquest, with each new conquest providing additional resources for further expansion. The great commercial cities and republics of early modern Europe created mercenary armies of *condottieri*. They were expensive and poorly trained, and fighting largely consisted of mock encounters between small forces. As competition reduced the number of political units, and kings asserted more authority over feudal lords, larger and more capable states emerged. The wars between them were fewer, and those that occurred betrayed the still fragmentary nature of national cohesion.

Gradually, national unity was established, and by the end of the seventeenth century, the age of Louis XIV, the standing army reached maturity. But if war gained in power and effectiveness, it became entirely divorced from the people. Governments "parted company with their peoples and behaved as if they were themselves the state." The means of war were the resources they could extract from populations and the rag-tag collection of mercenaries this allowed them to buy. Knowing their own limits and those of their adversaries, leaders understood that they were reasonably safe from total defeat but had to restrict their aims. If their army was annihilated they would not have the resources to raise another one, and this constraint enjoined the greatest caution in the limited campaigns that did occur. War became increasingly positional, a contest in maneuver, with battle avoided whenever possible. Even gifted commanders like Gustavus Adolphus, Charles XII and Frederick operated under these constraints. They recognized that military success was almost certain to provoke countervailing coalitions. "War was thus deprived of its most dangerous feature – its tendency toward the extreme, and of the whole chain of unknown possibilities which would follow."[112]

"All Europe rejoiced in this development," Clausewitz wryly observes. The decline in inter-state violence was considered "a logical outcome of the enlightenment." In fact, it reflected the survival of antiquated political structures and ways of thinking that the French Revolution was about to challenge, and in some places, sweep away. "In 1793," Clausewitz wrote,

> a force appeared that beggared all imagination. Suddenly war again became the business of the people – a people of thirty millions, all of whom considered themselves to be citizens .... The people became a participant in war; instead of governments and armies as heretofore, the full weight of the nation was thrown into the balance. The resources and efforts now available for use surpassed all conventional limits; nothing now impeded the vigor with which war could be waged, and consequently the opponents of France faced the utmost peril.

This change did not happen all at once. At the outset, French revolutionary armies had serious deficiencies in leadership, tactics and supply. "Once these imperfections were corrected by Bonaparte, this juggernaut of war, based on the strength of the entire people, began its pulverizing course through Europe."[113]

At the time of the French Revolution, the Prussians and most other continental armies relied on conscripts and foreign mercenaries. They were poorly paid, inadequately trained, largely unmotivated and likely to desert at the first sign of serious combat. Armies maneuvered in shallow but tightly packed lines because these formations, while awkward, made it possible for officers to exercise control and enforce discipline. Cavalry were used as shock troops to probe flanks, disrupt enemy attacks and harass retreating forces. Logistics and command and control problems limited the size of operational units to battalions, or regiments at most. French conscripts were on the whole ideologically committed, more responsive to training and less likely to desert when out of sight of their officers. Even before the Revolution, the French had begun to experiment with maneuver and attack columns, both of which included skirmishers allowed to fire at will, and the use of cavalry and foot soldiers to forage for supplies. The Revolution and subsequent efforts to construct a politically reliable officer corps temporarily degraded the quality of the army because so many qualified officers were lost and replaced by

[112] Clausewitz, *On War*, Book VIII, ch. 3, pp. 586–89. [113] Ibid., pp. 502–03.

incompetents, but radical measures – including the occasional beheading – improved the quality of leadership at every level. Better officers, Bonaparte among them, integrated close order and open forces and artillery into large and maneuverable armies which they used to close with and destroy the more traditional forces of the conservative monarchies. Bonaparte's Italian campaign of 1800 was merely the harbinger of things to come.[114]

French successes compelled their adversaries to adopt their methods or find effective counter-strategies. This happened first in Spain, where resistance to France developed almost spontaneously among the people and took the form of a people's war. In 1809, after a series of crushing defeats at the hands of Napoleon, the Austrian government made an unprecedented effort to mobilize new forces and reserves. In 1812, the Russians exploited their vast spaces to conduct a strategic retreat and lay waste to towns, cities and resources that might otherwise have sustained Napoleon's advancing army. The French retreat from Russia encouraged Prussia to change sides and without money or credit and a population half its pre-war size, was able to mobilize a force twice the size of its 1806 army. By 1814, the German states and Russia between them put about a million men in the field.[115] Clausewitz observed that war again

> became the concern of the people as a whole and took on an entirely different character, or rather closely approached its true character, its absolute perfection. There seemed no end to the resources mobilized; all limits disappeared in the vigor and enthusiasm shown by governments and their subjects. Various factors powerfully increased that vigor; the vastness of the available resources, the ample field of opportunity, and the depth of feeling generally aroused. The sole aim of war was to overthrow the opponent. Not until he was prostrate was it considered possible to pause and try to reconcile the opposing interests.[116]

Clausewitz credited Napoleon with genius, but genius of a particular kind. He perfected a genre of warfare that the French Revolution and related economic and administrative advances had made possible. Napoleon's armies overran Europe because he and his countrymen were willing to expend men and material on a scale never before witnessed in Europe. France fielded large, well-supplied armies of conscripts who identified with the Revolution, and in its name were willing to risk their lives in costly battles far from their homeland. Clausewitz reasoned that

[114] John A. Lynn, *The Bayonets of the Republic: Motivation and Tactics in the Army of Revolutionary France, 1791–94* (Boulder: Westview, 1996).
[115] Clausewitz, *On War*, Book VIII, ch. 3, pp. 502–03.
[116] Ibid., p. 593, and a similar statement in "On the Life and Character of Scharnhorst" (1817), in Paret and Moran, *Historical and Political Writings*, p. 102.

the tremendous effects of the French Revolution abroad were caused not so much by new military methods and concepts as by radical changes in policies and administration, by the new character of government, altered conditions of the French people, and the like. That other governments did not understand these changes, that they wished to oppose new and overwhelming forces with customary means: all these were political errors.... In short, we can say that twenty years of revolutionary triumph were mainly due to the mistaken policies of France's enemies.[117]

What about the future? With Napoleon safely out of the way would warfare once again become rare, or at least limited and restrained? This would only happen, Clausewitz insisted, if "we again see a gradual separation taking place between government and people." This was highly unlikely for many reasons, not the least of which was the precedent set by the Napoleonic Wars. "Once barriers – which in a sense consist only in man's ignorance of what is possible – are torn down, they are not so easily set up again." "When major interests are at stake," Clausewitz warns readers, "mutual hostility will express itself in the same manner as it has in our own day."[118]

Clausewitz's history of warfare embeds an implicit theory of modernization. Progress, if that is the right word, can be measured along two dimensions: the ability of a political unit to extract resources and mobilize its population in support of domestic and foreign goals, and the extent to which the people become involved in the affairs of state. For Clausewitz, the two are related, although, as Frederick the Great showed, states that rely on coercion and efficient bureaucracies can extract considerable resources while keeping the masses disenfranchised. The French Revolution and Napoleon demonstrated that popular participation dramatically increases the power of the state, while at the same time making it vulnerable to the vagaries of domestic politics. Unlike Herder, who believed that the rise of national consciousness throughout Europe would promote peaceful coexistence among states, or Kant, who hoped that the emergence of republican states everywhere would do away with war, Clausewitz had no such illusions. Based on the experience of France, he worried that democracies would be more violent than their authoritarian predecessors. His argument resonates with those critics of the democratic peace who contend that democratizing states may be the most war-prone kind of regime.[119]

[117] Clausewitz, *On War*, Book VIII, ch. 6, p. 609. [118] Ibid., p. 593.
[119] Edward Mansfield and Jack Snyder, "Democratization and the Danger of War," in Michael E. Brown, Sean M. Lynn-Jones and Steven E. Miller, eds., *Debating the Democratic Peace* (Cambridge, Mass.: MIT Press, 1996), pp. 301–36.

War and politics

Clausewitz's analysis of Napoleonic warfare reaffirmed Scharnhorst's contention that warfare and political modernization could not be analyzed independently; the latter was the underlying cause of the former. Clausewitz pondered this problem over the course of his career, although not with the same intensity and detachment that he did the military manifestations of modernization.

Prussia was a backward, authoritarian monarchy, and Clausewitz began his career uncritical of this state of affairs. Not surprisingly, he assimilated the values of those around him. He was a Prussian patriot, unswervingly loyal to the monarchy, in favor of dynastic expansion, opposed to the French Revolution, and the French more generally, and disliked democrats and unassimilated Jews.[120] He shared the traditional Prussian outlook on the state: it existed to serve the army, and the function of the army was to expand the territory and power of the state. His early writings and notebooks exhibit a certain callousness about the exploitation of human capital for these ends, and very high expectations about the role of the king and his commitment to defend not only the interests of the state but its "sacred honor."[121]

Under the tutelage of Scharnhorst, and in response to his own observations, Clausewitz began to reflect more deeply upon problems of the state and political organization. In the course of his first campaign, he had been struck by the pockets of extreme poverty he encountered in the Prussian countryside. Scharnhorst convinced him that charity was not the solution, and that the limited and entirely paternalistic concern the Prussian state displayed toward its poor benefited neither the poor nor the state. The condition of the peasantry and urban poor could only be ameliorated through education and opportunities for self-betterment.[122]

Clausewitz gradually moved beyond the Frederician conception of the state in important ways. In keeping with the tenor of his age, he thought of Germany as a cultural community that transcended political borders and looked to Prussia and its king to play a leading role in national regeneration. Citizens in turn should subordinate their individual goals to this collective end. They should have the right to judge the morality of the state's policies, and it was incumbent upon them, especially public men, to prepare themselves through education to exercise this responsibility.

[120] Clausewitz, *Politische Schriften und Briefe*, p. 2; "The Germans and the French" (1807), in *Historical and Political Writings*, pp. 251–62; Paret, *Clausewitz and the State*, pp. 128–36 on France and the French, and pp. 212–13 on the distinction Clausewitz seemed to make throughout his life between assimilated Jews, with whom he had good relations, and unassimilated German and Polish Jews whom he described as vermin.

[121] Paret, *Clausewitz and the State*, pp. 94–95. [122] Ibid., p. 73.

Toward this end, Clausewitz committed himself to a life-long course of self-improvement by means of reading and discussion.

Clausewitz projected his own yearnings for accomplishment and recognition on to Prussia. Paret suggests that the state became "an all-powerful, feared person, with whose authority he could identity and from whom he could gain the self-confidence he required to attain his goals."[123] This was an obvious psychological strategy for a sensitive, ambitious young man of low social standing, separated from his family at age twelve and nurtured from birth in an environment that identified service to the monarch as the highest goal. The twin defeats of Jena and Auerstädt, the near-collapse of the Prussian state and the equanimity by which these developments were regarded by the majority of the populace, were a serious blow to Clausewitz's self-esteem. Some of his essays and letters of the period border on near-hysteria, and dwell on the shame he felt for himself and his country. We had "magnificent hopes," he wrote, but now "our whole beautiful relationship to Germany has been destroyed. We have been deprived of our civic happiness, our careers are ended, our strength lies idle, and the unjust judgment of the whole of Europe rests heavily upon us... Yet I want to call out to all Germans: *Honor yourselves* – that is – *Don't despair at your fate!*"[124]

Clausewitz attributed Prussia's defeat to the poverty and lassitude of the people's spirit. He saw this as the inevitable result of a paternalist state governed by incompetent leaders. "Had those who led the nation shown themselves to be better men, then the nation would have been animated by a different spirit." External strength was a function of internal unity; the people needed to submerge their private goals in favor of those of the state. Clausewitz was prepared to adopt the most extreme measures: "With whips I would stir the lazy animal and teach it to burst the chains with which out of cowardice and fear it permitted itself to be bound. I would spread an attitude throughout Germany, which like an antidote would eliminate with destructive force the plague that is threatening to decay the spirit of our nation."[125] In light of German history in the twentieth century, Clausewitz's apotheosis of the state and call for a strong leader seems a chilling portent.

When the Napoleonic threat receded and Clausewitz felt personally more secure, he developed a more moderate and psychologically detached

[123] Ibid., p. 131.

[124] "Historische Briefe," *Minerva* II (April 1807), pp. 25–26, quoted in Paret, *Clausewitz and the State*, p. 128; "Notes on History and Politics" (1803–1807) and from the "Political Declaration" (1812) in *Historical and Political Writings*, pp. 239–49, 287–303.

[125] Clausewitz to Marie Brühl, 28 February and 5 October 1807, *Correspondence*, pp. 91, 141–44, quoted in Paret, *Clausewitz and the State*, p. 129.

view of the state. He still insisted that the state required a powerful army to provide security and respect for its citizens in an anarchic and dangerous world. But he increasingly emphasized its internal responsibilities, and especially the use of its regulative and supportive powers to stimulate economic development and provide mass education. By such means, citizens could improve themselves, physically and morally. Clausewitz's thinking shows a progressive affinity toward Humboldt, who was entrusted with the reform of Prussia's educational system in the aftermath of Jena and Auerstädt. He viewed rational governance and education as the principal mechanisms to help individuals develop their *Humanität*. "The true end of Man," he wrote, was "the highest and most harmonious development of his powers to a complete and consistent whole."[126] Humboldt conceived of *Bildung* as a transformative process that overcame "one-sidednesss" and inculcated a strong sense of social morality. It was intended to generate civic spirit, loyalty to the state and acceptance of a society based on merit.[127] Following Humboldt – who in turn, was inspired by Plato – Clausewitz distinguished between knowledge and skill (*technē*) and education and training, and conceived of education as the harmonious development of aptitudes that would allow individuals to attain their full human potential. In his later years, Clausewitz gave precedence to the cultural mission of the state over and above its political one.[128] This represented a total reversal of his youthful conception of the state.

Clausewitz did not live long enough to finish *On War*, let alone develop a coherent statement of his evolving views on political structure. As with Thucydides, this has allowed scholars to draw contrasting portraits of Clausewitz by emphasizing different periods of his life and giving different weight to his actions or his writings.[129] The first serious study of his political views, published in 1920, was written by German historian, Hans Rothfels. It focused on Clausewitz's role in the Napoleonic war, and especially the crisis of 1812 which prompted Clausewitz and a coterie of fellow officers to enter Russian service to continue the struggle against France. For Rothfels, Clausewitz was the quintessential Prussian patriot who risked a promising career to perform great services for his

[126] Wilhelm von Humboldt, *The Limits of State Action*, ed. J. W. Burrow (Cambridge: Cambridge University Press 1969 [1791]), p. 16.

[127] Ibid., p. 16. See Walter Harris Bruford, *The German Tradition of Self-Cultivation* (Cambridge: Cambridge University Press, 1975), pp. 1–28; Suzanne L. Marchand, *Down from Olympus: Archeology and Philhellenism in Germany, 1750–1970* (Princeton: Princeton University Press, 1996), pp. 24–31.

[128] On Fichte's influence, see Paret, *Clausewitz and the State*, pp. 177–81.

[129] The point about time period is made by Paret and Moran in their "Introduction to Part Two" of *Historical and Political Writings*, pp. 223–35.

country.[130] The most prominent postwar study, by American historian Peter Paret, also privileges the Napoleonic era, but examines Clausewitz's subsequent career and writings. Paret emphasizes Clausewitz's commitment to reform and his frustration at the post-Napoleonic reaction in Prussia that halted reform and sidetracked his career. He depicts Clausewitz's youthful idealization of the state and emotional patriotism as giving way to a more mature, balanced and "realist" understanding of the state. Clausewitz's emotional detachment from the state and withdrawal from active politics were essential preconditions for his superb intellectual contributions to the study of war.[131] In her review of Paret, C. B. A. Behrens offers a third interpretation that focuses on the later Clausewitz and makes much of his 1831 essay, "Europe Since the Polish Partitions."[132] Behrens maintains that Clausewitz became increasingly conservative in response to the rise of democratic and national movements, and believes that had he not succumbed to cholera in 1831, he would have supported the forces of reaction in 1848.[133]

Clausewitz was a curious amalgam of the old and the new, but he was hardly the would-be reactionary that Behrens suggests. He had little regard for the aristocracy, which he pilloried as a largely parasitical class. In an unpublished manuscript written in the early 1820s, Clausewitz traced the historical development of the three principal classes of society: the nobility, the middle class and the subjects of the nobility. The noble "possessed his property through the sword .... and knew no other means of supporting himself." Once individual conquest became impractical, nobles "sought employment in military service of the state, which was the basis of the entire feudal system." But gunpowder and skillful foot soldiers did away with knights, and the noble's identification with the profession of arms was transformed from an honorable "corporate duty" into an unjustifiable "corporate prerogative." Together with administrative sinecures, it led to a system of "abuses and privileges" and profligate "extravagances" that continued into modern times. "We still remember from our youth the troop of servants, the ostentatious show of livery, clothing, and arms, without which a noble house was thought unable to

130 Rothfels, *Carl von Clausewitz*.

131 Paret, *Clausewitz and the State*; "Bemerkungen zu dem Versuch von Clausewitz, zum Gesandten in London ernannt zu werden," *Jahrbuch für die Geschichte Mittel-und Ostdeutschlands* 26 (1977), pp. 161–72; "Die politischen Ansichten von Clausewitz," in Ulrich de Mazière, ed., *Freiheit ohne Krieg?* (Bonn: Dümmler, 1980), pp. 333–48; "Gleichgewicht als Mittle der Friedenssicherung bei Clausewitz und in der Geschichte der Neuzeit," *Wehrwissenschaftliche Rundschau* 29 (1980), pp. 83–86.

132 *Historical and Political Writings*, pp. 369–76.

133 C. B. A. Behrens, "Which Side Was Clausewitz On?," *New York Review of Books*, 14 October 1976, pp. 41–44.

survive." Only recently, Clausewitz noted, "do we see noblemen managing their property according to commercial principles and turn, when necessary, to manufacturing and trade in agricultural products."[134]

The middle class, by contrast, "has never been able to contemplate any activity apart from increasing its wealth through diligence and hard work." Its collective wealth "could not fail to increase substantially over the centuries, and this, together with its growing numbers, inevitably made this estate more significant." By the end of the eighteenth century, the middle class "had become four or five hundred times larger than *l'ancien peuple* [the nobility], and in the eyes of philosophy, as of ordinary common sense, the enormity of its majority was the essential basis for its [political] claims." The peasant is also motivated by the same acquisitive drive, "because the peasant is also a *worker*." However, serfdom made it difficult, and often impossible, for the peasant to improve his condition. Where the conditions of serfdom have changed, or where the peasant has gained his freedom, Clausewitz observed, he has achieved much greater prosperity. The numbers and wealth of the peasantry have accordingly increased everywhere in Western Europe, and as a class, "It has drawn closer to the middle class, and the gap between them has narrowed."[135]

Clausewitz argues that the conflict between the nobility and the middle class in France led to revolution because of extraordinary abuses of their power by the nobility and its great oppression of the peasantry. German estates, by comparison, were administered prudently and paternalistically. Internal tensions were correspondingly less acute and "the impulse to revolution basically did not exist." The French example nevertheless inspired the German people and all the more so because it coincided with the corrupt and incompetent regimes of Joseph II in Austria and Frederick Wilhelm II in Prussia. The former's "wastefulness, his mistresses, his immoral officials, his absurd visions, and religious edicts were all things that recalled the worst epochs of other lands, cost the government the respect of the people, and made the benefits of revolution more understandable to many." People thus "approved *this goal* of the French Revolution even if they rejected its means."[136]

Clausewitz defends the key reforms implemented by Prussia and the south German states: abolition of serfdom and guild restrictions, opening the offices of state to the middle classes and, in some southern states, ending the tax-exempt status of the nobility. They were beneficial to these

[134] Carl von Clausewitz, "Agitation" (early 1820s), *Historical and Political Writings*, pp. 338–68.
[135] Ibid. [136] Ibid.

societies and essential to prevent revolution. Two important demands remained: unification and a constitution. Unification, he reasoned, could only come about through conquest because none of the German princes would voluntarily give up their sovereignty. The constitution was a more complex question. "The deliberations of a parliament can reinforce a government's policy, but they can also cripple it, and the one is as likely as the other." Geography is the determining factor. In the United States, Britain and Holland, constitutions strengthen the bonds between governments and people. But the German states, "surrounded on all sides by dangers" can only survive "by means of secrecy, resolution and diplomatic dexterity, and these are not the natural attributes of parliamentary bodies."[137]

Clausewitz struggled to find some way of reconciling the conflicting requirements of the modern age. Perhaps influenced by his friend Hegel, or vice versa, he regarded a monarch as essential to provide overall direction to the state, but had no illusions about the capabilities of the Hohenzollerns. He despaired at their preference to confine the circle of advisors to high-ranking nobility. The king was under the "constant influence of weaklings, profligates, and shirkers" and isolated from public opinion, the very conditions that led to disaster in 1806.[138] Clausewitz was equally horrified by the excesses of democracy, which in France had led to turmoil, violence and quasi-dictatorship. In postwar Germany it encouraged crude expressions of nationalism. Everywhere, it deflected public opinion from consideration of important issues. He nevertheless considered some form of popular participation in government essential to mobilize the energy of the people and to limit the abuses and incompetence of absolutist rulers.[139] Toward this end he favored a free press and some kind of franchise, limited by property, professional and gender qualifications. In 1819, he suggested that

> the government gather around it representatives of the people, elected from those who share the true interests of government and are known to the people. Let this be the government's main support, friend, and ally, as Parliament has been for a century the support of the king of England. With this institution let the government mobilize the energies of a valiant people against its external enemies and rivals; with this institution let the government enchain reckless forces if they turn against their own community in frenzy and ferment.[140]

137 Ibid.
138 From the "Political Declaration" (1812), p. 290; Taylor, *Hegel*, pp. 398–403, 339–40–44, 50, on his views on the monarchy and the estates.
139 "Agitation," and "Letter to Fichte," in *Historical and Political Writings*, pp. 338–68, 280–84.
140 Carl von Clausewitz, "On the Political Advantages and Disadvantages of the Prussian *Landwehr*" (1819), in *Historical and Political Writings*, pp. 331–34.

Clausewitz's argument mirrored that of Friedrich Schlegel, who wrote that in a republican democracy, the "people" would select the most learned and virtuous men and women to represent them.[141] Neither Schlegel nor his avid reader, Clausewitz specified how either the authorities or the people could identify candidates who shared "the true interests of the government," as Clausewitz put it or how such a limit on political representation would allow for the kind of constitution he thought essential to restrain the aristocracy.

Clausewitz's arguments imply that all European governments would have to reach some kind of accommodation with their middle classes. Those that failed to do so would remain backward, in a state of growing turmoil and invite revolution or conquest by more ambitious and efficient neighbors. Most European states would also have to confront the national question, and Clausewitz expected it to take one of two forms. As in Germany, nationalists would demand a political unit more or less coterminous with their conception of the nation. Alternatively, oppressed nationalities would demand their independence from one or more states of which they were part. The Polish rebellion of 1830 was the paradigmatic illustration of the latter, and had threatened the stability of the three great Eastern European powers. Clausewitz was dubious that these problems could be resolved peacefully because they often represented a conflict between two seemingly irreconciliable principles: national determination and state interests. He came down decisively on the side of state interests, even though he recognized elsewhere that they stood in the way of the transformation of Europe into a continent of nation states.[142]

The transition from absolute monarchies to some form of representative governments had equally important implications for the peace of Europe. Clausewitz described warfare as the *raison d'être* of the nobility, but it did not follow, as Joseph Schumpeter would argue a century later, that this class had to inflate international tensions and fight wars to preserve its prerogatives.[143] The nobility had proven remarkably adept at securing and exploiting a privileged position within the state, and its smarter representatives recognized that serious warfare would put them in jeopardy. Nor did Clausewitz subscribe to Kant's optimistic belief that

[141] Friedrich Schlegel, "The Concept of Republicanism," in Frederick C. Beiser, ed. and trans., *The Early Political Writings of the German Romantics* (Cambridge University Press, 1966), pp. 102, 108.

[142] His pessimism is most forcefully expressed in "Europe since the Polish Partitions," and "On the Basic Question of Germany's Existence," both written in 1831. *Historical and Political Writings*, pp. 372–76, 378–84.

[143] Clausewitz, "Agitation"; Joseph Schumpeter, *Imperialism and Social Classes*, trans. Heinz Norden (New York: Meridian Books, 1961). First published in two parts in *Archiv für Sozialwissenschaft und Sozialpolitik* in 1919 and 1927.

republicanism would reduce the incidence of war.[144] The French Revolution convinced him that more democratic states could be extraordinarily aggressive and more successful in mobilizing the physical and human resources necessary to wage war. The emergence of republics, or constitutional monarchies with popular backing, would not necessarily make Europe more peaceful but it certainly held out the prospect of making warfare more deadly. In Book I, chapter 1 of *On War*, Clausewitz had described improvements in weaponry as a natural consequence of warfare. The pace of improvements had quickened in the course of Clausewitz's lifetime, a development that caught his attention.[145] For this reason too, warfare could be expected to become more destructive in the course of the nineteenth century.

Clausewitz did not predict 1914, and certainly did not foresee the extent to which industrialization would transform war into a numbing contest of attrition between entire societies. He was nevertheless among the first to understand that popular participation in the life of the nation propelled warfare toward its extreme and raised at least the theoretical possibility of a conflict like World War I. A key goal of *On War* was to alert readers to the increasing difficulty of keeping modern war limited in its means and ends. I believe he would have made this warning more explicit had he lived long enough to finish the planned revisions of his manuscript. Given the way *On War* was read, it is doubtful that even explicit warnings would have had their intended effect. The principal lesson military men took away from the volume was the need to destroy an enemy's armed forces through a *Vernichtungsschlacht* [battle of envelopment and annihilation]. Prussia's success in fighting such a battle at Sedan in 1870 enhanced Clausewitz's standing and created expectations of a *frisch und frölich* [brisk and merry] war in 1914. It is one of the ironies of history that Clausewitz, a proponent of reform and a defensive foreign policy, became a source of inspiration and legitimacy for the most reactionary forces in Germany.

[144] Immanuel Kant, *Zum ewigen Frieden; Ein philosophischer Entwurf* (Königsberg: Friedrich Nicolovius, 1795).
[145] Clausewitz, *On War*, Book I, ch. 1, p. 76, and Book II, ch. 1, p. 127.

6 Hans J. Morgenthau

> The probing of the theorist of the moral pretension of the national interest puts him an awkward position by making him suspect of being indifferent to all truth and morality. This is why there are so many ideologies and so few theories.
>
> Hans J. Morgenthau[1]

Hans Morgenthau is the intellectual father of postwar realism and arguably the most important international relations theorist of his generation. His textbook went through six editions, one of them posthumous, and was almost universally read by undergraduate and graduate students of international relations over a span of three decades. Because of Morgenthau, realism became the dominant paradigm in the field and maintained this position throughout the Cold War. In the 1980s, neorealism gained wide currency, and graduate students increasingly read Kenneth Waltz in lieu of Morgenthau as their introduction to the study of international relations.[2] In the aftermath of the Cold War, scholars interested in power and its consequences are looking to more traditional forms of realism for insights. Morgenthau and his ideas are once again timely and need to be put into historical and intellectual context for a new generation of readers.

Like Thucydides and Clausewitz, Morgenthau has been misinterpreted. Critics misread his insistence on the enduring and central importance of power in all political relationships as an endorsement of European-style *Realpolitik* and its axiom that might makes right.[3] His

[1] *Politics in the Twentieth Century*, I, *The Decline of Democratic Politics* (Chicago: University of Chicago Press, 1962), p. 60.

[2] Kenneth N. Waltz, *Theory of International Politics* (Reading, Mass.: Addison-Wesley, 1979). The *Social Sciences Citation Index* reveals 500 citations for Waltz, *Theory of International Politics* between 1986 and 1995. Morgenthau's highest count in this period was 364, for *Scientific Man vs. Power Politics* (London: Latimer House, 1947 [1946]). Cited in Nicholas Greenwood Onuf, *The Republican Legacy* (New York: Cambridge University Press, 1998), pp. 222–23.

[3] Most of this criticism was made in the late 1940s and 1950s by scholars and activists committed to achieving world peace through world law. A more recent and equally misguided

advocates – and here I have in mind Kenneth Waltz and his disciples – purged his approach of its tensions and nuance in a misguided effort to construct a more scientific theory. In the pages that follow, I reconstruct the core of Morgenthau's thinking about international relations and situate it in a discussion of his broader understanding of politics and human nature. I argue that power was the starting point – but by no means the end point – of his analysis of international affairs. He believed that successful foreign policy depended more on the quality of diplomacy than it did on military and other capabilities, and had to be tempered by ethical considerations. International relations theory could neither predict nor serve as a template for foreign policy, but it could provide a useful starting point for statesmen to structure the problems and choices they confronted. In the second half of the twentieth century, the most important goal of international relations theory was to enlighten statesmen about the need to transcend the national state and accept some form of supranational authority.

Biography

Unlike Thucydides and Clausewitz, Morgenthau had no military experience and was not a member of an elite family. He was born in 1904 in Coburg, in the duchy of Saxe-Coburg, into a middle-class Jewish family. Part of Bavaria after 1920, Coburg was a relatively prosperous small city of 20,000 with about 300 Jewish residents.[4] Coburg's Jews were overwhelmingly middle class and assimilated, and generally described themselves as *deutsche Staatsbürger Jüdischen Glaubens* [Germans of the Jewish faith]. Morgenthau's paternal grandfather was a rabbi, and his father, Ludwig, a doctor and a conservative nationalist, who gave him the middle name of Joachim after the kaiser's youngest son. His father was cold, distant, "neurotic and oppressive," and young Hans was relieved when he left to serve in the war. He was close to his mother, who was warm and protective

attempt to tar Morgenthau with the brush of *Realpolitik* is Jan Willem Honig, "Totalitarianism and Realism: Hans Morgenthau's German Years," in Benjamin Frankel, ed., *Roots of Realism* (Portland, Or.: Frank Cass, 1996), pp. 283–313. Honig reviews Morgenthau's early legal writings, and exaggerates his idealism in this phase of his career. He also overdraws the similarities between Morgenthau's later writings on realism and the works of German jurist nationalist, Carl Schmitt. A more convincing discussion of the relationship between the two is to be found in Martti Koskenniemi, *The Gentle Civilizer of Nations: The Rise and Fall of International Law 1870–1960* (Cambridge: Cambridge University Press, 2002), ch. 6.

[4] Jürgen Erdmann, *Coburg, Bayern und das Reich, 1918–1933* (Coburg: Rossteutscher, 1969), pp. 79–158; N. F. Hayward and D. S. Morris, *The First Nazi Town* (Aldershot: Avebury, 1988), for Coburg between the wars.

and whom he credits with "saving him." He spent all his holidays with his much beloved maternal grandparents in Munich.[5]

Coburg politics in the Weimar period were characterized by escalating tensions between the left-center *Zentrum*-SDP (Social Democratic Party) coalition and the nationalist right, in which the Nazis came to play a dominant role. Hitler made his first public speech in Coburg in October 1922, and helped to make anti-Semitism a prominent issue in the *Landtag* (provincial parliament) election of 1924. The *Völkischer Block*, an alliance of right-wing parties, won the election, and one of their campaign promises was to strip Jews of all their rights as citizens. In June 1929, in elections for the *Stadtrat* [municipal council], Coburg voted a Nazi majority into power and earned the dubious distinction of becoming the first Nazi-governed town in Germany.[6]

Morgenthau was the only Jewish student in the Ducal Gymnasium Casimirianum, and was constantly exposed to anti-Semitic taunts and punishment. In 1922, his fourth and penultimate year in Gymnasium, the school commemorated its founding by Prince Johann. By tradition, the outstanding student in the school laid a wreath of bay leaves at the foot of the prince's statue, and Morgenthau was accorded this honor, much to the annoyance of many Coburg residents. On the day of the event leaflets appeared all over town denouncing him as a *gottverdammter Jude* [goddamn Jew]. The former prince, Carl Eduard, attended the ceremony and held his nose throughout Morgenthau's speech, a well-known anti-Semitic gesture intended to suggest that all Jews stank.

> Nobody would speak to me . . . And people would spit at me and shout at me. People would shake their fists at me and shout imprecations or antisemitic insults and so forth. It was absolutely terrible . . . probably the worse day of my life.[7]

Outside of school he fared no better. Forced by his father to join the German equivalent of the Boy Scouts, he was treated as a despised outsider. "I remember once, I marched in a group with people behind me and people in front of me. The people behind me would all spit on my back."[8] He could not wait to leave Coburg.

Morgenthau subsequently studied philosophy and law at the Universities of Frankfurt, Munich and Berlin. He practiced criminal and labor law in Frankfurt, and in 1931 was appointed acting president of the regional Labor Law Court. From 1932 to 1935, he taught public law at the

[5] Interviews with Bernard Johnson, Hans J. Morgenthau Papers, Library of Congress, B208; Christoph Frei, *Hans J. Morgenthau: An Intellectual Biography* (Baton Rouge: Louisiana State University Press, 2001 [1994]), pp. 12–16, citing additional materials.

[6] Erdmann, *Coburg, Bayern und das Reich*, pp. 65–58.

[7] Interviews with Bernard Johnson. [8] Ibid.

University of Geneva, and, unwilling to return to Nazi Germany, taught for a year in Madrid before emigrating to the United States. His first job was as an elevator boy, but he subsequently taught political science at Brooklyn College (1937–39), the University of Kansas City (1939–43), the University of Chicago (1943–71), The City College of New York (1971–75) and the New School for Social Research (1975–81). His most productive years were at the University of Chicago, where he became the Albert A. Michelson Distinguished Service Professor and a major intellectual figure on the campus.

Morgenthau was shy and reluctant to initiate conversations for fear of rejection, a neurosis he attributed to his earlier experiences in Germany.[9] He enjoyed the company of other intellectuals and relished the free exchange of ideas, preferably with a Cuban cigar in his mouth and a brandy snifter in his hand. He was protective of his personal life, and questions about his German past were taboo. Late in life he decided it was important to record some of his younger experiences and produced a short, 16 page, "Fragment of an Intellectual Autobiography," published in 1978. In it he acknowledged an early fascination with national liberation and war. During the Balkan War of 1912 he sympathized with Turkey's enemies, read about the Bulgarian siege of the fortress of Adrianople and purchased the sheet music of the Bulgarian national anthem to play on the piano. As a teenager he was drawn to philosophy and literature and dreamed of becoming a writer, a professor or a poet. He entered the University of Frankfurt with the intention of studying philosophy but was disappointed by the narrow, "rationalistic pretenses" of his professors and went off to Munich to read law. His father would not let him study literature, and he chose law as a fallback because it "appeared to make the least demands on special skills and emotional commitment." It gave him time to attend lectures on philosophy and literature. His autobiographical essay pays homage to the history and law professors who shaped his intellectual development and early legal career in Frankfurt.[10]

The most revealing part of this document is a lengthy excerpt from a senior German class assignment that Morgenthau wrote in *Gymnasium* in September 1922. He acknowledges an impending choice between two fields of activity. One in which "men year in year out, in eternally, repetitive, monotonous rhythm, sow and harvest, save and consume," and become happy by raking in more than others. The other in which "men, too work indefatigably . . . in the service of a higher cause." Here too

[9] Interview with Bernard Johnson; Frei, *Hans J. Morgenthau*, pp. 22–25.

[10] Hans J. Morgenthau, "Fragment of an Intellectual Autobiography: 1904–1932," in Kenneth W. Thompson and Robert J. Myers, *A Tribute to Hans Morgenthau* (Washington, DC: New Republic Book Co., 1977), pp. 1–17.

happiness can be achieved, through "the virtue of the deed," and its contribution to posterity. The idealistic Morgenthau wanted to "work in the service of a great idea, on behalf of an important goal." He saw two obstacles in his path: his untested abilities, and Germany's anti-Semitism. With respect to the former he took consolation in Goethe's observation that "Our desires are presentiments of the abilities that lie within ourselves, harbingers of what we shall be able to accomplish."[11]

Morgenthau could not respond to anti-Semitism with the same optimism. He was embittered by the blatant bias of the socially dominant groups of German society who "sanction and promote social ostracism and brutal insults that are destructive of ties of love and friendship." He felt doubly humiliated: by the insults to which he was directly exposed; and, indirectly, by the effects of a life time of such harassment on his parents and Jews of their generation. In what must have been a painful admission, he acknowledged that

> Men who have gotten accustomed to submitting to insults in silence and to patiently bear injustices; who have learned to grovel and duck; who lost their self-respect – such men must have spoiled their character, they must have become hypocritical, false and untrue. The moral resistance of people whose sense of honor and justice is day by day trod underfoot is being slowly but fatally crushed . . .[12]

The young Morgenthau insisted that "Free, straight personalities grow only in pure, fresh air." He vowed to struggle openly against anti-Semitism, never to accommodate to it. "The stronger the pressure from the outside becomes, the more violent and one-sided will be my reaction to this movement and its representatives." He nevertheless imagined a time in the not too distant future when he might be "Embittered by loneliness . . . excluded from all the pleasures of youth, [and] expelled from my Fatherland."[13]

The intellectual

Morgenthau's experience in Germany encapsulates the Janus face of modernity. The spirit of rational inquiry, secularization and concomitant desires for upward mobility liberated human beings from social and physical constraints and offered them myriad ways to fulfill their individual and collective potential. These developments constituted a challenge to the existing order and generated acute insecurity among individuals and classes who were threatened by economic and social change. Both

[11] Ibid., pp. 2–3. [12] Ibid., p. 2. [13] Ibid., p. 2.

consequences of modernity were readily apparent in the Second Reich and the Weimar Republic. Economic development, education and national unification fostered prosperity, extraordinary artistic and scientific achievements and inclusion of Germany's Jews into the cultural and political life of the nation. The decline of traditional values, defeat in World War I and the twin economic hardships of inflation and depression provided fertile ground for revolutionary mass movements. The corresponding rise of anti-Semitism and the triumph of Hitler deprived Germany's Jews of their rights, their property, and ultimately, their lives, if they did not emigrate.

Morgenthau's *Gymnasium* essay recognized the two faces of modernity and their divergent implications for his future. His theoretical writings, beginning with shorter wartime pieces and culminating in *Scientific Man vs. Power Politics*, published in 1946, build on this understanding.[14] The argument common to all these works is that modernity has encouraged a naive faith in the power of reason that has blinded well-meaning men to the darker side of human nature – with disastrous consequences for themselves, their institutions and the peace of the world. In an unpublished article, written on the eve of America's entry into the war, Morgenthau attributed isolationism to liberalism's rejection of power politics and its tendency to ignore or downplay the political element in both domestic and foreign politics. Anglo-American liberalism, in particular, "argues against war as something irrational, unreasonable, an aristocratic pastime or totalitarian atavism which has no place in the modern world."[15] This ideology, he insisted, blinded liberals to the true nature of the fascist challenge and left their countries unprepared to deal with it.

Morgenthau's critique of liberalism was part of his broader assault on the Enlightenment. In *Scientific Man vs. Power Politics* he described the prerationalist age as aware of two forces – god and the devil – who struggled for dominance of the world. There was no expectation of progress, only of continuing and undecided conflict. From this everlasting conflict came a tragic sense of life. Christianity introduced the idea of progress; good would ultimately triumph over evil and the second coming would usher in a new paradise. The rationalist philosophy of the Enlightenment

[14] Hans J. Morgenthau, "Liberalism and War," unpublished manuscript, 1941, Hans J. Morgenthau Papers, Library of Congress; Review of George Schwarzenberger, *Power Politics* (London: Jonathan Cape, 1941), in *American Journal of International Law* (April 1942), pp. 351–52; "The Limitations of Science and the Problem of Social Planning," *Ethics* 54: 3 (April 1944), pp. 174–85; "The Scientific Solution of Social Conflicts" (New York: Conference on Science, Philosophy and Religion and their Relations to the Democratic War of Life, 1945); *Scientific Man vs. Power Politics*, pp. 10, 174–78. Initially published by the University of Chicago Press in 1946.

[15] "Liberalism and War," unpublished article, 1941, p. 7. Morgenthau Papers.

secularized this vision; progress in the form of man's mastery over nature and social organization now had the potential to produce a happy and just society. Remarkable success in harnessing nature for productive ends encouraged equal optimism about the efficacy of social engineering. Man and the world were assumed to be rational, an assumption, Morgenthau insisted, that was flatly contradicted by the experiences of the age.[16]

He considered the Enlightenment's misplaced faith in reason the underlying cause of the twentieth century's horrors. Reason undermined religion, and with it, the values and norms that had previously restrained individual and collective behavior. At the same time, it made possible advances in technology and social organization that brought about the modern industrial state. That state became the most exalted object of loyalty on the part of the individual, and the most effective organization for the exercise of power over the individual. "While the state is ideologically and physically incomparably more powerful than its citizens, it is free from all effective restraint from above. The state's collective desire for power is limited, aside from self-chosen limitations, only by the ruins of an old, and the rudiments of a new, normative order, both too feeble to offer more than a mere intimation of actual restraint."[17]

The power of the state, Morgenthau suggested, feeds on itself through a process of psychological transference. Impulses constrained by ethics and law are mobilized by the state for its own ends. By transferring their egotism to the nation, people gain vicarious release for their otherwise repressed impulses. What was formerly egotism, and ignoble and immoral, now became patriotism, and noble and altruistic. The Bolsheviks and Nazis took this process a step further, and encouraged direct violence by citizens against communities and classes they identified as enemies of the state. Elimination of the Kulaks, forced collectivization, Stalin's purges, World War II and the Holocaust were all the result of the transference of private impulses on to the state and the absence of any limits, domestic or international, on the exercise of state power.[18]

Morgenthau considered the absence of constraints on state power *the* defining characteristic of international politics in the twentieth century. The failure of well-meaning statesmen between the wars to grasp this reality greatly exacerbated its negative consequences. The Western democracies neither maintained their military power nor balanced against the threat posed by Germany, Italy and Japan. "They took refuge instead in meaningless pronouncements and agreements, non-aggression

[16] Morgenthau, *Scientific Man vs. Power Politics*, pp. 10, 174–78. [17] Ibid., p. 168.

[18] Ibid., p. 169. The psychological component of this analysis relied heavily on the earlier work of Morgenthau's Chicago colleague, Harold Lasswell, *World Politics and Personal Insecurity* (New York: McGraw-Hill, 1935).

treaties, and international organizations that were incapable of collective action."[19] Misplaced faith in the efficacy of law, international agreements and the League of Nations encouraged aggressive states to encroach on their neighbors and launch a second and more costly world war.

This line of argument was hardly surprising coming from someone who had lived through the Great War, the Nazi rise to power, World War II and had lost family in the Holocaust.[20] Leo Strauss, a colleague and fellow German *emigré* whom Morgenthau helped to bring to the University of Chicago, was even more hostile to the Enlightenment. He saw the Nazis as the ultimate expression of rationalism, and sought to resurrect natural law as a defense against moral relativism. Similar arguments about the Enlightenment were made by Karl Popper, Jacob Talmon and Isaiah Berlin.[21] But many pioneers of the behavioral revolution were also refugee scholars (e.g., Kurt Lewin, Oskar Morgenstern, Franz Neuman, Karl W. Deutsch).[22] Personal, and often harrowing, encounters with communists and Nazis enhanced their faith in reason and belief that science was the best means of making the world a better and safer place. Morgenthau was troubled that so many of his colleagues, especially those with similar life experiences, clung to what he regarded the illusion of progress in international affairs. He turned to psychology for an explanation, and came to the conclusion that the modern mind cannot come "face with this immutable character of international politics. It revolts and takes refuge in the progressivist conviction that what was true in the past

[19] Hans J. Morgenthau, *The Decline of Democratic Politics* (Chicago: University of Chicago Press, 1958), p. 66.

[20] Morgenthau's friend, Reinhold Niebuhr, *Moral Man, Immoral Society: A Study in Ethics* (New York: Scribner's, 1932), ch. 9, and "The Myth of World Government," *The Nation*, 16 March 1949, and *The Structure of Nature and Empires* (New York: Scribner's, 1959), also attacked the naive expectations of the Enlightenment, especially its belief in the power of reason to better the human condition. He had a strong belief in absolute values, and in the possibility of cooperation across social classes. See Robin W. Lovin, *Reinhold Niebuhr and Christian Realism* (Cambridge: Cambridge University Press, 1995); Richard W. Fox, "Reinhold Niebuhr and the Emergence of the Liberal Realist Faith, 1930–45," *Review of Politics* 38 (April 1976), pp. 244–65. Max Horkheimer and Theodor W. Adorno, *Dialectic of Enlightenment* (New York: Continuum, 1944), p. 13, made a similar argument about the Nazis. "The Hitler youth is not a return to barbarism but the triumph of repressive equality, the disclosure through peers of the parity of the right to justice." All of these arguments hark back to Hegel's claim, in the *Phenomenology of the Spirit*, that the leveling effects of abstraction encouraged by the Enlightenment ultimately lead to the creation of the "herd."

[21] Karl Popper, *The Open Society and its Enemies* (London: Routledge, 1945); Jack Talmon, *The Origins of Totalitarian Democracy* (New York: Praeger, 1960); Isaiah Berlin, "Freedom and its Betrayal," unpublished lecture, cited in Michael Ignatieff, *A Life: Isaiah Berlin* (New York: Vintage, 2000), pp. 201–03.

[22] Lewis A. Coser, *Refugee Scholars in America: Their Impact and their Experience* (New Haven: Yale University Press, 1984), provides brief personal and intellectual autobiographies of scholars on both sides of this divide.

cannot be true in the future; for, if it were, mankind would be in desperate straits."[23]

International relations

Morgenthau is best known for *Politics Among Nations*, the first edition of which appeared in 1948. It was intended to be an original theoretical statement and a text, and had an extraordinary print run. The sixth and posthumous edition, revised by Kenneth W. Thompson, appeared in 1985.[24] Reviews of the book were largely positive, and it quickly gained adoption in college courses around the country. Critics objected to the central place of power in the argument. Barrington Moore thought Morgenthau's analysis had a "shaky psychological underpinning." With no empirical evidence beyond questionable parallels with animal societies, he asserts that the drive for power is both strong and universal. He was also irritated "by the author's device of substituting an apt quotation – preferably from an author dead at least a hundred years – for rigorous proof."[25]

The first edition of *Politics Among Nations* is another broadside against the early post-war hope – rapidly waning by the time Morgenthau's book was published – that the struggle for power could be eliminated through international law and institutions.[26] The lust for power, according to Morgenthau, is an inherent quality of human beings and "inseparable from social life itself." The struggle for power is, therefore, "a constitutive element of all human associations, from the family through fraternal and professional associations and local political organizations to the state."[27]

[23] Morgenthau, *Decline of Domestic Politics*, pp. 62–66.

[24] Hans J. Morgenthau, *Politics Among Nations: The Struggle for Power and Peace* (New York: Alfred Knopf, 1948).

[25] Barrington Moore, Jr., "Review of *Politics Among Nations*," *American Sociological Review* 14 (April 1949), p. 326.

[26] On the so-called realist–idealist debate, see Cecelia Lynch, *Beyond Appeasement: Interpreting Interwar Peace Movement in World Politics* (Ithaca: Cornell University Press, 1999); Brian C. Schmidt, "Anarchy, World Politics and the Birth of a Discipline: American International Relations, Pluralist Theory and the Myth of Interwar Idealism," *International Relations* 16 (April 2002), pp. 9–32; Lucian M. Ashworth, "Did the Realist–Idealist Great Debate Ever Happen? A Revisionist History of International Relations," *International Relations* 16 (April 2002), pp. 33–52. The consensus here is that Morgenthau and E. H. Carr offered a caricature of their opponents. Leonard Woolf, Konni Zilliacus, David Mitrany and Alfred Zimmern never ignored human nature or claimed that law was a panacea to international conflict. They were also among the earliest and most outspoken opponents of fascism.

[27] Morgenthau, *Scientific Man vs. Power Politics*, p. 16; Morgenthau, *Politics Among Nations*, pp. 17–18. Martti Koskenniemi, private communication with author, 14 March 2002,

While "there is no escape from the evil of power," context may mute its expression.[28] In many societies, norms, institutions and laws direct the struggle for power into ritualized and socially acceptable channels that prevent its otherwise violent and destructive consequences. In the international sphere, the struggle for power cannot so readily be tamed. The destructive potential of power politics can only be constrained by enlightened statesmen who work with rather than against the forces that motivate states.[29]

All politics is a contest between those who want more and those who want to hold on to what they have. States, like individuals, seek to increase, maintain or demonstrate their power. A state that aims at acquiring more power, pursues a policy of "imperialism." A state whose foreign policy has the goal of maintaining its power, pursues "a policy of the status quo." A state can also choose to demonstrate power and pursue "a policy of prestige." A policy of prestige is not an end in itself, but a strategy for supporting or challenging the status quo; its outward manifestations are easy to identify, but its underlying purpose may be difficult to fathom.[30]

Morgenthau brackets his typology of states with several important caveats. All three foreign policies are simplistic representations of more complex patterns of behavior. The status quo can be challenged or defended with varying degrees of intensity; challengers are sometimes reconciled by accommodation, and defenders are sometimes willing to make minor adjustments in the status quo to accommodate them. Statesmen may be unaware of the actual character of their own foreign policy. They can pursue a policy of imperialism and convince themselves they are defending the status quo; the Roosevelt administration believed that its "Good Neighbor Policy" toward Latin America represented a shift in orientation, when in reality it substituted one method of domination for another. None of the three patterns of foreign policy are inherent attributes of states or types of states. Leaders adopt different policies in response to their circumstances and goals; there are no easy markers to help statesmen predict or identify the motives and policies of their neighbors.[31]

suggests that Morgenthau's interest in power and the *Lustprinzip* reflect the influence of Nietzsche on him.

28 Morgenthau, *Politics Among Nations*, p. 172.

29 Ibid., *Decline of Democratic Politics*, p. 80.

30 Morgenthau, *Politics Among Nations*, 21–25, and the subsequent chapters devoted to the three foreign policies. Morgenthau had first introduced the threefold distinction among states in *La notion du 'politique' et la théorie des différends internationaux* (Paris: 1933), pp. 42ff., 61.

31 Ibid., pp. 21–25, 58–60.

For Morgenthau the status quo is the benchmark against which all foreign policies can be assessed. The status quo is a well-established concept in legal-diplomatic practice; peace treaties often require combatants to evacuate foreign territory and to restore the *status quo ante bellum*. Morgenthau is more interested in the distribution of power in the aftermath of wars as codified in the territorial clauses of peace treaties, subsequent alliances or special bi- and multilateral treaties. Examples include the Treaty of Paris of 1815 and the Holy Alliance after the Napoleonic Wars, and the Treaties of Versailles and Petit Trianon following World War I. In each case, victors used these treaties and agreements to establish new states or frontiers and procedures for conducting international relations.[32]

Morgenthau's use of peace treaties as reference points reflects his recognition that major shifts in territory and the creation and demise of states are almost always the result of war. War in turn is often the result of shifts in the balance of power in favor of rising powers with imperialist aims.[33] Such states can sometimes be accommodated peacefully; Great Britain gave way to the United States in the nineteenth century, and successfully transformed an adversary into an economic and political partner. More often, concessions whet the appetite of imperialist states and encourage new challenges that lead to war, as did appeasement of Italy and Germany in the 1930s.[34]

The universality of the power drive means that the balance of power is "a general social phenomenon to be found on all levels of social interaction."[35] Individuals, groups and states inevitably combine to protect themselves and their interests from predators. The international balance of power is "only a particular manifestation of a general social principle to which all societies composed of autonomous units owe the autonomy of their component parts."[36] It can deter war when status quo powers can muster more military capability than imperialist challengers and demonstrate their resolve to go to war in defense of the status quo. Balancing can also intensify tensions and make war more likely. This is because neither the motives of states, their military capability or their willingness to use it in defense of the status quo can be assessed with certainty. States accordingly seek a margin of safety in their military capabilities. When opposing states or alliances do this, tensions and suspicions ratchet up – the baneful consequences of what John Herz would call

[32] Ibid. [33] Conversation with the author, October 1959.
[34] Morgenthau, *Politics Among Nations*, pp. 43–45.
[35] Morgenthau, *Decline of Democratic Politics*, pp. 49, 81.
[36] Morgenthau, *Politics Among Nations*, p. 125.

the "security dilemma."[37] In this circumstance, status quo powers may be tempted to launch preventive wars to preserve their position against rising challengers. Morgenthau nevertheless considered the balance of power on the whole beneficial because even when it failed to prevent war it might limit its consequences and preserve the existence of states, small and large, that comprise the political system. He credited the balance with having served these ends throughout the eighteenth and nineteenth centuries.[38]

Morgenthau has rightly been criticized for using several definitions of the balance of power without effectively distinguishing among them.[39] He uses the concept in the most general sense to describe the configuration of power at any given moment. He also uses it to describe the relative balance between status quo and imperialist states, a preponderance of power in favor of status quo states, or a policy aimed at achieving the latter. To compound this confusion, he is inconsistent in his expectations that status quo powers would balance against imperialist states. In *Politics Among Nations*, he asserts "that the balance of power and policies aimed at its preservation are not only inevitable, but an essential stabilizing factor in a society of sovereign nations."[40] Elsewhere in this book, and in other publications, he describes the balance of power as only "a general tendency." In the *Decline of Domestic Politics*, he observes that balancing does not occur automatically, but happens often enough to give "a repetitive character" to international politics, and this in turn allows for "theoretical systematization."[41] Some of these apparent contradictions can be reconciled if we recognize the distinction Morgenthau intended between the *principle* of the balance of power and the *practice* of balancing.[42] The principle applied to all political situations, and balancing was thus a universally appropriate strategy. But balancing did not always occur, or achieve its ends, because of "the particular conditions under which the

[37] John Herz, "Idealist Internationalism and the Security Dilemma," *World Politics* 2: 12 (1950), pp. 157–80.
[38] Morgenthau, *Politics Among Nations*, pp. 155–59, 162–66.
[39] Ernest B. Haas, "The Balance of Power: Prescription, Concept, or Propaganda," *World Politics* 5 (1953), pp. 442–77; Bruno Wasserman, "The Scientific Pretensions of Professor Morgenthau's Theory of Power Politics," *Australian Outlook* 12 (March 1959), pp. 55–70; Martin Wight, "The Balance of Power," in Herbert Butterfield and Martin Wight, eds., *Diplomatic Investigations: Essays in the Theory of International Politics* (London: Allen & Unwin, 1966), pp. 149–75; Inis L. Claude, *Power and International Relations* (New York: Random House, 1962), pp. 25–37, identifies four different uses of the balance of power in *Politics Among Nations* and *In Defense of the National Interest*.
[40] Morgenthau, *Politics Among Nations*, p. 125. Also, *Decline of Domestic Politics*, pp. 80–81.
[41] Morgenthau, *The Decline of Democratic Politics*, p. 65.
[42] Robert W. Tucker, "Professor Morgenthau's Theory of Political 'Realism'," *American Political Science Review* 46 (March 1952), pp. 214–24; Wasserman, "The Scientific Pretensions of Professor Morgenthau's Theory of Power Politics," pp. 55–70.

principle must operate in a society of sovereign states."[43] Leaders might fail to grasp the nature or severity of a challenge, lack the capability or will to oppose an imperialist state, be constrained by domestic or foreign circumstances from collaborating with other status quo powers, or decide to pursue a policy of appeasement.

Morgenthau analyzed the general conditions under which a balance of power is most likely to promote peace and stability. It was most successful, he maintained, in the seventeenth through nineteenth centuries when there were many great and not so great powers, which allowed many possible combinations of alignment. Britain frequently played the role of balancer and gave considerable naval and financial support to the status quo powers. The existence of a colonial frontier also permitted compensation at the expense of third parties outside of the system. But most important of all was the sense of community that constrained the ends and means of power. In the tradition of Montesquieu, Voltaire, Burke and Kant, Morgenthau understood Europe to be something more than a collection of autonomous states motivated by pure self-interest. It was "one great republic" with common standards of "politeness and cultivation" and a common "system of arts, and laws, and manners." As a consequence, the "mutual influence of fear and shame imposed moderation on the actions of states and their leaders and instilled in all of them "some common sense of honor and justice." However much leaders desired to increase their power at the expense of their neighbors, they limited their ambitions, because for the most part they recognized the right of the others to exist and the fundamental legitimacy of the international political order.[44]

For Morgenthau, the success of the balance of power for the better part of three centuries was less a function of the distribution of capabilities than it was the underlying values and sense of community that bound together the actors in the system. When the European value consensus broke down, as it did from the first partition of Poland through the Napoleonic Wars, the balance of power no longer functioned to preserve

[43] Morgenthau, *Politics Among Nations*, p. 125.

[44] Ibid., pp. 159–66, 270–84; Hans J. Morgenthau, *In Defense of the National Interest: A Critical Examination of American Foreign Policy* (Lanham, Md.: University Press of America, 1982 [1951]), pp. 60–61. Similar arguments were subsequently made by the so-called English school, especially Hedley Bull, *The Anarchical Society: A Study of Order in World Politics* (New York: Columbia University Press, 1977). See also John Gerard Ruggie, "International Regimes, Transactions, and Change: Embedded Liberalism in the Postwar Economic Order," *International Organization* 36 (Spring 1982), pp. 379–415, and Friedrich V. Kratochwil and John Gerard Ruggie, "International Organization: A State of the Art on the Art of the State," in Edward D. Mansfield, ed., *International Organization: A Reader* (New York: Harper Collins, 1994), pp. 4–19.

the peace or integrity of the members of the system.[45] The consensus broke down again in the twentieth century with even more disastrous consequences. At mid-century, Morgenthau was deeply pessimistic about the future. The balance of power was at its nadir. There were two great powers instead of many, Britain no longer had the capability to play the role of balancer, the colonial frontier had disappeared and one of the principal powers rejected the very premises of the international order. International politics had been reduced "to the primitive spectacle of two giants eyeing each other with watchful suspicion."[46]

Morgenthau's theory is descriptive *and* prescriptive. "Realism," he insists in *Politics Among Nations*, is superior to "idealist" approaches on both counts. It is more rigorous because its axioms are logically derived from its starting assumptions. It is empirically valid because "the facts as they are actually lend themselves to the interpretation the theory has put upon them."[47] Morgenthau makes much of the latter claim, contrasting his theory with "idealist" theories and related strategies that fly in the face of political reality. He offers Neville Chamberlain's strategy of appeasement as a paradigmatic example. In doing so, he risks being hoist on his own petard. Woodrow Wilson's pursuit of idealist goals at the Versailles peace conference, or British and French appeasement of Germany, followed by half-hearted attempts at balancing after Hitler occupied Czechoslovakia in March 1939, indicate that leaders do not always pursue realist foreign policies. Morgenthau considered this kind of criticism beside the point; the purpose of *Politics Among Nations* was not an "indiscriminate description of political reality," but an attempt to develop a "rational theory of politics." The balance of power was "an ideal system," and in his more pessimistic moments Morgenthau was willing to admit that it was "scarcely found in reality." Realism provided a benchmark against which actual policies could be understood and evaluated. For the same reason, it contained a strong normative element. It was a "theoretical construct" of a fully rational and informed foreign policy that "experience can never completely achieve," but which can be used as a guide for making and assessing policy.[48]

Morgenthau's rejoinder is far from satisfactory. He made unabashed empirical claims for his theory, and behavior at variance is anomalous. All

45 Morgenthau, *Politics Among Nations*, pp. 160–66; Morgenthau, *In Defense of the National Interest*, p. 60. Paul W. Schroder, "A. J. P. Taylor's International System," *International History Review* 23 (March 2001), pp. 3–27, makes the same point.

46 Morgenthau, *Politics Among Nations*, p. 285.

47 Hans J. Morgenthau, *Politics Among Nations*, 3rd ed. (New York: Alfred A. Knopf, 1960), p. 1.

48 Ibid., p. 8; Morgenthau, *Decline of Domestic Politics*, p. 49.

social theories encounter anomalies, and the telling question is whether Morgenthau's theory provides a better account of international behavior than competitors. Morgenthau would insist on a second empirical criterion: the outcome of foreign policies at odds with realism. He maintained that "idealist" policies fail to promote peace and stability. But two decades later, we shall see, he was equally critical of realist approaches that failed to recognize moral and practical limitations on power. Most of us would probably agree that appeasement, as practiced by the Western democracies in the 1930s, rewarded Hitler's appetite for aggression and helped to provoke a long and costly war. Woodrow Wilson's policies find more support in the scholarly community, although all but his most ardent supporters admit that he may have been naive in the execution of some of his most important initiatives. A good case nevertheless can be made for the principles he espoused; the peace and prosperity of present-day Europe rest on a foundation of national self-determination, democratic government and international organization. Morgenthau conceded as much late in his career.

Realism vs. neorealism

International relations scholars of the neopositivist persuasion find Morgenthau stimulating but frustrating. They are impressed by his efforts to build a deductive theory but are put off by his invocation of causes at multiple levels of analysis and failure to present his theory in the categories and language of modern social science. Kenneth Waltz sought to overcome these "weaknesses" in his *Theory of International Politics*.[49] Any comparison of their approaches should start with their respective understanding of power.[50]

For Morgenthau, politics is about power. "The concept of interest defined in terms of power" sets politics apart as an autonomous sphere and made possible a theory of international relations.[51] He conceives of power as an intangible quality that had many diverse components.[52] Waltz appears to agree; he offers a definition of power almost identical to Morgenthau's. But he goes on to assert the overwhelming importance of material capabilities, especially military capabilities, because "force remains the final arbiter" of international affairs. The superpowers are "set apart from the others . . . by their ability to exploit military technology

[49] Waltz, *Theory of International Politics*.

[50] For a more extensive critique of Waltz, see Richard Ned Lebow and Thomas Risse-Kappen, *International Relations Theory and the End of the Cold War* (New York: Columbia University Press, 1995), chs. 1 and 2.

[51] Morgenthau, *Politics Among Nations*, 3rd ed., p. 5.

[52] Ibid., pp. 131, 180–81.

on a large scale and at the scientific frontiers."[53] Morgenthau, by comparison, describes "armed strength" as the most important *material* component of power. National power has material *and* political components, among them territory, population, national resources, industrial capacity, military preparedness, national character, morale and the quality of diplomacy and government. None of these attributes translate directly into power because power is "a psychological relation[ship]" that gives those who exercise it control over certain actions of others "through the influence which the former exert over the latter's minds." "Of all the factors which make for the power of a nation, the most important is the quality of diplomacy." The other attributes of national power are the raw materials out of which the power of a nation is fashioned. Diplomacy "combines those different factors into an integrated whole, gives them direction and weight, and awakens their slumbering potentialities by giving them the breath of actual power."[54]

Politics Among Nations offers many examples of states whose political power far exceeded their material capabilities because they had astute leaders (e.g., Germany between 1935 and 1939), and states whose power was well below what might have been expected due to incompetent leaders or domestic divisions (e.g., the United States between the wars, France in 1940). Morgenthau believed that power was so much a function of leadership and morale that explanations or predictions based on estimates of material capability were meaningless. Even in extreme cases, where giants confronted pygmies, material capabilities did not always determine behavior or outcomes. It had been utterly impractical for Melos to resist Athens, but the Melians did so with fatal consequences because they were moved by honor and inspired by their leaders. The Greeks, outnumbered on land and at sea, defeated the Persian invader, just as Israel, in 1947–48 and again, in1967, overcame adversaries with vastly greater material capabilities because of their internal cohesion, organizational capability and astute leadership.[55]

Morgenthau recognized that the strategies and tactics that leaders used to transform the potential attributes of power into influence are just as important – and far more intellectually interesting – than the attributes themselves. If power is "a psychological relationship," leaders need to know not only what resources are at their disposal but which ones to use and how to use them in any given circumstance. It follows that there is no absolute measure of state power, because it is always relative and

[53] Waltz, *Theory of International Politics*, pp. 131, 153, 180–81.
[54] Morgenthau, *Politics Among Nations*, 1st ed., pp. 14, 105.
[55] These two examples come from Morgenthau lectures at the University of Chicago in 1960 and The City College of the City University of New York in 1973.

situation specific. States possess different strengths and weaknesses and distributions of capabilities, and what gives one influence over another may not confer the same advantage over other states or with the same state in a different context. Influence might usefully be compared to the children's game of rock, scissors and paper. Each of the two protagonists makes a fist behind its back and decides whether to be a rock, scissors or a piece of paper. At the count of three, they thrust out and open their fist and reveal one (rock), two (scissors) or three (paper) fingers. The rock triumphs over the scissors because it can smash them, but is trumped by the paper that wraps the rock. The scissors in turn defeat the paper because of its ability to cut it. The game highlights the relational nature of power. The American rock (nuclear and local conventional superiority) triumphed in Cuba because Khrushchev was desperate to avoid a humiliating military defeat. But American compellence failed against North Vietnam because Hanoi, although at a serious military disadvantage, did not fear war. North Vietnamese paper (willingness to suffer) wrapped the American rock. Theories of international relations, and especially those of deterrence and compellence, need to consider capabilities – and counter-capabilities – beyond usable military force. Policymakers in turn must remember that material capabilities only translate into bargaining leverage when they enable one actor to inflict meaningful loss or confer meaningful gain on another. Power is intransitive.

The successful exercise of power demands a sophisticated understanding of the goals, susceptibilities and vulnerabilities of allies, adversaries and third parties. Like Thucydides, Morgenthau believed that power is most effective when masked. "Man is born to seek power, yet his actual condition makes him a slave to the power of others."[56] Human beings repress this unpleasant truth, and those who want to exercise power must help them do so. Clever leaders come up with justifications or invoke ideologies that make "interests and power relations . . . appear as something different than what they actually are." Whenever possible, they must convince others who must submit to their will that they are acting in their own interest or that of the community.[57] For all of these reasons, Morgenthau insisted that "What is required for mastery of international politics is not the rationality of the engineer but the wisdom and moral strength of the statesman."[58] Martti Koskenniemi observes with justification that for all Morgenthau's claims to have developed a sociological theory of international relations, he never deviated from his belief that

[56] Morgenthau, *Scientific Man vs. Power Politics*, p. 145.
[57] Morgenthau, *The Decline of Democratic Politics*, p. 59.
[58] Morgenthau, *Politics Among Nations*, p. 172.

all important outcomes depended on the ethical sensibility and good judgment of leaders.[59]

Power was the currency of international relations, but, unlike money, it could not be given numerical value and counted. Here too, the judgment of statesmen was critical. Morgenthau argued that it was easier to calculate the balance of power when there are only two major powers, and that alliances, and defections from them, are less important in bipolar systems because of the greater relative power of the two poles. Morgenthau's thinking about the structure of the international system evolved over the decades, but at no point did he consider polarity the most important determinant of peace or war. The first edition of *Politics Among Nations* noted the gradual decline in the number of sovereign states and great powers since the Thirty Years War and how, after 1945, only three states qualified as great powers on the basis of their material capabilities. A few years later, Morgenthau calculated that only two great powers were left because Britain had become distinctly inferior in power to both the United States and the Soviet Union. If Russian power had a weight of seventy on a scale, the United States had a weight of one hundred, to which Britain contributed a weight of ten and other allies, twenty. The power of the United States and the Soviet Union had become so "overwhelming" in comparison to allies and third parties that "through their own preponderant weight they determine the balance of power between them." The balance of power could no longer be "decisively affected" by changes in the alignments of their allies, at least for the foreseeable future. Nor could a lesser power readily defect from alliances, because "the two giants" had the power to "hold them there even against their will."[60]

Morgenthau argued that in the eighteenth century, when alliances were flexible and unreliable, and when defections could have serious, if not decisive, consequences for the power balance, the great powers had to exercise "constant vigilance, circumspection and caution."[61] In a bipolar world – a concept introduced by William T. R. Fox in 1944, but not used by Morgenthau until 1950 – the two superpowers were so powerful relative to other states that they did not have to worry about the possible consequences of allied defections or shifts in alliances.[62] The flexibility of the balance of power and its restraining influence upon power aspirations

[59] Koskenniemi, *The Gentle Civilizer of Nations*, p. 467.

[60] Morgenthau, *Politics Among Nations*, 1st ed., pp. 270–74; *In Defense of the National Interest*, pp. 48, 52–54.

[61] Ibid., p. 273.

[62] Morgenthau, *Politics Among Nations*, pp. 270–78. William T. R. Fox, *The Super-Powers* (New York: Harcourt, Brace, 1944). For Morgenthau's uses of the term bipolarity, see *In Defense of the National Interest*, p. 45, *Politics Among Nations*, 2nd ed. (New York: Alfred A. Knopf, 1954), Table of Contents and p. 325.

of the main protagonists had disappeared. The superpowers were free to define their respective positions as vital interests and engage each other with every means at their disposal in every arena in which they competed. In this novel situation, "the give and take of compromise becomes a weakness which neither side is able to afford."[63] Under bipolarity, Clausewitz's classic dictum had been reversed, because "the art of diplomacy is transformed into a variety of the art of warfare."[64]

Morgenthau was clearly uncomfortable with the pessimistic implications of his analysis, and sought to hold out a ray of hope for the future. "The changed structure of the balance of power has made the hostile opposition of two gigantic power blocs possible," he argued, "but it has not made it inevitable." Bipolarity has the potential for "unheard-of good as well as for unprecedented evil." Morgenthau buttresses this claim with a long quote from the seventeenth-century French philosopher, François Fénelon – one of those long-dead "authorities" to whom Barrington Moore objected – who hypothesized that an equilibrium between two major powers should reconcile both to the status quo and thereby preserve the integrity of smaller powers. Morgenthau worried that the character of modern war and nationalist universalism would prevent these putative advantages from being realized.[65]

In the third edition of *Politics Among Nations*, Morgenthau recognized additional incentives for superpower restraint. He speculated that the experience of the Korean War might have taught Moscow and Washington that they had to adapt their policies to the wishes of their allies "if they wanted to draw the maximum of strength from their support."[66] The emergence of a number of newly independent and unaligned states might also serve the cause of restraint.[67] The second and third editions continued to describe bipolarity as on the whole inimical to peace.[68] In the fifth edition, published in 1972, Morgenthau expressed cautious optimism. Détente, explicit recognition of the territorial status quo in Europe, a corresponding decline in ideological confrontation, the emergence of third forces (e.g., Japan, China, West Germany), and the damaging effects of Vietnam on American power had made both superpowers more cautious and respectful of the status quo. For all practical purposes, their

[63] Morgenthau, *Politics Among Nations*, p. 285.
[64] Ibid., pp. 270–86, 430. Quote on p. 285. *In Defense of the National Interest*, pp. 45–52, repeats the arguments of *Politics Among Nations* cited in this paragraph, sometimes word for word.
[65] Ibid., pp. 285–86, and "World Politics in the Mid-Twentieth Century, *Review of Politics* 19 (April 1948), pp. 154–73.
[66] Morgenthau, *Politics Among Nations*, 3rd ed., p. 351.
[67] Morgenthau, *Politics Among Nations*, 2nd ed., Preface and p. 337; 3rd ed., pp. 351–52.
[68] Ibid., 2nd ed., p. 338, 3rd ed., pp. 362–63.

de facto acceptance of the postwar division of Europe had ended the Cold War.[69]

Because of his emphasis on power and the balance of power, Morgenthau is commonly considered a structural theorist. In contrast to neorealism, his theory considers state-level attributes to be of critical importance. He also considered agency decisive at every level of interaction. Morgenthau characterized states as status quo, imperialist and prestige-seeking, but considered these orientations fluid and not inherent attributes of states or their regimes. The relevant chapters in *Politics Among Nations* indicate that they are a function of circumstances; rising powers are more likely to be imperialist, while declining powers are almost certain to be defenders of the status quo. States like post-World War I Germany, which have been deprived of territory but not the industrial base or population that gives them the potential to become great powers again, will be imperialist regardless of the character of their governments. Foreign policy orientations also reflect leadership choices. The Second German Reich under Bismarck was a status quo power, a policy that changed dramatically under his successors, and was unrelated to any significant change in the balance of power.[70]

Foreign policy orientations give rise to a balance of power, but the pattern of alignments is far from mechanical. This too depends on the choices made by leaders. The balance of power is more likely to preserve the peace when status quo powers possess a preponderance of power. This requires leaders of status quo powers to recognize the imperialist designs of would-be challengers and muster the resolve and diplomatic skill to forge an alliance powerful enough to hold them in check. Leaders of imperialist states must allow themselves to be deterred; they must exercise restraint when they are outgunned by an opposing coalition of status quo powers. The failure of status quo *and* imperialist leaders to behave appropriately was responsible for World War II and the system transformation it brought about.[71] Morgenthau believed that key decisions by the superpowers and third parties would also determine the consequences and future of bipolarity. Peace and stability did not depend on the nuclear balance, but on the moral quality of leaders and their willingness to place the common goal of survival over the pursuit of unilateral advantage.[72] Bipolarity could give way to multipolarity if China, Japan and West Germany acquired nuclear weapons. This too was a decision independent of the balance of power.[73]

[69] Ibid., 5th ed., 1972, preface. pp. 355–56 still reflect the pessimism of earlier editions.
[70] Ibid., 1st ed., chs. 2–4. [71] Ibid.
[72] Ibid., pp. 285–86. [73] Ibid., 5th ed., Preface and pp. 252–53.

Neorealists describe anarchy as the defining characteristic of the international system; it makes international politics a "self-help" system and qualitatively different from domestic politics. Morgenthau acknowledged differences between domestic and international politics; "cultural uniformity, technological unification, external pressure, and, above all, a hierarchic political organization," combined to make polities more stable and less subject to violent change than "the international order."[74] He nevertheless recognized that states varied enormously in their cohesion and ran the gamut from the highly integrated and peaceful societies of Scandinavia to the Hobbesian worlds of civil war Russia, Stalin's Soviet Union and Hitler's Germany. An enormous potential for violence existed in domestic societies, just as the potential for harmony existed in international life. "The difference between domestic and international politics in this respect is one of degree and not of kind."[75]

Morgenthau would have accused neorealists of basing their theory on a narrow slice of human experience.[76] He considered the twentieth century atypical because there were fewer limitations on state power than "at almost any time since the Thirty Years War." International politics had not always been this way and was "not likely to be so forever."[77] The second big difference was nuclear weapons. They "transcend the ability of any nation-state" to control and harness them, and rendered the sovereign nation state an atavism.[78] The late twentieth-century world required "a principle of political organization transcending the nation-state and commensurate with the potentialities for good or evil of nuclear power itself." While Waltz and neorealists sought to explain the status quo, Morgenthau struggled to look beyond it. The primary responsibility of statesmen was to avoid a nuclear Holocaust, and the task of international relations theorists was to help them to by laying the groundwork "for a new international order radically different from that which preceded it."[79]

Ethics and politics

In *Scientific Man vs. Power Politics*, Morgenthau offers a rather confusing discussion of ethics in which he describes three different views of public morality. The traditional approach of *Salus publica suprema lex* acknowledges that states can temporarily set aside normal legal, and perhaps,

[74] Ibid., p. 21; *Scientific Man vs. Power Politics*, p. 105.
[75] Morgenthau, *Politics Among Nations*, p. 21.
[76] Morgenthau, *The Decline of Democratic Politics*, p. 47; Norman A. Graebner, "Morgenthau as Historian," in Thompson and Myers, eds., *Truth and Tragedy*, pp. 66–76.
[77] Morgenthau, *Decline of Democratic Politics*, pp. 60, 59.
[78] Ibid., p. 76. [79] Ibid.

other norms as well, to protect the republic. He somewhat inaccurately associates Machiavelli and Hobbes with this view, and the European tradition of *Realpolitik*.[80] From the time of the Greeks, he insists, it was widely acknowledged that people were not allowed to act in the political sphere as they pleased. State actions had to conform to a higher standard of morality than simple interest. In modern times, he continues, two distinct strategies developed to reconcile private and public morality. Wilsonian liberalism sought to compel states to conform to the standards of private morality through the application of international law. This effort failed, as Morgenthau believed any such effort must, and helped to bring about the kind of aggressive behavior it was expected to prevent. Lenin and the Bolsheviks embraced a third strategy: they justified state actions in terms of the beneficial ends they were intended to achieve. Behavior at odds with conventional standards of private morality was legitimized with reference to a higher principle. Morgenthau dismissed this strategy, what philosphers call "consequentialist ethics," as a perfidious sleight of hand because we can never know the longer-term consequences of our actions. The claim that the end justifies the means is nothing more than an attempt to escape moral responsibility.[81] *Pace* Kant, Morgenthau clearly subscribes to a "deontological" view of ethics, although he nowhere makes this explicit.

For Morgenthau, politics is "the paradigm and the prototype of all possible corruption." It "is a struggle for power over men," and "degrades man" by using him as a means to achieve fundamentally corrupt ends. As this is equally true of domestic and international politics, there is no basis for a double moral standard. "One and the same ethical stand applies to the private and public sphere."[82] Morgenthau is adamant that morality – defined in the Hegelian sense in terms of the historically significant conventions of the epoch – should limit both the ends that power seeks and the means employed to achieve those ends. Certain ends and means are unacceptable because of the opprobrium that attaches to them. Morality puts the stamp of its approval on other ends and means. It not only makes them more acceptable, but more attainable because of the positive value others attach to them.[83]

Morality has prescriptive and descriptive value. It defines a code of behavior that states *ought* to follow but not infrequently violate. It is

[80] Morgenthau did not consider Machiavelli the forerunner of power politics. He merely gave advice on how to succeed in politics without glorifying power or those who exercise it. "Philosophy of International Relations," Lecture Notes, 1952, Hans J. Morgenthau Papers, Container 81.

[81] Morgenthau, *Scientific Man vs. Power Politics*, pp. 151–68.

[82] Ibid., p. 167.

[83] Morgenthau, *The Decline of Democratic Politics*, p. 59.

descriptive in that foreign policy often conforms to the prevalent moral code, even when it conflicts with short-term interests or has power-related costs. States routinely "refuse to consider certain ends or to use certain means, either altogether or under certain circumstances, not because in the light of expediency they appear impractical or unwise, but because certain moral rules interpose an absolute barrier."[84] Leaders also recognize that policies that reflect existing moral codes are more likely to gain at home and abroad.

Morgenthau's commitment to ethical imperatives might appear puzzling in light of his rejection of Wilsonian liberalism and assertions that politics is about power. He vehemently denied any contradiction, and criticized E. H. Carr for trying to divorce power from morality.[85] Wilson's error was not his concern for morality, but his failure to grasp the immutable character of human beings and the role of power in domestic and international politics. It is proper and realistic to be bound by moral constraints, but naive and dangerous to believe that morality, expressed through law and international institutions, can consistently restrain the pursuit of relative advantage.[86] Any analysis of international morality must "guard against the two extremes either of overrating the influence of ethics upon international politics or of denying that statesmen and diplomats are moved by anything else but considerations of material power."[87]

During the Vietnam War, Morgenthau made an interesting admission about the centrality of power in his theory of international relations. Politics was undeniably about power, but in the 1940s he had emphasized it to the point of excluding other features of politics as a reaction to the liberal idealist emphasis on law and morality. This had been a strategic as much as an intellectual choice. "When the times tend to depreciate the elements of power," he wrote in 1966, international relations theory

> must stress its importance. When the times incline toward a monistic conception of power in the general scheme of things, it must show its limitations. When the times conceive of power primarily in military terms, it must call attention to the variety of factors which go into the power equation and, more particularly, to the subtle psychological relations of which the web of power is fashioned.

[84] Morgenthau, *Politics Among Nations*, 1st ed., pp. 174–75.
[85] Hans J. Morgenthau, "The Political Science of E. H. Carr," *World Politics* 1 (October 1948), pp. 127–34.
[86] Hans J. Morgenthau, *La réalité des normes, en particulier des normes du droit international. Fondements d'une théorie des normes* (Paris: 1934), and "Théorie des sanctions internationales," *Revue de droit international et de législation comparé*, 3rd series, 16 (1935), pp. 474–503, 809–836.
[87] Morgenthau, *Politics Among Nations*, 1st ed., p. 174.

When the reality of power is being lost sight of over its moral and legal limitations, it must point to that reality. When law and morality are judged as nothing, it must assign them their rightful place.[88]

By the mid-sixties, the political culture of national security in the United States had undergone an about-face. The role of morality and law now needed to be brought to the attention of policymakers and theorists alike.

Following Kant and Hans Kelsen, Morgenthau treated law as a system of norms (*nomos*), and argued that international society had evolved to encompass a wide range of norms that states for the most part obeyed.[89] "The influence of civilization [has made] some policies that are desirable and feasible ethically reprehensible and, hence, normally impossible of execution."[90] *Politics Among Nations* devotes a chapter to restraints on the use of violence that emerged since the Thirty Years War. These include the understanding that war is a struggle between competing armed forces, and not a contest between entire populations; conventions that protect prisoners of war and keep them from being tortured or killed; the prohibition of certain weapons, and limitations on the use of others; the responsibilities and rights of neutrals; and general acceptance of the view that violence should be restricted to the minimum level compatible with the goals of war. Laws and conventions also proscribe behavior (e.g., territorial violations, bugging embassies) in which states routinely engage. "The protestations of innocence or of moral justification by which accusations in such matters are uniformly met" are, Morgenthau maintains, "indirect recognition of the legitimacy of these limitations."[91] He considered the twentieth century enigmatic in this respect; more new norms had been created by international treaties than ever before, but adherence to norms of all kinds had declined. International morality had reached its high-water point in the eighteenth century, and had receded subsequently in response to the rise of nationalism and the growing dependence of leaders on public opinion.[92]

Morgenthau's concern for ethics undergirded his opposition to the Indochina war. He was an early critic of American intervention and equally skeptical of subsequent escalations. Beginning in November 1963 he produced a steady stream of articles for *Commentary* and the *New Republic* as well as letters to the editors of the *Washington Post*

[88] Hans J. Morgenthau, "The Purpose of Political Science," in James C. Charlesworth, ed., *A Design for Political Science: Scope, Objectives and Methods* (Philadelphia: American Academy of Political and Social Science, 1966), p. 77.

[89] Morgenthau, *La réalité des normes*, makes the case for three types of norms: morality, customs (*moeurs*) and law. Legal norms were the only type of norms that regulated relations among states and would have more weight if supported by these other norms.

[90] Ibid., pp. 176–77. [91] Ibid., p. 180. [92] Ibid.

and *New York Times*.[93] Behind the scenes, he provided anti-war arguments to Frank Church, one of the principal Senate opponents of intervention.[94] Morgenthau was deeply troubled that American policymakers had jettisoned idealism only to adopt European-style *Realpolitik*. Vietnam was being fought in the name of realism, but represented a perversion of that philosophy. Realism had a moral basis. It was not merely a self-serving justification for the status quo.[95] Morgenthau's opposition to Vietnam cost him the much coveted presidency of the American Political Science Association; its conservative pro-war administrator quietly mobilized pro-war professors to block his nomination.

In 1965, Morgenthau published a book on Vietnam in which he excoriated American intervention on practical and moral grounds. He insisted that the use of military force to shore up an unpopular, oppressive government of absentee landlords was certain to fail. It was an "improvident and foolish use of power" that would inevitably lead to a "serious loss of prestige."[96] A "foreign power" has no business "defending the status quo against a national and social revolution."[97] Morgenthau was particularly offended by Washington's military strategy. "Counterinsurgency" was a "mechanical connivance" that differed from traditional warfare in that it was directed against the population rather than identifiable armed forces.

[93] Hans J. Morgenthau, "The Impotence of American Power," *Commentary* 36 (November 1963), pp. 384–86; Letter to the *Washington Post* (a rejoinder to an earlier article by Zbigniew Brzezinski in favor of military intervention in Vietnam, 15 March 1964); "We are Deluding Ourselves in Vietnam," *New York Times Magazine*, 18 April 1965, pp. 24, 85–87; "Russia, the US and Vietnam," *The New Republic*, 1 May 1965, pp. 12–13; unpublished letter to the *New York Times*, 18 August 1965, Morgenthau Papers, container 43; "Johnson's Dilemma: The Alternatives Now in Vietnam," *The New Republic*, 28 May 1966, pp. 12–16; "Truth and Power: The Intellectual and the Johnson Administration," *The New Republic*, 26 November 1966, pp. 8–14; "To Intervene or Not to Intervene," *Foreign Affairs* 45 (April 1967), pp. 425–36; "Bundy's Doctrine of War Without End," *The New Republic*, 2 November 1968, pp. 18–20; "Between Hanoi and Saigon: Kissinger's Next Test," *The New Leader*, 13 November 1972, pp. 5–6; "The New Escalation in Vietnam," *The New Republic*, 20 May 1972, pp. 9–11; "Explaining the Failures of US Foreign Policy: Three Paradoxes," *The New Republic*, 11 October 1975, pp. 15–18.

[94] On 31 December 1964, Morgenthau urged Church to pressure the administration to seek a withdrawal by means of a neutralization agreement. In January 1967, he provided Church with a critique of a Department of Defense film justifying American intervention. This letter and subsequent correspondence between Morgenthau, Church and the Senator's office is in containers 12 and 43 of the Morgenthau Papers.

[95] Richard A. Falk, "Normative Constraints on Statecraft: Some Comments on Morgenthau's Perspective," and Marcus Raskin, "The Idealism of a Realist," Thompson and Myers, eds., *Truth and Tragedy*, pp. 77–84, 85–94.

[96] Hans J. Morgenthau, *Vietnam and the United States* (Washington, DC: Public Affairs Press, 1965), Preface, p. 12.

[97] Hans J. Morgenthau, "US Misadventure in Vietnam," *Current History* 54 (January 1968), pp. 29–30; Hans J. Morgenthau, *A New Foreign Policy for the United States* (New York: Praeger, 1969), pp. 134–35.

"Military action aimed at the destruction of guerrilla forces entailed the destruction of entire villages, people and crops alike."[98]

When air and ground operations did not produce the expected results, Washington sent more forces, carried out more extensive air operations, bombed Hanoi and Haiphong and extended the ground and air war into the rest of Indochina. Morgenthau worried – needlessly, as it turned out – that such escalation risked a wider war with China and the Soviet Union. He was equally disturbed by the moral implications of escalation. If South Vietnam survived long enough, he conceded, the United States might compel the Viet Cong and North Vietnamese to halt their military campaign in the South. Victory would not be achieved by breaking the enemy's will to resist, but "by killing so many of the enemy that there is nobody left to resist." Such a strategy was a perversion of Clausewitz, who conceived of killing in war as a means to bend or break an adversary's will. In Vietnam, "killing becomes an end in itself." The physical elimination of the enemy and victory "become synonymous." Hence, the "body count," however fictitious, became the metric of success.[99]

Morgenthau warned that "No civilized nation" could wage such a war "without suffering incalculable moral damage." The resulting opprobrium would be all the more severe because most of the world saw no military or political benefit that could warrant the kind of widespread, indiscriminate killing and destruction the United States was inflicting on Indochina. Such behavior stood in sharp contrast to American claims to be "a novel experiment in government, morally superior to those that went before it," and made a mockery of its claim to be "performing a uniquely beneficial mission not only for itself but for all mankind."[100] Vietnam was costing the United States its *hēgemonia*.

Morgenthau elaborated this theme in a subsequent article in the *New Republic* in which he accused the United States of trying to suppress the symptoms of instability rather than addressing its causes. Throughout the Third World, and especially in Vietnam, successive administrations had consistently supported the side of repression in an on-going struggle over social, economic and political reform. American leaders pursued short-term stability at the expense of their long-term interests. "The United States has found itself consistently on the wrong side of the great issues, which in retrospect will appear to have put their stamp upon the present period of history."[101]

[98] Morgenthau, *A New Foreign Policy for the United States*, pp. 134–35.
[99] Ibid., p. 137. [100] Ibid., pp. 137–38.
[101] Morgenthau, "Explaining the Failures of US Foreign Policy." In a 1974 letter to the *New York Times*, 10 October 1974, protesting American involvement in the coup in Chile, Morgenthau referred to the United States as "the foremost counterrevolutionary power on earth."

There was also a domestic component to Vietnam. Leaders of democracies are frequently pulled in opposite directions by state and political interests. Postwar American presidents had repeatedly mobilized public opinion to support foreign policies based on uncompromising opposition to world communism. Over time, this strategy made the government the prisoner of the passions it had aroused and had compelled it to intervene in Vietnam. It threatened to destroy the give and take of "pluralistic debate through which errors can be corrected and the wrong policies set right."[102] There had been no meaningful public debate prior to American intervention, and once committed, it became impossible for the Johnson administration to extricate itself when its policy had failed. The decline of American democracy was at its core a problem of ethics.

In his lectures and conversations, Morgenthau drew the parallel between the ill-fated Athenian expedition in Sicily and the United States in Vietnam. Both failures were attributable to hubris and the lack of prudence it engendered. The biggest difference between the two conflicts, Morgenthau hastened to point out, was that Thucydides thought that a more serious effort by Athens to reinforce and support its military operation in Sicily might have resulted in victory. By 1967, Morgenthau was adamant that further buildups of American forces could not materially affect the outcome, and that the only way to end the war, in the absence of wise leadership, was through domestic opposition that would convince the Congress to halt funding for the war.[103]

Morgenthau saw obvious parallels in the methods and goals of ethics and international relations theory. Philosophers and theorists alike should search for underlying, universal truths through the study of history, and adapt them to contemporary circumstances. It is the task "for every age, and particularly a scientific one, to rediscover and reformulate the perennial problems of political ethics and to answer them in the light of the experience of the age."[104] In ethics as in politics, Morgenthau attempted to perform this service for his adopted country.

War, peace and system transformation

One of the tragedies of the post-World War I era, Morgenthau maintained, was that Wilsonians read the limited success of law in restricting violence as evidence that international agreements could outlaw war and resolve, or at least regulate, the kinds of conflicts that had led to war in the past.

[102] Hans J. Morgenthau, *Truth and Power: Essays of a Decade, 1960–1970* (New York: Praeger, 1970), pp. 40–44.
[103] Conversations with Hans Morgenthau, 1961–78.
[104] Morgenthau, *Scientific Man vs. Power Politics*, p. 146.

American and British foreign policy reflected these ideals at a time when Germany, Italy and Japan were riding roughshod over all civilized values and practices. This juxtaposition of naivete and evil brought about World War II.[105]

At mid-century, Morgenthau feared that the world had escaped the frying pan of fascism only to risk the fire of nuclear conflagration. He agreed with Bernard Brodie that the atomic bomb had changed the nature of warfare.[106] As it required "only a limited number of atomic bombs to destroy the military potential of the United States," war against a nuclear-capable Soviet Union would be irrational no matter how much damage the American air force could inflict on that country.[107] Morgenthau reasoned that nuclear weapons were "the only real revolution which has occurred in the structure of international relations since the beginning of history" because they radically changed the relationship between the means and ends of foreign policy. War between nuclear powers was no longer an extension of politics by other means but mutual suicide.[108] Morgenthau worried that the superpowers, although they recognized this truth, would back themselves against the wall or lose control in a crisis and stumble into a catastrophic war.[109]

The principal threat to peace was political. The superpowers were "imbued with the crusading spirit of the new moral force of nationalistic universalism," and "face each other in inflexible opposition." They had transformed what should have been a run-of-the-mill power struggle into a Manichean conflict between good and evil in which persuasion had become "tantamount to trickery, compromise means treason, and the threat of force spells war."[110] Unlike many of his colleagues, Morgenthau was equally critical of the United States. American leaders confused their professed values and morality. Their foreign policy had become increasingly divorced from any conception of the national interest and had assumed the character of a crusade in the name of universal, but really parochial,

105 Morgenthau, "Liberalism and War"; "Review of *Power Politics*"; *Politics Among Nations*, 1st ed., Part 9.

106 Bernard Brodie, *The Absolute Weapon: Atomic Power and World Order* (New York: Harcourt, Brace, 1946), is cited in the bibliography of the first edition of *Politics Among Nations*.

107 Morgenthau, *Politics Among Nations*, 1st ed., p. 319; "World Politics in the Mid-Twentieth Century," pp. 154–73.

108 Morgenthau, *The Decline of Democratic Politics*, p. 76; *Politics Among Nations*, 3rd ed., p. 326, also noted the mass destructive potential of bacteriological weapons.

109 Hans J. Morgenthau to Helen Fuller, managing editor of the *New Republic*, 24 December 1956, commenting on his article published in the *New Republic* on 10 and 17 December 1956, Morgenthau Papers, container 43; "Has Atomic War Really Become Impossible?," *Bulletin of the Atomic Scientists* 12 (January 1956), pp. 7–9.

110 Morgenthau, *Politics Among Nations*, 1st ed., p. 430.

values. McCarthyism and Vietnam were indications of the extent to which American leaders and public opinion had become "equally hostile to the middle ground of subtle distinctions, complex choices, and precarious manipulations, which is the proper sphere of foreign policy."[111]

By the early 1970s Morgenthau thought the threat of nuclear war had receded but considered the overall problem of world peace no closer to solution.[112] He remained convinced that attempts to banish war through laws and international agreements were doomed to failure so long as the fundamental character of international relations remained unchanged. "To improve the world one must work with existing forces, not against them." In keeping with his tragic understanding of politics, Morgenthau maintained that moral principles can never fully be realized, but only approximated through the ever temporary balance of interests and equally precarious management of conflicts. A wise statesman "aims at achievement of the lesser evil rather than of the absolute good."[113] "Power," Morgenthau acknowledged, "is a crude and unreliable method of limiting the aspirations for power on the international scene," but the balance of power may be a good *short-term* strategy for preserving the peace.[114] For the same reason, he became a strong, public advocate of nuclear arms control in light of the near-term impossibility of nuclear disarmament.[115]

An enduring solution to the problem of war required a fundamental transformation of the international system. In 1948, Morgenthau castigated fellow realist E. H. Carr for wanting to substitute the "utopia of supranationalism for liberal internationalism."[116] He gradually moved in

[111] Morgenthau, *Vietnam and the United States*, p. 81.

[112] Francis Boyle, *World Politics and International Law* (Durham: Duke University Press, 1985), pp. 72–73, reports an interview with Morgenthau on 10 November 1979 in which he expressed great pessimism about the future. He told Boyle that "In my opinion the world is moving ineluctably towards a third world war – a strategic nuclear war. I do not believe that anything can be done to prevent it." This statement stands in sharp contrast to his published statements and other conversations, and Morgenthau himself confessed that "I am in a pessimistic mood today, so perhaps you should come back at another time and ask me that question again."

[113] Morgenthau, *Decline of Democratic Politics*, p. 80.

[114] Morgenthau, *Politics Among Nations*, 1st ed., p. 169.

[115] Letter to the *New York Times*, 19 June 1969, describing a speech of President Richard Nixon as a demagogic attack on the concept of arms control. Morgenthau distinguishes between conventional and nuclear arms control, and argues that "Mr. Nixon is completely wrong with respect to nuclear weapons, for the conventional modes of thought are not applicable to them. While conventional arms control and disarmament indeed depend upon the settlement of issues which give rise to the arms race in the first place, nuclear arms control and disarmament are rational necessities regardless of the settlement of international conflicts, once both adversaries have reached the optimum of nuclear sufficiency."

[116] Morgenthau, "The Political Science of E. H. Carr," *World Politics* 1 (October 1948), pp. 127–34.

that direction himself because he came to believe that sovereign nation states could not cope with nuclear weapons and the threat to human survival they posed. By 1962, he would insist that the long-term well-being of the human race required "a principle of political organization transcending the nation-state."[117] His commitment to some form of supranational authority deepened in the 1970s. Humanity was now threatened by a population explosion, world hunger and environmental degradation in addition to the continuing danger of a nuclear Holocaust. Nation states seemed incapable of ameliorating any of these problems.[118] But if they were so zealous about safeguarding their sovereignty, how could the international system possibly evolve toward a new order? Progress would only take place, Morgenthau reasoned, when enough national leaders became convinced that it was in their respective national interests. In the 1950s, he was dubious about the virtues of European federation, and the Schumann Plan in particular. He insisted at the time that the key to a European peace was "the calculated and determined intervention on the part of the United States."[119] By the 1960s he had reversed himself, and considered the European Coal and Steel Community a striking example of what was possible when leaders reconceptualized their interests. The process of European integration illustrated the apparent paradox that "what is historically conditioned in the idea of the national interest can be overcome only through the promotion in concert of the national interest of a number of nations."[120]

For Morgenthau, the European Community did not reflect a change in the distribution of power but in the organizing principles of a regional system. He hoped that state sovereignty would be superseded by some kind of supranational authority, ultimately, on a global basis. He never elaborated any institutional framework or seriously addressed the problem of transformation, but remained adamant that learning would have to be the catalyst for such a transformation. The national interest is a fluid concept, and leaders' understandings of it change over time. The failures of the past and the challenges of the present might convince leaders that

[117] Morgenthau, *Decline of American Politics*, pp. 75–76.

[118] Kenneth W. Thompson, "Introduction," in Morgenthau, *In Defense of the National Interest*, p. v; personal communications with Hans Morgenthau.

[119] "Building a European Federation," reprinted from 46 *Proceedings of the American Society of International Law* (1952), pp. 130–34. Morgenthau reviews efforts to create a European peace through the Schumann Plan. Aims to bind Germany to France. Key is a viable balance of power, which "cannot be created by preaching the virtues of European federation, but only by the calculated and determined intervention on the part of the United States."

[120] Morgenthau, *Decline of American Politics* p. 93. *Decline of Democratic Politics* was published in 1962, but this essay was originally published in 1958 in *Decline of American Politics*.

national interests are better served by less, rather than more sovereignty. In the long run, ideas trump structure. Morgenthau was a Weberian at heart.

He would have been pleased by Gorbachev's foreign policy revolution. He would have explained it, and the subsequent rapprochement of Russia and the West in terms of learning and the changed conception of the national interest that it promoted. He would have been greatly amused by the efforts of neorealists, caught off-guard by these developments, to attribute them *ex post facto* to changes in the balance of power.

Morgenthau on theory

Scientific Man vs. Power Politics appeared at the beginning of the postwar "behavioral revolution" and represents one of the most cogent contemporary critiques of efforts to construct predictive theories in political science. Toward this end, Morgenthau drew on the writings of Max Weber and other participants in the turn of the century *Methodenstreit*, made analogies to quantum physics and advanced arguments that will resonate with contemporary reflexivists.[121]

Morgenthau insisted that the social world differed from the physical world in fundamental ways that confounded attempts to determine causation and make predictions. There was no single cause in the social sphere that would produce a given outcome under a wide range of circumstances. Single causes invariably had multiple, often contradictory, effects depending on the circumstances. Similar outcomes could also have multiple, different causes. It was impossible "to foresee with any degree of certainty which effects will be brought about by this particular cause, nor is it possible to state in retrospect with any degree of certainty what particular cause has produced this effect."[122]

Social complexity was attributable in large part to the reflexive nature of human beings. Unlike atoms, people had goals, emotions and histories that affected their understanding and responses to external stimuli. Social behavior is a composite of many human actions, and groups of people will react differently to an identical stimulus under different physical, psychological and social conditions.[123] Social complexity is also the outcome of the multiplicity of stimuli that act on individuals and groups and make it impossible to isolate any one stimulus and test its effects. Every

[121] Morgenthau reaffirmed his epistemology two decades later in "Common Sense and Theories of International Relations," *International Affairs* 21 (Summer 1967), pp. 207–14.

[122] Morgenthau, *Scientific Man vs. Power Politics*, p. 112. [123] Ibid., pp. 112–13.

stimulus, present and past, ripples through the organism or body politic and affects its frame of references, sensitivity to information, emotional state, repertory and behavior. Because all so-called causes "are interwoven with the crosscurrents and intricacies of social causation," the best the social sciences can do is to "present a series of hypothetical possibilities, each of which may occur under certain conditions – and which of them will actually occur is anybody's guess."[124]

Morgenthau maintained that the process of social inquiry differed in important ways from research into the natural world. Macro physical phenomena could be studied from a distance; a geologist could fly over a desert and take photographs without disturbing a single grain of sand. The social scientist stands in the streams of social causation as an acting and reacting agent. "What he sees and what he does are determined by his position in those streams; and by revealing what he sees in terms of his science he directly intervenes in the social processes." Gallup polls transcend theoretical analysis and influence how people vote. Karl Marx's writings about class struggle and proletarian revolution influenced Russian intellectuals and helped to bring about a revolution. Marx's writings might also convince Western capitalists to treat their workers differently and make revolution less likely. Social knowledge becomes a stimulus for behavior and can change the way people act. Morgenthau thought the social world more like that part of the physical world governed by the laws of quantum mechanics, in which any human attempt to measure the location, spin or charge of particles significantly affects these same parameters.[125]

The social world shapes social inquiry. Investigators are products of their cultures and epochs. They are subjected to all kinds of pressures emanating from groups and society as a whole, that largely "determine the objects, methods, and results of scientific investigation." Influence of this kind is not limited to contracts and research grants. The government, directly, and through the universities, disposes of a wide range of professional rewards that help to determine the status of professors.[126] Social science is a reflection of the power structure, and, not surprisingly, its findings most often justify that structure and buttress its legitimacy. "Truth itself becomes relative to social interests and emotions." Claims of objectivity indicate how little awareness social scientists have of their real role in society. Few investigators have the ability and courage to step outside their cultures or challenge the institutions upon which they depend

[124] Ibid., pp. 114–15; *Decline of American Politics*, p. 71.
[125] Morgenthau, *Scientific Man vs. Power Politics*, pp. 123–26.
[126] Morgenthau, "The Purpose of Political Science," pp. 71–72.

for publication, tenure, salary increases and other forms of professional recognition.[127]

Because prediction is impossible, social scientists fall back on explanation. "They prove that France was bound to fall in 1940 because of certain trends in her social and political structure which were obvious to anyone. Yet nobody was able to predict before the event that those trends would materialize instead of others which were quite as much in the public eye. The seeming proof that what happened was bound to happen argues *post hoc ergo propter hoc* and has no scientific value."[128] Morgenthau was bemused by how events, some of which were, or would, have been rejected as impossible beforehand because they were at odds with reigning theories, were made consistent with those same theories in retrospect. By such sleights of hand the social scientists indulge their "inveterate tendency to stick to their assumptions and to suffer constant defeat from experience rather than to change their assumptions in the light of contradicting facts."[129]

For someone who disparaged prediction, Morgenthau made two of his own that seem right on the money six decades later. He expected social science to "retreat ever more from contact with the empirical world into a realm of self-sufficient abstractions." It would become a new form of scholasticism that "dissolves the substance of knowledge into the processes of knowing." Social scientists would "think about how to think and to conceptualize about concepts, regressing ever further from empirical reality until [they] find the logical consummation of [their] endeavors in mathematical symbols and other formal relations." Their patently false claims to objectivity would sooner or later provoke a strong reaction among a younger generation of academics who "would take flight in a subjective dogmatism that identifies the perspective and preferences of the observer with . . . the truth."[130] The social science parody of modernism – would provoke postmodernism.

A quintessential feature of the Enlightenment from Voltaire on was its rejection of the past as an unrelieved record of error and superstition. Morgenthau lamented that behavioral social science, and rationalism more generally, threw out the baby with the bath water when they turned their backs on the cumulative wisdom of humankind. Hostility to history introduced a dichotomy between political science and political philosophy, and Morgenthau correctly foresaw that political science

[127] Ibid., pp. 140–44. [128] Ibid., p. 120.

[129] Morgenthau, *The Decline of Democratic Politics*, p. 282.

[130] Ibid., pp. 28, 44. In 1940, Morgenthau, "Positivism, Functionalism and International Law," *American Journal of International Law* 34 (1940), pp. 260–84, had used similar language to make a similar prediction of positivist international law.

departments would marginalize or gradually eliminate political philosophy courses and faculty. This would make political theory sterile by cutting it off from contact with current issues, and deprive political science of a working knowledge of the Western tradition.[131] History and political theory were both essential to political science because the real task of theory is "to separate in the intellectual tradition at their disposal that which is historically conditioned from that which is true regardless of time and place, to pose again the perennial problems of politics, and to reformulate the perennial truths of politics, in the light of the contemporary experience."[132]

Morgenthau had a very different conception of theory than his behavioralist colleagues, and one that was strikingly reminiscent of Clausewitz. Because social reality is "complicated, incongruous and concrete," the best reason and empirical analysis can do is "discover universal motives and strategies associated with them that give rise to certain patterns of behavior." These patterns are never determined because all politics is contextual (*Standortsgebunden*) and depends on the subjective understandings, goals and skills of actors.[133] Abstract theories, moreover, are never ends in themselves, but means toward framing foreign policy choices. Theories, even valid ones, are only the *starting points* for such analysis. They provide conceptual categories and tools of analysis that investigators can use to analyze specific cases, and alert them to the possibility that certain kinds of behavior may occur. To understand or forecast actual behavior, investigators must ask additional questions specific to the case and independent of the theory; even physical theories require knowledge of initial conditions. We must work back and forth between the general and the specific in an attempt to develop a better understanding of the world.

The deeper purpose of social science, and of international relations theory, is to identify problems and propose and evaluate possible solutions to them and bring this knowledge to the attention of the public and policymakers. "All good theory," Morgenthau insisted, "is practical theory, which intervenes in a concrete political situation with the purpose of change through action."[134]

[131] Ibid., pp. 3–4. [132] Morgenthau, *The Decline of Democratic Politics*, p. 48.

[133] Morgenthau's use of the terms *Standortsgebundenheit* (situational determination) and *Sitz im Leben* (seat in life) reflect the influence of the historicist, Wilhelm Dilthey, *Der Aufbau der geschichtlichen Welt in den Geisteswissenschaften* (Stuttgart: Teubner, 1958). The sociology of knowledge, to which Morgenthau was exposed in his university years, reflected this perspective and the importance of a historical frame of reference in understanding social behavior. On the relationship between historicism and sociology, see H. Stuart Hughes, *Consciousness and Society* (New York: Knopf, 1958), esp. pp. 183ff.

[134] Morgenthau, *Scientific Man vs. Power Politics*, pp. 72–73, 119–22.

Morgenthau among nations

Morgenthau scholars disagree about the relative importance and continuity of his German and American experiences. Christoph Frei argues for the primacy of Morgenthau's European experiences and the continuity of his writings. He interprets his American books on international politics as extensions of his European investigations into international law.[135] Jan Willem Honig emphasizes the debt that Morgenthau, and American realism more generally, owe to German totalitarian ideologies.[136] Martti Koskenniemi also stresses Morgenthau's intellectual debt to Carl Schmidt, and finds striking similarities in their objections to international law and the "decadence" of twentieth-century liberalism.[137] Andreas Söllner sees a sharp break between the German and American Morgenthau; the Weimar liberal became a postwar conservative.[138] Niels Amstrup adopts a middle position; he finds the genesis of some of Morgenthau's postwar concepts in his prewar writings.[139]

None of these interpretations adequately capture the evolution of Morgenthau's thinking about ethics, politics and international affairs. Koskenniemi and Amstrup are the closest to the mark. Morgenthau's prewar writings already disparaged the naivete of those who believed that war could effectively be outlawed. He was adamant that states will always disagree about the proper organizing principles of the international environment, and that disputes with "high political content" cannot be resolved by judicial means. He also developed the three-fold characterization of states out to change the status quo, maintain it or just display their power.[140] In a more fundamental sense, all of Morgenthau's written work reveals a continuous commitment to social justice and world order, but some discontinuities in the means by which these ends might be achieved.

Morgenthau was a self-conscious amalgam of three different cultural traditions: Jewish, German and American. He began his 1922 *Gymnasium* essay by observing that his "relationship to the social environment is

135 Frei, *Hans J. Morgenthau*, chs. 5–8.

136 Honig, "Totalitarianism and Realism."

137 Koskenniemi, *The Gentle Civilizer of Nations*, pp. 459–65.

138 Andreas Söllner, "Hans J. Morgenthau: ein deutscher Konservativer in Amerika?," in Rainer Erb and Michael Schmidt, eds., *Antisemitismus und jüdische Geschichte: Studien zu Ehren von Herbert A. Strauss* (Berlin: Wissenschaftlicher Autorenverlag, 1987), pp. 243–66.

139 Niels Amstrup, "The 'Early' Morgenthau: A Comment on the Intellectual Origins of Realism," *Cooperation and Conflict* 13 (1978), pp. 163–75; personal communication with the author.

140 Hans J. Morgenthau, *La notion du "politique" et la théorie des différends internationaux* (Paris: Sirey, 1933).

determined by three facts: I am a German, I am a Jew, and I have matured in the period following the war." He was a self-identified Jew in Germany and America, and proud of his heritage, although he led a secular life.[141] Judaism puts great emphasis on social justice and communal solidarity. A grandson of a rabbi, Morgenthau imbibed these values, and they were reflected in the his commitment to dedicate his life to do something worthwhile for humanity.[142] This commitment helped to sustain and motivate Morgenthau during the most difficult periods of his life in Germany, subsequent emigration and long search for personal and professional security.

Morgenthau's *Gymnasium* essay expressed concern that it might not be possible to reconcile his religious-cultural and national identities. Unlike many of his contemporaries, he was unwilling to hide or renounce his Jewish identity or otherwise accommodate to bigotry. He suffered keenly from the practical and psychological consequences of rejection in Coburg. He must have encountered prejudice on a daily basis in Munich and Frankfurt as well, as anti-Semitism became increasingly pronounced during the course of the 1920s. By the time he left Germany, less than a year before Hitler came to power, the worst fear expressed in his essay had materialized; he was *ausgeschlossen* and *ausgetossen* [excluded and expelled].[143] The experience of being driven from his homeland by prejudice deepened his commitment to social justice.

The cultural and intellectual milieu of the Weimar Republic constituted the second strand of Morgenthau's development. Here, German and Jew came together. The French revolution had made it possible for Jews to become full citizens and participants in the national culture while retaining their traditional religious affiliation. Elsewhere in Europe, Jews struggled to achieve similar rights and supported political movements and parties that promised to make this possible. For Morgenthau, it was natural for Jews to adopt "the optimistic outlook that the emancipation of German Jewry though the application of liberal principles was tantamount to the permanent solution of the Jewish problem in Germany."

141 Morgenthau was involved with Jewish questions throughout his career and was a strong supporter of Israel. He engaged in a public polemic with C. L. Sulzberger, who wrote a column in the *New York Times* on 1 July 1970 in which he argued that Jews were just a religious sect, and that if the Soviet Union treated them that way the "Jewish problem" would diminish. Morgenthau objected strenuously in a letter to the editor published on 7 July. His draft letter was an even more strongly worded defense of the concept of Jewish nationality, of Zionism and of Soviet Zionists. Morgenthau Papers, container 43.

142 Morgenthau, "Fragment of an Intellectual Autobiography," pp. 1–4.

143 Ibid., p. 2. Quotation from the German original, "Was ich von meiner Zukunft erhoffe, und worauf sich diese Hoffnung gründet," September 1922.

When rabid nationalism threatened the fruits of emancipation, many Jews clung desperately to liberalism as a psychological defense.[144]

The German Morgenthau was squarely in the liberal Jewish tradition. Looking back on his university experience he remembered that it was "impossible to visualize the ignorance, confusion, meanness and general moral and intellectual degradation that dominated German public life and upon which the authority of great scholars bestowed a semblance of moral and intellectual legitimacy." Max Weber was an exception, and "was everything most of his colleagues pretended to be but were not." Morgenthau also admired Professor Karl Rothenbücher and attended his lectures on Weber's political and social philosophy. Rothenbücher lacked Weber's ability for creative synthesis, but "approached political problems with the same detachment, objectivity, and penetrating intelligence in which Weber excelled." Morgenthau was moved by his extraordinary courage. Following the unsuccessful Nazi putsch of November 1923, Rothenbücher wrote a pamphlet excoriating Bavarian prime minister Gustav von Kahr for his initial support of the Nazis. He became a marked man, and died prematurely in 1932.[145]

Morgenthau's short legal career gave practical and academic expression to his liberal commitments. In Frankfurt, he had several professional possibilities but chose to clerk for Hugo Sinzheimer, a prominent Social Democrat who had helped to draft the Weimar constitution and expose the "stab-in-the-back" legend.[146] Morgenthau was not so much attracted to labor law as he was to Sinzheimer who was "passionately and eloquently devoted to the legally defined interests of the underdog – the worker exploited and abused and the innocent helplessly caught in the spiderweb of criminal law."[147] The labor court was an eye opener for Morgenthau. He regularly stood in for his mentor, and was occasionally asked to serve as a temporary member of the court. He was appalled to discover how partisan and hostile to the Republic some of the judges were, and how deeply ingrained their anti-Semitism was. He learned the sobering lesson that "What was decisive was not the merits of the legal interpretation, but the distribution of political power."[148] This micro encounter with politics, and the Weimar experience more generally, stripped away his liberal illusions and convinced him that power and self-aggrandizement

144 Hans J. Morgenthau, "The Tragedy of German-Jewish Liberalism," originally given as The Leo Baeck Memorial Lecture in 1961; *Decline of Democratic Politics*, pp. 247–56, quote on p. 249.

145 Morgenthau, "Fragment of an Intellectual Autobiography," pp. 8–9.

146 Ernst Fraenkel, "Hugo Sinzheimer," in Falk Esche and Frank Grube, eds., *Reformismus und Pluralismus: Materialen zu einer ungeschriebenen politischen Autobiographie* (Hamburg: Hoffmann and Campe, 1973), pp. 131–42.

147 Ibid., pp. 9–10. 148 Ibid., pp. 9–12.

lay at the heart of politics. It was probably not coincidental that during this period – the late 1920s – he immersed himself in the writings of Freud and Nietzsche, and read and annotated the complete works of the latter. Morgenthau was personally depressed at the time, and confided to his diary that he found solace in Nietzsche and his concept of *Blick des Sehers* – the free, analytic spirit who has the courage to look deeply into the soul. It seems evident that Morgenthau hoped to model himself on such a Promethean hero.[149]

Through Sinzheimer, Morgenthau met prominent Weimar intellectuals, including Martin Buber, Otto Kahn-Freund, Franz Neuman and Paul Tillich. He also came to know the leading luminaries of the Frankfurt School (*Institut der Sozialforschung*), but was put off by what he considered their preoccupation with fine points of Marxist theory at a time when the Republic was under acute threat from the extremist forces on the right and the left.[150] Morgenthau's own scholarly publications in this period, which others have analyzed in detail, addressed the role of international law and its relationship to politics.[151] His 1929 dissertation, *Die internationale Rechtspflege, ihr Wesen und ihre Grenzen* [The International Administration of Justice: Its Character and Limits], was a response to the arguments of Carl Schmitt, a noted conservative intellectual and international lawyer.[152] Morgenthau sought to answer the question of why so few international conflicts were resolved by legal means. He distinguished between disputes [*Streitigkeiten*] that lend themselves to legal language and resolution, and tensions [*Spannungen*] that cannot be redressed by legal means because the goals of at least one of the parties demanded a change in legal rights or transformation of the legal order.[153] He found that even in *Streitigkeiten*, states often refused to bring their disputes before third party mediators or courts on the grounds of honor and vital interest.

Morgenthau's second book, published in Paris in 1933, continued his attack on the positivist distinction between the political and the legal. He argued that law stood in sharp contrast to the will to power [*volonté de puissance*], and could not maintain order when imperialist powers were on the rise and status quo powers on the decline.[154] His third and final

149 Frei, *Hans J. Morgenthau*, pp. 95–113.

150 Morgenthau, "Fragment of an Intellectual Autobiography," p. 14.

151 Frei, *Hans J. Morgenthau*, chs. 5–7; Honig, "Totalitarianism and Realism"; Koskenniemi, *The Gentle Civilizer of Nations*, pp. 440–65.

152 Hans J. Morgenthau, *Die internationale Rechtspflege, ihr Wesen und ihre Grenzen* (Leipzig: Noske, 1929). The 1934, 2nd ed., of Carl Schmitt, *Das Begriff der Politischen*, is available in English with an introduction by George Schwab and a foreword by Tracy B. Strong, *The Concept of the Political* (Cambridge, Mass.: MIT Press, 1966).

153 Morgenthau, *Die internationale Rechtspflege*, pp. 73–84.

154 Morgenthau, *La notion du "politique" et la théorie des différends internationaux*; Frei, *Hans J. Morgenthau*, chs. 5–6; Koskenniemi, *The Gentle Civilizer of Nations*, pp. 453–55.

prewar book, *La réalité des normes*, was published in Geneva in 1934. It addressed the problem of sanctions, and its argument was deeply influenced by, but also critical of, Hans Kelsen's abstract approach to international law. He submitted it as his *Habilitationschrift* at the University of Geneva, but it was rejected by the first examination board. A second board, chaired by Hans Kelsen, whose formalist conceptions Morgenthau attacked in his book, accepted the manuscript primarily because the ever-magnanimous Kelsen made such a strong statement on Morgenthau's behalf.[155] Morgenthau's last major work on international law was an article, written after he had taken up residence in Kansas City. It was highly critical, not of international law *per se*, but of unreasonable expectations so many scholars and liberal politicians had of its ability to regulate international conflicts. Morgenthau lamented that they paid "almost no attention to the psychological and sociological laws governing the actions of men in the international sphere."[156]

Andreas Söllner considers Morgenthau a Weimar liberal and American conservative. This is a fundamental misreading of Morgenthau's intellectual and political orientation in the United States. His rejection of rationalism made him appear conservative, or even reactionary. This stance and his general political pessimism were most pronounced in his early postwar works, notably *Scientific Man vs. Power Politics*. Morgenthau's views underwent considerable evolution, and by the 1970s he had become much more optimistic about the prospects of avoiding nuclear war, restoring America's purpose and even transforming the international system. His optimism was based on his renewed belief in the power of experience and reason to serve as engines for progress.

Morgenthau wrote *Scientific Man vs. Power Politics* in the immediate aftermath of the worst irruption of barbarism spawned by Western civilization. Nazi Germany and Soviet Russia rode roughshod over laws, norms and conventions intended to restrain hateful and self-destructive passions. His marginal life in Germany, academic humiliation in Geneva, loss of position and possessions in Madrid, anxious wanderings in Europe in search of a visa to a safe haven, struggles to survive economically in New York and Kansas City and loss of family, including grandparents, in the Holocaust, darkened his mood and sapped his faith in human reason. But Morgenthau was too intellectually curious, reflective and open-minded to allow his *Weltanschauung* to ossify. His intellectual growth did not stop with his early postwar books, but continued throughout his career. I described his changing views of the Cold War, and how by the 1970s he

155 Frei, *Hans J. Morgenthau*, pp. 45–49.
156 Morgenthau, "Positivism, Functionalism and International Law," pp. 261–84.

became convinced that the conflict had been resolved *de facto* by mutual acceptance of the postwar political and territorial status quo in Europe. He also regarded with interest and approval Western European efforts to build a more peaceful continent on the twin foundations of parliamentary democracy and supranational institutions. Both transformations, he explicitly recognized, were based on learning and reason.

Morgenthau's rekindled optimism was also the result of his experiences in his adopted homeland. Quotidian life in America, especially in the Middle West, helped to restore his faith in human beings and their ability to create and sustain a productive, egalitarian, tolerant and largely peaceful society. *The Purpose of American Politics*, published in 1960, is a biting critique of Cold War American leadership, but its opening chapters are a paean of praise to America's experiment with democracy. The conclusion is a reaffirmation of Morgenthau's faith in the political system. His idealism had reasserted itself, but in a more sophisticated form that might be described as a synthesis of his European and American experiences. He was painfully aware that the practice of American politics and foreign policy did not live up to its ideals. He considered McCarthyism a prominent but temporary failure of the American system, and racism a more enduring and fundamental contradiction of the country's purpose. In 1964 he wrote that "the unequal condition of the American Negro" was "an endemic denial of the purpose for which the United States was created..."[157] Vietnam was another big failure, and, as we have seen, it prompted lectures, articles and a book in which he diagnosed the causes of intervention, some of them structural. But he came to regard the domestic crisis provoked by the war as a catalyst for positive social and political change, especially in the area of civil rights.[158] An early and ardent supporter of the civil rights movement and an early and outspoken critic of Vietnam and member of a score of liberal-activist organizations cannot be described as a conservative.[159]

Morgenthau's mature theoretical work also represents a creative and thoughtful synthesis of Europe and America. His European experience taught him that status quo powers needed the military capability to deter or defeat adversaries intent on expanding their territory or imposing their social systems through conquest. From his reading of European history and experience of American politics he learned that the wide dispersion

[157] Hans J. Morgenthau, "The Coming Test of Democracy," *Commentary* (January 1964), pp. 61–63.

[158] Conversations with Morgenthau.

[159] Morgenthau belonged to Academic Committee on Soviet Jewry, the Kurdish–American Society, Americans for Democratic Action, Council for a Livable World, National Council for Civic Responsibility, Turn Toward Peace.

of power and authority and the operation of a balance of power among these actors was the most efficacious mechanism for maintaining liberty and advancing the public welfare. He recognized that balances did not automatically form when their material conditions were present, but depended on the understanding and political skill of actors. It was the responsibility of international relations specialists to make actors aware of their interests in general and how they applied in specific instances.

Politics Among Nations can be read as an attempt to apply the *Federalist Papers* and the American Constitution to international relations. Both documents represent self-conscious attempts to harness "private vice" to build "public virtue" through separation of powers, checks and balances and representative institutions. Morgenthau made the analogy explicit in his lectures where he attributed the success of democratic societies to their checks and balances and talked at length about the need to apply the same principles, although not in institutional form, to international relations.[160] These principles appealed to Morgenthau because in his view they were based on a realistic understanding of the nearly universal human drives for power and self-aggrandizement and the corrupting consequences of all authority.

America taught Morgenthau a more important lesson than constitutional engineering: it is possible to create a society that minimizes violent conflict by providing security and equal opportunity to its citizens. Here too, he tried to extrapolate from the American experience to the international environment. A secure international order, like its domestic counterpart, would depend on

> social pressure which is able to contain the selfish tendencies in human nature within socially tolerable bounds; conditions of life creating a social equilibrium which tends to minimize the psychological causes of social conflict, such as insecurity, fear, and aggressiveness; and, finally, a moral climate which allows man to expect at least an approximation to justice here and now and thus offers a substitute for strife as a means to achieve justice.[161]

Morgenthau welcomed progress toward these goals in Western societies and looked forward to the day when these conditions might become realized on a regional and even global scale.

[160] "Philosophy of International Relations," Lecture notes, 1952, pp. 55–58, Morgenthau Papers, container 81.

[161] Morgenthau, *Scientific Man vs. Power Politics*. 183.

7 The wisdom of classical realism

> Many wonders are there, but none is more *deinon* (wondrous, strange, powerful, awful) than man.
>
> Sophocles[1]

Chapters 3 through 6 analyzed the writings of Thucydides, Clausewitz and Hans Morgenthau in historical context. Here, I offer a comparative analysis that emphasizes the fundamental unity of classical realism across a span of nearly 2,500 years. It is organized around the themes of order, justice and change, the central dimensions of politics for all three thinkers. Classical realists have holistic understandings of politics that stress the similarities, not the differences, between domestic and international politics, and the role of community in promoting stability in both. They recognize that communal bonds are fragile and easily undermined by the unrestrained pursuit of unilateral advantage by individuals, factions and states. When this happens, time-honored mechanisms of conflict management like alliances and the balance of power may not only fail to preserve the peace but may make domestic and international violence more likely.

The importance of community directs our attention to the ever-present tensions between the interests of the community and those of its members, whether individuals or states. I have already discussed Thucydides' understanding of this polarity, and in this chapter I show the fundamental similarity between his views and those of Clausewitz and Morgenthau. All three classical realists believed that the tensions between individuals and communities could be understood and in part reconciled at a deeper level of understanding. This is because a well-functioning community is essential to the intelligent formation and pursuit of individual interests. Principles of justice on which viable communities must be based, also allow the efficient translation of power into influence. Membership in a community imposes limits on the ends and means of power. And failure to subordinate goals to the requirements of justice leads to self-defeating

[1] Sophocles, *Antigone*, 332.

policies of overexpansion. Classical realists recognized that great powers are often their own worst enemies because success and the hubris it engenders encourage actors to see themselves outside of and above their community, and this in turn blinds them to the need for self-restraint.

The third section of the chapter explores change and transformation. Classical realists think of political systems in terms of their principles of order, and the ways in which they help to shape the identities of actors and the discourses they use to frame their interests. For classical realists, changes in identities and discourses are associated with modernization, and hegemonic war is more often a consequence than a cause of such a transformation. This different understanding of cause and effect has important implications for the kinds of strategies classical realists envisage as efficacious in maintaining or restoring order. While recognizing the importance of power, they put more weight on values and ideas.

Thucydides constructed no theories in the modern sense of the term, but he is widely regarded as the first theorist of international relations. Clausewitz and Morgenthau are explicitly theoretical. The fourth section of the chapter shows the similarities in their understanding of the nature and purpose of theory. All three classical realists are united in their belief that theoretical knowledge is not an end in itself, but a starting point for actors to work their way through contemporary problems and, in the process, come to deeper forms of understanding.

I conclude the chapter with a brief reprise of tragedy. For reasons I have previously elaborated, Thucydides must be considered the fourth great tragedian of fifth-century Athens. Neither Clausewitz nor Morgenthau wrote tragedies, but they shared his tragic understanding of life and politics. It lay at the core of their theories, their understanding of theory and their strategies for reconstituting or renegotiating order.

Order and stability

Most realists have a straightforward answer to the problem of order: effective central authority. Governments that defend borders, enforce laws and protect citizens make domestic politics more peaceful and qualitatively different from international politics. The international arena remains an anarchical, self-help system, a "brutal arena where states look for opportunities to take advantage of each other."[2] Survival depends on a state's material capabilities and its alliances with other states.[3] Thucydides,

[2] John Mearsheimer, "The False Promise of International Institutions," *International Security* 19 (1994–95), pp. 5–49.

[3] Kenneth N. Waltz, *Theory of International Politics* (Reading, Mass.: Addison-Wesley, 1979), pp. 103–04; Robert Gilpin, *Global Political Economy: Understanding the International*

Clausewitz and Morgenthau are not insensitive to the consequences of anarchy, but do not make this kind of generic distinction between international and domestic politics, such a distinction did not come into use until after Jeremy Bentham coined the term "international." For classical realists, *all* politics is an expression of the same human drives and subject to the same pathologies. They see more variation in order and stability *within* domestic political orders and international systems than they do between them. They explain this variation with reference to the cohesiveness of society, domestic or international, and the channels into which it directs human drives.

In ancient Greece, the contemporary realist distinction between domestic and international politics was altogether inappropriate because there were no police forces to maintain domestic order. Citizens had to protect themselves, and for this reason, the traditional *oikos* (household) was built like a fortress. In the polis, technically a state of anarchy, people for the most part depended on the good will and support of their neighbors.[4] If someone raised a hue and cry in the night, it was customary for neighbors to come running. Cities like Athens ultimately developed courts for citizens to bring complaints, and they were very active in the fifth century. But good will and an atmosphere of trust (*pistis*) were the foundation of order.[5] Such a system worked best in small communities, as it does today, where everybody knows everybody else.

Thucydides devotes equal attention to internal developments in Athens and external developments in the diverse theaters of war. He describes parallel developments in both realms and encourages us to understand them as the outcomes of similar and reinforcing processes. His city states run the gamut from highly ordered and consensual to those racked by

Economic Order (Princeton: Princeton University Press, 2001), p. 16, writes that "all realists share a few fundamental ideas such as the anarchic nature of the international system and the primacy of the state in international affairs." Waltz, *Theory of International Politics*, p. 113, offers a more extreme characterization of the differences between domestic and international life: "In international politics force serves, not only as the *ultima ratio*, but indeed as the first and constant one." G. John Ikenberry, *After Victory: Institutions, Strategic Restraint, and the Rebuilding of Order after Major Wars* (Princeton: Princeton University Press, 2001), p. 21, is more sensitive to the empirical variation that exists within both domestic and international orders.

4 Fifth-century Athens had a rudimentary police force of about 300 Scythian slaves who helped the magistrates maintain order at public meetings, control crowds, arrest criminals and control prisoners. There were no public prosecutors, and the Athenian police force may have been unique.

5 Andrew Lintott, *Violence, Civil Strife and Revolution in the Classical Ciity* (Baltimore: Johns Hopkins University Press, 1982), pp. 13–33; Paul Rahe, *Republics Ancient and Modern* (Chapel Hill: University of North Carolina Press, 1994), I, *The Ancien Régime in Classical Greece*, p. 55.

anarchy and civil war. These differences have nothing to do with the presence or absence of a Leviathan, but with the cohesiveness of the community (*homonoia*). When communal bonds are strong, as in Periclean Athens, and in Greece more generally before the Peloponnesian War, *nomos* restrained actors, whether individuals or city states. When community breaks down, as in Corcyra in the 420s, so does order. The introduction of a Leviathan in Corcyra, in the form of an Athenian expeditionary force, actually made matters worse. It provided the cover for the democratic faction to seek out and slaughter its real or imagined enemies.[6] Thucydides would have agreed with Aristotle's observation that law "has no power to compel obedience beside the force of habit."[7]

Thucydides was interested not only in the connections between domestic politics and foreign policy, but between domestic and international structures. We have previously examined these relationships in the context of Athens. The rise of demagogues prolonged and extended the war, and the suffering and costs of war helped to undermine community at home and intensify factional divisions. Athenian economic-military power and its democratic constitution also transformed the structure of international relations, an interaction I examine later in this chapter.

The same tale can be told about Sparta, but here the arrow of causation points in the opposite direction. To achieve victory, Spartiates had to break with their traditions, something resisted by citizens of all political persuasions who wanted to remain steadfast to the ways of their fathers (*meletai*).[8] The extent to which Spartiates felt cross-pressured is illustrated by their wartime treatment of helots. Hard-pressed for additional forces, they created the special status of ex-helot for slaves willing to bear arms. But, upon reflection, Spartiates felt even more threatened by the prospect of a combat-hardened underclass, and slaughtered all the helots who had volunteered.[9] They were then compelled to enlist free Greek *perioikoi* (literally, dwellers around) as mercenaries, acquire a navy with Persian money and conduct campaigns far afield from the Peloponnesus. By 404, Sparta's values had been thoroughly compromised. Victorious Spartiates succumbed to hubris, and behaved in increasingly despotic and "un-Greek ways." They deprived other poleis of their independence and handed over some Ionian cities to enslavement by the Persian king.[10] They ultimately provoked a coalition against them that included some of their most important former allies. Thucydides might with

[6] Thucydides, IV.46.4–IV.48.5. [7] Aristotle, *Politics*, 1269a20.
[8] Thucydides, I.19–28, VIII.5–44, on Spartan innovation.
[9] Thucydides, V.34, IV.80.2–4.
[10] Xenophon, *Hellenica*, III.5.13, *De Vectigalibus*, V.1.14; Isocrates, *Areopagiticus*, 4, 122, *On the Peace*, 8.67.

some justification be considered the original "second image reversed" theorist.[11]

By the nineteenth century, domestic and foreign policy were distinct categories of analysis. In *On War*, Clausewitz begins by treating them as analytically distinct domains. He defines warfare as an activity of organized political units, but this association becomes blurred in practice. In early modern Europe, private quarrels, and even brigandage, were part and parcel of the process of state building. In the seventeenth and eighteenth centuries, he concedes, public and private goals were fused, as many of the dynastic wars of Europe's leading powers were fought to advance the personal interests of their rulers. In the nineteenth century, guerrilla warfare, conducted by irregular and unofficial units, was also motivated by political goals. People's war could create the conditions for a successful counter-offensive by the defender's own army, or compel a militarily undefeated enemy to withdraw by making occupation too costly to bear psychologically and politically.

Like Thucydides, Clausewitz describes parallel processes in domestic and international affairs, and is interested in the relationships between them. He analyzes domestic politics in terms of his defining characteristic of international relations: the drive of actors to expand their power until opposed by equal and opposite forces. He depicts Europe's aristocracy as a parasitical class that appropriated its property by the sword, and when conquest was no longer feasible, found employment in the military service of the state. Aristocrats transformed the profession of arms into an unjustifiable "corporate prerogative," and used their control of the state to award themselves administrative sinecures, repress the peasantry and, later, to exclude the commercial classes from political power. In France, the "abuses and privileges" and profligate "extravagances" of the aristocracy were so extreme, and the resentment of the peasantry so great, that it allied with the increasingly prosperous bourgeoisie to make a revolution. The aristocracy overreached itself and was finally opposed by a coalition of superior forces.[12]

On War describes complex relationships among domestic structure, foreign policy and international relations. The French Revolution made efficient central administration possible, and with it, the *levée en masse*

[11] The second image refers to the impact of domestic structures on the international system, and second image reversed to the impact of the international system on domestic structures. See Peter Gourevitch, *Politics in Hard Times: Comparative Responses in International Economic Crises* (Ithaca: Cornell University Press, 1986).

[12] Carl von Clausewitz, "Agitation" (early 1820s), in *Historical and Political Writings*, ed. and trans. Peter Paret and Daniel Moran (Princeton: Princeton University Press, 1992), pp. 338–68.

and large and well-equipped armies. Popular support for the revolution conferred enormous military advantages. All night marches could be conducted without fear of mass desertion. Soldiers could be trained to use their initiative to exploit ground cover and other tactical opportunities. They were also willing to risk their lives in defense of the revolution and France. In the hands of a military genius like Napoleon, the French army swept all opposition from the field and transformed the nature of warfare.[13]

International relations also influenced domestic structures. Following Prussia's catastrophic defeat, a desperate king and his advisors turned to the reformers for help. The newly created Military Reorganization Commission, dominated by Scharnhorst and his disciples, worked closely with the new first minister, Baron von Stein, to reform the internal structure of the army, impose universal conscription and open the officer corps to qualified commoners, all with an eye toward building bridges between the army and the people. The military reformers adapted the structure and tactics of the army to modern warfare, and the new army performed well in early engagements and at the Battle of Leipzig, where Napoleon was routed. When the allied victory at Waterloo removed the threat of Napoleon, domestic concerns again became paramount. The king and Junkers reasserted control over the officer corps, purged the reformers and scrapped pending legislation that left democracy still-born with tragic consequences for Germany and Europe.[14]

Like Thucydides, Clausewitz is particularly interested in the connections between domestic structure and foreign policy. He attributed France's expansionist policy to the revolution and the leadership struggle it spawned. As in post-Periclean Athens, competition for power encouraged contestants to outbid each other in appealing to the basest motives of the masses. They invoked the omnipresent foreign threat to justify an internal war against the aristocracy and draconian measures against their domestic opponents, branded traitors to the revolution. Clausewitz portrays Napoleon as a successful Alcibiades and the ultimate perversion of French revolutionary principles; he had himself crowned emperor and imposed tyranny at home and abroad. Once again, power divorced from principle found expression in limitless and self-defeating military expansion.

[13] Carl von Clausewitz, *On War*, ed. and trans. Michael Howard and Peter Paret (Princeton: Princeton University Press, 1976), Book VIII, ch. 3, pp. 502–03.

[14] Gordon A. Craig, *The Politics of the Prussian Army, 1640–1945* (New York: Oxford University Press, 1955), pp. 54–81; Walter M. Simon, *The Failure of the Prussian Reform Movement, 1807–1819* (Ithaca: Cornell University Press); Thomas Nipperdey, *Germany from Napoleon to Bismarck, 1800–1866*, trans. Daniel Nolan (Princeton: Princeton University Press, 1996), pp. 237–80.

For Clausewitz, the differences between Frederick I and Napoleon were revealing. The Great Elector was also an ambitious leader; he organized the Prussian state around its army, and began the long-standing German tradition of making state structure subservient to foreign policy needs (*der Primat der Aussenpolitik*). But Frederick was restrained in his pursuit of territorial expansion. In the first instance, this was due to the inherent limitations of a relatively small state and the effective operation of a European balance of power. More fundamentally, Frederick considered himself a member of the European community of princes, and this identity shaped his goals. Territorial expansion was not an end in itself, but a means toward higher standing within his community. Unlimited territorial aims were not only impractical, but would have undermined the very status that he sought.[15] Napoleon was thunderstruck by *The Marriage of Figaro* and exclaimed: "*C'est déja la révolution en action.*"[16] One can only wonder at how he would have responded to Don Giovanni, a figure, like himself, who is outside of community, unrestrained in his ambitions and destructive to himself and everyone around him. For Clausewitz, Napoleon was the modern reincarnation of the tragic Greek hero whose self-willed break with his community initially empowers him but ultimately leads to personal and national tragedy.

Morgenthau's understanding of the relationship between domestic and international politics mirrors that of Thucydides and Clausewitz. At the outset of *Politics Among Nations* he introduces a sharp distinction between international and domestic politics which he then systematically undermines. *All* politics, he insists, is a struggle for power that is "inseparable from social life itself."[17] In many countries, laws, institutions and norms direct the struggle for power into ritualized and socially acceptable channels. In the international arena, the struggle cannot so readily be tamed.[18] The character of international relations nevertheless displays remarkable variation across historical epochs. In the eighteenth century, Europe was "one great republic" with common standards of "politeness and cultivation" and a common "system of arts, and laws, and manners." Although

[15] Carl von Clausewitz, *Nachrichten über Preussen in seiner grossen Katastrophe: Kriegsgeschichtliche Einzelschriften* (Berlin: 1888), was nevertheless clear that Frederick's absolutism had frozen the structure of the state and so stifled the creative energies of the Prussian people that subsequent disaster was all but inevitable.

[16] Quoted in Mladen Dolar, "If Music Be the Food of Love," in Slavoj Žižek and Mladen Dolar, *Opera's Second Death* (New York: Routledge, 2002), p. 40.

[17] Hans J. Morgenthau, *Scientific Man vs. Power Politics* (London: Latimer House, 1947), p. 16, and *Politics Among Nations: The Struggle for Power and Peace* (New York: Alfred A. Knopf, 1948), pp. 17–18.

[18] Morgenthau, *Politics Among Nations*, p. 172, *The Decline of Democratic Politics* (Chicago: University of Chicago Press, 1958), p. 80.

Morgenthau did not make the analogy in print, he often spoke of the parallel between international relations in the eighteenth century and pre-Peloponnesian War Greece.[19] In both epochs, "fear and shame" and "some common sense of honor and justice" induced leaders to moderate their ambitions.[20] The sense of community was ruptured by the French Revolution, and only superficially restored in its aftermath. It broke down altogether in the twentieth century when the principal powers became divided by ideology as well as by interests. In the 1930s, four major powers – Germany, the Soviet Union, Japan and Italy – rejected the very premises of the international order. The Soviet Union continued to do so in the postwar era, reducing international politics "to the primitive spectacle of two giants eyeing each other with watchful suspicion."[21]

Morgenthau recognized the same variation in domestic politics. In strong societies like Britain and the United States, norms and institutions muted the struggle for power, but in weak societies like Nazi Germany and Stalin's Soviet Union, they broke down. Politics in these countries was every bit as violent and unconstrained as in any epoch of international relations. For Morgenthau, as for Thucydides and Clausewitz, communities and the identities and norms they help to create and sustain are the most critical determinants of order, at home and abroad.

Balance of power

Contemporary realists consider military capability and alliances the very foundation of security. They regard the balance of power as a universally applicable mechanism, although most effective in a multipolar system. The Greeks were by no means insensitive to the value of alliances. Aristotle observed that "When people are friends, they have no need for justice, but when they are just they need friends as well."[22] Thucydides, and classical realists more generally, nevertheless recognized that military

[19] Class notes, "Introduction to International Relations," 4 October 1960.

[20] Morgenthau, *Politics Among Nations*, pp. 159–66, 270–84; Hans J. Morgenthau, *In Defense of the National Interest: A Critical Examination of American Foreign Policy* (Lanham, Md.: University Press of America, 1982 [1951]), p. 60. Similar arguments were subsequently made by the so-called English school, especially Hedley Bull, *The Anarchical Society: A Study of Order in World Politics* (New York: Columbia University Press, 1977). See also John Gerard Ruggie, "International Regimes, Transactions, and Change: Embedded Liberalism in the Postwar Economic Order," *International Organization* 36 (Spring 1982), pp. 379–415, and Friedrich V. Kratochwil and John Gerard Ruggie, "International Organization: A State of the Art on the Art of the State," in Edward D. Mansfield, ed., *International Organization: A Reader* (New York: Harper Collins, 1994), pp. 4–19.

[21] Morgenthau, *Politics Among Nations*, p. 285.

[22] Aristotle, *Nicomachean Ethics,* 1155a24–26.

power and alliances are double-edged swords; they are as likely to provoke as to prevent conflict.

Book I of Thucydides leaves no doubt that Athenian efforts to obtain a favorable balance of power were an instrumental cause of war. The alliance with Corcyra led to a violent encounter with the Corinthian fleet and raised the prospect of a wider war with Sparta. Athens then took peremptory action against Megara and Potidaea, and made war difficult to prevent. Sparta's alliance with Corinth dragged it in turn into a war with Athens that many Spartiates would have preferred to avoid. Nowhere in his text does Thucydides provide a single example of an alliance that deterred war, and by the logic of the balance of power some of them should have. His speeches and narrative suggest several reasons for this unrelieved pattern of deterrence failure. Arrogance and stupidity (*amathia*) lead the list.[23] The Spartan war faction offers a striking example. Ignoring all the evidence to the contrary, it was convinced of Sparta's invincibility and clung to the unreasonable expectation that it could fight and win a short war.[24]

Deterrence was also defeated by arrogance and intelligence. Pericles welcomed the Corinthian–Corcyrean conflict as a low-cost opportunity to enhance Athenian power. He appears to have reasoned that Athenian support of Corcyra would deter Corinth from attacking, but that, if deterrence failed, Sparta would nevertheless remain neutral. A thoughtful planner, he had a fall-back strategy to cope with the worst-case outcome of war with Sparta. He would not oppose the expected Spartan invasion of Attica, but conduct a low-key campaign of naval harassment in and around the Peloponnese. Spartiates would become increasingly frustrated by their inability to engage Athens and tire of war and the peace party would return to power. He and Archidamus would then conclude a more enduring peace. Pericles miscalculated every step of his elaborate scenario, and his alliance with Corcyra was the initial *hamartia* of the Athenian tragedy. A careful reading of Thucydides indicates that he was by no means blind to Pericles' failings. He also understood that Pericles' hubris was emblematic of that of Athens, just as Sthenelaïdas' was of Sparta.

Deterrence was also defeated by the breakdown of community and the conventions it sustained. Athenians increasingly succumbed to the impulses of self-aggrandizement (*pleonexia*). In the Sicilian debate, the sensible and cautious Nicias tries to educate Athenians about the size and

[23] Thucydides, I.84.3. Archidamas attempts to put *amathia* in a positive light by claiming it restrains Spartans from ever thinking of themselves as above the laws.

[24] Ibid., I.80–85, pp. 46–50.

population of Sicily and the military readiness of its largest city, Syracuse, and warms of the dangers of sailing against an island so far away when there are undefeated enemies close to home.[25] Alcibiades dismisses these risks out of hand and appeals to the greed of his audience.[26] Recognizing that direct arguments against the expedition will not succeed, Nicias now tries to dissuade the assembly by insisting on a much larger force and more extensive provisions than were originally planned. To his surprise, the more he demands, the more eager the assembly becomes to support the expedition, convinced that a force of such magnitude will be invincible.[27] Carried away by the prospect of gain, Athenians became immune to the voice of reason, and committed the second *hamartia* of the Athenian tragedy, and the one that provoked *nemesis* (the wrath of the gods).

Clausewitz did not discuss the concept of the balance of power in any detail, but acknowledged its failure to deter Prussia from challenging France in 1806, and Napoleon from invading Russia. The former was reminiscent of the Spartan decision for war. Like Sthenelaïdas and the war party, King Friedrich Wilhelm and his generals were so irrationally confident of success and correspondingly blind to the evidence of their shortcomings in previous campaigns against the French that they were positively lackadaisical in their preparations. Napoleon's invasion of Russia was more like the Sicilian expedition. By 1812, Napoleon had become immune to the voice of reason, succumbed to *hubris* and committed the *hamartia* that provoked *nemesis* in the form of defeat and exile. Against such a figure, powerful and outside the bonds of community, deterrence, even based on a favorable balance of power, offered no guarantee against attack. The most military capability could do – and here Clausewitz would agree with Hermocrates – was to provide a good defense.

For Morgenthau, the universality of the power drive meant that the balance of power was "a general social phenomenon to be found on all levels of social interaction."[28] Individuals, groups and states inevitably combined to protect themselves from predators. At the international level, the balance of power had contradictory implications for peace. It might deter war if status quo powers outgunned imperialist challengers and demonstrated their resolve to go to war in defense of the status quo. Balancing could also intensify tensions and make war more likely because of the

[25] Ibid., 6.9; W. Robert Connor, *Thucydides* (Princeton: Princeton University Press, 1984), pp. 158–68, for an insightful discussion of the debate, and 159, n. 5 which notes another parallel between the Persian and Sicilian invasions: leaders' lack of experience; Kurt von Fritz, *Die Geschichte Geschichtsschreibung* (Berlin: Walter de Gruyter, 1968), I, p. 728, on Nicias as advisor.

[26] Thucydides, VI: 16–18. [27] Ibid., VI: 20–24.

[28] Morgenthau, *Decline of Democratic Politics*, pp. 49, 81.

impossibility of assessing with any certainty the motives, capability and resolve of other states. Leaders understandably aim to achieve a margin of safety, and when multiple states or opposing alliances act this way, they ratchet up international tensions. In this situation, rising powers may be tempted to go to war when they think they have an advantage, and status quo powers to launch preventive wars against rising challengers. Even when the balance of power failed to prevent war, Morgenthau reasoned, it might still limit its consequences and preserve the existence of states, small and large, that constitute the political system. Like Clausewitz, Morgenthau credited the balance with having served these ends for much of the eighteenth and nineteenth centuries.[29]

For Morgenthau, the success of the balance of power for the better part of two centuries was less a function of the distribution of capabilities than it was of the existence and strength of international society that bound together the most important actors in the system. When that society broke down, as it did from the first partition of Poland through the Napoleonic Wars, the balance of power no longer functioned to preserve the peace or the existence of the members of the system.[30] International society was even weaker in the twentieth century, and its decline was an underlying cause of both world wars. Morgenthau worried that its continuing absence in the immediate postwar period had removed all constraints on superpower competition. By the 1970s, he had become more optimistic about the prospects for peace. Détente, explicit recognition of the territorial status quo in Europe, a corresponding decline in ideological confrontation, the emergence of Japan, China and West Germany as possible third forces and the effects of Vietnam on American power had made both superpowers more cautious and tolerant of the status quo.[31] But, perhaps most importantly, their daily contacts, negotiations and occasional agreements had gone some way toward normalizing their relations and creating the basis for a renewed sense of international community.

Thucydides, Clausewitz and Morgenthau understood politics as a struggle for power and unilateral advantage. The differences between domestic politics and international relations were merely differences of degree. Military capability and alliances were necessary safeguards in the rough-and-tumble world of international relations, but could not be

[29] Morgenthau, *Politics Among Nations*, pp. 155–59, 162–66, 172, and *Decline of Democratic Politics*, p. 80.

[30] Morgenthau, *Politics Among Nations*, pp. 160–66; Morgenthau, *In Defense of the National Interest*, p. 60. Paul W. Schroder, "A. J. P. Taylor's International System," *International History Review* 23 (March 2001), pp. 3–27, makes the same point.

[31] Morgenthau, *Politics Among Nations*, 5th ed., 1972, Preface. But pp. 355–56 still reflect the pessimism of earlier editions.

counted on to preserve the peace or the independence of actors. Order, domestic and international, ultimately rested on the strength of the community. When states and their rulers were bound by a common culture, by conventions and personal ties, competition for power was restrained in its ends and its means. Under such conditions, a balance of power might prevent some wars and limit the severity of others. In the absence of community, military capability and alliances were no guarantee of security, and could provoke wars they were intended to prevent. States like Athens, and leaders like Napoleon and Hitler, could not be deterred. As Morgenthau recognized, the balance of power works best when needed least.

For classical realists order is the result of identities and the internal constraints they generate, both directly, on behavior, and indirectly, by the manner in which identities shape interests. Order is only secondarily attributable to the external constraints imposed by governments, alliances and superior military capabilities. International society – conceived of as community at the international level – is of critical importance to classical realists. It is not something they theorize; the concept is implicit in Thucydides, noted by Clausewitz and explicitly acknowledged by Morgenthau, who never defines it, but offers eighteenth-century Europe as its defining manifestation. For all three it appears to be something different from and largely independent of any political authority that may or may not exist in the system.

The idea of international society was envisaged by Montesquieu, Vattel, Burke and Gentz, all of whom grasped the possibility of a rule-governed international relations independent of any overarching institutions.[32] This concept was given sharper conceptual form by the so-called English school of international relations. Hedley Bull, arguably its most important representative, defined it as the set of rules, norms and procedures that govern diplomatic activity.[33] In the tradition of Grotius, Bull and Adam Watson contend that these practices emerge through dialogue among the members of the society, all of whom come to recognize their "common interest in maintaining these arrangements." The English school makes state actors ontologically prior to international society and defines society narrowly by equating it with the organizing principle of the system (sovereignty) and the procedures governing diplomatic and official

[32] Bull, *The Anarchical Society*, pp. 13–14. See also, C. A. W. Manning, *The Nature of International Society* (London: London School of Economics, 1962); Martin Wight, *System of States* (Leicester: Leicester University Press, 1977); Hedley Bull and Adam Watson, eds., *The Expansion of International Society* (Oxford: Oxford University Press, 1984); Adam Watson, *The Evolution of International Society* (London: Routledge, 1992).

[33] Bull and Watson, *The Expansion of International Society*, p. 1.

interactions.[34] Thucydides and Morgenthau would have found both features troubling. They would have felt comfortable with the broader, proto-constructivist conception of Karl W. Deutsch, for whom the identities of actors and their societies are mutually constitutive.[35] Christian Reuss-Smit has recently argued that sovereignty cannot be the foundation of international society because different kinds of societies have developed in systems of sovereign political units. To explain this variation scholars need to look beyond sovereignty to normative components of society, especially to beliefs about the moral purpose of the state.[36]

Their differing focus on the normative values of international society versus the structure of the international system accounts for important differences between classical and many modern realists. Because they conceive of anarchy as the defining characteristic of international systems, modern realists consider security the principal, although by no means the exclusive, concern of foreign policy. Looking at international relations through the prism of international society led classical realists to consider a multiplicity of motives, any one of which may be paramount, depending on the circumstances.

Invoking a common fifth-century understanding of human motivation, Thucydides explains the outbreak and the course of the Peloponnesian War in terms of fear, honor and interest.[37] In their unsuccessful effort to justify their foreign policy, the Athenian envoys told the Spartan assembly that "the nature of the case first compelled us to advance our empire to its present height; fear being our principal motive, though honor and interest afterwards came in."[38] They assert that fear is once again foremost in their minds:

> And at last, when almost all hated us, when some had already revolted and had been subdued, when you had ceased to be the friends that you once were, and had become objects of suspicion and dislike, it appeared no longer safe to give up our empire; especially as all who left us would fall to you. And no one can quarrel with a people for making, in matters of tremendous risk, the best provision that it can for its interest.[39]

Not for the last time, Athenian words contradict Athenian behavior. Book I indicates that in 431 Athenians had few fears for the security of their

[34] The problem of ontology has important implications for how we think about cooperation and how it develops, some of which I address in Chapter 8.

[35] Karl W. Deutsch *et al.*, *Political Community and the North Atlantic Area* (Princeton: Princeton University Press, 1957).

[36] Christian Reus-Smit, *The Moral Purpose of the State: Culture, Social Identity, and Institutional Rationality in International Relations* (Princeton: Princeton University Press, 1999).

[37] Isocrates, *Antidosis*, 15,217, *To Philip*, 5.135, writes that men will do anything for pleasure (*hēdonē*), gain (*kerdos*) and honor (*timē*).

[38] Thucydides, I.75.2–3. [39] Ibid., I.75.4–5.

empire, but rather welcomed the opportunity to augment their power relative to Sparta and Corinth. The Athenian speech can be read either as a *prophasis* – a self-conscious attempt to justify a policy being pursued for other reasons – or, as I think more likely, an indication of the extent to which Athenians are not yet ready to acknowledge their real motives, even to themselves. Morgenthau made a similar observation in the context of the American imperium in Latin America; the Roosevelt administration was unable to see the contradiction between its proclaimed motives and its behavior. Its "Good Neighbor Policy," intended to reconcile the two, increased the perceived dissonance south of the border.[40]

Thucydides leads thoughtful readers to a parallel conclusion about Sparta. Its decision for war had less to do with fear than it did with honor. *Timē* refers to honor in the sense of standing or status, but it also encompasses dignity and self-respect, which requires people to act in the right way, regardless of their standing.[41] Most Spartiates saw both on the line in 431. If they stood aside, Athens would increase its absolute power and relative standing at their expense. Failure to come to the aid of their allies – independent of any outcome – would be dishonorable. Sparta's standing as a hegemon and its reliability as an ally were twin pillars of its identity, and made the decision for war a foregone conclusion for most Spartiates. The Melians also put their honor – conceived as freedom (*eleutheria*) and independence (*autonomia*) above security. So did the Athenians when they first opposed Persia, in sharp contradiction to their later assertion that they were activated by fear. Athens could easily have stood aside when the Ionians revolted against Persian rule in 499, but rashly intervened on a limited, symbolic scale – they sent a mere twenty ships – to show support for people felt to be their kinsmen.[42] That intervention was the catalyst for the subsequent invasions of Greece.[43] Corcyra, Corinth and other key third parties who twice pushed the two hegemons into war were motivated by a combination of honor and interest (the pursuit of advantage, often economic). A single-minded focus on security, which guides most realist readings of Thucydides, misses the

[40] Morgenthau, *Politics Among Nations*, pp. 57–58.

[41] Bernard Williams, *Shame and Necessity* (Berkeley and Los Angeles, University of California Press, 1993), p. 103, contends that Sophoclean characters are presented to us as people who have a conviction that they need to act in a certain way. They are moved by their understanding or view of themselves. They are often moved by self-respect. They could not look at others (or the gods in the case of Antigone) if they did – or did not do – certain things. They are grounded in *ēthos*.

[42] Herodotus, V.98–104; Russell Meiggs, *The Athenian Empire* (New York: Oxford University Press, 1972), pp. 24–28.

[43] Meiggs, *The Athenian Empire*, p. 32.

complexity of his story – and of international relations – when it becomes the sole lens through which foreign policy is refracted.

We need not dwell on interest, the second of Thucydides' motives, because it is extensively discussed in the international relations literature. It is as central to the liberal and Marxist paradigms as fear is to the realist. Honor is the neglected member of the motivational triad. It is both an important motive for actors and an ordering principle in international relations. As we have observed, there is structure even in anarchy; all international systems, regardless of their degree of order, are highly stratified.[44]

Honor was an important issue for Clausewitz, personally and professionally. I described his emotional response to Prussia's defeat in 1806, and how, like Spartiates before him, his sense of self-esteem was linked to the honor and standing of his state. Honor drove Prussia to war, and the goal of regaining that honor through victory motivated Scharnhorst, Gneisenau, Clausewitz and their circle. Clausewitz appealed to other Germans, urging them to "Honor themselves" by not collaborating with the French occupation.[45] Morgenthau was also deeply concerned with the question of honor in his youth, reflected in his critical remarks about how turning a blind eye to anti-Semitism had deprived his parents' generation of German Jews of their self-respect and "character."[46] His mature work recognizes honor, along with interest and fear, as an important motive of foreign policy. He treats it as a source of restraint in the eighteenth century – the period when the balance of power was most effective. He offers no reason for this judgment, but it is not difficult to fathom.

These examples indicate that honor has internal and external dimensions. As anthropologist Julian Pitt-Rivers puts it, "honour is the value of a person in his own eyes, but also in the eyes of his society."[47] Continental jurists introduced a similar distinction: between "objective honor," which refers to a person's reputation (an odd use of the term because there is

[44] This point is also made by Ian Clark, *The Hierarchy of States: Reform and Resistance in the International Order* (Cambridge: Cambridge University Press, 1989), p. 2.

[45] Carl von Clausewitz, "Notes on History and Politics", (1803–1807) and from the "Political Declaration" (1812), in *Historical and Political Writings*, pp. 239–49 and 287–303.

[46] Hans J. Morgenthau, "Fragment of an Intellectual Autobiography: 1904–1932," in Kenneth W. Thompson and Robert J. Myers, *A Tribute to Hans Morgenthau* (Washington, DC: New Republic Book Co., 1977), pp. 1–17.

[47] Julian Pitt-Rivers, "Honour and Social Status," in J. G. Peristiany, ed., *Honour and Shame: The Values of Mediterranean Society* (Chicago: University of Chicago Press, 1966), p. 22. See also Frank Henderson Stewart, *Honor* (Chicago: University of Chicago Press, 1994), for a general review of the concept of honor, with particular reference to Europe and North Africa, and an interesting chapter on honor in Arthur Schopenhauer, "Aphorisms on the Wisdom of Life," in *Parerga and Paralipomena*, trans. E. F. J. Payne (Oxford: Oxford University Press, 1974), I, esp. ch. 4, "What a Man Represents," pp. 353–403.

nothing objective about such assessment), and "subjective honor," which is a person's sense of self-worth.[48] It may be more useful to think of external and internal honor, and to recognize that they are related. In the case of Sparta, "objective" or external honor – conceived as coequal standing as a hegemon – and "subjective" or internal honor – doing the right thing by one's allies – were intertwined because failure to come to the support of the allies also would have damaged Sparta's standing. External honor is always a relational concept, and when it feeds back on internal honor, as it did in Sparta, external competition is likely to become more acute.[49] John Finley observes that "it is the nature of honour that it must be exclusive, or at least hierarchic. When everyone attains equal honour, then there is no honour for anyone. Of necessity, therefore, the world of Odysseus was fiercely competitive, as each hero strove to outdo the others."[50] As the *Iliad* makes abundantly clear, honor was the root cause of a mutually destructive ten-year conflict between extended kinship groups. For the polis to emerge, the concept of the hero as an identity and honor as his motivation had to be reframed in communal terms. Honor became more political than personal, and a cause of conflict among states rather than individuals. But it was also a potent source of solidarity at the individual and communal levels. External honor can only be earned through membership in society and behavior in conformity with its values. By the fifth century in Greece, *timē* was not only won through skill in combat, but by the benefits that bravery and sacrifice conferred on the community at large by guaranteeing its freedom and independence. This was the basis of Athens' *hēgemonia*.

Not only in Greece, but in modern Europe, competition among the great powers was from the very beginning a struggle for rank and honor. Thomas Hobbes described it as a continuation of earlier dynastic rivalries, driven almost entirely by considerations of personal standing.[51] In the eighteenth century, the *philosophes* redefined honor to make it appropriate

[48] Moritz Liepmann, "Die Beleidigung," in Karl Birkmeyer *et al.*, eds., *Vergleichende Darstellung des deutschen und ausländischen Strafrechts: Besonder Teil* (Berlin: Otto Liebmann, 1906), IV, pp. 217–373.

[49] This is not always the case, as the World Cup indicates. Honor, in the sense of standing, is competitive, and a zero sum game. But honor in the sense of dignity is independent of how many rounds of competition a team survives or where it ends up in the rankings. It is a function of treating the game and other soccer teams with respect, and of following the rules and the informal norms that govern the *agōn*. A team can finish high in the rankings and low in honor in the eyes of other teams and fans.

[50] Moses I. Finley, *The World of Odysseus* (New York: Viking Press, 1954), p. 126.

[51] For Hobbes, this was a quintessential preoccupation of the leisure classes, and by extension, wealthier states: "All men naturally strive for honour and preferment; but chiefly they who are least troubled with caring for necessary things," *English Works*, II, p. 160, cited in Keith Thomas, "The Social Origins of Hobbes' Political Thought," in K. C. Brown, ed., *Hobbes Studies* (Oxford: Blackwell, 1965), p. 191.

to a rationally organized society.[52] In the nineteenth century, it found expression in the scramble for Africa, the construction of battle fleets, and, more recently, in the acquisition of nuclear weapons, the launching of satellites, inclusion in the elite club of the most developed economies (G-6 and G-7) and seats on major United Nations' bodies and committees. During the Cold War, the Soviet Union and the United States engaged in intense, and often, dangerous, competition for influence in Europe and the Third World. The Cold War may have begun as part of a quest for security, but over time it became something of a "game" played for reasons of status. There is strong evidence that the Soviet Union put such a vast percentage of its resources into its military because, by the 1980s, it was the only domain in which it could compete successfully with the United States and maintain its superpower status. We know too that one of Brezhnev's most important goals in seeking détente was recognition by the United States of its equal standing as a superpower.[53] Post-1945 French foreign policy makes no sense whatsoever unless we factor in standing as a principal motivation.

"Subjective" or internal honor appears to be a near-universal attribute of warrior classes. It was central to the identity of aristocrats in both bronze age Greece and in Europe, and in southern Europe seems to have trickled far down the social hierarchy. The most cursory glance at the politics of the twentieth century reveals the critical importance of this kind of honor in foreign policy.[54] It was key to the decisions that led to war in 1914.[55] For Austria's leaders, the assassination was not just a pretext to invade Austria, but an attempt to preserve the honor of the empire and its leaders.[56] The German kaiser also framed the problem

[52] John Pappas, "La campagne des philosophes contre l'honneur," *Studies on Voltaire and the Eighteenth Century* 205 (1982), pp. 31–44; Stewart, *Honor*, pp. 32–33; Charles Taylor, *The Ethics of Authenticity* (Cambridge, Mass.: Harvard University Press, 1992), pp. 46–47.

[53] Raymond L. Garthoff, *Détente and Confrontation: American–Soviet Relations from Nixon to Reagan*, rev. ed. (Washington, DC: Brookings, 1994), pp. 40–63; Richard Ned Lebow and Janice Gross Stein, *We All Lost the Cold War* (Princeton: Princeton University Press, 1994), pp. 152–56.

[54] Honor is also emphasized by Oran Young, "International Regimes: Toward a New Theory of Institutions," *World Politics* 39 (October 1986), pp. 104–22; Barry O'Neill, *Honor, Symbols, and War* (Ann Arbor: University of Michigan Press, 1999).

[55] Avner Offer, "Going to War in 1914: A Matter of Honor?," *Politics & Society* 23 (June 1995), pp. 213–41.

[56] Samuel R. Williamson, Jr., "Influence, Power, and the Policy Process: The Case of Franz Ferdinand," *The Historical Journal* 17 (1974), pp. 417–34, "The Origins of World War I," *Journal of Interdisciplinary History* 18 (Spring 1988), pp. 795–818, and *Austria-Hungary and the Coming of the First World War* (London: Macmillan, 1990); R. J. Evans, "The Habsburg Monarchy and the Coming of War," in R. J. Evans and Hartmut Pogge von Strandmann, eds., *The Coming of the First World War* (Oxford: Oxford University Press, 1988), pp. 33–56.

this way, and it made him willing to issue his so-called "blank check" to Austria.[57] Russian leaders recognized the likely consequences of their mobilization but nevertheless felt compelled to back Serbia as a matter of honor. Like the Austrians – and the Spartans – they believed they could not sacrifice their honor and retain their standing as a great power.[58] The British Cabinet would never have mustered a majority behind intervention if at least some of its members had not felt compelled to honor their country's pledge to defend Belgium's neutrality.[59] In the interwar period, Bolsheviks and Nazis tried, without much success, to adapt honor to their social orders, an indication of the importance to which these self-declared opponents of the existing order nevertheless attached to the concept.[60]

By identifying fear, honor and interests as key motives, and associating different kinds of behavior with each, classical realists offer us a useful – but largely ignored – framework for the study of foreign policy.[61] When honor and interest are important motives, conflict and war are likely, but the ends and means of foreign policy will be limited. Interests, especially economic ones, often depend on the well-being, even prosperity of other actors, just as honor requires the preservation of society and its members.[62] The frequency of war in such a world will vary inversely with its perceived destructiveness and the functioning of the balance of power. Fear will become the dominant motive when international society weakens or dissipates. The security dilemma is most appropriate to this latter kind of world. But, as we have observed, deterrence may fail because actors who are outside of society are unlikely to behave rationally. Wars in this circumstance are likely to be more general in their goals and destructive in the prosecution and consequences.

[57] Holger H. Herwig, *The First World War: Germany and Austria-Hungary, 1914–1918* (London: Arnold, 1998), pp. 8–18; F. R. Bridge, *From Sadowa to Sarajevo: The Foreign Policy of Austria-Hungary, 1866–1914* (London: Routledge & Kegan Paul, 1972), pp. 335–36.

[58] D. C. Lieven, *Russia and the Origins of the First World War* (New York: St. Martin's Press, 1983); D. W. Spring, "Russia and the Coming of War," in Evans and Pogge von Strandmann, eds., *The Coming of the First World War*, pp. 57–86.

[59] Luigi Albertini, *The Origins of the War of 1914*, trans. Isabella M. Massey (London: Oxford University Press, 1957), III, pp. 364–71, 405–11; Zara S. Steiner, *Britain and the Origins of the First World War* (New York: St. Martin's Press, 1977), pp. 233, 236–37.

[60] S. Tackmann, "Die moralische Begriffe Ehre und Würde in der sowjetischen Ethikliteratur, *Deutsche Zeitschrift für Philosophie* 23 (1975), pp. 172–77; Markus Brezina, *Ehre und Ehrenschutz in nationalsozialistischen Recht* (Augsburg: AV-Verlag, 1987).

[61] Robert E. Osgood, *Ideals and Self-Interest in America's Foreign Relations* (Chicago: University of Chicago Press, 1953), pp. 5–6, defines the national interest and the goals of statecraft as security, standing (honor) and wealth.

[62] For a recent statement of this long-understood relationship, see Alexander Wendt, *Social Theory of International Politics* (Cambridge: Cambridge University Press, 1999), pp. 248, 319, argues that agents whose interests are constituted by a social structure have a stake in that structure.

Interest and justice

Contemporary realists define interest in terms of power. For the most part, they equate power with material capabilities. According to Kenneth Waltz, "the political clout of nations correlates closely with their economic power and their military might."[63] Many contemporary realists also believe in the primacy of self-interest over moral principle, and regard considerations of justice as inappropriate, if not dangerous foundations on which to base foreign policies.[64] At best, appeals to justice can serve to justify or mask policies motivated by more concrete material interests. Classical realists do not present a united front on the role of power. They value it to varying degrees along a continuum that progresses from Thucydides through Clausewitz to Morgenthau. Their conception of power is nevertheless different from their modern counterparts, especially neorealists, although Morgenthau's and Waltz's definitions of power are deceptively similar.[65] Classical realists consider capabilities to be only one source of power and do not equate power with influence. Influence for them is a *psychological* relationship, and like all relationships, based on ties that transcend momentary interests. Justice enters the picture because it is the foundation for relationships and of the sense of community on which influence and security ultimately depend.

As we have seen, the first level of Thucydides' history depicts the tension between interest and justice and how it becomes more acute in response to the exigencies of war. It also reveals how interest and justice are inseparable and mutually constitutive at a deeper level. In his funeral oration, Pericles described Athens as a democracy (*dēmokratia*), but Thucydides considered the constitutional reforms of 462–461 to have created a mixed form of government (*xunkrasis*).[66] Behind the facade of democracy, he tells us, lay the rule of one man (*ergōi de hupo tou prōtou andros archē*) – Pericles.[67] The democratic ideology, with which he publicly associated himself, moderated class tensions and reconciled the *dēmos* to the economic and political advantages of the elite in a Gramscian manner. When the gap between ideology and practice was exposed by the behavior of post-Periclean demagogues, class conflict became more acute and

63 Waltz, *Theory of International Politics*, p. 153.

64 Forde, "Classical Realism," p. 62; Terry Nardin, "Ethical Traditions in International Affairs," in Terry Nardin and David R. Mapel, *Traditions of International Ethics* (New York: Cambridge University Press, 1992), pp. 14–16.

65 For a comparison and discussion, see Richard Ned Lebow, "The Long Peace, the End of the Cold War, and the Failure of Realism," *International Organization* 48 (Spring 1994), pp. 249–78.

66 Thucydides, II.37.1; Plutarch, *Cimon*, 15.2; Plato, *Menexenus*, 238c–d.

67 Thucydides, I.37.1 and II.65.9–10; Plutarch, *Cimon*, 15.2; Plato, *Menexenus*, 238c–d.

politics more vicious, leading to the violent overthrow of democracy by the Dictatorship of the Thirty in 404 and its equally violent restoration a year later. Justice, or at least a belief in justice, was the foundation for community.

Athenian imperialism underwent a similar evolution. The empire was successful when power was exercised in accord with the social conventions governing Greek speech and behavior. Post-Periclean Athens consistently chose power over principle, lost its *hēgemonia*, alienated allies and weakened its power base. In 425, during the Mytilenean debate, Cleon tells the assembly to recognize that their empire (*archē*) is a despotism (*turannis*) based on military power and the fear it inspires.[68] In 416, the Athenian commissioners in the Melian Dialogue divide people into those who rule (*archē*) and those who are subjects (*hupēkooi*).[69] To intimidate allies and adversaries alike, they acknowledge their need to expand. Runaway imperialism of this kind stretched their resources to breaking point. Interest defined outside of the language of justice is irrational and self-defeating.

Thucydides' parallel accounts of Athenian domestic politics and foreign policy indicate his belief that coercion is a grossly inefficient and ultimately self-defeating basis of influence. The sophist Gorgias (*circa* 430) personified *logos* as a "great potentate, who with the tiniest and least visible body achieves the most divine works." Employed in tandem with persuasion, it "shapes the soul as it wishes." Thucydides leads us to the same conclusion. Persuasion (*peithō*) can maintain the position of the "first citizen" (*stratēgos*) of Athens *vis-à-vis* the masses and that of the hegemon *vis-à-vis* its empire and effectively mask the exercise of power. To persuade, leaders and hegemons must live up to the expectations of their own ideology. For Athens, this meant providing benefits to citizens and allies, and upholding the principles of order on which the polis and its empire were based.[70]

Thucydides' characterization of Athens and its empire is rooted in the traditional Greek understanding of the relationship between interest and justice. According to a founding myth of Greek society, that Plato has Protagoras relate, the first humans were able feed, house and clothe themselves by relying on their instincts. Because they lived isolated lives, they were vulnerable to attack from wild animals. They banded together for self-protection, but treated each other so badly (*adikein*) that they soon sought refuge again in their individual caves. Zeus took pity on them and sent Hermes to give them *aidōs* (respect, reverence) and *dikē* (justice) so they could live together harmoniously.[71] *Dikē* is an ordering principle

[68] Thucydides, III.37.2. [69] Ibid., 5: 95. [70] Gorgias, DK, frg. 82, B II, 8, 13–14.

[71] Plato, *Protagoras*, 322c8–323. A version of the myth can also be found in Hesiod, *Works and Days*, 274–80.

that required people to treat others as equals, attempt to see things from their point of view and to empathize with them. *Aidōs* enforces justice through shame. Together, they create the ties of affection (*desmoi philias xunagōgoi*) that bring order to cities.[72] In the fifth century, the tragedians – and Thucydides – describe this relationship in reverse. They attribute *stasis* and war to private quarrels that destroy *philia*, leading Aristotle to observe that "even the smallest disputes are important when they occur at the centers of power."[73] In the most fundamental sense, justice enables identities and interests.

At least as far back as Homer, Greeks believed that people only assumed identities – that is, became people – through membership and participation in a community. Its practices and rituals gave individuals their values, created bonds with other people and, at the deepest level, gave meaning and purpose to their lives.[74] Community also performed an essential cognitive function. To take on an identity, people not only had to distinguish themselves from others, but "identify" with them. Without membership in a community, they could do neither, for they lacked an appropriate reference point to help determine what made them different from and similar to others. This was Oedipus' problem; because of his unknown provenance, he did not know who he was or where he was heading. His attempt to create and sustain a separate identity through reason and aggression was doomed to failure, and may have been intended by Sophocles as a parable for Periclean Athens.[75]

Community originally took the form of a household (*oikos*), and later, of the city state, or polis.[76] In both forms of community, security and

[72] *Dikē* is usually translated as justice, but Charles Segal, *Oedipus Tyrannus: Tragic Heroism and the Limits of Knowledge* (New York: Oxford University Press, 2001), p. 58, suggests that a more accurate rendering is "path of retribution." It implies a process that undoes violence with more violence.

[73] Aristotle, *Politics*, 1303b19–20, 31–32.

[74] Marcel Mauss, *The Gift: the Form and Reason for Exchange in Archaic Societies*, trans. W. D. Halls (New York: Norton, 1990 [1925]).

[75] Like Oedipus, Athens' intellectual prowess becomes impulsiveness, its decisiveness becomes thoughtlessness, and its sense of mastery finds expression as intolerance to opposition. His fall presages that of Athens, and for the same reasons. Bernard Knox, *Oedipus at Thebes* (New York: Norton, 1970), p. 99; J. Peter Euben, *The Tragedy of Political Theory: The Road Not Taken* (Princeton: Princeton University Press, 1990), pp. 40–41.

[76] Thucydides, II.35–47, for Pericles funeral oration, in which he makes clear that men fight and die for the city, not for their individual *kleos*. In this regard it is telling that in the casualty lists men are listed by name according to Cleisthenic tribal divisions, without patronymic or demotic. See Nicole Loraux, "Mourir devant Troie, tomber pour Athènes: De la gloire du héros à l'idée de la cité," in G. Gnoli and Jean-Pierre Vernant, eds., *La mort, les morts dans les anciennes sociétés* (Cambridge: Cambridge University Press, 1982), p. 28. For comparisons between life in an actual *oikos* and later Greek literary and philosophical idealizations of it, see Nicholas Cahill, *Household and City Organization at Olynthus* (New Haven: Yale University Press, 2002).

sustenance were principal ends, and the interest of the individual was advanced through the group's attainment of common goals.[77] All communities were organized around the principles of hierarchy and *philia*. The latter embraced affection, friendship and belonging, and at its core signified some form of freely chosen association.[78] *Philia* was routinely used to describe the bonds of marriage and the political "friendship" of citizens who choose to associate with one another in a political community.[79] In the last third of the fifth century, the term was also used to characterize a citizen's relationship to his polis, and responsibility for its well-being.[80] Without any intended irony, Athenian playwrights describe as "demos-lovers," people who had the same degree of affection for their polis as for their family and friends.[81]

In his funeral oration, Pericles exhorts Athenians to think of themselves as lovers (*erastai*) of their polis.[82] Sara Monoson suggests that Pericles

[77] Aristotle, *Politics*, 1252a1, notes that "Every state is a community of some kind, and every community is established with a view to some good." Moses I. Finley, *The Ancient Economy*, 2nd ed. rev. (Berkeley and Los Angeles: University of California Press, 1999), and The *World of Odysseus* (New York: Viking, 1978); Pierre Vidal-Naquet, *The Black Hunter: Forms of Thought and Forms of Society in the Greek World*, trans. Andrew Szegedy-Maszak (Baltimore: Johns Hopkins University Press, 1986); William James Booth, *Households: On the Moral Architecture of the Economy* (Ithaca: Cornell University Press, 1993).

[78] Aristotle, *Nicomachean Ethics*, 1155a14, 1159b25, 1161a23, 1161b12, and *Politics*, 1280b39, observes that for Greeks, political community is a common project that requires affection and a common commitment among citizens, and that friendship is often considered more important than justice.

[79] On the meaning of *philia*, see Aristotle, *Nicomachean Ethics*, Books 8–9, and *Eudemian Ethics*, 7; W. Robert Connor, *The New Politicians of Fifth-Century Athens* (Princeton: Princeton University Press, 1971), ch. 2; Horst Hunter, *Politics as Friendship: The Origins of Classical Notions of Politics in the Theory and Practice of Friendship* (Waterloo, Ont.: Wilfrid Laurier University Press, 1978); David Konstan, "*Philia* in Euripides' *Electra*," *Philologos* 129 (1985), pp. 176–85; Walter K. Lacey, *The Family in Classical Greece* (Ithaca: Cornell University Press, 1984 [1968]); Jean Pierre Vernant, *Mythe et pensée chez les grecs, études de psychologie historique* (Paris: Maspero, 1966), pp. 208–09; John M. Cooper, *Reason and Emotion* (Princeton: Princeton University Press, 1999), chs. 14 and 15.

[80] Aristotle, *Politics*, 1320B7–11, 1329b39–1330a2, cites Archytas with favor. He contends that property should be private, but that everybody's needs should be looked after. In the tradition of good friends (*philikos*), citizens should share their wealth.

[81] In *Antigone*, Sophocles uses *philia* in a double sense: as kinship and as affection toward the polis. See R. P. Winnington-Ingram, *Sophocles: An Interpretation* (Cambridge: Cambridge University Press, 1980), p. 129; Connor, *The New Politicians of Fifth-Century Athens*, pp. 99–100.

[82] Thucydides, II.43.1. Susan Guettel Cole, "Oath, Ritual and the Male Community in Athens," in Josiah Ober and Charles Hedrick, eds., *Dēnokratia: A Conversation on Democracies, Ancient and Modern* (Princeton: Princeton University Press, 1996), pp. 227–48, shows that the metaphor of kinship was widely used to create the impression that Athens was "one family." Plato, *Laws*, 708c, 738d; Aristotle, *Politics*, 1280b37, indicate that Athenians regarded participation in ceremonial rites and sacrifice as a basis for reciprocal ties. Those rites were often conducted by *phratria*, or brotherhoods, and membership was an essential component of citizenship.

had a specific kind of relationship in mind.[83] Greeks categorized sexual relationships in terms of roles, not gender preferences. *Erastai*, used in the plural form by Pericles, referred to the dominant, active penetrating partner. Those who were submissive, passive and penetrated – male or female – were described, pejoratively, as *erōmenoi*. For Greeks, masculinity was something to be achieved and defended through a combination of active and energetic but self-controlled behavior.[84] When Pericles urges Athenians to act as *erastai*, he is telling them to assume the masculine role with respect to their city (*erōmenos*) and, by extension, to the rest of Greece.[85]

There is an important homoerotic dimension to this metaphor. The Greek conception of masculinity was difficult to reconcile with one of the most common and highly valued relationships for citizens: love affairs with young males, whom older men pursued and cultivated with gifts. The bonds of affection they established and the responsibility they assumed were expected to endure beyond the young man's maturation, induction into the citizenship rolls and concomitant termination of sexual relations with his *erastos*. Citizenship implied active, dominant participation in the life of the polis. To be passive and submissive and allow oneself to be penetrated like a woman or male prostitute would undercut an adolescent's self-esteem and make his subsequent transition to the dominant role more problematic. The solution was to valorize the *erastos–erōmenos* relationship as a form of friendship (*charis*), sustained by reciprocal gift exchange in which the youth rewards his pursuer with sexual favors in return for mentoring, support, affection and gifts of a non-monetary nature.[86] The ideal *erōmenos* – honored, perhaps, more in the breach than in practice – avoided submission

[83] S. Sara Monoson, *Plato's Democratic Entanglements: Athenian Politics and the Practice of Philosophy* (Princeton: Princeton University Press), pp. 64–87; Victoria Wohl, *Love Among the Ruins: The Erotics of Democracy in Classical Athens* (Princeton: Princeton University Press, 2002), pp. 30–73.

[84] Eva C. Keuls, *The Reign of the Phallus: Sexual Politics in Ancient Athens* (New York: Harper & Row, 1985); Martha Nussbaum, *The Fragility of Goodness: Luck and Ethics in Greek Tragedy and Philosophy* (New York: Cambridge University Press, 1986), chs. 6 and 7; K. J. Dover, *Greek Homosexuality, Updated with a New Postscript* (Cambridge Mass.: Harvard University Press, 1989); David Cohen, "Sexuality, Violence and the Athenian Law of *Hubris*," *Greece and Rome* 38 (1991), pp. 171–88; John J. Winkler, *The Constraints of Desire: The Anthropology of Sex and Gender in Ancient Greece* (New York: Routledge, 1990).

[85] See also Wohl, *Love Among the Ruins*, pp. 30–72. In his *Menexenus*, Plato explicitly rejects Pericles' use of erotic relationships as a model for citizenship in favor of one based on family relations.

[86] As friendship and reciprocity were inextricably linked in the Greek mind, *charis* actually encompassed both concepts.

by suppressing any display of passion and engaging only in intercrural intercourse.[87]

Charis (friendship, gratitude) encouraged loyalty, self-restraint and generosity based on the principle of reciprocity. It was the foundation of traditional interpersonal and inter-*oikos* relations.[88] Scholars disagree about whether reciprocity survived the transition from *oikos* to *polis*, and the extent to which it was supplanted by the new ideal of communal solidarity.[89] One incentive for this transition was the high political cost of reciprocity. While hospitality and gifts elicited friendship and return gifts, transgression against oneself or family required vengeance, which led to escalating family and political feuds. The wealthy were expected to give more, and their *charis* was the principal source of funding for the Dionysia, and later, for warships. But reciprocity also encouraged expectations of private gifts and rewards, and was thus a source of corruption in the polis.[90] Pericles's funeral oration and his lifestyle indicate that he, at least, considered *charis* and reciprocity an appropriate model for Athens. He solved the corruption problem by living a simple and relatively isolated life. He was famous for his refusal to socialize with his peers, presumably to avoid becoming enmeshed in any personal relationships and

[87] Dover, *Greek Homosexuality*; Winkler, *The Constraints of Desire*; Monoson, *Plato's Democratic Entanglements*, pp. 74–85; Nick Fisher, "Gymnasia and Democratic Values of Leisure," in Paul Cartledge, Paul Miller and Sitta von Reden, eds., *Kosmos: Essays in Order, Conflict and Community in Classical Athens* (Cambridge: Cambridge University Press, 1998), pp. 84–104.

[88] Hesiod, *Works and Days*, 349–52, advised Greeks to "Measure carefully when you must borrow from your neighbor, then, pay back the same, or more, if possible, and you will have a friend in time of need."

[89] Richard A. S. Seaford, *Reciprocity and Ritual: Homer and Tragedy in the Developing City State* (Oxford: Oxford University Press, 1991), suggests that solidarity largely replaced reciprocity. The case for continuing reciprocity in social, economic and political relationships is made by Paul Millett, "The Rhetoric of Reciprocity in Classical Athens," in Christopher Gill, Norman Postlethwaite and Richard Seaford, *Reciprocity in Ancient Greece* (Oxford: Oxford University Press, 1998), pp. 227–54, and *Lending and Borrowing in Ancient Athens* (New York: Cambridge University Press, 1991), esp. pp. 24–52, 109–26, 148–59; Danielle Allen, *The World of Prometheus: The Politics of Punishing in Democratic Athens* (Princeton: Princeton University Press, 2000); Malcolm Schofield, "Political Friendship and the Ideology of Reciprocity," in Cartledge, Miller and von Reden, *Kosmos*, pp. 37–51.

[90] On bribery and reciprocity, see A. W. H. Adkins, *Merit and Responsibility: A Study in Greek Values* (Oxford: Oxford University Press, 1960); K. J. Dover, *Greek Popular Morality in the Time of Plato and Aristotle* (Berkeley: University of California Press, 1974), pp. 180–84; Mary Whitlock Blundell, *Helping Friends and Harming Enemies: A Study in Sophocles and Greek Ethics* (Cambridge: Cambridge University Press, 1989), ch. 2. Gregory Vlastos, *Socrates: Ironist and Moral Philosopher* (Cambridge: Cambridge University Press, 1991), pp. 194–99, argues that there was an explicit rejection of reciprocity in the democratic polis, especially of its retaliatory aspects, because of their destructive consequences. Thucydides, VIII.54, and Xenophon, *Memorabilia*, II.4.6., note the damaging aspect of reciprocity as used by politicians to buy votes for undemocratic ends.

their concomitant obligations.[91] He insisted on having his house burned when Athenians took refuge behind their walls for fear that Archidamus would spare it as an act of friendship.[92] Outside his household, his only meaningful relationship was with his city, toward which he directed his love as an *erastos*. He did in practice what he urged others to do metaphorically. In return for dedicating his life to the city, he expected its citizens to reciprocate and sustain him in power by supporting his policies.

In modern liberal democracies, one of the principal political tensions is between the authority of the state and the freedom of the individual. Eighteenth-century political philosophers looked for means of keeping governments from exceeding their constitutional authority and transgressing against the rights of individuals. The Federalist Papers sought to solve this problem through the separation of power and checks and balances.[93] Thucydides has Pericles offer a different solution to this problem. Greeks recognized that *erastos–erōmenos* relationships were subject to abuse; not infrequently, the *erastos* acted shamefully and penetrated his *erōmenos*. Monoson suggests that Pericles' choice of metaphor signals his concern about similar abuse in the political sphere, manifest as corruption and demagogic appeals to the assembly by politicians to advance their parochial goals.[94] I read it as having equally important foreign policy implications, perhaps foremost in Pericles' mind in the wartime conditions of his funeral oration. Athens must assume, as it already had, the dominant, masculine role in its relations with allies. But, Pericles adds, these relations must also be governed by *charis* and reciprocity; Athens must exercise the degree of restraint toward its allies expected of an *erastos*. Only in this way, could Athens maintain their respect and loyalty.[95]

Clausewitz addresses the question of interest and justice only peripherally, but Morgenthau tackles it head on. Perhaps the most frequently

[91] Plutarch, *Pericles*, 7.5, reports that Pericles only traveled on one street in the city: the road leading to the agora and the assembly. The only social event he is known to have attended was the wedding feast of his kinsman Euryptolemos, and he left immediately after the libations were made. Thucydides, II.60.5, II.65.8

[92] Thucydides, II.13.

[93] Alexander Hamilton, John Jay and James Madison, *The Federalist: A Commentary on the Constitution of the United States* (New York: Modern Library, n.d.), especially numbers 10, 47, 48 and 51.

[94] Monoson, *Plato's Democratic Entanglements*, pp. 82–83.

[95] J. T. Hooker, "χάρις and ἀρετή in Thucydides," *Hermes* 102: 1 (1974), pp. 164–69, suggests that Thucydides has Pericles use *charis* in an ironic sense, just as the Corcyreans did, because both are really acting out of motives of self-interest. Periclean hypocrisy would not be inconsistent – and might even strengthen – any contrast intended by Thucydides between the proper way of behaving and Pericles behavior and its ill-fated consequences.

quoted line from *Politics Among Nations* is the assertion in its opening pages that "the concept of interest defined in terms of power" sets politics apart "as an autonomous sphere of action," and in turn makes a theory of politics possible.[96] Morgenthau goes on to subvert this formulation to develop a more nuanced understanding of the relationship between interest and power. These contradictions can be reconciled if we recognize that Morgenthau, like Clausewitz, distinguished between the realms of theory and practice. The former aspired to create an abstract, rational ideal based on the underlying and unchanging dynamics of international politics. Such a theory represented the crudest of templates. Policy, and its analysis, were concrete, not always rational, and had to take into account many considerations outside the sphere of politics.

The contrast between theory and practice is equally apparent in Morgenthau's conceptualization of power. Like Clausewitz, he thought of power as an intangible quality with many diverse components, which he catalogs at some length. But, in the real world, the strategies and tactics leaders use to transform the raw attributes of power into political influence were just as important as the attributes themselves. Because influence is "a psychological relationship," leaders need to know not only what buttons are at their disposal but which ones to push in any circumstance. There were no absolute measures of state power, because it was always relative and situation-specific. Levers of influence that *A* could use against *B* might be totally ineffectual against *C*. The successful exercise of power required a sophisticated understanding of the goals, strengths and weaknesses of allies, adversaries and third parties. But, above all, it demanded psychological sensitivity to the others' needs for self-esteem.

People seek domination but most often end up subordinate to others.[97] They try to repress this unpleasant truth, and those who exercise power effectively employ justifications and ideologies that facilitate this process. Whenever possible, they attempt to convince those who must submit to their will that they are acting in their interests or those of the wider community.[98] "What is required for mastery of international politics," Morgenthau insisted, "is not the rationality of the engineer but the wisdom and moral strength of the statesman."[99]

Like Thucydides, Morgenthau understood that adherence to ethical norms was just as much in the interest of those who wielded power as it was for those over whom it was exercised. He made this point in his critique of American intervention in Indochina, where he argued that

[96] Morgenthau, *Politics Among Nations*, 3rd ed., p. 5.
[97] Morgenthau, *Scientific Man vs. Power Politics*, p. 145.
[98] Morgenthau, *The Decline of Democratic Politics*, p. 59.
[99] Morgenthau, *Politics Among Nations*, p. 172.

intervention would fail and erode America's influence in the world because the ends and means of American policy violated the morality of the age. There was a certain irony to Morgenthau's opposition. Two decades earlier, he had written *Politics Among Nations*, in large part to disabuse an influential segment of the American elite of its naive belief that ethics was an appropriate guide for foreign policy and that international conflicts could be resolved through the application of law. Intervention in Indochina indicated to him that American policymakers had "over learned" the lesson; they had embraced *Realpolitik* and moved to the other end of the continuum. Morgenthau was adamant that morality, defined in terms of the conventions of the epoch, imposes limits on the ends that power seeks and the means employed to achieve them.[100]

For classical realists, justice is important for two different but related sets of reasons. It is the key to influence because it determines how others understand and respond to you. Policy that is constrained by accepted ethical principles and generally supportive of them provides a powerful aura of legitimacy and helps to reconcile less powerful actors to their subordinate status. Influence can also be bought through bribes or compelled by force, but influence obtained this way is expensive to maintain, tenuous in effect and usually short lived. By contrast, a demonstrable commitment to justice can create and maintain the kind of community that allows actors to translate power into influence in efficient ways.[101]

Justice is important in a second fundamental way. It provides the conceptual scaffolding on which actors can intelligently construct interests. Classical realists recognize that interests are subjective in nature, and that individuals and states are often moved by fear, honor or greed, or a combination of these motives, to define their interests in ways that bring them into unnecessary conflict with other people and states. John Herz attributed the security dilemma to this kind of thinking.[102] So, above all else, a commitment to justice is a powerful source of self-restraint, and restraint is necessary in direct proportion to one's power. Weak states must

[100] Morgenthau, *Scientific Man vs. Power Politics*, pp. 151–68.

[101] Nor is that other great realist, Machiavelli, as Machiavellian as he is sometimes described. He opposed unprincipled conduct on the grounds that it is inefficient and often ineffective. J. G. A. Pocock, *The Machiavellian Moment* (Princeton: Princeton University Press, 1975), and H. F. Pitkin, *Fortune Is a Woman* (Berkeley and Los Angeles: University of California Press, 1984), p. 300, portray him as a civic "activist." Like Morgenthau and Thucydides, he saw law and justice as resources of power, and demands contrary to law and justice as likely to meet with great resistance because they would be perceived as contrary to the interests of the community. The most insightful analysis is Mary Dietz, "Trapping the Prince: Machiavelli and the Politics of Deception," *American Political Science Review* 80 (September 1986), pp. 777–800.

[102] Herz, "Idealist Internationalism and the Security Dilemma," *World Politics* 2, 12 (1950), pp. 157–80.

generally behave cautiously because of external constraints. But powerful states are not similarly bound, and the past successes that made them powerful breed hubris, encourage their leaders to make inflated estimates of their ability to control events and seduce them into embracing risky ventures. As in Greek tragedies, these *hamartiai* often lead to catastrophe, as they did for Athens, Napoleon and Hitler. Internal restraint and external influence are thus closely related. Self-restraint that prompts behavior in accord with the acknowledged principles of justice both earns and sustains the *hēgemonia* that makes efficient influence possible.

Modernization

Modern realists differentiate systems on the basis of their polarity (uni-, bi- and multipolar).[103] System change occurs when the number of poles changes. This is often the result of hegemonic wars, brought on in turn by shifts in the balance of material capabilities. Rising powers may go to war to remake the system in their interests, and status quo powers to forestall such change. For some realists, this cycle is timeless and independent of technology and learning. Others believe that nuclear weapons have revolutionized international relations by making war too destructive to be rational. In their view, this accounts for the otherwise anomalous peaceful transformation from bi- to multipolarity at the end of the Cold War.[104]

For classical realists, transformation is a much broader concept, and one they associate with processes that we have come to describe as modernization. Modernization brings about shifts in identities and discourses and, with them, changing conceptions of security. The late bronze age world of the heroes of Greek epic poetry was the starting point for attempts by fifth-century Greeks to understand and respond to the development of the polis and emergence of the money economy. The *oikos* (household) had been the traditional political, economic and social unit. Its members lived in a hierarchical relationship that was maintained and softened – in theory, anyway – by bonds of affection and loyalty. A major

[103] Randall L. Schweller, *Deadly Imbalances: Hitler's Tripolarity and Strategy of World Conquest* (New York: Columbia University Press, 1998), tries to make the case for tripolarity.

[104] Waltz, *Theory of International Politics* and "The Emerging Structure of International Politics," *International Security* 18 (Fall 1993), pp. 5–43; John J. Mearsheimer, "Back to the Future: Instability in Europe After the Cold War," *International Security* 15 (Summer 1990), pp. 5–56; William C. Wohlforth, "Realism and the End of the Cold War," *International Security* 19 (Winter 1994–95), pp. 91–129; Kenneth A. Oye, "Explaining the End of the Cold War: Morphological and Behavioral Adaptations to the Nuclear Peace?," in Richard Ned Lebow and Thomas Risse-Kappen, *International Relations Theory and the End of the Cold War* (New York: Columbia University Press, 1995), pp. 57–84.

goal of the *oikos* was to generate enough wealth to free the lord from work and enable him to live a life of leisure. Economic exchange, mostly barter of agricultural produce for tools, weapons and luxury goods, was essential to attain self-sufficiency (*autarkeia*). Gifts served to cement relationships and establish hierarchy within and across households.[105] The *Iliad* and *Odyssey* provide numerous illustrations of how this worked in practice.[106]

In the late eighth century, the polis replaced the *oikos* as the unit of political and economic life.[107] Thucydides attributes this shift to conquest, but it must also have been a response to the perceived economic and security benefits of the amalgamation of small communities into larger units. Not surprisingly, the political structure of the early polis copied the *oikos*; it was hierarchical and centered on the king, his retainers, servants and slaves.[108] By 700 BCE, most kingdoms had given way to aristocratic rule. This was a major transformation because the ruling class, although small, was conceived of as a group of equals. Henceforth, expanding political rights to more, or even all, citizens, as in the case in Athens, became a change in degree, not of kind.

There is as much disagreement about the extent to which Greeks understood economics as a separate field of inquiry as there is agreement about the nature of social-economic changes that accompanied the emergence of the polis.[109] The individual gradually replaced the extended

105 Homer, *Iliad* and *Odyssey*; Mauss, *The Gift*; Vidal-Naquet, *The Black Hunter*; Booth, *Households*; Marshall Sahlins, *Stone Age Economics* (Chicago: Aldine-Atherton, 1972); Seaford, *Reciprocity and Ritual: Homer and Tragedy in the Developing City State*; Sitta von Reden, *Exchange in Ancient Greece* (London: Duckworth, 1995); Walter Donlon, "Reciprocities in Homer," *Classical World* 75 (1981–82), pp. 137–85, and "Political Reciprocity in Dark Age Greece: Odysseus and his *hetairoi*," Graham Zanker, "Beyond Reciprocity: The Akhilleus–Priam Scene in *Iliad* 24," and Norman Postlethwaite, "Akhilleus and Agamemnon: Generalized Reciprocity," in Gill, Postlethwaite and Seaford, *Reciprocity in Ancient Greece*, pp. 51–72, 73–92 and 93–104, 201–02.

106 At the end of the Cyclops episode, Homer, *Odyssey*, IX.549–52, describes how Odysseus and his followers (*hetairoi*) break up in to groups to hunt. They share the spoils, with each man getting ten goats, except for Odysseus, who gets eleven, including the ram that was Cyclops' favorite. He promptly gives the ram as a gift to his companions, and they roast it and feast together. The leader (*basileus*) has accepted a gift and bestowed one in return, acknowledging his primacy and *charis*. By contrast, the conflict between Agamemnon and Achilles, which drives the narrative of the *Iliad*, is the result of Agamemnon's violation of the norm of reciprocity.

107 There were intermediate forms of social organization – the *deme* and *ethnos*, and social-political-religious organizations like phratries – most of which endured into the fifth century.

108 This is well illustrated by Aeschylus in *Seven Against Thebes* and the *Oresteia*.

109 Until recently, scholars regarded the ancient economy as so embedded in social context as to prevent any systematic reflection on purely economic matters by the Greeks. Karl Polanyi, "Aristotle Discovers the Economy," in Karl Polanyi, Conrad Arensberg and H. C. Pearson, eds., *Trade and Market in the Early Empires* (Glencoe: Free Press, 1957), pp. 65–94; Joseph Schumpeter, *History of Economic Analysis*, ed. Elizabeth Brady

family of oikos as the basic economic unit, and the goal of production and exchange increasingly became the pursuit of wealth. The economy was disembedded from the *oikos* and put on a contractual basis. Economic exchanges were more likely to be evaluated independently of past exchanges and the relationships they had established or maintained. This change in thinking was facilitated by the spread of writing and the use of coinage; the latter is thought to have appeared in the third quarter of the seventh century. The money economy hastened the decline of traditional social relations and the values on which they rested.[110] Before

Schumpeter (Oxford: Oxford University Press, 1954), pp. 53–54, dismissed the ancient economy so primitive as to be without value for study. Finley, *The World of Odysseus*, is a little more open to the idea of ancient consciousness about economics as a separate sphere of activity. See also Booth, *Households*; June W. Allison, "*Axiosis*, the New *Arēte*: A Periclean Metaphor for Friendship," *Classical Quarterly* 51: 1 (2001), pp. 53–64, maintains that Thucydides engages in artful manipulation of a class of terminology that can only be considered economic. Ian Morris, "Foreword," to Finley, *The Ancient Economy*, pp. ix–xxxvi, for a good overview of the controversy, and differences among Weber, Polanyi and Finley. There is also considerable controversy about the economic importance of an exchange versus money economy. On this subject, see Polanyi, "Aristotle Discovers the Economy"; Sarah C. Humphreys, "History, Economics and Anthropology: The Work of Karl Polanyi," in Humphreys, *Anthropology and the Greeks*, 2nd ed. (Boston: Routledge & Kegan Paul, 1983), pp. 31–75.

110 On the dating of coinage, see E. S. G. Robinson, "The Coins from the Ephesian Artemision Reconsidered," *Journal of Hellenic Studies* 71 (1951), pp. 156–67; Colin M. Kraay, "Hoards, Small Change and the Origin of Coinage, *Journal of Hellenic Studies* 84 (1964), pp. 76–91; S. Karweise, "The Artemisium Coin Hoard and the First Coins of Ephesus," *Revue belge de numismatique et de sigillographie* 137 (1991), pp. 1–28; C. J. Howgego, *Ancient History from Coins* (New York: Routledge, 1995). There is a large literature on the social-political consequences of money, including Fustel de Coulanges, *La cité antique. Étude sur le culte, le droit, les institutions de la Grèce et de Rome* (Paris: Hachette, 1888); Max Weber, *Economy and Society*, ed. Guenther Roth and Claus Wittich, trans. Ephriam Fischoff *et al.*, 3 vols. (New York: Bedminister, 1968 [1925]); Moses I. Finley, *Economy and Society in Ancient Greece* (New York: Viking, 1982); Michel Austin and P. Vidal-Naquet, *Economic and Social History of Ancient Greece: An Introduction*, trans. and rev. M. M. Austin (London: B. T. Batsford, 1977); Vernant, *Mythe et pensée chez les grecs*; von Reden, *Exchange in Ancient Greece*, and "Money, Law and Exchange: Coinage in the Greek Polis," *Journal of Hellenic Studies* 117 (1997), pp. 154–76; Leslie Kurke, *The Traffic in Praise: Pindar and the Poetics of Social Economy* (Ithaca: Cornell University Press, 1991), and *Coins, Bodies, Games, and Gold* (Princeton: Princeton University Press, 1999). There is also disagreement about the extent to which the introduction of coinage was a destructive revolutionary event or easily integrated into a preexisting patterns of commercial exchange, and the changing nature of the relationship between short-term exchanges pursued for individual gain and longer-term exchanges intended to perpetuate the social order. Controversy also surrounds their broader political and philosophical consequences. Von Reden contends that coinage strengthened the hand of the polis and of civil versus religious forms of justice. Vernant hypothesizes that the move from an exchange to a money economy allowed people to think about human behavior, especially politics, independently of religion, and that this in turn encouraged the development of positivist thought and its application to a novel set of problems. He further suggests, as does Seaford, *Reciprocity and Ritual*, pp. 220–28, that the evolution of Greek cosmology mirrored political developments and the new realities of the polis.

the introduction of money, gifts often had no precise equivalent, creating the expectation of future exchanges and ongoing relationships. Money equalized exchange and allowed for one-time transactions.[111] In the traditional economy, giver and recipient had also been linked by the stories attached to their objects of exchange. In the modern economy, objects were inanimate goods.[112] The "individual" gradually emerged as an identity, acquisition became his end, and profit (*kerdos*) the means to this end.[113]

If money became the currency of economic exchange, Thucydides leads us to understand that power now became the currency of politics.[114] Affective bonds and the commitment to the good of community they encouraged gave way to the goal of individual self-advancement. Politicians used any available means to attain power, just as unscrupulous individuals did to obtain wealth. For Thucydides and Aristophanes, the economic and political realms come together in the figure of Cleon, son of a leather factory owner, who spread his wealth lavishly and openly to buy votes in the assembly.[115]

[111] Gabriel Herman, *Ritualised Friendship and the Greek City* (Cambridge: Cambridge University Press, 1987), pp. 80–82; Paul Millett, "Sale, Credit and Exchange in Athenian Law and Society," in Paul A. Cartledge, Paul Millett and S. Todd, *Nomos: Essays in Athenian Law, Politics and Society* (Cambridge: Cambridge University Press, 1990), pp. 15–48; Seaford, *Reciprocity and Ritual*, pp. 203–05, and Kurke, *Coins, Bodies, Games, and Gold*, pp. 7–11 note that exchange and payment were possible before the introduction of coinage, and that early coinage was heavy, not well suited as a medium of exchange and generally circulated only locally.

[112] Mauss, *The Gift*; Sahlins, *Stone Age Economics*, 204–10.

[113] The market economy did not so much supplant reciprocity as supplement it. Economic exchange for profit was well established in the late bronze age, and in the fifth and fourth centuries exchange coexisted with the market economy of the polis. The two systems tended to shade into one another. Exchange for profit was frequently – and still is – embedded in social relationships. See, James C. Scott, *The Moral Economy of the Peasant* (New Haven: Yale University Press, 1976). Conversely, reciprocity in Greece, as in other societies, was often conducted for profit. Homer provides several examples of Odysseus acting this way to increase his own *kleos* at the expense of his group of followers (*hetairoi*). Bernard S. Cohen, "Representing Authority in Victorian India," in Eric Hobsbawm and Terence Ranger, eds., *The Invention of Tradition* (Cambridge: Cambridge University Press, 1983), pp. 165–211, provides a fascinating example of how the British interpreted all exchanges as economic in nature and missed how the offering of *nazar* and *pashkash* were ritual acts of incorporation.

[114] J. H. Kroll and N. M. Waggoner, "Dating the Earliest Coins of Athens, Corinth and Aegina," *American Journal of Archeology* 88 (1984), pp. 325–40, date the earliest Athenian currency, the so-called *Wappenmünzen*, to the last quarter of the sixth century.

[115] Moses I. Finley, "Athenian Demagogues," *Past & Present* 21: 1 (1962), pp. 3–24; G. E. M. de Ste. Croix, "The Character of the Athenian Empire," *Historia* 3 (1954), pp. 1–41, and *Origins of the Peloponnesian War* (Ithaca: Cornell University Press, 1972); Virginia Hunter, *Thucydides the Artful Reporter* (Toronto: Hakkert, 1973); Donald Kagan, *The Archidamian War* (Ithaca: Cornell University Press, 1974), pp. 156–60; A. J. Woodman, *Rhetoric in Classical Historiography: Four Studies* (London: Croon,

Thucydides' language encourages readers to draw an analogy between the individual pursuit of wealth and Athenian pursuit of power. The empire was based on the power of money (*chrēmatōn dunamis*). It generated revenue (*chrēmatōn prosodoi*) to build and maintain the largest navy in Greece. Athens was so powerful relative to other city states that it could dominate them (*allōn archē*) by force.[116] Tyrants were rulers without any constitutional basis who dispensed with reciprocity and took what they wanted. Gyges of Lydia was the first known tyrant, and, not coincidentally, Lydia was thought to be the first city to have introduced money.[117] Other notable tyrants included Polycrates of Samos, Peisistratus of Athens and Hieron of Syracuse, all of whom were notable for their intelligence, confidence and aggressiveness. Like tyrants, Athens no longer needed to legitimize its rule or provide the kind of benefits that normally held alliances or poleis together.[118] Wealth encouraged the "orientalization" of Athens, a perspective common to Herodotus and Thucydides. It led to a deep shift in Athenian values, superficially manifested in an increasing reliance on force. This pattern of behavior was a reflection of changing goals; the goal of honor (*timē*) increasingly gave way to that of acquisition. And *hégemonia* was replaced by *archē*.

Thucydides' account of the Peloponnesian War is rich in irony. Athens, the tyrant, has jettisoned the traditional bonds and obligations of reciprocity in expectation of greater freedom and rewards only to become trapped by a new set of more onerous obligations. As Pericles recognizes in his funeral oration, Athens had maintained its *hegemonia* by demonstrating *charis* to its allies. "In generosity," he told the assembly, "we are equally singular, acquiring our friends by conferring not by receiving favors."[119] The post-Periclean empire must maintain its *archē* by

Helm, 1988). Thucydides appears to have been made the scapegoat for Cleon's defeat at Delium, and was exiled from Athens for twenty years. This would provide grounds enough for his hatred of Cleon. Cleon is portrayed as a villain by Aristophanes in his comedy, *Knights*, produced in 424, and parodied in *Wasps*. See Niall W. Slater, *Spectator Politics: Metatheatre and Performance in Aristophanes* (Philadelphia: University of Pennsylvania Press, 2002), pp. 68–69, 88–103, 115–66.

[116] Thucydides, I.5.

[117] The word *turannos* (tyrant) is of Asian, and perhaps even of Lydian origin. Thucydides, I.13.1, maintains that tyranny was made possible by the increase in state revenues brought about by trade, money and increased wealth. Herodotus, 3.80.5, says a tyrant is someone who "moves ancestral laws and forces himself on women and kills men who have not been tried." Thucydides, VI.15, considered Alcibiades a potential tyrant. Arlene W. Saxonhouse, "The Tyranny of Reason in the World of the Polis," *American Political Science Review* 82 (December 1988), pp. 1261–75, argues that the tyrant became the paradigm of the free individual, who broke away from what was old and limiting.

[118] Plato makes a similar argument in *Gorgias* where Socrates argues that tyrants and their henchmen are the least powerful, least free and least happy people in the world because to retain power they must become slaves of the opinions of others.

[119] Thucydides, II.40.4.

constantly demonstrating its power and will to use it. It must keep expanding, a requirement beyond the capabilities of any state.[120] There is a double irony in that Corcyra, which dragged Athens into war, did nothing to help its ally during the long course of the conflict. It outdid Athens in pursuing its interest of the moment by making a seemingly irresistible offer but not living up to its end of the bargain once its partner was committed. The fate of the Athenian empire illustrates the truth of what at first appeared to be the naive Corinthian claim on the eve of war that what is just is also in the long run expedient (*sumphora*). Thucydides has much sympathy for this argument but no sympathy at all for the Corinthians who make it. They never practiced what they preached, and their remarkably short-sighted and patently expedient behavior led to the war with Corcyra that put Athens and Sparta on a collision course.

The contrast between Corinthian words and deeds is an instance of a more general phenomenon. Thucydides documents the hypocrisy and injustice of Sparta at Plataea, of Athenian demagogues and of allies who make the most principled appeals to Athens and Sparta in support of the crassest of interests. Even the Melians are mealy-mouthed.[121] Their protestations of friendship are belied by their previous support of Sparta and acts of piracy against allied trade.[122] The pattern is clear: the loftiest and most compelling statements about justice and its practical benefits are made by the worst transgressors. This is more than irony. It is an indication of the transitional nature of fifth-century Greek society. Traditional values and practices of all kinds were rapidly being abandoned but have not yet been replaced by a new discourse. People caught in a liminal epoch generally want to believe that the old ways remain reliable cultural

[120] There is another parallel to Sophocles here. In *Antigone*, Creon insists on total authority in order to be able to maintain order and save his city. He ignores the pleas – and interests – of his family, advisors and the gods, and brings the city to the verge of disaster. Seeking domination, he ends up helpless. As J. Peter Euben, *The Tragedy of Political Theory*, p. 38, observes, Creon's failure points to the need to reconstitute an order without believing that order is all there is or that it can be restored without the cooperation of others. Socrates makes much the same point in his critique of Polemarchus in Book I of the *Republic*. The idea resurfaces in Hobbes, for whom the drive for security brings about absolute insecurity, and finds resonance in the John Herz's modern conception of the security dilemma, in "Idealist Internationalism and the Security Dilemma," pp. 157–80.

[121] The Plataean episode is described in four stages by Thucydides: II.2–6 for the attack on Plataea, II.71–78 for the blockade and siege, III.20–24 for the escape of some of the Plataeans, and III.52–69 for the surrender, antilogy and murder of the remaining Plataeans. See Peter Pouncey, *The Necessities of War: A Study of Thucydides' Pessimism* (New York: Columbia University Press, 1980), pp. 17–19 for a good discussion of the importance of Plataea and the parallel it offers to Melos.

[122] Thucydides makes no mention of their most un-neutral behavior, presumably because the Melians are needed as a sympathetic foil and contrast to the Athenians.

and emotional anchors. Sophisticated actors accordingly honor and pay lip-service to these values and practices in proportion to their violation of them. At Melos, the Athenians shocked their contemporaries – and subsequent generations of readers – by openly articulating their actual motives and calculations. Our shock, and theirs, is not a reaction to what the words of the commissioners tell us about the Athenians, but what they reveal about ourselves and our world.

Modernization and its consequences drive Clausewitz's analysis of war and politics. Although he does not use the term, our concept of modernization captures the various processes that Clausewitz believed push war toward its theoretical definition: a reciprocal, escalating effort of adversaries to overthrow each other by all the means at their disposal. His overview of the history of warfare in Book VIII of *On War* attributes this growing capability to a reinforcing series of economic, technological and organizational advances that facilitated the emergence of well-organized political units in which war and politics were the concern of the people, not just of their rulers.

For Clausewitz, modernization was a gradual process with dramatic manifestations. It took the form of incremental improvements in armaments, logistics and tactics, the pace of which quickened or slowed as a function of political organization, technology and battlefield incentives. Dramatic manifestations were unpredictable in timing and nature, and transformed politics and warfare, and, more importantly, how people thought about them. They required agency, in the form of genius, to intuit new possibilities and bring them to concrete realization. The French Revolution is a case in point. It created a new political culture and institutions that allowed the government to mobilize the French people in support of its foreign policy goals.[123] In the hands of a genius like Napoleon, the French Army transformed the nature of warfare and overran Europe.

Clausewitz's analysis is reminiscent of Thucydides. His France, like Athens, was a large, dynamic society whose radical commitment to egalitarianism and political experimentation constituted at least as great a threat to its neighbors as did its impressive military capabilities. France's continental adversaries, like Sparta, fought to maintain the traditional order and insulate their societies from revolutionary contagion. They were equally slow to grasp the sources of their opponent's strength, and then deeply ambivalent about becoming more like their opponent even though they recognized this was to some degree necessary to survive and prevail. In the flush of victory, Prussia, Austria and Russia were more successful

[123] Book VIII, ch. 3, pp. 502–03.

than Sparta in turning back the political clock; they excluded from power, or actively suppressed, bourgeois intellectuals and progressive aristocrats. With Napoleon in exile, continental monarchs and their principal advisors expected warfare to return to the limited and restrained form that had characterized it in the eighteenth century.

Clausewitz thought this response unrealistic and indicative of the old regime's continued unwillingness to confront the challenge of modernity. Like Thucydides, he recognized that "Once barriers – which in a sense consist only in man's ignorance of what is possible – are torn down, they are not so easily set up again." Political logic pointed to the same conclusion. Limited wars in which maneuver substituted for battle could only take place in a world in which "we again see a gradual separation taking place between government and people." This was not going to happen. Modernization had given rise to a new class with the wealth, education and self-confidence to consider itself the core of the nation and demand a commensurate share of political power. "When major interests are at stake," Clausewitz warned, "mutual hostility will express itself in the same manner as it has in our own day."[124]

Clausewitz and Thucydides put equally great emphasis on community as the foundation of political-military power, but they also considered it a source of hubris. For Thucydides, the two faces of community come together in Pericles' decision to risk war with Sparta in the belief that his political skills together with his city's cohesion and resilience would lead to a favorable outcome. Clausewitz regarded Napoleon's hijacking of the French Revolution for his personal ends and the willingness of the French people to follow him as a graphic illustration of the downside of community. Like Thucydides, he attributed this phenomenon to the factional squabbling of democratic governments and the kinds of people they propel into power.[125]

Morgenthau's understanding of modernization recapitulates another aspect of Thucydides. Modernization led to a misplaced faith in reason, undermined the values and norms that had restrained individual and state behavior. Morgenthau drew more directly on Hegel and Freud. Hegel warned of the dangers of the homogenization of society arising from equality and universal participation in society. It would sunder traditional communities and individual ties to them without providing an

[124] Ibid., p. 593.

[125] Kurt A. Raaflaub, "Democracy, Power and Imperialism in Fifth-Century Athens," in J. Peter Euben, John R. Wallach and Josiah Ober, eds., *Athenian Political Thought and the Reconstruction of American Democracy* (Ithaca: Cornell University Press, 1994), pp. 103–48, for Thucydides' understanding of the link between democracy and imperial expansion.

alternative source of identity.[126] Hegel wrote on the eve of the industrial revolution and did not envisage the modern industrial state with its large bureaucracies and modern means of communication. These developments, Morgenthau argued, allowed the power of the state to feed on itself through a process of psychological transference that made it the most exalted object of loyalty. Libidinal impulses, repressed by the society, were mobilized by the state for its own ends. By transferring these impulses to the nation, citizens achieved vicarious satisfaction of aspirations they otherwise could not attain or had to repress. Elimination of the Kulaks, forced collectivization, Stalin's purges, World War II and the Holocaust were all expressions of the projection of private impulses onto the state and the absence of any limits on the state's exercise of power.[127] Writing in the aftermath of the great upheavals of the first half of the twentieth century, Morgenthau recognized that communal identity was far from an unalloyed blessing: it allowed people to fulfill their potential as human beings, but also risked turning them into "social men" like Eichmann who lose their humanity in the course of implementing the directives of the state.[128]

The intellectual transformation Morgenthau attributes to the Enlightenment bears striking similarities to the proto-Enlightenment of fifth-century Greece. In both epochs, the self-definition of human beings, widespread belief in the power of reason and the triumph of secular over religious values had far-reaching political implications. The principal difference between the two periods was in the area of technology; the modern Enlightenment made possible the industrial revolution and machine age warfare. Nuclear weapons are an outgrowth of this process, and for Morgenthau, "the only real revolution which has occurred in the structure of international relations since the beginning of history." War between nuclear powers was no longer an extension of politics by other means but mutual suicide.[129]

Morgenthau can also be read against Clausewitz. In the 1830s, Clausewitz envisaged the modern state – a political unit in which leaders and

[126] Hegel develops these arguments in the *Phenomenology of Spirit* (1807) and *Philosophy of Right* (1821). Charles Taylor, *Hegel* (Cambridge: Cambridge University Press, 1975), pp. 403–21.

[127] Ibid., p. 169. The psychological component of this analysis relied heavily on the earlier work of Morgenthau's Chicago colleague, Harold Lasswell, *World Politics and Personal Insecurity* (New York: McGraw-Hill, 1935). Morgenthau also drew on Hegel.

[128] Hannah Arendt, *Eichmann in Jerusalem: A Report on the Banality of Evil* (New York: Viking, 1964). Morgenthau and Arendt were friends and colleagues, and their extensive correspondence suggests that they drew on each other's insights in their work.

[129] Morgenthau, *The Decline of Democratic Politics*, p. 76; *Politics Among Nations*, 3rd ed., p. 326, also noted the mass destructive potential of bacteriological weapons.

people were bound together by a common purpose and loyalty – as a positive development that would allow human beings to express their *Humanität*. The French Revolution and its excesses nevertheless alerted him to the possibility that such a state, in the hands of a maniacal leader, could be used for perverse ends. In the 1930s, when Morgenthau began writing about international relations, two powerful variants of Clausewitz's nightmare – Stalin's Soviet Union and Hitler's Germany – threatened the survival of Western civilization. Clausewitz's nineteenth-century solution had become the twentieth century's nightmare. For all three classical realists, order required a balance between individual and communal identities. Thucydides thought the balance had swung too far in the direction of the individual. Clausewitz also lamented this shift, and the focus of people on their own advancement at the expense of the state and the community it was intended to represent. For Morgenthau, the pendulum had swung in the other direction. State power had become so great that it was able to mold individuals to its needs, with consequences that were disastrous for both domestic and international order.

Restoring order

Thucydides, Clausewitz and Morgenthau wrote in the aftermath of destructive wars that undermined the communities and conventions that had sustained order at home and abroad. None of them thought it feasible to restore the old way of life, aspects of which had become highly problematic even before the onset of war. They searched instead for some combination of the old and the new that could accommodate the benefits of modernity while limiting its destructive potential.

Thucydides can be read as a critic of modernity. By the time he wrote, there was a long-standing tradition of attacking change, stretching at least as far as far back as Hesiod and Pindar. Pindar warned that monetary exchange threatened to turn the Muse into a whore because it placed her outside of personal relationships.[130] Scorn of trade and of the low born (*kakoi*) who profited from it was a sign of the increasing insecurity of the aristocracy. By mid-fifth century, *agoraios* (merchants and traders who set up shop every day in the agora) had become a general term of contempt.[131] Sophocles repeatedly uses the word *kerdos* (profit) to denigrate Creon's materialistic conceptions of politics and life.[132] Xenophon, Plato and Aristotle, all of whom wrote in the fourth century, opposed

[130] Pindar, *Isthmian Odes*, II.1–11; Kurke, *The Traffic in Praise*, pp. 240–56.
[131] Herodotus, II.167; Connor, *New Politicians of Fifth Century Athens*, pp. 153–54.
[132] Robert F. Goheen, *The Imagery of Sophocles's Antigone* (Princeton: Princeton University Press, 1941), p. 97, for Creon and "profit."

the money economy on more philosophical grounds.[133] Wealth provided the leisure for a man to engage in politics, seek wisdom and lead a virtuous life, none of which would happen if the desire for wealth became unlimited and self-reinforcing. Plato's *Laws* represents the intellectual highpoint of the conservative reaction to modernity. It envisaged a rural community on Crete – the most traditional part of Greece – modeled, at least in part, on old Sparta. Private property was to be regulated and restricted, and no money, industry, commerce or foreign contacts would be permitted.[134]

Thucydides' response to modernity is harder to adduce. He produced no texts like the *Republic* or the *Laws*. He wrote no conclusion to his history, nor is it clear that he would have if he had lived longer. In Chapter 4, I described his meta-theme as the rise and fall of civilization. Communities arose as the result of a positive feedback cycle between language (*logos*) and conventions (*nomos*), and the precondition for their restoration was the reconstitution of *logos* – here intended to mean reason as well as language – and the conventions it enabled. Thucydides approached language and society differently than Plato who wanted to recapture the "true meanings" of words as a means of approximating the ideal forms.[135] Thucydides was not interested in some theoretical ideal, but what might be attainable in practice. His model, to the extent that he had one, may have been Aeschylus. Their diagnoses and responses appear quite similar.

The *Oresteia* is about justice, and how it restrains the passions that would otherwise tear apart families and cities. Justice traditionally took the form of revenge, carried out by family members or their friends.[136] Young Orestes is encouraged by Apollo to avenge the death of his father, Agamemnon, who had been murdered by his mother, Clytemnestra. Orestes has an additional motive for slaying Clytemnestra and her

[133] Xenophon, *Oeconomicus*, VII.29; Aristotle, *Politics*, I.8–11, on the dangers of unlimited acquisition, and VII.8.1329a on the importance of leisure.

[134] Plato, *Laws*, IV.704d–705b, V.739c–745b, IX.855a–856e, 877d, XI.923a–924a, 929b–e, proposed wealth be controlled by legislation aimed at sustaining equality. He would outlaw dowries and restrict the acquisition of disposable forms of wealth. The city should also be some distance from the sea to reduce contact with money and trade.

[135] Plato's views on language and speech are developed over the course of his opus. Building on the Socratic concept of dialogue, Hans-Georg Gadamer reaches a diametrically opposed conclusion: language allows a community to thrive precisely because words do not have exact meanings. People can accordingly start from different understandings and fuse their perspectives. Diversity in meaning is a sign of cultural growth and richness, and something to be treasured.

[136] Douglas M. McDowell, *Athenian Homicide Law in the Age of the Orators* (Manchester: Manchester University Press, 1963), chs. 1, 14; Peter A. French, *The Virtues of Vengeance* (Lawrence: University of Kansas Press, 2001), on how traditional Greek conceptions of vengeance animate the Western genre of films.

consort: reclaiming his citizenship, membership in a phratry (clan association) and his father's throne and estates. All three confer identity, without which he leads a meaningless life in exile. To reclaim his identity he must transgress the laws of man and god and carry the curse of the House of Atreus into the next generation. In the *Eumenides*, the last play of the trilogy, Orestes is pursued by the Furies, or Erinyes, the goddesses of vengeance. They are among the oldest of the Greek gods, and embodied humanity's most primal instincts. Athena intervenes to end the cycle of murder and revenge by means of a trial in the Areopagus, a court of citizens that she creates. The jurors are deadlocked, and Athena casts her decisive ballot in favor of Orestes, who is now free to return to Argos without further harassment. The furies are only reconciled to the judgment when Athena arranges for them to have a respected place in the city. In a solemn procession, citizens escort the now renamed "Eumenides," or well-wishers, to their new home, a chamber beneath the polis. There they remain, forever a reminder of the destructive nature of human impulses not repressed or appropriately channeled by a civic culture. The *Oresteia* shows how the new and innovative – i.e., the polis and its institutions – must be built on the old and the inherited. By dramatizing the disruptive consequences of primal urges, Aeschylus encourages respect for the ancient traditions and the new civic arrangements that can tame the reckless lust, aggression and pride of mortals, even harness them to promote equality and justice.[137]

Like Aeschylus, Thucydides wanted his readers to recognize the need for a synthetic order that would combine the best of the old and the new, and avoid, as far as possible, their respective pitfalls. The best of the new was its spirit of equality (*isonomia*), and the opportunity it offered to all citizens to serve their polis.[138] The best of the old was its

[137] John Jones, *On Aristotle and Greek Tragedy* (New York: Oxford University Press, 1962), p. 98; Robert Fagels, introduction to his translation of the *Oresteia* (New York: Bantam Books, 1977), pp. 13, 44; Euben, *The Tragedy of Political Theory*, pp. 76–77, for the overview of the argument and the quote.

[138] *Isos* means fair or equal, and *nom*, from *nomos*, as noted earlier, refers to law and custom. It appears to have been coined by Alcmaeon of Croton, frg. 24B4, a medical writer, to describe a constitution in which all citizens were subject to the rule of law and had equal rights of participation in communal decisions. There is general agreement that *isonomia* signified equality in a double sense: equal participation by all in the creation of laws, and fair and equal treatment of all by the laws. Herodotus, III.142, uses the metaphor of the circle and the center to describe *isonomia*, by which he means democratic equality. *Isonomia* was a notable Athenian slogan from the time of Cleisthenes and implied "political equality under the law." Martin Ostwald, *Nomos and the Beginnings of the Athenian Democracy* (Oxford: Oxford University Press, 1969). See also, Ober, *Mass and Elite in Democratic Athens: Rhetoric, Ideology, and the Power of the People* (Princeton: Princeton University Press, 1989), pp. 74–75; Monoson, *Plato's Democratic Entanglements*, p. 32, n. 42.

emphasis on excellence and virtue (*aretē*), which encouraged members of the elite to suppress their appetite for wealth and power, and even their instinct for survival, in pursuit of valor, good judgment and public service. The Athenians displayed *aretē* at Marathon and Salamis where they risked their lives for the freedom of Greece.[139] By the end of the fifth century, *aretē* had progressed through three stages of meaning: from its original Homeric sense of fighting skill, to skill at anything and to moral goodness.[140] Thucydides uses all three meanings, and has Pericles introduce a fourth in his funeral oration where *aretē* now describes the reputation a state can develop by generous behavior toward its allies.[141] Thucydides offers an idealized view of Periclean Athens as an example of the kind of synthesis he envisages.[142] It is the very model of a mixed government (*xunkrasis*) that allowed the capable to rule and the masses to participate in government in meaningful ways. It successfully muted tensions between the rich and the poor and the well-born and men of talent, and stood in sharp contrast to the acute class tensions and near stasis of *fin de siècle* Athens.[143]

Thucydides may have hoped that inter-city relations could be reconstituted on similar foundations. The same kinds of inequalities prevailed between poleis as within them. If the power of tyrants could give way to aristocracy and mixed democracy, and the drive for power and wealth be constrained by the restoration of community, the same might be done for inter-polis relations. Powerful states might once again see it as in their

[139] Thucydides, II.20, II.25, II.41, II.43, and IV.81.2; Hooker, "χάρις and ἀρετή in Thucydides," suggests that Pericles' use of both *aretē* and *charis* should be cross-referenced with the earlier use of terms by the Corcyreans, and suggests that Thucydides is parodying the hypocritical "Newspeak" of fifth-century politicians.

[140] The sophists contributed to this evolution by freeing *aretē* from its class base. In the seventh century Tyrtaeus extended the concept of *aretē* to the citizens fighting as hoplites. Pericles, II.42.2, uses it to describe all citizens who fight and die for Athens. On Tyrtaeus, Werner Jaeger, "Tyrtaeus on True *Aretē*," in *Five Essays* (Montreal: Casalini, 1966), pp. 103–42. Socrates and Plato widened its lexical field, employing *aretē* to describe the excellence of the human soul. For Plato, it signified the kind of reflection and knowledge that provides a clear grasp of human ends and the appropriate means of attaining them. He used this conception to critique the conventional understanding of virtue.

[141] Ibid. II.34.5. Hooker, "χάρις and ἀρετή in Thucydides."

[142] Thucydides praise of Pericles stands in sharp contrast to Plato. He has Socrates criticize Pericles for uprooting Athenians from the land during the plague, and for failing to display or teach *aretē*. The more fundamental disagreement is about the nature of *aretē*, which, for Plato, is achieved by suffering injustices instead of committing them, and conquering one's own tyrannical impulses, and by doing so, helping to build a more just Athens.

[143] In the fourth century, Democratus, frgs. 68B245, B255, would make the same argument. Great disparities in wealth aroused jealousy (*phthonos*), which was the cause of stasis.

interest to wield influence on the basis of *hegemonia*. Power imbalances could be "equalized" through the principle of proportionality (*to analogon*); the more powerful states receiving honor (*timē*) in degree to the advantages they provided for less powerful poleis.[144] Aeschylus points toward a solution along these lines in his *Promethia*. The "tyrant" Zeus is strong and nasty enough to contemplate annihilation of human beings and punishment of their benefactor, Prometheus. Their conflict is resolved by Zeus' realization that he can only hold on to power by exchanging favors (*charis*) with Prometheus. This outcome leads to justice for humankind. I believe that Thucydides favored a similar balance, or isonomy. His history was intended to educate the wealthy and powerful as to the baneful consequences of acting like tyrants, on the individual or state level, and the practical benefits, indeed the necessity, of maintaining the appearance, if not the substance, of the older forms of reciprocity in the political arena.

Thucydides is a stern skeptic and rationalist, but one who supported religion because he considered it to be a principal pillar of morality and conventions. In his view, the radical sophists had done a disservice to Athens by arguing that *nomos* is arbitrary and a justification for various forms of inequality. Thucydides wrote for a small, intellectually sophisticated elite, who, like himself, were unlikely to accept *nomos* as gods-given. He appeals to them with a more sophisticated defense of *nomos* that does not require rooting it in *phusis*. By demonstrating the destructive consequences of the breakdown of *nomos* and the conventions it upheld, he makes the case for its necessity and the wisdom of those in authority to act *as if* they believed it derived from nature. For Thucydides, language and conventions are arbitrary but essential.[145] His history, like a tragedy, provides an "outside perspective" for elites to generate a commitment to work "inside" to restore what is useful, if not essential, to justice and order.[146]

[144] By the fourth century, the notion of proportionality had become widely accepted. Aristotle, *Nicomachean Ethics*, 1158b23–28, 1162b11–12, 32–33, *Eudemian Ethics*, 1163b32–33; A. W. Price, *Love and Friendship in Plato and Aristotle* (Oxford: Oxford University Press, 1989); N. Sherman, *The Fabric of Character: Aristotle's Theory of Virtue* (Oxford: Oxford University Press, 1989), pp. 128–36; Christopher Gill, "Altruism or Reciprocity in Greek Ethical Philosophy," in Gill, Postlethwaite and Seaford, *Reciprocity in Ancient Greece*, pp. 303–28.

[145] Democritus, frgs., 2490–50, would later offer the same defense of *nomos*. Nicole Loraux, "Thucydide et la sédition dans les mots," *Quaderni di Storia* 23 (January–June 1986), pp. 95–134, argues, incorrectly, in my view, that Thucydides assumes an invariant language, and that this is what makes an outside, objective perspective possible.

[146] In contrast to Thucydides, for whom the reader is an observer, Plato, in *Gorgias* and the *Republic*, tries to involve the reader quite directly in the process of breaking down and restoring language. Their goals are not dissimilar.

The extension of Thucydides' domestic project to foreign policy would be in keeping with Greek practice. Relations between *poleis*, and before that, between households, were traditionally regarded as extensions of domestic relations. There was a strong sense of "pan-Hellenic" community going back at least as far as the seventh-century poetry of Archilochus. A century later, Herodotus tells us, the Athenians resisted the Persians in the name of "our common brotherhood with the Greeks: our common language, the altars and sacrifices of which we all partake, the common character which we bear."[147] In the aftermath of the Peloponnesian War, this sentiment was still very much alive.[148] Plato described the "natural relationship" between Greeks as a form of kinship.[149]

Greek political theory was rich in expectations and poor in results. Statesmen were supposed to conform to high standards, but rarely did so. The war and death of Pericles revealed the fragile nature of this commitment and how much it was the expression of the *aretē* of a single, talented leader. Was it really possible to resurrect a strong sense of community in a world dominated by a market economy in which the concept of self-interestedness had emerged so forcefully? Of all the historical figures in the text, Hermocrates may come the closest to speaking for Thucydides, and his speech at Gela suggests that he was cautiously optimistic.[150] His Syracuse offers a nice parallel to Athens in that it was a large, bustling democracy in which, judging from Hermocrates, many traditional values had been preserved. But Syracuse would have to learn to live with success, and might yet follow in the footsteps of Persia and Athens and repeat the cycle of *hubris, atē, hamartia*, and *nemesis*.

Along with Plato, Thucydides recognized that the "ancient simplicity" they both admired could no longer be reproduced through everyday practice.[151] The old ways were no longer natural once alternatives had emerged. Grammatical acquisition illustrates this point, and is an

[147] Herodotus, VIII.144. Pan-Hellenism was initially inspired by the Olympic and Pythian Games at Delphi.

[148] Isocrates, frg. 4.3, 15–17, 199–23, 126, 130, called for an all-Greek effort to conquer the Persian empire, distribute its wealth and give its richest land to poor Greeks to colonize. *Lysistrata* (produced in 411) pleads for Greeks to unite against barbarians instead of killing one another and destroying each other's cities. In Euripides' *Iphigenia at Aulis*, written in about 407, Iphigenia declares that it is noble to die for Greece, and that Greeks are superior to barbarians because they are free, not enslaved. Thrasymachus makes the first use of *homonoia* in 411. But it was also a central idea for Sophists.

[149] Plato, *Republic*, 469b–471c. When Greeks fight Greeks, he writes, Hellas is sick. When such fighting occurs, it should be kept within strict limits because of the underlying relationship of kinship. And unlike barbarians, Greeks should not be sold into slavery.

[150] Thucydides, IV.59–64.

[151] Plato's pessimism about the power of convention is manifest in his design of the Republic. The Guardians are educated to have conceptions of justice that restrain them, but the other classes need the Guardians to restrain them through the imposition of

appropriate analogy given both men's fascination with words. Children learn to speak unselfconsciously through imitation and repetition, but adults must make conscious efforts to learn new languages, and often find it helpful or necessary to start with the conceptual framework offered by a grammar. Thucydides offered his account of the Peloponnesian War as a grammar to aid in the reconstruction of the language of politics.[152]

Money and profit were reprehensible well into modern times. In the Middle Ages, commercial activities were contrasted unfavorably with chivalry and its emphasis on honor and glory. As late as the seventeenth century, avarice was routinely described as the "foulest" of all passions.[153] Max Weber wrote *The Protestant Ethic and the Spirit of Capitalism* to explain why an activity that for millennia "was at best ethically tolerated" turned somehow into a valued "calling."[154] The acceptance of profit paralleled growing dissatisfaction with honor as a motive. A long line of prominent writers, among them, Thomas Aquinas and Dante, condemned glory seeking as sinful, but the tradition remained alive, in practice and literature, and reached its apotheosis in the writings of Machiavelli and Corneille. A major seventeenth-century project was "the demolition of the hero," and writers like LaRochefoucauld, Racine and Pascal sought to discredit glory seeking as crass self-interest, self-love or an escape from the real world.[155] Clausewitz embodied the older tradition; he heaps scorn on money making as a source of corruption, but, interestingly, drew a parallel between war and commerce. It focuses individuals on their self-interest at the expense of communal solidarity and service to the state. Morgenthau acknowledged the pursuit of profit as a legitimate activity, but personally rejected such a life for himself.

Clausewitz also sought to restore domestic and international order by creating a synthesis between the old and the new. In the decades after Napoleon's defeat his thinking about the state evolved considerably.

right opinion (*orthodoxa*). In the *Laws*, 653b, he recognizes that obedience to the laws for most people is not based on reasoned acceptance but is the result of habituation and conditioning.

[152] Plato, recognizing that traditional forms of reciprocity had disappeared, sought to establish justice on the basis of rational principles that were understood and enforced by the guardians.

[153] Albert O. Hirschman, *The Passions and the Interests: Political Arguments for Capitalism before its Triumph* (Princeton: Princeton University Press, 1977), pp. 41–42. See also, E. Sutcliffe, *Guez de Balzac et son temps – littérature et politique* (Paris: Nizet, 1959), pp. 120–31; Morton Bloomfield, *The Seven Deadly Sins* (East Lansing, Mich.: Michigan State College Press, 1954), p. 95.

[154] Max Weber, *The Protestant Ethic and the Spirit of Capitalism*, trans. Talcott Parson (New York: Scribner's, 1958 [1904–05]).

[155] Hirschman, *Passions and Interests*, pp. 10–11.

He embraced Humboldt's view of the state as a mechanism to help the individual to develop his *Humanität*.[156] He emphasized the internal responsibilities of the state and especially the use of its regulative and supportive powers to stimulate economic development and provide public education. Both forms of intervention would enable citizens to improve themselves, physically and morally, and to realize their human potential. Clausewitz continued to regard the monarchy as essential to provide overall direction to the state, but had no illusions about the capabilities of the Hohenzollerns. He despaired at their unwillingness to extend their circle of advisors beyond high-ranking nobility.[157] He was also dismayed by the excesses of democracy, but considered involvement of the people as essential to limit the abuses and incompetence of absolute rule. He wanted to open the highest levels of the civil service and military to capable men of all class backgrounds.[158]

Clausewitz differed from Thucydides in two important respects. He left a written record of his views on politics, although, as we observed in Chapter 4, they were not nearly as developed or as insightful as his analysis of war. He was much less enamored of the traditional order than Thucydides, but just as fearful of modernity. Frederick William was no Pericles, and Clausewitz considered the Prussian aristocracy narrow in its outlook, unreasonably jealous of its prerogatives and irrationally hostile to progress. Men like Hardenberg, Scharnhorst, and Clausewitz himself, had been excluded from power once the danger of Napoleon had passed. Clausewitz was impressed by the industry of the middle classes, but did not share Herder's expectation that nationalism would promote peace, or Kant's optimism that republicanism would reduce the incidence of war and possibly lead to a universal republic.[159] The French Revolution had convinced him that democratic states could be extraordinarily aggressive. The emergence of republics, or constitutional monarchies with popular backing, also held out the prospect of making warfare more prolonged and deadly because they were that much more successful in mobilizing the physical and human resources necessary to wage war.

Looking to the future, Clausewitz thought that all European governments would have to reach some kind of accommodation with their middle classes. Those that failed to do so would remain backward, in a state of growing political turmoil that would invite revolution or conquest by

[156] In 1809, Clausewitz wrote a letter to Fichte commenting favorably on his article on Machiavelli. Reprinted in *Historical and Political Writings*, pp. 280–84.

[157] From the "Political Declaration" (1812), p. 290.

[158] "Agitation," and "Letter to Fichte," *Historical and Political Writings*, pp. 338–68, 280–84.

[159] Immanuel Kant, *Zum ewigen Frieden; Ein philosophischer Entwurf* (Königsberg, 1795).

more ambitious and efficient neighbors. It was possible, even likely, that aristocratic regimes motivated by the goal of dynastic expansion would be replaced by national governments with foreign policies subject to the vagaries of democratic politics. Europe would become organized on a vertical, national basis instead of a horizontal, aristocratic one, and ties of blood and friendship would no longer cut across political boundaries. The sense of community that had limited eighteenth-century warfare above and beyond the limits imposed by financial and technical constraints would disappear altogether. This transformation posed a great danger to the peace and stability of Europe because of the increasing prominence of the national question. Nationalists of all kinds would demand political boundaries that encompassed their nationality, as was already happening in Germany. Oppressed minorities would also demand independence from the states of which they were part. The Polish rebellion of 1830 offered a graphic illustration, and had seriously threatened the peace among the three great powers of Eastern Europe. Clausewitz was dubious that these problems could be resolved peacefully because they represented a conflict between two seemingly irreconcilable principles: national determination and state interest.[160]

Clausewitz's ability to look into the future far exceeded his ability to devise any solution for the problems he envisaged. His failure could be attributed at least in part to his recognition of the intractable nature of the national problem and the domestic political constraints that were likely to preclude compromise solutions. But it also reflected unresolved tensions in Clausewitz's mind between the competing world views of the Enlightenment and counter-Enlightenment. He shared the Enlightenment belief in the power of reason to liberate human beings from servitude and create a society in which they could fulfill their potential and find individual and collective fulfillment. He also acknowledged the validity of the counter-Enlightenment critique, with its emphasis on the holistic nature of man, his emotions and passions, and view of the world as complex, contradictory and composed of social entities in a state of constant flux and conflict. He hoped that reason and compromise would triumph, but feared that passion and greed would prove more powerful. His inability to reconcile these orientations at the philosophical level, or find a way of controlling their most dangerous manifestations at the political level foreshadowed the problem that subsequent generations of continental intellectuals and politicians would face and fail to solve with tragic consequences for Europe.

[160] His pessimism is most forcefully expressed in "Europe since the Polish Partitions," and "On the Basic Question of Germany's Existence," both written in 1831. *Historical and Political Writings*, pp. 372–76 and 378–84.

For Morgenthau, the absence of external constraints on state power was *the* defining characteristic of international politics at mid-century. The old normative order was in ruins and too feeble to restrain great powers.[161] Against this background, the Soviet Union and the United States were locked into an escalating conflict, made more ominous by the unrivaled destructive potential of nuclear weapons. The principal threat to peace was nevertheless political: Moscow and Washington were "imbued with the crusading spirit of the new moral force of nationalistic universalism," and confronted each other with "inflexible opposition."[162] The balance of power was a feeble instrument in these circumstances, and deterrence was more likely to exacerbate tensions then to alleviate them. Bipolarity could help to preserve the peace by reducing uncertainty – or push the superpowers toward war because of the putative advantage of launching a first strike. Restraint was needed more than anything else, and Morgenthau worried that neither superpower had leaders with the requisite moral courage to resist mounting pressures to engage in risky and confrontational foreign policies.

Realism in the context of the Cold War was a plea for statesmen, and above all, American and Soviet leaders, to recognize the need to coexist in a world of opposing interests and conflict. Their security could never be guaranteed, only approximated through a fragile balance of power and mutual compromises that might resolve, or at least defuse, the arms race and the escalatory potential of the various regional conflicts in which they had become entangled. Morgenthau insisted that restraint and partial accommodation were the most practical *short-term* strategies for preserving the peace.[163] A more enduring solution to the problem of war required a fundamental transformation of the international system that made it more like well-ordered domestic societies. By 1962, the man who twenty years earlier had heaped scorn on the aspirations of internationalists, would insist that the well-being of the human race now required "a principle of political organization transcending the nation-state."[164]

Morgenthau's commitment to some form of supranational authority deepened in the 1970s. Beyond the threat of nuclear holocaust, humanity was also threatened by the population explosion, world hunger and environmental degradation. He had no faith in the ability of nation states

[161] Morgenthau, *The Decline of Democratic Politics*, p. 60, and *Political Man vs. Scientific Politics*, p. 168.
[162] Morgenthau, *Politics Among Nations*, 1st ed., p. 430.
[163] Ibid., p. 169; *The Decline of Democratic Politics*, p. 80; Letter to the *New York Times*, 19 June 1969.
[164] Morgenthau, *Decline of American Politics*, pp. 75–76.

to ameliorate any of these problems.[165] But if leaders and peoples were so zealous about safeguarding their sovereignty, what hope was there of moving them toward acceptance of a new order? Progress would only occur when enough national leaders became convinced that it was in their respective national interests. The series of steps Europeans had taken toward integration illustrated the apparent paradox that "what is historically conditioned in the idea of the national interest can be overcome only through the promotion in concert of the national interest of a number of nations."[166]

Thucydides, Clausewitz and Morgenthau grappled with successive phases of modernization and their social, political and military consequences. They understood these consequences, and modernization itself, as an expression of evolving identities and discourses. Human beings were never entrapped by their culture or institutions, but constantly reproducing, changing and reinventing them. For Thucydides, modernization and discourse are mutually constitutive. Their relationship is captured by the feedback loop between *logoi* (words) and *erga* (deeds) that I described in Chapter 4. Thucydides' *Archeology* puts him in the same camp as Karl Polanyi, who also considered the market economy at least as much a consequence as a cause of changing identities.[167] Morgenthau, more influenced by Weber here than by Thucydides, also gives primacy to the realm of ideas: the intellectual changes associated with the Enlightenment – especially belief in the power of reason – precede and enable the economic, political and military developments associated with modernity.

The central problem for classical realists was that old procedures were being abandoned or not working, and were being replaced by new and dangerous practices that had entered without much warning. They were as yet unnamed and had no language to define or situate them. All three thinkers sought to put the problem of modernization into historical and conceptual perspective as a first step toward making sense of ongoing change and its associated threats. They recognized that stable domestic orders, and the security that they might enable, could only be restored by some synthesis that blended the old with the new. This synthesis had to harness the power of reason, but make allowance for the disruptive passions that often motivated individuals, classes and political units. It had

[165] Kenneth W. Thompson, "Introduction," in Morgenthau, *In Defense of the National Interest* (Lanham, Md.: University Press of America, 1982), p. v; conversations with Hans Morgenthau.

[166] Morgenthau, *Decline of American Politics* p. 93. *The Decline of Democratic Politics* was published in 1962, but this essay was originally published in 1958 in *Dilemmas of Politics*.

[167] Karl Polanyi, *The Great Transformation* (New York: Holt, Rinehart, 1944).

to build community, but could not ignore powerful centrifugal forces, especially self-interest at the individual, group and national levels, that modernization had encouraged and legitimated. The biggest challenge of all was to construct the new order through the willing agency of representatives of the old order in cooperation with the newly empowered agents of modernity.

Given the nature of the challenge, it is not surprising that classical realists were better at diagnosis than treatment, to use Thucydides' medical metaphor. Thucydides was the most sophisticated of the three thinkers. Perhaps by design, he offered no explicit synthesis, but contented himself with identifying an earlier synthesis – Periclean Athens – that might serve as a model, or at least a starting point, for thinking about the future. Clausewitz gives us nothing more than the outlines of a synthesis – a national state that looked after the needs of its citizens and won their loyalty in return – but remained rightly pessimistic about the ability of his contemporaries to reach this goal. Morgenthau addressed the problem of order at two levels: he sought stop-gap political measures to buy time for statesmen to grasp the need to transcend the state system. Their works remain possessions for all time, not only because of their insights into war, politics and human nature, but because of something they may never have consciously recognized: unresolved tensions that indicate the necessity, but also, the great difficulty of reconciling tradition and modernity by conscious, rational designs.

Theory

Aristotle thought it unlikely that human investigations could ever produce *epistēmē*, defined as knowledge of essential natures reached through deduction from first principles. Like some critics of neo-positivism, he was more inclined to accept the possibility of generalizations that held true for the most part (*epi to polu*) under carefully specified conditions.[168] Thucydides does not directly engage questions of epistemology, but one can readily infer that he shared this understanding of the limits of social inquiry. One of his recurrent themes is the extent to which human behavior is context-dependent; similar external challenges provoke a range of responses from different political cultures. As those cultures evolve, so do their foreign policies, a progression I documented in the case of Athens. There is also variation within culture. Thucydides' accounts of the Spartan decision to go to war, the plague in Athens, the Mytilenian

[168] Aristotle, *Nicomachean Ethics,* 1141a–b, on the contrast between theoretical and practical wisdom.

Debate and *stasis* in Corcyra all reveal that individuals respond to the same or similar situation in very different ways.

Clausewitz and Morgenthau explicitly deny the possibility of general laws and of predictions based on more limited kinds of generalizations. Clausewitz describes international relations as a constant struggle for dominance in which states expand their power until opposed by equal and opposite political-military forces. State expansion is a law of politics, but unlike laws of physics it is tempered in practice by a range of constraints that keep states from expanding as far as their power might allow and others from checking them in accord with their interests. The same is true of war. In theory, reciprocal escalation [*Wechselwirkung*] propels it to its maximum potential, but, in practice, it is held in check by political, organizational and human limitations. Context made every case unique, and the interconnectedness of all social behavior made every case different in terms of the broader context in which it assumed meaning for actors.

Both men nevertheless believed that theory could help to order the world. Clausewitz found the dialectic useful to express this understanding. Thesis represented theory, antithesis everything in practice that defied the application of theory, and synthesis, the blending of theoretical and practical wisdom to achieve real world goals in the most practical way. Morgenthau conceived of the social world as "a chaos of contingencies," but "not devoid of a measure of rationality." The social world could be reduced to a limited set of social choices of uncertain outcome because of the irrationality of actors and the inherent complexity of the social world. The best a theory could do "is to state the likely consequences of choosing one alternative over another and the conditions under which one alternative is more likely to occur or to be successful than the other."[169]

Theōria, theōrein and *theōros*, are all post-Homeric words having to do with seeing and visiting. The noun (*theōros*) meant "witness"or "spectator." A *theōrōs* was dispatched to Delphi by his polis to bring back a full account of the words of the oracle. He might also be sent to religious and athletic festivals, and it is here that the word picked up its connotation of spectator. Over time, the role of the *theōros* became more active; a *theōros* was expected not only to describe what he had seen but to explain its meaning. This was a formidable conceptual task when it involved the customs of non-Greek peoples. All of the activities of a *theōros* were

[169] Hans J. Morgenthau, "The Purpose of Political Science," in James C. Charlesworth, ed., *A Design for Political Science: Scope, Objectives and Methods* (Philadelphia: American Academy of Political and Social Science, 1966), pp. 63–79.

undertaken on the behalf of the polis, but in the course of the fifth century theory took an inward turn, and gradually became divorced from practice. Socrates and Plato were key figures in this transition, but their theoretical inquiries, while now conducted as ends in themselves, still had as their goal knowledge relevant to civic life.[170] Plato insisted that a philosopher would always choose the mixed life of contemplation and political activity because it would be more fulfilling (*eudaimōn*).[171]

Classical realists continue this tradition. Thucydides comes closest to the model of the *theōros*; he provides readers with a description of events that has interpretations of their meaning embedded in it. Clausewitz and Morgenthau are post-transition figures; they conduct independent theoretical inquiries in which brief historical accounts, more properly described as examples, are used for the purposes of illustration. But in the best tradition of the Greeks, they aspire to develop a framework that actors can use to work their way through contemporary problems. Morgenthau insisted that "All lasting contributions to political science, from Plato, Aristotle, and Augustine to the *Federalist*, Marx and Calhoun, have been responses to such challenges arising from political reality. They have not been self-sufficient theoretical developments pursuing theoretical concerns for their own sake."[172] Great political thinkers confronted with problems that could not be solved with the tools on hand developed new ways of thinking to use past experience to illuminate the present. Beyond this, Thucydides, Clausewitz and Morgenthau sought to stimulate the kind of reflection that leads to wisdom, and with it, appreciation of the need for *sōphrosunē*. For all three classical realists history was the vehicle for tragedy and the teacher of wisdom.

The tragic vision

The plot of *Antigone* revolves around the discovery by Creon, king of Thebes, that his nephew, the traitor Eteocles, has been buried in violation of his orders that his body be left as carrion on the outskirts of the city. He is convinced that the soldiers guarding the body were bribed, and that the gods themselves were the source of the growing discontent of the citizenry. Creon's threats of violent reprisals provoke the chorus to sing

[170] J. Peter Euben, "Creatures of a Day: Thought and Action in Thucydides," in Terence Ball, *Political Theory and Praxis: New Perspectives* (Minneapolis: University of Minnesota Press, 1977), pp. 28–56. Euben's book laments the baneful consequences for modern political theory and politics of the severance of the ties between them.

[171] *The Republic*, 420b4–5. Aristotle, *Nicomachean Ethics*, 1094b7, and *Politics*, 1278a40–b5, makes a similar argument.

[172] Hans J. Morgenthau, "The Purpose of Political Science," in Charlesworth, *A Design for Political Science*, p. 77.

praises to man. They acknowledge human beings as the most inventive of all creatures who reshape the goddess earth with their ploughs, yoke horses and bulls, snare birds and fish in the twisted mesh of their nets and make paths through the turbulent seas with their ships. But they destroy what they create, kill what they love most and seem incapable of living in harmony with themselves and their surroundings.[173] The juxtaposition of man's achievements and transgressions is a central theme of Greek tragedy and classical realism. Like the chorus in *Antigone*, Thucydides, Clausewitz and Morgenthau recognized the extraordinary ability of human beings to harness nature for their own ends, and their propensity to destroy through war and civil violence what took them generations to build. Their writings explored the requirements of stable orders, but they remained pessimistic about the ability of the powerful to exercise self-restraint. Like Aeschylus, they saw a close connection between progress and conflict. They understood that violent challenges to the domestic and international orders are most likely in periods of political, economic, social and intellectual ferment.

Thucydides was a contemporary of Sophocles and Euripides, and the only one of our three authors who wrote a tragedy. For reasons that I explored in Chapter 2, he chose to develop a new form for his tragedy, what we today call a history. In the early fourth century BCE, history and philosophy began to emerge as separate genres, and were well established by the modern era. Tragedy declined, and no significant Athenian tragedies were performed after the death of Sophocles and Euripides in 406. The Renaissance resurrected the tragic form, and gave us the plays of Shakespeare. In the late eighteenth century, German intellectuals turned to tragedy as a model for reconstituting ethics and philosophy. Clausewitz and Morgenthau were deeply influenced by this latter development. Clausewitz was a contemporary of many of the major figures of the German counter-Enlightenment, and friends with some of them, including Hegel. Morgenthau was better read, and intimately familiar with the corpus of ancient and modern literature and philosophy. His intellectual circle included his colleague and fellow *émigré* Hannah Arendt, who had studied with Heidegger, wrote about tragedy and applied its lessons to contemporary politics, as did American-born theologian Reinhold Niebuhr.

[173] J. T. Sheppard, *The Wisdom of Sophocles* (London: Allen & Unwin, 1947), pp. 46–48; Goheen, *The Imagery of Sophocles's Antigone*, pp. 53, 141; Aya Betensky, "Aeschylus' Oresteia: The Power of Clytemnestra," *Ramus* 7 (1978), pp. 21–22; Charles Segal, "Sophocles' Praise of Man and the Conflicts of the Antigone," *Arion* 3 (1964), pp. 46–66; Euben, *The Tragedy of Political Theory*, pp. 34–35.

Early twentieth-century German social science was deeply influenced by tragedy, largely through exposure to Hegel and Nietzsche.[174] Morgenthau immersed himself in Nietzsche in the late 1920s, and came to understand tragedy, he later wrote to his British colleague, Michael Oakeshott, as "a quality of existence, not a creation of art."[175] His post-war writings, beginning with *Scientific Man vs. Power Politics*, repeatedly invoke tragedy and its understanding of human beings as the framework for understanding contemporary international relations. The principal theme at which he hammers away is the misplaced faith in the powers of reason that has been encouraged by the Enlightenment. But he is equally wary of emotion freed from the restraints of reason and community. "The *hybris* of Greek and Shakespearean tragedy, the want of moderation in Alexander, Napoleon, and Hitler are instances of such an extreme and exceptional situation."[176] Although he never used the Greek word, *sōphrosunē*, his German and English writings and correspondence make frequent use of its equivalents: *Urteilskraft* [sound judgment] and prudence. He offers them, as did the Greeks, as the antidotes to hubris. Tragedy, and its emphasis on the limits of human understanding, also shaped his approach to theory. Like politics, it had to set realistic goals, and recognize the extent to which its vision was shaped and constrained by its political and social setting.

Clausewitz makes no references to the classics, and we have no evidence that he read either Greek tragedies or Thucydides. His writings are nevertheless infused by a tragic vision, which he picked up second hand through his familiarity with the writings and figures of the German counter-Enlightenment. This vision finds expression in an understanding of war – and the social world more generally – in terms of polarities and the tensions between them. *On War* is built around the polarities between theory and practice, but it and Clausewitz's other writings recognize and embrace other polarities, including those between tradition and modernity, democracy and order, the nation and the state. Like Thucydides and the tragic playwrights, he looked for another level of understanding at which the tensions these polarities generate might be overcome. His synthesis of the soldier-statesman represents such an attempt, but as Clausewitz acknowledged, it was an ideal, difficult to achieve in practice and even more difficult to sustain. He struggled, without success,

[174] Kurt Lenk, "Das tragische Bewusstein in der deutschen Soziologie," *Kölner Zeitschrift für Soziologie und Sozialpsychologie* 10 (1964), pp. 257–87.
[175] Hans J. Morgenthau to Michael Oakeshott, 22 May 1948, Morgenthau Papers, B-44.
[176] Morgenthau, *Scientific Man vs. Power Politics*, p. 135; Christopher Frei, *Hans J. Morgenthau: An Intellectual Biography* (Baton Rouge: Louisiana State University Press, 2001 [1994]), pp. 185–89.

to find some strategy for bridging the political tensions that had become more acute as a result of the development of the modern state and nationalism. In this sense, he is closer in his pessimism to Sophocles and Euripides than to Aeschylus, for whom such a renegotiated order was a real possibility.

The deepest lesson that Clausewitz took away from history and the events through which he lived was the need to know one's own limits. This is, of course, the core insight of tragedy, and equally central to the writings of Thucydides and Morgenthau. It is a lesson, they would insist, that cannot be assimilated in the detached, intellectual way we so often think associate with learning. It serves as a starting point for reflection about our relationships with the wider world, and comes to infuse our beings in a way that it shapes our goals and behavior. This kind of learning is not only essential for individuals, but for scholarly communities and nations. And it is to this dimension of tragedy that I now turn.

8 Running red lights and ruling the world

> Ancient Hubris breeds, again and again,
> Another Hubris, young and stout.
>
> Aeschylus[1]

I now turn to contemporary international relations and social science, and exploit my analysis of classical realism to offer a critique of both. I begin with post-Cold War American policy, and examine some of the striking similarities – and important differences – between the United States and Athens. Like mid-fifth-century Athens, Washington gives evidence of breaking free from the traditional constraints which served its broader interests so well in the past. For the United States, these constraints arise from international law, institutional obligations, norms of consultation and policy by consensus among close allies and more general norms associated with the country's frequently proclaimed commitment to a democratic and peaceful world order. For classical realists, this is well-trodden path, down which ancient tyrants, Xerxes' Persia, Periclean Athens, numerous tragic heroes, and many subsequent empires have trod. Success and power breed hubris and now raise the disturbing possibility of America becoming a tragedy.

Current realist theories are blind to this possibility because they are focused on power and external threats. In addition, they tend to equate material capabilities with power and power with influence, ignoring the extent to which the latter is a psychological relationship. Classical realists recognize that the most efficient way to wield influence is through consent, not coercion, and that consent is greatly facilitated by *hegemonia* and convincing others of the benefits of following one's lead. Since the end of the Cold War, the unilateral foreign policy of the Clinton and Bush administrations has been increasingly at odds with the principles on which American *hegemonia* had been based, has antagonized allies and important third parties alike and has compelled Washington to rely increasingly on bribes and threats to get its way. The standing of the United States

[1] *Agamemnon* 763ff.

may be much more precarious that most realists and members of the national security community recognize. Worse still, modern realist categories of analysis blind their adherents to the reasons why American influence could undergo a precipitous decline in the decades ahead. This will be because the United States proves itself to be its own worst enemy.

The second part of the chapter segues from policy to theory and tackles the problem of cooperation. It is the prerequisite of international order and should be the core concern of post-Cold War American foreign policy. Realists, liberal institutionalists and constructivists, among others, have attempted to explain international cooperation. The literature stresses the differences among these competing explanations, but I draw attention to what they have in common. With the exception of some "thick" constructivist approaches, they are rooted in an ontology that takes as its starting point a world populated by egoistic, autonomous actors. These approaches frame cooperation as a collective action problem and invoke variants of the same mechanisms to explain why anything beyond momentary, issue-based cooperation occurs. But more extensive cooperation undeniably exists and may be close to the norm at every level of human interaction from inter-personal to international. Thucydides, some anthropologists, sociologists in the tradition of Durkheim, and "thick" constructivists offer a more compelling explanation for this empirical regularity. This is "every day" practice – what Thucydides called *nomos* – that makes compliance the default and non-compliance at times difficult even to imagine.

The contortions rational choice theories must go through to try to account for cooperation highlights the inadequacy of their starting assumptions. The next section of the chapter critiques these assumptions. It draws on insights and findings from classics, literature, philosophy, sociology and international relations, as well as empirical evidence, to argue that sociopaths aside, actors are neither egoistic nor autonomous as those terms are understood by rational choice theories. The same body of materials suggests that cooperation is ultimately based on understandings actors develop about themselves, in particular, recognition of the importance of relationships to fulfillment of their deepest needs. Cooperation is more a response to internal imperatives than it is to external constraints and opportunities.

In the final section of the chapter, I build on this conclusion to offer a social theory of ethics. It is rooted in the linkages that classical realists, especially Thucydides, the Greek playwrights, many philosophers and the world's great religious traditions posit or find among interest, identity, community and justice. The outlines of this theory – I go no further than an outline – offer a theoretical solution to the problem posed at the outset of the book: how to address the seeming conflict between interests and ethics, and my assertion that they might be reconcilable at a deeper level of understanding.

Athens achieved *hegemonia* – a form of legitimate authority conferred on one by others – because of its courage and sacrifice on behalf of Hellas in the long struggle against the Persian invader. Its standing and honor were augmented by its extraordinary economic, political and cultural dynamism, a way of life that was emulated or resisted by other *poleis*. The United States earned its *hegemonia* for much the same reasons. It liberated much of Europe and Asia from invaders, and its powerful economy, democracy and popular culture appeal to or horrify the rest of the world. Washington managed at least parts of its informal empire in accord with its proclaimed principles. Arguably, its most enduring success was the introduction of institutions in Germany, Italy and Japan that set all three countries on the road toward democratization and economic development. American aid was the catalyst for a wider European economic recovery and sparked the phenomenal growth of the economies of the Pacific rim. In all these countries the United States retains considerable good will, especially among the first postwar generation.[2] Like Athens, Washington also pursued policies at odds with its ideology. Successive administrations supported a score of repressive, authoritarian regimes in Asia, Africa, Europe and Latin America that were economic partners or political allies in the struggle against communism. The United States also waged a costly and unsuccessful war in Indochina that alienated public opinion at home and tarnished its reputation abroad.

The United States differs from Athens in important ways. It never pursued a policy of limitless military expansion, treats its allies differently than it does its enemies and bounced back from defeat in Indochina to become militarily even more powerful, unlike Athens in the aftermath of its Sicilian expedition. Following its earlier victory over Persia, Athens imposed tighter control over its allies, sparking several rebellions. The United States chose to wield influence over its allies by informal and largely indirect means, and its ability to do so depends at least as much on ideological affinity, common interest and respect for American leadership

[2] G. John Ikenberry and Charles A. Kupchan, "Socialization and Hegemonic Power," *International Organization* 44 (Summer 1990), pp. 283–315; G. John Ikenberry, "Liberal Hegemony and the Future of American Postwar Order," in T. V. Paul and John A. Hall, eds., *International Order and the Future of World Politics* (Cambridge: Cambridge University Press, 1999), pp. 123–45, and *After Victory: Institutions, Strategic Restraint, and the Rebuilding of Order After Major Wars* (Princeton: Princeton University Press, 2001), contend that the legitimacy of American leadership abroad is based on its economic openness, reciprocity and multilateral management, and for these reasons, has survived the end of the Cold War.

as it does on material capabilities and the occasional coup. For this reason, *hegemonia* may be an even more important asset to Washington now that the Cold War is over.

For most of the Cold War the United States exercised considerable restraint *vis-à-vis* its most important allies in its both its rhetoric and policies. After the Berlin Wall came down and the Soviet Union and its empire imploded, Americans basked in the euphoria of what Charles Krauthammer called the "unipolar moment."[3] The United States wielded unprecedented power, measured in terms of military capability, and the Pentagon quickly proposed a new grand strategy to preserve unipolarity.[4] Thoughtful members of the academic security community disagree about how long this extraordinary position can be maintained, with some arguing that it is transitory and even dangerous.[5] A minority holds that American preeminence can endure. William Wohlforth, who makes the most persuasive case for this position, contends that the United States is the first state in modern history "with decisive preponderance in all the underlying components of power: economic, military, technological, and geopolitical." He sees no reason why the United States should lose its relative advantages in any of these domains. Unipolarity, moreover, benefits other major powers by minimizing security competition among them, while providing incentives to minor powers to bandwagon.[6] Joseph Nye, Jr. makes a parallel argument about the survival of American primacy that emphasizes the importance of "soft power" – the leadership resources, cultural and ideological attractions, and norms and institutions that have

[3] Charles Krauthammer, "The Unipolar Moment," *Foreign Affairs* 70 (Winter 1990/91), pp. 23–33.

[4] Patrick Tyler, "The Lone Superpower Plan: Ammunition for Critics," *New York Times*, 10 March 1992, p. A12.

[5] Christopher Layne, "The Unipolar Illusion: Why New Great Powers Will Arise," *International Security* 17 (Spring 1993), pp. 5–51; Douglas Lemke, "Continuity of History: Power Transition Theory and the End of the Cold War," *Journal of Peace Research* 34 (February 1996), pp. 203–36; Michael Mastanduno, "Preserving the Unipolar Moment: Realist Theories and US Grand Strategy after the Cold War," *International Security* 21 (Spring 1997), pp. 44–98; Charles A. Kupchan, "After Pax Americana: Benign Power, Regional Integration, and the Sources of Stable Multipolarity," *International Security* 23 (Fall 1998), pp. 40–79; Samuel P. Huntington, "The Lonely Superpower," *Foreign Affairs* 78 (March–April 1999), pp. 35–49.

[6] William C. Wohlforth, "The Stability of a Unipolar World," *International Security* 24 (Summer 1999), pp. 5–41, cite from p. 7. Ikenberry, "Liberal Hegemony and the Future of American Postwar Order"; Mastanduno, "Preserving the Unipolar Moment," and "Economics and Security in Statecraft and Scholarship," *International Organization* 52 (Autumn 1998), pp. 825–54. Stephen G. Brooks and William C. Wohlforth, "American Primacy in Perspective," *Foreign Affairs* 81 (July–August 2002), pp. 20–33, offers more evidence in support of the dominance of the United States, but notes that by 2002, public opinion polls revealed that 40 percent of Americans had come to see the United States as merely one of several leading powers.

become increasingly important means of influencing international behavior. Nye suggests that the United States has an even greater lead in "soft power," and that the importance of soft power is increasing relative to more traditional forms of power that rely on coercion.[7]

The debates about hard versus soft power and the duration and value of unipolarity address only one component of political influence as understood by Thucydides and other classical realists. Such capabilities, whether hard or soft, are the raw materials of *archē*, power based on control. To achieve or sustain *hegemonia*, capabilities must be used to the perceived benefit of allies and third parties to help reconcile them to their subordinate status. There has been little recognition of this political truth in Washington, and no real discussion in the scholarly literature of the concept of *hegemonia*, its basis, current standing or future.[8] Judging from their public statements, American leaders appear to take their *hegemonia* for granted. Former President Bill Clinton and Secretary of State Madeline Albright were in the habit of referring to the United States as the "leader" and "indispensable nation."[9] The Bush administration repeatedly asserted its right to lead, and did not hesitate to express its frustration with and hostility toward the leaders of France and Germany when they would not fall in line.

Realist scholars made parallel claims. For Wohlforth, the United States is "the global security manager," and "indispensable nation in all matters of importance" because the international system is built around American power.[10] "Scholars and policymakers" alike, he insists, "should do more to advertise the attractions of unipolarity."[11] The very title of Joseph Nye's book, *Bound to Lead*, exudes *hubris*.[12] According to Joshua Muravchik, the United States did not chose hegemony; it was forced to accept this responsibility, and, the French aside, "the only people who are averse to American leadership are the Americans."[13] John Ikenberry contends

[7] Joseph S. Nye, Jr., *Bound to Lead: The Changing Nature of American Power* (New York: Basic Books, 1990), pp. 173–201.

[8] Academics are more alert to this problem. See Richard Ned Lebow and Robert Kelley, "Thucydides on Hegemony: Athens and the United States," *Review of International Studies* 27 (October 2001), pp. 593–609; Brooks and Wohlforth, "American Primacy in Perspective," who warn against using power to make short-term gains at the expense of long-term interests.

[9] Quoted in Alison Mitchell, "Clinton Urges NATO Expansion in 1999," *New York Times*, 23 October 1996, p. A20.

[10] Wohlforth, "The Stability of a Unipolar World," p. 40.

[11] *Ibid.*, p. 41.

[12] Nye, *Bound to Lead*, p. xviii.

[13] Joshua Muravchik, *The Imperative of American Leadership: A Challenge to Neo-Isolationism* (Washington, DC: American Enterprise Institute Press, 1996). The citations are from the AEI book summary available at http://www.aei.org/bs/bs6297.htm.

that "the most pointed European criticism of the United States has not been about coercion or heavy handedness but rather about perceptions of American willingness to lead."[14]

From almost any vantage point outside the United States, Ikenberry's assertion appears increasingly questionable. Not that allies deny American power. In 1999, the French foreign minister, Hubert Védrine, admitted that the technological, economic and even cultural power of the United States was unlike "anything known in modern history."[15] German Foreign Minister Joschka Fischer, while distancing himself from anti-Americanism, warned that "alliances between free democracies should not be reduced to following. Alliance partners are not satellites."[16] The Netherlands' minister of foreign trade, Anneke van Dok van Weele warned that "Washington should stop bossing its friends."[17] In Canada, anti-Americanism has increased in response to perceived American bullying of Cuba.[18] As a prominent British diplomat put it, "One reads about the world's desire for American leadership only in the United States. Everywhere else one reads about American arrogance and unilateralism."[19] These comments were directed at the Clinton administration. The Bush administration drew considerably more criticism abroad for its arrogance and unabashed unilateralism.[20]

Modern realists insist that order is created and maintained by the power of a hegemon. Classical realists understood that subordinates are never really reconciled to their status and are readily angered by treatment that brings it to mind.[21] A single glaring example of hegemonic

[14] G. John Ikenberry, *After Victory: Institutions, Strategic Restraint, and the Rebuilding of Order After Major Wars* (Princeton: Princeton University Press, 2001), p. 253.

[15] Craig R. Whitney, "NATO at 50: With Nations at Odds, Is it a Misalliance?," *New York Times*, 15 February 1999, p. A7.

[16] Steven Erlanger, "Germany Joins Europe's Cry that the US Won't Consult," *New York Times*, 13 February 2002, p. A14.

[17] "Washington Should Stop Bossing its Friends," *New Straits Times*, 2 July 1997, p. 37, reprinted from the *International Herald Tribune*.

[18] Preston Jones, "Our Canadian Cousins," *Weekly Standard*, 19 October 1998, p. 36 and Craig Turner, "Canada: 'America the Bully' Is Media's New Tune," *Los Angeles Times*, 2 August 1996, p. A5.

[19] Fareed Zakaria, "Loves Me, Loves Me Not," *Newsweek*, 5 October 1998, p. 55.

[20] Brian Knowlton, "Bush's Marks Rise in Europe, *International Herald Tribune*," 18 April 2002, pp. 1, 6; Michael Wines, "In Czar Peter's Capital, Putin Is Not as Great," *New York Times*, 20 May p. A9; Steven Erlanger, "Protests, and Friends Too, Await Bush in Europe," *New York Times*, 22 May 2002, p. A8; Todd S. Purdum, "A Wider Atlantic: Europe Sees a Grotesque US," *New York Times*, 16 May 2002, p. A3; Sean Kay, "Security in Eurasia: Geopolitical Constraints and the Dynamics of Multilateralism," unpublished paper, April 2002.

[21] Thucydides, I.76; Hans J. Morgenthau, *Scientific Man vs. Power Politics* (London: Latimer House, 1947), p. 145; *Politics Among Nations: The Struggle for Power and Peace* (New York: Alfred Knopf, 1948), and *Politics in the Twentieth Century*, I, *The Decline of*

self-aggrandizement can offset multiple instances of self-restraint and sensitivity to allied needs and interests.[22] Only rarely, does a dramatic example of self-restraint achieve the same effect in reverse.[23] A decade after the end of the Cold War, it is no exaggeration to suggest that while the United States still considers itself as a *hegemonia*, most of the rest of the world regards it as an *archē*. The powerful arouse opposition just by being powerful, and some of the opposition to the United States reveals more about the psychology of those who feel themselves to be powerless than it does about American motives and behavior. However, much of it is attributable to American arrogance.

The perceptual asymmetry between American self-perceptions and those of others has already had detrimental consequences for American foreign policy. Seemingly at the zenith of its power, the United States has been increasingly unsuccessful in imposing its strategic, political and economic preferences on allies, adversaries and third parties.[24] What we witness everywhere is something else: growing reluctance to accept American leadership on a range of strategic, political and economic issues and growing resentment at American efforts to impose its preferences by fiat, bribes and rhetorical coercion. In the not too distant future, American leaders and public opinion may have to reconcile themselves to playing a less influential role on the world stage or do so by relying more on rewards

Democratic Politics (Chicago: University of Chicago Press, 1962), p. 99. More recently, Robert Gilpin, *War and Change in World Politics* (New York: Cambridge University Press, 1981), p. 31, and Robert Keohane, *After Hegemony: Cooperation and Discord in the World Political Economy* (Princeton: Princeton University Press, 1984), p. 39, have acknowledged the need to consider the prestige and legitimacy of the hegemonic power as a sustaining source of cooperation.

[22] George Orwell, *Inside the Whale and Other Essays* (Harmondsworth: Penguin, 1962), pp. 95–96, provides a revealing example of how this worked in the framework of colonialism.

[23] Richard Ned Lebow and Janice Gross Stein, *We All Lost the Cold War* (Princeton: Princeton University Press, 1994), pp. 317–19, on Kennedy's self-restraint in the Cuban missile crisis, and how it redefined the context of relations with the United States for Khrushchev.

[24] The paradox of power was first conceptualized by John Herz, *International Politics in the Atomic Age* (New York: Columbia University Press, 1959), pp. 22, 169, who observed that absolute power was the same thing as absolute impotence because nuclear weapons could not be used to advance any political goal. Kenneth N. Waltz, *Theory of International Politics* (Reading, Mass.: Addison-Wesley, 1979), p. 192, strongly objects to the relational definition of power used by Hans Morgenthau, Robert Dahl and others. "Power is a means," Waltz insists, "and the outcome of its uses is necessarily uncertain." It follows that "The paradox that some have found in the so-called impotence of American power disappears if power is given a politically sensible definition." This conceptual sleight of hand reduces power to some measure of capabilities, and deprives it of any analytical value it might have for the study of foreign policy and international relations. See Robert A. Dahl, "The Concept of Power," *Behavioral Science* 2 (July 1957), pp. 2–1–15; David A. Baldwin, "Power Analysis and World Politics: New Trends versus Old Tendencies," *World Politics* 31 (January 1979), pp. 161–94.

and coercion. The former would be a serious blow to the foreign policy establishment, and the latter is probably unacceptable to American and world opinion.[25]

Modern realism defines security as protection against external threats, principally of a military nature. Some realists recognize that external threats can take diverse forms (e.g., economic sanctions, denial of raw materials, interference with trade, unwanted and uncontrollable immigration, violence against one's nationals abroad, or their expulsion from another country, penetration of the homeland by pathogens with the potential to cause serious epidemics). Cold War security policy was nevertheless defined almost entirely in terms of opposition to the Soviet Union, its communist satellites and Third World allies. Perceived domestic threats to security (e.g., communist penetration of American society and government) were generally extensions of the external threat. Post-Cold War American foreign policy operates in what is widely recognized to be a far more diverse threat environment. There is no consensus about the principal threat; analysts and officials offer a range of threat hierarchies, and periodically rearrange them. At various times over the last decade, the emphasis has been on China as a possible great power challenger, so-called rogue states (e.g., Afghanistan, Iraq, North Korea), nuclear proliferation and regional conflict that has the potential for nuclear escalation (e.g., the Middle East, India–Pakistan), and, more recently, non-state-sponsored terrorism. A less influential strand of academic and policy opinion has tried without notable success to focus attention on democratization, economic development, the AIDS epidemic and humanitarian intervention and to argue that success in these domains is critical to American security in the longer term.

What is strikingly absent from the post-Cold War security debate is any recognition of domestic threats to security that are not simply offshoots of external ones. Rightly or wrongly, the latter have drawn a lot of attention, particularly in the aftermath of the events of 11 September. Classical realists offer a broader perspective on security. Conventional readings of Thucydides and Morgenthau, and even of Clausewitz, stress their concern for external threats and the need to balance against them. This is an important theme of both Morgenthau and Clausewitz, but, as I have shown, represents a serious misreading of Thucydides. His narrative leaves no doubt that alliances are more likely to provoke war than

[25] The same point has been made by Huntington, "The Lonely Superpower"; Gary Wills, "Bully of the Free World," *Foreign Affairs* 78 (March–April 1999), pp. 50–59; Richard N. Haas, "What to Do with American Primacy," *Foreign Affairs* 78 (September–October 1999), pp. 37–49; Stephen M. Walt, "Two Cheers for Clinton's Foreign Policy," *Foreign Affairs* 79 (March–April 2000), pp. 63–79.

to deter. Athens' defensive alliance with Corcyra led to war with Corinth and Sparta, the Lacedaemonian Confederacy propelled Sparta into war with Athens, and Hermocrates' successful effort to cobble together a Syracusan-led coalition failed to dissuade an increasingly irrational Athenian assembly from voting credits for the Sicilian expedition.

Thucydides draws our attention to the internal threats to security, which he, Morgenthau and Clausewitz consider at least as serious as external ones. For all three classical realists, great powers are likely to be their own worst enemies because of their hubris, and not unrelated over- and underestimation of external threats. The Peloponnesian War came about in part because Pericles, and Athenians more generally, succumbed to hubris. They underestimated the power of their adversaries and overestimated their power and ability to control events. They were unrealistically confident that their military and economic power could be used to deter or compel adversaries and allies, and win any ensuing war, if coercive diplomacy failed. After the plague and a long and costly war, Athenians should have become more cautions and reflective, but they displayed even greater overconfidence. They allowed the hard-won peace to collapse and committed the second and disastrous *hamartia* of the Sicilian expedition. Defeat led to near-*stasis* at home, which further sapped Athenian power.

Clausewitz tells a parallel story. Napeoleonic France constituted a serious threat to Prussia but hubris prevented the Prussian political and military leadership from recognizing the gravity of the threat. Even after the War of the First Coalition revealed the military potential of the "nation in arms," Prussia's military adhered to outmoded Fredrician tactics and failed to develop any serious war plan, while the king and his advisors blundered into a second challenge of France that led to their country's defeat and occupation. Hubris was also responsible for Napoleon's increasingly unlimited ambitions, and led to the same kind of disastrous overextension, in this case, the invasion of Russia, that had been responsible for Athens' defeat.

Morgenthau had two stories to tell. The first involved hubris, overweaning ambition and related overconfidence. Periclean Athens, Philip II of Spain, Louis XIV, Napoleonic France, Wilhelminian and Nazi Germany were his prime examples. They provoked coalitions against them, although often not in a timely enough manner to avoid costly wars. Morgenthau regarded the failure of Britain and France to put together an effective anti-Nazi coalition in the 1930s as one of the tragedies of the twentieth century. This was the principal lesson many of his readers took away from *Politics Among Nations*. That book and subsequent writings put even greater emphasis on the dangers of hubris and overestimation of threats. Morgenthau came to believe that the American national security establishment exaggerated both the Soviet threat and its own power. This almost oxymoronic combination led to Vietnam, which he considered a moral and political disaster.

In *We All Lost the Cold War*, Janice Stein and I tried to draw out and expand upon both of Morgenthau's stories. We argued that the triumphalism associated with the end of the Cold War and collapse of the Soviet Union was unwarranted and dangerous. Soviet communism was not defeated by American military power, alliances and intervention around the world, but by it own internal contradictions and the growing awareness of them among the Soviet elite. The Reagan arms build-up and Star Wars might actually have prolonged the Cold War rather than ending it. It is now well documented that it is the strength of European and American peace movements and Euro-socialism, not the military might of NATO, that convinced Gorbachev and his advisors that they could take the risks of making the kind of concessions necessary to set the peace process in motion without fear of the West stepping up the military pressure on them.[26] More importantly, triumphalism obscured the very real domestic and foreign policy costs associated with fifty years of Cold War, including the development of powerful military-industrial complex, McCarthyism, intervention in Vietnam and a pattern of widespread support for repressive, right-wing dictatorships around the world.

Triumphalism was riding high, and our counter-arguments were not well received. Indeed, critics rarely engaged our analysis or evidence, but simply dismissed our position out of hand.[27] Little has changed in the intervening ten years. The national security debate, to the extent there has been one, has concerned the nature of the external threat. In moments when something of a consensus has emerged, as in the aftermath of 11 September, controversy has shifted to the question of the best tactics for meeting this threat. The kind of criticism, and downright hostility, that Washington increasingly encounters abroad, the growing gap between the perception of the United States as a *hegemonia* by its political leadership and national security elite, and the contrasting perception of it by

[26] On this issue, see Jacques Lévesque, *The Enigma of 1989: The USSR and the Liberation of Eastern Europe*, trans. Keith Martin (Berkeley: University of California Press, 1997); Matthew Evangelista, *Unarmed Forces: The Transnational Movement to End the Cold War* (Ithaca: Cornell University Press, 1999); Robert D. English, *Russia and the Idea of the West: Gorbachev, Intellectuals and the End of the Cold War* (New York: Columbia University Press, 2000); Richard K. Herrmann and Richard Ned Lebow, eds., *Learning from the Cold War* (New York: Palgrave, 2003).

[27] Some reviews were sympathetic, and the *Atlantic* invited us to contribute an article. But, more typical, were the negative responses of the *New Republic, Wall Street Journal, National Review*, and realist academics. The *National Review*, to its credit, sought at least to engage our argument.

foreigners, including our closest allies, as an *archē*, suggests the need for a national debate about the nature of the *internal* threats to our security. From the perspective of classical realism, it raises the prospect that yet another great power has become its own worst enemy, and may be heading down a well-trodden path that ultimately leads to *nemesis*. Readers, and Americans more generally, might usefully ponder the proposition readily distilled from the writings of classical realists, that it is not might that makes right but right that makes might.

The extent of the gap between American power and influence and the varied reasons for it are amenable to empirical investigation. Many realists are not cognitively disposed to ask these questions because they define power in terms of military and economic capability. And even those who do not, tend to equate power with influence.[28] Classical realists, by contrast, consider material capabilities to be only one component of power, and power, whether hard or soft, only the raw material of influence. When influence derives from respect and legitimacy, it becomes easier to convince others that what you want them to do is in the common interest. Failing this, influence must be based on carrots and sticks, and its costs increase sharply. By denuding classical realism of its conceptual complexity, failing to recognize the psychological basis of influence and divorcing the concept of interests from that of justice, contemporary realism has deprived itself of a vocabulary that could help make sense of the current international environment and offer a useful starting point for thinking about national interests and the strategies best calculated to protect and advance them.

The conceptual poverty of contemporary realism may help to explain why its predictions about the post-Cold War world have been at odds with the reality that has emerged.[29] In the absence of external threat, balance of power theory predicts that alliances will weaken, if not break up, as suppressed rivalries among their members reemerge and drive foreign policy.[30] Some realists went so far as to predict (and recommend) that Japan and Germany would (should) acquire their own nuclear arsenals

[28] For a recent example of the "interests equals power" thesis, see Stephen van Evera, *Causes of War: Power and the Roots of Conflict* (Ithaca: Cornell University Press), p. 7.

[29] Conversations with realist colleagues indicate that to the extent they are willing to recognize that their predictions have been off the mark, they attribute them to the continued unipolarity of the international system.

[30] Ronald Steel, "NATO's Last Mission," *Foreign Policy* 74 (Fall 1989), pp. 83–95; Christopher Layne, "Superpower Disintegration," *Foreign Policy* 78 (Spring 1990), pp. 3–25; John Mearsheimer, "Back to the Future: Instability of Europe after the Cold War," *International Security* 15 (Summer 1990), pp. 5–57, and "Why We Will Soon Miss the Cold War," *Atlantic* 266 (August 1990), pp. 35–50; Pierre Hassner, "Europe Beyond Partition and Unity: Disintegration or Reconstruction?," *International Affairs* 66 (July 1990), pp. 561–75; Hugh DeSantis, "The Graying of NATO," *Washington Quarterly* 14

to cope with the kind of security threats that would arise in a multipolar world.[31] NATO has not fragmented, but grown. Germany and Japan have not gone nuclear and the perceived risk of war among developed countries has not increased.[32] Equally striking is the success of the Japanese–American alliance, and post-Cold War efforts of the partners to enhance their military cooperation in a number of ways.[33]

Hegemonic stability theory asserts that the dominant state will set up an international economic and political order that will serve its interests and induce or compel other states to conform to this order. When the power of the hegemon wanes, other states will challenge the leader and attempt to change or transform the order in accord with their interests.[34] In the late 1980s, some realists maintained that the United States was a declining power and predicted that rising powers like Japan and Germany would challenge American hegemony.[35] That did not happen, but neither did

(Autumn 1991), pp. 51–65; Kenneth A. Waltz, "The Emerging Structure of International Relations," *International Security* 18 (Fall 1993), pp. 44–79; Layne, "The Unipolar Illusion," and "From Preponderance to Offshore Balancing"; Josef Joffe, "'Bismarck' or 'Britain'? Toward an American Grand Strategy after the Cold War," *International Security* 19 (Spring 1995), pp. 94–117; Stephen Walt, "The Ties that Fray: Why Europe and America Are Drifting Apart," *National Interest* 54 (Winter 1998/99), pp. 3–31.

31 Mearsheimer, "Back to the Future"; Waltz, "The Emerging Structure of International Relations."

32 James Davis, "What Fallout? Victory and the Phenomenon of Alliance Collapse," forthcoming; John Duffield, "NATO's Functions after the Cold War," *Political Science Quarterly* 119 (Winter 1994/95), pp. 763–87.

33 Mike M. Mochizuki, "A New Bargain for a Stronger Alliance," in Mike M. Mochizuki, ed., *Toward a True Alliance: Restructuring US–Japan Security Relations* (Washington, D.C.: Brookings, 1997); Michael Green, *Japan's Reluctant Realism* (New York: Palgrave, 2001); Richard Armitage *et al.*, "The United States and Japan: Advancing Toward a Mature Partnership" (Washington, D.C.: Institute for National Strategic Studies, National Defense University, 11 October 2000); Steven C. Clemons, "The Armitage Report: Reading Between the Lines," Japan Policy Research Institute, Occasional Paper No. 20, February 2001.

34 Charles Kindleberger, *The World in Depression, 1929–1939* (Berkeley: University of California Press, 1973); Robert Gilpin, *US Power and the Multinational Corporation: The Political Economy of Foreign Direct Investment* (New York: Basic Books, 1975); Stephen D. Krasner, "State Power and the Structure of International Trade," *World Politics* 28 (April 1976), pp. 346–77, and *Structural Conflict* (Berkeley: University of California Press, 1985); Robert Keohane, "The Theory of Hegemonic Stability and Change in International Economic Regimes, 1967–1977," in Ole R. Holsti, Randolph M. Sieverson and Alexander L. George, eds., *Change in the International System* (Boulder: Westview, 1980), pp. 131–62; Susan Strange, "The Persistent Myth of Lost Hegemony," *International Organization* 41 (Autumn 1987), pp. 551–74, and *States and Markets* (London: Pinter, 1994); David Rapkin, ed., *World Leadership and Hegemony* (Boulder: Lynne Rienner, 1990). For a review of this literature, see David A. Lake, "Leadership, Hegemony, and the International Economy: Naked Emperor or Tattered Monarch with Potential," *International Studies Quarterly* 37 (December 1993), pp. 459–89.

35 Robert Gilpin, "American Policy in the Post-Reagan Era," *Daedalus* 116 (Summer 1987), pp. 33–67; Paul Kennedy, *The Rise and Fall of the Great Powers: Economic Change and Military Conflict from 1500–2000* (New York: Random House, 1987).

American economic or military power decline relative to that of its major allies. Other realists, especially since the end of the Cold War, consider the United States a rising power, or a state with such a preponderance of power, that they characterize the international system as unipolar. In this circumstance, some realist theories predict that we should witness balancing against the dominant power.[36] This has not happened either. Allies have resisted specific American initiatives (e.g., sanctions against Iraq, ballistic missile defense, opening their markets to genetically modified produce) but give no evidence of either balancing or bandwagoning.

In a recent and important book, John Ikenberry argues that shifts in the balance of power are less important in an environment in which institutions play an important regulatory role. Economic, political and juridical institutions tend to restrain powerful actors and reward weaker ones, providing the latter with strong incentives to retain close relations with the dominant power. In the aftermath of World War II, the United States organized an international order that is unprecedented in the number and strength of its institutions and the way in which American power is both wielded and constrained through these institutions. American hegemony is based on the sophisticated recognition that the most stable orders are those "in which the returns to power are relatively low and the returns to institutions are relatively high."[37] It accordingly depends on restraint as much as it does on power. Constructivists carry the institutional argument a step further and contend that over time successful institutions not only structure behavior and interests, but also identities. They do so by creating normative and cognitive pathways the structure the frames of reference actors use to work their way through problems, and thereby lead them to accept the underlying premises of the institutions as their own.[38]

[36] Joseph S. Nye, Jr., *The Paradox of American Power* (New York: Oxford University Press, 2002), argues that if the United States provokes others through its unilateral behavior, a countervailing coalition will form. For relevant theoretical literature on balancing, see Morgenthau, *Politics Among Nations*, part IV; Arnold Wolfers, "The Balance of Power in Theory and Practice," in Arnold Wolfers, ed., *Discord and Collaboration: Essays in International Politics* (Baltimore: Johns Hopkins University Press, 1962), pp. 117–31; Waltz, *Theory of International Politics*; Barry R. Posen, *The Sources of Military Doctrine: France, Britain, and Germany Between the World Wars* (Ithaca: Cornell University Press, 1984); Stephen Walt, *The Origins of Alliances* (Ithaca: Cornell University Press, 1987). For critiques, Inis L. Claude, Jr., *Power and International Relations* (New York: Random House, 1962) and Ernst B. Haas, "Regime Decay: Conflict Management and International Organizations, 1945–1981," *International Organization* 37 (Spring 1983), pp. 189–256; Mastanduno, "Preserving the Unipolar Moment."

[37] Ikenberry, *After Victory*, esp. pp. 248, 257–73.

[38] See Alexander L. Wendt, "Identity Formation and the International State," *American Political Science Review* 99 (June 1994), pp. 384–98; Peter J. Katzenstein, "United Germany in an Integrating Europe," in Katzenstein, ed., *Tamed Power: Germany in Europe*

A legitimated order based on clearly articulated principles is a double-edged sword. It can sustain the influence of the hegemon in the manner Ikenberry describes. However, it creates the expectation that the hegemon will uphold those principles. Failure to do so encourages and legitimizes opposition. Ikenberry acknowledges numerous instances over the decades when the United States acted, or appeared to act, in an arrogant manner. These include the corporate "invasion" of Europe in the 1950s, Eisenhower's response to the Suez crisis of 1956, the "Nixon shocks" of 1971, the sudden closure of the gold window and the Euro-missile controversy of the early 1980s. Ikenberry nevertheless insists that Washington generally acted in a restrained way because it was compelled to do so by the very institutions it had established. These institutions, he points out, have survived the Cold War and have been strengthened and extended. Allies carp whenever Washington fails to live up to its professed values, but the current situation is merely an extension of the past and "it is difficult to argue that the level of conflict has risen."[39]

I see a qualitative shift in American behavior; post-Cold War administrations have been less constrained, acted more unilaterally, and threaten to undermine the conditions in which American leadership is acceptable. European calls for American leadership, cited by Ikenberry and Mastanduno as evidence that all is well within the alliance, might also be understood as appeals to Washington to consult more frequently and take into account the views and interests of others. On occasion, they represent pleas by self-interested actors who want the United States to do their bidding. Survey research, elite interviews and the mere passage of time are likely to make clear if a new pattern of American behavior and allied responses is emerging.

The nature of cooperation

Institutionalists make fundamental claims about the nature and causes of cooperation. They contend that institutions reduce contractual uncertainty. They create strong incentives for cooperation by providing more information to actors, helping them to resolve the "shadow of the future"

(Ithaca: Cornell University Press, 1996), pp. 1–48; Martha Finnemore, "Norms, Culture, and World Politics: Insights from Sociology's Institutionalism," *International Organization* 50 (Spring 1996), pp. 325–48, for an emphasis on the cognitive and enabling versus constraining features of institutions; Craig Parsons, "Showing Ideas as Causes: The Origins of the European Union," *International Organization* 56 (Winter 2002), pp. 47–84, reverses the arrow of causation for the European Community, arguing that ideas and the community they helped to create explain why strong institutions were developed in lieu of other political choices.

[39] Ikenberry, *After Victory*, p. 252.

and reducing the likelihood of defection. The latter benefit is achieved in the first instance by providing mechanisms that allow, or even compel, actors to make binding commitments, thus increasing the costs of defection. Over time, the rewards of working through institutions also reduce the benefits of defection. Ikenberry's work represents the most sophisticated attempt to apply this argument to the Western alliance, but he is by no means alone in suggesting that the institutions set up by the United States and its partners have set down deep roots and shape their domestic political, economic and military practices in ways that make the costs of their disruption extraordinarily high and the benefits of competing orders most uncertain.[40]

Institutions crystalize emerging patterns and shore them up in times of change. They presuppose common interests or the existence of a community with common values, and become the custodians of the procedures and values they represent and help to congeal in practice.[41] In ancient Greece, citizens called on their neighbors for assistance. Today, we call the police.[42] When people leave the regulation of order to institutions, everyday social control is likely to decline, and with it, the strong sense of community it sustains.

The interplay of institutions and culture is enormously complex and still poorly understood. Here, I want to draw attention to one aspect of this relationship that has been extensively theorized. Beginning with Plato, philosophers and social scientists have considered how authority both limits and expands freedom. Anthropologists, not only the structural-functionalists among them, have explored the many ways in which

[40] Robert O. Keohane, *International Institutions and State Power: Essays in International Relations Theory* (Boulder: Westview, 1989); Arthur A. Stein, *Why Nations Cooperate: Circumstance and Choice in International Relations* (Ithaca: Cornell University Press, 1990); Cheryl Shanks, Harold K. Jacobson and Jeffrey H. Kaplan, "Inertia and Change in the Constellation of International Governmental Organizations, 1981–1991," *International Organization* 50 (Autumn 1996), pp. 593–628; Peter I. Hajnal, *The G7/G8 System: Evolution, Role and Documentation* (Brookfield, Vt.: Ashgate, 1999); Ikenberry, *After Victory*, esp. pp. 248, 257–73. For similar arguments that explain the failure of institutions, see Barry Eichengreen, *Golden Fetters: The Gold Standard and the Great Depression 1919–1939* (New York: Oxford University Press, 1992); Beth A. Simmons, *Who Adjusts: Domestic Sources of Foreign Economic Policy During the Interwar Years* (Princeton: Princeton University Press, 1994), who argue that institutional success is a function of state policy convergence. Institutions collapse when those preferences diverge.

[41] Following Friedrich V. Kratochwil, *Rules, Norms, and Decisions: On the Conditions of Practical and Legal Reasoning in International Relations and Domestic Affairs* (New York: Cambridge University Press, 1989), p. 64, I define values as more general than either norms or rules. Whereas rules prescribe specific actions, values inform attitudes. Instead of addressing the cost-calculus of actors, they strengthen the will and emotional attachments.

[42] People still call on their neighbors in locales where the police are feared, the local community is tight-knit and state institutions are considered foreign.

societies are repressive of the individual. In this connection, they distinguish between society and its formal instantiations, which may take the form of institutions. The latter control the visible, outward forms of behavior. They repress at the level of practice, but may free people at the level of belief.[43] Even at the level of practice, they often allow for considerable slack, and sometimes deliberately, as a kind of safety valve to ensure greater outward compliance to more critical rules. In a paradoxical way, institutions are liberating. Social control, by contrast, demands inward acquiescence. It attempts to shape the discourse of a culture, and thus, the way people think and feel and conceive of themselves. Such control can be stultifying, as both Nietzsche and Freud insisted it was the case in Victorian Europe.[44] Foucault, a modernist for all his disclaimers, maintains, like Plato, Rousseau and Nietzsche, that institutions regulate consciousness through the same disciplinary mechanisms.[45] Proponents of the strong formulation of institutionalism closely mirror Foucault in their belief in the power of institutions to feed back into society and shape its discourses and, by extension, the way in which actors frame their identities and interests.

Liberal institutionalists tend to have a more restricted definition of an institution than anthropologists and many of their colleagues in comparative politics. The latter are interested in kinship, social and other ties that regulate behavior, and may lead to compliance with norms in the absence of any enforcement authorities.[46] Liberal institutionalists direct their attention to formally established bodies (e.g., NATO, IMF, GATT) and the environments created by their rules and procedures. They make far-reaching claims for such institutions, not dissimilar from those made by

[43] See James C. Scott, *Domination and the Arts of Resistance: Hidden Transcripts* (New Haven: Yale University Press, 1990), for an insightful comparative treatment of how subordinates and the oppressed create and defend social spaces in which to express dissent. Friedrich Nietzsche, *The Will to Power*, trans. Walter Kaufmann and R. J. Hollingdale (New York: Random House, 1967), para 864, observed that slaves employ "the instincts of cowardice, cunning, and canailles," to undermine the power structure.

[44] Sigmund Freud, *Civilization and its Discontents*, trans. James Strachey (New York: Norton, [1929]1961); Friedrich Nietzsche, *Daybreak*, trans. R. J. Hollingdale (Cambridge: Cambridge University Press), para 112.

[45] Michel Foucault, *The Archeology of Knowledge*, trans. A. M. Sheridan Smith (New York: Pantheon, 1972), pp. 31–38, 126–31, 166–77; Plato, *Laws*, 663, insists that "The legislator . . . can persuade the minds of the young of anything, so that he only has to reflect and find out what belief will be of the greatest public advantage."

[46] M. Fortes and E. E. Evans-Pritchard, *African Political Systems* (Oxford: Oxford University Press, 1940); John Middleton and David Tait, eds., *Tribes Without Rulers, Studies in African Segmentary Systems* (London: Routledge & Kegan Paul, 1958); Bull, *Anarchical Society*, pp. 59–65; Jack Snyder, "Anarchy and Culture," *International Organization* 56 (Winter 2002), pp. 7–46. Roger D. Masters, "World Politics as a Primitive Political System," *World Politics* 16 (July 1964), pp. 595–619, draws the analogy in reverse.

anthropologists for the collective institutions of a society (which include a wide range of informal social practices). Their emphasis on instrumental reason as opposed to habit divides modern from classical realists, just as to some degree it does the Anglo-American, liberal tradition from continental philosophy. I first encountered these different understandings as a graduate student at Yale in the early 1960s. Karl W. Deutsch, a Central European socialist, made a strong case to our seminar for the power of *nomos*. Stopping at red lights, he explained, had begun as a convention of convenience, but over time had become internalized so that a driver coming down a country road at night would stop at a red light even if nobody else was in sight. My classmate Nick Onuf had heard Robert Tucker, a prominent realist and quintessential American liberal, use the same example in his class at Johns Hopkins. Tucker insisted that drivers only honored red lights for fear of the consequences of not stopping. In the middle of the night, at a deserted intersection, the average driver would not hesitate to run a red light. Onuf convinced a couple of friends that the moment had come for empirical research. Armed with several six-packs of cold beer, they drove out to a suburb well past midnight, found a crossroads with an unimpeded view of the road and hid behind some low-lying bushes. Several hours and many beers later, they had their answer: the dozen or so drivers who came by slowed down – some came to a full stop – had a careful look for other cars or the dreaded police cruiser, and then ran the light. The truth lay somewhere between the predictions of Deutsch and Tucker.[47] The power, and lack of power, of institutions, and *nomos* more broadly, is another polarity of social life that people – and social scientists – must learn to negotiate.

In this connection, Eastern Europe provides a nice counterpoint to Western Europe. The web of institutions established by the Soviet Union was every bit as broad and encompassing as those set up or encouraged by the United States in the postwar period. They did not survive the emergence of a reformist regime in the Soviet Union, and their collapse helped to bring about the collapse of the Soviet Union itself. As long as institutional compliance was enforced by the Soviet Union, member states acquiesced in their outward behavior, just as individual citizens did within states where communist governments were in power. The German Democratic Republic went to Orwellian lengths of impressing almost one-third of its adult citizens into the role of informer in the hope of denying any private spaces and enforcing institutional control in every nook and cranny of life. Efforts at achieving outward compliance were

[47] Personal communication from author, 8 March 2002. Onuf swears that this is the only piece of empirical research he has ever carried out in the course of his career.

largely successful throughout the Soviet bloc, but did not readily translate into "mind control." Even in the absence of a functioning civil society, East Europeans especially, kept alternative conceptions of history and society alive.[48] Opponents of communist regimes also learned how to exploit the outward manifestations of conformity for their own ends.[49] In the Soviet Union, almost from the beginning, historians, social scientists, writers, and artists of all kind wrote fiction and non-fiction, or created works of representational or performing art that superficially reproduced, and even appeared to reaffirm, the official discourse and its associated interpretations, while actually subverting them in subtle ways. Readers, viewers and audiences became increasingly adept in their ability to pick up these cues and read, so to speak, between the lines. In the last decade of the Soviet Union, the practice of "double discourse" became increasingly open, with social scientists sometimes able to criticize existing assumptions or policies provided they opened and closed their books and articles with appropriate genuflections to the Marxist canon.[50]

The Soviet, Eastern European cases – and more recently, Afghanistan – suggest, *pace* Aristotle, that there are clear limits to the power of institutions.[51] When foisted on a hostile populace, they may secure outward compliance, but little else. The Athenian alliance, the communist governments in Eastern Europe, the Warsaw Pact and the Taliban endured only as long as the power propping them up.[52] Nor do institutions fare well in environments where community is weak or lacking, as evidenced by the failure of some Russian stock markets, so many Third

[48] Lésveque, *The Enigma of 1989*; Matthew Evangelista, *Unarmed Forces: The Transnational Movement to End the Cold War* (Ithaca: Cornell University Press, 1999); Robert D. English, *Russia and the Idea of the West: Gorbachev, Intellectuals and the End of the Cold War* (New York: Columbia University Press, 2000); Claudio Fogu, Wulf Kansteiner and Richard Ned Lebow, eds., *The Politics of Memory in Postwar Europe*, forthcoming.

[49] Czeslaw Milosz, *The Captive Mind* (New York: Vintage, 1990 [1951]), pp. 54–81, describes the concept of Ketman, and how it allowed people to develop inner lives while showing outward compliance.

[50] An early example is the Malevich painting entitled "Soviet Cavalry." Painted in 1918, it was well received by Soviet officialdom. It shows a solid, unmovable earth, represented in dark layers, like geological strata, with a dividing line between earth and sky two-thirds up the canvas. Racing across the ground is a tiny group of Red cavalry. The message is here today, gone tomorrow. Just hang in there.

[51] Aristotle, *Poetics*, 660, writes "the true legislator will persuade – and if he cannot persuade, will compel."

[52] This conclusion is supported by work in reactance theory, which suggests that compliance can be coerced by means of threats and careful surveillance, but once surveillance ceases, compliance will as well. The reaction against the order (and the authority behind it) may be in proportion to the degree to which it was imposed, not negotiated. Sharon S. Brehm and Jack W. Brehm, *Psychological Reactance: A Theory of Freedom and Control* (New York: Academic Press, 1981).

World governments and the League of Nations.[53] Institutions cannot introduce order into societies that most closely resemble the world of institutional theorists: an anarchical one populated by self-interested actors. This is not to deny the importance of institutions; they can consolidate and sustain communities, but in and of themselves they are incapable of creating them.

Other scholars have looked beyond institutions to societies themselves – at the domestic and international level – to discover underlying reasons for order and cooperation. Robert Putnam's research on social capital is a well-received example. Deploying Mauss' thesis about exchange in ancient Greece, Putnam argues that "networks of community engagement foster sturdy norms of reciprocity." "Generalized reciprocity" relieves the recipient of having to balance any particular exchange, and creates expectations of further exchanges.[54] For the ancient Greeks, as understood by Emile Durkheim and Marcel Mauss, participation in a network of ritual exchange and mutual obligation built community by creating affective ties among individuals, providing important shared experiences, and stretching their identities into what Durkheim called *la conscience collective*.[55] Collective identities transformed the meaning of cooperation for members of a community. Working within the dominant ontology, Putnam reframes cooperation as a narrow collective action problem, and looks to micro-economics for explanations of why autonomous, rational actors cooperate. Not surprisingly, he comes up with the same mechanisms as institutionalists: transparency and the shadow of the future. Economic and political transactions "in dense networks of social interactions" reduce the incentives people might otherwise have for free-riding and malfeasance by helping increase the flow of information and reducing transaction costs.[56]

[53] On the stock markets, Timothy Frye, *Brokers and Bureaucrats: Building Market Institutions in Russia* (Ann Arbor: University of Michigan Press, 2000).

[54] Robert D. Putnam, *Bowling Alone: The Collapse and Revival of American Community* (New York: Simon & Schuster, 2000), esp. pp. 21–25, 288–89.

[55] Emile Durkheim, *The Division of Labor in Society*, trans. W. D. Halls (New York: Macmillan, 1984 [1893]), 229–30; Robert Connor, "Civil Society, Dionysiac Festival, and the Athenian Democracy," in Josiah Ober and Charles Hedrick, eds., *Dēmokratia: A Conversation on Democracies, Ancient and Modern* (Princeton: Princeton University Press, 1996), pp. 217–26, makes this argument in the case of fifth-century Athens.

[56] Putnam, *Bowling Alone*, pp. 21–25; Durkheim, *The Division of Labor in Society*, pp. xxii–xxiii, 38–39, who insists that contracts cannot lay the foundation for a social order, and could only be created and sustained on the basis of a prior existing order. Marcel Mauss, *The Gift: the Form and Reason for Exchange in Archaic Societies*, trans. W. D. Halls (New York: Norton, 1990 [1925]).

"Thin" constructivist accounts of cooperation also incorporate individual ontologies and consequential choice mechanisms.[57] Alexander Wendt, an atypical "thick constructivist," offers us a parallel understanding of cooperation at the international level. He describes the international system as a social construction, with a structure that is more cultural than material. The system nevertheless comprises objective identities: friend, rival, enemy. They are not produced by agents, although their behavior determines the distribution of these identities, and *pace* Bull, can produce three different kinds of anarchy. A Hobbesian or realist world is one in which enemies predominate, and where actors accordingly have unlimited aims, resort to worst-case analysis and preemptive behavior and formulate their interests in terms of relative gains. Lockean or liberal anarchy is populated by rivals who accept the right of other actors to exist, allow for neutrality, pursue more limited aims and engage more successfully in balancing and other strategies of conflict management. Kantian or constructivist anarchy, which, Wendt speculates, may be in the process of emerging, is dominated by friendly behavior, security communities and the practice of collective security. The degree of cooperation and its causes differ from one kind of anarchy to another; norms may be observed because of coercion, self-interest or legitimacy.[58] Wendt ignores what many social theorists, including Aristotle and Hegel, saw as the most powerful source of normative compliance: everyday practice that makes non-compliance almost difficult to imagine.[59]

While critical of existing theories of cooperation, Wendt fully buys in to their ontology. Like Waltz, he assumes the prior existence of materially constituted, uncomplicated and fully autonomous actors whose "only determinable interest, as they enter the arena of interaction, is survival." They have no identity until they interact with other actors at the system level. Wendt, however, fails to distinguish adequately between

[57] See Thomas Risse, Stephen C. Ropp and Kathryn Sikkink, eds., *The Power of Human Rights: International Norms and Domestic Change* (Cambridge: Cambridge University Press, 1999); Margaret Keck and Kathryn Sikkink, *Activists Beyond Borders: Advocacy Networks in International Politics* (Ithaca: Cornell University Press, 1998). This observation has also made by Donald P. Green and Ian Shapiro, *Pathologies of Rational Choice Theory: A Critique of Applications in Political Science* (New Haven: Yale University Press, 1994), pp. 17–19; Jeffrey T. Checkel, "Why Comply? Social Learning and European Identity Change," *International Organization* 55 (Summer 2001), pp. 553–88.

[58] Alexander L. Wendt, *Social Theory of International Politics* (Cambridge: Cambridge University Press, 1999). The three forms of anarchy come from Hedley Bull, *Anarchical Society* (London: Macmillan, 1977), pp. 24–27.

[59] This point is made by Ted Hopf, "Constructivism All the Way Down," *International Politics* 37 (September 2000), pp. 369–78. See also, Steve Smith, "Wendt's World," *Review of International Studies* 26 (January 2000), pp. 151–63.

cooperation and community. The former refers to collaboration on a case-by-case basis, and the latter to a common "we feeling" that provides an enduring basis for continuing cooperation.[60] At times Wendt appears to be saying that the international system can promote the emergence of community by transforming identities, but at other times he seems to suggest that it merely strengthens cooperation by recasting interests. Wendt differs from Waltz in that he allows for three different kinds of anarchy, each of which corresponds to a different understanding of international relations. But once he acknowledges such variation, he needs to account for it. The most obvious explanation would be that actors have pre-social identities (whatever that might be), or at least experiences, that generate the expectations and frames of reference they use to interpret the behavior and motives of others. These identities and cognitive predispositions can only come from domestic or international society. Both remain outside his theory.[61]

A world of autonomous, egoistic individuals – even the fiction of such a world – when used as a starting point of analysis, fosters the belief that cooperation and commitments should serve purely selfish ends. Working from such an assumption, which rules out other reasons for community, it is easy to see why social scientists working in the rational choice tradition must resort to the most extreme forms of intellectual prestidigitation to explain how anything beyond the most short-lived and instrumental kind of collaboration ever occurs. Having coaxed the rabbit of individualism out of their analytical hat, social scientists are now unsuccessfully casting about for tricks to put it back inside.

Are actors individuals?

The realist, liberal and social capital approaches are generally considered distinct and competitive. But it is their similarities I find striking and troubling. All three approaches share a common ontology and logic. Their starting point is the liberal assumption of the autonomous, egoistic actor who, in the words of C. B. Macpherson, is "the proprietor of his person and capacities." Society is conceived of as "a lot of free individuals

[60] The expression is from Karl W. Deutsch, *Nationalism and Social Communication* (Cambridge, MA: MIT Press, 1953).

[61] Some of these points are made by Naeem Inayatullab and David L. Blaney, "Knowing Encounters: Beyond Parochialism in International Relations Theory," in Lapid and Kratochwil, *The Return of Culture and Identity in IR Theory*, pp. 65–84; Sujata Chakrabarti Pasic, "Culturing International Relations Theory: A Call for Extension," in Lapid and Kratochwil, *The Return of Culture and Identity in IR Theory*, pp. 85–104; Hopf, "Constructivism All the Way Down."

related to each other as proprietors of their own capacities and of what they have acquired by their exercise."[62] Proponents of these approaches explain cooperation (or the lack of it, in the case of neorealism) with reference to the incentives (or lack of them) offered by the environment. This ontology, imported into the discipline from economics, has now metastasized through the social sciences and is found at the core of all theories of rational choice. The self-contained individual as the unit of analysis is a socially conditioned choice, and one that imposes serious conceptual limitations on scholarship. It also raises troubling ethical issues.

There is nothing natural about people acting primarily on the basis of individual self-interest. Individual identity is historically conditioned, took millennia to emerge and has been regarded as *un*natural by most people for most of its existence.[63] In traditional societies, people were – and still are – more tightly integrated into communities, and more likely to define their identities in communal terms.[64] They do not lack a concept of self, but that concept is relationally defined; it is likely to be the sum of socially assigned roles.[65] *Persona* is the Latin word for mask and describes

[62] C. B. Macpherson, *The Political Theory of Possessive Individualism: Hobbes to Locke* (Oxford: Oxford University Press, 1962), p. 3. Aafke E. Komter, *The Gift: An Interdisciplinary Perspective* (Amsterdam: Amsterdam University Press, 1996), for a recent compilation of literature on gifts and the norms of reciprocity.

[63] During the fifth century, the individual achieved an identity in Athenian law, but it remained poorly defined. These changes were reflected in tragedy, which became more psychological, especially in the hands of Sophocles and Euripides. Jean-Pierre Vernant, "Intimations of the Will in Greek Tragedy," in Jean-Pierre Vernant and Pierre Vidal-Nacquet, *Myth and Tragedy in Ancient Greece*, trans. Janet Lloyd (New York: Zone Books, 1990), pp. 49–84. For Aristotle, in the fourth century, decision was *hairesis*, and reflected intention, in contrast to older, Homeric conceptions of action, that emphasized external constraints over internal volition.

[64] Bernard Yack, *The Fetishism of Modernities: Epochal Self-Consciousness in Contemporary Social and Political Thought* (Notre Dame: University of Notre Dame Press, 1997), reminds us that this is something of an overstatement. T. K. Fitzgerald, *Metaphors of Identity* (Albany: State University of New York Press, 1993), p. 190, rightly observes that identity and culture are not synonymous. Yosif Lapid, "Culture's Ship: Returns and Departures in International Relations Theory," in Yosef Lapid and Friedrich Kratochwil, *The Return of Culture and Identity in IR Theory* (Boulder: Lynne Rienner, 1997), pp. 3–20, notes that collectivities come in many flavors, and to describe them as "identities" is to substitute one loose concept for another.

[65] Durkheim, *The Division of Labor in Society*, Preface and pp. 219–22, characterized identities in traditional societies as "mechanical solidarity," in which individuals are completely socialized into the beliefs and values of the group and assume socially determined roles. In modern society, characterized by a division of labor, "organic solidarity" bonds people together who perform specialized roles and are accordingly dependent on one another. Moses I. Finley, *The World of Odysseus* (New York: Viking Press, 1954), p. 134, describes identities in ancient Greece as a form of mechanical solidarity. Kinship and status were determining. "The basis values of the society were given, predetermined and so were a man's place in the society and the privileges and duties that followed from his status."

the outer face that one presents to the community.[66] The face defines the self in others' eyes and in one's own mind's eye. This understanding resonates in the modern understanding of identity as a set of meanings "that an actor attributes to itself while taking the perspectives of others."[67] At the collective level, identities are often defined, and perhaps, even constructed, with reference to "others" and what our understanding of them says about ourselves.[68]

In ancient Greece, there was no conception of individual self-interest, and none of "self-interestedness" prior to the late fifth century. Unfortunate individuals such as slaves and outcasts who did not belong to a community, were thought of as liminal people and objects of pity and fear. Durkheim observed that the replacement of the collectivity by the individual as the object of ritual attention is one of the hallmarks of transitions from traditional to modern societies. Indeed, from Rousseau on, Enlightenment and Romantic ideologies emphasized the uniqueness and autonomy of the inner self.[69] Modernity created a vocabulary that recognizes

[66] Thomas Hobbes, *Leviathan*, ed. C. B. Macpherson (Harmondsworth: Penguin, 1968), Part I, xvi, p. 112, notes the derivation of *persona*, which he compares to an actor on stage. The person – the individual who has become part of the commonwealth and lost some of his will in the process – is such an actor. Onuf, "The Rise of the Liberal World: Conceptual Developments from Thomas Hobbes to Henry Wheaton," paper presented at Center of International Studies, University of Southern California, 17 October 2001; Jean-Christoph Andrew, *Worlds Apart: The Market and the Theater in Anglo-American Thought, 1550–1750* (Cambridge: Cambridge University Press, 1986), pp. 98–103, for Hobbes on persons, the actors and the stage.

[67] G. McCall and J. Simmons, *Identities and Interactions* (New York: Free Press, 1978), pp. 61–100.

[68] Lars-Eric Cederman, *Constructing Europe's Identity: The External Dimension* (London: Lynne Rienner, 2001), argues that this is increasingly the case for the identity of the European Union, where its identity is being defined by reference to "non-Europe" as opposed to its constitutive units, member states. Bull, *The Anarchical Society*, pp. 33–34, 44, made a similar argument about European international society in the eighteenth century.

[69] Romantics rejected obedience to some general moral law in favor of being "true to oneself." Rousseau considered this a difficult process requiring continuous struggle because in modern society there is often little relationship between who we are and whom we appear to be. Marshal Berman, *The Politics of Individualism: Radical Individualism and the Emergence of Modern Society* (London: Allen & Unwin, 1971). For Hegel, the "authentic" romantic was a "beautiful soul," pure in its inwardness and uncorrupted by modernity's divisiveness. *Phenomenology*, Bb, Cc; Robert E. Norton, *The Beautiful Soul: Aesthetic Morality in the Eighteenth Century* (Ithaca: Cornell University Press, 1995). On Durkheim, see *The Elementary Forms of Religious Life* (London: George Allen & Unwin, 1915), and *The Division of Labor in Society*; Talcot Parsons, *The Structure of Social Action* (New York: Mc-Graw-Hill, 1937), pp. 378–90; Steven Lukes, *Emile Durkheim. His Life and Work. A Historical and Critical Study* (Palo Alto: Stanford University Press, 1973); Steven Collins, "Categories, Concepts or Predicaments? Remarks on Mauss' Use of Philosophical Terminology," in Michael Carrithers, Steven Collins and Steven Lukes, *The Category of the Person: Anthropology, Philosophy, History* (Cambridge: Cambridge University Press, 1985), pp. 46–82.

tensions between inner selves and social roles but encourages us to cultivate and express our "inner selves" and original ways of being.[70] As products of this ideology, we tend to take for granted that our desires, feelings and choices are spontaneous and self-generated, but there is good reason to believe that they are in large part socially constituted. This was certainly the perspective of Thucydides, Plato and even Thomas Hobbes.[71] Hegel maintained that human beings oriented themselves and were guided by social practices that they learned pre-reflexively. More recently, Erving Goffman, in the tradition of Hegel and Durkheim, sought to document the extent to which everyday life is structured by an astonishing variety of rituals that construct and reinforce identities and render the very notion of an autonomous inner self highly problematic.[72] Goffman's implicit message is that most modern people, like their traditional counterparts, are also the sum of the social roles they learn to perform, but delude themselves into believing that their identities and behavior largely reflect personal choice. Additional empirical support for the social construction of identity comes from psychological research that finds that people have a great sense of their own uniqueness, but then when asked to describe what makes them unique, come up with generally shared

[70] The concept of self is treated as unproblematic by positivists, as a socially created identity by constructivists and as a collective delusion by many postmodern and postcolonial scholars for whom it can only be achieved by creating the denigrating identity of "otherness" for others. Nicholas Onuf, "Parsing Personal Identity: Self, Other, Agent," observes that despite the centrality of the self for modern scholarship, it remains an "unexamined primitive." Many concepts of self rely on the idea of interpellation developed by Louis Althusser, "Ideology and Ideological State Apparatuses (Notes Toward an Investigation)," in *Lenin and Philosophy and Other Essays*, trans. Ben Brewster (New York: Monthly Review Press, 1971), pp. 127–88. For commentary and subsequent development of the concept of the relational self, see John Shotter, "Social Accountability and the Social Construction of 'You,'" in John Shotter and Kenneth J. Gergen, *Texts of Identity* (London: Sage, 1989), pp. 133–51; Judith Butler, *Excitable Speech: The Politics of the Performative* (New York: Routledge, 1997); Paul John Eakin, *How Our Lives Become Stories: Making Selves* (Ithaca: Cornell University Press, 1999); Kenneth Gergen, *An Invitation to Social Construction* (London: Sage, 1999).

[71] Hobbes, *Leviathan*, I, xiii, pp. 86–87. Inhabitants of the state of nature have only limited faculties, consisting of strength, form and prudence. While some men excel in one or the other faculty, *in toto* there is little difference among them. They are equal and interacting on a bare stage, so without real identities which depend on differentiation. Hobbes has created the state of nature in part to show the social construction of identity.

[72] Erving Goffman, *Presentation of Self in Everyday* Life (New York: Doubleday, 1959), *Behavior in Public Places: Notes on the Social Organization of Gatherings* (New York: Free Press, 1962), and *Stigma: Notes on the Management of Spoiled Identity* (New York: Simon & Schuster, 1963), suggests that by engaging in a behavior, in this case cooperative, the actor projects an image consistent with this behavior. John Ruggie, "International Regimes, Transactions, and Change: Embedded Liberalism in the Postwar Economic Order," in Stephen D. Krasner, ed., *International Regimes* (Ithaca: Cornell University Press, 1983), pp. 195–232, makes the case for embedded liberalism working in this manner.

or widely valued attributes like honesty, dedication to family, artistic or athletic talent.[73]

We also think of ourselves as unique because of our idiosyncratic pasts and the ways in which they make us who we are. There may be some biological basis for this claim: Gerald Edelman proposes a theory of neural nets that describes how the nervous system evolves in response to life experiences and becomes a physical representation of the uniqueness of every individual.[74] But memories are not hard-wired. As Vico suspected, many of our most important memories turn out to be social constructions.[75] Modern psychological work on collective memory begins with Maurice Halbwachs, who argued that "social organization gives a persistent framework into which all detailed recall must fit, and it very powerfully influences both the manner and matter of recall."[76] Decades of accumulating research finds autobiographical memory largely unreliable, even so-called "flashbulb memories" which involve recall of shocking events along with considerable details of one's personal circumstances at the time the news was received.[77] Accumulating evidence suggests that to some degree we remake our memories and life narratives over time in response to our psychological needs and group identifications.[78]

[73] Jerome Bruner, "The 'Remembered' Self," in Ulric Neisser and Robyn Fivush, *The Remembering Self: Construction and Accuracy in the Self Narrative* (Cambridge: Cambridge University Press, 1994), pp. 41–54; Kenneth J. Gergen, "Mind, Text, and Society: Self-Memory in Social Context," in Neisser and Fivush, *The Remembered Self*, pp. 78–104.

[74] Gerald M. Edelman, *Bright Air, Brilliant Fire: On the Matter of the Mind* (New York: Basic Books, 1992).

[75] Giambattista Vico, *The New Science*, trans. T. G. Bergin and M. H. Fisch (Ithaca: Cornell University Press, 1948 [1725]), distinguished among memory (*memoria*), memory as imagination (*fantasia*) and memory as invention (*ingegno*).

[76] Maurice Halbwachs, *The Collective Memory*, trans. Francis J. Ditter, Jr. and Vida Yazdi Ditter (New York: Harper & Row, 1980 [1941]), p. 296. The other founding fathers of collective memory are Lev S. Vygotsky, *Mind in Society: The Development of Higher Psychological Processes*, ed. Michael Cole (Cambridge, Mass.: Harvard University Press, 1978); and F. C. Bartlett, *Remembering: A Study in Experimental and Social Psychology* (New York: Macmillan, 1932).

[77] R. Brown and J. Kulik, "Flashbulb Memories," *Cognition* 5 (1977), pp. 73–99; J. N. Bohannon and V. L. Symons, "Flashbulb Memories: Confidence, Consistency, and Quantify," in E. Winograd and U. Neisser, eds., *Affect and Accuracy in Recall* (New York: Cambridge University Press, 1992), pp. 65–91.

[78] The psychological literature emphasizes the temporal nature of identity. This consensus is reflected in Polkinghorne's observation that "Self, then, is not a static thing or a substance, but a configuration of personal events into an historical unity which includes not only what one has been but also anticipation of what one will be." Donald E. Polkinghorne, *Narrative Knowing and the Human Sciences* (Albany, N.Y.: State University of New York Press, 1988). See also Craig R. Barclay, "Composing Protoselves Through Improvisation," in Neisser and Fivush," *The Remembering Self*, pp. 55–77; W. F. Brewer, "What is Autobiographical Memory?," in D. C. Rubin, ed., *Autobiographical Memory* (Cambridge: Cambridge University Press, 1986), pp. 34–49; Robyn Fivush, "The Function of Event Memory," in Ulrich Neisser and E. Winograd, eds., *Remembering Reconsidered: Ecological and Traditional Approaches to the Study of Memory* (Cambridge:

Psychologists find multiple "remembered selves," with evocation of any one of them depending on the social milieu in which the person is situated at the time.[79] Memory studies indicate that the concept of the authentic self is deeply problematic. We evolve over time, in response to internal and external stimuli, and the best we can do is call up imperfect and selective representations of what we once were – or would like to think we were.[80]

In traditional societies identities are undifferentiated from social roles.[81] In the *Iliad*, Achilles must choose between an early death with honor or a long, peaceful life, and chooses the death of a hero. Achilles is always described as the "best of the Achaeans" because he expresses the values of his society to a superlative degree. His choice of a hero's death is a reflection of the extent to which his identity is a product of his culture. As the events of 11 September indicate, we find it inexplicable, and positively horrifying, that anyone today would choose a martyr's death over a long, prosperous life. But we still model ourselves on "heroes" who personify cultural values. Public opinion polls indicate that Americans want

Cambridge University Press, 1988), pp. 277–82; Dorothy Holland and Naomi Quinn, eds., *Cultural Models in Language and Thought* (Cambridge: Cambridge University Press, 1987); R. D'Andrade, "Some Propositions About the Relation Between Culture and Human Cognition," in James W. Stigler, Richard. A. Shweder and Gilbert H. Herdt, eds., *Cultural Psychology: Essays in Comparative Human Development* (Cambridge: Cambridge University Press, 1990), pp. 65–129; Rubin, ed., *Autobiographical Memory*; A. E. Collins, S. E. Gathercole, M. A. Conway and P. E. M. Morris, eds., *Theories of Memory* (Hillsdale, N.J.: Lawrence Erlbaum, 1993); Winograd and Neisser, eds., *Affect and Accuracy in Recall*; Ulric Neisser, ed., *The Perceived Self: Ecological and Interpersonal Sources of Self-Knowledge* (Cambridge: Cambridge University Press, 1993); Neisser and Fivush, *The Remembering Self*; James W. Pennebaker, Dario Paez and Bernard Rimé, *Collective Memory of Political Events: Social Psychological Perspectives* (Mahwah, N.J.: Lawrence Erlbaum, 1997). For broader studies, that relate changes in memory to life histories and political events, see Erik H. Erikson, *Childhood and Society* (New York: Norton, 1950); Alessandro Portelli, "Uchronic Dreams: Working-Class Memory and Possible Worlds," in *The Death of Luigi Trastulli and Other Stories: Form and Meaning in Oral History* (Albany: State University of New York Press, 1991).

[79] Ulric Neisser, "John Dean's Memory: A Case Study," *Cognition* 9 (1981), pp. 1–22; D. P. Spence, *Narrative Truth and Historical Truth: Meaning and Interpretation in Psychoanalysis* (New York: Norton, 1982); R. T. White, "Recall of Autobiographical Events," *Applied Cognitive Psychology* 18 (1989), pp. 127–35; D. E. Polkinghorne, "Narrative and Self-Concept," *Journal of Narrative and Life History* 1 (1991), pp. 135–53; Neisser, *The Perceived Self*; Neisser and Fivush, *The Remembering Self*.

[80] Paul John Eakin, *Making Selves: How Our Lives Become Stories* (Ithaca: Cornell University Press, 1990), p. x.

[81] Hermann Fränkel, *Early Greek Poetry and Philosophy*, trans. M. Hadas and J. Willis (Oxford: Oxford University Press, 1975), p. 80; James M. Redfield, *Nature and Culture in the Iliad* (Chicago: University of Chicago Press, 1975), pp. 20–24; Jean-Pierre Vernant, *L'individu, la mort, l'amour: Soi-même et l'autre en Grèce ancienne* (Paris: Gallimard, 1989), p. 55; Walter Benjamin, *The Origin of German Tragic Drama*, trans. John Osborne (London: New Left Books, 1977), pp. 106–08. Bernard Williams, *Shame and Necessity* (Berkeley: University of California Press, 1993), maintains there is no contrast between self and non-self because in the *Iliad*, "man is completely part of his world."

to be affluent, hold high-paying and high-status jobs, be slim-waisted, and athletically accomplished. We adopt behavioral attributes and consumer preferences consistent with many of these goals. It is the rare individual who rejects outright the pressures that begin at birth to mold "him"or "her" into a him or her and typical representative of society, or of one of its sub-groups. And people who "drop out" often drop in to subcultures where identities, dress and behavior are at least as socially imposed. Our inner selves and associated desires may be almost as socially determined as those of Achilles. The major difference, I will argue in Chapter 9, is that we are exposed to multiple discourses, which give us some choice, allow for synthetic identities, and in turn encourage the more rapid evolution of the discourses that shape our identities.

Identities and interests at the state level depend heavily on international society. Leopold von Ranke, a nineteenth-century precursor of Kenneth Waltz, defined a great power in terms of its capabilities.[82] But since the modern state system emerged, many more authorities have considered great power status something akin to *hegemonia* in that it can only be conferred by other powers. Membership in the international system, and even more, great power status, carries certain responsibilities.[83] Grotius, Pufendorf, Vattel, Wolff, and more recently, the English School and some constructivists, elaborated these responsibilities and the rules to which member states must adhere.[84] In the words of Hedley Bull,

[82] A great power had to possess the capability to maintain itself against all other powers, even when they united against it. Theodore H. Von Laue, *Leopold von Ranke: The Formative Years* (Princeton: Princeton University Press, 1950), p. 203.

[83] F. H. Hinsley, *Power and the Pursuit of Peace* (Cambridge: Cambridge University Press, 1963), pp. 4–5, 133–37, 142–44, 160–61, 180–82, 191–93, on the evolution of European understandings of the "great powers." Herbert Butterfield, "The Balance of Power," in Herbert Butterfield and Martin Wight, *Diplomatic Investigations: Essays in the Theory of International Politics* (Cambridge: Harvard University Press, 1966), pp. 132–48; Bull, *Anarchical Society*, p. 203.

[84] Onuf, *The Republican Legacy,* on Pufendorf, Grotius, Vattel and Wolff. On the English school, see Chris Brown, "World Society and the English School. An International Society Perspective on World Society," *European Journal of International Relations* 7 (December 2001), 423–42; Barry Buzan, "From International System to International Society: Structural Realism and Regime Theory Meet the English School," *International Organization* 47 (Summer 1993), pp. 327–52. Core works of the English School include C. A. W. Manning, *The Nature of International Society* (London: London School of Economics, 1962); Butterfield and Wight, *Diplomatic Investigations*; Martin Wight, *Systems of States* (Leicester: Leicester University Press, 1977); Bull, *Anarchical Society*; Michael Donelan, ed., *The Reason of State* (London: Allen & Unwin, 1978); Adam Watson, *The Evolution of International Society* (London: Routledge, 1992). The English School is generally perceived as hewing a middle path between realism and utopianism. The principal theorists in this school felt themselves part of classical realism. Bull's treatment of international society has Aristotelian and Kantian roots in its stress on states as agents of the good and society as an arrangement for realizing the common good of humanity. This argument has been taken up in the United States by Terry Nardin, *The Ethics of War and Peace: Religious and Secular Perspectives* (Princeton: Princeton University Press, 1998).

member states conceive of themselves as "bound by a common set of rules in their relations with one another, and share in the working of common institutions."[85] International society theorists acknowledge that these rules and norms have a rhetorical component, but insist that they are for the most part obeyed because they enable states to pursue their interests in a more efficient and less violent way.[86] Oran Young has observed that new states have little choice but to participate in these practices and institutional arrangements.[87] In Bull's judgment, rules and norms make anarchy more a Lockean than a Hobbesian world because they enable trade, civilized social relations and some degree of security without a sovereign authority.[88]

The seventeenth- and eighteenth-century jurists, statesmen and philosophers who wrote about international society considered it coterminous with Christian Europe. For Fichte, "Christian Europe" was a single nation whose "common culture and civilisation" set it apart from other regions and cultures.[89] Postwar theorists have directed their attention to the emergence of a community among the developed democracies, constructed around a core "North Atlantic Community."[90] Building on John Searle's distinction between "brute" and "social" facts, Kratochwil and some other constructivists contend that international society must, of necessity, precede the state system because it creates the constitutive

[85] Bull, *Anarchical Society*, p. 16.

[86] Kratochwil, *Rules, Norms, and Decisions,* offers the most analytically sophisticated explanation for compliance with rules, norms and principles. In the first instance, they reduce the complexity of choice-situations and are guidance devices that bring conceptual order to the environment. Secondarily, they serve as means to facilitate goals, share meanings, justify behavior and enable communication in the broadest sense. At a deeper level, they influence choices by helping to structure processes of categorization, deliberation and interpretation.

[87] Oran Young, """International Regimes: Toward a New Theory of Institutions," *World Politics* 39 (October 1986), pp. 104–22.

[88] Bull, *Anarchical Society*, pp. 46–51; Barry Buzan, "From International System to International Society"; Ian Clark, *The Hierarchy of States: Reform and Resistance in the International Order* (Cambridge: Cambridge University Press, 1989), p. 2.

[89] Hinsley, *Power and the Pursuit of Peace,* pp. 4–5; Bull, *Anarchical Society,* pp. 16–17; Nardin, *Law, Morality, and the Relations of States,* pp. 62–63; Nicholas Greenwood Onuf, *World of Our Making: Rules and Rule in Social Theory and International Relations* (Columbia: University of South Carolina Press, 1989), pp. 167–68, and *The Republican Legacy*, pp. 163–67. The boundaries of this system gradually expanded, and came to include non-Christian powers like the Ottoman Empire. There is much discussion in the postwar literature cited above about the extent to which there is anything approaching an international society now that regional political systems have been subsumed into an international one with a growing set of common practices and institutions.

[90] Karl W. Deutsch *et al.*, *Political Community and the North Atlantic Area* (Princeton: Princeton University Press, 1957). For recent elaborations, see Emanuel Adler and Michael Barnett, *Security Communities* (Cambridge: Cambridge University Press, 1998); Bruce Cronin, *Community Under Anarchy: Transnational Identity and the Evolution of Cooperation* (New York: Columbia University Press, 1999).

frameworks in terms of which actors relate. These rules – particularly those surrounding sovereignty – also determine who qualifies as an actor.[91] Identities come through naming and participation in society. States, like people, can be socialized into membership and its attendant responsibilities. Germany and Japan went through such a process in the aftermath of World War II, and some other former dictatorships are in varying stages of transformation.[92] It is not too much of a stretch to interpret the evolution of the Soviet Union in the same light. At the outset, Bolsheviks conceived of the Soviet Union as a temporary political unit and world revolutionary force utterly antagonistic to the existing state system. After Stalin's death, Soviet leaders came to accept the state system, their membership in it and sought external recognition as a superpower. By the time of Gorbachev, membership in international society had helped to undermine traditional communist identities, making an end to the Cold War possible.[93]

Hedley Bull conceived of international society as "thin" in comparison to domestic societies. For the English School as a whole, it was not a halfway house between anarchy and world government, but a Pareto-optimal solution to the problem of balancing cultural diversity against the need for

[91] John Searle, *Speech Acts: An Essay in the Philosophy of Language* (Cambridge: Cambridge University Press, 1969), and *The Construction of Social Reality* (New York: Free Press, 1995); Kratochwil, *Rules, Norms, and Decisions*, pp. 25–28; John Gerard Ruggie, "Embedded Liberalism and the Postwar Economic Regimes," and *Constructing the World Polity: Essays on International Institutionalization* (New York: Routledge, 1998), pp. 22–25, 32–36, and ch. 2.

[92] Thomas U. Berger, "Norms, Identity, and National Security in Germany and Japan," in Peter J. Katzenstein, ed., *The Culture of National Security: Norms and Identity in World Politics* (New York: Columbia University press, 1996), pp. 317–56; Amy Gurowitz, "Mobilizing International Norms: Domestic Actors, Immigrants and the Japanese State," *World Politics* 51 (April 1999), pp. 413–45; Etel Solingen, "The Political Economy of Nuclear Restraint," *International Security* 19 (Fall 1995), pp. 126–69, and *Regional Orders at Century's Dawn: Global and Domestic Influences on Grand Strategy* (Princeton: Princeton University Press, 1998); Audie Klotz, *Norms in International Regimes: The Struggle Against Apartheid* (Ithaca: Cornell University Press, 1995); Jeffrey T. Checkel, "Norms, Institutions and National Identity in Contemporary Europe," *International Organization* 51 (Winter 1997), pp. 31–63. Andrew P. Cortell and James W. Davis, Jr., "Understanding the Domestic Impact of International Norms: A Research Agenda," *International Studies Review* 2 (Spring 2000), pp. 65–90, for a good review of this literature.

[93] Jeffrey T. Checkel, *Ideas and International Political Change: Soviet/Russian Behavior and the End of the Cold War* (New Haven: Yale University Press, 1997). Robert G. Herman "Identity, Norms, and International Security: the Soviet Foreign Policy Revolution and the End of the Cold War," in Katzenstein, *The Culture of National Security*, pp. 271–316; Jacques Lévesque, *The Enigma of 1989: The USSR and the Liberation of Eastern Europe*, trans. Keith Martin (Berkeley: University of California Press, 1997); Robert D. English, *Russia and the Idea of the West: Gorbachev, Intellectuals, and the End of the Cold War* (New York: Columbia University Press, 2000); Richard K. Herrmann and Richard Ned Lebow, eds., *Learning from the Cold War* (New York: Palgrave, 2004).

order.[94] The postwar transformations of Germany, Japan and the Soviet Union, and more recently, of South Africa and the countries of Eastern Europe, suggest that international society, especially Western regional society, is thicker than Bull and his colleagues imagined. A commitment to a thicker version of international society by at least some Western powers has provoked vocal opposition from some Asian countries, most notably, China, and it remains to be seen whether a thick or thin version will prevail in the long run.

There are also striking parallels between individual and collective actors in the realm of memory. I previously noted the connection between memory and identity, and how individual memories are at least in part socially constructed. Individuals have a tendency to rewrite their pasts, generally, but not always unconsciously, in response to cues from peer groups and the wider society. Psychologists speculate that one important incentive for doing so is the expected rewards of group membership and solidarity.[95] There is growing evidence that collective memory is also socially constructed. The events that people recall as well as the emotions and meanings attributed to them are significantly affected by commemorations and discourses propagated by authorities and other institutions and groups.[96] A recent cross-national study of the politics of memory

[94] Bull, *Anarchical Society*; Tim Dunne, *Inventing International Society: A History of the English School* (New York: St. Martin's Press, 1998), p. 11; Andreas Osiander, "Sovereignty, International Relations, and the Westphalian Myth," *International Organization* 55 (Spring 2001), pp. 251–87, observes that for Bull, individual states act as the "custodian" of the common good in a way that the more limited international society cannot.

[95] J. A. Robinson, "Sampling Autobiography," *Cognitive Psychology* 8 (1976), pp. 588–95; W. F. Brewer, "What is Autobiographical Memory?," in D. C. Rubin, ed., *Autobiographical Memory* (Cambridge: Cambridge University Press, 1986), pp. 24–49; Ulric Neisser, "Self-Narratives: True and False," in Neisser and Fivush, *The Remembering Self*, pp. 1–18; Craig R. Barclay, "Composing Protoselves Through Improvisation," in Neisser and Fivush, *The Remembering Self*, pp. 55–77; Derek Edwards and Jonathan Potter, "The Chancellor's Memory: Rhetoric and Truth in Discursive Remembering," *Applied Cognitive Psychology* 6 (1992), pp. 187–215; Derek Edwards, Jonathan Potter and D. Middleton, "Toward a Discursive Psychology of Remembering," *The Psychologist* 5 (1992), pp. 441–46; Kenneth J. Gergen, "Mind, Text, and Society: Self-Memory in Social Context," in Neisser and Fivush, *The Remembered Self*, pp. 78–103. For the critics, see A. Baddeley, "Is Memory all Talk?," *The Psychologist* 5 (1992), pp. 447–48; I. E. Hyman, Jr., "Multiple Approaches to Remembering," *The Psychologist* 5 (1992), pp. 450–51; Ulric Neisser, "The Psychology of Memory and the Socio-Linguistics of Remembering," *The Psychologist* 5 (1992), pp. 451–52.

[96] For a sampling of this mushrooming literature, see Helmut Peitsch *et al.*, eds., *European Memories of the Second World War* (New York: Berghahn, 1999); Peter Novick, *The Holocaust in American Life* (New York: Houghton-Mifflin, 1999); Istvan Deak *et al.*, eds., *The Politics of Retribution in Europe: World War II and its Aftermath* (Princeton: Princeton University Press, 2000); Jeffrey Herf, *Divided Memory: The Nazi Past and the Two Germanies* (Cambridge: Harvard University Press, 1997); Lisa Yoneyama, *Historical Traces: Time, Space and the Dialectics of Memory* (Berkeley: University of California Press,

in postwar Europe, found that postwar memories of World War II and the Holocaust evolved considerably over the course of five decades, and were shaped by a complex interplay between top-down and bottom up forces, both of which were significantly influenced by international, cross-national and trans-national discourses and interventions. External influences were most important in Germany, seeking to regain its standing in Western and international society, and more recently, in those Eastern European countries admitted to, or seeking admission to, the European Union and NATO. Some of the Eastern European states are in the process, often self-consciously, of bringing their memories and the identities they help to construct into line with those sanctioned and promoted by the European Union (EU) and NATO.[97]

Modern society's emphasis on individualism and free choice creates an entrenched predisposition to exaggerate the uniqueness of the inner self. But uniqueness can only exist as distinction, so identity is relational by definition. *Kleos* (fame) derived from the verb *kluein* (to hear). It indicates recognition, as Homer knew so well. Fame requires heroic deeds, bards to sing about those deeds and folk willing to listen and be impressed by them. Modern people need each other just as much as benchmarks against which to define themselves and to acknowledge, praise or vilify their behavior and achievements.[98] Kant captured this tension nicely when he observed that each person seeks "to achieve a rank among his fellows,

1999); Michael Molasky, *The American Occupation of Japan and Okinawa: Literature and Memory* (London: Routledge, 1999); Iyunolu Folayan Osagie, *The Armistad Revolt: Memory, Slavery, and the Politics of Memory in the United States and Sierra Leone* (Athens: University of Georgia Press, 2000); John Berry and Carol Berry, eds., *Genocide in Rwanda: A Collective Memory* (Washington, D.C.: Howard University Press, 1999); Stacy Beckwith, ed., *Charting Memory: Recalling Medieval Spain* (New York: Garland, 2000); Peter Bradley and David Cahill, *Habsburg Peru: Images, Imagination and Memory* (Liverpool: Liverpool University Press, 2000). For general reviews, see Jeffrey Olick and Joyce Robbins, "Social Memory Studies: From 'Collective Memory' to the Historical Sociology of Mnemonic Practices," *American Review of Sociology* 24 (1998), pp. 105–40, Richard Ned Lebow and Janice Gross Stein,"Memory, Democracy and Reconciliation," in Fogu, Kansteiner and Lebow, *The Politics of Memory in Postwar Europe*; Wulf Kansteiner, *Postmodern Historicism: The Liberation of History in the Age of Memory Studies*," forthcoming.

[97] Fogu, Kansteiner and Lebow, *The Politics of Memory in Postwar Europe*.

[98] One of my favorite Jewish jokes is about an avid golfer whose ambition is to play eighteen uninterrupted holes of golf. He belongs to a largely Jewish golf club and on Yom Kippur, instead of going to *shul*, suitably disguised, he sneaks onto the course with his bag of clubs. As he approaches the first hole, G-d and Moses, watching from on high, are not pleased. Our golfer tees off and his ball flies 300 yards down the fairway. As it comes to a halt, a rabbit grabs it and bolts for the woods. The golfer is enraged, but then watches in amazement as an eagle swoops down, snatches up the rabbit who disgorges the ball as they fly over the green. It lands an inch from the hole, where a startled chipmunk tips it in for a hole in one. A baffled Moses turns to G-d, and asks: "I thought you were going to punish him?" A smiling deity replies: "So, who can he tell?"

whom he cannot stand, but also cannot stand to leave alone."[99] Some decades back, the authors of *The Lonely Crowd* distinguished between "inner" and "other" direction. Inner-directed people acted in response to their own set of values and goals. Other-directed people had goals and values shaped by others and behaved in the ways intended to gain their approval.[100] But this distinction is exaggerated because even inner-directed people need to define themselves in opposition or in contrast to the identities and roles being foisted on them by society. Inner selves and individual identities cannot exist apart from society because membership and participation in society – or its rejection – is essential to the constitution of the self.

Homer, the Old Testament and the sacred texts of Hinduism recognized that societies are held together by narrative discourses. The stories we hear about others, and those we tell about ourselves, convey, reinforce and interpret values and roles. They define our values, goals and identities, encourage us to view the world or one another in certain ways, and make it difficult, sometimes impossible, to conceive of alternatives. In Book IX of the *Iliad*, Achilles spurns the gifts of Agamemnon as described to him by Odysseus. In effect, Achilles rejects the war, and with it, honor and the other motives that have spurred him to action in the past. He gives vent to rage because he lacks an alternative vocabulary that would allow him to formulate a new identity, desire or plan of action. Once his anger subsides, he is vulnerable to the pleadings of Odysseus to return to the fray. Beginning with Gramsci, modern thinkers picked up on this theme, but with a twist. Homer says nothing about the evolution of discourses, only about their defining consequences. Left-wing critics of capitalism have stressed the ability of elites and their publicists to shape discourses that effectively consolidate and preserve their economic and political hegemony by creating a "false consciousness" among the working class.[101] Their opponents assert that the concept of

[99] Immanuel Kant, *Ideas Toward a Universal History* in *Cambridge Edition of the Writings of Immanuel Kant* (Cambridge: Cambridge University Press, 1992–), 1, 8:20–21. Unless otherwise noted, all citations to Kant are from this edition.

[100] David Riesman in collaboration with Ruel Denney and Nathan Glazer, *The Lonely Crowd: A Study of the Changing American Character* (New Haven: Yale University Press, 1950).

[101] Antonio Gramsci, *Selections from the Prison Notebooks*, ed. and trans. Quintin Hoare and Geoffrey Nowell Smith (London: Wishart, 1971); Ralph Miliband, *The State in Capitalist Society* (London: Weidenfeld and Nicholson, 1969); Louis Althusser, *Reading Capital* (London: New Left Books, 1970); Frank Parkin, *Class, Inequality and the Political Order* (New York: Praeger, 1971); Jürgen Habermas, *Legitimation Crisis* (Boston: Beacon Press, 1975); Anthony Giddens, *The Class Structure of Advanced Societies* (New York: Harper, 1975); Nicos Poulantzas, *State, Power, Socialism* (London: New Left Books, 1978).

false consciousness mistakes public for hidden transcripts, and ignores all the evidence of behind-the-scenes, and not so hidden resistance to dominant discourses. They theorize that the more constrained subordinated classes are at the level of public practice, the freer they may be in the realm of thought and private practice.[102] Ironically, this practice may have become most pronounced in the socialist world where local literary figures and Western scholars have commented on the extent to which citizens made a show of loyalty and enthusiasm about things to which they were indifferent or actively abhorred to protect their private selves.[103]

Theories of institutionalism and hegemonic discourses claim to operate at the level of social control; their critics contend that the most they do is regulate practice. This distinction nicely parallels that between *hegemonia* and *archē*. The former uses power to shape a discourse that legitimizes authority and maintains it by behavior in accordance with the expectations of that discourse. The latter relies on institutions and police to compel outward compliance. The collapse of Soviet-imposed governments and institutions in Eastern Europe was the result of a failure to transform *archē* into *hegemonia*. When it became clear that Mikhail Gorbachev would not use the Red Army to maintain communist regimes in Eastern Europe, their days became numbered.[104] Compliance with the more extreme social and religious edicts of the Taliban disappeared almost overnight as their power crumbled throughout Afghanistan. The success of NATO and the EU – witnessed by the desires of Eastern Europeans for membership – does not necessarily mean that these institutions have reshaped the identities of their members.[105]

[102] Paul Willis, *Learning to Labour* (Westmead: Saxon House, 1970); Nicholas Abercrombie, Stephen Hill and Brusan S. Turner, *The Dominant Ideology Thesis* (London: Allen & Unwin, 1980); James C. Scott, *Weapons of the Weak: Everyday Forms of Peasant Resistance* (New Haven: Yale University Press, 1985), and *Hidden Transcripts*, pp. 70–107; Barrington Moore, Jr., *Injustice: The Social Bases of Obedience and Revolt* (White Plains, NY: M. E. Sharpe, 1987).

[103] Milosz, *The Captive Mind*, pp. 54–81; Ken Jowitt, *The New World Disorder: The Leninist Extinction* (Berkeley: University of California Press, 1992), pp. 79–80, 134–37. Oleg Kharhkhordin, *The Collective and the Individual in Russia: A Study of Practices* (Berkeley: University of California Press, 1999), contends that public performance, and more generally, the strategies required to negotiate public life, were reproduced in private life and became the basis for a distinct individuation that makes Russians very different from their Western counterparts.

[104] Lévesque, *The Enigma of 1989*; Evangelista, *Unarmed Forces*; English, *Russia and the Idea of the West*.

[105] There is growing and diverse literature on the subject of European identities. See, for example, Jacques Lenoble and Nicole Dewandre, eds., *L'Europe au soir du siècle: Identité et démocratie* (Paris: Éditions Espirt, 1992); Ole Waever, Barry Buzan, Morten Kelstrup and Pierre Lemaitre, eds., *Identity, Migration and the New Security Agenda in Europe*

To this point in my argument I have not questioned the conventional description of modern society as a collection of independent individuals. But it too mistakes ideology for practice. The Bill of Rights and the Constitution – a quintessential Enlightenment project – take the individual as their unit, as does the American legal system. The courts have extended this concept to corporations and other groups like trade unions who, for legal purposes, are treated as individuals. Unlike some other Western countries – Canada, for example – Congress and the courts have generally resisted the claims of groups qua groups for legal standing. Our laws and legal decisions are an important indicator of how we see ourselves, but there is always a gap, often a large one, between self-image and reality.

In practice, neither the United States nor any other developed country has ever come close to resembling a society of egoistic individuals. Sociopaths aside, the rest of us are embedded in a web of relationships – a *social habitus*, to use Mauss' language – that begins with families and personal relationships and extends out to business or professional ones and some mix of social, sporting, civic or religious groups and generally go beyond this to ethnic, regional and national identifications. We enter into these relationships, because we find purpose and fulfillment by sharing and acting in concert with other people.[106] Relationships and the affective ties, obligations and loyalties they generate give our lives meaning and direction. They not only constitute the cement of community, they teach us who we are. We have multiple identities – something well documented by psychologists – and many of them collective in the sense that we equate our well-being with that of others.[107] As Norbert Elias puts

(London: Pinter, 1993); Klaus Dieter Wolf, ed., *Projekt Europa im Übergang? Probleme, Modelle und Strategien des Regierens in der Europa* (Baden-Baden: Nomos, 1997); Reinhold Viehoff and Rien T. Siegers, eds., *Kultur, Identität, Europa: Über die Schwierigkeiten und Möglichkeiten einer Konstruktion* (Frankfurt: Suhrkampf, 1999); and Lars-Erik Cederman, "Political Boundaries and Identity Trade-Offs," in Cederman, ed., *Constructing Europe's Identity: The External Dimension*, pp. 1–34.

[106] In his *Philosophy of Right*, Hegel argued that the modern world consisted of three overlapping spheres of *Sittlichkeit* (ethical life). Together, they formed a social whole in which people found virtue and satisfaction through the obligations they developed in each sphere.

[107] Durkheim, *The Division of Labor in Society*, pp. xl–xli, 172–74. Henri Tajfel, *Human Groups and Social Categories* (Cambridge: Cambridge University Press, 1981); Henri Tajfel and John Turner, "The Social Identity Theory of Intergroup Behavior," in S. Worchel and W. Austin, eds., *Psychology of Intergroup Relations* (Chicago: Nelson-Hall, 1986), pp. 7–24; Marilynn Brewer, "The Social Self: On Being the Same and Different at the Same Time," *Personality and Social Psychology Bulletin* 17 (1991), pp. 475–82; Marilynn Brewer and Norman Miller, *Intergroup Relations* (Pacific Grove: Brooks-Cole, 1996); Stuart Kaufman, *Modern Hatreds: The Symbolic Politics of Ethnic War* (Ithaca: Cornell University Press, 2001); Richard Herrmann, Thomas Risse and Marilynn Brewer, *Identities in Europe and the Institutions of the European Union*, forthcoming.

it, the "I" is embedded in the "we." Scholars must start from the structure of relations *between* individuals in order to understand the identity of any of them.[108] The most compelling proof that the world is not composed of egoistic actors is the behavior of people who actually separate themselves from all social ties. For Greek playwrights, the individual freed from the bonds of family and community was something to be feared and pitied. Ajax, Antigone, and Electra were destructive to themselves, their families and their societies. We observe the same phenomenon at the international level. From Nazi Germany to North Korea, states that reject world society and seek to become truly autonomous actors have became self-destructive pariahs.

Thucydides casts Athens as a tragic hero whose power and hubris led it to break free from the traditional web of relationships and reciprocal obligations that bound cities to one another and restrained their foreign policy goals. Having severed these ties, Athens pursued a policy of unlimited expansion that led to loss of empire, defeat and near *stasis* at home. Since the end of the Cold War the United States has gone some way down the same perilous path – and for much the same reasons. So too have many Americans. For most of the time I worked on this book I lived in Columbus, Ohio, a prosperous Middle Western city whose self-image is one of hard-work, family values and community, all wrapped in a buckeye-studded American flag. I was constantly struck by the disparity between ideology and practice. Nowhere was this more apparent than on the roads where drivers no longer signal when they turn, showing flagrant disregard for other drivers and the idea of community. Running red lights is also routine. I frequently observed not one, but two and three drivers in a row go through a traffic signal that had already turned red. Accident statistics indicate that such behavior is extraordinarily dangerous; each year, more than 900 Americans die, and another 20,000 are injured in accidents arising out of cars running red lights.[109] It also risks an expensive traffic citation, and all for momentary gain – assuming that you do not have to stop at the next light. It is a perfect example of egoism run amok, and illustrates the general point, first made by Thucydides, that

[108] Norbert Elias, *The Society of Individuals*, ed. Michael Schröter, trans. Edmund Jephcott (Oxford: Basil Blackwell, 1991), pp. 61–62. Ian Burkitt, *Social Selves: Theories of the Social Formation of Personality* (London: Sage, 1991), for a thoughtful review of the literature that challenges the concept of the autonomous individual.

[109] These figures were provided by the Insurance Institute for Highway Safety, cited in W. G. Jurgensen, "Traffic-cop Cameras are Solid Idea," *Columbus Dispatch*, 9 October 2001, p. A 11. This is part of a general decline in courteous driving. The American Automobile Association's Foundation for Traffic Safety found more than a 50 percent rise in aggressive driving between 1990 and 1996. Cited in Putnam, *Bowling Alone*, pp. 142–43.

rational self-interest cannot exist outside a community and the language of justice on which it is based.

My examples are related. Bourgeois culture puts as much emphasis on the outward as the inward independence of the individual. Social hierarchy is not determined by kinship, but conceptualized in terms of dependence and independence. For the English political theorists, dependency – being at the mercy of another's will – deprives one of "completeness" as a human being.[110] Charlotte Brontë's novels elaborate this understanding and show how a dependent person is seen by society to be included in another's identity. In bourgeois society, people must strive to achieve and assert their independence, and the latter is frequently synonymous with control over others. Such a culture has become increasingly dominant in the United States, and the need of people who resent the extent to which they are at the mercy of others to establish their independence in symbolic ways has become correspondingly greater. The roads and highways offer a daily opportunity to proclaim one's independence, just as passionate support for sports teams offer the prospect of delicious, if vicarious and short-lived, moments of domination. The same psychological process may help account for why an increasing percentage of the population see no reason for taxes, and oppose programs that may benefit the society as a whole but have no immediate personal payoffs. American social science contributes to this trend by placing individuals and their narrowly constructed self-interest at the center of its analytical world. It makes the current state of affairs appear a reflection of the natural order, and, by doing so, helps to make it self-fulfilling.

The concept of individual identity emerged only gradually from collective conceptions of identity based on roles.[111] According to Amartya Sen, self-interest was not used as the first principle of an economic model until the late nineteenth century.[112] Other economists insist that this did not happen until the publication in 1942 of Joseph Schumpeter's influential

[110] Macpherson, *The Political Theory of Possessive Individualism.*

[111] Norbert Elias, *The History of Manners: The Civilizing Process*, I (Oxford: Basil Blackwell, 1978), and *State Formation and Civilization: The Civilizing Process*, II (Oxford: Basil Blackwell, 1882), contends that the self-perception of individuals developed among the aristocracy during the late Middle Ages and the early Renaissance in response to the emergence of the state and its imposition of abstract rules of behavior. These rules gradually become internalized and the concomitant emergence of the individual "ego" encouraged individual self-perception. The idea of self then found expression in the writings of Renaissance philosophers, and later, of René Descartes (1596–1650).

[112] Amartya K. Sen, "Rational Fools: A Critique of the Behavioral Foundations of Economic Theory," in H. Harris, ed., *Scientific Models and Men* (Oxford: Oxford University Press, 1978), pp. 317–44, attributes this innovation to F. Y. Edgeworth, *Mathematical Psychics: An Essay on the Application of Mathematics to the Moral Sciences* (London: C. K. Paul, 1881).

theory of political and economic behavior.[113] Readers might object that some of the greatest modern philosophers, including Hobbes, conceived of the state of nature as composed of fully autonomous, egoistic and rational individuals who negotiated social contracts to escape from violence and disorder. This would be a misreading of Hobbes. For Enlightenment philosophers, contracts were convenient fictions that allowed them to reconcile self-interest with authority and provide a logical foundation for order. None of them, with the possible exception of Locke, conceived of human beings as autonomous and rational, or believed that contracts could be negotiated in a state of nature. Hobbes was adamant that contracts required trust, the very condition that was lacking in the state of nature. Order could only be imposed by a Leviathan.[114] He was equally certain that any analogy between the state of nature and international politics was inappropriate. States do not have the same incentives to leave the state of nature. While even the strongest man needs to sleep, states can keep a constant watch by having people work in shifts.

For liberal philosophers, autonomous rational agents and the contracts they negotiated performed the same role that such agents do for contemporary theories of rational choice – with one big difference. Grotius, Hobbes and Locke used contracts as thought experiments to help them construct deductive foundations for political orders. They never intended or expected that their systems, or the assumptions on which they were based, would be taken literally as recipes for community, or used to explain or predict political behavior. Modern social science, and rational choice in particular, is an expression, product, and even vehicle of modernity. It crystalizes modernity's constitutive pathology of trying to turn abstract discourse into concrete reality. Its proponents *believe* that their assumptions, if not fully descriptive of reality, provide a close enough fit for them to model complex human behavior. Modern realism may be the most extreme example of this conceit, but it is only one example of a class of approaches that dominate international relations and social science more generally.

[113] Joseph Schumpeter, *Capitalism, Socialism and Democracy* (New York: Harper & Row, 1963 [1942]); Jane J. Mansbridge, "The Rise and Fall of Self-Interest in the Explanation of Political Life," in Mansbridge, ed., *Beyond Self-Interest* (Chicago: University of Chicago Press, 1990), pp. 3–24.

[114] Hobbes, *Leviathan*, II, xvii, p. 117, writes that "Covenants, without the sword, are but Words, of no strength to secure a man at all." Christopher Jencks, "The Social Basis of Unselfishness," in Herbert J. Gans, Nathan Glazer, Joseph Gusfield and Christopher Jencks, eds., *On the Making of Americans: Essays in Honor of David Riesman* (Philadelphia: University of Pennsylvania Press, 1979), pp. 63–86, notes that for Hobbes, moral ideas, not compulsion, also explain why we abide by the social contract. Kratochwil, *Rules, Norms and Decisions*, pp. 113–17.

Internal motivation vs. external constraint

The dominant ontology has a second core assumption: actors respond primarily to external stimuli. Realist, liberal and institutionalist approaches all focus on the constraints and opportunities created by the environment. They reward certain kinds of behavior and punish others, and shape actors indirectly through a process of natural selection, or directly by influencing their cost calculus. The latter may be accomplished by creating a "shadow of the future," lowering information costs or establishing a pattern of interactions that makes coordination more efficient for everyone. Cooperation may emerge as the unintentional outcome of cumulative self-interested behavior.[115] "Tit-for-tat," considered by many one of the most robust theories of cooperation, is a prominent representative of this approach; it assumes that actors will cooperate or defect in response to the previous choices of others with whom they interact.[116] As we have seen, this premise is also central for Alexander Wendt, for whom behavior is shaped by external incentives and constraints. His "alter" and "ego" construct their system on the basis of mutual interactions, and once that system is established, it creates strong incentives for both the founders and other actors to conform.[117] Theories of this kind sometimes allow for differences in the character of actors; Bueno de Mesquita, for example, introduces a distinction between risk-prone and risk-averse actors – but these actor level characteristics are second-level refinements for theories that rely on environmental cues as their principal mechanisms.[118]

By contrast, theories of foreign policy at the state level are based on differences among actors. They build typologies of strong and weak states

[115] For influential research of this kind, see Mancur Olson, *The Logic of Collective Action* (Cambridge, Mass.: Harvard University Press, 1965); George Stigler and Gary Becker, "De Gustibus Non Est Disputandum," *American Economic Review* 67: 2 (1977), pp. 76–90; William Gamson, "The Social Psychology of Collective Action," in Aldon D. Morris and Carol McClurg Mueller, *Frontiers in Social Movement Theory* (New Haven: Yale University Press, 1992), pp. 53–76.

[116] Robert Axelrod, *Evolution of Cooperation* (New York: Basic Books, 1984), starts from the premise that actors are autonomous and egoistic and that cooperation can emerge from entirely self-interested behavior. Tit-for-tat assumes at least part of the cooperation it attempts to explain. Actors all play the game according to the rules, and part of the reason they do is that the tournament is run by an outsider who compels them to abide by the rules. Alexander Wendt, "Collective Identity Formation and the International State," *American Political Science Review* 88 (June 1994), pp. 384–96 observes, Axelrod's formulation of tit-for-tat also ignores the way in which repeated interactions can transform identities and interests in the course of the game.

[117] Wendt, *Social Theory of International Politics*, pp. 326–36.

[118] Bruce Bueno de Mesquita, *The War Trap* (New Haven: Yale University Press, 1981), pp. 34–35.

and societies, modernizing and traditional elites or democracies versus other forms of government. Morgenthau's theory is founded on a threefold typology of foreign policy goals. The democratic peace is the most recent effort to explain cooperation – or at least the absence of war – in terms of state level characteristics. This burgeoning literature developed largely in response to the empirical finding that democracies do not fight one another, and much of the discussion is about the robustness and significance of this finding. The democratic peace remains undertheorized, and there is no agreement about the mechanisms responsible. Building on Kant, Michael Doyle contends that democracies have liberal cultures that eschew war and violence, putting a premium on peaceful conflict resolution. They value what Kant calls "the spirit of commerce," which structures cooperation and community through trade. Other scholars suggest that elections make leaders answerable to public opinion. Democratic states thus expect their counterparts to behave more peacefully, and are more confident about monitoring their military preparations.[119] Most of these explanations, by reinforcing economic and political costs, also take the form of external constraints on leaders. Only the Kantian explanation stresses the *internal* causes of peace: common practices that construct common discourse and identities which have subtle but powerful influences on expectations and behavior.[120] As currently formulated, democratic peace theory, like its institutionalist counterpart, may mistake symptoms for causes.[121]

[119] The literature on this subject is vast. A relevant sampling includes, Bruce Russett, *Grasping the Democratic Peace: Principles for a Post-Cold War World* (Princeton: Princeton University Press, 1993); John Owen, "How Liberalism Produces the Democratic Peace," *International Security* 19 (Fall 1994), pp. 87–125; James Lee Ray, *Democracy and International Conflict: An Evaluation of the Democratic Peace Proposition* (Columbia: University of South Carolina Press, 1995); "How Liberalism Produces the Democratic Peace," *International Society* 20 (1994), pp. 87–125; Michael Williams, "The Discipline of the Democratic Peace: Kant, Liberalism and the Social Constructivism of Security Communities," *European Journal of International Relations* 7 (December 2001), pp. 525–54.

[120] Bonnie Honig, *Political Theory and the Displacement of Politics* (Ithaca: Cornell University Press, 1993), argues that recognition (of who is a democratic state) is part of process of subject-construction and identity formation within and between liberal-democratic states. For Kant, the concept of respect lies at the core of this social recognition. Respect is extended to actors who recognize and act on the categorical imperative and the moral law (*Achtung*) within themselves. It comes about through emotion and reason. Williams, "The Discipline of the Democratic Peace," pp. 525–54, extends this argument to the democratic peace and NATO.

[121] William R. Thompson, "Democracy and Peace: Putting the Cart Before the Horse?," *International Organization* 50 (Winter 1996), pp. 141–74, offers a more extreme formulation of this argument. He argues that "Zones of peace" may be a necessary antecedent for democratic states to emerge. Such zones also depend on the construction of some degree of common identity.

Philosophers, ancient and modern, have sought the explanation for cooperation *within* the minds of actors.[122] Grotius, Pufendorf, Hobbes, Hume and Smith recognized that people need each other to achieve their individual goals, and that recognition of this need impels them toward society and the social life.[123] Feelings were central for the liberal philosophers. Hobbes considered "fellow-feeling" and the sympathy for others it engendered to be natural proclivities of human beings.[124] Adam Smith thought that moral ideas derived from feelings of empathy. Our ability to experience the pain and pleasure of others, and our desire to have them experience ours, keeps us from being entirely selfish. Feelings are responsible for ethics because they provide the incentive to understand and evaluate our behavior as others see, experience and judge it.[125] While not insensitive to the role of emotions, Kant emphasized the central role of reason in producing knowledge and self-enforcing ethics. Social antagonism provides an incentive for us to develop our rational faculties. We use these faculties to advance our own selfish ends, primarily by means of calculation and communication with others.[126] When our reason fully

[122] The strongest formulation of internal motivation is Rousseau, who writes in *Emile* that "the heart receives laws only from itself." *Oeuvres*, IV.521; *Emile*, p. 234. The most important exceptions may be Hume and Hegel. David Hume, *The Philosophical Works*, ed. Thomas H. Green and Thomas H. Grose (Aalen: Scientica, 1964), II, p. 105, explains society entirely in terms of the selfish motives of actors. Hegel, *Philosophy of Right*, trans. T. M. Knox (Oxford: Oxford University Press, 1942), Sections190, 199, 209E, for whom the family is a unit of feeling, held together by affection. But cooperation in what he calls "civil society" is brought about by the "cunning of reason," which, like Smith's "invisible hand," is an external mechanism. J. B. Schneewind, *The Invention of Autonomy: A History of Modern Moral Philosophy* (New York: Cambridge University Press, 1998), p. 4, reminds us that the emphasis on internal motivation is part of the general assault, during the seventeenth and eighteenth centuries, on traditional conceptions of morality based on obedience. Enlightenment moral philosophers conceived of morality as self-governance, and this in turn provided the justification for people to assume control of their lives in a wide range of domains. Reid, Bentham and Kant are all important figures in this transition. Charles Taylor, *Sources of the Self: The Making of Modern Identity* (Cambridge: Harvard University Press, 1989), p. 83, makes a similar argument.

[123] Hugo Grotius, *De jure belli ac pacis libri tres*, trans. Frances W. Kelsey (Oxford: Oxford University Press, 1925), Prolegomena, § 6, p. 11, quoting Marcus Aurelius; Samuel Pufendorf, *De jure naturae et gentium libri octo*, trans. C. H. Oldfather and W. A. Oldfather (Oxford: Oxford University Press, 1934), I, ii, pp. 154–78; Adam Smith, *The Theory of Moral Sentiments*, ed. D. D. Raphael and A. L. Macfie (Oxford: Oxford University Press, 1976), I, 1, i, §§ 3–5, p. 10, and II, ii–iii § 1, p. 85.

[124] Hobbes, *Leviathan*, I, vi, p. 126; Onuf, *The Republican Legacy* and "Normative Frameworks for Humanitarian Intervention," forthcoming.

[125] Adam Smith, *The Theory of Moral Sentiments* (Oxford: Oxford University Press, 1976 [1759]), Section I.1–2, II, 4, III, 2.33.

[126] In Kant's terminology, human experience results from intuitions (*Anschauungen*) and concepts (*Begriffe*). Objects are given to us through sensibility (*Sinnlichkeit*), which produces intuitions. Objects are also thought about, leading to understanding (*Verstand*),

develops, it grasps the fundamental law of humanity: the absolute equality and dignity of all human beings. Reason now becomes the vehicle for helping us overcome our competitive propensity and cooperate with other human beings on the basis of equality to achieve common goals. For Kant, like the liberal philosophers, cooperation is not a function of external stimuli, but an expression of the *internal* moral development of human beings.[127] He alleged that this was true of states as well as individuals, and the basis for a "perpetual peace" founded on a *civitas gentium*.[128]

The German idealist and, to a lesser extent, the Anglo-American liberal traditions looked back to Aristotle and his conception of human beings as political animals who could only find fulfillment in the life of the polis. Poleis were created and sustained by affection and friendship (*philia*), because these bonds encourage us to define our happiness in terms of the well-being of our family, friends and fellow citizens. *Philoi* constitute expanding circles of affective networks that cumulatively add up to the civic project (*koinōnia*).[129] Citizenship is the active sharing of power among equals in contrast to the hierarchical relations of the *oikos*.[130] Plato also considered friendship the foundation of community because it created an atmosphere of trust in which meaningful dialogue and justice became possible. Plato's dialogues allow Socrates to demonstrate in practice that it is the surest route for reaching common conclusions in a cooperative way. For Plato and Aristotle, philosophy also encouraged the kind of introspection that had the potential of turning the soul toward

and through understanding to concepts. *Critique of Pure Reason* [1881], Axi–xii, A19–20/B33–34, 738–39, B766–67; *What Does it Mean to Orient Oneself in Thinking?* [1786], 8:144–6, in *Religion and Rational Theology*; *Critique of the Power of Judgment*, 5:293–8; *Ideal Toward a Universal History*, I, 8:20–21. Allen W. Wood, *Kant's Moral Religion* (Ithaca: Cornell University Press, 1970).

127 Kant, *Groundwork of Metaphysics*, 4:428–9, 435; *Conjectural Beginning of Human History*, 8:114; *Metaphysics of Morals*, 6:314, 27.463, in *Lectures on Ethics*; Schneewind, *The Invention of Autonomy* p. 521; Allen W. Wood, "Kant's Practical Philosophy," in Karl Ameriks, ed., *The Cambridge Companion to German Idealism* (Cambridge: Cambridge University Press, 2000), pp. 57–75.

128 Michael W. Doyle, "Kant, Liberal Legacies, and Foreign Affairs: Part 1," and "Kant, Liberal Legacies, and Foreign Affairs: Part 2," *Philosophy and Public Affairs* 12 (1983), pp. 205–35 and 323–53, and "Liberalism and World Politics," *American Political Science Review* 80 (December 1986), pp. 1151–169; Onuf, *The Republican Legacy*; pp. 230–32; Reinhard Kosseleck, *Critique and Crisis: The Enlightenment and the Pathogenesis of Modern Society* (Oxford: Berg, 1988).

129 Aristotle, *Politics*, 1253a2–3, and Chapter 7, this vol. for a discussion of *philia*.

130 For Plato, *Republic*, 419a–421a, the ideal community is one in which benefits are distributed fairly, according to some generally accepted principle of justice. See also, Aristotle, *Nicomachean Ethics*, Books 9, 10 and 1155a23, and b29–31, and *Politics*, 1280b29–40.

justice.[131] Hannah Arendt has argued that the absence of *philia*, and a resulting inability to see the world through the eyes of other people, is what made Adolf Eichmann into one of the greatest criminals of the twentieth century.[132]

These philosophical arguments are prefigured by Sophocles, whose *Philoctetes* emphasized the difference between persuasion (*peithō*), achieved by consultation about mutual interests, and deceit (*dolos*). *Philoctetes* is about who we are and who we can become through honest dialogue with others. Odysseus, the master of deceitful stratagems, fails to grasp the essential truth that our principal wealth is not material, but social and cultural. It consists of the relationships of trust we build with neighbors and friends and the reciprocity generated, and helps sustain these relationships and the broader communities to which we all belong.[133] In Chapter 7 I described one of the founding myths of ancient Greece in which Zeus sent Hermes to give cavemen *aidōs* (respect, reverence) and *dikē* (justice) so they could live together harmoniously. *Dikē* is an ordering principle that requires people to treat others as equals, attempt to see things from their point of view and empathize with them. *Aidōs* enforces justice through shame. Together, they create the ties of friendship (*desmoi philias sunagōgoi*) that bring order to cities.[134]

Kant thought that *xenia* was probably the one universal standard of honorable conduct.[135] Many of the world's great moral-philosophical traditions share more fundamental understandings of human beings, among them the belief that affection and reciprocity are the basis for cooperation and community. The Mishnah says that "The reward for a good deed is another good deed; and the penalty for a transgression is another transgression."[136] Kung Fuzi (Master Kung), known as Confucius in the West, insisted that rulers treat people as they would like to be treated.

[131] *Dialektikē* derives from *dialegesthai* (to engage in conversation). Plato, *Republic*, 509d–511d and 531d–534e. Aristotle stresses the role of reason in leading one to virtue and a good life, an argument he develops in the *Eudemian* and *Nicomachean Ethics*. John M. Cooper, "Contemplation and Happiness: A Reconsideration," and "Reason, Moral Virtue, and Moral Value," both in Cooper, *Reason and Emotion*, pp. 212–36, 253–80.

[132] Hannah Arendt, *Eichmann in Jerusalem: A Report on the Banality of Evil* (New York: Viking, 1964), pp. 287–88; J. Peter Euben, "Reading Democracy: 'Socratic' Dialogues and the Political Education of Democratic Citizens," in Ober and Hedrick, *Dēmokratia*, pp. 327–59.

[133] James Boyd White, *Heracles' Bow: Essays on the Rhetoric and Poetics of the Law* (Madison: University of Wisconsin Press, 1985), pp. 3–27; Alasdair MacIntyre, *After Virtue*, 2nd ed. rev. (Notre Dame: Notre Dame University Press, 1984), p. 134.

[134] Plato, *Protagoras*, 322c8–322d5.

[135] Immanuel Kant, "Perpetual Peace," in Hans Reiss, ed., *Kant's Political Writings*, trans. H. B. Nisbet (Cambridge: Cambridge University Press, 1991), pp. 105–08.

[136] *Pikey Avot*, 4.2.

He believed that cooperation was sustained by filial devotion, humaneness and ritual; these sentiments and practices give rise to loyalty and reciprocity.[137]

Experimental economists have found empirical support for the universality of reciprocity as a principle. One of their more robust findings is the extent to which people are willing to forgo material gain to punish others who would deny their equality.[138] The standard format for this research is a game in which two players must decide how to share $100 or an equivalent sum of money. A coin toss determines the roles of proposer and responder. The proposer makes a single offer to share the money on any basis he or she wants, and the responder can accept or reject the offer. The two players are kept apart and both are informed beforehand that no further communication will be allowed beyond the initial offer and response. If the proposer's offer is accepted, the $100 is distributed in accordance with the terms of that offer. If it is rejected, neither side receives any money. In almost all cultures, two-thirds of the proposers offer the responder 40–50 percent of the total; only four out of a hundred offer less than 20 percent. More than half of all responders reject offers of less than 20 percent. They prefer to forego any gain to prevent proposers from making what, in their judgment, is an unfair gain. A review of the literature concludes that the experiments "all point to one conclusion: we do not adopt a purely self-centered viewpoint but take account of our co-player's outlook. We are not interested solely in our own payoff but compare ourselves with the other part and demand fair play."[139]

[137] Benjamin I. Schwartz, *The World of Thought in Ancient China* (Cambridge: Harvard University Press, 1985), pp. 56–134; Irene Bloom, "Confucius and the Analects," in Wm. Theodore de Bary and Irene Bloom, eds., *Sources of Chinese Tradition*, I: *From Earliest Times to 1600* (New York: Columbia University Press, 1999), pp. 41–44; "Selections from the Analects," in de Bary and Bloom, *Sources of Chinese Tradition*, 4:15, p. 49.

[138] Karl Sigmund, *Games of Life: Explorations in Ecology, Evolution and Behavior* (Harmondsworth: Penguin, 1995); Kenneth G. Binmore, *Game Theory and the Social Contract: Just Playing* (Cambridge, Mass.: MIT Press, 1998); Armin Falk, Ernst Fehr and Urs Fischbacher, "On the Nature of Fair Behavior," Institute for Empirical Research in Economics, University of Zurich, Working Paper No. 17, August 1999; Martin A. Nowak, Karen M. Page and Karl Sigmund, "Fairness versus Reason in the Ultimatum Game," *Science* 289, 8 September 2000, pp. 980–94. Joseph Henrich *et al.*, "In Search of Homo Economicus: Behavioral Experiments in 15 Small-Scale Societies," *American Economic Review* 91 (May 2001), pp. 73–78, report on the conduct of a variety of related games in fifteen hunter-gatherer, nomadic and other small-scale societies. Economic man finds no support in any of the games or societies, but variation across groups is best explained by the degree of market integration and the more real life economic payoffs for participants are dependent on cooperation. Both findings suggest that people can to some degree be socialized into behaving in accord in the expectations of economic man, but that important residual commitments to fairness and reciprocity remain.

[139] Karl Sigmund, Ernest Fehr and Martin A. Nowak, "The Economics of Fair Play," *Scientific American* 286 (January 2002), pp. 82–87.

Experimental economists and game theorists have struggled to come up with explanations for behavior seemingly so at odds with the logic of *homo economicus*. Some acknowledge a widespread concern for fairness and reciprocity, but others suggest that participants fail to understand the game, and incorrectly expect a second round. Still others hypothesize that the game reveals an evolutionary atavism; for millions of years people lived in small groups whose functioning depended on trust and openness. "Our emotions are thus not finely tuned to interactions occurring under strict anonymity."[140] Sophisticated social scientists can look the truth in the face and not see it – when it violates their cherished assumptions.

Greek and modern philosophers, the Jewish and Confucian traditions, classical realism, and at least some social scientists, point us toward a similar, if not the same, understanding of the origins of cooperation and civil order.[141] Cooperation is possible when people recognize its benefits. These benefits are not only material, and this recognition is not brought about by external constraints and opportunities, but by introspection and experience. They bring some of us – individuals, communities and states – to deeper understandings of our interests and the recognition that we cannot become ourselves outside of close relations with other people. At every level of interaction, from personal relationships to business and politics, we become willing to forego certain short-term gains to sustain these relationships and the principles of justice on which they rest. Viewed in this light, the emergence of the EU, the end of the Cold War and the survival of NATO represent triumphs of higher-order learning.[142] By contrast, the foreign policies of the Clinton and Bush administrations, like the policies of Enron, Arthur Anderson and WorldCom, are a retrogression to a more primitive, self-centered and inevitably counterproductive way of thinking about oneself and the world.

There is a deeper philosophical point here having to do with the nature of reason. The Enlightenment installed reason at the apex of its Pantheon

[140] Ibid., p. 85.

[141] For a sampling of literature on reciprocity and collective identity, see Craig Calhoun, "The Problem of Identity in Collective Action," in Joan Huber, ed., *Macro-Micro Linkage in Sociology* (Beverly Hills: Sage, 1991), pp. 51–76; Alberto Melucci, *Nomads of the Present* (London: Hutchinson, 1989); Aldon Morris and Carol McClura Mueller, eds., *Frontiers in Social Movement Theory* (New Haven: Yale University Press, 1992); Amartya Sen, "Goals, Commitments and Identity," *Journal of Law, Economics, and Organization* 20 (1992), pp. 341–55; Robyn Dawes, Alphons J. C. Van der Kragt and John Orbell, "Cooperation for the Benefit of Us – Not Me, or My Conscience," in Mansbridge, *Beyond Self-Interest*, pp. 97–110.

[142] I have developed this argument in more detail in "The Long Peace, the End of the Cold War, and the Failure of Realism," *International Organization* 48 (Spring 1994), pp. 249–77, Richard Ned Lebow and Janice Gross Stein, *We All Lost the Cold War* (Princeton: Princeton University Press, 1994), and Herrmann and Lebow, eds., *Learning from the Cold War*.

while at the same time reducing it to a mere instrumentality. For Plato, reason had desires of its own; its purpose was to discover the ends of life and educate the spirit and appetite so they would want to collaborate harmoniously to achieve these ends. For Hume, the quintessential Enlightenment philosopher, this relationship was reversed. Reason became "slave to the passions," and its assignment was finding efficient means of attaining goals – what Max Weber would later call "instrumental reason."[143] In accord with this understanding, modern social science, in contrast to ancient philosophy, is overwhelmingly focused on means instead of ends. It treats ends as either exogenous (as with most preference structures) or something that reason readily infers from the environment (e.g., the putative concern for relative gain in an anarchical international system). Unlike classical realism, modern realism and much of social science, largely misses or ignores the ways in which reason can promote new understandings, reshape ends and constrain or rechannel appetites and the spirit. It is this kind of learning that brings about cooperation at the individual and international levels and is thus a proper subject of social science.

Interests, order and ethics

For Thucydides, Plato and Aristotle and some modern philosophers, cooperation and the civic project (*koinōnia*) are ultimately an expression of our *innate* sociability. Man is a political animal, as Aristotle so aptly put it, and we are driven by our instincts to associate with others to realize our own needs and potential. However, the instinctual sociability of human beings is insufficient to bring about or sustain a functioning social order.[144] Relationships and the commitments they entail are not simply instrumental means to selfish ends, but important ends in their own right. Instinctual and rational processes are mutually reinforcing. We become who we are through close association with others. As Charles Taylor observes, "we become full human agents, capable of understanding ourselves, and hence of defining our identity," only through dialogue with others.[145] Our interests depend on identity, and identity in turn depends on community. One of the reasons that Hobbes invoked the state

[143] David Hume, *A Treatise of Human Nature*, eds., David Fate Norton and Mary Norton (Oxford: Oxford University Press, 2000), 2.3.3.4. See also *An Inquiry Concerning the Principles of Morals*, ed. Tom L. Beauchamp (New York: Oxford University Press, 1998), Appendix I, p. 163.

[144] Aristotle, *Politics*, 1253a30, is contrasting human beings to other gregarious animals, and 1252b28–1253a39 on the city (*politeia*) as being necessary to allow people to fulfill their purposes as human beings.

[145] Charles Taylor, *The Malaise of Modernity* (Toronto: Anansi Press, 1991), p. 33.

of nature was to show that deprived of an identity, we all become more or less identical, and our only interests are the fundamental requisites of survival – food, clothing, shelter and sex.[146] Identity confers interests because it gives us social purpose and allows for differentiation.

My argument has implications for ethics. Before I elaborate them, I want to clarify what I mean by ethics. In modern discourse we generally distinguish between morality and ethics. Morality derives from *moralis*, Cicero's rendering of the Greek *ēthikos*. For fifth- and fourth-century Greeks, *ēthikos* was the set of character traits that influenced behavior.[147] Modern usage transforms ethics from an expression of our identities into formally constituted sets of rules, often based on some claim of universal validity. I use the term in the Greek sense in the expectation that restoring the connection between ourselves and our ethics may finesse an otherwise unsolvable metaphysical problem. Once we recognize that we cannot have identities and interests in the absence of justice – an argument I shall presently make – it follows that we have a deeper interest in upholding these principles of justice.

The Enlightenment rejected the Aristotelian conception of *telos* as unfounded superstition. Prominent Enlightenment and counter – Enlightenment thinkers were committed to a praxis based on individual differentiation and mutual respect. Hobbes, a prominent exponent of this outlook, denies that there is a "finis ultimus, utmost aim, or summum bonum, highest good, such as is spoken of in the books of the ancient philosophers."[148] But without *telos*, there was no longer any empirical benchmark for assessing the good. Philosophers from Kant on struggled to build an alternative foundation for traditional moral codes, but failed because they could not find any incontrovertible first principles. Attempts to base such systems on reason or sentiment invite rejection on the grounds that they are arbitrary and culturally biased.[149] But it may be possible to root ethics, although not a particular code, in observable empirical regularities. This was the approach of the pre-Aristotelian Greeks for whom primordial world experience, mediated by language, was the foundation for all philosophy.

My argument is ontological, and based on the connections we have discovered linking interest, identity, community and justice. Interest requires identity, because it confers social purpose. Identity is a form of differentiation, without which people would not have particular social interests.

[146] My colleague Alexander Stephan rightly insists that I add tennis to the list.
[147] MacIntyre, *After Virtue*, p. 38.
[148] Thomas Hobbes, *Leviathan*, 1.11.
[149] Ibid., pp. 48–49, 54–55, 58–59. For a recent, thoughtful attempt to ground ethics in our intuitions, see Taylor, *Sources of the Self*.

Identity in turn depends upon the existence of community. Communities construct identities through their discourses, which embed values, social roles and expectations concerning their performance. They also establish the hierarchies on which social differentiation depends. Viable communities rest on some conception of justice, acceptable to most members of the community, without which hierarchy would not be tolerated. Thucydides understood this fundamental political truth. He praises Pericles for creating a constitution in which one man in effect ruled, but in the interest of the many, making his rule palatable to them. He recognizes the important difference between a society's recognition of the inherent equality of all citizens, and the degree to which this equality is actually implemented in the political, economic and social spheres. The former is an essential building block of community, while the latter varies from society to society, and within societies over time.[150]

Thucydides also recognized that all communities are bounded, that the Greek community was distinct from the non-Greek world, and that Greeks behaved, and were expected to behave, differently toward non-Greeks. The boundaries of community were less problematic in Clausewitz's time, where they were generally thought to be coterminous with Christian Europe. But boundary issues again emerged as critical in the post-war and post-Cold War era. This is not the place to delve into this question in any detail, but only to note that the concept of a European and North Atlantic identity has assumed real substance, and a larger community of developed nations may be in the process of taking shape. It is an open question as to whether those communities can cohere in as meaningful a way as pan-Hellenism in the fifth century BCE, and if they do, whether they require the existence of a similar demonized "other." Justice in turn is almost always based on recognition of the fundamental equality of human beings, honored in practice to varying degrees. Most of the world's religions and ethical traditions describe this equality as an outgrowth of *philia* or affection that people develop toward one other. Such affection appears to be both a natural attribute of our species but also something that comes about through the use of our rational faculties. Reasoning in reverse, it follows that all of us have a strong, even primary, interest in maintaining community and the general principles of equality on which it is based. Without it, we cannot have societies, identities or interests.

Moving from these ontological claims to the meaning of justice in any social context is an altogether different matter. It has proven impossible

[150] For a modern discussion of this difference, see Stuart Hampshire, *Justice as Conflict* (Princeton: Princeton University Press, 2001).

to establish by logic first principles on which ethical systems can be based. Ethical orders must develop within societies and become legitimized through practice over the course of time. There is nothing organic, natural or mystical about ethical orders, but at any given time they represent the culmination of a long and complicated historical process. They are the result of a multitude of decisions by people, acting unilaterally or collectively, with consequences that may be unintended or unforseen. These orders sanction certain pathways for attaining or justifying one's goals, and by doing so, create incentives for people to use them. Well-trodden paths give the appearance of being natural and in turn help to legitimize and maintain the orders that created them. It was this recognition that prompted Heraclitus to insist that "the people must fight for the law just as for the city wall."[151] One of the distinguishing features of modern society is the extent to which people have become aware of this process, and try to free themselves from inherited identities – or impose new identities on others through control of the state and its institutions, especially the educational system and the media.

Such a process began in Greece. The political system of Athens was the result of multiple experiments at constitutional engineering. The reforms of Solon, Cleisthenes and Pericles were all efforts to adapt the political system to changing circumstances.[152] They attempted to reduce internal divisions and strengthen loyalty to the polis by removing onerous economic burdens on the underprivileged, breaking up traditional patterns of affiliation that competed with the polis for loyalty and extending the class base of political participation. Classical realists are part of this tradition; Thucydides, Clausewitz and Morgenthau believed that political orders, and the pattern of social relations they support, must periodically be renegotiated, especially in the aftermath of destructive wars.

None of our classical realists said very much about the *process* by which social orders should be renegotiated. For this we must turn to turn to their contemporaries. Gorgias (*circa* 430 BCE) summed up the Greek *logos* as a "great potentate, who with the tiniest and least visible body achieves the most divine works." When employed in tandem with persuasion, he proclaimed, it "shapes the soul as it wishes."[153] Thucydides recognized the power of language, but also the danger of rhetoric when

[151] Frg. 44, Dennis Sweet, *Heraclitus: Translation and Analysis* (Lanham, Ms.: University Press of America, 1995), p. 19.

[152] Solon's reforms (*c*. 594–93) and those of Cleisthenes (510–500) made every Athenian a freeman and citizen. The restriction of the powers of the Areopagus Council in 462 had the effect of vesting political authority in the assembly (*ekklēsia*). By 431, large numbers of citizens took an active role in government through participation in the assembly and the courts (*dikastēria*) where they served as judge and jury.

[153] DK, frg. 82, B II, 8, and 13–14.

employed by clever people seeking selfish ends. Plato's Socrates had a similarly low opinion of rhetoric, and developed dialogue as an alternative. Quite apart from its ability to produce a consensual outcome through reason, the free exchange of ideas among friends and the give-and-take of discussion strengthened the bonds of friendship and respect that were the foundation of community. Such a process might even be possible – indeed, was all the more essential – in a society in which individuals have become increasingly autonomous. Plato portrays Socrates' life as a dialogue with his polis, and his acceptance of its death sentence as his final commitment to maintain the coherence and principle of that dialogue. Plato structures his dialogues to suggest that Socrates' positions do not represent any kind of final truth. His interlocutors often make arguments that Socrates cannot fully refute, or chooses not to, pointing readers towards a holistic contemplation of dialogue and the understanding that its tensions can lead to more comprehensive and tolerant understandings.[154]

Socrates' emphasis on dialogue has been revived in the twentieth century, and is central to the thought and writings of figures as diverse as Mikhail Bakhtin, Hans-Georg Gadamer and Jürgen Habermas. Bakhtin suggests that even solitary reflection derives from dialogues with others against whom or with whom we struggle to establish ourselves and our ideas.[155] Habermas' "critique of ideology" leads him to propose a coercion-free discourse that departs from human praxis.[156] For Gadamer, dialogue "is the art of having a conversation, and that includes the art of having a conversation with oneself and fervently seeking and understanding of oneself."[157] It is not so much a method, as a philosophical enterprise that puts people in touch with themselves and others, and reveals to them the prior determinations, anticipations, and imprints that reside in their concepts. Experiencing the other through dialogue can lead to *ekstasis*, or the experience of being outside of oneself. Dialogue

154 This last point is made by John M. Cooper, "Socrates and Plato in Plato's Gorgias," in Cooper, *Reason and Emotion*, pp. 28–75.

155 Mikhail Bakhtin, *Problems of Dostoevsky's Poetics* (Minneapolis: University of Minnesota Press, 1984); Michael Holquist and Katerina Clark, *Mikhail Bakhtin* (Cambridge, MA: Harvard University Press, 1984); James Wertsch, *Voices of the Mind* (Cambridge: Harvard University Press, 1991).

156 Jürgen Habermas, *Moral Consciousness and Communicative Action*, trans. Christian Lenhardt and Shierry Weber Nicholsen (Cambridge: MIT Press, 1990); J. Donald Moon, "Practical Discourse and Communicative Ethics," in Stephen K. White, ed., *The Cambridge Companion to Habermas* (New York: Cambridge University Press, 1995), pp. 143–66.

157 Hans-Georg Gadamer, "Reflections on My Philosophical Journey," in Lewis Edwin Hahn, ed., *The Philosophy of Hans-George Gadamer* (Chicago: Open Court, 1997), pp. 3–63, quote on p. 33; Johannes Fabian, "Ethnographic Objectivity Revisited: From Rigor to Vigor," in Allan Megill, ed., *Rethinking Objectivity* (Durham: Duke University Press, 1994), pp. 81–108.

can help people who start with different understandings to reach a binding philosophical or political consensus, although Gadamer is far from optimistic about achieving this end in practice. Critical hermeneutics in its broadest sense is an attempt to transgress culture and power structures through a radical break with subjective self-understanding.[158] Whether these are feasible strategies, or fantasies of intellectuals who are at odds with and powerless to effect the course of events is another question, and one I will address in the next chapter.

[158] On Gadamer and dialogue, see Hans-George Gadamer, *Truth and Method*, 2nd ed. rev., trans. Joel Weinsheimer and Donald G. Marshall (New York: Crossroad, 1989 [1960]); "Plato and the Poets," in *Dialogue and Dialectic*, trans. P. Christopher Smith (New Haven: Yale University Press, 1980), pp. 39–72, and "Reflections on My Philosophical Journey," in Lewis Edwin Hahn, ed., *The Philosophy of Hans-George Gadamer* (Chicago: Open Court, 1997), pp. 17, 27; Robert Sullivan, *Political Hermeneutics: The Early Thinking of Hans-Georg Gadamer* (University Park: Pennsylvania State University Press, 1990); Georgia Warnke, *Gadamer: Hermeneutics, Tradition, and Reason* (Stanford: Stanford University Press, 1987); Hans Herbert Kögler, *The Power of Dialogue: Critical Hermeneutics after Gadamer and Foucault*, trans. Paul Henrickson (Cambridge, MA: MIT University Press, 1999 [1992]). Gadamer's approach to dialogue informs the arguments of Hannah Arendt, "The Crisis in Education," in *Between Past and Future: Eight Exercises in Political Thought* (New York: Penguin, 1968), pp. 190–91, and J. Peter Euben, "Reading Democracy: 'Socratic' Dialogues and the Political Education of Democratic Citizens," in Ober and Hedrick, *Dēmokratia*, pp. 327–59, both of whom stress the partial nature of our knowledge, our ability to learn and to learn about ourselves through open discussions with others.

9 Tragedy and scholarship

> But man can be at odds with himself in two ways: either as savage, when feeling predominates over principle; or as a barbarian, when principle destroys feeling.
>
> Friedrich Schiller[1]

This final chapter of the book continues my exploration of ontology. In contrast to rational choice theories that work on the assumption of egoistic, autonomous actors, I offer the outlines of an ontology that builds on the polarities of life that are problematized by Greek tragedies and Thucydides. I contend that they are a better starting point for social analysis because they more accurately reflect the human condition. Egoistic, autonomous actors are a fiction of Enlightenment philosophy. So too is the possibility of altruistic communal actors envisaged by Marxist theory. In practice, individuals and their societies are distributed somewhere along a continuum between these two extremes. This is true for all polarities that capture important attributes of human orientation and behavior.

Tragedy and classical realism also offer us important epistemological insights. They raise serious doubts about the principal conceit of social science: the feasibility of developing a general, theoretical understanding of human behavior that bridges culture and time. Tragedy suggests, and classical realists affirm, that all knowledge is local, temporally bound and quickly negated because of the feedback loop between *logos* and *erga*. Such understandings, moreover, should never be confused with wisdom, which represents a holistic understanding of the human condition and the possible ends of human life. Tragedians and classical realists make no pretence about knowing the ends of life, but believe that such a question is approached by integrating the understandings we derive from theory, experience and the arts. Some of this knowledge is reflective, and some takes the form of understandings that go beyond words. Knowledge of

[1] *Über die Ästhetische Erziehung des Menschen*, Vierter Brief, para. 6, in Friedrich Schiller, *On the Aesthetic Education of Man* (bilingual ed), trans. Elizabeth M. Wilkinson and L. A. Willoughby (Oxford: Oxford University Press, 1967), p. 21.

both kinds can feed back into our theoretical inquiries and help create a positive, reinforcing cycle of discovery.

The final section of the chapter revisits ethics. Chapter 8 proposed a social theory of ethics, but did not respond to the normative questions that I raised at the beginning of the book. Do Nixon and the pope really belong in hell? And, more generally, to what ethical standards should our leaders be held accountable? I offer an instrumental defense of public ethics based on the more sophisticated understanding of interest common to classical realists. Following classical realists, I contend that behavior at odds with the accepted morality of the age undermines the standing, influence and even the hegemony of great powers. In the longer term, great powers – and institutions of all kinds – benefit more from respect and legitimacy in the eyes of allies and third parties than they do from most kinds of short-term gains that unethical methods might attain. If such behavior is most generally inimical to the real interests of states and institutions, there is no political justification for it. It follows that unethical behavior, and those responsible for it, ought to be judged by the same standards of morality to which private citizens are expected to conform.

The original form of public dialogue was Greek tragedy, which was emulated by Thucydides and rejected by Plato.[2] Tragedy sought to create dialogue on multiple levels. It was a conversation between playwright and audience, and almost certainly stimulated post-performance discussions among citizens about the issues that it raised on stage. Tragedy frequently took the form of an extended dialogue between characters who personified competing world views about personal, family, civic and religious relations and responsibilities.[3] Tragic conversations are self-defeating when protagonists talk past each other, fail to develop empathy and learn nothing new about themselves. Antigone and Creon interact in this way with catastrophic consequences for themselves and their family. Sophocles' Oedipus, by contrast, conducts an internal dialogue with himself after his reversal of fate. In *Oedipus at Colonus*, he has become a man of wisdom and inner peace.

[2] Plato's assault on poetry, especially tragic poetry, in the *Republic* and the *Laws*, constitutes an implicit admission of its importance, not only for Athens, but for his project, which might be described as an alternative. A good case can be made that Plato considered himself that last and greatest of the tragic poets, and the only one who sought to use tragedy to direct attention away from the level of visible objects and semblances to that of mathematics and thinking.

[3] Jean-Pierre Vernant, "Greek Tragedy: Problems of Interpretation," in Richard Macksey and Eugenio Donato, eds., *The Structuralist Controversy: The Languages of Criticism and the Sciences of Man* (Baltimore: Johns Hopkins University Press, 1972), pp. 273–88, suggests that the very logic of tragedy is that of polarity, or the tension between opposites. It can also be found in the *dissoi-logoi* of the sophists.

Like Oedipus, Greek tragedy reveals a deepening in its understanding of dialogue and also of progress. Aeschylus, born about 525, wrote in the decades after the victory at the Salamis and during the political struggle leading up to the restriction of the powers of the Areopagus Council in 462. His plays suggest that reason and dialogue could mute conflict, build bonds of solidarity and find ways of accommodating old and new conceptions of justice, family and communal obligations. His *Oresteia* and *Promethia* have happy endings, worked out after both sides have the opportunity to make thorough presentations of their respective positions. Sophocles also recognized rival truths, but these plays suggest that they could only be reconciled at some deeper level. The conflicts are multiple and cross-cutting. Both Aeschylus and Sophocles rely on *dei ex machinae*; gods appear, or otherwise use their authority, to put an end to strife, but never by resolving underlying value conflicts.[4]

Euripides, born in about 485, like Sophocles, witnessed two decades of war, the plague, the breakdown of Athens' political culture and reemergence of intense factional conflict. *Hecuba, Trojan Women, Electra, Orestes* and *Bacchae* track the descent of Athens into barbarism.[5] Sophocles and Euripides searched for some way of *restoring* a civilizing discourse in an intensely partisan and conflictual environment in which much of the population had become wary of politics and increasingly focused on their narrow self-interest. Sophistic teachings, moreover, had made great inroads among the elite and we may surmise that many were now convinced that all conventions were man-made and self-serving.

The German idealists who embraced tragedy at the end of the eighteenth century resembled Aeschylus in their optimism, although they tended to be drawn more to the works of Sophocles. They hoped to use tragedy as a model for a new discourse that would promote a moral and political transformation of their society. For Gadamer and Habermas, their twentieth-century descendants, the problem was once again reconstruction, and this time in the aftermath of wars, dictatorships and civil upheavals that surpassed anything witnessed by Sophocles, Euripides and Plato. Like their Greek predecessors, these advocates of dialogue faced the daunting task of recreating community in an environment where individual conceptions of the good were at war with one another. The situation was parallel in another respect: the Enlightenment and fifth-century

[4] Alasdair MacIntyre, *After Virtue*, 2nd ed. rev. (Notre Dame: Notre Dame University Press, 1984), p. 144, on the *deus ex machina*.

[5] Charles Segal, *Tragedy and Civilization: An Interpretation of Sophocles* (Norman: University of Oklahoma Press, 1981); Simon Goldhill, "The Great Dionysia and Civic Ideology," in John J. Winkler and Froma I. Zeitlin, *Nothing to Do with Dionysos?: Athenian Drama in its Social Context* (Princeton: Princeton University Press, 1990), pp. 97–129.

proto-Enlightenment undermined the authority of conventions. In the Enlightenment, this took the form of the rejection of Aristotelian *telos*, and, with it, destruction of the *sensus communis* (common understanding of the good). Fundamental questions of meaning and order became the focus of intellectual and political contention.

Like most traditional literary forms, tragedy reworked myth to convey or problematize ethics. It did so in a public forum, sponsored by the state and with much of the citizenry in attendance. Tragedy was a situationally specific political art form, and this was one reason, I have argued, that Thucydides chose to write his tragedy as a history. Although culturally bound in form and language, tragedies have universal import. They are relevant today as they were to fifth-century Athenians because we also live in a transitional era where old and new values are often in conflict in our minds, in our society and increasingly in the world at large due to the spread of Western cultural and economic practices.

Tragedies reveal that at some level all recognized character traits, roles and conceptions of justice are problematic. Generosity carried to excess makes one vulnerable to exploitation, a sense of adventure blinds one to risks and healthy self-esteem can shade into arrogance. *Ajax* and *Oedipus* show how single-minded efforts to excel in particular roles (e.g., warrior, leader) risk failure, loss of status and annihilation. Oedipus' downfall was the result of his unswerving commitment to follow his curiosity and intellect to wherever they led him. He considered this course of action in the best interests of his city, as indeed it was, when it led to his triumph over the Sphinx. In many tragedies, this point is driven home by the use of a *hamartia*, or miscalculation, that sets the hero on the road to self-destruction. A *hamartia* is a judgment error that results from the unchecked indulgence of laudable character traits.[6]

Traditional identities and their related roles were rooted in a series of concepts like *aretē* (honor and excellence), *kudos* (glory), *dikē* (justice), *aidōs* (shame), *kratos* (power), *sōphrosunē* (the restraint imposed on desires by reason) and *xenia* (guest friendship), all of whose meanings were

[6] John Jones, *On Aristotle and Greek Tragedy* (London: Chatto & Windus, 1962); Suzanne Saïd, *La faute tragique* (Paris: Maspero, 1978), pp. 26–31, 212–16, 452–54, with particular reference to Oedipus; Amélie Oksenberg Rorty, "The Psychology of Aristotelian Tragedy," in Rorty, ed., *Essays on Aristotle's Politics* (Princeton: Princeton University Press, 1992), pp. 1–23. Antigone, as Hegel notes, is not responsible for any *hamartiai*; she calculates with accuracy the likelihood of her action. Neither is Oedipus' downfall, strictly speaking, caused by *hamartiai*. Philoctetes improves his situation as a result of his. The *Persians* of Aeschylus is the one play that is squarely based on a *hamartia*. The very focus on the hero is distorting for understanding tragedy. This last point is also made by H. D. F. Kitto, *Form and Meaning in Drama: A Study of Six Greek Plays and of Hamlet* (London: Methuen, 1956), p. 233.

well established. During the fifth century, many of these words took on extended or even new meanings, and some of their old meanings were contested and rendered problematic. These changes reflected the tensions, and many incompatibilities, between the old, hierarchical order of the *oikos* with its ascribed roles, and the new, democratic order of the polis and its unprecedented degree of economic and political mobility. *Dikē*, for example, meant not only justice, but, more fundamentally, the order of the universe. The man who respects that order is *dikaios*.[7] *Antigone* reveals that order and justice no longer correspond and can be in sharp conflict. In Sophocles' *Philoctetes*, Neoptolemus and Odysseus both claim *dikaiosunē* for their arguments. They go on to disagree about the nature of wisdom (*sophia*) and the kinds of actions that are disgraceful (*aischros*).[8] The Mytilenian and Melian Debates of Thucydides explore contrasting visions of justice and their implications for policy. The tragedians exposed the conflict between old and new at the linguistic level to alert citizens to the need to find accommodations in real life that would forestall the destructive conflicts to which these differences of interpretation led.[9]

Tragedy does not offer specific policy lessons – although the implications of Athens' decline for American foreign policy seem reasonably clear. By making us confront our limits and recognize that chaos lurks just beyond the fragile barriers we erect to keep it at bay, tragedy can help keep our conceptions of ourselves and our societies from becoming infused with hubris.[10] As I have shown, it also provides the basis for an ethical and intellectual framework with which to confront life. In modern discourses, ethics and behavior are generally addressed as distinct subjects of inquiry because they are understood to derive from different principles. Many modern realists consider these principles antagonistic; not all the time to be sure, but frequently enough to warrant the establishment

[7] Hugh Lloyd-Jones, *The Justice of Zeus* (Berkeley: University of California Press, 1971), p. 161.

[8] Sophocles, *Philoctetes*, 1245–51; MacIntyre, *After Virtue*, p. 134.

[9] There is an interesting parallel here to the Enlightenment and Romanticism. The Enlightenment's assault on the old order undermined background meanings of words, metaphors and images in terms of which people communicated. Earl Wasserman, *The Subtler Language* (Baltimore: Johns Hopkins University Press, 1968), contends that this made it necessary for Romantic writers like Wordsworth, Shelley and Hōlderlin to articulate a new sensibility.

[10] The arbitrariness of fate and the inability of human beings to escape their condition goes back to the archiac age. In the *Iliad*, XXIV, Achilles laments that "the gods have spun the thread for pitiful humanity, that the fate of Man should be sorrow, while themselves are exempt from care." E. R. Dodds, *The Greeks and the Irrational* (Berkeley: University of California Press, 1951), pp. 29–30, contends that the sense of helplessness became more intense in the late fifth century. It certainly continued well past the Peloponnesian War.

of a clear hierarchy with interest-based considerations at the apex. For the Greek tragedians, and I number Thucydides among them, there was no separation between ethics and behavior. Sophocles and Euripides examine this problem at the individual level, and Thucydides does so at both the individual and state levels. Their writings show how individuals or states that sever identity-defining relationships enter a liminal world where reason, freed from affection, leads them to behave in self-destructive ways.[11] Rational interests presuppose ethical commitments.[12]

Tragedies and Thucydides' history also reveal the importance of dialogue. Through intimate discussions with others we open ourselves up to new perspectives on life and its problems and develop affection and respect for our interlocutors. Dialogue promotes civic peace by helping to keep us from adopting the kind of extreme positions so typical of tragic characters. Greek tragedy drives homes the unpleasant truth that there is no relationship between suffering and justice. Virtuous people are victims of disease, death and every kind of social misfortune. No amount of knowledge or power can protect against the kind of reversals tragic heros encounter or the suffering they bring on.[13] Knowledge and power make reversals more likely by encouraging hubris. For the Greeks, hubris is a category error. It is the mistake of believing that we can transcend our status and limitations; the worst form of hubris is comparing oneself to the gods. Aeschylus regularly associates hubris with tyrants.[14]

The tragic playwrights understand hubris as the result of otherwise commendable character traits and commitments. Thucydides links hubris to cleverness, self-confidence, forethought, decisiveness, initiative and risk taking, the very qualities that lead to political success. For Pericles, and the citizens of Athens, success stimulates the appetite for further successes while blinding them to the attendant risks. It breeds overconfidence in one's own judgment and ability to control events. It

[11] The chorus in *Antigone*, 404–410, exclaims: "When he obeys the laws and honors justice, the city stands proud . . . But when man swerves from side to side, and when the laws are broken, and set at naught, he is like a person without a city, beyond human boundary, a horror, a pollution to be avoided."

[12] I have elaborated this argument at some length in Chapters 3, 4 and 7.

[13] Aristotle, *De Anima*, 1100b30–33, observes that the virtuous cannot protect themselves against tragedy any more than other people, but they can retain their nobility (*kalos*).

[14] Hubris is another Greek concept that is well established in archaic times. Agamemnon's hubris helps to propel the plot of the *Iliad* and it is the offense of Penelope's suitors in the *Odyssey*. Aristotle, *Rhetoric*, 1378b28–29, defines hubris as "the serious assault on the honor of another, which is likely to cause shame, and lead to anger and attempts at revenge." N. R. E. Fisher, *Hybris: A Study in the Values of Honour and Shame in Ancient Greece* (Warminster: Aris & Phillips, 1992), p. 493, notes that hubris was considered a major crime because of its deleterious effects on the self-esteem of individuals and the cohesion of the community.

encourages leaders and followers to mistake temporary ascendancy for a permanent state of affairs. Hubris makes people victims of their own success.

Sōphrosunē is the antonym and antidote for *hubris*. It is a word of aristocratic origin that gradually developed an exceptionally wide semantic field. It came to encompass common sense, restraint, self-control, prudence and balanced judgment, and for women, chastity.[15] *Sōphrosunē* is a state of mind, not a course of conduct, although it is expected to govern behavior. It did not necessarily imply limiting one's goals, but did require restraint in the methods used to attain them. For this reason, Pericles felt justified in using *sōphrosunē* to describe Athens in his funeral oration. *Sōphrosunē* is a particularly appropriate attribute for those of us who live, work and influence the policy of the world's greatest power. It builds on the fundamental message of tragedy that human beings and their societies alike must recognize their limits and learn to live within them.

Thucydides was pessimistic that leaders and states could become *sōphrōn* and escape the cycle of *hubris-atē-hamartia-nemesis*. He nevertheless wrote his account of the Peloponnesian War in the hope that familiarization with the time-worn script would encourage future actors to become wise enough to write new endings. It was not his aim – nor mine – to suggest that we model ourselves on the best of the Greeks. Modernity has so changed our lives and our perspective on life that direct emulation of the Greeks would be impossible. Our task is rather to find a language appropriate to our time in which the lessons of tragedy can be expressed and speak meaningfully to us and our contemporaries.

Tragedy and ontology

We think of cooperation as an anomaly because social science has constructed an imaginary of autonomous, self-interested actors. If it emphasized the communal side of human beings, and, with it, our propensity to form and maintain rewarding relationships, conflict would appear anomalous. In this counter-factual academy scholars could garner international reputations by explaining how violent and self-aggrandizing behavior, so seemingly at odds with human nature, could nevertheless arise as the unintentional outcome of efforts to advance the common good. But most people, most communities and most states live in relative harmony with

[15] Helen North, *Sophrosyne: Self-Knowledge and Self-Restraint in Greek Literature* (Ithaca: Cornell University Press, 1966). Aristotle, *Nicomachean Ethics*, 1145a, contends that *sōphrosunē* is necessary to avoid *pleonexia*.

one another most of the time – although this is often achieved at some cost to the intellectual, social and political independence of individuals. If humanity has a default condition, it may be concord. It does not follow that social science should do a flip-flop in its ontology – although a good half-dozen provocative studies that devised ingenious explanations to show how violent conflict can arise within highly integrated communities would be refreshing.

The tragic understanding of human nature is like a bean bag filled with diverse and even contradictory traits that rub up against each other and shift location in response to internal dynamics and outside forces. Social science does its best to ignore, even deny, this diversity. Simplistic assumptions about human nature – the equivalent of having one kind of bean always on top – are an essential precondition for deductive, parsimonious theory. The choice of autonomous, self-interested human beings with no history – the most extreme characterization possible – reflects uncritical acceptance of Enlightenment ideology. But sophisticated Enlightenment philosophers, unlike their social scientist descendants, never mistook their ideological goals for social reality.

Chapter 8 emphasized the cooperative side of human nature and the social construction of human identity. It did so to highlight the unreality and negative social consequences of the dominant ontology's core assumptions. But similar criticisms could be voiced about the continental tradition of privileging society, and considering the identities of actors the creations of their societies. Paradigms and theories that build on only one pole of any social tension are based on unrealistic portrayals of human nature and encounter serious ontological problems. Most theories of cooperation, especially those of international cooperation, fall into what Ian Burkitt calls the trap of "double reduction." Individual actors behave, as indeed they must, on the basis of preexisting identities or roles, but then create a social structure or system that, to varying degrees, reshapes their identities and roles.[16] Waltz and Wendt are guilty of such reduction, but so too are social and critical theorists like Durkheim, Goffman and Foucault.[17] They merely enter the process at different locations: realists and liberals begin with individual actors, and constructivists and Marxists with the society or its structure.

The most important difference among all these theorists may be the extent to which their actors end up prisoners of the structures they, or

[16] Ian Burkitt, *Social Selves: Theories of the Social Formation of Personality* (London: Sage, 1991), pp. 44–45.

[17] Maja Zehfuss, "Constructivism and Identity: A Dangerous Liaison," *European Journal of International Relations* 7 (September 2002), pp. 315–48, on Wendt.

their predecessors, have created. Some, like Waltz and Althusser, conceive of structure as maximum security prisons from which neither parole nor escape is possible.[18] Others, like Marx, Foucault, Ruggie and Wendt, acknowledge to varying degrees the potential of actors to reshape their identities and the structures that give rise to them. Marx and Foucault do both. They consider actors the products of deeply entrenched power structures or discourses, but allow considerable independence of mind to a few rebels like themselves.[19] Just how does a privileged minority liberate itself from a power structure or discourse? And if it can do it, why not others? Goffman, Milosz and Scott allow a wider range of people to free their mental selves, as long as they show outward compliance. This opens up another dualism: between the character as role or mask, and the self as performer manipulating this mask.[20]

Wendt and Ruggie recognize the possibility, as Ruggie puts it, of "reflective acts of social creation, within structured constraints to be sure."[21] But Wendt leaves only a little more room for independent actors than his neo-realist counterparts. His "alter" and "ego" establish a modus vivendi which they subsequently sustain through practice. This is a rational strategy for both parties, and other actors who join their system, and an efficient one, because stable societies depend on predictable patterns of interactions. Once these patterns are established, Wendt contends, actors will struggle to retain them because they fear disorder, and, more importantly, they become committed to identities which this order sustains. Having boxed himself into a structural corner, Wendt struggles to fight free and considers several routes of escape: the creation of trust through self-restraint, changes in domestic structure and self-binding.

[18] Kenneth N. Waltz, *Theory of International Politics* (Reading, Mass.: Addison-Wesley, 1979); Louis Althusser, *Lenin and Philosophy and Other Essays*, trans. Ben Brewster (New York: Monthly Review Press, 1971). The strongest claims by constructivists in international relations for the primacy of society as the source of state agency and identity are made by Richard K. Ashley, "Untying the Sovereign State: A Double Reading of the Anarchy Problematique," *Millennium* 17 (1988), pp. 227–62, and David Campbell, *Writing Security: United States Foreign Policy and the Politics of Identity* (Minneapolis: University of Minnesota Press, 1992).

[19] Michel Foucault, "The Subject and Power," in Hubert Dreyfus and Paul Rabinow, *Michel Foucault: Beyond Structuralism and Hermeneutics* (Chicago: University of Chicago Press, 1983), pp. 208–26; Steven Lukes, *Essays in Social Theory* (New York: Columbia University Press, 1977), pp. 3–29, on the diversity of understandings of agent-structure in the Marxist tradition, and Hans-Herbert Kögler, *The Power of Dialogue: Critical Hermeneutics After Gadamer and Foucault*, trans. Paul Henrickson (Cambridge: MIT Press, 1966), pp. 264–65, on Foucault.

[20] Burkitt, *Social Selves*, pp. 70–71. See the previous discussions of Axelrod, Goffman and Scott.

[21] John G. Ruggie, *Constructing the World: Polity: Essays on International Institutionalization* (New York: Routledge, 1998), p. 4.

He acknowledges that all of his explanations are problematic, as indeed they are, for even more fundamental reasons that he considers.[22]

Constructivists need to adumbrate the mechanisms by which actors free themselves from dominant discourses and possibly transform the culture that is otherwise responsible for their identities. Cecilia Lynch has grappled with this problem in her well-documented study of how social agents – peace and anti-Apartheid groups – delegitimated existing international norms and substituted new ones in their place by creating new narratives that exposed more sharply the contradictions between emerging domestic practices and well-entrenched international ones. Rodney Hall has taken another promising step in this direction. In contrast to Wendt, he pays considerable attention to the domestic life of states. He theorizes that changes in collective identities at the state level change the legitimating principles and composition of the international system. International systems reproduce themselves until they become impediments to actors at the state and international levels. According to Hall, pressures from actors to make the system reflective of their identities prompted a series of changes in the European and then the international system. The European system evolved from feudal theocracy through dynastic, territorial and national sovereignty – and is possibly undergoing a transition to liberal globalism. Hall offers a theory to explain the construction of domestic identities that has to do with how a regime legitimizes itself and where its population considers sovereignty to reside.[23]

Ted Hopf's *Social Construction of International Politics* also looks inside states. He finds that state identities are rooted in internal identity discourses. Every society is composed of a number of discursive formations, and every individual has multiple identities that may or may not reflect these formations. Discursive formations consist of "logics of intelligibility, un/thinkability, and un/imaginability," that operate much like linguistic structures and lead people to conceptualize in certain ways. They are reproduced through verbal, textual and physical practices that become naturalized and take the form of habit and custom. Individuals can think independently of these structures, but the topography of domestic identities is usually concentrated in a relatively small number of discursive formations. Hopf uses newspapers, novels, films, journals, textbooks and journals to establish inductively the dominant formations in Moscow in 1955 and in 1999. The predominant discourse in 1955 was post-Stalinist,

[22] Alexander Wendt, *Social Theory of International Politics* (New York: Cambridge University Press, 1999), pp. 313–69. Steve Smith, "Wendt's World," *Review of International Studies* 26 (January 2000), pp. 151–63, offers similar criticism.

[23] Rodney Bruce Hall, *National Collective Identity: Social Constructs and International Systems* (New York: Columbia University Press, 1999).

but pre-Khrushchev, and centered on the project of the "New Soviet Man." Four discourses emerged in 1999: New Western Russians, who understand their country as part of the West; New Soviet Russians, who understand Russia as the successor to the Soviet Union; Liberal Essentialists, who reflect the Slavophil tradition and consider Russia unique; and Liberal Relativists, who dismiss the other discourses as flawed efforts to find or create an illusory self. From each discourse in the two time periods, Hopf deduces a series of hypotheses about how Soviets or Russians should see other states and tests them against different data.[24]

Hopf and Hall identify a progression of domestic identities but tell us little about the process by which they wax and wane. This is a central concern of Thucydides, who, as we have seen, attributes such change to an ongoing interplay of *logoi* (words) and *erga* (acts), propelled by goal-seeking behavior. The closest modern understanding to Thucydides may be that of the American pragmatists, especially of George Herbert Mead for whom "mind" and "self" take shape in the course of interpersonal communications. People alter their behavior, linguistic and physical, to adjust to one another, and by doing so form groups held together by affective bonds and hostility to other groups. Groups may form alliances, and this leads to further behavioral adjustments which can transform hostile into friendly feelings. Human behavior is never a direct replica of what went before, but changes in response to new social challenges. Changes are reflective acts, mediated by language, and through this process, individual and communal identities evolve along parallel tracks.[25]

For Thucydides, Mead, Hopf and other "thick constructivists," individual identities and societies are mutually constitutive.[26] Social reality begins as a conversation among individuals that ultimately leads to the creation of societies, and they in turn socialize individuals into their discourses.[27] Individuals nevertheless retain a degree of autonomy. This

[24] Ted Hopf, *Social Construction of International Politics: Identities and Foreign Policies, Moscow, 1955 and 1999* (Ithaca: Cornell University Press, 2002).

[25] George Herbert Mead, *Mind, Self, and Society* (Chicago: University of Chicago Press, 1934); Morris Rosenberg, "The Self-Concept: Social Product and Social Force," in Morris Rosenberg and Ralph H. Turner, *Social Psychology: Sociological Perspectives* (New York: Basic Books, 1981), pp. 593–624; Peter L. Berger and Thomas Luckmann, *The Social Construction of Reality: A Treatise in the Sociology of Knowledge* (New York: Anchor Books, 1966); Anthony Giddens, *The Constitution of Society* (Berkeley: University of California Press, 1984); Burkitt, *Social Selves*, pp. 28–54.

[26] For similar formulations, see Rom Harré, *Social Being: A Theory for Social Psychology* (Oxford: Basil Blackwell, 1979), and *Personal Being: A Theory for Individual Psychology* (Oxford: Basil Blackwell, 1983); Anthony Giddens, *Central Problems in Social Theory* (Berkeley and Los Angeles: University of California Press, 1979), pp. 69–73, *Profiles and Critiques in Social Theory* (Berkeley and Los Angeles: University of California Press, 1982), pp. 7–11, *The Constitution of Society*, pp. 1–40.

[27] Such an account is, of course, as unrealistic as societies arising from a contract.

is due in the first instance to the cognitive processes that mediate individual understandings of the values, rules, norms and practices of society. Contrary to the Enlightenment assumption of universal cognition, people perceive, represent and reason about the world in different ways.[28] These processes entail reflection, and this may lead individuals to some awareness of the extent to which they are products of their society. Such recognition is greatly facilitated by the existence of alternative discourses. In their absence, as Achilles discovered, it is difficult, if not impossible, to construct a different identity for oneself even when highly motivated to do so. For Thucydides, alternative discourses are initially the products of other societies (e.g., other Greek *poleis* and non-Greek states), which may become role models for disaffected individuals or the raw material from which new individual and social identities are constructed. Modern societies, as Shawn Rosenberg observes, are composed of many "locales of social change," each with discourses that are to some degree distinct.[29] This heterogeneity makes choices available, and this recognition, if and when it occurs, sets other processes in motion. It encourages, if not compels, individuals to evaluate their beliefs, values and practices in light of available alternatives. They may end up more committed to their original identities, gravitate toward existing alternatives or attempt, like imaginative California chefs, to create various kinds of satisfying fusions.

According to Thucydides, the starting points of transformation are behavioral and linguistic. Previously stable patterns of social interaction become uncertain and ill-defined, and this weakens the social norms that support them. Discourses also become unstable when identity and practice diverge. Language is subverted because people who reject old practices, or pioneer new ones, generally feel the need to justify them with reference to older values. They need to offer a *prophasis* (justification), as Thucydides so brilliantly demonstrated in the speeches of Book I. Concepts that impart meaning to words and conventions need to be stretched, distorted or entirely reformulated to justify practices at odds with the traditional ones, or traditional practices carried out for hitherto unacceptable purposes.[30]

[28] Shawn W. Rosenberg, *The Not So Common Sense: Differences in How People Judge Social and Political Life* (New Haven: Yale University Press, 2002), pp. 252–62.

[29] Rosenberg, *The Not So Common Sense*, pp. 3–4.

[30] Especially the speeches of the Corcyreans and Corinthians before the Athenian Assembly, the Mytilenian Debate and the Melian Dialogue. Following Goethe, Ludwig Wittgenstein, *Philosophical Investigations*, trans. G. E. M. Anscombe (Oxford: Blackwell, 1953), §546, insisted that in the beginning was the deed, and that words were a form of deed. Like Thucydides, he maintained that we come to understand the meaning of the words by examining the activities associated with them.

Changes in practice constitute challenges to various kinds of authorities, who, if they are in a position to, usually insist on compliance with established practices. But once these practices lose legitimacy, enforcement becomes increasingly difficult, if not ultimately impossible. Over the course of sixty-one years of life in the United States, I have witnessed the collapse of social practices as diverse as the doffing of hats and the opening of doors for women, dress codes at public schools (which still exist, but are periodically relaxed), segregation by "race" of public facilities, and the emergence of others such as the recreational use of marijuana and cohabitation by unmarried couples, now of any gender. All of these transitions were gradual, and some of them were marked by repeated confrontations between defenders of the old practices and practitioners of new ones. Others, like the decline in doffing hats (made easier by the decline in the wearing of hats), or failure to signal for turns, were stealthy; they were characterized by a quiet, reinforcing cycle of non-observance and non-expectations of observance. The changes I described occurred in a democratic society, and most of them came from below. Authoritarian regimes reveal somewhat different patterns because public challenges of dominant discourses are not allowed. When they do happen, they often take the form of a sharp phase transition of the kind described by chaos theory. In the Democratic Republic of Germany, a police state in which citizens learned to keep their thoughts to themselves, a chain of events beginning in the summer of 1989 – Gorbachev's visit to Berlin, the exodus of large numbers of East Germans to the West, the Politburo's removal of Honecker, demonstrations in Leipzig, and then at the Wall in East Berlin – suddenly made everyone aware of the extent of opposition to the regime. This realization, which the *Stasi* had struggled for years to prevent, created a groundswell of protest that quickly led to a collapse of the regime and then of the country.[31]

The breakdown of practices and the patterns of social interaction they sustain, cause problems for people who have reproduced those patterns as a matter of habit; it compels them to reflect on their practices, and by extension, their own identities. Such a process is likely, at least initially, to lead to social fragmentation through a proliferation of locales of social exchange. In due course, one or more of these discourses may emerge as dominant. But blending can also occur, as existing discourses undergo change to accommodate new practices and participants. This evolution may be unguided and the result of numerous accommodations

[31] Jacques Lévesque, *The Enigma of 1989: The USSR and the Liberation of Eastern Europe* (Berkeley: University of California Press, 1997), pp. 143–64; Charles S. Maier, *Dissolution: The Crisis of Communism and the End of East Germany* (Princeton: Princeton University Press, 1997), pp. 120–67.

at the lowest levels of interpersonal interaction, as is often the case with language. It can also entail deliberate policy choices, like those made by the medieval Catholic church in its efforts to bring pagans into the fold.

The transformation of individual and social identities is an ideational process, but it is significantly affected by the material world. For Thucydides, as we observed in Chapters 2, 3 and 8, traditional identities were greatly stressed by the transformation from a barter to a money economy and the subsequent rise of Athens as a regional economic and political-military power. These developments gave rise to new practices, at odds with traditional ones, and helped to set in motion the process that I described in the paragraphs above. Thucydides' understanding of the story is not linear. Economic and political developments also had ideational roots; they were facilitated by changes in the ways in which people thought about themselves and their society. Of equal importance, ideas and language are the medium through which any kind of change takes place. The development of philosophy, access through travel to alternative discourses, the questioning of *nomos*, and the rise of skepticism were both causes and effects of material change, and vehicles that made it possible. The Peloponnesian War began long after this process was under way, and is understood by Thucydides as a consequence of modernization. The war set in motion a different kind of ideational-material interaction: between the physical consequences of war and plague on the one hand, and the social world of language, conventions and social identity on the other. Through speeches, dialogues and narrative he shows us how the war transformed language and undermined conventions and community, and how these changes made the war more unrestrained and destructive. Ideas expressed in words are in constant tension with ideas expressed in action. For Thucydides and the tragic playwrights, the material and ideational worlds are related in ways that make it difficult to assign primacy to either. The tension between them is another polarity of human existence.

The dominant, liberal ontology and its constructivist alternative both tap into truths about human beings and their societies. As all the post-Kantian German idealist philosophers recognized, modern people have developed individual identities and interests, but they and their interests are also the products of their societies. People have interests as individuals, but they also have strong affiliative needs that are reflected in their collective identities. Tragedy is based on these dualisms. By dramatizing extreme situations, it encourages us to see how even ordinary human beings in the course of their quotidian lives are pulled in opposite directions by conflicting needs, multiple identities and different loyalties to which they give rise. As a general rule, these conflicts become more acute in periods of transition when discourses, and the values, conventions and practices they sustain, are questioned or breaking down. At most times and in most societies – as responses to traffic lights on deserted roads suggests – human behavior is arrayed somewhere along the continuum between the polar extremes that tragedy describes. Very rarely, does it reflect any of these poles, and when it does, the consequences are usually destructive. Any ontology worthy of attention must start from the premise that these polarities define the extremes of the human condition. Social theories must represent, not suppress, the diversity and inherent instability of human identities, interests and motives, and their complex interactions with the discourses, social practices and institutions they generate and sustain.

Tragedy is relevant to this problem in a double sense. It tells us where to look for vocabularies that help us get outside our own identities and the discourses from which they are derived. One of the reasons Athenian playwrights set plays in the heroic age and most often in other cities was to offer a distant perspective on contemporary life.[32] Froma Zeitlin contends that Thebes – the setting for plays by Aeschylus, Sophocles and Euripides – was the dramatic "other" that provided a negative model of society and government in contrast to the Athenian self-image.[33] Thucydides' account of the Peloponnesian War recognizes that alternative vocabularies make change possible. Sparta and Persia (and Asia, more generally) were the principal alternative discourses available to Athens. Sparta was an atavism and the polis whose culture came closest to the values and language of the heroic age. It became the benchmark for comparison, consciously invoked by the Corinthians, and implicitly by Thucydides, to show how far the Athenians had moved away from traditional values, practices and identities.

Athenians – especially aristocratic Athenians – respected Spartan military prowess and communal solidarity, but many of them also dismissed Spartiates as a bunch of needlessly self-sacrificing country bumpkins. Pericles had close ties with Sparta, and both Thucydides and Alcibiades took up residence there after being ostracized. Asian tyrannies, and above all Persia, were constructed as mirror images to Athenian democracy. In contrast to the Athenian idea of self-mastery and restraint, the tyrant indulges his political, material and sexual desires without moderation.

[32] The *Persians* of Aeschylus is the only extant play based on what was a contemporary theme.

[33] Froma I. Zeitlin, "Thebes: Theater of Self and Society in Athenian Drama," in Winkler and Zeitlin, eds., *Nothing to Do with Dionysos?*, pp. 130–67. Plays set in Thebes include *Seven Against Thebes* by Aeschylus, the *Bacchae, Suppliant Women* and the *Phoenissae* of Euripides, and *Oedipus, Oedipus at Colonus* and *Antigone*.

He is corrupt, beyond the law and more interested in luxury than public service.[34] But Persia was privately admired – especially by more ambitious Athenians.[35] Miltiades and Alcibiades both spent time in the employment of Persian monarchs. In his funeral oration, Pericles admits that Athens has come to resemble a tyranny. Cleon openly acknowledges that Athens is a tyranny, and Thucydides uses the Melian Dialogue to suggest that Athenians have become like the Persians. From Thucydides' perspective, neither Sparta nor Persia was a satisfactory model for Athens, and this may be a fundamental reason why he was committed to a synthetic alternative that built on the best of the old and the new.

Beginning in the late eighteenth century, tragedy and Greek art, and the image of the Greek world they conveyed, served as an alternative discourse for many German intellectuals. They constructed an idealized picture of Greek life based on a supposed harmony of man and nature and ethics and behavior, the very things they found lacking in their culture. German writers and philosophers attempted, without notable success, to use this discourse to bring about social and political change, and, when that failed, took refuge in it as an alternate cultural space. Greek tragedy was also a model for some intellectuals in the post-war period; Hannah Arendt, Hans Morgenthau and Reinhold Niebuhr among them. Once again, it offered an alternative discourse from which to critique and understand one's own society. For many German intellectuals of their generation, Marxism was a more attractive alternative. The Frankfurt School embarked on a project that was a conscious parallel to the nineteenth-century evocation of tragedy and Greece; it drew on the German philosophical tradition, primarily Marx and Freud, to generate a space of critique.

It is not surprising that tragedy was relegated to a relatively obscure place in the post-war cultural landscape. Tragedy, as I noted in Chapter 2, seeks to understand nature and human beings with the goal of reducing human suffering and pain. The Enlightenment project was about mastering and dominating nature. Past failures were considered the results of ignorance and stupidity, and history is no longer tragedy but comedy. This orientation became even more pronounced in the twentieth century,

[34] Herodotus, III.80.5; Plato, *Republic*, 577d7–9, 579b3–c2; Aristotle, *Politics*, 1311a28–b23; Rebecca W. Bushnell, *Tragedies of Tyrants: Political Thought and Theater in the English Renaissance* (Ithaca: Cornell University Press, 1990), p. 9; Victoria Wohl, *Love Among the Ruins: The Erotics of Democracy in Classical Athens* (Princeton: Princeton University Press, 2002), pp. 219–25.

[35] Kurt Raaflaub, "Stick and Glue: The Function of Tyranny in Fifth Century Athenian Democracy," in K. Morgan, ed., *Popular Tyranny: Sovereignty and its Discontents* (Austin: University of Texas Press, forthcoming).

as comedy increasingly addressed the kinds of problems and themes that in the past would have been the subjects of tragedy.

Schelling, Hegel, Nietzsche, Morgenthau, Arendt and the Frankfurt School all understood tragedy to be more than a language. It was a collective effort to adapt Athenian society to changing political, economic and social realities. This was, after all, a fundamental purpose of the playwrights, Aeschylus especially, and of the authorities who made the Great Dionysia a publicly supported and prominent occasion. We cannot use tragedy for this purpose, and the closest equivalent today may be popular culture. It is an admittedly unstructured and multiple set of locales where new discourses and practices take shape, are reflected upon and widely disseminated. To be sure, this observation would almost certainly be greeted with indignation by two of the more prominent representatives of the Frankfurt School who attacked American popular culture as mass culture and the enemy of the intellectual and high cultural discourses they envisaged as the alternative to capitalist domination. Horkheimer and Adorno were not wrong in stressing the commercial nature of American popular culture and its steamrolling effects. Later cultural critics have lamented that market needs have both coopted and watered down minority and oppositional cultures.[36] Cultural leavening has also accompanied globalization, and may be one of its defining characteristics. It has aroused widespread concerns that the gene pool of cultural diversity is being depleted, but critics tend to ignore the extent to which many attributes of threatened cultures are being assimilated into the mainstream.

Horkheimer, Adorno and their successors have been more sensitive to the costs of mass culture than to its possible benefits. They see mass culture spread by what we might call a "Grisham's Law" in which bad literature drives out the good, and "fakelore" supplants authentic practice. This focus obscures what may turn out to be the most important consequence of mass culture. American popular culture, unlike high culture, reaches out to marginal groups, their discourses and verbal and non-verbal means of expression. The resulting synthesis waters down, partially "defangs" and coopts the voices of resistance.[37] It nevertheless brought greater awareness of oppression to white, middle-class America,

[36] Max Horkheimer and Theodor W. Adorno, *Dialectic of Enlightenment*, trans. John Cumming (New York: Continuum 2001 [1944]).

[37] This is a principal claim of the "Situationists," pre-1968 representatives of the Frankfurt school tradition. See Guy Debord, *Panégyrique. Tome premier* (Paris: Gallimard, 1993), *Panégyrique. Tome second* (Paris: Fayard, 1997), and *The Society of the Spectacle* (New York: Zone Books, 1995); Sadie Plant, *The Most Radical Gesture: The Situationist International in a Postmodern Age* (London: Routledge, 1992).

and to some degree transformed its discourses. By creating what Johannes Fabian has called "terrains of contestation," it not only opened a space where marginal groups were free to maneuver, but brought them and their discourses into contact with representatives of high culture, especially in the arts and the academy.[38] It helped to create the very challenge to the power structure that the Frankfurt School feared it would prevent. The one exception, Herbert Marcuse, was equally wrong in his expectation that the counter culture could be taught the language of Marxism and mobilized to advance a "new left" agenda.[39] Dissident intellectuals, on the whole, have tended to adopt the language, manners, dress and modes of resistance of the oppressed.

This American dynamic has been partially reproduced on a global scale because the culture industries need new material and new markets to expand. As local cultural traditions enter the global media, local actors and their agendas acquire extra-local stages and come into contact with each other as well as with the supposedly dominant Western tradition.[40] Like the Internet, the global entertainment media creates a space open to the broadest possible public. And thanks to the Internet, that space has become more difficult for commercial or political authorities to monitor, let alone control. This raucous, undisciplined and diffuse reality stands in sharp contrast to the intimate fora of rational-instrumental debate envisaged by Habermas.[41] Such debate is premised on a liberal society in which not only the elite, but a significant component of the broader society, have mastered the Enlightenment code and reside in political units in which free speech is unrestricted. These conditions are only met in a select number of developed democracies. There is, nevertheless, a "dialogue" going on in the public fora of the world, making it take a more symbolic than linguistic form. Global popular culture may be the closest functional equivalent we have to the Athenian theater.

[38] Dick Hebdige, *Subculture: The Meaning of Style* (London: Methuen, 1979); Johannes Fabian, *Moments of Freedom: An Anthropology of Popular Culture* (Charlottesville: University Press of Virginia, 1998).

[39] Morton Schoolman, *The Imaginary Witness: The Critical Theory of Herbert Marcuse* (New York: Free Press, 1980); Barry Katz, *Herbert Marcuse and the Art of Liberation: An Intellectual Biography* (London: Verso, 1982).

[40] Néstor Garcia Canclini, *Hybrid Cultures: Strategies for Entering and Leaving Modernity*, trans. Christopher L. Chiappari and Silvia L. López (Minneapolis: University of Minnesota Press, 1995), and *Consumidores y ciudadanos: conflictos multiculturales de la globalization* (Mexico City: Grijalbo, 1995).

[41] Jürgen Habermas, *The Structural Transformation of the Public Sphere: An Inquiry into a Category of Bourgeois Society*, trans. Thomas Burger (Cambridge: MIT Press, 1991); Craig Calhoun, ed., *Habermas and the Public Sphere* (Cambridge: MIT Press, 1997); Simone Chambers, "Discourse and Democratic Practices," in Stephen K. White, ed., *The Cambridge Companion to Habermas* (Cambridge: Cambridge University Press, 1995), pp. 233–62.

The combination of economic globalization and the world-wide international political system have brought different political cultures into closer contact than ever before. It may be, as critics contend, that the secular, commercial and hedonist values of the West are being foisted on local cultures. Fundamentalist movements around the world – including those in the United States – also make this claim.[42] But the West's expanding influence has also exposed it to new ideas and discourses. Thanks to the kinds of norms to which Habermas has directed our attention, international society, at least in theory, and nominally in practice, confers equal standing on its members. Western elites are accordingly compelled to address alternative points of view more seriously and respectfully. In the early twentieth century, international socialism was the principal alternative discourse to Western liberal imperialism. Today, multiple languages and discourses exist, and they have interpenetrated one another, and not only at the elite level. People increasingly live in more than one discourse, and more insiders are able to adopt more outsider perspectives. Multiple identities are once again the norm in developed societies, something well documented in Russia and Western Europe.[43] Alternative discourses encourage multiple identities, which are inherently unstable and make change more feasible at the domestic and international levels of society.

Tragedy is comfortable with this kind of diversity. In contrast to most theories that take stable structures, societies and identities as the norm, tragedy emphasizes the dynamism of social life. It recognizes that the accommodations individuals and societies make with the tragic polarities are always temporary. They are uneasy compromises that can never be adequately justified by logic, may be difficult to legitimize politically and are likely to encounter a succession of moral and political dilemmas. Like the moon's tug and pull on the oceans, they give rise to inner tides that find outward expression in breaking waves of conflicting obligations and loyalties. Our search for ontological stability must give way to acceptance of the truth that social life, and our understandings of it, are, and always must be, in a state of flux.[44]

[42] Susan Friend Harding, *The Book of Jerry Falwell: Fundamentalist Language and Politics* (Princeton: Princeton University Press, 2000).

[43] Hopf, *Social Construction of International Politics*. On Western Europe, see Richard Herrmann, Thomas Risse and Marilynn Brewer, *Identities in Europe and the Institutions of the European Union*, forthcoming. This volume makes use of survey and electoral data. For a micro study that makes many of the same points, see Dorothy Noyes, *Fire and the Plaça: Community, Self and Performance in Catalonia After Franco* (Philadelphia: University of Pennsylvania Press, 2003).

[44] This point is made nicely by Yosef Lapid, "Introduction. Identities, Border, Orders: Nudging International Relations Theory in a New Direction," in Mathias Albert,

Individuals and societies adapt to changing circumstances – and create new social circumstances – by ever-shifting understandings and accommodations to the polarities of life. Very occasionally, such transitions may be peacefully negotiated by entire communities. This was the immediate goal of Greek tragedy, and of Aeschylus in particular. Such an adjustment may have profound consequences for individual and collective identities and behavior. There are only so many quasi-stable sites along any continuum, so a shift may have to travel some distance from its prior location. Polarities are also interconnected like the springs of a mattress. Changes in the pressure on any spring affect the tensions of adjacent springs and their accommodations ripple through all the other springs in the mattress. The outward spread of the force diminishes in proportion to distance, but, depending on the existing distribution of forces, even minute pressures can produce large readjustments. Attempts at new accommodations to polarities may, accordingly, result in something akin to what physical scientists refer to as a phase transition, a transformation in the state of a system. Thucydides' account of the Peloponnesian War represents the first self-conscious analysis of such a transformation.

Tragedy and epistemology

The instability of identities and the dynamism of societies indicate that all understanding of human behavior must be local in place and time. Building on this understanding, Clausewitz and Morgenthau distinguished between universal and particular knowledge. They developed theories at the most general level of abstraction to describe the dynamics that characterize war and international relations and make them distinct spheres of activity. They recognized that their theories were useless for purposes of practice because in the real world war and foreign policy were embedded in social contexts and therefore subject to influence by a host of other complex processes (e.g., understandings of the past, organizational capabilities, domestic politics) as well as purely idiosyncratic factors such leadership and chance. In contrast to neopositivism, they did not see theory as the holy grail of scholarly activity, but only a means to an end. They understood theory as *epistēmē*, and never confused it with *sophia*. The latter required a holistic knowledge that integrated the conceptual insights of theory with the practical understanding.

David Jacobson and Yosef Lapid, eds., *Identities, Border, Orders: Rethinking International Relations Theory* (Minneapolis: University of Minnesota Press, 2001), pp. 1–20. See also, Arjun Appadurai, *Modernity at Large* (Minneapolis: University of Minnesota Press, 1997); William Leach, *Country of Exiles* (New York: Pantheon Books, 1999).

Homer, Aeschylus, Sophocles, Euripides, Thucydides and Plato chose to communicate abstract knowledge through the vehicles of epics, plays, dialogues and history. Clausewitz and Morgenthau are transitional figures in that they embrace theory but embed it in quasi-historical narratives that have as one of their purposes the demonstration of the limits of theory. Modern social science has adopted a style of presentation that opens with a statement of propositions and methods followed by the presentation of data and discussion of findings. Does this mode of analysis and its associated style of presentation advance our understanding of the social world? The tragic vision would lead us to understand narrative and more scientific forms of presentation, and ideographic and nomothetic approaches, as capturing another tension, in this case in the production of knowledge. Each form of inquiry and expression makes us aware of the limits of the other, and, together, might prompt deeper insights than either can produce alone. Inquiry and praxis and art and science might also be understood as components of an underlying unity of the sort that guides practice and sustains communities and identities. Classical realists understood this truth, and many social scientists do not. Thucydides, Clausewitz and Morgenthau wrote for doers as well as thinkers, and understood that dramatic and narrative forms speak to task-oriented people in a way that the language of social science never can. They conceived of theory as a means to help such people organize and make explicit sense of the insights and sensitivities they had gleaned through experience and reading.[45] Theory was to help free people from the concerns of the moment, and, like the double vision of tragedy, provide them with another perspective from which to assess their situation.

The Enlightenment elevated reason as the source of all knowledge and science as its most perfect expression. History, art, poetry and the world of feelings were deeply suspect and dismissed as props of the church and the aristocracy. Voltaire, like Plato, condemned poetry as a form of dangerous "figurative" language.[46] The counter-Enlightenment understood positivistic reason as a pernicious force that divided man from nature, and sought to reverse this tend by restoring respect for feeling and art as its principal form of expression, and restoring nature as a warrant for knowledge, truth and spiritual integrity. Much of the German philosophical enterprise from Kant on must be understood as a response to science. Schelling, Fichte and Hegel refused to concede that everything outside of

[45] This is, of course, another tension. Theory divorced from politics will develop nonpolitical aims and forums distant from centers of political life. Politics uninformed by theory will be guided entirely by the quest for power, wealth and standing.

[46] Voltaire, *Philosophical Dictionary*, trans. Theodore Besterman (Baltimore: Penguin, 1971).

science was mere poetry, and knowledge of a lesser order. They rejected the emerging model of science as the benchmark for knowledge, developed the alternative conception of *Geisteswissenschaft* – which became the "Humanities" or "interpretative sciences" of the English-speaking world – and sought philosophical foundations for and standards appropriate to its evaluation. This was a goal of Kant's *Critique of Judgment*, and Schiller's essay on "Aesthetic Education of Man," and also a major theme of Hegel's *Phenomenology*.[47]

The counter-Enlightenment fought a largely unsuccessful rear-guard action for most of the nineteenth and twentieth centuries. The progress of science, and the growing belief that it was a force for physical and spiritual betterment, helped to diffuse and legitimize the hierarchy of knowledge established by Enlightenment philosophers. Although resisted by a diverse array of forces, this outlook found institutional expression in the universities, especially in Germany and the United States, where classics, and humanities more generally, lost their primacy to the sciences, engineering and other forms of *epistēmē* and *technē*. In the second half of the twentieth century, the so-called behavioral revolution sought to transform political science, psychology, sociology and economics, the core of what was now called the "social sciences," to distance it from the "soft knowledge" of the humanities and bind it as closely as possible with the "hard sciences." In the United States this was a successful institutional strategy; social scientists on the whole are paid less than physical scientists but considerably more than humanists, and have their own sub-sections in the National Science Foundation. Within the social sciences, there is a pecking order with economics, the most mathematical and "scientific" of the disciplines, at the top, and cultural anthropology, the least, at the bottom.

There have been intellectual payoffs, and many costs, associated with this strategy. As Hans Morgenthau predicted back in the 1940s, political philosophy has been largely marginalized, and even in political science departments where it still exists, its courses are rarely required. There is little intellectual interchange between political philosophers and their colleagues in other fields, who increasingly describe – inaccurately – what they do as "normal science." As social science seeks to emulate the physical sciences, political scientists seek to emulate economics in the hope of upgrading their status, and have established a preference structure in the discipline that rewards game theorists, formal modelers and other

[47] G. W. F. Hegel, *Elements of the Philosophy of Right*, trans. H. B. Nisbet (Cambridge: Cambridge University Press, 1991 [1821], 7, puts equal emphasis on reason, and rejects sentiment as a guide.

applications of rational choice. This can go to absurd lengths. At a mid-Western university I know all too well, "physics envy" prompted the dean of social sciences to purge anthropology of its cultural anthropologists.

There are numerous critiques of the behavioral revolution and its methods, and it is not my intention to author yet another one. I want to offer an equally critical but different perspective on the trajectory of the social sciences and its intellectual consequences. Once again, my starting point is Greek tragedy. As I noted earlier, it employed the strategy of double vision to draw spectators into the drama emotionally while distancing themselves from it intellectually to develop a more profound understanding of its dynamics and meaning. Thucydides used the same strategy, as did Plato in a way with his dialogues. While trashing the poets, Plato slyly invented a new art form to convey his insights because, like the tragedians and Thucydides, he recognized that wisdom is best developed and communicated through the interplay of art and reason. Aristotle developed his concept of *catharsis* to show how emotional anguish could lead to knowledge. Shakespeare and Goethe wrote in this tradition, the latter quite self-consciously.

Romanticism made artistic creation the vehicle of self-discovery, and the artist the model human being. It rejected Aristotle's concept of *mimēsis*, of art as imitation, in favor of art as *poiēsis*, or the act of creation itself. The idea of self-realization through the aesthetic was successfully propagated by Schiller, for whom life and form come together in the beauty of the living form [*lebende Gestalt*].[48] Goethe's Werther is presented as someone who lives the life of feeling and sensibility. This approach to life found its most forceful statement in the writings of Nietzsche, where it became the basis for his radical critique of Christianity and science. He posits a sharp opposition between the Apollonian art of sculpture and the non-plastic Dionysian art of music. The world of the intellect is Apollonian, and has dominated Western philosophy and culture since the time of Socrates. For the Apollonian, everything must be intelligible to be beautiful. Nietzsche insists there is intelligence beyond the intelligible, and it finds expression in the emotions, communal solidarity and the "oneness" with nature, all made possible by Dionysian ecstasy. Dionysian art convinces us of the joy of existence, and we come to this realization

[48] "If man is ever to solve the problem of politics in practice, he will have to approach it through the problem of the aesthetic, because it is only through beauty that man makes his way to freedom." Friedrich Schiller, *Letters on the Aesthetic Education of Man* (bilingual ed.), trans. Elizabeth Wilkinson and L. A. Willoughby (Oxford: Oxford University Press, 1967), *Essays*, 90. The move from mimesis to expression really began in the eighteenth century, but gained wider currency during the Romantic period. M. H. Abrams, *The Mirror and the Lamp* (New York: Oxford University Press, 1953); Charles Taylor, *Hegel* (Cambridge: Cambridge University Press, 1975), pp. 17–10, 36–40.

by grasping the truth that lies behind its representation. Music offers a practical illustration. It exists in a realm that is beyond and before all phenomena. Language and the concepts its spawns can never capture the cosmic symbolism of music because language itself is a symbol. It can have superficial contact with music – it can describe its structure, rhythm, instrumentation and evolution – but it cannot disclose its innermost heart. That speaks to us directly, unmediated by language.[49]

Nietzsche held the triumph of the Apollonian responsible for the ills of Western culture. It spawned science, defined as "the belief in the explicability of nature and in knowledge as a panacea." Science and reason were "seductive distractions" that solidified knowledge into constraining concepts that stifled creativity. For Nietzsche, the task of art is to interrogate and undermine all perspectives to keep them from hardening into life-restricting concepts. He urged his contemporaries to "frolic in images" and recognize that creative life consists of replacing one set of metaphors and illusions with another. Aristotle understood art as an imitation of nature. For Nietzsche, it is "a metaphysical supplement, raised up beside it to overcome it." Tragic art, in particular, creates and destroys its own illusions. By doing so, it destroys old dreams and makes way for new ones.[50]

Nietzsche insisted on the need for a new aesthetic consciousness to free people from the limitations of conventions and accepted discourses, of which Christianity and science were the most deeply entrenched and constraining. Such a consciousness would enable and facilitate self-expression and self-knowledge, although it too would have to be

[49] *The Birth of Tragedy*, in *Basic Writings of Nietzsche*, trans. and ed. Walter Kaufmann (New York: Modern Library, 1962), Sections 1 and 3; Walter Kaufmann, *Nietzsche*, 3rd ed., rev. (Princeton: Princeton University Press, 1968); Hayden White, *Metahistory: The Historical Imagination in Nineteenth Century Europe* (Baltimore: Johns Hopkins University Press, 1973), pp. 331–74. Nietzsche builds on Hegel's conception of art as a mode of consciousness that is not representation. Scott Burnham, *Beethoven Hero* (Princeton: Princeton University Press, 1995), argues that Beethoven offers a concrete example of this process. His "Eroica" and some of the early piano sonatas were conscious efforts to affirm his identity and to provoke listeners, through their identification with the music, to understand themselves as self-legislating human beings.

[50] *Birth of Tragedy*, sections 2, 18 and 23. Ironically, Nietzsche's project closely parallels that of John Locke, one of the founding fathers of the Enlightenment to which he so strongly objected. Locke proposes an extreme form of demolition based on the recognition, shared by Nietzsche, that our understanding of the world is an amalgam of sensations and reflections. These syntheses are constructed on a foundation of passions, customs and the beliefs of the age which we assimilate in the course of our education. Locke, like Nietzsche, urged us to distance ourselves from these influences to understand the social order and our role within it. For Locke, disengaged, procedural reason was the key to enlightenment. For Nietzsche, reason was another mechanism of enslavement. On Locke, see Charles Taylor, *Sources of the Self: The Making of Modern Identity* (Cambridge: Harvard University Press, 1989), pp. 165–73, 242–43.

challenged and replaced before it solidified and became life-restricting. Humanity, its art and other creations – as Greek tragedy recognized – could at best hope to achieve a precarious balance between perfect form and utter chaos. To achieve this recognition, it was first necessary to approach chaos, and Nietzsche anticipated the arrival of a Zarathustra-like Superman (*Übermensch*) who would lead the way to a new barbarism. Unlike the savage life of the prehistoric past, the new barbarism would free the human spirit and empower man to lead a more creative life.

Nietzsche's rejection of reason is every bit as dangerous as the Enlightenment's rejection of emotions. While Nietzsche cannot be held responsible for Hitler, *Der Führer* had an eerie resemblance to his *Übermensch*.[51] Nor, *pace* Morgenthau, Strauss and Jean François Lyotard, can the horrors of Bolshevism and its sister regimes be laid at the feet of the Enlightenment – even though they were quintessential Enlightenment projects based on the assumption that scientific principles would promote the perfectability of humankind.[52] The relationship between reason and sentiment has been framed as one of antagonism by the Enlightenment and its critics. Aeschylus, Sophocles and Thucydides understood it as another human tension, perhaps the greatest tension of all. They recognized that imbalance in either direction could have destructive consequences; the mind and the emotions had to work together to produce and sustain civil order.[53]

The same is true of knowledge. Our ability to predict, explain, control or manipulate social phenomena has been consistently confounded by the complexity and openness of social systems, and the ability of human beings to plan around and undermine any temporarily valid generalization.[54] The positivistic idealization of "the scientific enterprise"

[51] On this question see, Steven E. Ascheim, *The Nietzsche Legacy in Germany 1890–1990* (Berkeley: University of California Press, 1992), and the various essays in Jacob Golomb and Robert S. Wistrich, *Nietzsche, Godfather of Fascism? On the Uses and Abuses of Philosophy* (Princeton: Princeton University Press, 2002).

[52] Jean François Lyotard, *The Post Modern Condition*, ed., Geoff Bennington and Brian Massumi (Minneapolis: University of Minnesota Press, 1994), p. 82. See also, Zygmunt Baumann, *Modernity and the Holocaust* (Ithaca: Cornell University Press, 1989).

[53] Kant's *Critique of the Power of Judgment*, ed. Paul Guyer, trans. Paul Guyer and Eric Matthews (Cambridge: Cambridge University Press, 2000) also suggests that we cannot position ourselves fully on either side of this divide; and indeed, our classical realists – and Wittgenstein, Dewey, Heidegger and the Frankfurt School are all extensions of the Enlightenment project they criticize. Anthony J. Cascardi, *Consequences of Enlightenment* (Cambridge: Cambridge University Press, 1999), offers an updated variant of this argument, insisting that we do not need an anti-Enlightenment stance to pursue constructive social and ethical goals.

[54] For a more extensive development of this argument, see Steven Bernstein, Richard Ned Lebow, Janice Gross Stein and Steven Weber, "Physics Got All the Easy Problems: Adapting Social Science to an Unpredictable World," *European Journal of International Relations* 6 (March 2000), pp. 43–76.

is not well equipped to confront the social world because, by its very nature, it must fragment the world into artificially isolated components. It also strives to find laws that are true in all times and places. Ironically, the pace of social evolution is quickened by our efforts to understand behavior and its context.

Science claims objectivity, and many of its practitioners have succumbed to this comforting illusion. They do not realize – as have critics from Nietzsche through Morgenthau – that science, especially social science, is embedded in a social context and often serves to legitimate and uphold the power structure of which it is a part. The language and concepts of contemporary realism are eminently suited to justifying American power and foreign policies and largely incapable of providing a critique of those policies and the assumptions on which they are based. Nothing proves as much support for this contention as the opposition to American intervention in Iraq expressed by many realists and neorealists. None of their arguments, with the possible exception of the claim that intervention might help provoke balancing against us in the long term, derived from their theories. Rather, they expressed a widely shared view, held just as strongly by many non-realists, that the United States was overextending itself, that the administration had proof neither of Iraqi possession of weapons of mass destruction nor of Saddam's alleged ties to Al Qaeda, and that intervention was likely to invite more, not less, terrorism against the United States. These criticisms are quite independent of realist theories. Classical realism, by contrast, can offer a powerful critique of intervention in Iraq, the starting point of which is the need to act in accord with principles of consultation and consensus that sustain the institutions and broader community. For this is what ultimately allows the United States to translate its power efficiently into influence.

Social science can also develop discourses that are subversive of the dominant order, but it is no accident that they tend to be marginalized by the dominant scholarly discourse supportive of the status quo. American social science desperately needs to develop a reflexive understanding to grasp its inherently subjective and intensely political nature.

At the outset of the book, I introduced the ancient Greek distinction between *technē* and *epistēmē* on the one hand, and *sophia* on the other. For the Greeks, *epistēmē* was conceptual knowledge that offered a useful but incomplete understanding of the world. *Sophia*, by contrast, represented a holistic wisdom that could place the components of the universe, especially human beings, in their broader context, and by doing so understand their limitations and the extent to which, like driftwood on a turbulent sea, they are buffeted by forces over which they have no control. Socrates was dismayed to discover that many masters of the productive arts (*technē*) equated their knowledge with wisdom, and that politicians, who lacked even *technē*, were even more convinced of their wisdom.[55] If Socrates made his inquiries today, I suspect he would find craftsmen more cautious in their claims, but encounter unbridled arrogance from producers of *epistēmē*.

Prominent physical scientists have come to recognize this truth more readily than their social scientist counterparts. This may be because twentieth-century science, while immensely more successful, has become even more fragmented and mathematical. It is impossible for physicists to develop a broad conceptual understanding of their field as a whole, and increasingly difficult for them to do so even in the segments of it relevant to their particular research. Quantum mechanics and relativity, whose concepts are not readily, if at all, explicable verbally, accelerated the already existing tendency to conceptualize physical knowledge in the language of mathematics. James Jeans went so far as to suggest that "the Great Architect of the Universe" had to be a mathematician.[56] Werner Heisenberg maintained that the only role of imagination and intuition was to provide mental images of mathematical realities.[57] Their conception of nature was diametrically opposed to that of Nietzsche, for whom mathematical symbols were reflections – shadows in the Platonic sense – of deeper truths.[58] In recent years, many scientists have called for a more conceptual and holistic understanding of their enterprise. Others are coming to understand that creativity is an artistic process, and often inspired, as it was in the case of Einstein, by art, life experience and emotions.[59] Insights often come into being as a fleeting images or inchoate feelings that only later find expression in symbolic language. Historians of science have also pointed to the importance of dialogue among a network of open-minded interlocutors as essential to the development of modern physics.[60]

[55] Plato, *Charmides*, 165a – 167c, 170c – 171c.

[56] James Jeans, *The Mysterious Universe* (New York: Cambridge University Press, 1930), p. 134.

[57] A. Miller, *Imagery in Scientific Thought* (Boston: Birkhäuser, 1984), pp. 173–74.

[58] Hans-Georg Gadamer, "Reflections on My Philosophical Journey," in Lewis Edwin Hahn, ed., *The Philosophy of Hans-George Gadamer* (Chicago: Open Court, 1997), p. 9, upholds the Nietzschian tradition. "From the Greeks," he writes, "one could learn that thinking in philosophy does not, in order to be responsible, have to adopt as system-guiding the thought that there must be a final grounding for philosophy in a highest principle; on the contrary it stands always under the guiding thought that it must be based on primordial world experience, achieved through the conceptual and intuitive power of the language in which we live."

[59] See, for example, David Bohm and F. David Peat, *Science, Order, and Creativity*, 2nd ed. (New York: Routledge, 1989).

[60] Mara Beller, *Quantum Dialogue: The Making of a Revolution* (Chicago: University of Chicago Press, 1999).

I went through such a process in the course of this project. I wrote my Nixon story in the midst of my research on Thucydides. The impetus was intense dislike for Richard Nixon and the need to think about something other than my book for a week. I was rewarded on both counts; I returned to my research with renewed vigor and a very satisfying sense of *Schadenfreude*. I had not only sentenced Nixon to a post-lifetime of hard labor, but Pope Pius too. I recognized from the outset – I think – that the choice of characters and the plot was directly relevant to one of the principal themes of my book: the destructive implications of building firewalls between personal and institutional ethics and domestic and foreign policy. President and pope are put in an environment where they have the opportunity to contemplate their moral responsibility for behavior they believed at the time to be in the interests of the institutions they directed. My plot developed a logic of its own and wiggled free of the outline I had in mind. Pope Pius emerged as a pitiable figure who has grown in moral stature during the course of his decades in Hell. He is reconciled to his punishment because he has come to recognize the gravity of his crimes, and has penetrated the many layers of defenses he had previously erected to deny responsibility and choice, and most importantly, the applicability of conventional standards of morality to people who act on behalf of global institutions. Nixon begins to take his first steps down this path, and by the end of the story the reader, and even the author – much to his annoyance – have developed some sympathy for him.

Only later, with enough distance from the act of creation to reflect upon the story from the perspective of a reader, did I grasp the dynamics of this progression. In life, the president and pope were loners who found intimacy of any kind difficult. To the extent that Nixon felt affection for other people, he hesitated to express it, perhaps for fear of making himself vulnerable. Ironically, that vulnerability became more apparent when he expressed hostility and anger, which he had few compunctions about doing, even in public. Nixon not only built a barrier between public and private life, but between himself and his humanity, and this may help to explain why he, and people like him, are able to carry out the acts they do – and often sleep at night. Pius' defenses gradually fell away because Hell provided the catalyst for him to regain his humanity, something he could only do by opening himself up to feelings. Initially, these feelings were of horror and self-pity, but later, they also encompassed affection for other people. Affection leads to empathy, which makes it possible to see oneself through the eyes of other people. The interaction of inside feelings and outside perspectives, of sentiment and intellect, is both the foundation of ethics and the path to redemption. Nixon is only setting out on this journey, but even in the course of the short time we visit him in Hell, his range of emotions widens, and progresses from anger, envy and hostility to desire to make connections with other people, ideas and the beauty and the companionship he associates with music. Empathy is still beyond him, but we get the sense that he may ultimately come to experience it.

The bottom line of my story – and of my book, my story taught me – is that compartmentalization is blinding and dangerous. In the case of Oedipus, the blinding was literal. Like pope and president, the king of Thebes had a powerful intellect that was neither constrained nor channeled by affection and commitment to other people. Oedipus became the victim of his own arrogance, a realization that came to him only after entering a hell of his own making. In light of the title of Chapter 8, it is interesting to note that his arrogance found its initial expression in what may be the first recorded instance of road rage. On foot at a crossroads, Oedipus encountered a carriage. The old man inside wanted Oedipus ejected from the road to make way for him, but Oedipus bested the coachman when he assaulted him. The old man – whom we know to be Laius, Oedipus's father – struck him on the head with his two-pointed goad. Oedipus pushed him out of the carriage with his walking stick and killed him without further ado.[61] In the introduction, I compared Nixon to other tragic heroes, and argued that the fit was imperfect in every case. The pope of my story comes to resemble the wise if pathetic hero of *Oedipus at Colonus*, and we sense that Nixon has the potential to reach this state.

As the Schiller epigraph indicates, our intellects need to be connected to our emotions, and our emotions need to be disciplined by our intellects. Social science, as currently formulated, not only sustains this compartmentalization, it encourages us to view it as natural and beneficial. This is the most fundamental reason why it is in need of renewal. It may also explain why empirical anomalies have on the whole not prompted many social scientists to question their basic framework, but rather to search for new ways of extending it to address them. Their work is often imaginative, and occasionally even elegant, but a different kind of creativity is required if social science, and my field of international relations, is to remain relevant and helpful in a rapidly changing world. This can only be accomplished by stepping outside of the dominant ontology. Paradigms, Kuhn reminds us, are not merely abstract formulations, but subjective ways of thinking and communicating about how we see the world.[62] The deeper we embed ourselves in a paradigm, the more difficult it becomes

[61] Sophocles, *Oedipus The King*, 801–814.
[62] Thomas Kuhn, *The Structure of Scientific Revolutions* (Chicago: University of Chicago Press, 1970).

to abstract ourselves from it and look at the world afresh.[63] Art may be essential as a vehicle to transport scholars to a distant vantage point from which they can reassess their enterprise – and themselves. It can also put us in touch with our feelings, and by doing so, generate new insights or reacquaint us with old ones that can subsequently find expression in new ways of conceiving the world and ultimately, in new research programs.[64] This kind of "tacking" between holistic visions and discrete research projects, between the "frolic in images" and bench science, can build creatively on the tensions that social science has until now largely ignored. In keeping with the tragic vision, it can build unity through diversity and wisdom through uncertainty.

Tragedy and Ethics

"Nixon in Hell" condemned the president to the underworld for his sin of commission, and the pope for his sin of omission. Traditional views of hell and judgment are rooted in transcendental realism – the belief in an absolute good. For many of the world's religions, this good and its associated moral codes have been legislated by a supreme being. A majority of American Christians believe that people who fail to conform to these codes are consigned by g-d to purgatory or hell.[65] Dante's *Inferno*, undeniably the most famous fictional description of hell, offers exquisite details about the nature and severity of punishments associated with different sins. I do not doubt that Dante would approve of sending Nixon and Pius XII into the inferno. After all, he populated his netherworld with several emperors and popes and a score of lesser officials.

I consigned Nixon and Pius XII to a figurative hell, but not on the basis of their failure to live up to the Ten Commandments. Nor do I appeal to secular forms of transcendental realism that attempt to deduce universal codes of ethics from first principles based on reason or sentiment. I am well disposed toward such efforts but find them deeply problematic. I have developed a different justification based on the instrumental merit

[63] For this very reason, William James argued that multiple approaches were always essential, and that science should progress by a gradual growth, extension and reformulation in thinking based on interaction among these different approaches and their research programs.

[64] Niels Bohr and Werner Heisenberg provide two striking examples from the world of physics. Bohr was deeply influenced by the writings of William James and James Joyce. "Stream of consciousness" led him to think about quantum mechanics in terms of ambiguity and complementarity. Heisenberg's love of Plato encouraged his belief in the primacy of mathematics in representing the physical world. Bohn and Peat, *Science, Order and Creativity*, p. 101.

[65] For Gallup and other polls, see http://www.religioustolerance.org/chr_poll3.htm#salv.

of ethics. It is best illustrated by the fate of Athens as understood by Thucydides. Success bred hubris, which took the form of exaggerated ambition and, with it, rejection of the constraints, obligations and other norms traditionally associated with inter-polis relations. Like a tyrant, Athens freed itself of these restraints in the expectation that it would gain greater freedom of action and thereby augment its power and wealth. By the time of the Melian Dialogue, Athenians had come to the sober realization that they escaped traditional obligations only to become ensnared by a more onerous one. Their *archē* is sustained by fear of the consequences of revolt, and they must constantly demonstrate that power. But continued expansion is beyond the means of any state and leads to overextension and defeat.

Clausewitz tells a similar story about Napoleonic France, as does Morgenthau about Hitler's Germany. Once again, rejection of the ethical norms and international obligations of the era led to aggressive polices that ended in defeat, at enormous human cost to the aggressor and his victims alike. Nixon and Kissinger were not out to conquer continents. Their escalation of the Vietnam War and expansion of the ground fighting into Cambodia nevertheless ended in disaster, and a great human cost. Their conduct of the war – also true of their predecessor, the Johnson administration – entailed actions strikingly at odds with accepted standards of morality, even wartime morality. Morgenthau and other critics of intervention offered numerous examples, including the support of a dictatorial regime in Saigon, undermining political order in Laos and Cambodia, indiscriminate destruction of villages, aerial bombardment of civilians and the bombing and invasion of Cambodia.

The Johnson and Nixon administrations either denied these violations of conventional morality – and in some cases of international law – or defended them as necessary to protect American interests and security. It is apparent that none of these actions, nor intervention in Indochina more generally, served American interests – quite the reverse. Vietnam went communist in the end, and American prestige suffered a serious setback, and not only in Asia, but in Western Europe, where it fueled the kind of political and cultural opposition to the United States that has since become the norm among a sizeable segment of the population.

All these judgments benefit from the advantage of hindsight. However, the outlines of failure were already apparent to Nixon and Kissinger when they escalated the war. They did so, not with victory in mind, but to prolong the existence of their puppet regime in the South. They hoped to keep it and South Vietnam afloat long enough to perhaps strike some acceptable deal with Hanoi and, failing that, to escape any domestic political retribution for losing Vietnam. In the end, they negotiated the regime away behind the back of its leader, and President Ford was left to face the consequences. Many of their most morally reprehensible actions were motivated less by perceived national interest than by parochial political ambition. This makes them even less defensible.

This has not been a book about the Indochina War, but about political ethics more generally. I have dwelt on that war because, like the Peloponnesian, Napoleonic and Second World Wars, and arguably, the narrow unilateralism of the Bush administration, it is emblematic of a more general political and ethical truth. This is the likelihood and danger of great power hubris. Power and success breed more far-reaching ambitions and overconfidence. When not constrained by strong cultural norms, they lead to the kind of self-defeating and destructive ventures we have encountered in this volume. The ethical precepts and practices of our age, when adhered to, function as barriers to hubris and behavior that undermines the standing, influence and even the hegemony of great powers. In the long run, great powers, indeed, all states and institutions, benefit more from respect and legitimacy in the eyes of allies and third parties than they do from the kinds of short-term gains that unethical methods might attain. If such behavior is most generally inimical to the real interests of states and institutions, there is no political justification for it. It follows that unethical behavior, and those responsible for it, ought to be judged by the same standards of morality to which individual citizens are expected to conform.

Great power hubris does not occur in a cultural vacuum. Nor is it always associated with evil leaders. Hitler and Stalin, both of whom gave evil new meaning, were nevertheless products of political cultures that facilitated both their rise to power and the implementation of their horrendous projects. Nixon, Kissinger and Pius XII are more compelling exemplars of political hubris because they are not evil men. Whatever their flaws, they never sought to harm or destroy people as an end in itself or as a means of satisfying pathological personal needs. This in no way absolves them from responsibility for their actions, but they did what they did – and could only have done what they did – because they also operated within a political and institutional framework in which power trumped principle. Expediency had increasingly become an acceptable practice, and even preferable to more traditional, even mandated, procedures that appeared costlier and more constraining. Domestic politics and foreign policy generally become corrupt in tandem and contaminate one another, as Thucydides so brilliantly described in the case of Athens. It is no accident that Watergate, the Nixon coverup and Kissinger's wiretaps of his subordinate followed hard on the heels of their Indochina policy.

Thucydides attributed the decline and breakdown of *nomos* to a negative reinforcing cycle of *logos* and *erga*. Words changed or lost their meanings, and altered the way people thought about themselves and their obligations, undermining longstanding conventions and the constraints they enforced. The behavior this enabled further eroded the meaning of words, leaving Athenians with the language of power and self-interest, narrowly defined. It is sobering to consider that such a process is underway in the United States – in our culture, not just our foreign policy – although we are still some distance from the mentality of the Melian Dialogue. There are many causes for this transformation, but one of them is surely the negative feedback loop that has characterized American thinking about foreign policy and its practice. The language of classical realism, with all its subtlety, commitment to caution and respect for conventions, has been replaced by the cruder language of modern realism and its emphasis on power and expediency. These maxims, which have become conventional wisdom, guide policymakers, and their behavior in turn appears to confirm the assumptions of the modern realist discourse.

This feedback look has been under way for some time, for decades in the deterrence literature, where amoral analysis of the use of conventional and nuclear attacks to signal resolve was already pronounced in Thomas Schelling's highly influential *Arms and Influence*, published in 1964.[66] "Hard-nosed" realism gradually replaced classical realism, and gained an aura of intellectual legitimacy with the development of neorealism. As previously noted, many contemporary realists and neorealists opposed the war in Iraq, and none of them can be held responsible for American foreign policy. Nevertheless, the discourse they sustain is surprisingly influential and illustrates the dangers of divorcing political analysis from ethical discourse. It has the potential to turn American hegemony into another tragedy.

[66] On the amorality of Schelling's conceptions of coercive bargaining, see Richard Ned Lebow, "Thomas Schelling and Strategic Bargaining," *International Studies* 51 (Summer 1996), pp. 555–76.

Name index

Achilles, 56, 101, 127, 335–336, 341, 371
Adolphus, Gustavus, 48, 177–178, 179, 181, 182, 197, 205
Adorno, Theodor, 376
Aeschylus, 20, 21, 25, 52, 96, 115, 116, 135–137, 139, 140, 151, 158, 294–295, 297, 307, 309, 310, 361, 362, 365, 374, 376, 379, 380, 384
Agamemnon, 101, 127, 131, 294
Ajax, 23, 140, 344
Akousilaos of Argos, 128
Albright, Madeline, 314
Alcibiades, 42, 105, 120, 131, 134–135, 153, 262, 266, 374, 375
Alcmeonidae, the, 68
Alexander the Great, 308
Allison, June, 108
Althusser, Louis, 368
Anaxagoras, 68
Anaximander, 128
Ancillon, Johann Peter von, 176
Andromache, 151
Antigone, 23, 137–138, 139, 140, 344, 361
Apel, Karl, 57
Apollo, 294
Aquinas, Thomas, 299
Archidamus, 82, 85–86, 88, 91, 93, 138, 265–266
Archilochus, 298
Archytas of Tarentum, 166
Arendt, Hannah, 24, 307, 351, 375, 376
Aristophanes, 71, 134, 158, 287
Aristotle, 264, 293, 306, 327, 350–351, 354, 355
  Ethics, 62
  Knowledge, 60, 304
  Law, 165
  Literature, 21, 77
  Practice, 329–333
  Property, 166
  Tragedy, 43–44, 46, 58, 77, 382
Artabanus, 135
Athena, 95, 127, 141, 150, 294–295
August, Prince of Prussia, 172–173
Augustine of Hippo, 306
Austin, John L., 121

Bacon, Francis, 27
Bakhtin, Mikhail, 57, 358
Behrens, C. B. A., 211
Benjamin, Walter, 46
Bentham, Jeremy, 259
Berenhorst, Georg Heinrich von, 184
Berkeley, George, 30
Bismarck, Otto von, 235
Blücher, Gebhard Lebracht von, 174, 200
Böckh, August, 14–16
Bowersock, G., 118
Boyen, Hermann von, 173
Brasidas, 70, 102
Brezhnev, Leonid, 5, 257
Briseis, 101
Brodie, Bernard, 243
Brontë, Charlotte, 345
Brühl, Marie von, 172, 173, 176
Brunswick, Karl Wilhelm Ferdinand, 171, 200
Bueno de Mesquita, Bruce, 347
Bull, Hedley, 268, 330, 336
Bülow, Heinrich Dietrich von, 179, 182, 183
Burckhardt, Jacob, 34
Burkitt, Ian, 367
Burke, Edmund, 32, 228

Calhoun, John C., 263–264
Carl Eduard, Duke of Saxe-Coburg, 218
Carr, E. H., 14, 26, 238, 243
Chamberlain, Neville, 229
Charles XII (of Sweden), 205
Charon of Lampsakos, 128
Chrysothemis, 74
Church, Frank, 240

Cimon, 69, 80, 92, 100
Clausewitz, Carl von, 58, 94, 234, 357–358, 379, 380
  biography, 170–176
  community, 267–268
  counter-Enlightenment, relation to, 183
  democracy, 212–215
  domestic politics and foreign policy, 261–263
  early writings, 173, 179–182
  Enlightenment, relation to, 177–178, 181, 296–301
  escalation, 305
  future of war, 214–215
  Jews, 208
  limits of theory, 168–169, 180, 183, 281–282, 305
  misinterpretation, 35–38
  modernization, 26, 290–291
  my interpretation, 44–48
  order, 291, 299–301
  polarities, 308
  philosophical tradition, 31–32
  state, 169–170, 208–214, 291–293, 297–302, 304
  synthesis, 33, 211
  Thucydides, comparison to, 171
  tragedy, 20, 307–309
Cleisthenes, 79, 357
Cleomedes, 124
Cleon, 115, 123, 134, 153–154, 375
Clinton, Bill, 314
Clytemnestra, 294
Cobden, John, 33
Condé, Louis II de Bourbon, 4th Prince of, 196
Condillac, Etienne Bonnot de, 30
Connor, W. Robert, 51, 65, 68, 104, 110, 118–119, 121–122
Cornford, F., N., 127
Courbière, Wilhelm H. de'H., 200
Crane, Gregory, 105, 120, 152
Crawley, Richard, xiv, 72, 106
Creon, 23, 137, 139, 140, 293, 306, 361
Critias, 161
Croesus, 130, 133, 150

Daley, Richard, 5
Dante Alighieri, 389
Davout, Louis Nicolas, 200
De Gaulle, Charles, 23
Deianira, 138, 344
Democritus, 160, 166, 188
Demosthenes, 134
Descartes, René, 27, 29, 30, 185
Deutsch, Karl W., x, 223, 269, 326
Devil, the, 1
Diodorus Siculus, 70
Diodotus, 115, 138
Dionysius of Halicarnassus, 125
Dodds, E. R., 139
Dohna, Alexander von, 174
Dok van Weele, Anneke von, 315
Doyle, Michael, 66, 112, 113, 348
Duchacek, Ivo, x
Dumas, Mathieu, 179
Durkheim. Emile, 328–332, 333, 367

Edelman, Gerald, 334
Eichmann, Adolph, 292–293, 351
Einstein, Albert, 386
Eisenhower, Dwight D., 323
Electra, 74, 344
Elias, Norbert, 343
Engels, Friedrich, 33
Ephorus, 70
Erinyes, the, 295
Euben, Peter, 52, 127
Euler, Leonhard, 196
Euripides, 20, 25, 75, 115, 116, 119, 127, 135, 137, 139, 140, 150, 307, 309, 362, 365, 374, 380

Fabian, Johannes, 377
Fénelon, François de Salignac de la Mothe, 234
Ferdinand, Prince of Prussia, 172
Fichte, Johann Gottlieb, 170, 176, 177, 186, 188, 337, 380
Finley, John, 69, 272
Finnemore, Martha, 162
Fischer, Joschka, 315
Fish, Stanley, 52
Foch, Ferdinard, 36
Forde, Steven, 120
Foucault, Michel, 51, 325, 365, 368
Fox, William T. R., 233
Frederick Wilhelm II (King of Prussia), 48–50, 170, 173, 174–181, 202–203, 212, 266, 300
Frederick, II (the Great), 48, 169, 180, 181–182, 192, 196, 197, 198–199, 205, 207, 263
Friedrich Wilhelm, II (German emperor), 273
Freud, Sigmund, 54, 57, 150, 253, 291, 325, 375

Gadamer, Hans-Georg, 51, 55, 57, 358, 362–380

Galileo Galilei, 185
Garst, Daniel, 119–120
Gibbon, Edward, 46
Gilpin, Robert, 15
Gneisenau, August Wilhelm Neidhardt von, 175–176, 201, 271
Goethe, Johann Wolfgang von, 177, 188, 382
Goffman, Erving, 333, 367, 368
Gorbachev, Mikhail S., 246, 338, 342, 372
Gorgias, 73, 276, 357
Graham, Billy, 5
Gramsci, Antonio, 275, 341
Grey, Edward, 94
Grolman, Karl Wilhelm von, 175, 201
Grotius, Hugo, 62, 268, 336, 346, 349
Grouchy, Emmanuel de, 175
Guthrie, W. K. C., 147
Gyges, 288

Habermas, Jürgen, 57, 358, 362, 380
Haemon, 140
Halbwachs, Maurice, 334
Hall, Rodney, 369
Hamann, Johann Georg, 177
Hanson, Victor, 37–38
Hardenberg, Karl August von, 201, 300
Hegel, Georg Wilhelm Friedrich, 46–49, 57, 138–139, 177, 213, 291–293, 307–308, 376, 380, 381
  art, 47
  Antigone, 53–54
  dialectic, 188, 189
  Greece, 34, 52
  state, 170
  Thucydides, 46–54
Heidegger, Martin, 46, 307
Heisenberg, Werner, 386
Hekataios of Miletos, 128
Helen, 101
Heracles, 138
Heraclitus, 65, 68, 76, 111, 128, 129, 357
Herder, Johann Gottfried, 46, 176, 177, 188, 207, 300
Hermes, 276, 351
Hermocrates, 33, 153, 154, 266, 298
Herodotus, 54, 72, 73, 106, 110, 115, 116, 125, 128–129, 130–131, 132, 133, 135, 140, 142, 150, 163, 288, 298
Herz, John, 226, 283
Hesiod, 21, 293
Hieron of Syracuse, 288
Hippocrates, 104, 107, 143
Hippodamus, 109
Hiss, Alger, 13
Hitler, Adolph, 49, 218, 229, 230, 260, 284, 308, 384
Hobbes, Thomas, 26, 237, 329–332, 333, 346, 349, 354
  Leviathan, 165
  sociability, 62, 346, 349, 354
  Thucydides, 51, 58, 66, 110
Hohenlohe, Prince Friedrich Ludwig, 173, 200
Hölderlin, Friedrich, 46, 52
Homer, 58, 74, 101, 108, 163, 277, 340, 341, 379
  structure of text, 20–21, 129, 130
Honecker, Erich, 372
Hopf, Ted, 162–166, 369–370
Hornblower, Simon, 104
Horkheimer, Max, 376
Howard, Michael, 38
Humboldt, Wilhelm von, 45, 210, 300
Hume, David, 46
  knowledge, 30, 185
Husserl, Edmund, 193

Ikenberry, John, 314, 324

Jaeger, Werner, 118–119
Jeans, James, 386
Johnson, Lyndon B., 5, 22
Jomini, Antoine-Henri de, 179, 182
Joseph II (of Austria), 212

Kagan, Donald, 67
Kahn, Herman, 37
Kant, Immanuel, 33, 176, 177, 181, 185, 186, 228, 329–333, 340, 348, 349, 351, 355, 380, 381
  democratic peace, 207, 214, 300
  ethics, 62, 239
  genius, 181
  knowledge, 30
  state, 170
  tragedy, 33, 46–49
Keegan, John, 37
Kelsen, Hans, 239
Kennedy, John F., 5
Khrushchev, Nikita S., 232
Kierkegaard, Søren, 48
Kissinger, Henry, 5, 6, 7, 14, 22, 23, 37
Knesebeck, Karl Friedrich von, 200
Knox, Bernard, 22, 132
Kong Fuzi (Confucius), 351
Koskenniemi, Martti, 232–233
Kratochwil, Friedrich V., 337

Krauthammer, Charles, 313
Kuhn, Thomas, 182, 388
Kutuzov, Prince Michael Laironovich, 174

Laius, 388
LaRochefoucauld, 17, 299
Lavater, Johann Casper, 177
Le Duc Tho, 19
Lehrer, Tom, 19
Leibniz, Gottfried Wilhelm, 30
Lenin, V. I., 33, 237
  Clausewitz, 36
Leonidas, 161
Lewin, Kurt, 223
Liddell Hart, B. H., 37
Locke, John, 30, 329, 346
Louis XIV, 204
Louise, Queen of Prussia, 172
Luttwak, Edward, 37
Lyotard, Jean-François, 384

Machiavelli, Niccolò, xii, 26, 39, 176, 180, 237, 283, 299
MacIntyre, Alasdair, 61
MacPherson, C. B., 330
Mao Zedong, 5, 6–7, 49
Marcuse, Herbert, 377
Mardonius, 133, 135
Marx, Karl, 29, 33, 57, 188, 306, 368, 375
  Clausewitz, 57
Mauss, Marcel, 328, 343
Mead, George Herbert, 370
Meinecke, Friedrich, 39
Menelaus, 101
Metternich, 32
Milosz, Czeslaw, 25, 368
Miltiades, 106, 375
Moltke, Helmuth von, 35
Monoson, Sara, 278, 281
Montesquieu, Charles-Louis de Secondat de la Brède et de, 176, 228
Moore, Barrington, 224, 234
Morgenstern, Oskar, 223
Morgenthau, Hans, x–xi, 14, 58, 61, 121, 357–358, 376, 379, 380, 384, 385
  balance of power, 266–268
  biography, 217–224, 255
  Decline of Domestic Politics, 226–227
  domestic politics and foreign policy, 263–264
  early writings, 217–218, 221, 253–254
  Enlightenment, 221–222, 308
  ethics, 236–242
  In Defense of the National Interest, 38
  Indochina war, 239–242
  international society, 267–268
  interest and justice, 281–283
  Judaism, 250
  justification for inclusion in book, 26–27
  leadership, 232–233
  limits of theory, 229–230, 246–249, 305
  misinterpreted, 38–39, 216–217
  modernity, 218, 219–220
  modernization, 291–293
  nuclear weapons, 236, 243, 244
  order, 293, 301–303, 304
  philosophical tradition, 31–32, 375, 381
  polarity, 234–235
  policy focus, 33
  power, 224–225, 226–229, 230–233
  Politics Among Nations, 26, 38–39, 256, 262–264, 282, 283
  Purpose of American Politics, 255
  status quo, 225–226
  Scientific Man vs. *Power Politics*, 38, 221–223, 236, 246, 254, 308
  supranationalism, 245–246, 298–300, 302
  system transformation, 242–246
  tragedy, 20, 48–50, 307–309
  typology of states, 225, 348
Möser, Johann Jakob, 177
Müller, Adam von, 179
Müller, Johannes von, 176
Muravchik, Joshua, 314

Napoleon, 48, 169, 170, 173, 174–185, 196, 197, 200–203, 204, 205–207, 261–308
Neoptolemus, 23, 364
Neuman, Franz, 223
Newton, Isaac, 180, 185
Nicias, 42, 105, 131, 134–135, 138, 164, 265–266
Niebuhr, Reinhold, 307
Nietzsche, Friedrich, 11, 14, 46, 253, 308, 325, 382
  art, 385, 386
  Greece, 52
  hermeneutics, 57
  tragedy, 53–54, 376
Nixon, Richard, 1–13, 14, 387
  tragic figure, 19, 22–24
Novalis (Friedrich von Hardenberg), 177
Nye, Jr. Joseph, 313–314

Oakeshott, Michael, 308
Ober, Josiah, 121, 146, 153
Odysseus, 23, 95, 127, 137, 141, 150, 272, 341, 351, 364
Oedipus, 25, 30, 54, 76, 96, 132, 277, 361–362, 363, 388
O'Etzel (von Etzel), Franz August, 187
Onuf, Nicholas, 162, 326
Orestes, 74, 294–295, 362
Orwin, Clifford, 120–121
Osgood, Robert, 62

Paine, Thomas, 33
Paret, Peter, 38, 172, 179, 193, 209, 211
Paris, 101
Pascal, Blaise, 299
Pausanias, 100, 164
Peisistratus, 288
Pericles, 33, 104, 116, 122–124, 126, 134, 155, 265, 268–275, 291, 298, 300, 357, 365–366, 374, 375
  funeral oration, 119, 121, 126, 150, 278, 280, 281, 288, 296
  responsibility for war, 77–94, 95, 104
  strategy, 122–124, 135
  Thucydides on, 68, 70, 73, 131, 153–155
Pestalozzi, Johann Heinrich, 174
Phaedra, 150
Phidias, 68
Pindar, 141, 293
Pitt-Rivers, Julian, 271
Pius XII, 2–13, 387, 388
Plato, 25, 188, 210, 293, 298, 306, 361, 362, 380
  dialogue, 59–60, 324, 357–358
  ethics, xiii, 62, 121
  interpretations, 32–33
  institutions, 325
  knowledge, 77, 112
  Laws, 166, 294
  literature, 58
  philia, 350–351
  Protagoras, 142, 161
  Republic, 32, 142, 294
  speech, 294
  synthesis, 25
  written word, 43
Plutarch, 70, 91
Polanyi, Karl, 303
Polanyi, Michael, 59
Polycrates of Samos, 288
Polyneices, 137
Pouncey, Peter, 105
Prodicus, 41–44
Prometheus, 297
Protagoras, 109, 160, 166, 276
Pufendorf, Samuel von, 62, 336, 349
Putnam, Robert, 328

Racine, Jean, 299
Rahe, Paul, 120, 149
Ranke, Leopold von, 34, 336
Rapoport, Anatol, 37
Rawlings, III, Hunter, 107–108
Reus-Smit, Christian, 269
Ricoeur, Paul, 57
Rosenberg, Shawn, 371
Rothfels, Hans, 210
Rousseau, Jean-Jacques, 176, 325, 329–332
Ruggie, John, 162, 368–369

Searle, John, 337
Scharnhorst, Gerhard von, 171–172, 174, 175, 178–179, 180–182, 183, 199–200, 203, 208, 262–263, 271, 300
Schell, Johnathan, 65
Schelling, Friedrich Wilhelm Joseph, 45–49, 52, 189, 376, 380
Schelling, Thomas, 37
Schiller, Johann Christoph Friedrich von, 177, 186, 360, 381, 382, 388
Schlegel, August Wilhelm, 174, 177
Schlegel, Friedrich, 177
Schleieremacher, Friedrich, 45, 177
Scott, James C., 368
Schumann, Frederick, 14
Schumpeter, Joseph, 345
Searle, John, 121
Segal, Charles, 59, 96
Sen, Amartya, 345
Shakespeare, 20, 49, 307, 382
Shawcross, William, 13
Sicard, Roch-Ambroise Cucurron, 173
Smith, Adam, 62, 349
Socrates, 25, 109, 306, 382, 385
  dialogue, 59–60, 350, 357–358
  written word, 43
Solon, 21, 79, 130, 357
Sophocles, 20, 21, 25, 52, 53, 68, 73, 96, 115, 116, 127, 135–137, 142, 257, 265–307, 309, 362, 365, 374, 380, 384
  agency, 30–31
Sphinx, the, 363
Staël, Anne-Louse-Germaine de, 174
Stahl, Hans-Peter, 118

Stalin, Joseph, 36, 49, 222, 292–298, 338
Stein, Heinrich Friedrich Karl von und zum, 201, 203, 262
Sthenelaïdas, 86, 95, 102–104, 138, 265, 266
Strauss, Leo, 32–33, 223, 384

Taylor, Charles, 354
Teiresias, 139
Tell, William, 48, 181
Tellis, Ashley, 113
Themistocles, 68, 92, 132
Thielmann, Johann Adolph von, 175
Thompson, Kenneth W., 224
Thucydides, 357–358, 361, 364, 370, 371, 373, 379, 380, 381, 384, 387
  Archeology, 75, 148–149, 155, 298
  Athenian realism, 122
  Athens as tragedy, 126, 344
  biography, 68–70, 127
  community, 259–261, 267–268
  constructivist, 159–167, 371, 373
  dialogue, 58
  ethics, 365
  epistemology, 304–305
  honor, 270–271
  inconsistency, 104–114
  interest and justice, 275, 281
  justification for inclusion in book, 26
  knowledge, 366
  logos and *erga*, 146–155, 298–301, 303, 379
  misinterpreted, 34–35, 188
  modernization, 285, 303–304
  my interpretation, 40–44, 115–118
  money, 287–290
  order, 292–298
  origins of war, 77–104
  Pericles, 126, 296
  philosophical tradition, 31–32
  sophia, 60
  speeches, 129
  structure of text, ix–x, 21, 56, 129, 382
  synthesis of old and new, 33, 152
  tragedy, 20, 307–309
Thucydides, son of Melesias, 69
Tieck, Christian Friedrich, 177
Tisias, 124
Trotsky, Leon, 36
Tucker, Robert, 326

Vattel, Emmerich de, 336
Védrine, Hubert, 315
Vellacott, Philip, 96
Vernant, Jean-Pierre, 24
Vico, Giambattista, 334
Voltaire (François Marie Arouet), 228, 248, 380

Wallace, W. P., 118
Wallenstein, Albrecht von, 48, 181
Waltz, Kenneth, 39, 61, 113, 216, 230, 236, 275, 329–333, 336, 367, 368
Warner, Rex, 72, 106
Watson, Adam, 268
Weber, Max, 29, 299, 303
Wendt, Alexander, 329–330, 347, 367, 368–369
White, James Boyd, 119, 126
William of Orange, 181
Wilson, Woodrow, 33, 229, 230, 237–238
Wincklemann, Johann Joachim, 45
Wohlforth, William, 313
Wolf, Friedrich August, 45
Wolff, Christian, 336
Woodhead, Arthur, 108

Xenophon, 70, 293
Xerxes, 116, 125, 130, 133–134, 135, 142, 150, 164

Yack, Bernard, 27–28
Yorck, Hans David Ludwig von, 120–121
Young, Oran, 337

Zeitlin, Froma, 374
Zeno, 154
Zeus, 276, 297, 351

Subject index

Abydus, 135
Aegina, 82, 87–88
Afghanistan, 342
agency and structure, x, 95–96, 367–373
agōn (contest), 24, 139
aidōs (respect), 276–293, 351, 380
Ajax, 127, 140, 363
Allgemeine Kriegsschule, 172, 175, 176, 179, 187, 199
Amphipolis, 70
anangkē (constraint), 106
Anti-Ballistic Missile Treaty (ABM), 18, 315
Antigone, 20, 53, 137, 140, 306, 364
antilogic, 154
anti-Semitism, 218, 219–220
appeasement, 226–229, 230
Archidamian War, *see* Peloponnesian War
Areopagus, 79, 295, 361, 362
aretē (virtue), 160–163, 296–300, 301, 302, 363
Argonne Forrest, 171
Argos, 98, 269
archē (control), 122, 142, 160, 288–289, 314, 316, 340–342
arms control, 50
Arthur Anderson, 353
atē (seduction), 116, 131, 150
Athens (*see* Pericles and other figures and the Melian Dialogue)
  address to Spartan assembly, 269
  assembly (*ekklēsia*), 79, 115, 156
  Corcyra, 90–91, 105
  courts, 259
  deterrence, 265–266
  Dictatorship of the Four Hundred, 165
  Egyptian expedition, 80, 133
  empire, 78–82, 122–125, 152, 327, 374–375
  eve of war, 78–82
  identity, 42, 365
  military, 99
  Mytilenian debate, 98, 126, 137, 149, 304
  plague, 71, 304, 362
  power, 28, 33–35, 155
  Second Confederacy, 125–128
  "war party,", 40–41
Auerstädt, Battle of, 173, 200, 209, 210
Auschwitz-Birkenau, 1, 12
Austria-Hungary, 273, 290
autonomous actors (*see* individuals), 329–333
axiōsis (reciprocity), 157

Bacchae, 137, 362
balance of power, 112, 264–267, 297–298, 300–302
Balkan War of 1912–13, 219
battle of envelopment (*Vernichtungsschlacht*)., 36, 215
Belgium, 274
Berlin, 174
Berlin Wall, 313, 372
Bildung, 45
Black Sea, 81
Borodino, Battle of, 174
Breitenfeld, Battle of, 181
Breslau, 176
Brooklyn College, 219
Bush administration (George W. Jr.), 18–19, 315, 353

Cambodia, invasion of, 13, 22
Canada, 343
Chalcidice, 87, 123
charis (generosity), 156, 279–281, 288
China, 234, 235, 241, 267
Christianity, 221, 382, 383

City College of New York, 219
Clinton administration, 18, 315, 353
Coblenz, 186
Coburg, 217–218, 251
coinage (*see* money), 286–288
Cold War, ix, 16–18, 50, 65–66, 246, 254, 255, 273, 310, 313, 316, 322, 338, 353
Columbus, Ohio, 344
Commentary, 239
community, 355–357
compellence, 232
conscience collective, 328
Constitution, US, 53
constitutional engineering, 357
constructivism, 51, 159, 322, 328–330
  of identities, 367–375
cooperation, 350–353
Corcyra, 42, 73, 78, 83, 89–93, 97–99, 103–104, 107, 113–114, 120, 134, 144, 145, 146–147, 155, 159, 165, 260, 265, 270, 289, 304
Corinth, 28, 42, 78, 82–85, 87–93, 103, 113, 114, 120, 156, 157–158, 265, 270, 289, 374
Coronea, Battle of, 80
counter-Enlightenment, 25, 33, 45, 176–178, 183, 381
counterfactuals, 95
Cuban missile crisis, 232
Czechoslovakia, 229

Delian League, 122
Delium, 70
Delphic Oracle, 81, 84, 86
democratic peace, 214–215, 348
détente, 234, 267, 273
deterrence, 232, 265–266
deus ex machina, 362
dialectic, 47, 188–189
dialogue, 21, 51–52, 350–351, 357–359, 361, 362, 365, 381–382
Die Zeit
dikē (justice), 147, 156–157, 276–277, 293, 351, 363
Dionysia, 24, 136, 280
dirty hands debate, xii, 15
Don Giovanni, 263
double discourse, 327
double vision, 42
dualism, 378
Ducal Gymnasium Casimirianum, 218, 221, 250–251
dunamis (power), 108

Eastern Europe, 327, 339, 340, 342
economics, experimental, 352–353
Eion, 70
Eisenhower administration, 17
Electra, 74, 137, 362
elpis (hope), 116–135
Enlightenment (*see also* proto-Enlightenment), 25, 28, 29–32, 33, 50, 176–178, 185, 221–222, 248, 332, 343, 363, 367, 371, 380
Enron, 353
epic poetry, 21
Epidamnus, 89–93, 97, 98, 107, 113–114
epistēmē (knowledge of essential natures), 60, 61, 299–304, 379, 381, 385–386
erastos-erōmenos relationship, 278–281
erōs (desire), 120
Erythrae, 80, 133
ethics, xi–xii, 58–64, 364–365
  international, 22, 236–242
  social theory of, 354–359
ethikos (set of character traits), 355
euēthēs (ancient simplicity), 120, 151–152
European Coal and Steel Community, 245
European Community, 246
European Union, 340–342, 353
extasis (out of body experience), 358
exchange, (*see axiōsis*), 157

false consciousness, 56, 340–342
Federalist Papers, 256, 281, 306
First Peloponnesian War, 80
flashbulb memories, 334
Frankfurt, 218, 219, 251, 252
Frankfurt School, 253, 375, 377
France (*see* French Revolution, Napoleon, Napoleonic Wars), 231, 248, 266, 273, 290
French Revolution, 25, 27, 33, 168, 185, 205–206, 207, 251, 261–262, 297, 300–302
fundamentalism, 51–52, 377–378

Geisteswissenschaft (humanities), 381
genius, 48, 169, 181–182, 184
General Agreement on Trade and Tariffs (GATT), 325
Geneva, 174, 254
Germany, 222–227, 229, 230, 231, 234, 235, 236, 243, 254, 262–264, 267, 293, 298–301, 312, 320–321, 326, 338, 339, 340–342, 344, 372
Globalization, 377

Great Britain, 226–228, 229, 233, 243, 264, 274
Good Neighbor Policy, 225, 270
Grossgörchen, 174, 175
Gulf War

hamartia (missing the mark), 47, 116, 132, 134, 150, 266
Hanover, 178
hapax legomena, 72
Hecuba, 137, 362
hēgemonia, 122, 126, 276–289, 292, 297–302, 312, 313, 314, 316, 336, 342
Hegemonic Stability theory, 321–322
Hellenica, 70
Hellespont, 81, 133
Hermeneutics, 52–58
hēsuchia (rest, tranquility), 148–149, 158
Hinduism, 341
Hippocratic corpus, 106, 107, 145
historia (history), 73
History of the Peloponnesian War
  Athens as tragedy, 116, 126–141
  Archeology, 75
  as history, 42–44
  causes, 40–41, 77–104
  interpretations, 33–35, 118–122
  inevitability, 89–96
  modernization, 28
  overview of my interpretation, 39–42, 115–118
  structure of text, 110–111
  third parties, 82–89
Holocaust, 3, 25, 222, 223, 254, 292, 340–344
Holy Alliance, 32, 226–228
homonoia (community), 39, 166–167, 257–258, 260, 277–281
honor, 271–274
House Committee on Un-American Activities, 13
hubris, 47, 150, 266, 298–303, 314, 365, 366
Humanität, 45, 210, 297–300, 302
hypocrisy, 17–18

identity, 277, 287, 324–325, 338, 345–346, 354–357
  Multiple, 378–379
  transformation, 371–377
Iliad, 56, 101, 128, 129, 150, 272, 335, 341
Indochina War, 21–23, 26, 50, 65, 238, 239–242, 244, 255, 267, 282
individual self interest, 330, 332, 354–359
  as unit of analysis, 366
institutionalism, 322–328, 340–342, 347
interest, 122–126
International Criminal Court, 316
international law, 223, 238–239, 242, 336–339
International Monetary Fund, 325
international society, 226–228, 267–269
Internet, 377–378
Ionian revolt, 270
Iraq, 322
isolationism, 221
isonomia (equality), 295
Israel, 231
Italy, 222, 243, 264, 312

Japan, 222, 234, 235, 243, 264, 312, 320–321, 338, 339
Japanese–American Alliance, 321
Jena, Battle of, 173, 200, 209
Jews, 2, 3, 12–13, 208, 217–218, 251–252, 271
Johns Hopkins University, 326
justice, 120–166, 355–357

kairos (making the most of an opportunity), 143
Kansas City, 254
katharsis (catharsis), 43, 47, 382
kerdos (profit), 287, 293
kinēsis (movement), 147, 148–149
kleos (fame), 340
koinōnia (the civic project), 350, 354
Königsberg, 174
Korean War, 34–39, 234
kratos (power), 108, 363
Kriegschuldfrage, 111
kūdos (glory), 363
Kyoto Protocol, 18, 315

Lacedaemonian Confederacy, 84, 97–98
League of Nations, 223
Leipzig, 173, 372
Leipzig, Battle of, 203, 262–264
Leucimme, 89, 90
levels of analysis, 96
Leviathan, 165, 260, 346
lexis eiromenē, 128
liberalism, 221, 238, 347
literature and wisdom, 21

logos (word), 41, 117–118, 146–155, 276–293, 294, 357, 370
Lonely Crowd, 341
Lützen, Battle of, 181
Lydia, 288

Macedon, 28
Madrid, 254
Magna Graecia, 28
Mainz, 173
Marathon, Battle of, 80, 106
Marriage of Figaro, 263
Marshall Plan, 17
Marxism, 253, 271, 375, 377–378
Mass culture, 376–377
McCarthyism, 244, 255
Megara, 77, 80, 82, 83–84, 88, 265
Megarian Decree, 77–78, 87, 105, 107
Melian Dialogue, x, 26, 65, 113, 115, 119, 124, 126, 129, 145, 147–148, 161, 270, 290, 364
Melos, 116, 289
memory, 334–335, 339–340
metabolai (upheavals), 143
Methodenstreit, 159, 246
Miletus, 80, 133
Militärische Gesellschaft, 172
military technology, 28
mimēsis (imitation), 43, 382
Mishnah, 351
mind–body problem, 378
modernity, 27–28, 293, 332, 366
modernization, 25, 284, 298–304
  fifth-century Greece, 27–34, 152
  nineteenth century, 218, 219–220
money (*see* coinage), 75
Moscow, 174
Munich, 219, 251
music, 383
Mytilene, 364

Nancy, 173
Napoleonic Wars, 25, 27, 32, 168, 179, 226–228, 267
narrative, 20–21, 72–73, 341–342
National Science Foundation, 381–382
NATO, 17, 340, 342, 353
Nazis, 31, 165, 219, 223, 252, 274
nemesis (catastrophe), 116, 132, 133, 134, 149, 150, 266
neopositivism, 379
neural nets, 334
Neuruppin, 171
New Republic, 239
New School for Social Research, 219
Newton's Laws, 180
New York City, 254
New Yorker, 65
New York Times, 240
nihilism, 161
"Nixon Shocks" (1971), 323
Nobel Peace Prize, 19
nomos (conventions, laws), 49, 117, 141–146, 239, 294, 297, 300–302, 326
North Atlantic Community, 337
North Korea, 344
nous (insight), 76–77
nuclear weapons, 236, 243, 244, 276–292, 297–300, 302

Odyssey, 285
Oedipus at Colonus, 53, 388
Oedipus complex, 54
Oedipus Tyrannus, 20, 45, 54, 76, 132, 139
oikos (household), 29, 259, 277, 284, 350
ōmos (raw), 149
On War, 186–198, 204–205, 261, 290, 297–302, 308
  chance, 195
  dialectic, 47, 188–189
  emotions, 195
  friction, 194–195
  future of warfare, 207
  history of warfare, 204–205
  ideal types, 193–194
  interpretation, 35–38
  my interpretation, 44–48
  definition of war, 189–192
  reception, 26
  synthesis, 195–198
  typology of wars, 192–193
  war in practice, 47
  war in theory, 47
order, 258–264, 276–293, 354–359
Oresteia, 127, 136, 139, 294–295, 362
  Agamemnon, 149, 151

Pacific Rim, 312
Pan-Hellenism, 297–298, 300–302
Paros, 106
Parthenon, 69, 123
pathei mathos, 150–151
Peace of Nicias, 98
Pentecontaētia, 122

peripeteia (reversal), 30
Persia, 28, 80, 98, 133, 135, 150, 164, 231, 270, 298–301, 303, 312, 374, 375
Persians, 132
persona (public face), 331
philia (affection, friendship), 125, 166, 278–281, 350–351, 356–357
Philoctetes (Sophocles), 23, 351, 364
Philoctetes (Euripides), 137
phusis (nature), 129, 141–146, 160, 297–298, 300–302
Pius XII, 2–13
Plataea, x, 98, 100, 164, 289
pleonexia (ambition), 128, 142, 158, 265
poiēsis (making), 60, 382
Poland, 176, 200, 211, 212–214, 226–228, 267, 301, 303
polarity, 233–234, 284, 297, 300–302, 313–315
Posen, 176
Potidaea, 83–84, 87–88, 105, 107, 265
power, 122–126, 364–365
power transition, 35–38
praxis (human action), 26, 60
Prometheus, 297, 362
Promethia, 297, 362
prophasis (justification), 77, 106–108, 111, 124, 159, 270, 371
prospect theory, 154
Proto-Enlightenment, 29–31, 276–292, 363
Prussia (*see* Wars of the the First and Second Coalitions and associated battles), 174, 175, 266, 271
  army, 199, 203
  Junkers, 203, 264
  on eve of war, 198–199
  occupation of, 200–201
  reform, 199–200, 201, 204, 262, 290
psuchē (soul), 21, 58
Pylos, 134

Quantum mechanics, 386

realism, xi, 112–113, 125, 275, 311, 385
  classical, 39–40, 63, 216, 257–258, 275, 283, 284, 315, 320, 348, 357
  ethics, xi–xii, 14–16
  neorealism, 66, 121, 216
  and Thucydides, 115
  Thucydides and, 41
Realpolitik, 15, 19, 23, 39, 237, 240, 283
reciprocity (*see axiōsis*), 351–353
relativity, 386
Renaissance, 307
rhetoric, 357
road rage, 388
romanticism, 332
Roosevelt (Franklin) administration, 225, 270
Russia (*see also* Soviet Union)
  Civil War, 49
  Napoleonic Wars, 200, 206, 266, 290
  World War I, 274
Russo-Turkish War (1736–39), 179

Saalfeld, Battle of, 200
Saigon, 23
Salamis, 69, 116, 122, 133
salus publica, 236
Samian Rebellion, 81, 83, 120
Scandinavia, 236
Schumann Plan, 245
security dilemma, 66, 226–227, 229, 274
September 11, 20
Serbia, 274
Seven Years War, 199
shadow of the future, 347
Sicilian Debate, and expedition, 50, 115, 119, 123, 126, 131, 146, 242, 265, 266, 312
signs, 75, 140
Sinta, 2
social capital, 328
social contracts, 346
social habitus, 343
social roles, 335
social science, 345–348, 366–367, 381–382, 388–389
soft power, 313–314
Soissons, 173
sophia (wisdom), 32, 59–60, 61, 364, 379, 385
sophism, 150–151, 362
  and Athens, 109–110
  epistemology, 160
  rhetoric, 154
  Thucydides and, 41
sōphrosunē (self-control), 158, 306, 308, 363, 366
South Africa, 339
Soviet Union, 222, 233, 234, 236, 241, 243, 264, 274, 293, 302, 310, 313, 326–328, 339, 372
Spain, 206

Sparta (*see also* Lacedaemonian Confederacy), 28, 32, 74, 265, 269, 374
army, 97, 99
character, 99–103, 260–261, 290
decision for war, 78
efforts to avert war, 86–89
ephors, 82–89
gerousia, 82–89
helots, 100, 260
"Peace party," "war party,", 40–41, 101, 265
way of life, 152, 158
stasis (civil strife), 41, 137, 143–144, 152, 153, 165, 166–167
Suez Canal Crisis, 323
Suppliant Women, 136, 139
supranationalism, 245–246
Sybota, 87, 92
Syracuse, 28, 98, 135, 153, 266, 298

Tadzhikstan
Taliban, 327, 342
Talmud, 53
Tanakh, 50
technē (skill), 59–60, 61, 141, 148, 210, 381, 385
telos (purpose), 355, 363
Testament, old (*see Tanakh*)
Tet Offensive, 21
texts, 50–58
Thasos, 69
Thebes, 23, 98, 374
theōros (witness), 305–306
therapy, 150, 151, 154
Thermopylae, 164
Thirty Years Truce, 28, 80, 81, 87–88, 91, 134
Thirty Years War, 179, 181, 182, 233, 236, 239
Thrace, 69
Thurii, 81
thucydideische Frage, 104
Tilsit, Treaty of, 200
timē (honor), 101, 103, 122, 270, 272, 288, 312
tit-for-tat, 347
Tokyo fire bombing, 3
tolma (daring), 149
tragedy, 20–25, 361–367, 373–376, 378
basis for ontology, 63–64
epistemology, 379–386
ethics and, 58–64
heroes, 96, 116, 131
Renaissance, 45
Morgenthau and, 49
ontology, 366–367
plot line, 125–128
Thucydides and, 41–44
Treaty of Basel, 171
Treaty of Paris, 226–227
Treaty of Petit Trianon, 226–228
Treaty of Tilsit, 173, 174
Treaty of Versailles, 226–227, 229
Trojan Women, 137, 362
Troy, 95
Truman administration, 17
Turkey, 200, 219
tyranny, 123, 148, 155, 276, 288, 293, 297–300, 302, 374, 375–376
Tyranny of the Thirty, 161, 276

United Nations, 273
United States (*see also* Indochina War), 372, 377–378
Athens, 312–313, 344–345
Bill of Rights, 343
civil war, 164–165
civil society, 264
foreign policy, 65, 233, 234–235, 245, 273, 297–302, 315
University of Berlin, 218
University of Chicago, 219, 223
University of Frankfurt, 218, 219
University of Geneva, 219, 254
University of Kansas City, 219
University of Madrid, 224–225
University of Munich, 218

Vatican, 5, 12–13
Vicenza, 45
Viet Cong, 21
Vietnam War, *see* Indochina War,
Vietnam, 17, 232

War of the First Coalition, 172–184
War of the Second Coalition, 200
warfare
in ancient Greece, 163–164
nineteenth century, 168, 172–184
Warsaw Pact, 327
Washington Post, 12–13, 239

Watergate, 8
Waterloo, Battle of, 171, 175, 203, 262
Weimar Republic, 251
  politics of, 218, 221, 252–253
Women of Trachis, 138
WorldCom, 353
World War I, 27, 49, 94, 111, 165, 215, 221, 223, 273–274
World War II, 3, 25, 27, 31, 49, 222, 223, 235, 243, 292, 322, 338, 340

xenia (guest friendship), 160–163, 351, 363

Zahlbach, 171